The Tax Law of Associations

Update Service

BECOME A SUBSCRIBER!
Did you purchase this product from a bookstore?

If you did, it's important for you to become a subscriber. John Wiley & Sons, Inc. may publish, on a periodic basis, supplements and new editions to reflect the latest changes in the subject matter that you *need to know* in order to stay competitive in this ever-changing industry. By contacting the Wiley office nearest you, you'll receive any current update at no additional charge. In addition, you'll receive future updates and revised or related volumes on a 30-day examination review.

If you purchased this product directly from John Wiley & Sons, Inc., we have already recorded your subscription for this update service.

To become a subscriber, please call **1-877-762-2974** or send your name, company name (if applicable), address, and the title of the product to:

mailing address: | **Supplement Department**
John Wiley & Sons, Inc.
One Wiley Drive
Somerset, NJ 08875

e-mail: | **subscriber@wiley.com**
fax: | **1-732-302-2300**
online: | **www.wiley.com**

For customers outside the United States, please contact the Wiley office nearest you:

Professional & Reference Division
John Wiley & Sons Canada, Ltd.
22 Worcester Road
Etobicoke, Ontario M9W 1L1
CANADA
Phone: 416-236-4433
Phone: 1-800-567-4797
Fax: 416-236-4447
Email: canada@wiley.com

John Wiley & Sons, Ltd.
The Atrium
Southern Gate, Chichester
West Sussex PO 19 8SQ
ENGLAND
Phone: 44-1243-779777
Fax: 44-1243-775878
Email: customer@wiley.co.uk

John Wiley & Sons Australia, Ltd.
33 Park Road
P.O. Box 1226
Milton, Queensland 4064
AUSTRALIA
Phone: 61-7-3859-9755
Fax: 61-7-3859-9715
Email: brisbane@johnwiley.com.au

John Wiley & Sons (Asia) Pte., Ltd.
2 Clementi Loop #02-01
SINGAPORE 129809
Phone: 65-64632400
Fax: 65-64634604/5/6
Customer Service: 65-64604280
Email: enquiry@wiley.com.sg

The Tax Law of Associations

Bruce R. Hopkins

WILEY

John Wiley & Sons, Inc.

For general information on our other products and services, or technical support, please contact our Customer Care Department within the United States at 800-762-2974, outside the United States at 317-572-3993 or fax 317-572-4002.

Wiley also publishes its books in a variety of electronic formats. Some content that appears in print may not be available in electronic books.

For more information about Wiley products, visit our Web site at http://www.wiley.com.

Library of Congress Cataloging-in-Publication Data:

Hopkins, Bruce R.
  The tax law of associations / by Bruce R. Hopkins.
    p. cm.
  Includes bibliographical references and index.

  ISBN 978-0-470-45548-7

  1. Nonprofit organizations—Taxation—Law and legislation—United States.
  2. Associations, institutions, etc.—Taxation—Law and legislation—United States. I. Title.
  KF6449.H665 2006
  343.7305'266—dc22

                              2006008033

10 9 8 7 6 5 4 3 2 1

This book is dedicated to all who lead and manage the associations
I am privileged to represent.

Americans of all ages, all conditions, and all dispositions constantly form associations. They have not only commercial and manufacturing companies, in which all take part, but associations of a thousand other kinds, religious, moral, serious, futile, general or restricted, enormous or diminutive. The Americans make associations to give entertainments, to found seminaries, to build inns, to construct churches, to diffuse books, to send missionaries to the antipodes; in this manner they found hospitals, prisons, and schools. If it is proposed to inculcate some truth or to foster some feeling by the encouragement of a great example, they form a society. Wherever at the head of some new undertaking you see the government in France or a man of rank in England, in the United States you will be sure to find an association.

—Alexis de Tocqueville, *Democracy in America* (1835)

About the Author

Bruce R. Hopkins is the country's leading authority on the law of tax-exempt organizations and is a lawyer with the firm Polsinelli Shalton Welte Suelthaus PC. He is also the author of 19 books, including *The Law of Tax-Exempt Organizations, Eighth Edition*; *Planning Guide for the Law of Tax-Exempt Organizations*; *The Tax Law of Unrelated Business for Nonprofit Organizations*; *Nonprofit Law Made Easy*; *650 Essential Nonprofit Law Questions Answered*; *The Law of Fundraising, Third Edition*; *Private Foundations: Tax Law and Compliance, Second Edition*; *The Tax Law of Charitable Giving, Third Edition*; *The Law of Intermediate Sanctions*; and *The Law of Tax-Exempt Healthcare Organizations, Second Edition*; all published by John Wiley & Sons. Mr. Hopkins also writes the monthly newsletter *Bruce R. Hopkins' Nonprofit Counsel*, also published by John Wiley & Sons.

Contents

CONTENTS

Appendices

Tables

CONTENTS

Preface

A lawyer with a fulltime tax-exempt organizations practice, spanning many years (decades), is privileged to represent several categories of exempt organizations, including colleges, universities, and schools; health care institutions; churches and other religious organizations; other public charities; private foundations; advocacy organizations; associations; social clubs; and fraternal and veterans' organizations. Lawyers in this circumstance may also have the opportunity to serve a cemetery company, a crop operations financing organization, or a state-sponsored workers' compensation entity. Each exempt organization presents unique problems, issues, and forms of gratification (particularly if the problems and issues are satisfactorily resolved).

Tax-exempt organizations lawyers (or, if you will, nonprofit lawyers) know better than to publicly favor one type of exempt organization client over another. Yet favorites are inevitable, because of the nature of the work generated (depth, complexity, variety) and/or the individuals involved (personalities, intelligence, challenges).

Take, for example, associations. The exempt organizations lawyer will find, at these organizations, interesting, energetic, dedicated, and motivated individuals (on the board and on the staff), who preside over a dazzling array of substantive questions and issues of law. As to the latter, the entire panoply of the law of tax-exempt organizations is presented: eligibility for exemption, private inurement, legislative activities, political activities, related foundations, for-profit subsidiaries, partnerships and other joint ventures, annual reporting issues, unrelated business rules, and more. And that is just the federal tax law. A lawyer representing an association and/or affiliated entity can also feast on law concerning antitrust, campaign finance, charitable solicitation, contracts, employee benefits, insurance, intellectual property, and a host of other issues.

* * *

Your author has had, and is having, the pleasure of writing and updating (through editions and supplements) *The Law of Tax-Exempt Organizations*. Some subjects in that book are too expansive to be contained within its pages, generating other law books, such as those directly relating to private foundations and the unrelated business rules. So, too, with the matter of associations. There is a chapter in the exempt organizations book on these entities (business leagues), but it has proved to be insufficient. There was so much more to explore and analyze.

Thus, this book. Here, the association executive, board member, lawyer, accountant, and anyone else interested in the tax law of associations will find full discussions of topics common (and often unique) to tax-exempt associations: the concept, evolution, forms, and roles of associations (Chapter 1); requirements for tax exemption (Chapter 2); private inurement, private benefit, and excess benefit transactions (Chapter 3); lobbying and political campaign activities (Chapter 4); the unrelated business rules (Chapter 5); for-profit subsidiaries and limited liability companies (Chapter 6); partnerships and joint ventures (Chapter 7); association-related foundations (Chapter 8); charitable giving and fundraising (Chapter 9); annual reporting and disclosure requirements (Chapter 10); and non-tax association law (Chapter 11). There is even a little bit of history.

* * *

The Internal Revenue Service, a few years ago, embarked on an ambitious project to examine, on a statistical analysis basis, the entire tax-exempt sector. The agency conceived of the sector as consisting of around 40 market segments; the plan was to analyze each one and use the resulting data to support regulation projects, examination criteria, public and private rulings, and perhaps proposed legislation. Summary data from these analyses was to be made public, the first in early 2004. The project has not been faring well, with IRS resources diverted to other ends.

One of the first of the market segment studies concerned business leagues. When this book was conceived, there was to be an epilogue, which was to be based on the market segment analysis of the nation's tax-exempt associations. As of mid-2006, that report has not materialized; the same fate befell the epilogue. Perhaps, some day, that analysis will emerge and when it does it will be incorporated into this book, in a supplement, cumulative supplement, or edition.

* * *

This book is infused with (and, in part, stimulated by) admiration and appreciation for those who lead and manage associations. Your author has been representing associations for nearly four decades, and is grateful for the tough legal problems, all the air travel, and sheer fun. Association conventions, conferences, seminars, and board meetings generate many memorable occurrences, some of which ought not to be recounted here. Association representation can even lead to marriage.

* * *

I wish to express my deep and sincere thanks for the help and support on this project provided by senior editor, Susan McDermott, and senior production editor, Kerstin Nasdeo.

BRUCE R. HOPKINS
June, 2006

The Tax Law of Associations

CHAPTER ONE

Associations, Society, and the Tax Law

The term *association* does not have legal efficacy; although used constantly, it is, like many other terms bandied about in the nonprofit sector (such as *fund*, *foundation*, or *society*), not a formal term of law (as opposed to *corporation* or *trust*). Niceties of the law aside, however, associations are plentiful, powerful, increasing in number, and a significant component of a free society and a democratic state. Current estimates are that there are over 140,000 associations in the United States; there are thousands more in other countries.[1]

§ 1.1 INTRODUCTION TO *ASSOCIATIONS*

Dictionaries provide many definitions of the word *association*; the one that casts the term, as a noun, to mean a form of organization in essence states that an association is an organization of persons having a common interest. Synonyms are *society*, *league*, and *union*. The term, of course, derives from the verb *associate*, which means (in this context) "to join, share, or unite with others."

The principal advocate for associations in the United States is the American Society of Association Executives (ASAE), located in Washington, D.C. This organization, generally regarded as the "association of associations," defined the term *association* as a nonprofit organization that is "membership-based," "private" (as opposed to for-profit or governmental), and "legally incorporated," and has a "public benefit purpose."[2] This definition is essentially correct,[3] and thus, for purposes of this book:

> *Association* is defined as a nonprofit membership organization that provides services to its members in achievement of an objective of enhancing conditions within a trade, industry, or profession, and, in the process, provides substantial benefits to the public.[4]

Members of an association can be individuals, organizations (for-profit and/or nonprofit, tax-exempt or taxable), or both.

Most associations in the United States are exempt from federal income taxation. State income taxation exemption is usually also available. The federal tax law, since 1913,[5] characterizes most of these organizations as *business leagues*.[6]

---

[1] The Union of International Associations, headquartered in Brussels, Belgium, states that it is a clearinghouse for information on over 40,000 "international organizations and constituencies" (www.uia.org).

[2] This definition is in a brochure prepared by ASAE titled "How Associations Make a Better World," available at www.asaenet.org/betterworld (referenced throughout as ASAE, "How Associations Make a Better World").

[3] A finicky lawyer will take issue with the third of these elements, noting (1) that the phrase "legally incorporated" is redundant, in that an entity is either incorporated pursuant to a statute or it is not (and it is difficult for an organization to be "illegally incorporated") and, more important, (2) an organization can be an association without being incorporated.

[4] The Department of Commerce once defined a *trade association* as a "nonprofit, cooperative, voluntarily joined, organization of business competitors designed to assist its members and its industry in dealing with mutual business problems" (Judkins, *National Associations of the United States* vii (1949)). This definition, however, excludes from the ambit of the term *association* professional societies and associations the members of which are tax-exempt organizations.

[5] Tariff Act of October 3, 1913, 38 Stat. 114, 172.

[6] Internal Revenue Code of 1986, as amended, section (IRC §) 501(c)(6).

(The term *association* is broader than the term *business league*.[7]) The definition of a business league in the federal tax regulations closely parallels the preceding definition of an association: a business league is an "association of persons having some common business interest, the purpose of which is to promote such common interest."[8] These regulations add that the activities of a business league "should be directed to the improvement of business conditions of one or more lines of business."[9]

The case law supports this definition of a tax-exempt business league, largely in connection with analyses of the *line of business requirement*. The U.S. Supreme Court observed[10] that exempt business leagues represent either an entire industry[11] or all components of an industry within a geographic area.[12] The Court favorably referenced an observation of the appellate court, where it was stated that it was the "manifest intention" of Congress in writing this statute to "provide an exemption for organizations which promote some aspect of the general economic welfare."[13] The Court also noted another opinion from the same court, where tax exemption as a business league was denied an organization because "[n]othing is done to advance the interests of the community or to improve the standards or conditions of a particular trade."[14] Another federal court of appeals reviewed these characteristics of a business league and concluded that, since Congress has left this definition undisturbed over the decades, it has been given the "imprimatur of Congress and is thus entitled to the effect of law."[15]

The case law, from the outset, teaches that the essential function of an association is to be educational and informational, for its members and for others, particularly others in the line of business involved. Thus, one association, comprised of individuals engaged in shoe repair, was portrayed by a court (writing in 1947) as an entity "designed to teach the shoe repair man to be a better artisan and business man, to show him the advantages of modern advertising and the use of machinery and of proper shop layout, and in general how to render better services to the public."[16] The association was formed because "it was recognized by its members that only through improving the conditions of the shoe repair men, the quality of their workmanship, and the relations with the public could its purpose of promoting the welfare of the entire industry be accomplished."[17] This court subsequently characterized an association as a "conduit for an industrywide

---

[7] See § 1.6.

[8] Income Tax Regulations (Reg.) § 1.501(c)(6)-1.

[9] *Id.* See § 2.7.

[10] Nat'l Muffler Dealers Ass'n, Inc. v. United States, 440 U.S. 472, 482-483 (1979).

[11] Citing American Plywood Ass'n v. United States, 267 F. Supp. 830 (W.D. Wash. 1967); Nat'l Leather & Shoe Finders Ass'n v. Comm'r, 9 T.C. 121 (1947).

[12] Citing Comm'r v. Chicago Graphic Arts Fed'n, Inc., 128 F.2d 424 (7th Cir. 1942); Crooks v. Kansas City Hay Dealers Ass'n, 37 F. 83 (8th Cir. 1929); Washington State Apples, Inc. v. Comm'r, 46 B.T.A. 64 (1942).

[13] Nat'l Muffler Dealers Ass'n, Inc., 565 F.2d 845, 846-847 (2d Cir. 1977).

[14] Produce Exchange Stock Clearing Ass'n v. Helvering, 71 F.2d 142, 144 (2d Cir. 1934). This approach is also reflected in United States v. Oklahoma City Retailers Ass'n, 331 F.2d 328 (10th Cir. 1964); Retailers Credit Ass'n of Alameda County v. Comm'r, 90 F.2d 47 (9th Cir. 1937).

[15] The Engineers Club of San Francisco v. United States, 791 F.2d 686, 689 (9th Cir. 1986).

[16] Nat'l Leather & Shoe Finders Ass'n v. Comm'r, 9 T.C. 121, 126 (1947).

[17] *Id.*

cooperative exchange of . . . information."[18] A federal court of appeals observed that a tax-exempt association engages in activities consisting of "professional programming."[19]

§ 1.2 HISTORY AND EVOLUTION OF ASSOCIATIONS

A term that is infrequently used these days is *guild*. The dictionary advises that a guild is an association of individuals engaged in kindred pursuits or having common objectives; the word is often preceded by the adjective *medieval*. The contemporary association (along with certain other membership groups, such as labor unions and chambers of commerce) traces its history to these medieval guilds.

Historically, these guilds were in the nature of societies or small business associations, with members being self-employed artisans or part of a small craft shop or cooperative. It has been written that "[o]ne's view of guilds tends to be heavily colored by one's view of political economy, since the whole history of trade, technology, intellectual property, regulated professions, social security, and professional ethics are entwined with the history of the guilds in Europe."[20]

Merchant guilds are thought to be the first of these entities to emerge; they began to appear in the tenth century.[21] These organizations were formed for the mutual protection of the member merchants' horses, wagons, and goods while traveling. As industries became more specialized, *craft guilds* came into being. This type of entity would have as its members artisans engaged in the same occupation (i.e., bakers, cobblers, stone masons, and carpenters) who associated for protection and mutual aid. These craft associations became important, to the point that individuals in a town could not practice their craft without belonging to the appropriate guild. The essential purpose of these guilds, believed to have been highly regimented in operation, was to create and maintain a monopoly with respect to particular crafts.

The guilds performed other services for their members and their families, including the provision of funeral expenses for poorer members and aid to survivors, supplying of dowries for poor girls, coverage of members with a type of health insurance, building of chapels, donating of windows to local churches and cathedrals, and watching over the morals of members (i.e., those who engaged in gambling and usury). These guilds also contributed to the emergence of Western lay education; previously, the only schools were those sponsored by monastic or cathedral institutions.

Yet, while protecting their members, the guilds also provided certain forms of protection to the consumer. Thus, craft regulations prevented poor workmanship; manufacturing processes and other trade secrets were guarded; advertising and price-cutting were forbidden; prices were regulated; sales by foreign artisans were prohibited; and the number of masters in individual guilds was limited.

---

[18] MIB, Inc. v. Comm'r, 80 T.C. 438, 453 (1983).

[19] The Engineers Club of San Francisco v. United States, 791 F.2d 686, 690 (9th Cir. 1986).

[20] www.en.wikipedia.org/wiki/Guild.

[21] The following discussion is based in large part on a paper available at www.public.iastate.edu/~gbetcher/373/guilds.htm.

From a political viewpoint, a guild was neither sovereign nor unrelated to society outside the guild and town organization. As a collective unit, a guild might be a vassal to a bishop, lord, or king. The extent of vassalage was dependent on the degree of independence between a guild and the town in which it was located. The guilds had a close connection with the city authorities. The city council could intervene in the event of trouble between guilds; these councils could establish the hours of work, fix prices, and establish weights and measures. Guild officials were frequently appointed to serve in civic government because the guilds usually voted as a unit, raised troops for the civic militia, and paid taxes as a group. Guilds were required to perform public services, such as policing the streets and constructing public buildings and walls to defend the town or city.

The members of these guilds were called *confraternities*—brothers helping one another. By the thirteenth century, to become a member of a guild, individuals went through three stages: apprentice, journeyman, and master. An apprentice would so serve for two to seven years, living with the master and his family, and learning the rudiments of his trade. The apprentice progressed to journeyman, who became entitled to work for compensation. A journeyman who produced a masterpiece could become a master craftsman and be voted into membership in the guild.

Others regard these guilds as less public service oriented and more focused on creating monopolies. The guilds regulated technical processes, hours of labor, wages, the number of workmen to be employed, prices, and trade practices. The number of men employed was regulated in order to keep the production of all guild shops approximately equal. The employment of improved methods of manufacture, due to new inventions or the use of water power, was discouraged unless all producers shared alike in the benefits. This type of "close supervision of trade and industry, which today is called planned economy and is branded as communism, was obviously designed to benefit not so much the consumers as the producers organized in the guilds."[22]

The guild system began to decline around the close of the 1700s, because guilds were believed to be in opposition to free trade and a hindrance to technological innovation, technology transfer, and business development.[23] Critics such as Jean-Jacques Rousseau and Adam Smith (and even Karl Marx) helped fuel the free market (laissez-faire) movement that made its way into the political and legal system. Because of industrialization and modernization of trades and industries, and the rise of powerful nation-states that could issue patent and copyright protections (often, in the process, revealing the trade secrets), the guilds' power faded. By the 1800s, many former handicraft workers had been forced to seek employment in the emerging manufacturing industries, using not closely guarded techniques but standardized methods controlled by corporations.

Modern antitrust law[24] can be said to be derived in some respects from the statutes by which the guilds were abolished in Europe. Nonetheless, these

---

[22] These observations are based in large part on a paper available at www.mars.acnet.wnec.edu/~grempel/courses/wc1/lectures/24guilds.html.

[23] The following analysis is based on material available at www.en.wikipedia.org/wiki/Guild.

[24] See § 11.6.

guilds are the precursors of the contemporary association, which generally has as its membership a group of persons who have joined the entity voluntarily and believe that their career in their trade, industry, or profession will be enhanced by this form of cooperation with their colleagues and their involvement with the association. Also, today's tax-exempt association usually engages in member-focused activities that also provide considerable benefits to the public.

§ 1.3 ROLE OF ASSOCIATIONS IN SOCIETY

ASAE has an awareness campaign, called Associations Advance America, that is designed to impress the value of associations not just to their individual and corporate members, but to the larger society.[25] ASAE also has an Associations Make a Better World Campaign that seeks to promote understanding of the association model as a significant contributor to societies and economies worldwide.[26]

(a) Professional Development and Continuous Skill-Building

ASAE observed that education is often the single most common association function. In many industries and professions, associations are the only source of continuing education.[27] Associations educate their members on technical and scientific matters, business practices, and legal issues; ASAE views this as elevating the quality of publicly delivered goods and services.[28] ASAE observed that, because of associations, the nation's workforce remains competitive and skilled in the latest techniques, trends, and technologies.

(b) Information

Associations collect and disseminate information on industries, issues, and trends, providing valuable background for policy, regulatory, and legislative decisions. By informing the public about the efficiency, quality, and safety of products and services, associations help bolster public confidence in the marketplace.

(c) Standards-Setting, Codes of Ethics, and Certification

Associations play a prominent role in setting performance, technical and safety standards, ethical codes, and professional certification programs.[29] These efforts help reduce the risks that consumers face in the marketplace.[30] Associations also save taxpayers money by engaging in these vital functions that government would otherwise have to perform. Standardization provides an international language to help shrink barriers to trade. If adopted throughout the world, standards create a large market instead of many fragmented markets.

---

[25] The following analysis is based on information available on the ASEA Web site (www.asaenet.org).

[26] This campaign is reflected in ASAE, "How Associations Make a Better World."

[27] There is an interesting parallel between the facts that the guilds were instrumental in introducing lay education (that is, education provided by an institution other than a religious one) to the public (see § 1.2) and associations as a principal or only source of continuing education in the modern era.

[28] This rationale underlies, for example, the special tax treatment for associations' trade shows. See § 5.9(a).

[29] Associations invest over $1.1 billion annually setting and enforcing standards and certifications, according to an ASAE Foundation study, referenced on the ASAE Web site.

[30] Cf. discussion in text accompanied by *infra* note 35.

(d) Research and Statistics

Associations develop and disseminate valuable data that might otherwise be unavailable. Policymakers, regulators, researchers, journalists and other representatives of the media, consumer groups, and others use this information to enhance a broad understanding and analysis of the economy. Governments are often dependent on research and statistics provided by associations.

(e) Volunteerism and Community Service

Founded on the principles of volunteerism and cooperation,[31] associations nurture involvement in society and community service. By pooling their talents and resources, association members help the needy, provide disaster relief, mentor youth, and clean up the environment. Association activities generate what is known as *social capital*—features of social organization such as networks, norms, and social trust that facilitate coordination and cooperation for mutual benefit. ASAE observed that it is not just the sum of the institutions that underpin a society, they are the glue that holds society together. Social networks can increase productivity by reducing the costs of doing business. Increasing evidence shows, ASAE reported, that social cohesion is critical for societies to prosper economically and for development to be sustainable.[32]

(f) Constituent Contact

Associations are important, sometimes indispensable, intermediary organizations linking individuals and businesses with governments. Associations serve as a dual gateway: as a mechanism to convey their views to government officials and as a conduit by means of which government stays in touch with constituents.

(g) Giving Voice to Citizens

Government relations activities conducted by associations give members a voice in government decisions impacting their profession, trade, and cause. Associations collect and disseminate information on public policy issues, forecast how public policy issues affect their members, and help members understand and reach consensus for positions on issues. By educating legislators and regulators about issues affecting members' businesses, professions, and causes, associations help government officials make informed decisions.

(h) Economic Impact

ASAE observes that associations are "economic engines that fuel America's prosperity."[33] Associations pump billions of dollars into the economy and create hundreds of thousands of good jobs. Association meetings and conventions generate billions more in revenue for cities. Although associations are almost

---

[31] See § 1.2, last paragraph.

[32] Americans devote more than 173 million volunteer hours each year—time valued at more than $2 billion—to charitable and community service programs through their associations, according to an ASAE Foundation study, referenced on the ASAE Web site.

[33] ASAE Web site.

always tax-exempt organizations,[34] their operating expenditures generate billions of dollars in tax revenues annually—from property taxes, payroll taxes, sales taxes, and 35 other types of taxes.

(i) Social and Networking Functions

The ASAE analysis barely mentions the point that associations provide social and networking opportunities that enhance individuals' work and growth within their trade, industry, or profession. While this can augment the quality of goods and services produced, and improve the development of individuals' competence, there is an entertainment and social component to association life that can also lead to personal development. Associations are not supposed to be social clubs[35]; nonetheless, associations' annual and other meetings, trade shows, and the like can spawn terrific social events, long-lasting friendships, and other interesting and enlightening experiences. Members often enjoy the inevitable board, committee, and other politics and eagerly anticipate the camaraderie found at each annual conference. Associations tend to attract the best of humanity and, for that reason alone, make wonderful clients for lawyers and other consultants.

§ 1.4 RATIONALES FOR ASSOCIATIONS' TAX EXEMPTION

There are different forms of associations.[36] One measure as to these distinctions is the composition of these organizations' membership. When the members of an association are entirely or primarily individuals, the presumption generally is that the entity is a business league (an IRC § 501(c)(6) organization). That is, the Internal Revenue Service[37] or a court will presume that an association of individuals is an organization that has the personal and career development of these members as its principal purpose, with benefits to society at large secondary at best.

Certification programs are classic illustrations of this point. It is the judgment of the IRS that the primary purpose for certification of individuals is to improve the reputation and business interests of the members of the certifying organization (or other related constituency) and the industry or profession of which they are a part. In a rare pronouncement on the point, the IRS stated that a certification program (at least the one the agency reviewed) was designed and operated principally to achieve professional standing for the profession involved and to enhance the respectability of those who become certified; benefits to the larger society were dismissed as incidental.[38] Moreover, the IRS concluded that

---

[34] See § 2.16.

[35] Social clubs can be tax-exempt by reason of IRC § 501(c)(7). See § 1.6(f).

[36] See § 1.5.

[37] The Internal Revenue Service is referenced throughout as the "IRS" or the "agency."

[38] IRS General Counsel Memorandum (Gen. Couns. Mem.) 39721. In general, Hopkins, "The Meaning of Tax-Exempt Status in the Work of Certification Organizations," as Chapter 1 of Schoon & Smith (eds.), *The Licensure and Certification Mission: Legal, Social, and Political Foundations* (New York: Professional Examination Service, 2000). See § 1.3(c).

such a certification program conducted by a charitable organization[39] was an unrelated business for that organization.[40]

Congress has determined that business leagues are entitled to federal income tax exemption. As noted, these are entities with a membership that have a common business interest, their purpose is to promote that interest, and their activities are directed to the improvement of business conditions of one or more lines of business.[41] The policy reasons underlying this exemption have not been well articulated, but it may be presumed that Congress believed—and continues to believe—that these organizations provide sufficient community and public benefits to warrant exemption.[42]

Not all tax-exempt associations are business leagues, however. As ASAE observed, associations "represent a wide range of collective interests including professions, industry, business, and philanthropic causes."[43] This reference to *philanthropic* objectives embraces associations the purposes of which are charitable, educational, religious, and/or scientific (IRC § 501(c)(3) organizations).[44] Some associations qualify for federal income tax exemption as social welfare organizations (IRC § 501(c)(4) entities).[45]

There are several ways an entity can qualify as a tax-exempt charitable organization.[46] Most pertinent to the association model, however, are the *advancement* categories of charitable organizations: those that advance education, science, and/or religion.[47] For example, associations in the education context include alumni and alumnae associations,[48] honor societies,[49] gem and mineral clubs,[50] garden clubs,[51] and professional societies.[52] Associations in the scientific setting include scientific research cooperatives. Exempt religious organizations include associations and conventions of churches, and conferences of churches.[53]

ASAE observed that, by "[b]ringing together disparate individuals, businesses, academia, and government, associations wield a collective power that is much greater than the sum of their parts." The work of associations is "woven throughout the fabric of society; citizens, the business sector, and governments have come to depend on the social and economic benefits that associations afford."[54]

---

[39] That is, an organization described in IRC § 501(c)(3).

[40] IRS Private Letter Ruling (Priv. Ltr. Rul.) 200439043.

[41] See § 1.1, text accompanied by notes 8–9.

[42] Often the views of "management" are reflected in association policies. Thus, there is a corresponding tax exemption for "labor"-oriented entities (see § 1.6(c)). On occasion, the distinction between an association of individuals and a labor organization is blurred.

[43] ASAE, "How Associations Make a Better World."

[44] See Hopkins, *The Law of Tax-Exempt Organizations, Eighth Edition* (Hoboken, NJ: John Wiley & Sons, 2003) (*Tax-Exempt Organizations*), Chapters 6–10.

[45] See § 1.6(a).

[46] See *Tax-Exempt Organizations*, Chapter 6.

[47] Reg. § 1.501(c)(3)-1(d)(2).

[48] Rev. Rul. 60-143, 1960-1 C.B. 192; Rev. Rul. 56-486, 1956-2 C.B. 309.

[49] Rev. Rul. 71-97, 1971-1 C.B. 150.

[50] Rev. Rul. 67-139, 1967-1 C.B. 129.

[51] Rev. Rul. 66-179, 1966-1 C.B. 139.

[52] Rev. Rul. 71-506, 1971-2 C.B. 233.

[53] IRC § 170(b)(1)(A)(i).

[54] ASAE Web site.

§ 1.5 FORMS OF ASSOCIATIONS

There are essentially four forms of nonprofit organizations that the IRS recognizes as tax-exempt entities: corporation, unincorporated association, trust, and limited liability company.[55] Only the first two of these four forms are suitable for tax-exempt associations. The main distinction between the two entities is the protection against personal liability that the corporate form provides.[56]

Nearly all tax-exempt associations have a common feature: a membership. The members of an exempt association may be individuals, for-profit businesses, tax-exempt organizations, or a combination of these entities. If the membership of an association is primarily or solely comprised of individuals, then, as noted, it will likely be regarded as a business league. Nonetheless, if the primary purpose[57] of such an association is charitable, educational, and/or scientific, the organization may be exempt as a charitable, educational, and/or scientific entity in the nature of a *professional society*.

If the members of an association are all or principally for-profit businesses, the entity will unavoidably constitute a business league. Where all or most of the members of an association are tax-exempt organizations, the association will likely have the same federal tax exemption as its members (assuming the members all have the same exempt status). As examples, an association of exempt colleges and universities will itself be a charitable and/or educational organization; an association of exempt scientific research organizations will be a charitable and/or scientific organization.

Associations sometimes are cast as representing a trade, an industry or business, or a profession. Thus, often there are references to *trade associations*, *business associations*, and *professional associations*. The federal tax law, however, does not make these distinctions, and the concepts of the business league usually apply equally to all three categories of entities. In some circumstances, nonetheless, a professional association may be organized and operated so that it is charitable, educational, and/or scientific in nature, in which case it may be portrayed as a *professional society*.

§ 1.6 OTHER EXEMPT "ASSOCIATIONS": A COMPARATIVE ANALYSIS

There are at least 68 types of organizations that are tax-exempt pursuant to federal law.[58] About one-third of these categories of entities are likely to have a membership—a structural element that is almost always obligatory for a business league.[59] Narrowing the range of federal tax exemption, then, there are about 25 types of exempt organizations (including business leagues,[60] chambers

---

[55] *Tax-Exempt Organizations*, § 4.1.

[56] In general, Hopkins, *Planning Guide for the Law of Tax-Exempt Organizations: Strategies and Commentaries* (Hoboken, NJ: John Wiley & Sons, 2004), Chapter 1.

[57] See *Tax-Exempt Organizations* § 4.4.

[58] *Tax-Exempt Organizations*, App. C.

[59] The statute, after all, refers to a business league as an "association of persons" (IRC § 501(c)(6)).

[60] See § 2.4.

of commerce,[61] boards of trade,[62] real estate boards,[63] and professional football leagues[64]) that tend to have and serve a membership, that is, that usually confer services and/or other benefits on a collective basis. Generically, they are all *associations*.

(a) Social Welfare Organizations

Federal statutory law provides tax exemption for "[c]ivic leagues or organizations not organized for profit but operated exclusively for the promotion of social welfare."[65] The term *social welfare* is commensurate with the "common good and general welfare" and "civic betterments and social improvements."[66] The promotion of social welfare does not include activities that primarily constitute "carrying on a business with the general public in a manner similar to organizations which are operated for profit."[67] An organization is not operated primarily for the promotion of social welfare if its "primary activity is operating a social club for the benefit, pleasure, or recreation of its members."[68] To qualify as an exempt social welfare organization, the activities of the organization must be those that benefit a community in its entirety, rather than merely benefit the organization's membership or other select group of individuals or organizations.[69]

Tax-exempt social welfare organizations and exempt business leagues have three shared characteristics: a prohibition on the provision of benefits to particular persons, on for-profit business activities, and on private inurement. The fundamental difference between them is that the exempt social welfare organization must have the primary purpose of serving a *community*,[70] while the primary purpose of an exempt business league is to provide services to those within a *line of business*.

Indeed, a membership structure can preclude tax exemption as a social welfare organization. That is, an organization can be found to not qualify as an exempt social welfare organization because it is operating primarily for the benefit of its members rather than for the purpose of benefiting the community as a

---

[61] See § 2.11.

[62] See § 2.12.

[63] See § 2.13.

[64] See § 2.14.

[65] IRC § 501(c)(4). See *Tax-Exempt Organizations*, Chapter 12.

[66] Reg. § 1.501(c)(4)-1(a)(2)(i).

[67] Reg. § 1.501(c)(4)-1(a)(2)(ii).

[68] *Id.* See § 1.6(f).

[69] Reg. § 1.501(c)(4)-1(a)(2)(i). A tax-exempt social welfare organization must reflect a "community movement designed to accomplish community ends" (Erie Endowment v. United States, 316 F.2d 151, 156 (3rd Cir. 1962)).

[70] In practice, this requirement of services to a *community* is often ignored; prime examples of this are the national advocacy organizations that are exempt by reason of IRC § 501(c)(4). Nonetheless, this element of exemption continues to be invoked by the IRS on occasion; in one instance, an organization that claimed to be an agency providing home health care services to residents of five facilities was in fact merely a registry that matched the needs of residents with independent service providers for a fee, causing the IRS to deny recognition of tax exemption in part on the ground that the entity did not serve a requisite community (Priv. Ltr. Rul. 200544020).

whole.[71] Consequently, where organizations provide substantially different benefits to the public as compared to its members, they are not *primarily* devoted to the promotion of social welfare.[72] In essence, even though there may be aspects of the organization that greatly benefit society, "if the majority of the organization's services benefit private members," the organization cannot qualify under this category of exemption.[73]

Thus, a membership-based organization involved in the provision of housing for veterans did not qualify as a tax-exempt social welfare organization. A court wrote that the entity "does, of course, furnish housing to a certain group of citizens but it does not do so on a community basis"; this activity was cast as a "public-spirited but privately devoted endeavor."[74] The court continued: "Its work in part incidentally redounds to society but this is not the 'social welfare' of the tax statute."[75] It added that classification as "'civic' or 'social' depends upon the character—as public or private—of the benefits bestowed, of the beneficiary, and of the benefactor."[76]

(b) Local Associations of Employees

Federal statutory law provides tax exemption for "local associations of employees, the membership of which is limited to the employees of a designated person or persons in a particular municipality."[77] The net earnings of these organizations must be devoted primarily to charitable, educational, and recreational purposes.

Thus, this type of organization provides services for local groups of employees. Organizations that provide services primarily for the convenience of members, serve as a cooperative buying service, or function as an employee benefit organization cannot qualify for tax exemption as local associations of employees.

(c) Labor Organizations

Federal statutory law provides tax exemption for "labor organizations."[78] The principal purpose of an exempt labor organization is the betterment of working conditions of individuals engaged in a common pursuit and the development of

---

[71] E.g., Contracting Plumbers Co-op Restoration Corp. v. United States, 488 F.2d 684 (2d Cir. 1973) (where a plumbers' cooperative was denied exemption pursuant to IRC § 501(c)(4) because its benefits were proportional to its members' financial involvement); American Women Buyers Club, Inc. v. United States, 338 F.2d 526 (2d Cir. 1964) (where an association was held to not be exempt by reason of IRC § 501(c)(4) inasmuch as a majority of its benefits were provided to its members and it did not promote social welfare).

[72] Vision Service Plan v. United States, 2006-1 U.S.T.C. ¶ 50,173 (E.D. Cal. 2005) (where the organization's benefits it provided to the public were found to be incidental; its primary purpose was held to be to serve its paying members (subscribers)).

[73] *Id.*

[74] Comm'r v. Lake Forest, Inc., 305 F.2d 814, 818 (4th Cir. 1962).

[75] *Id.*

[76] *Id.* Tax exemption pursuant to IRC § 501(c)(4) is sometimes accorded to organizations that promote health or are part of the health care field, yet that fact alone does not guarantee this category of exemption (e.g., IHC Health Plans, Inc. v. Comm'r, 325 F.3d 1188 (10th Cir. 2003)).

[77] IRC § 501(c)(4). See *Tax-Exempt Organizations*, § 18.3.

[78] IRC § 501(c)(5). See *Tax-Exempt Organizations*, § 15.1.

a higher degree of efficiency in the particular occupation.[79] The most common of these organizations is the labor union. The private inurement doctrine is applicable with respect to labor organizations.

Thus, just as the tax-exempt business league works to improve conditions within a line of business, the exempt labor organization works to better the working conditions of groups of workers. From the larger perspective, the management-labor dichotomy is reflected in these two types of exempt organizations: the business league represents the employers, and the labor organization serves the employees.

(d) Agricultural Organizations

Federal statutory law provides tax exemption for "agricultural" organizations.[80] This category of organization must have as its principal object the betterment of the conditions of those involved in the exempt pursuits, the improvement of the grade of their products, and the development of a higher degree of efficiency in the particular occupation.[81] The private inurement doctrine is applicable in this setting.

A tax-exempt agricultural organization usually has a membership; those served by the entity must represent a significant portion of the interested agricultural community. As is the case with the exempt business league, the performance of services directly on behalf of an individual member is not improvement of the grade of a person's product or development of a higher degree of efficiency in a person's agricultural-related pursuits. Nonetheless, as is true for exempt business leagues, where an activity only incidentally benefits individual members, tax exemption as an agricultural entity is available.

(e) Horticultural Organizations

Federal statutory law provides tax exemption for "horticultural organizations."[82] This type of exempt organization essentially has the same characteristics as the exempt labor and agricultural organizations.[83] An illustration of an exempt horticultural organization is a garden club formed for the purpose of betterment of the conditions of individuals engaged in horticultural pursuits and improving their products.

(f) Social Clubs

Federal statutory law provides tax exemption for "[c]lubs organized for pleasure, recreation, and other nonprofitable purposes, substantially all of the activities of which are for such purposes."[84] Generally, this exemption is extended to social and recreational clubs that are supported primarily by membership fees, dues, and assessments. These entities must have a membership comprised of individuals, personal contacts, and fellowship; a commingling of the members

---

[79] Reg. § 1.501(c)(5)-1(a)(2).
[80] IRC § 501(c)(5). See *Tax-Exempt Organizations* § 15.3.
[81] Reg. § 1.501(c)(5)-1(a)(2).
[82] IRC § 501(c)(5). See *Tax-Exempt Organizations* § 15.3.
[83] See §§ 1.6(c) and 1.6(d), respectively.
[84] IRC § 501(c)(7). See *Tax-Exempt Organizations*, Chapter 14.

must constitute a material part in the operation of this type of organization. The private inurement doctrine is applicable in this context.

The primary purpose of a tax-exempt social club, then, is to provide a range of social and recreational services to its members, who are individuals. While country clubs, dinner clubs, and swim, tennis, and golf clubs set the norm for the exempt social club, the concept of this type of exempt entity is considerably broader and embraces organizations such as flying clubs, collegiate fraternities and sororities, and gem and mineral clubs.

(g) Fraternal Beneficiary Societies

Federal tax statutory law provides tax exemption for certain "[f]raternal beneficiary societies, orders, or associations."[85] These entities generally operate under the lodge system and pay life, sick, accident, or other benefits to their members and their dependents.[86] The use of the words *fraternal* and *beneficiary* in this context connote an organization—that is, an association of individuals—who have the same or similar calling, avocation, or profession, or who are otherwise working in unison to achieve some worthy objective.

(h) Voluntary Employees' Beneficiary Associations

Federal tax statutory law provides tax exemption for "[v]oluntary employees' beneficiary associations providing for the payment of life, sick, accident, or other benefits to the members of such association or their dependents or designated beneficiaries."[87] This type of entity, more an employee benefit fund than an authentic association, must be an association of employees having a common employer (or affiliated employers).[88] Eligibility for membership in a voluntary employees' beneficiary association may be restricted by geographic proximity or by objective conditions or limitations reasonably related to employment. The private inurement doctrine is applicable.

(i) Domestic Fraternal Societies

Federal tax statutory law provides tax exemption for certain "[d]omestic fraternal societies, orders, or associations."[89] These entities operate under the lodge system, and devote their net earnings exclusively to religious, charitable, scientific, literary, educational, and fraternal purposes; they do not provide life, sick, or similar benefits to their members.[90]

(j) Teachers' Retirement Fund Associations

Federal tax statutory law provides tax exemption for "[t]eachers' retirement fund associations of a purely local character."[91] This exemption is available as long as

---

[85] IRC § 501(c)(8). See *Tax-Exempt Organizations* § 18.4(a).
[86] Reg. § 1.501(c)(8)-1.
[87] IRC § 501(c)(9). See *Tax-Exempt Organizations* § 16.3.
[88] Reg. § 1.501(c)(9)-2(b).
[89] IRC § 501(c)(10). See *Tax-Exempt Organizations* § 18.4(b).
[90] Reg. § 1.501(c)(10)-1.
[91] IRC § 501(c)(11). See *Tax-Exempt Organizations* § 16.7.

there is no private inurement (other than through payment of retirement benefits) and the organization's income consists wholly of amounts received from public taxation, amounts received from assessments on the teaching salaries of members, and investment income.

(k) Benevolent Life Insurance Associations

Federal tax statutory law provides tax exemption for "[b]enevolent life insurance associations of a purely local character."[92] These associations basically operate to provide life insurance coverage to their members, albeit at cost because of the requirement that income be collected solely for the purpose of meeting losses and expenses.

(l) Cemetery Companies

Federal tax law provides tax exemption for "[c]emetery companies owned and operated exclusively for the benefit of their members."[93] Generally, this type of exempt organization owns a cemetery, sells lots in it for burial purposes, and maintains these lots (along with any unsold ones) in a state of repair and upkeep appropriate for a final resting place. Its members are owners of the lots who hold them for bona fide burial purposes and not for purposes of resale. The private inurement doctrine is applicable to these types of organizations.

(m) Veterans' Organizations

Federal tax law provides tax exemption for a "post or organization of past or present members of the Armed Forces of the United States" that satisfy certain criteria.[94] An exempt veterans' organization must operate primarily to promote the social welfare of a community; assist disabled and needy veterans and members of the U.S. armed forces and their dependents, and the widows, widowers and orphans of deceased veterans; provide entertainment, care, and assistance to hospitalized veterans or members of the U.S. armed forces; carry on programs to perpetuate the memory of deceased veterans and members of the armed forces, and comfort their survivors; conduct programs for religious, charitable, scientific, literary, or educational purposes; sponsor or participate in activities of a patriotic nature; provide insurance benefits for their members or dependents thereof, or both; and/or provide social and recreational activities for their members.[95] The private inurement doctrine is applicable to these organizations.

(n) State-Sponsored Medical Care Organizations

Federal tax law provides tax exemption for certain state-sponsored membership organizations to provide medical care coverage for certain uninsurable individuals.[96] To qualify for exemption, these individuals, who must be residents of the

---

[92] IRC § 501(c)(12)(A). See *Tax-Exempt Organizations* § 18.5(a).
[93] IRC § 501(c)(13). See *Tax-Exempt Organizations* § 18.6.
[94] IRC § 501(c)(19). See *Tax-Exempt Organizations* § 18.10.
[95] Reg. § 1.501(c)(19)-1(c).
[96] IRC § 501(c)(26). See *Tax-Exempt Organizations* § 18.14.

state involved, must be unable to acquire medical care coverage for their medical condition through insurance or from a health maintenance organization, or able to acquire the coverage only at a rate that is substantially in excess of the rate for the coverage through the membership organization. The private inurement doctrine is applicable to these organizations.

(o) State-Sponsored Workers' Compensation Entities

Federal tax law provides tax exemption for certain state-sponsored organizations that reimburse their members for losses arising under workers' compensation acts.[97] To be eligible for this exemption, an organization must be established before June 1, 1996.

(p) Religious or Apostolic Organizations

Federal tax law provides tax exemption for certain "[r]eligious or apostolic associations or corporations."[98] These entities must have a common treasury or community treasury. These associations may engage in business for the common benefit of their members. The members must include in their annual gross income their entire pro rata shares, whether distributed or not, of the taxable income of the association.

(q) Farmers' Cooperatives

Certain farmers' cooperatives are eligible for exemption from federal income taxation.[99] These cooperatives are farmers', fruit growers', or like associations organized and operated on a cooperative basis for the purpose of (1) marketing the products of members or other producers and returning to them the proceeds of sales, less the necessary marketing expenses, on the basis of either the quantity or the value of the products furnished by them; or (2) purchasing supplies and equipment for the use of members or other persons and turning over the supplies and equipment to them at actual cost plus necessary expenses.[100]

(r) Shipowners' Protection and Indemnity Associations

Federal tax law provides tax exemption for nonprofit "shipowners' mutual protection and indemnity associations."[101] The private inurement doctrine is applicable with respect to these organizations.

(s) Homeowners' Associations

Federal tax law provides tax exemption for certain condominium management associations, residential real estate management associations, and timeshare associations.[102] These associations enable their members (usually individual homeowners) to act together in managing, maintaining, and improving areas where they live.

---

[97] IRC § 501(c)(27)(A). See *Tax-Exempt Organizations* § 18.15(a).
[98] IRC § 501(d). See *Tax-Exempt Organizations* § 8.7.
[99] IRC § 521. See *Tax-Exempt Organizations* § 18.11.
[100] Reg. § 1.521-1.
[101] IRC § 526. See *Tax-Exempt Organizations* § 18.12.
[102] IRC § 528. See *Tax-Exempt Organizations* § 18.13

(t) Quasi-Governmental Entities

The concept of tax exemption extends to a variety of governmental and quasi-governmental organizations. These entities range from the states to nonprofit organizations that have a unique relationship with one or more governmental departments, agencies, or instrumentalities. There are essentially four ways an organization can achieve exemption in this context: (1) by constituting a state or a political subdivision of a state; (2) by reason of having its income excluded from federal income taxation, when the income is derived from the exercise of an essential governmental function and the income accrues to a state or political subdivision of the state[103]; (3) by classification as an instrumentality of a state; or (4) by reason of being an integral part of a state, city, or similar governmental entity.[104]

For these organizations that are structured as associations, the most likely basis for tax exemption is the third one. The IRS frequently classifies entities pursuant to the exclusion rule, such as associations of public school districts, other units of state and local governments, and political subdivisions.

(u) Other Membership Organizations

Still other tax-exempt organizations have a membership (or patronage) structure. This is the case, for example, for college and university alumni and alumnae associations,[105] cooperative hospital service organizations,[106] cooperative service organizations of operating educational organizations,[107] and charitable risk pools.[108] Still other exempt organizations may have a membership structure, such as charitable, educational, scientific, and religious entities[109] and political organizations.[110]

§ 1.7 COMPARISONS TO OTHER EXEMPT ORGANIZATIONS

The tax exemption category (if any) that is most suitable for a particular collective-type organization is obviously dependent in large part on application of the primary purpose test.[111] Various cooperative entities, employee benefit funds, advocacy organizations, fraternal and veterans' groups, and other entities are, as noted, eligible for tax-exempt status. Often the entirety of what an organization does operationally will dictate the availability of any exemption. An organization may have more than one category of exempt function, with the principal one leading to any exemption, such as an entity that has some educational activities but predominant social and recreational functions.

---

[103] IRC § 115.
[104] See *Tax-Exempt Organizations* § 18.17.
[105] These entities are tax-exempt by reason of IRC § 501(c)(3).
[106] IRC § 501(e). See *Tax-Exempt Organizations* § 10.4.
[107] IRC § 501(f). See *Tax-Exempt Organizations* § 10.5.
[108] IRC § 501(n). See *Tax-Exempt Organizations* § 10.6.
[109] IRC § 501(c)(3). See *Tax-Exempt Organizations*, Chapters 6–10.
[110] IRC § 527. See *Tax-Exempt Organizations*, Chapter 17.
[111] See § 2.3.

Many collective organizations are clearly not business leagues. Those that are generically the closest to business leagues are labor, agricultural, and horticultural organizations. This is because, just as business leagues have the primary purpose of promoting a common business interest, these other three types of organizations must have as their principal object the betterment of the conditions of those engaged in the exempt pursuits, the improvement of the grade of their products, and the development of a higher degree of efficiency in the particular occupation.[112]

---

[112] Reg. § 1.501(c)(5)-1(a)(2).

CHAPTER TWO

Tax Exemption for Business Leagues and Similar Organizations

Federal tax law provides exemption from federal income tax for "[b]usiness leagues . . . not organized for profit and no part of the net earnings of which inures to the benefit of any private shareholder or individual."[1] This exemption is also extended to chambers of commerce, real estate boards, boards of trade,

---

[1] IRC § 501(c)(6). The second component of this provision is a recitation of the doctrine of private inurement (see Chapter 3).

and professional football leagues (whether administering a pension fund for football players or not).

§ 2.1 CONCEPT OF *TAX EXEMPTION*

Every element of gross income received by a person, including a corporation or trust, is subject to the federal income tax.[2] The presumption is that all income is taxable; income, to not be taxable, must be exempt by virtue of a specific tax law provision. Examples of this are the provisions for tax-exempt organizations.

An organization is not exempt from the federal income tax merely because it is organized and operated as a *nonprofit* entity.[3] Tax exemption is achieved only where the organization satisfies the requirements of a particular provision in the Internal Revenue Code.[4] Thus, in general, an organization that meets the appropriate statutory criteria qualifies—for that reason alone—as a tax-exempt organization. That is, whether an organization is entitled to tax exemption, on an initial or ongoing basis, is a matter of statutory law. It is Congress that, by statute, defines the categories of organizations that are eligible for federal income tax exemption,[5] and it is Congress that determines whether a type of tax exemption should be continued.[6]

§ 2.2 RECOGNITION OF TAX EXEMPTION

An organization's tax-exempt status may be *recognized*. This is a function of the IRS, which it exercises, where appropriate, by making a written determination that an entity constitutes an exempt organization. (The role of the IRS in recognizing the tax-exempt status of organizations is part of its overall practice of evaluating the tax status of organizations.[7]) Eligibility for exempt status, however, is different from recognition of that status. Thus, Congress, as noted, and not the IRS, is responsible for *granting* tax-exempt status.

As a general rule, an organization desiring tax-exempt status pursuant to the federal tax law is not required to secure recognition of exemption from the IRS.[8]

---

[2] IRC § 61(a).

[3] See discussion at *Tax-Exempt Organizations* § 1.1.

[4] IRC §§ 501(c), 521, 526–529; Reg. § 1.501(a)-1(a)(1).

[5] E.g., HCSC-Laundry v. United States, 450 U.S. 1 (1981) (where the Supreme Court held that Congress had the authority to exclude nonprofit laundry organizations from the scope of the tax exemption accorded to cooperative hospital service organizations (see *Tax-Exempt Organizations* § 10.4)).

[6] E.g., Maryland Sav.-Share Ins. Corp. v. United States, 400 U.S. 4 (1970) (where the Supreme Court held that Congress did not exceed its power to tax nor violate the Fifth Amendment to the Constitution in denying tax-exempt status to nonprofit insurers of deposits in savings banks and similar entities where the insurers were organized after September 1, 1957 (see *Tax-Exempt Organizations* § 18.5)). Likewise, for example, IRC § 501(c)(18) (see *Tax-Exempt Organizations* § 16.6) is applicable only to trusts created before June 25, 1959; IRC § 501(c)(20) is available to provide tax exemption for trusts under a qualified group legal services plan for tax years beginning before July 1, 1992; IRC § 501(c)(27)(A) (see *Tax-Exempt Organizations* § 18.15) is applicable only to entities established before June 1, 1996; and IRC § 501(c)(23) (see *Tax-Exempt Organizations* § 18.10(b)) is available only to an organization organized before 1880.

[7] Reg. §§ 601.201(a)(1), 601.201(d)(1).

[8] E.g., Savings Feature of Relief Dep't of B&O R.R. Co. v. Comm'r, 32 B.T.A. 295 (1935); Rev. Rul. 80-108, 1980-1 C.B. 119 (reflecting the fact that an organization qualifying for tax exemption as a social welfare organization (see § 1.6(a)) is not required to seek recognition of tax exemption). The current tax regulations are incorrect on this point (Reg. § 1.501(a)-1(a)(3)).

Nonetheless, an organization in this position may seek recognition of exempt status and often is well advised to do so (following standards used in ascertaining whether to seek any type of ruling from the IRS[9]). By contrast, in order for an organization to be granted tax exemption as a charitable entity or as an employee benefit organization, it must file an application for recognition of the exemption with the IRS and receive a favorable determination.[10] Likewise, for an organization to be treated as a tax-exempt political organization, it must give notice to the IRS of its existence.[11] Consequently, when an organization makes application to the IRS for a determination as to exempt status, it is requesting the IRS to recognize its tax exemption, not to grant tax exemption.

Subject only to the authority of the IRS to revoke a ruling for good cause (usually a change in the facts or law), an organization whose tax-exempt status has been recognized by the IRS can rely on that determination as long as there are no substantial changes in its character, purposes, or methods of operation.[12] (On the occurrence of any one of these changes, the organization is expected to notify the IRS and obtain a reevaluation of its exempt status.[13])

§ 2.3 APPROPRIATE EXEMPTION CATEGORY

A fundamental concept of the law of tax-exempt organizations is the *primary purpose rule*.[14] This principle is formally explicated, by use of the word *exclusively*, in the context of exempt charitable organizations,[15] exempt social welfare organizations,[16] exempt cemetery companies,[17] exempt medical care coverage organizations,[18] and exempt workers' compensation coverage organizations,[19] and by use of the word *substantially* in the case of exempt social clubs.[20] This principle of law is generally applicable to all categories of exempt organizations.[21] This, then, is one of the fundamental bases for determination of the appropriate category of tax exemption (if any) for an organization.

The primary purpose test looks to an organization's purposes rather than its activities (although courts from time to time focus only on activities[22]).[23] The emphasis should not be on the nature of an organization's primary activities as

---

[9] In this context, the advantages to be gained by obtaining recognition of tax-exempt status include acknowledgment by the IRS that the entity qualifies for tax exemption, exemption from certain state taxes, and eligibility for preferential mailing rates (see § 11.4).

[10] IRC § 508(a).

[11] IRC § 527(i).

[12] Reg. § 1.501(a)-1(a)(2).

[13] See § 4.5(a).

[14] See *Tax-Exempt Organizations* § 4.4.

[15] IRC § 501(c)(3); Reg. § 1.501(c)(3)-1(c)(1).

[16] IRC § 501(c)(4).

[17] IRC § 501(c)(13).

[18] IRC § 501(c)(26).

[19] IRC § 501(c)(27).

[20] IRC § 501(c)(7).

[21] E.g., Orange County Agric. Soc'y, Inc. v. Comm'r, 55 T.C.M. 1602 (1988), *aff'd*, 893 F.2d 647 (2d Cir. 1990).

[22] E.g., Church in Boston v. Comm'r, 71 T.C. 102 (1978).

[23] Reg. § 1.501(c)(3)-1(c)(1).

the test of tax exemption but on whether the activities accomplish one or more exempt purposes.[24]

The general rule, as stated by the Supreme Court in the context of charitable organizations, is that the "presence of a single . . . [nonexempt] purpose, if substantial in nature, will destroy the exemption regardless of the number or importance of truly . . . [exempt] purposes."[25] A federal court of appeals held that nonexempt activity will not result in loss or denial of tax exemption where it is "only incidental and less than substantial" and that a "slight and comparatively unimportant deviation from the narrow furrow of tax approved activity is not fatal."[26] In the words of the IRS, the rules applicable to charitable organizations in general have been "construed as requiring all the resources of the organization [other than an insubstantial part] to be applied to the pursuit of one or more of the exempt purposes therein specified."[27] Consequently, the existence of one or more authentic exempt purposes of an organization will not be productive of tax exemption as a charitable entity—or, for that matter, any other type of nonprofit organization—if a substantial nonexempt purpose is present in its operations.[28]

The proper approach to be taken, therefore, when ascertaining whether a nonprofit organization qualifies as a tax-exempt entity, is to assume *arguendo* one or more exempt purposes and then endeavor to determine whether the organization has a commercial or other nonexempt purpose. On finding a nonexempt purpose, an inquiry should be made as to whether it is primary or incidental in relation to the exempt purposes. Then, if there is a nonexempt purpose that is substantial in nature, exemption would be precluded or revoked.[29]

This approach was adhered to by a court, in concluding that a policemen's benevolent association could not qualify for tax exemption as a charitable organization because the payment of retirement benefits to its members was a substantial nonexempt function.[30] This approach was again followed by the court in a case holding that a religious organization was ineligible for tax exemption because a substantial portion of its receipts was expended for the nonexempt function of medical care of its members.[31] The latter of these two decisions was reversed, however, with the appellate court holding that the medical aid plan was carried out in furtherance of the church's religious doctrines and therefore was in furtherance of an exempt purpose.[32]

Sports organizations can present this issue. For example, when an organization promotes, advances, and sponsors recreational and amateur sports, with a

---

[24] E.g., Aid to Artisans, Inc. v. Comm'r, 71 T.C. 202 (1978).

[25] Better Business Bureau of Washington, D.C. v. United States, 326 U.S. 279, 283 (1945).

[26] St. Louis Union Trust Co. v. United States, 374 F.2d 427, 431-432 (8th Cir. 1967).

[27] Rev. Rul. 77-366, 1977-2 C.B. 192.

[28] E.g., Stevens Bros. Found. v. Comm'r, 324 F.2d 633 (8th Cir. 1963), *cert. den.*, 376 U.S. 969 (1964); Scripture Press Found. v. United States, 285 F.2d 800 (Ct. Cl. 1961), *cert. den.*, 368 U.S. 985 (1962); Fides Publishers Ass'n v. United States, 263 F. Supp. 924 (N.D. Ind. 1967); Edgar v. Comm'r, 56 T.C. 717 (1971); The Media Sports League, Inc. v. Comm'r, 52 T.C.M. 1093 (1986).

[29] E.g., American Inst. for Economic Research, Inc. v. United States, 302 F.2d 934 (Ct. Cl. 1962); Pulpit Resource v. Comm'r, 70 T.C. 594 (1978).

[30] Policemen's Benevolent Ass'n of Westchester County, Inc. v. Comm'r, 42 T.C.M. 1750 (1981). It was because of this rationale that tax exemption for professional football leagues had to be created by statute (see § 2.14).

[31] Bethel Conservative Mennonite Church v. Comm'r, 80 T.C. 352 (1983).

[32] Bethel Conservative Mennonite Church v. Comm'r, 746 F.2d 388 (7th Cir. 1984)

significant emphasis on training and education, the organization can qualify as an exempt charitable and educational entity.[33] If, however, the principal purpose of the organization is the advancement of the social and recreational interests of the players, the organization cannot constitute that type of exempt organization.[34]

Likewise, an organization may not achieve public charity status as an operating educational institution[35] where it is engaged in both educational and non-educational activities (for example, a museum operating a school), unless the museum activities are incidental.[36] Thus, the IRS denied public charity status to an organization the primary function of which was not the presentation of formal instruction but the maintenance and operation of a museum.[37] The IRS denied recognition of exempt status to any organization seeking qualification as a social club,[38] in part because its primary purpose was to further "business arrangements" with its members.[39] An organization having religious broadcasting as its predominant activity was ruled by the IRS as ineligible to be a church.[40]

There is no formal definition of the term *insubstantial* in this setting. Thus, application of the primary purpose test entails an issue of fact to be determined under the facts and circumstances of each case.[41] A court opinion suggested that, where a function represents less than 10 percent of total efforts, the primary purpose test will not be applied to prevent exemption.[42] Another court opinion stated that an organization that received approximately one-third of its revenue from an unrelated business could not qualify for exempt status, in that the level of nonexempt activity "exceed[ed] the benchmark of insubstantiality."[43] Yet the IRS allowed a charitable organization to remain exempt where it derived two-thirds of its income from unrelated businesses, inasmuch as the net income from the businesses was used to further exempt purposes.[44]

The primary purpose test, therefore, is one of the principal means for determining whether a collective-type organization qualifies as a tax-exempt business league, constitutes another type of exempt organization, or is not exempt.

§ 2.4 BUSINESS LEAGUES IN GENERAL

The term *business league* is unclear and rather antiquated; at best, the word *league* suggests an association of persons united by common interests or for the achievement of common ends. Synonyms include *alliance, association, coalition, federation,* and *network;* from a historical standpoint, as noted, another synonym is *guild.*[45] Today, this word is usually associated with groupings of sports teams

---

[33] E.g., Hutchinson Baseball Enters., Inc. v. Comm'r, 73 T.C. 144 (1979), aff'd, 696 F.2d 757 (10th Cir. 1982).

[34] E.g., Wayne Baseball, Inc. v. Comm'r, 78 T.C.M. 437 (1999).

[35] See § 8.2(b).

[36] Reg. § 1.170A-9(b).

[37] Rev. Rul. 76-167, 1976-1 C.B. 329.

[38] See § 1.6(f).

[39] Priv. Ltr. Rul. 200450041.

[40] IRS Technical Advice Memorandum (Tech. Adv. Mem.) 200437040.

[41] E.g., Kentucky Bar Found. v. Comm'r, 78 T.C. 921 (1982).

[42] World Family Corp. v. Comm'r, 81 T.C. 958 (1983).

[43] Orange County Agric. Soc'y, Inc. v. Comm'r, 55 T.C.M. 1602, 1604 (1988), aff'd, 893 F.2d 647 (2d Cir. 1990).

[44] Tech. Adv. Mem. 200021056.

[45] See § 1.2.

(baseball, basketball, football, and hockey leagues) or less formal arrangements in the sport context (such as, a bowling league).

As the Supreme Court observed, the phrase *business league* "has no well-defined meaning or common usage outside the perimeters" of the federal tax law.[46] Another court wrote that these two words do not have a "special significance."[47] On another occasion, the Supreme Court said that *business league* is a term "so general . . . as to render an interpretive regulation appropriate."[48] The six components of the contemporary tax regulation defining business leagues are referenced next. Nonetheless, the word *association* endures as the term far more commonly employed when referencing a business league.[49]

(a) General Principles

A court held that a business league is an association of persons having some common business interest. It quickly added, nonetheless, that "[a]ll business leagues are not exempt."[50] Those that are tax-exempt have six discrete characteristics.

(i) Tax Law Characteristics.   A tax-exempt business league is an association of persons having some common business interest, the purpose of which is to promote that common interest and not to engage in a regular business of a kind ordinarily carried on for profit. Its activities must be directed to the improvement of business conditions of one or more lines of business, as distinguished from the performance of particular services for individual persons. An organization the purpose of which is to engage in a regular business of a kind ordinarily carried on for profit, even though the business is conducted on a cooperative basis or produces only sufficient income to be self-sustaining, cannot be an exempt business league.[51]

This definition of a tax-exempt business league, "[h]aving been left undisturbed despite numerous reenactments" of the exemption provision, "is deemed to have been given the imprimatur of Congress and is thus entitled to the effect of law."[52] A parsing of this definition shows that a business league, to be exempt, must be an association:

1.   Of persons having a common business interest;

2.   The purpose of which is to promote that common business interest;

3.   That is not organized for profit;

---

[46] Nat'l Muffler Dealers Ass'n, Inc. v. United States, 440 U.S. 472, 476 (1979).

[47] Retailers Credit Ass'n of Alameda County v. Comm'r, 90 F.2d 47, 50 (9th Cir. 1937).

[48] Helvering v. Reynolds Co., 306 U.S. 110, 114 (1939).

[49] A *trade association* was defined as a "nonprofit, cooperative, voluntarily-joined, organization of business competitors designed to assist its members and its industry in dealing with mutual business problems" (Judkins, *National Associations of the United States* vii (U.S. Dep't of Commerce 1949)).

[50] Retailers Credit Ass'n of Alameda County v. Comm'r, 90 F.2d 47, 50 (9th Cir. 1937).

[51] Reg. § 1.501(c)(6)-1.

[52] The Engineers Club of San Francisco v. United States, 791 F.2d 686, 689 (9th Cir. 1986). Also United States v. Oklahoma City Retailers Ass'n of Alameda County, 331 F.2d 328 (10th Cir. 1964).

4. That does not engage (other than incidentally) in a business ordinarily conducted for profit;[53]

5. The activities of which are directed to the improvement of business conditions of one or more lines of business, as distinguished from the performance of particular services for individual persons; and

6. Of the same general class as a chamber of commerce, board of trade, or the like.[54]

To be exempt as a business league, an organization must meet all six of these criteria. For example, an entity that satisfied only the first four of these elements was held to not be entitled to tax exemption as a business league.[55] If, however, an otherwise disqualifying activity is merely incidental or subordinate to an entity's principal purpose, exemption as a business league will not be defeated.[56]

Even though it is almost always essential to qualification as a tax-exempt business league that the organization be an association of persons having a common business interest, the persons do not necessarily have to be engaged in a business at the time they are acting in association. As an illustration of this point, an organization of persons studying for a degree in a particular profession can qualify as an exempt business league if the purpose of the organization is to promote their common business interests as future members of that profession.[57] Also, an exempt association will not jeopardize its business league status if it characterizes as nonvoting associate members persons who are merely sponsors of the organization and lack a common business interest with the regular members.[58]

(ii) Members. The typical exempt business league has a membership; this element is reflected in the preceding six-part definition that references an "association of persons." Usually this membership is comprised of individuals, for-profit businesses, or both. A tax-exempt business league may, however, have exempt organizations as members (although that fact can change the basis for the tax exemption[59]), even where there are only two entities as members. For example, the IRS held that a trust created by an exempt labor union and an exempt business league qualified as an exempt business league.[60] Likewise, a trust created pursuant to collective bargaining agreements between an exempt labor union and several exempt business leagues was ruled to be exempt as a business league.[61]

---

[53] Although the tax regulation is absolute on the point, it has been held that a business undertaken by a business league will not lead to revocation of its exemption if the activity is "merely incidental" to the organization's main purposes (e.g., Retailers Credit Ass'n v. Comm'r, 90 F.2d 47, 51 (9th Cir. 1937)).

[54] E.g., Credit Union Ins. Corp. v. United States, 896 F. Supp. 1166 (D. Md. 1995, aff'd, 86 F.3d 1326 (4th Cir. 1996)).

[55] The Engineers Club of San Francisco v. United States, 791 F.2d 686 (9th Cir. 1986).

[56] E.g., Comm'r v. Chicago Graphic Arts Fed'n, Inc., 128 F.2d 424 (7th Cir. 1942); Retailers Credit Ass'n of Alemeda County v. Comm'r, 90 F.2d 47 (9th Cir. 1937).

[57] Rev. Rul. 77-112, 1977-1 C.B. 149.

[58] In one instance, the requirement that there be an *association of persons* was deemed met solely because the organization was created by three incorporators and had a board of directors (North Carolina Ass'n of Ins. Agents, Inc. v. United States, 83-2 U.S.T.C. ¶ 9445 (E.D.N.C. 1983)), although that decision was reversed (739 F.2d 949 (4th Cir. 1984)).

[59] See § 1.6.

[60] Rev. Rul. 70-31, 1970-1 C.B. 130.

[61] Rev. Rul. 82-138, 1982-2 C.B. 106.

There can be situations, however, where an exempt business league does not have members. For example, an association of individuals that is exempt as a charitable organization and that wants a certification program should place the program in a separate entity, which would be a business league.[62] This type of business league can gain tax-exempt status, even though it lacks a membership. Of course, for this purpose, the membership of the association may be imputed to the business league.

(iii) Dues. Inherent in the concept of a membership organization is the expectation that the organization is supported primarily by dues, although this requirement is not among the formal elements of the definition of a business league. Nonetheless, the IRS has observed that an exempt business league must be "financed, at least in part, through membership dues." The agency, notwithstanding the absence of the point in the tax regulation, wrote that an organization "which is not in fact membership supported lacks the most significant characteristics common to" exempt business leagues. An organization that has "demonstrated a pattern of nonmembership support must necessarily fail a critical test of exemption" for business leagues, the IRS added.[63]

Nonetheless, the IRS considered the tax-exempt status of a membership organization, the primary activity of which was provision of the requisite certifications of origin, in the form of "clearing documents" for shipping purposes, to U.S. suppliers of goods and services to another country. The organization was the only entity in the United States authorized to certify commercial and legal documents related to transactions between the two countries. The certification fees provided more than 95 percent of the organization's total revenue. In this case, however, the IRS resolved the dues issue by concluding that the certification fees were received for an activity that contributed importantly to the accomplishment of the organization's exempt functions and that this income had a "substantial causal relationship to the achievement of exempt purposes."[64] The IRS then ruled that the certification fee income is "therefore considered to be membership support."[65]

An exempt business league is not required to promote the betterment of general commercial welfare.[66]

(b) Varieties of Exempt Business Leagues

Varieties of tax-exempt business leagues abound. Consider these:

- An organization that made recommendations concerning the establishment and revision of regulations and rates for its members who were regulated by a federal agency.[67]

---

[62] See §§ 1.3(c), 2.4(c).
[63] Priv. Ltr. Rul. 200020056.
[64] This is phraseology imported from the unrelated business context (see § 5.7).
[65] Priv. Ltr. Rul. 200020056.
[66] Rev. Rul. 59-391, 1959-2 C.B. 151.
[67] Rev. Rul. 67-393, 1967-2 C.B. 200.

- An organization that provided its member small loan companies with information concerning borrowers.[68]

- An organization composed of advertising agencies that verified the advertising claims of publications selling advertising space and made reports available to members of the advertising industry generally.[69]

- An organization composed of members of a particular industry formed to develop new and improved uses for existing products of the industry.[70]

- An organization formed to improve the business conditions of financial institutions by offering rewards for information leading to the arrest and conviction of individuals committing crimes against its members.[71]

- An organization that operated a "plan room" and published a news bulletin that contained information about plans available at the plan room, bid results, and activities of concern to persons in the industry.[72]

- An organization created pursuant to state statute to pay claims against (act as guarantor for) insolvent insurance companies, where the companies were mandatory members of the organization. [73]

- An organization of representatives of diversified businesses that owned or leased one or more digital computers produced by various manufacturers.[74]

- An organization, the members of which were involved in the commercial fishing industry in a state, that published a monthly newspaper of commercial fishing technical information and news and that derived its income primarily from membership dues and sales of advertising.[75]

- An association of insurance companies created pursuant to a state's no-fault insurance statute to provide personal injury protection for residents of the state who sustain injury and are not covered by any insurance. [76]

- An organization that collected contributions to further an industry's programs.[77]

---

[68] Rev. Rul. 67-394, 1967-2 C.B. 201.

[69] Rev. Rul. 69-387, 1969-2 C.B. 124.

[70] Rev. Rul. 69-632, 1969-2 C.B. 120.

[71] Rev. Rul. 69-634, 1969-2 C.B. 124.

[72] Rev. Rul. 72-211, 1972-1 C.B. 150, clarifying Rev. Rul. 56-65, 1956-1 C.B. 199. The IRS held that the organization was serving a "quasi-public function imposed by law which is directed at relieving a common cause of hardship and distress of broad public concern in the field of insurance protection." Also Builder's Exch. of Tex., Inc. v. Comm'r, 31 T.C.M. 844 (1972).

[73] Rev. Rul. 73-452, 1973-2 C.B. 183.

[74] Rev. Rul. 74-147, 1974-1 C.B. 136. The IRS found that the "primary objective of the organization is to provide a forum for the exchange of information which will lead to the more efficient utilization of computers by its members and other interested users, and thus improves the overall efficiency of the business operations of each."

[75] Rev. Rul. 75-287, 1975-2 C.B. 211.

[76] Rev. Rul. 76-410, 1976-2 C.B. 155. The IRS held that its activities "promote the common business interests of its members by fulfilling an obligation that the state has imposed upon the insurance industry as a prerequisite for doing business within the state and by enhancing the image of the industry."

[77] Priv. Ltr. Rul. 8422170.

- An organization that promoted convention and tourism business in a town.[78]

- An organization that effected improvement in public awareness of thoroughbred racing.[79]

A merger, consolidation, or other reorganization of business leagues can result in one or more exempt business leagues.[80]

(c) Certification Programs

As noted, some appropriate functions of an exempt business league are, when considered alone, charitable, educational, and/or scientific activities.[81] There can be a dispute, nonetheless, as to what the primary purpose[82] of a particular activity is, that is, for example, whether the primary purpose of an activity is charitable or otherwise, such as promotion of a common business interest. This dichotomy of view is amply apparent in connection with programs of exempt organizations that entail the certification of individuals.

Certification of individuals, product testing, and the like is a tax-exempt function for a business league. In a speech in 1973, the commissioner of Internal Revenue, analogizing to organizations that accredit television repairers and automobile mechanics, commented that organizations that accredit physicians in their fields of specialization will be classified as exempt business leagues rather than exempt charitable or educational organizations.[83] Thus, in the view of the IRS, enhancement of the medical profession, not delivery of adequate health care, is the primary objective of these organizations. These views of the agency were memorialized in a ruling published that year.[84]

Similarly, the IRS ruled that an organization formed by physicians who are members of a state medical society to operate peer review boards for the purpose of establishing and maintaining standards for quality, quantity, and reasonableness of the costs of medical services qualified as a tax-exempt business league.[85] The agency recognized that these organizations were established in response to concern over the rising costs of health care, in an effort to curtail these expenses by reviewing medical procedures and utilization of medical facilities. Nonetheless, ruled the IRS, "[a]lthough this activity may result in a measurable public benefit, its primary objective is to maintain the professional standards, prestige, and independence of the organized medical profession and thereby further the common business interest of the organization's members."[86] The promotion of health, however, is a charitable purpose,[87] and some courts are

---

[78] Priv. Ltr. Rul. 9032005.
[79] Priv. Ltr. Rul. 9050002.
[80] E.g., Priv. Ltr. Rul. 9003045.
[81] See § 2.3.
[82] See *Tax-Exempt Organizations* § 4.4.
[83] Speech on Aug. 29, 1973, before the American Society of Association Executives (IR-1326).
[84] Rev. Rul. 73-567, 1973-2 C.B. 178.
[85] Rev. Rul. 74-553, 1974-2 C.B. 168.
[86] *Id.* at 169.
[87] See *Tax-Exempt Organizations* § 6.3.

of the view that improvements in the delivery of health care is a charitable undertaking, even if the medical profession is somewhat benefited.[88]

§ 2.5 LEGISLATIVE AND REGULATORY HISTORY

The contemporary concept of the *business league* is rooted in its legislative and subsequent regulatory history.

(a) Legislative History

Tax exemption for business leagues has its genesis as part of the constitutionally permissible federal income tax system that was enacted into law in 1913.[89] The version of this legislation passed by the House of Representatives provided exemption for "labor, agricultural, or horticultural organizations." The Senate Finance Committee was importuned to amplify this phraseology to encompass nonprofit business entities. The Senate, and ultimately both houses of Congress, settled on the phrase *business league* as an addition to these categories of tax exemption. Nonetheless, the legislative history is silent as to the meaning of this term.[90]

The principal submission to the Senate Finance Committee in this regard was tendered by the Chamber of Commerce of the United States ("Chamber"). The Chamber's statement included:

> The commercial organization of the present day [association] is not organized for selfish purposes, and performs broad patriotic and civic functions. Indeed, it is one of the most potent forces in each community for the improvement of physical and social conditions. While its original reason for being is commercial advancement, it is not in the narrow sense of advantage to the individual, but in the broad sense of building up the trade and commerce of the community as a whole.[91]

The statement of the Chamber added:

> These organizations receive their income from dues . . . which business men pay that they may receive in common with all other members of their communities or of their industries the benefits of cooperative study of local development, of civic affairs, of industrial resources, and of local, national, and international trade.[92]

The Senate Finance Committee, while receptive to the Chamber's lobbying, rejected the Chamber's proposed language, which would have extended federal income tax exemption to all "commercial organizations not organized for profit." The term *business league* was utilized instead.

---

[88] E.g., San Antonio District Dental Soc'y v. United States, 340 F. Supp. 11 (W.D. Tex. 1972); Huron Clinic Found. v. United States, 212 F. Supp. 847 (S.D. 1962).

[89] Tariff Act of 1913, 38 Stat. 114.

[90] S. Rep. No. 80, 63rd Cong., 1st Sess. 25 (1913); H. Rep. No. 86 [conference report], 63rd Cong., 1st Sess. 26 (1913). At this time, tax exemption was also provided to chambers of commerce and boards of trade.

[91] "Briefs and Statements on H.R. 3321 Filed with the Senate Committee on Finance," 63rd Cong., 1st Sess. 2002 (1913). The word *commercial* had a much different connotation in 1913 than it does 90 years later (see § 5.2(b); *Tax-Exempt Organizations*, Chapter 25).

[92] "Briefs and Statements on H.R. 3321 Filed with the Senate Committee on Finance," 63rd Cong., 1st Sess. (2002) 2003 (1913).

(b) Regulatory History

The IRS first attempted a definition of the term *business league* in 1919, employing this regulation: "A business league is an association of persons having some common business interest, which limits its activities to work for such common interest and does not engage in a regular business of a kind ordinarily carried on for profit." The agency added: "Its work need not be similar to that of a chamber of commerce or board of trade."[93]

This language, however, proved to be too expansive, and the IRS soon began to narrow the scope of the definition. This effort was aided by invocation of the doctrine of *noscitur a sociis*, which means "it is known from its associates." That is, the meaning of a word is or may be known from the accompanying words.[94] More specifically, the doctrine means that general and specific words are associated with and take color from each other, restricting general words to a sense analogous to those that are less general.[95]

The first application of the doctrine in this context occurred in 1924, when tax exemption as a business league for a stock exchange was requested. The solicitor of Internal Revenue reasoned that, although a stock exchange conceivably could be embraced by the definition of *business league* or perhaps *board of trade*, it lacked the characteristics that a business league, chamber of commerce, and board of trade share in common and that form the basis for the exemption. Congress must have used these terms, the IRS reasoned, to "indicate organizations of the same general class, having for their primary purpose the promotion of business welfare." By contrast, the primary purpose of a stock exchange is to "afford facilities to a limited class of people for the transaction of their private interests."[96] Thereafter, the tax regulation was amended to exclude stock exchanges from treatment as exempt business leagues.[97]

Subsequently, a court applied this principle of statutory construction, denying exemption as a business league to a corporation organized by associations of insurance companies to provide printing services for member companies.[98] Thereafter, Congress amended the Internal Revenue Code to add tax exemption for real estate boards (but not stock exchanges).

The IRS then incorporated the doctrine of *noscitur a sociis* into the tax regulation. The sentence "Its work need not be similar to that of a chamber of commerce or board of trade" was deleted. Its replacement stated:

> It is an organization of the same general class as a chamber of commerce or board of trade. Thus, its activity should be directed to the improvement of business conditions or to the promotion of the general objects of one or more

---

[93] Reg. 45, Art. 518 (1919).

[94] Black's Law Dictionary.

[95] E.g., Dunham v. State, 192 So. 324, 325, 326 (Sup. Ct. Fl.). The doctrine has been applied by the Supreme Court on occasion (e.g., United States v. Leslie Salt Co., 350 U.S. 383 (1956)).

[96] L. O. 1121, III-1 C.B. 275, 280–281 (1924).

[97] T.D. 3746, IV-2 C.B. 77 (1925); Reg. 69, Art. 518 (1926). With the incorporation of the denial of exempt status to stock exchanges in the tax regulations, L.O. 1121, III-1 C.B. 275 (1924), was rendered obsolete (Rev. Rul. 68-207, 1968-1 C.B. 577).

[98] Uniform Printing & Supply Co. v. Comm'r, 9 B.T.A. 251 (1927), aff'd, 33 F.2d 445 (7th Cir. 1929), *cert. den.*, 280 U.S. 591 (1929).

lines of business as distinguished from the performance of particular services for individual persons.[99]

A court observed that, pursuant to this doctrine, a business league "to be exempt must possess the general characteristics of these other organizations [chambers of commerce and boards of trade] with which the statute groups it."[100] Another court thereafter wrote that the statute and regulations "so construed mean, therefore, that the purpose of the [exempt] league must be to promote [a] common interest, must be similar to those of a chamber of commerce or board of trade, and must not be to engage in a regular business of a kind ordinarily carried on for profit."[101]

Congress, in 1966, expanded this category of tax exempt organizations to include professional football leagues.[102] Nothing in the legislative history of that amendment, however, indicates that Congress objected to or endeavored to change the IRS's position as to the class of organizations included in this tax exemption provision. The then-chairman of the House Committee on Ways and Means stated, during debate on the amendment, that "no inference is intended by this change as to the application of section 501(c)(6) to other types of organizations."[103]

§ 2.6 DEFINITION OF *BUSINESS*

The term *business* is broadly construed and includes nearly every activity carried on for the production of income.[104] In this context, distinctions among trades, businesses, and professions are not, as such, observed. Thus, the fact that the membership of an organization is composed of individuals from professions does not preclude tax exemption as a business league, as long as the members all have a common business interest in a field.[105] The membership of an exempt business league may be individuals and/or other persons. Thus, an association of nonprofit consumer cooperatives that promoted the cooperative method of doing business was ruled to be an exempt business league,[106] as was an organization of individuals who advanced their spouses' profession.[107] The IRS concluded that an association that promoted a certain philosophy as to the conduct of business was an exempt business league, writing that "[u]pholding the integrity of a particular industry/profession is an activity properly engaged in by" exempt business leagues.[108]

Tax exemption as a business league has been denied for lack of a sufficient common business interest in situations involving an organization of individuals

---

[99] Reg. 74, Art. 528 (1929).
[100] Produce Exchange Stock Clearing Ass'n v. Helvering, 71 F.2d 142, 144 (2nd Cir. 1934).
[101] Retailers Credit Ass'n of Alameda County v. Comm'r, 90 F.2d 47, 50 (9th Cir. 1937) (internal quotation marks deleted).
[102] See § 2.14.
[103] 112 Cong. Rec. 28228 (1966).
[104] See § 5.2.
[105] Rev. Rul. 70-641, 1970-2 C.B. 119.
[106] Rev. Rul. 67-264, 1967-2 C.B. 196.
[107] Rev. Rul. 67-343, 1967-2 C.B. 198.
[108] Priv. Ltr. Rul. 200223067.

engaged in different trades or professions not in competition who exchanged business information.[109] Of course, if a group of persons are not engaged in a business at all—such as an association of motorists[110] and an association of dog owners most of whom were not in the business of raising dogs[111]—exemption in this context is not available. Thus, organizations that promote the common interests of hobbyists do not qualify as exempt business leagues.[112]

At a minimum, to qualify as an exempt business league, an organization must have some substantive program directed to the improvement of business conditions; for example, the mere provision of bar and luncheon facilities is insufficient.[113] Under certain circumstances, however, federal tax exemption may be available pursuant to another category of exemption.[114]

§ 2.7 LINE-OF-BUSINESS REQUIREMENT

The fundamental requirement for operation as a tax-exempt business league is that the organization engage in activities that are directed to the improvement of business conditions of one or more lines of business.

(a) Concept of *Line of Business*

A *line of business* is a trade, business (industry), or profession, or a segment of a trade, business, or profession. The IRS defines the phrase as a "trade or occupation, entry into which is not restricted by a patent, trademark, or similar device which would allow private parties to restrict the right to engage in the business."[115] A critical component of the *line of business* is that it is comprised of competitors within a trade, industry, or profession.[116]

A line of business may be thought of as, as noted, an entire industry (or trade or profession) or a segment (or slice) of an industry. This industry or slice thereof must be a horizontal classification, with no vertical limitation other than in terms of geography (such as a statewide association). While not every person (such as individuals or corporations) within the line of business must be a member of the business league, membership in the league must be available to all who are encompassed by the line of business. This horizontal line may be as narrowly drawn as the parties involved desire (within reason); the critical factor is that, once the organization has defined its membership criteria and thus defined the line of business, all who are eligible for membership and wish to be a member of the league must be admitted.

For example, a bar association is a tax-exempt business league. This type of entity can be national, regional, statewide, or local in scope. Thus, a lawyer may, simply by being a lawyer, be a member of at least four exempt bar associations

---

[109] Rev. Rul. 59-391, 1959-2 C.B. 151.
[110] American Automobile Ass'n v. Comm'r, 19 T.C. 1146 (1953).
[111] American Kennel Club v. Hoey, 148 F.2d 920 (2nd Cir. 1945).
[112] Rev. Rul. 66-179, 1966-1 C.B. 144.
[113] Rev. Rul. 70-244, 1970-1 C.B. 132.
[114] See § 1.6.
[115] IRS Exempt Organization Handbook (IRM 7751) § 652(1).
[116] See § 2.8.

(business leagues). Likewise, there may be an exempt association of lawyers where the line of business is more narrowly drawn, such as an association of litigators, antitrust lawyers, labor lawyers, or tax lawyers. As to the latter, for example, the line of business may be even more narrowly defined, such as an exempt association of tax lawyers whose primary practice is representing tax-exempt organizations, or (even more narrowly) lawyers who primarily represent exempt charitable organizations, or (even more narrowly), lawyers who primarily represent exempt private foundations. The line of business (industry slice) can therefore be rather thin but nonetheless valid as long as all who are eligible and wish to join are admitted to the league.

(b) Supreme Court Pronouncement

This line-of-business requirement was upheld by the Supreme Court as being consistent with the intent of Congress in granting tax exemption to business leagues. The occasion for the Court's review of the requirement was a case involving the exempt status of a trade organization of muffler dealers that confined its membership to dealers franchised by a particular company and that had as its principal activity bargaining with the company on behalf of its members. The Court held that the franchisees did not represent a line of business, in that their efforts did not benefit a sufficiently broad segment of the business community involved, as would the efforts of an organization functioning on behalf of the entire muffler dealer industry.[117]

The Court observed that "[m]ost trade associations fall within" one of two categories.[118] They either represent an "entire industry"[119] or "all components of an industry within a geographic area."[120] This characterization of the essence of tax-exempt associations was seen by the Court as "[t]rue to the representations made by the Chamber of Commerce, in its statement to the Senate [Finance Committee] in 1913,"[121] that benefits would be received "in common with all other members of their communities or of their industries."[122]

The Court wrote that, while the view of the IRS as to the necessity of the line-of-business requirement "perhaps is not the only possible one, it does bear a fair relationship to the language of the statute, it reflects the views of those who sought its enactment, and it matches the purpose they articulated."[123] Also, the agency "infrequently but consistently has interpreted [the definition] to exclude

---

[117] Nat'l Muffler Dealers Ass'n, Inc. v. United States, 440 U.S. 472 (1979), aff'g 565 F.2d 845 (2d Cir. 1977). The Supreme Court thus rejected the contrary view of the U.S. Court of Appeals for the Seventh Circuit, which held that an association composed solely of bottlers of a single brand of soft drink was an exempt business league (Pepsi-Cola Bottlers' Ass'n, Inc. v. United States, 369 F.2d 250 (7th Cir. 1966)).

[118] Nat'l Muffler Dealers Ass'n, Inc. v. United States, 440 U.S. 472, 483 (1979).

[119] Citing American Plywood Ass'n v. United States, 267 F. Supp. 830 (W.D. Wash. 1967); Nat'l Leather & Shoe Finders Ass'n v. Comm'r, 9 T.C. 121 (1947). The Court noted that the U.S. Court of Appeals for the Second Circuit earlier observed that an organization was not entitled to classification as an exempt business league because "[n]othing is done to advance the interests of the community or to improve the standards or conditions of a particular trade" (Produce Exchange Stock Clearing Ass'n v. Helvering, 71 F.2d 142,144 (2d Cir. 1934)).

[120] Citing Comm'r v. Chicago Graphic Arts Fed'n, Inc., 128 F.2d 424 (7th Cir. 1942); Crooks v. Kansas City Hay Dealers' Ass'n, 37 F. 83 (8th Cir. 1929); Washington State Apples, Inc. v. Comm'r, 46 B.T.A. 64 (1942).

[121] Nat'l Muffler Dealers Ass'n, Inc. v. United States, 440 U.S. 472, 482 (1979).

[122] See § 2.5(a)

[123] Nat'l Muffler Dealers Ass'n, Inc. v. United States, 440 U.S. 472, 484 (1979).

an organization . . . that is not industrywide" and therefore the IRS's view "merits serious deference."[124] The Court noted that the IRS "consistently has denied exemption to business groups whose membership and purposes are narrower,"[125] such as entities composed of businesses that market a single brand of automobile,[126] have licenses to a single patented product,[127] or bottle one type of soft drink.[128] The Court wrote that the IRS "has reasoned that these groups are not designed to better conditions in an entire industrial 'line,' but, instead, are devoted to the promotion of a particular product at the expense of others in the industry."[129]

Three arguments were presented to the Court as to why the line-of-business requirement should not be an essential element of the definition of an exempt business league, all of them predicated on the notion that the requirement unduly narrows the reach of the statute. One contention was that the Court need not defer to the content of the current tax regulation because it is not a contemporaneous construction of the statute and, moreover, is contrary to the regulation that was initially in force (1919–1929).[130] The Court, however, wrote that the change in 1929 "incorporated an interpretation thought necessary to match the statute's construction to the original congressional intent" and that the Court is "reluctant to adopt the rigid view that an agency may not alter its interpretation in light of administrative experience."[131]

The second argument, complementing the first one, was that the addition to the statute in 1966 of the reference to professional football leagues[132] made a new view of the doctrine of *noscitur a sociis* appropriate. This argument was rejected by the Court because nothing in the legislative history of this law expansion "indicates that Congress objected to or endeavored to change" the IRS's position in this regard and because, even if a different view of the doctrine were applied, the association in this case did not "share characteristics in common with a professional football league that would necessarily entitle it to exemption."[133]

The third argument was that, if this doctrine applies in this context, the Court should look beyond the range of the statutory definition of the term *business league* and take into account the fact that the bargaining function of the association in this case is comparable to that of a tax-exempt labor organization.[134] This contention had it that taxing an association like the one in this case (termed

---

[124] *Id.*

[125] *Id.* at 483.

[126] Rev. Rul. 67-77, 1967-1 C.B. 138.

[127] Rev. Rul. 58-294, 1958-1 C.B. 244.

[128] Rev. Rul. 68-182, 1968-1 C.B. 263 (announcing nonacquiescence in Pepsi-Cola Bottlers' Ass'n v. United States, 369 F.2d 250 (7th Cir. 1966)).

[129] Nat'l Muffler Dealers Ass'n, Inc. v. United States, 440 U.S. 472, 483-484 (1979), citing Rev. Rul. 76-400, 1976-2 C.B. 153, and Rev. Rul. 61-177, 1961-2 C.B. 117.

[130] See § 2.5(b).

[131] Nat'l Muffler Dealers Ass'n, Inc. v. United States, 440 U.S. 472, 485 (1979). This argument attracted the vote of three justices, who dissented from the majority opinion in part on the ground that the original regulation was "strong evidence of the understanding of the meaning of the law at the time it was enacted" (*id.* at 489).

[132] See § 2.14.

[133] Nat'l Muffler Dealers Ass'n, Inc. v. United States, 440 U.S. 472, 486-487 (1979).

[134] See § 1.6(c). The Court termed this exercise "searching for *socii*" beyond the confines of IRC § 501(c)(6) (Nat'l Muffler Dealers Ass'n, Inc. v. United States, 440 U.S. 472, 487 (1979)).

a *franchisee association*) "unreasonably will discourage joint action to improve shared business conditions and will yield only scant revenue to the Treasury."[135] The Court's rebuttal was that the association needed more than a "plausible policy argument" to prevail and that the "choice among reasonable interpretations" of the definition of a business league is for the IRS, not the courts.[136] The Court noted that the Senate Finance Committee, when drafting the law to include exemption for business leagues, rejected a broad proposal modeled on the exemption for labor organizations.[137]

"In sum," the Court concluded, the line-of-business requirement is "well grounded in the origin of [the statute] and in its enforcement over a long period of time" and the "distinction drawn here, that a tax exemption is not available to aid one group in competition with another within an industry, is but a particular manifestation of an established principle of tax [law] administration," which is that it is sufficient that the regulation implement congressional intent in "some reasonable manner."[138]

(c) Other Developments in Law

In the aftermath of the Supreme Court's opinion, the IRS ruled that tax exemption as a business league is not available for organizations that endeavor to improve business conditions in only "segments" of lines of business.[139] This development occurred when the agency, reviewing the status of an organization of users of a manufacturer's computers, formed to discuss computer use operational and technical problems (a computer users' group), ruled that the organization did not qualify as an exempt business league, in part because the organization helped provide a competitive advantage to the manufacturer and its customers.[140] This position of the IRS was endorsed by a federal district court, holding that a computer users' group did not constitute an exempt business league because it promoted a single manufacturer's computers, in that the group's activities "advance the interests of [the vendor] and fail to bestow a benefit upon either an entire industry or all components of an industry within a geographic area."[141] This decision was thereafter mirrored in another federal district court decision, finding a computer users' group to not be an exempt business league because the single manufacturer involved represented only a segment of the industry and because a group that "promotes a particular product at the expense of others in the industry necessarily fails the line of business requirement."[142] The second of these cases was affirmed, with the appellate court writing that the organization seeking exempt status was functioning as a "powerful marketing tool" for the computer manufacturer involved.[143]

---

[135] Nat'l Muffler Dealers Ass'n, Inc. v. United States, 440 U.S. 472, 488 (1979).
[136] *Id.*
[137] See § 2.5(a).
[138] Nat'l Muffler Dealers Ass'n, Inc. v. United States, 440 U.S. 472, 488 (1979).
[139] Rev. Rul. 83-164, 1983-2 C.B. 95.
[140] Another rationale is that this type of computer users' group is serving the private interests of its members (Rev. Rul. 74-116, 1974-1 C.B. 127).
[141] Nat'l Prime Users Group, Inc. v. United States, 667 F. Supp. 250 (D. Md. 1987).
[142] Guide Int'l Corp. v. United States, 90-1 U.S.T.C. ¶ 50,304 (N.D. Ill. 1990).
[143] Guide Int'l Corp. v. United States, 948 F.2d 360, 362 (7th Cir. 1991).

By contrast, an association was ruled by the IRS to be a tax-exempt business league where its diverse members own, rent, or lease computers of various manufacturers and its purpose is to facilitate their data processing; the primary objective of the organization was to provide a forum for the exchange of information that will lead to more efficient utilization of digital computers by its members.[144] Likewise, the IRS held that an organization formed by members of an industry that contracted with research organizations to develop new and improved uses for existing products was an exempt business league, in part because none of the organization's patents and trademarks was licensed to any member on an exclusive basis.[145]

§ 2.8 MEMBERSHIP SERVICES

As noted, nearly every exempt business league has a membership; the members pay dues in exchange for the services that the league provides.[146] Services provided by exempt business leagues, which promote a common business interest, typically are or include these activities:

- Conduct of annual conventions, educational seminars, and the like[147]

- Development and distribution of publications (e.g., journals and newsletters) of pertinence to the interests of an organization's members[148]

- Attempts to influence legislation germane to the members' common business interests[149]

- Presentation of information and opinions to government agencies

- Dissemination by other means of information (including advocacy) pertaining to the field involved

- Conduct of public relations and community relations programs

- Maintenance of a library

- Promotion of improved business standards and methods and uniform business practices[150]

- Holding of luncheon meetings for the purpose of discussing the problems of a particular industry[151]

- Conduct of an industry advertising program[152]

- Conduct of negotiations for members and nonmembers in an industry[153]

---

[144] Rev. Rul. 74-147, 1974-1 C.B. 136.
[145] Rev. Rul. 69-632, 1969-2 C.B. 120.
[146] See § 2.4(a).
[147] American Refractories Inst. v. Comm'r, 6 T.C.M. 1302 (1947); Atlanta Master Printers Club v. Comm'r, 1 T.C.M. 107 (1942). An organization gained exemption by advocating the open shop principle (Associated Indus. of Cleveland v. Comm'r, 7 T.C. 1449 (1946)).
[148] E.g., Nat'l Leather & Shoe Finders Ass'n v. Comm'r, 9 T.C. 121 (1947).
[149] Rev. Rul. 61-177, 1961-2 C.B. 117.
[150] Rev. Rul. 68-657, 1968-2 C.B. 218.
[151] Rev. Rul. 67-295, 1967-2 C.B. 197.
[152] Rev. Rul. 67-344, 1967-2 C.B. 199.
[153] American Fishermen's Tuna Boat Ass'n v. Rogan, 51 F. Supp. 933 (S.D. Cal. 1943).

- Sponsorship of other events, such as forums, sports tournaments, and holiday parties[154]
- Mediation and settlement of disputes affecting an industry[155]
- Operation of a bid registry[156]
- Investigation of criminal aspects of claims against members[157]
- Initiation and subsidization of litigation[158]
- Operation of an insurance rating bureau[159]
- Negotiation of the sale of broadcast rights[160]
- Conduct of fire patrols and salvage operations for insurance companies[161]
- Provision for equitable distribution of high-risk insurance policies among member insurance companies[162]
- Provision of credit information[163]
- Engage in research activities[164]
- Conduct of a trade show[165]
- Provision of certification programs[166]

In other instances, the IRS ruled that an organization formed to promote the acceptance of women in business and the professions was an exempt business league because it attempted to seek to improve conditions in one or more lines of business,[167] as was an organization formed to attract conventions to a city for the benefit of the economic interest of business throughout the community.[168]

§ 2.9 PROFESSIONAL ORGANIZATIONS

Some nonprofit membership organizations operate for the benefit of members of a profession rather than a trade or business. These entities are often known as

---

[154] Priv. Ltr. Rul. 9550001.

[155] Rev. Rul. 65-164, 1965-1 C.B. 238.

[156] Rev. Rul. 66-223, 1966-2 C.B. 224.

[157] Rev. Rul. 66-260, 1966-2 C.B. 225.

[158] Rev. Rul. 67-175, 1967-1 C.B. 139.

[159] Oregon Casualty Ass'n v. Comm'r, 37 B.T.A. 340 (1938).

[160] Priv. Ltr. Rul. 7922001.

[161] Minneapolis Bd. of Fire Underwriters v. Comm'r, 38 B.T.A. 1532 (1938).

[162] Rev. Rul. 71-155, 1971-1 C.B. 152.

[163] Oklahoma City Retailers Ass'n v. United States, 331 F.2d 328 (10th Cir. 1964); Rev. Rul. 70-591, 1970-2 C.B. 118; Rev. Rul. 68-265, 1968-1 C.B. 265.

[164] Rev. Rul. 69-106, 1969-1 C.B. 153; Glass Container Indus. Research Corp. v. United States, 70-1 U.S.T.C. ¶ 9214 (W.D. Pa. 1970).

[165] E.g., Texas Mobile Home Ass'n v. Comm'r, 324 F.2d 691 (5th Cir. 1963); American Woodworking Mach. & Equip. Show v. United States, 249 F. Supp. 392 (M.D. N.C. 1966); Nat'l Ass'n of Display Indus. v. United States, 64-1 U.S.T.C. ¶ 9285 (S.D. N.Y. 1964); American Inst. of Interior Designers v. United States, 204 F. Supp. 201 (N.D. Cal. 1962); Orange County Builders Ass'n, Inc. v. United States, 65-2 U.S.T.C. ¶ 9679 (S.D. Cal. 1956); Men's & Boys' Apparel Club of Fla. v. United States, 64-2 U.S.T.C. ¶ 9840 (Ct. Cl. 1964); Rev. Rul. 67-219, 1967-1 C.B. 212; Rev. Rul. 58-224, 1958-1 C.B. 242. See § 5.9(n).

[166] See §§ 1.3(c), 2.4(c).

[167] Rev. Rul. 76-400, 1976-2 C.B. 153.

[168] Rev. Rul. 76-207, 1976-1 C.B. 158.

professional societies. This can cause tax exemption classification tensions, inasmuch as there may be controversy as to whether the organization is properly cast as an exempt business league or an exempt charitable, educational, scientific, or like organization.

In many instances, a professional society will have as the basis for its tax exemption classification as a business league. For example, the IRS presumes that bar associations, medical societies, accounting institutes, and similar organizations are business leagues, notwithstanding their conduct of activities that are charitable, educational, scientific, and the like. The IRS applies the primary purpose test,[169] usually concluding that these organizations' activities, considered in the aggregate, are directed primarily at the promotion of the interests of members of the profession involved and thus that the entities are operated to further the common business purpose of their members.[170]

A tax-exempt medical society may engage in these charitable and educational activities: meetings where technical papers are presented, maintenance of a library, publication of a journal, provision of lectures and counseling services at medical schools, and support of public health programs. An exempt medical society may also convene an annual conference where members discuss practice issues, publish a membership journal and/or newsletter, provide a patient referral service, operate a grievance committee, conduct meetings concerned with the administration and enhancement of the practice of medicine, attempt to influence legislation, utilize an ethics committee, and conduct a public relations program. Where the latter category of activities predominates, the organization is deemed to have the essential characteristics and purposes of an exempt business league.[171]

A tax-exempt bar association may engage in charitable and educational activities, such as law institutes, moot court programs, speakers' bureaus, and provision of legal assistance to indigents. The bar association may also convene an annual membership conference, publish a membership journal and or/newsletter, publish studies on the economics of law office administration, conduct programs on enhancement of law practice profitability, and enforce standards of members' conduct.[172] Again, where the latter activities are primary, the organization is considered to have the purposes of and classification as an exempt business league. Some courts have implied, however, that bar associations may qualify as exempt charitable organizations.[173] Notably, a court held that the maintenance of "public confidence in the legal system" is a "goal of unquestionable importance in a civil and complex society" and that activities such as the operation of a client security fund, an inquiry tribunal, a fee arbitration plan, and a lawyer referral service are "devoted to that goal through various means of improving the administration of justice."[174]

---

[169] See § 1.4.

[170] It is because of this tax law outcome that many associations transfer their educational and similar functions to a separate organization (see Chapter 8).

[171] Rev. Rul. 71-504, 1971-2 C.B. 231. Also, Rev. Rul. 77-232, 1977-2 C.B. 71.

[172] Rev. Rul. 71-505, 1971-2 C.B. 232. Also Hammerstein v. Kelly, 349 F.2d 928 (8th Cir. 1965); Colonial Trust Co. v. Comm'r, 19 B.T.A. 174.

[173] St. Louis Union Trust Co. v. United States, 374 F.2d 427 (8th Cir. 1967); Dulles v. Johnson, 273 F.2d 362 (2d Cir. 1959); Rhode Island Hosp. Trust Co. v. United States, 159 F. Supp. 204 (D.R.I. 1958).

[174] Kentucky Bar Found., Inc. v. Comm'r, 78 T.C. 921 (1982). Also Fraternal Med. Specialist Sev., Inc. v. Comm'r, 59 T.C.M. 289 (1984).

If a professional society's dominant activities are noncommercial research, maintenance of a library, publication of a journal, and the like, it may qualify for tax exemption as being charitable, educational, scientific, or the like, as long as no substantial activities are directed at or are concerned with the protection or promotion of the professional practice or business interests of its membership.[175] A professional society, then, may fail to qualify as an exempt charitable organization and will be considered an exempt business league (or perhaps still another type of exempt entity) where it, other than incidentally, engages in public relations activities, polices a profession, seeks to improve the conditions of its members, seeks to develop goodwill or fellowship among its members, engages in social and recreational activities, maintains facilities (such as a restaurant, lounge, or club house) for its members, or engages in advocacy activities.[176] In one instance, an organization of individuals from various public health and welfare professions (seemingly charitable in nature) was ruled by the IRS to be an exempt business league, inasmuch as its activities "promote the business and professional interests of the members by increasing the effectiveness of the interaction among the various professions, by developing greater efficiency in the professions, and by solving problems common to the professions."[177] It is the position of the agency that activities such as the operation of certification programs and the maintenance of a code of ethics for members are suitable programs for professional organizations that are business leagues but not for professional organizations that are charitable, educational, scientific, and like organizations, because these programs are designed and operated to achieve professional standing for the line of business represented by the profession and to enhance the respectability of those who are certified.[178]

§ 2.10 DISQUALIFYING ACTIVITIES

There are four principal bases pursuant to which tax-exempt status may be denied an organization that otherwise qualifies as an exempt business league.

(a) Line-of-Business Requirement

One basis for nonqualification as a tax-exempt business league is a finding that the organization failed to satisfy the line-of-business requirement.[179]

(b) For-Profit Business Activities

As noted, one of the fundamental elements of the definition of an exempt business league is that it may not engage (other than incidentally) in a regular business of a kind ordinarily carried on for profit.[180]

---

[175] Rev. Rul. 71-506, 1971-2 C.B. 233.
[176] If advocacy activities are political campaign activities, even an incidental amount of these functions would preclude exempt status as a charitable (IRC § 501(c)(3)) organization.
[177] Rev. Rul. 70-641, 1970-2 C.B. 119.
[178] Gen. Couns. Mem. 39721.
[179] See § 2.7.
[180] See § 2.4(a).

(i) General Rule. One of the hallmarks of a for-profit business is that it is operated to generate profits for its owners.[181] Thus, an organization that issued shares of stock carrying the right to dividends was denied exemption as a business league.[182] Also, an association of insurance companies that provided medical malpractice insurance to physicians, nurses, hospitals, and other health care providers in a particular state, where that type of insurance was not available from for-profit insurers, was denied classification as an exempt business league on the ground that the provision of medical malpractice insurance is a business of a kind ordinarily carried on for profit.[183] Similarly, an association of insurance companies that accepted for reinsurance high-risk customers who would ordinarily be declined for coverage by the member companies was ruled to not qualify as an exempt business league, inasmuch as reinsurance is a business ordinarily carried on by commercial insurance companies.[184]

In one instance, a court held that an organization did not qualify as a tax-exempt business league because it engaged in a regular business of a kind ordinarily carried on for profit.[185] The court found that the organization was engaging in an insurance business to a substantial extent (measured in terms of time and finances), as its officers and employees were involved on a daily basis with record keeping, processing claims for benefits, paying claims, and performing other administrative duties in connection with the insurance activities. The court distinguished this insurance activity from that conducted by associations only on a passive basis (that is, mere sponsorship of the insurance program) and where a self-insurance program was not involved.[186]

A court concluded that a nonprofit organization that itself functioned as an insurance agent was a tax-exempt business league. The organization's sole client was a state, which it served in the purchase of all insurance and bonding coverage required by the state and its agencies. The court held that the organization functioned on behalf of agents in the state in that its competent handling of the state's insurance needs enhanced the image of the insurance industry from the standpoint of the public.[187] On appeal, however, it was held that the organization was not an exempt business league because it conducted a business of a kind ordinarily carried on for profit and did so more than incidentally.[188]

(ii) Incidental Business Activity. Notwithstanding the general rule, if the for-profit business activity is merely incidental to the organization's overall activities, the organization can be an exempt business league. Instead, the business activity is treated as one or more unrelated businesses.[189]

---

[181] See § 3.1.
[182] Northwestern Jobbers Credit Bur. v. Comm'r, 37 F.2d 83 (8th Cir. 1930). Cf. Crooks v. Kansas City Hay Dealers Ass'n, 37 F.2d 83 (8th Cir. 1929).
[183] Rev. Rul. 81-174, 1981-1 C.B. 335.
[184] Rev. Rul. 81-175, 1981-1 C.B. 337.
[185] Associated Master Barbers & Beauticians of America, Inc. v. Comm'r, 69 T.C. 53 (1977).
[186] Oklahoma Cattlemen's Ass'n, Inc. v. United States, 310 F. Supp. 320 (W.D. Okla. 1969); San Antonio District Dental Soc'y v. United States, 340 F. Supp. 11 (W.D. Tex. 1972).
[187] North Carolina Ass'n of Ins. Agents, Inc. v. United States, 83-2 U.S.T.C. ¶ 9445 (E.D. N.C. 1983).
[188] North Carolina Ass'n of Ins. Agents, Inc. v. United States, 739 F.2d 949 (4th Cir. 1984).
[189] See Chapter 5.

(c) Performance of Particular Services

As noted, an exempt business league may not (other than incidentally) perform particular services for individual persons.[190] This aspect of the law is the most developed of the bases for nonqualification of an organization as an exempt business league. Usually, for this purpose, these *individual persons* are, or are among, the organization's membership. Rather, an exempt business league is expected to function to improve business conditions in the trade, business, or profession involved.[191]

(i) Particular Services. The term *particular services* has not been accorded much attention. The term generally means services that are provided to an organization's membership that are either in addition to those that are exempt functions funded by dues (particularly where there is separate payment for them) or that provide what is sometimes termed a *convenience or economy* in connection with operation of members' businesses.

In one instance, an association of life insurance companies that operated an insurance underwriting information exchange among its members was ruled by a court to not qualify as a tax-exempt business league, despite its contention that its primary purpose was to benefit the entire life insurance industry by deterring fraud in the application process and that any benefits to its members were incidental.[192] The court agreed that the organization's activities advanced the members' interests generally but concluded that the member companies were also provided "particular services."[193] It was held that a major factor in determining whether services are *particular* is whether they are supported by fees and assessments in approximate proportion to the benefits received.

A court, in addressing this issue, concluded that an activity of a tax-exempt business league was an exempt function where the activity benefited its membership as a group, rather than the members in their individual capacities.[194] The benefit to the group occurred where the business league provided a product or service to its members (such as seminars and attempts to influence legislation) for a fee, with the benefit not directly proportional to the fees. This court wrote that "[s]ervices which render benefits according to the fee that is paid for them are taxable business activities, not tax exempt services."[195] The court continued: "Therefore, the activities that serve the interests of individual . . . [members] according to what they pay produce individual benefits insufficient to fulfill the substantial relationship test, since those activities generally do not generate inherent group benefits that inure to the advantage of its members as members."[196]

---

[190] See § 2.4(a).

[191] Southern Hardware Traffic Ass'n v. United States, 283 F. Supp. 1013 (W.D. Tenn. 1968), *aff'd*, 411 F.2d 563 (6th Cir. 1969).

[192] MIB, Inc. v. Comm'r, 734 F.2d 71 (1st Cir. 1984).

[193] *Id.* at 78–81.

[194] Professional Ins. Agents of Mich. v. Comm'r, 726 F.2d 1097 (6th Cir. 1984).

[195] *Id.* at 1104.

[196] *Id.*

Subsequently, the IRS grappled with these distinctions, differing between an "industry-wide benefit or a particular service to members." The agency held that activities that provide a benefit across an industry "usually possess certain characteristics," such as being an "activity for which individual members could not be expected to bear the expense and thus lends itself to cooperative effort" and that the benefits are "intangible and only indirectly related to the individual business."[197] Activities constituting particular services "can usually be characterized as either a 'means of bringing buyers and sellers together' or a 'convenience or economy' to members in conducting their business," added the IRS, which also cautioned that "[f]ull participation by industry components does not guarantee that the activity provides an industry-wide benefit."[198] Consequently, for example, the agency held that the operation, by an exempt association of members in the trucking industry, of an alcohol and drug testing program for members and nonmembers was a particular service for individual persons (as opposed to an incident of membership), notwithstanding the fact that the prevention of alcohol and drug abuse is a "legitimate goal" of trucking companies.[199]

It is frequently difficult in a specific instance to distinguish between the performance of particular services and activities directed to the improvement of business conditions. Perhaps the best illustration of this difficulty was the case of organizations that maintain a "plan room." In one case, an organization of contractors operated a plan room, containing information about plans available, bid results, and other activities of concern to persons in the industry. The IRS ruled that the organization was a tax-exempt business league because its activities improved the business conditions of the line of business served, inasmuch as it made the information on construction projects freely available to the construction industry in its entirety. Clearly, the existence of this type of a facility is a significant convenience or economy for the member contractors. The IRS, however, dismissed this aspect of the facts, on the ground that the information on file at the plan room generally duplicated the information already available to the organization's members.[200]

(ii) General Rule. Courts have, on several occasions, applied the rule that an organization cannot be an exempt business league if it provides particular services to individual persons. In one instance, an organization that operated a cold storage warehouse for its members on a cooperative basis was denied exemption as a business league because the organization's primary activities were found to constitute the performance of particular services for individual persons.[201] The court concluded that, even though the organization was not organized for profit and did not violate the private inurement doctrine, this combination of its members—done in order to save money—was not an appropriate function of an exempt business league.

---

[197] Priv. Ltr. Rul. 8524006.
[198] *Id.*
[199] Tech. Adv. Mem. 9550001.
[200] Rev. Rul. 72-211, 1972-1 C.B. 150, *clar.* Rev. Rul. 56-65, 1956-1 C.B. 199.
[201] Growers Cold Storage Warehouse Co. v. Comm'r, 17 B.T.A. 1279 (1929).

A stock clearing association was denied exemption as a business league where its purpose was to provide a business economy or convenience for individual traders.[202] Noting that serving as a convenience to members is not a characteristic of entities seeking recognition of exemption as a business league, the court stated that it could not find a reason to exempt an association that serves each member as a convenience or economy in the member's business.

Tax exemption as a business league was denied an organization formed to facilitate the purchase of supplies and equipment for, and to supply management services to, its members.[203] This court found that the organization did not appear to answer the description of an exempt business league. The association performed particular services for individual persons, as evidenced by activities that included the furnishing of credit information, the supplying of an apartment shopping service, and the making of arrangements for direct purchases by members at discount.

A court held that a real estate board, the primary purpose and activity of which was the operation of a multiple listing service for its members, did not qualify for this exemption.[204] It was stated that where this type of a service is "operated primarily for individual members as a convenience and economy in the conduct of their respective businesses, rather than for the improvement of business conditions within the [industry] generally . . . , the operation is not an activity warranting an exemption under the statute."[205]

An organization formed to facilitate the purchase of supplies and equipment, and to provide management services, for its membership was found to not be tax-exempt.[206] It was held by a court that the high percentage of income obtained by the organization from performing particular services for individuals as a convenience and economy in their business, along with its other income-producing activities, and the amount of time devoted by employees of the organization to the performance of these services was sufficiently substantial so that the income-producing activities could not be said to be merely incidental activities of the organization. In arriving at this conclusion, the court looked at the amount of time devoted to these activities by the organization's employees as compared with the time expended on activities for the members' common benefit.[207]

Another case involved a business league formed to promote the common business interest of its members by advancing the credit union movement. The organization endorsed and provided administrative services in connection with insurance, data processing, and debt collection for its member credit unions. According to the court involved, it is the "distinctiveness of the activity that cements the substantial relationship" between the activity and the exempt function.[208] The types of services provided to the organization's members, however,

---

[202] Produce Exchange Stock Clearing Ass'n v. Helvering, 71 F.2d 142 (2nd Cir. 1934).

[203] Apartment Operators Ass'n v. Comm'r, 136 F.2d 435 (9th Cir. 1943).

[204] Evanston-North Shore Board of Realtors v. United States, 320 F.2d 375 (Ct. Cl. 1963), *cert. den.*, 376 U.S. 931 (1964).

[205] *Id.*, 320 F.2d at 378.

[206] Indiana Retail Hardware Ass'n, Inc. v. United States, 366 F.2d 998 (Ct. Cl. 1966).

[207] Essentially the same result occurred in Uniform Printing & Supply Co. v. Comm'r, 33 F.2d 445 (7th Cir. 1929), *cert. den.*, 280 U.S. 69 (1929).

[208] Louisiana Credit Union League v. United States, 693 F.2d 525, 535 (5th Cir. 1982).

were not unique but rather were commercially available. Moreover, all of the services involved individual instead of group benefits because the benefits accrued only to the members who chose the services. Because they were neither unique in character nor inherently group-oriented, the services provided to the members were held to not be substantially related to the organization's exempt purposes.

In denying tax exemption as a business league to an organization, the activities of which consisted of providing particular services to its members in the form of transmittal of information that would be used in decisions affecting their business operations, a court held that the ultimate inquiry was whether the association's activities advanced the members' interests generally by virtue of their membership in the industry or whether they assist members in the pursuit of their individual businesses.[209] The fact that there may have been indirect and intangible benefits for the industry as a whole was held to not change the fact that the organization's services were in form and substance particular services for the members. The court reasoned that, without the exchange, members would themselves have to check insurance applications for their accuracy. It concluded that this organization performed particular services for individual persons, rather than for its members collectively, and thus was not exempt from income tax as a business league. The organization was distinguished from "classical" business leagues, namely entities that chiefly perform services for their members collectively rather than perform specific services for their members.[210]

In another instance, a court held that an organization did not qualify as a tax-exempt business league because its activities were directed to the performance of particular services for individual members.[211] The court observed that the organization offered its members, in addition to the many insurance programs, an eyeglass and prescription lens replacement service, and sold its local chapters and members various supplies, charts, books, shop emblems, and association jewelry. This court concluded that the organization was undertaking activities that "serve as a convenience or economy to . . . [its] members in the operation of their businesses" and was not promoting a common business interest or otherwise comporting itself like an exempt business league.[212]

In other court decisions, the performance of particular services for individual persons was found (and thus the organizations were denied tax-exemption as a business league) in instances of operation of a laundry and dry cleaning plant,[213] performance of services in connection with bond investments,[214] appraisal of properties,[215] promotion of the exchange of orders by wire,[216] estimation of quantities of building materials for an organization's members'

---

[209] MIB, Inc. v. Comm'r, 734 F.2d 71 (1st Cir. 1984).

[210] Id. at 78.

[211] Associated Master Barbers & Beauticians of America, Inc. v. Comm'r, 69 T.C. 53 (1977).

[212] Id. at 70.

[213] A-1 Dry Cleaners & Dyers Co. v. Comm'r, 14 B.T.A. 1314 (1929).

[214] Northwestern Mun. Ass'n, Inc. v. United States, 99 F.2d 460 (8th Cir. 1938).

[215] Central Appraisal Bur. v. Comm'r, 46 B.T.A. 1281 (1942).

[216] Florists' Telegraph Delivery Ass'n v. Comm'r, 47 B.T.A. 1044 (1942).

projects,[217] and the provision of food and beverage service by an engineering society to its members.[218]

The IRS likewise has not, over the decades, been reticent in applying this principle of law, holding that organizations were providing services to individual persons and thus denying tax exemption as a business league in these instances:

- An organization acting as a receiver and trustee for a fee.[219]

- An organization operating commodity and stock exchanges.[220]

- An organization, the principal activity of which consisted of furnishing particular information and specialized individual service to its individual members, through publications and other means to effect economies in the operation of their businesses.[221]

- An organization promoting and selling national advertising in members' publications.[222]

- An organization promoting its members' writings.[223]

- An organization operating a multiple listing service.[224]

- A nurses' registry. It was denied categorization as an exempt business league on the basis of a finding that it was no more than an employment service for the benefit of its members.[225]

- An organization conducting a trading stamp program.[226]

- An organization that provided its members with an economy and convenience in the conduct of their individual businesses by enabling them to secure supplies, equipment, and services at less cost than if they had to secure them on an individual basis.[227]

- An organization ensuring the discharge of an organization's members' obligations to pay taxes.[228]

- An organization maintaining a library for its members' use.[229]

- An organization providing services to members and nonmembers, principally operating a traffic bureau, which resulted in savings and simplified operations.[230]

---

[217] General Contractors Ass'n v. United States, 202 F.2d 633 (7th Cir. 1953).
[218] The Engineers Club of San Francisco v. United States, 791 F.2d 686 (9th Cir. 1986).
[219] O.D. 786, 4 C.B. 269 (1921).
[220] Reg. § 501(c)(6)-1. Cf. 55-715, 1955-2 C.B. 263.
[221] Rev. Rul. 56-65, 1956-1 C.B. 199.
[222] Rev. Rul. 56-84, 1956-1 C.B. 201.
[223] Rev. Rul. 57-453, 1957-2 C.B. 310.
[224] Rev. Rul. 59-234, 1959-2 C.B. 149.
[225] Rev. Rul. 61-170, 1961-2 C.B. 112.
[226] Rev. Rul. 65-244, 1965-2 C.B. 167.
[227] Rev. Rul. 66-338, 1966-2 C.B. 226.
[228] Rev. Rul. 66-354, 1966-2 C.B. 207.
[229] Rev. Rul. 67-182, 1967-1 C.B. 141.
[230] Rev. Rul. 68-264, 1968-1 C.B. 264.

- An organization, the principal activity of which was to provide its members with group workers' compensation insurance that was underwritten by a private insurance company. In carrying out this activity, the organization relieved its members of the burden of having to obtain insurance on an individual basis, resulting in a convenience in the conduct of their businesses.[231]

- An organization appointing travel agents to sell passage on members' ships.[232]

- A telephone answering service for tow truck operators, on the ground that it provided its members with economy and convenience in the conduct of their individual businesses.[233]

- An organization making interest-free loans to member credit unions.[234]

- An organization publishing and distributing a directory of an organization's members to businesses likely to require the members' services.[235]

- An independent practice association that provided health services through written agreements with health maintenance organizations (HMOs). Membership in the association was limited to licensed physicians engaged in the active practice of medicine and who were members of a county medical society. All members were required to enter into written service contracts that required (1) members to provide their services to the HMOs' patients in accordance with a compensation agreement negotiated between the association and the HMOs; (2) members to share medical and other records, equipment, and staff; and (3) members to limit referrals of HMOs' patients, to the extent feasible, to other participating members. The IRS concluded that the principal functions of the association was to provide an available pool of physicians who would abide by its fee schedule when rendering medical services to the subscribers of an HMO and to provide its members with access to a large group of patients who generally may not be referred to nonmember physicians. The IRS portrayed this organization as one that was akin to a billing and collection service, and a collective bargaining representative negotiating on behalf of its member physicians with HMOs. Additionally, the IRS stated that the association did not provide medical care to HMO patients that would not have been available but for the establishment of the association, nor did it provide such care at fees below what was customarily and reasonably charged by the members in their private practices.[236]

- An organization administering a welfare benefit plan pursuant to a collective bargaining agreement.[237]

---

[231] Rev. Rul. 74-81, 1974-1 C.B. 135.
[232] Rev. Rul. 74-228, 1974-1 C.B. 136.
[233] Rev. Rul. 74-308, 1974-2 C.B. 168.
[234] Rev. Rul. 76-38, 1976-1 C.B. 157.
[235] Rev. Rul. 76-409, 1976-2 C.B. 154.
[236] Rev. Rul. 86-98, 1986-2 C.B. 74.
[237] Gen. Couns. Mem. 39411 (revoking Gen. Couns. Mem. 38458).

- A network of physicians that entered into contracts with self-insured employers for the provision of health care benefits, with the major goal of minimizing administrative costs. The IRS ruled that this organization engaged in activities that provide a "convenience through an economy of scale" and relieved its member physicians of "having to conduct certain aspects of their businesses on their own." These services included the marketing of physicians' practices, negotiating the terms of their service contracts, referrals to other physicians, and facilitating physician contracts with patients that might not otherwise be available to them.[238]

The IRS held that a lawyer referral service was a tax-exempt business league, since (because of the manner in which it was operated) it was more than a mere business referral service and served to improve the image and functioning of the legal profession in general.[239]

The IRS denied tax exemption as a business league in the case of two types of associations of insurance companies because they were performing particular services for their members.[240] In one of these instances, an association of insurance companies in a state that provided medical malpractice insurance to health care providers where the insurance was not available from for-profit insurers in the state was held to be performing particular services for its member companies and policyholders because its "method of operation involves it in its member companies' insurance business, and since the organization's insurance activities serve as an economy or convenience in providing necessary protection to its policyholders engaged in providing health care."[241] This rationale was applied to the activities of an association of insurance companies that accepted for reinsurance high-risk customers who would ordinarily be declined for coverage by its member companies.[242] An association of insurance companies that assigns applications for insurance to member companies that perform the actual insurance functions can, however, qualify as an exempt business league inasmuch as it does not assume the risk on the policies.[243]

Under limited circumstances, a business league can—and be tax-exempt—operate a "warranty or guarantee" program, which is a program designed to assure purchasers of a product that it meets acceptable standards and to provide insurance and arbitration services, on the ground that it is providing services for the common benefit of its membership. These circumstances are that the program must primarily benefit the industry in its entirety rather than the private interests of its members, the advertisements do not have the purpose of giving members a competitive advantage over nonmembers (where the membership does not encompass an entire industry), and the activity is not ordinarily carried on for profit; also, the IRS favors an enforced policy of a business league of

---

[238] Priv. Ltr. Rul. 200522022.
[239] Rev. Rul. 80-287, 1980-2 C.B. 185.
[240] In these instances, the IRS also concluded that the associations were engaged in a business of a kind ordinarily carried on for profit (see § 2.10(b)).
[241] Rev. Rul. 81-174, 1981-1 C.B. 335.
[242] Rev. Rul. 81-175, 1981-1 C.B. 337.
[243] Rev. Rul. 71-155, 1971-1 C.B. 152.

obtaining reimbursement from the members responsible for defects.[244] The IRS, however, is likely to conclude that unwarranted private benefits are being conferred to an organization's members in this setting where only a small portion of the eligible sellers participate in the program.[245]

(iii) Particular Services Outside Membership. In most instances, the *individual persons* in this context are, or are among, the entity's membership. Occasionally, however, the *particular services* are provided not only to an organization's members, but also to others. For example, in an instance of a physicians' network that was denied exempt status as a business league, particular services were provided, in addition to the member physicians, to employers and an insurance company.[246]

(iv) Unrelated Business Activities. Despite an express prohibition as stated in the regulations, a tax-exempt business league will lose its exemption (or an organization will fail to gain exemption in the first instance) because it performs particular services for individual members only where the services are a principal or sole undertaking of the organization.[247] Where these services are less than a primary function of an exempt business league, the IRS will characterize them as a business of a kind ordinarily carried on for profit and treat the business as an unrelated activity.[248] For example, the IRS concluded that an executive referral service conducted by an exempt association constituted the performance of particular services for individual persons but, because other activities were the organization's primary ones, the agency ruled that the service was an unrelated business.[249] Similarly, a compensation consulting service, although performing particular services, did not jeopardize an association's exemption because it was not a primary activity of the organization.[250]

(d) Private Inurement

Still another basis for failure to qualify as a tax-exempt business league is violation of the doctrine of private inurement. That is, none of the income or assets of an exempt business league may be permitted to directly or indirectly unduly benefit an individual or other person who has a close relationship with the organization, when they are in a position to exercise a significant degree of control over it.[251]

§ 2.11 CHAMBERS OF COMMERCE

A tax-exempt chamber of commerce is a nonprofit association of individuals and businesses organized and operated to promote the commercial and industrial

---

[244] Gen. Couns. Mem. 34608.
[245] Gen. Couns. Mem. 39105.
[246] Priv. Ltr. Rul. 200522022.
[247] E.g., Rev. Rul. 68-265, 1968-1 C.B. 265; Rev. Rul. 68-264, 1968-1 C.B. 264. In general, Retailers Credit Ass'n of Alameda County v. Comm'r, 90 F.2d 47 (9th Cir. 1937).
[248] See Chapter 5.
[249] Priv. Ltr. Rul. 8524006.
[250] Priv. Ltr. Rul. 9128003.
[251] § 3.1.

interests of a community, state, or nation. This type of a business network, which usually has an advocacy component, typically functions to improve the business climate and advance the general economic welfare of a community. Thus, a chamber of commerce's efforts are directed at promoting the common economic interests of all of the commercial enterprises in a trade community.

A federal court of appeals noted, by reference to dictionaries, two similar definitions of the term *chamber of commerce*. One of these definitions is that a chamber of commerce is an association that promotes the commercial interests of a locality, country, or the like. The other definition is that such an organization is a society of a city that strives to promote the general trade and commerce of that community.[252]

The IRS observed, in a ruling, that a function of a local chamber of commerce was attempting to attract new industry to a community. This community had difficulty attracting new industry because of lack of suitable facilities and services. To help remedy this situation, the chamber of commerce undertook development of an industrial park, which the IRS found to be in furtherance of the organization's purpose of improving the general business conditions of the community.[253] Similarly, the IRS recognized an organization formed for the purpose of encouraging national organizations to hold their conventions in a city as an exempt chamber of commerce.[254] Membership in an exempt chamber of commerce must be voluntary and open to all business and professional persons in a community.[255]

The IRS ruled that a tenants' association—in this instance, an association of shopping center merchants—did not qualify as a tax-exempt chamber of commerce.[256] The agency noted that membership in the association was compulsory, imposed by the landlord owner of the shopping center, and that the requisite *community* was not being served, as the "community represented by the membership of the . . . organization is a closed, non-public aggregation of commercial enterprises having none of the common characteristics of a community in the usual geographic or political sense."[257] Moreover, the IRS invoked a private inurement doctrine rationale,[258] holding that the organization was designed to serve the tenants' business interests in the shopping center. Exempt status as a business league was denied because the association was not structured along particular industry or business lines.

A neighborhood community association may qualify for tax exemption in this context where the organization has a voluntary membership, it is not concerned with tenants' matters, and the organization is operated to improve the business conditions of a community (rather than a single one-owner shopping

---

[252] Retailers Credit Ass'n of Alameda County v. Comm'r, 90 F.2d 47, 51 (9th Cir. 1937). The second of these definitions was also cited in Crooks v. Kansas City Hay Dealers' Ass'n, 37 F.2d 83, 85 (8th Cir. 1929).

[253] Rev. Rul. 70-81, 1970-1 C.B. 131, *amplified by* Rev. Rul. 81-138, 1981-1 C.B. 358. The amplification of this ruling was for the purpose of noting that the debt financing of construction of a building to be leased to an industrial tenant at below-market rates was a related business, so that the rental function does not give rise to unrelated debt-financed income (see § 5.10).

[254] Rev. Rul. 76-207, 1976-1 C.B. 158.

[255] A self-insurer guaranty trust fund was held to be tax-exempt by reason of IRC § 501(c)(6) because it was "of the same general class" as a chamber of commerce or board of trade (Georgia Self-Insurers Guar. Trust Fund v. United States, 78 A.F.T.R. 2d 6552 (N.D. Ga. 1996)).

[256] Rev. Rul. 73-411, 1973-2 C.B. 180.

[257] *Id.* at 182. Also Rev. Rul. 59-391, 1959-2 C.B. 151.

[258] See Chapter 3.

mall).[259] This may be the case even though a majority of the association's member businesses is located in one shopping center.

Consequently, the principal distinction between a business league and a chamber of commerce is that the former must promote the common business interests of persons within a line of business, while the latter must promote the common business interests of persons within a community or similarly defined geographic area.

§ 2.12 BOARDS OF TRADE

A tax-exempt board of trade is a nonprofit organization organized and operated to regulate, promote, supervise, or protect commercial or business enterprises or interests in a community.

A federal court of appeals observed that the terms *chamber of commerce* and *board of trade* are "nearly synonymous," although there is a "slight distinction between their meanings." The court explained: "The former relates to all businesses in a particular geographic location, while the latter may relate to only one or more lines of business in a particular geographic location, but need not relate to all."[260] This court noted that a board of trade is an organization operated for the "advancement and protection of business interests."[261]

The above-referenced association of shopping center merchants was also denied tax-exempt status as a board of trade, essentially for the same reasons it failed to achieve exempt status as a chamber of commerce.[262] Similarly, an organization was precluded from exempt status as a board of trade principally because its predominant activity was the provision of services to individuals, in the form of grain analysis laboratory services to both members and nonmembers, and because the entity was supported almost entirely from the substantial profits of the laboratory.[263] Likewise, the concept of an exempt board of trade does not encompass organizations that "provide conveniences or facilities to certain persons in connection with buying, selling, and exchanging goods."[264] By contrast, an organization regulating the sale of an agricultural commodity to assure equal treatment of producers, warehousers, and purchasers was ruled to be an exempt board of trade.[265]

As is the case with tax-exempt business leagues and chambers of commerce, membership in an exempt board of trade must be voluntary and open to all trades and businesses in the particular community.

§ 2.13 REAL ESTATE BOARDS

Tax exemption for real estate boards, added to the federal tax law in 1928, came into being as an overturning of a court decision. The court, the year before,

---

[259] Rev. Rul. 78-225, 1978-1 C.B. 159.
[260] Retailers Credit Ass'n of Alameda County v. Comm'r, 90 F.2d 47, 51 (9th Cir. 1937).
[261] *Id.* at 51.
[262] Rev. Rul. 73-411, 1973-2 C.B. 180.
[263] Rev. Rul. 78-70, 1978-1 C.B. 159. Also Fort Wayne Grain & Cotton Exch. v. Comm'r, 27 B.T.A. 983 (1933).
[264] L.O. 1123, III-1 C.B. 275 (1924).
[265] Rev. Rul. 55-715, 1955-2 C.B. 263.

denied exemption as a business league to a corporation organized by associations of insurance companies to provide printing services for member companies.[266] Thereafter, the law was revised to specifically exempt real estate boards from federal income taxation.

§ 2.14 PROFESSIONAL FOOTBALL LEAGUES

Tax exemption for professional football leagues was added to the federal tax law in 1966. This was done to forestall a claim that the operation of a football league's pension plan would be considered private inurement in the form of provision of benefits to individuals in their private capacity. This addition to the statutory law was a component of a much larger legislative package that paved the way for a merger that created an "industry-wide" professional football league.

§ 2.15 APPLICATION FOR RECOGNITION OF EXEMPTION (FORM 1024)

To acquire recognition of tax exemption[267] as a business league or similar organization, the entity is required to file an application for recognition of exemption (Form 1024)[268] with the IRS. The portion of this application that is specifically applicable is Schedule C. There the applicant is requested to describe any services that it performs for its members or others, unless that information has been previously provided.

§ 2.16 NONEXEMPT MEMBERSHIP ORGANIZATIONS

Special rules apply in situations where a membership organization is not exempt from federal income tax and is operated primarily to furnish services or goods to its members. These rules allow deductions for a tax year attributable to the furnishing of services, insurance, goods, or other items of value to the organization's membership only to the extent of income derived during the year from members (including income derived during the year from institutes and trade shows that are primarily for the education of members).[269]

The purpose of these rules is to preclude a result earlier sanctioned by a court,[270] that is, to prevent a taxable membership organization from offsetting its business and investment income with deductions created by the provision of related services to members. Stated another way, these rules are designed to cause taxable membership organizations to allocate and confine their deductions to the corresponding sources of income. As a result, an organization that operated

---

[266] Uniform Printing & Supply Co. v. Comm'r, 33 F.2d 445 (7th Cir. 1929), *cert. den.*, 280 U.S. 69 (1929).
[267] See § 2.2.
[268] See Appendix B.
[269] IRC § 277.
[270] Anaheim Union Water Co. v. Comm'r, 321 F.2d 253 (9th Cir. 1963).

in a year at an overall loss may still have to pay tax if its unrelated business and investment activities produced net income. These rules are intended to deter the abandonment of tax-exempt status by membership organizations (so as to avoid the regulatory requirements) by entities that are serving their members at less than cost.[271]

---

[271] See *Tax-Exempt Organizations* § 13.6.

CHAPTER THREE

Private Inurement, Private Benefit, and Excess Benefit Transactions

The doctrine of *private inurement* is one of the most important sets of rules constituting the law of tax-exempt organizations; indeed, it is the fundamental defining principle of law that distinguishes *nonprofit organizations* from *for-profit organizations*.[1] The private inurement doctrine is a statutory criterion for federal income tax exemption for nine categories of exempt organizations. The doctrine is applicable to business leagues, chambers of commerce, real estate boards, boards of trade, and professional football leagues. The other classifications of exempt organizations to which the private inurement doctrine is applicable are

---

[1] See *Tax-Exempt Organizations* § 1.1.

charitable organizations,[2] social welfare organizations,[3] social clubs,[4] voluntary employees' beneficiary associations,[5] teachers' retirement fund associations,[6] cemetery companies,[7] veterans' organizations,[8] and state-sponsored organizations providing health care to high-risk individuals.[9]

Thus, aside from being organized and operated primarily for a tax-exempt purpose, and otherwise meeting the appropriate statutory requirements for exemption, an organization subject to the doctrine must comport with the federal tax law prohibiting private inurement. Despite the fact that this law is applicable to several categories of tax-exempt organizations, nearly all of the law concerning private inurement has been developed in connection with transactions involving charitable organizations. Thus, as discussed later, when applying the doctrine to a transaction or other arrangement involving an exempt association, most of the law involved will be that developed with respect to exempt charitable entities.

The oddly phrased and thoroughly antiquated language of the private inurement doctrine requires that the tax-exempt organization be organized and operated so that "no part of . . . [its] net earnings . . . inures to the benefit of any private shareholder or individual."[10] This provision reads as if it were proscribing the payment of the dividends. In fact, it is rare for a tax-exempt organization to have shareholders; it would certainly be a violation of the doctrine to make payments of dividends to them.[11] Moreover, the private inurement doctrine can be triggered by the involvement of persons other than individuals, such as corporations, partnerships, limited liability companies, estates, and trusts. The contemporary meaning of this statutory language is barely reflected in its literal form and transcends the nearly century-old formulation; what the doctrine means today is that none of the income or assets of a tax-exempt organization subject to the private inurement doctrine may be permitted to directly or indirectly unduly benefit an individual or other person who has a close relationship with the organization, when the individual or other person is in a position to exercise a significant degree of control over it.

The *private benefit doctrine* is considerably different from, although it subsumes, the private inurement doctrine. Being an extrapolation of the operational test applicable to tax-exempt charitable organizations,[12] this doctrine seemingly is applicable only to these entities. Nonetheless, the IRS appears to be of the view that the private benefit doctrine is applicable in connection with other categories of exempt organizations; the agency has so ruled in an instance involving

---

[2] That is, organizations described in IRC § 501(c)(3).

[3] See § 1.6(a).

[4] See § 1.6(f).

[5] See § 1.6(h).

[6] See § 1.6(j).

[7] See § 1.6(l).

[8] See § 1.6(m).

[9] See *Tax-Exempt Organizations* § 18.14.

[10] In a fine characterization, this phraseology was termed a "nondistribution constraint" (Hansmann, "The Role of Nonprofit Enterprise," 89 *Yale L.J.* 835, 838 (1980)).

[11] The law in a few states permits a nonprofit corporation to issue stock. This type of stock, however, does not carry with it rights to dividends. Thus, these rare bodies of law are not in conflict with the private inurement doctrine, although the IRS appears to believe they are.

[12] See *Tax-Exempt Organizations* § 4.5.

a social welfare organization.[13] Perhaps, then, the IRS believes that the doctrine is equally applicable to exempt business leagues, chambers of commerce, boards of trade, and the like.

The rules pertaining to *excess benefit transactions* are applicable with respect to public charitable organizations and social welfare organizations.[14] That is, a tax-exempt business league is not an *applicable tax-exempt organization*. An exempt business league can, however, be a disqualified person with respect to an applicable tax-exempt organization.[15]

§ 3.1 ESSENCE OF *PRIVATE INUREMENT*

The concept of *private inurement* lacks precision. One court wrote that the "boundaries of the term 'inures' have thus far defied precise definition."[16] Case law teaches that the doctrine is broad and wide-ranging. The rules concerning excess benefit transactions are introducing some exactitude to, albeit perhaps less application of, the doctrine. Further, the rules as to self-dealing involving private foundations[17] continue to bring many examples of private inurement transactions, as does the private benefit doctrine.

The word *inure* means to gravitate toward, flow to or through, or transfer to something. In the private inurement context, the emphasis is on a flowing, of income or assets, directly or indirectly, through a tax-exempt organization to a person who should not, as a matter of law, be receiving the economic benefit. The term *private* is used in this setting to mean unwarranted personal benefits and other forms of nonexempt uses and purposes. Consequently, the private inurement doctrine forbids (1) the flow or transfer of income or assets of an exempt organization, that is subject to the doctrine, through or away from the organization, and (2) the use of such income or assets by one or more persons closely associated with, or for the benefit of one or more persons with some significant relationship to, the organization, for inappropriate purposes.

A pronouncement from the IRS stated that private "i[n]urement is likely to arise where the financial benefit represents a transfer of the [tax-exempt] organization's financial resources to an individual solely by virtue of the individual's relationship with the organization, and without regard to accomplishing exempt purposes."[18] Another of these observations, more bluntly expressed, was that the "inurement prohibition serves to prevent anyone in a position to do so from siphoning off any of a charity's income or assets for personal use."[19]

The purpose of the private inurement rule is to ensure that the tax-exempt organization involved is serving exempt rather than private interests. It is thus necessary for an organization subject to the doctrine to be in a position to establish that it is not organized and operated for the benefit of persons in their private

---

[13] Exemption Denial and Revocation Letter 20044008E.

[14] See § 3.8(b).

[15] See § 3.8(c).

[16] Variety Club Tent No. 6 Charities, Inc. v. Comm'r, 74 T.C.M. 1485, 1494 (1997).

[17] IRC § 4941. See *Tax-Exempt Organizations* § 11.4(a).

[18] Gen. Couns. Mem. 38459.

[19] Gen. Couns. Mem. 39862. As noted, this summary applies not just to charitable organizations but to other tax-exempt organizations subject to the doctrine, including associations.

capacity, such as the organization's founders, trustees, directors, officers, members of their families, entities controlled by these individuals, or any other persons having a personal and private interest in the activities of the organization.[20]

In ascertaining the presence of private inurement, the law looks to the ultimate purpose of the organization involved. If its basic purpose is to benefit individuals in their private capacity—without thereby serving exempt purposes—then it cannot be tax-exempt, even though exempt activities may also be performed. Thus, a court, in concluding that an organization that purchased and sold products manufactured by blind individuals constituted an exempt charitable organization, was not deterred in reaching this finding because of the fact that the organization distributed a portion of its "net profits" to qualified workers at a state agency; the court in essence held that these distributions were in furtherance of exempt purposes.[21] Conversely, incidental benefits to private individuals will not defeat an exemption, as long as the organization otherwise qualifies for exempt status.[22]

The doctrine of private inurement does not prohibit transactions between a tax-exempt organization subject to the doctrine and those that have a close relationship with it. As the IRS wrote, "[t]here is no absolute prohibition against an exempt section 501(c)(3) organization dealing with its founders, members, or officers in conducting its economic affairs."[23] Rather, as is the case with the excess benefit transactions rules and the doctrine of private benefit, the private inurement doctrine requires that these transactions be tested against a standard of *reasonableness*.[24] The standard calls for a roughly equal exchange of benefits between the parties; the law is designed to discourage what the IRS termed a "disproportionate share of the benefits of the exchange" flowing to an insider.[25]

The reasonableness standard focuses essentially on comparability of data, that is, on how similar organizations, acting prudently, transact their affairs in comparable instances. Thus, the regulations pertaining to the business expense deduction, addressing the matter of the reasonableness of compensation, provide that it is generally "just to assume that reasonable and true compensation is only such amount as would ordinarily be paid for like services by like enterprises under like circumstances."[26] Consequently, the terms of these transactions are, in resolution of a private inurement issue, analyzed in relation to comparable practices at comparable exempt or for-profit organizations. Currently, the law generally holds that the relative insignificance of the private benefit provided to persons who should not have received it cannot serve as a valid defense

---

[20] Reg. §§ 1.501(a)-1(c), 1.501(c)(3)-1(c)(2). Also Ginsburg v. Comm'r, 46 T.C. 47 (1966); Rev. Rul. 76-206, 1976-1 C.B. 154.

[21] Industrial Aid for the Blind v. Comm'r, 73 T.C. 96 (1979).

[22] Reg. § 1.501(c)(3)-1(d)(1)(ii).

[23] Priv. Ltr. Rul. 9130002. Trustees and directors are also included in this group.

[24] By contrast, the private foundation self-dealing rules (IRC § 4941) generally and essentially forbid these types of transactions. In general, Hopkins & Blazek, *Private Foundations: Tax Law and Compliance, Second Edition* (Hoboken, NJ: John Wiley & Sons, 2003; annually supplemented) ("*Private Foundations*"), Chapter 5.

[25] Priv. Ltr. Rul. 9130002.

[26] Reg. § 1.162(b)(3).

to a claim of private inurement. That precept is undergoing reevaluation, in part because of the influence of the intermediate sanctions rules.

The core of the private inurement doctrine is the several ways to impermissibly confer private inurement.[27] Before reviewing private inurement transactions, however, it is necessary to summarize two other elements critical to the private inurement equation: the concepts of *net earnings*[28] and the *insider*.[29]

§ 3.2 CONCEPT OF *NET EARNINGS*

The term *net earnings* means gross earnings minus related expenses—a meaning that, as noted, seemingly applies the term, in the private inurement setting, in a technical, accounting sense.[30] For example, a state supreme court addressed this definition at length in the early decades of the federal tax law. In one opinion, this court wrote that, since the term is not defined in the statute, it "must be given its usual and ordinary meaning of what is left of earnings after deducting necessary and legitimate items of expense incident to the corporate business."[31] This approach was followed in the early years by other state courts and by federal courts.[32]

From the perspective of the law of tax-exempt organizations, however, this technical definition of the term was never quite adequate as to its sole meaning. Some courts applied the term in this constricted manner, where the facts particularly lent themselves to this approach,[33] but most court opinions on the point reflect the broader, and certainly contemporary, view that there can be inurement of net earnings in the absence of blatant transfers of all of an exempt organization's net income in the nature of dividend payments.[34]

An early proponent of this expansive view was another state supreme court, which observed that the *net earnings* phraseology "should not be given a strictly literal construction, as in the accountant's sense" and that the "substance should control the form," so that tax exemption should not be available where private inurement is taking place, "irrespective of the means by which that result is accomplished."[35] Likewise, early in the evolution of this body of law, a federal

---

[27] See 3 § 4. In one instance, however, the IRS refused to grant recognition of tax exemption, in part because the agency, while acknowledging that "there is no evidence of any inurement," speculated that the prospective "actual operations" of the organization may give rise to private inurement (Priv. Ltr. Rul. 200535029).

[28] See 3 § 2.

[29] See 3 § 3.

[30] The statute, as originally written in 1913, employed the term *net income*. In 1918, the word *earnings* was substituted for *income*. There is nothing in the legislative history to suggest that this change had any substantive significance, and the commonality of the meanings of the two terms indicates that none was intended.

[31] Bank of Commerce & Trust Co. v. Senter, 260 S.W. 144, 151 (Sup. Ct. Tenn. 1924). Likewise, Southern Coal Co. v. McCanless, 192 S.W. 2d 1003, 1005 (Sup. Ct. Tenn. 1946); Nat'l Life & Accident Ins. Co. v. Dempster, 79 S.W. 2d 564 (Sup. Ct. Tenn. 1935).

[32] E.g., United States v. Riely, 169 F.2d 542 (4th Cir. 1948); Winkelman v. General Motors Corp., 44 F. Supp. 960 (S.D.N.Y. 1942); Inscho v. Mid-Continent Development Co., 146 P. 1014 (Kan. 1915).

[33] E.g., Birmingham Business College, Inc. v. Comm'r, 276 F.2d 476 (5th Cir. 1960); Gemological Inst. of America v. Comm'r, 17 T.C. 1604 (1952), *aff'd*, 212 F.2d 205 (9th Cir. 1954); Putnam v. Comm'r, 6 T.C. 702 (1946).

[34] E.g., Edward Orton, Jr., Ceramic Found. v. Comm'r, 9 T.C. 533 (1947), *aff'd*, 173 F.2d 483 (6th Cir. 1949); Gemological Inst. of America v. Riddell, 149 F. Supp. 128 (S.D. Cal. 1957).

[35] Virginia Mason Hosp. Ass'n v. Larson, 114 P.2d 978, 983 (Wash. 1941).

court foresaw today's application of the term when it held that private inurement "may include more than the term net profits as shown by the books of the organization or than the difference between the gross receipts and disbursements in dollars" and that "[p]rofits may inure to the benefit of shareholders in ways other than dividends."[36] This view certainly represents the current application of the private inurement doctrine—as an overall standard assessing the use of a tax-exempt organization's income and assets[37]—although there is an occasional somewhat literal interpretation.[38]

In conclusion, the contemporary concept of private inurement goes far beyond any mechanical computation and dissemination of net earnings and embraces a much wider range of transactions and other activities.

§ 3.3 REQUISITE INSIDER

A private inurement transaction is one between a tax-exempt organization that is subject to the doctrine and a person (or persons) who has a special, close relationship with the organization. To put a name to the latter, the federal tax law appropriated the term *insider* from the federal securities laws.[39]

Generally, an *insider* is a person who has a unique relationship with the tax-exempt organization involved, by which that person can cause application of the organization's funds or assets for the private purposes of the person by reason of the person's exercise of control or influence over, or being in a position to exercise that control or influence over, the organization.[40] An insider includes an organization's founders, trustees, directors, officers, key employees, members of the family of these individuals, and certain entities controlled by them.[41] All of these persons have been swept into the insider category, from the starting point of the statutory language with its peculiar and incomplete reference to *private shareholder or individual*.[42]

---

[36] Northwestern Mun. Ass'n v. United States, 99 F.2d 460, 463 (8th Cir. 1938).

[37] E.g., Harding Hosp., Inc. v. United States, 505 F.2d 1068 (6th Cir. 1974).

[38] A federal court found that the term *net earnings* signified funds used for expenses over and above expenses that are "ordinary and necessary" in the operation of a charitable organization (Carter v. United States, 973 F.2d 1479, 1487 (9th Cir. 1992); Hall v. Comm'r, 729 F.2d 632, 634 (9th Cir. 1984)).

A less-than-literal interpretation of these rules occurred when a court held that "paying over a portion of *gross* earnings to those vested with the control of a charitable organization constituted private inurement as well," adding that "[a]ll in all, taking a slice off the top should be no less prohibited than a slice out of the net" (People of God Community v. Comm'r, 75 T.C. 127, 133 (1980) (emphasis in original)).

[39] These laws prohibit, for example, insider trading. See § 11.7.

[40] American Campaign Academy v. Comm'r, 92 T.C. 1053 (1989). It was subsequently stated that the "case law [as to private inurement] appears to have drawn a line between those who have significant control over the organization's activities and those who are unrelated third parties" (Variety Club Tent No. 6 Charities, Inc. v. Comm'r, 74 T.C.M. 1485, 1492 (1997)).

[41] In the excess benefit transactions context (see § 3.8) and in the private foundations context (IRC § 4946), the term *disqualified person* is used to describe an insider.

The IRS expressed the view that all persons performing services for a tax-exempt organization are insiders with respect to that organization (Gen. Couns. Mem 39670); this obviously is an overly expansive interpretation of the concept. It was the position of the IRS, for example, that all physicians on the medical staff of an exempt hospital are insiders in relation to the hospital (Gen. Couns. Mem. 39498); however, this stance was ameliorated in the aftermath of enactment of the intermediate sanctions law.

[42] It is, as noted (see *supra* note 11), uncommon for a nonprofit organization to have shareholders. When they exist, presumably they must be insiders for the private inurement doctrine to apply, although the IRS suggested that the status of a person as such a shareholder automatically makes that person an insider (Priv. Ltr. Rul. 9835001).

Case law is rich with court opinions concerning the involvement of insiders in private inurement transactions.

Five individuals leased property to a tax-exempt school, which constructed improvements on its property; of this group, one was the school's president, two were its vice-presidents, and one was its secretary-treasurer. These four individuals were also directors of the school and constituted its executive committee. Private inurement was found in the form of "excessive rent payments [by which] part of the net earnings of [the school] inured to the benefit of the members of the . . . group . . . and that part of the net earnings of [the school] also inured to their benefit because of the construction at its expense of buildings and improvements on real estate owned by them."[43]

A foundation failed to achieve tax-exempt status because part of its net earnings was determined to have inured to its founder. The foundation made loans for the personal benefit of this individual and his family members and friends, made expenditures to advance his personal hobby, and purchased stock in a corporation owned by a friend of his. A court concluded that the foundation was "organized in such a fashion that [its founder] held control of its activities and expenditures; it was operated to carry out projects in which [he] was interested and some of its funds were expended for [his] benefit or [for the benefit of] members of his family."[44]

Tax exemption was denied a college that had five family members as all of its trustees and three of them as its shareholders, because of private inurement in the form of "constant commingling of the funds of the shareholders and the [c]ollege."[45] A court concluded that this college was "operated as a business producing, or ultimately producing, substantial revenue for its operators[;] the net earnings, or substantial portions, were to be, and were in fact, distributed to these shareholders for their own personal benefit."[46]

A foundation, bearing the name of a radio personality, was established to provide musical instruction, proper living quarters, and medical assistance to young individuals interested in the field of entertainment, and who were featured in the shows of this entertainer. The foundation was found to be engaging in private inurement, inasmuch as in "these circumstances [the entertainer] received a great benefit by establishing an organization whereby the recipients of the organization's charitable services were in his employ and benefiting him" and that "it was to [his] advantage as a director of a radio program and as an employer to provide these services."[47]

A physician established an ostensible scientific research foundation; he and his father were two of the three trustees. A court found private inurement in the form of benefits to the physician in his medical practice. The foundation's laboratory, located next door to the physician's office, was, according to the government, used "on numerous occasions in his practice"; the foundation's principal activities were the treatment of patients (chiefly those of the physician). The

---

[43] Texas Trade School v. Comm'r, 30 T.C. 642, 647 (1958), aff'd, 272 F.2d 168 (5th Cir. 1959).

[44] Best Lock Corp. v. Comm'r, 31 T.C. 1217, 1236 (1959).

[45] Birmingham Business College, Inc. v. Comm'r, 276 F.2d 476, 479 (5th Cir. 1960).

[46] Id. at 480.

[47] Horace Heidt Found. v. United States, 170 F. Supp. 634, 638 (Ct. Cl. 1959).

court accepted the government's contention that the physician's "practice and the income therefrom were materially enhanced by the establishment of the laboratory."[48]

A church disbursed substantial sums to its founder and members of his family as fees, commissions, royalties, compensation for services, rent, reimbursements for expenses, and loans; the church maintained a personal residence for these individuals. Finding impermissible private inurement, a court observed that "[w]hat emerges from these facts is the inference that the . . . [founder's] family was entitled to make ready personal use of the corporate earnings . . . [N]othing we have found in the record dispels the substantial doubts the court entertains concerning the receipt of benefit by [this family] from [the church's] net earnings."[49] With respect to certain of these disbursements, the court stated that "logical inference can be drawn that these payments were disguised and unjustified distributions of [the church's] earnings."[50]

A court, in part because of the advantages obtained by the physicians who organized the institution, barred the tax exemption of a hospital. The founding physicians attended to most of the patients admitted to the hospital. The court's concern was over an arrangement for management services by which these physicians were paid and a lease of office space. The court concluded that the hospital was the "primary source of the doctors' professional income" and that this "virtual monopoly by the [physicians] of the patients permitted benefits to inure to . . . [them] within the intendment of the statute."[51]

The IRS revoked, on private inurement grounds, the tax-exempt status of a hospital organized and operated by a physician. The institution was held by a court to have distributed its earnings to the physician in the form of direct payments (compensation and loans), improvements to the property of a corporation he owned, administrative services relating to his private practice, and the free use of its facilities.[52] The same fate befell an organization established to study chiropractic methods, where the founding chiropractor sold his home, automobile, and medical equipment to the entity, and caused it to pay his personal expenses and a salary while he continued his private practice.[53] Likewise, the tax exemption of an organization was revoked because of several transactions, including the receipt of property from the founder's mother and payment to her of an annuity, payment of a child's college education, payment of the founder's personal expenses, and purchasing and leasing real estate owned by the founder.[54]

Private inurement precluded an ostensible religious organization from achieving tax-exempt status. Its governing board consisted of its founder, his spouse, and their child. It conducted some ministry through its founder (who

---

[48] Cranley v. Comm'r, 20 T.C.M. 20, 25 (1961).
[49] Founding Church of Scientology v. United States, 412 F.2d 1197, 1202 (Ct. Cl. 1969), cert. den., 397 U.S. 1009 (1970).
[50] Id. at 1201.
[51] Harding Hosp., Inc. v. United States, 505 F.2d 1068, 1078 (6th Cir. 1974).
[52] Kenner v. Comm'r, 33 T.C.M. 1239 (1974).
[53] The Labrenz Found., Inc. v. Comm'r, 33 T.C.M. 1374 (1974).
[54] Rueckwald Found., Inc. v. Comm'r, 33 T.C.M. 1383 (1974).

was also its principal donor) and made some grants to needy individuals selected by him. A court concluded that the founder's activities were "more personal than church oriented."[55] In similar circumstances, a court rejected an organization's claim of tax exemption because the organization provided its founder and his family with "housing, food, transportation, clothing and other proper needs as may from time to time arise."[56]

A court's finding that a church was ineligible for tax-exempt status was based in part on its conclusion that a portion of the net earnings of the church inured to the benefit of its founder and his family. Indicia of this private inurement included unreasonable increases in salaries and payments of directors' fees, management fees, and other payments in support of the family. The court also labeled as private inurement the founder's practice of marketing books and other items in the name of the church, and being paid royalties for the sales, as well as personally being paid royalties attributable to the literary efforts of employees of the church. Still other forms of private inurement were analyzed by the court, including "repayment of alleged debts in unspecified amounts and unfettered control over millions of dollars in funds" belonging to entities affiliated with the church.[57]

A community organization, with homeowners as members, was held to be engaging in private inurement transactions by providing "comfort and convenience" to the residents who, by reason of being the "intended beneficiaries" of the facilities and services of the organization, were found to have a "personal interest" in its activities.[58] The IRS has likewise adopted the view that the prohibition on private inurement relates only to circumstances where unwarranted benefits are provided by a tax-exempt organization to one or more insiders. Thus, the agency ruled that private inurement was not present where an exempt hospital compensated a hospital-based radiologist on the basis of a fixed percentage of the revenue of the radiology department; this conclusion was arrived at, in part, because the radiologist "did not control" the hospital.[59]

By contrast, a trust that was required to pay out its net income for tax-exempt purposes for a period of years or the lives of specified individuals was ruled by the IRS to not qualify for tax-exempt status. At the end of the income-payment period, the trust terminated and the principal reverted to the founder of the trust or his estate. The disqualifying feature in this regard was the reversionary interest, which resulted in inurement of investment gains over the life of the trust to the benefit of its creator.[60] The IRS observed that the "inurement issue . . . focuses on benefits conferred on an organization's insiders through the use or distribution of the organization's financial resources."[61]

---

[55] Western Catholic Church v. Comm'r, 73 T.C. 196, 211 (1979), aff'd, 631 F.2d 736 (7th Cir. 1980), cert. den., 450 U.S. 981 (1981).

[56] Parshall Christian Order v. Comm'r, 45 T.C.M. 488, 492 (1983).

[57] Church of Scientology of California v. Comm'r, 83 T.C. 381, 492 (1984), aff'd, 823 F.2d 1310 (9th Cir. 1987).

[58] Columbia Park & Recreation Ass'n, Inc. v. Comm'r, 88 T.C. 1, 24, 26 (1987), aff'd, 838 F.2d 465 (4th Cir. 1988).

[59] Rev. Rul. 69-383, 1969-2 C.B. 113, 114.

[60] Rev. Rul. 66-259, 1966-2 C.B. 214.

[61] Gen. Couns. Mem. 38459.

As the foregoing indicates, the focus on the concept of the *insider* in the private inurement area over the years has been on those who are the tax-exempt organization's founders, trustees, directors, officers, and family members. Recently, however, attention has been given to what may appear at the outset to be an independent entity, such as a vendor of services, and whether that person may be an insider with respect to an exempt organization. This development has been fueled in part by IRS-conceived examples of situations where ostensibly outside fundraising and similar companies are considered disqualified persons, under the intermediate sanctions rules, in relation to charitable organizations.[62]

The state of the law, as to this matter of vendors as insiders, is uncertain, largely because of litigation as to whether a fundraising firm can be an insider with respect to a charitable organization. A trial court found a fundraising firm to be an insider under these circumstances, because of the extent to which the firm took over, controlled, and manipulated the charity to its private ends.[63] By reason of the arrangement between the parties, the charity was funded and otherwise maintained in existence by the firm. This relationship was characterized as "substantial control" by the firm, which was portrayed as "in many ways analogous to that of a founder and major contributor to a new organization."[64] On appeal, however, this decision was reversed; the appellate court could not find anything in the facts of the case to support the "theory" that the fundraising firm "seized control" of the charity "and by doing so became an insider."[65] Said the court: "There is nothing that corporate or agency law would recognize as control."[66] Writing in obvious ignorance of the intermediate sanctions rules,[67] this appellate court wrote that the lower court used the word *control* "in a special sense not used elsewhere, so far as we can determine, in the law, including the federal tax law."[68]

This appellate court focused on the terms of the contract between the parties, because of its view that the lower court's classification of the fundraising firm as an insider with respect to the charity was based "on the fundraising contract."[69] This position, the court of appeals wrote, "threatens to unsettle the charitable sector by empowering the IRS to yank a charity's tax exemption simply because the Service thinks the charity's contract with its major fundraiser too one-sided in favor of the fundraiser, even though the charity has not been found to have violated any duty of faithful and careful management that the law of nonprofit corporations may have laid upon it."[70]

---

[62] See § 3.8(c).

[63] United Cancer Council, Inc. v. Comm'r, 109 T.C. 326 (1997).

[64] *Id.* at 387. The court wrote that, for purposes, of the private inurement doctrine, an insider is a person who has "significant control of the [exempt] organization's activities" (*id.*). Congress adopted the essence of this approach when it wrote the intermediate sanctions definition of *disqualified person* (see § 3.8(c)).

[65] United Cancer Council, Inc. v. Comm'r, 165 F.3d 1173, 1178 (7th Cir. 1999).

[66] *Id.*

[67] See § 3.8(c).

[68] United Cancer Council, Inc. v. Comm'r, 165 F.3d 1173, 1178 (7th Cir. 1999). The intermediate sanctions rules, embodying precisely that concept, had been in existence over three years when this was written.

[69] *Id.* at 1176.

[70] *Id.* at 1179. This court also observed: "If the charity's contract with the fundraiser makes the latter an insider, triggering the inurement clause of section 501(c)(3) and so destroying the charity's tax exemption, the charitable sector of the economy is in trouble" (at 1176). It was not the contract that made the fundraising firm an insider, however, but the actions and compensation amounts that resulted from it.

Consequently, a tax-exempt organization subject to the private inurement doctrine should be concerned with the doctrine only where there is a transaction or transactions involving one or more *insiders* with respect to the organization. The overall rule on this point was expressed this way: the "concept of private benefit [inurement] . . . [is] limited to the situation in which an organization's *insiders* . . . [are] benefited."[71] A modern definition of the term *insider* is a person who has a "significant formal voice in [an exempt organization's] activities generally and had substantial formal and practical control over most of [the organization's] income."[72]

At the same time, however, the IRS may elect to apply the intermediate sanctions penalties (when applicable) against the insider[73] rather than revoke tax-exempt status.[74] Moreover, even if it turns out that a transaction involving an exempt organization does not involve a person who is an insider, the analysis should not necessarily end, inasmuch as the transaction could nonetheless operate for the use or benefit of an insider/disqualified person[75] or be a transgression of the private benefit doctrine.[76]

§ 3.4 TYPES OF PRIVATE INUREMENT

The concept of the private inurement transaction has many manifestations. While the most common instance of private inurement is excessive compensation, there are several other forms of private inurement, most notably sales of assets, rental of property, lending of money, use of facilities or other assets, and involvement in partnerships or other joint ventures.

Although the precepts of private inurement and self-dealing in the private foundation setting are by no means precisely the same, this summary of self-dealing transactions offers a useful sketch of the scope of transactions that, in appropriate circumstances, amount to instances of private inurement[77]: (1) sale or exchange, or leasing, of property between a tax-exempt organization and an insider; (2) lending of money or other extension of credit between an exempt organization and an insider; (3) furnishing of goods, services, or facilities between an exempt organization and an insider; (4) payment of compensation (or payment or reimbursement of expenses) by an exempt organization to an

---

[71] Sound Health Ass'n v. Comm'r, 71 T.C. 158, 185 (1978). Occasionally, the overwhelming domination of a tax-exempt organization and wrongdoing by an insider can lead a court to a finding of private inurement, when in fact inurement is not present because the terms and conditions of the transactions involved were reasonable (e.g., Airlie Found., Inc. v. United States, 826 F. Supp. 537 (D.D.C. 1993), *aff'd*, 55 F.3d 684 (D.C. Cir. 1995)).

[72] Variety Club Tent No. 6 Charities, Inc. v. Comm'r, 74 T.C.M. 1485, 1493 (1997).

[73] As discussed, in the intermediate sanctions area, an insider is termed a *disqualified person* (see § 3.8(c)). The terms *insider* and *disqualified person* are essentially synonymous.

[74] See § 3.8(f).

[75] A discussion of transactions of this nature is in Hopkins, *The Law of Intermediate Sanctions: A Guide for Nonprofits* (Hoboken, NJ: John Wiley & Sons, 2003) ("*Intermediate Sanctions*"), § 4.8.

[76] See § 3.6.

[77] The definition of *self-dealing* as applied in the private foundation setting, written in 1969, is, in essence, a codification of much of the case law concerning private inurement. Yet, over 35 years later, Congress believed its specificity in this regard to be too limiting and chose, when once again legislating on the subject, to use an overarching definition when creating the excess benefit transaction (see § 3.8(d)).

insider; and (5) transfer to, or use by or for the benefit of, an insider of the income or assets of an exempt organization.[78]

A set of facts illustrating some of the distinctions between private inurement and self-dealing was provided in an instance involving a tax-exempt museum that, at the outset, was structured as a private foundation. The museum made a low-interest loan to an incoming director, who became a disqualified person with respect to the museum. The IRS determined that, for every year the loan principal remained outstanding, an act of self-dealing would occur, inasmuch as the extension of credit by a private foundation is, as noted, self-dealing. The museum thereafter, however, became qualified as a public charity, thus rendering the self-dealing rules inapplicable. The IRS valued the loan as part of the director's total compensation package and found the arrangement reasonable, thereby averting application of the private inurement doctrine.[79]

Occasionally the IRS, applying the doctrine of private inurement, denies an organization recognition of tax exemption[80] or revokes the exemption of an organization for engaging in a private inurement transaction or for some other form of private inurement arrangement.[81]

(a) Compensation for Services

A tax-exempt organization, subject to the private inurement doctrine, can, of course, make ordinary and necessary expenditures in furtherance of its operations without forfeiting its exempt status.[82] These expenditures include the payment of compensation for services rendered, whether to an employee or to a vendor, consultant, or other independent contractor. As a court observed, the law "places no duty on individuals operating charitable [or, for that matter, other exempt] organizations to donate their services; they are entitled to reasonable compensation for their efforts."[83] The legislative history of the intermediate sanctions rules states that an individual "need not necessarily accept reduced compensation merely because he or she renders services to a tax-exempt, as opposed to a taxable, organization."[84]

(i) Meaning of *Compensation*. The concept of *compensation* paid to an individual or other person by a tax-exempt organization is not confined to items such as a salary. All forms of compensation are aggregated for this purpose; in the case of an employee, the elements include salary, wages, bonuses, commissions, royalties,

---

[78] IRC § 4941 (d)(1)(A)–(E). The IRS applied the self-dealing rationale in one public pronouncement in an instance of a transaction involving a public charity and its directors (Rev. Rul. 76-441, 1976-2 C.B. 147); a court essentially did the same (without expressly using the term) in a case concerning a church and its ministers (Church by Mail, Inc. v. Comm'r, 48 T.C.M. 471 (1984), aff'd, 765 F.2d 1387 (9th Cir. 1985)).

[79] Priv. Ltr. Rul. 9530032. Today, a transaction of this nature would likely be sheltered, as to the intermediate sanctions rules, by the initial contract exception (see § 3.8(d)(iii)).

[80] E.g., Priv. Ltr. Rul. 200446025.

[81] E.g., Priv. Ltr. Rul. 200509027.

[82] E.g., Birmingham Business College, Inc. v. Comm'r, 276 F.2d 476 (5th Cir. 1960); Mabee Petroleum Corp. v. United States, 203 F.2d 872 (5th Cir. 1953); Broadway Theatre League of Lynchburg, Va., Inc. v. United States, 293 F. Supp. 346 (W.D. Va. 1968); Enterprise Railway Equipment Co. v. United States, 161 F. Supp. 590 (Ct. Cl. 1958).

[83] World Family Corp. v. Comm'r, 81 T.C. 958, 969 (1983).

[84] H. Rep. 104-506, 104th Cong., 2d Sess. 56, note 3 (1996).

fringe benefits, deferred compensation, severance payments, retirement and pension benefits, expense allowances, and insurance coverages[85]; in the case of an independent contractor, the elements include the payment of advances, fees, and expense reimbursements.[86]

(ii) Determining the Reasonableness of Compensation. The private inurement doctrine mandates that the compensation amount paid by most tax-exempt organizations be *reasonable*. In other words, the payment of *excessive* compensation can result in a finding of private inurement.[87] Whether an amount of compensation is reasonable is a question of *fact*, to be decided in the context of each case[88]; it is not an issue of *law*.

The process for determining the reasonableness of compensation is conceptually much like that entailed when valuing an item of property. It requires an appraisal—an evaluation of factors that lead to a determination of the value. It is an exercise of comparing a mix of variables pertaining to the compensation of others in similar circumstances. The basic standard has been in the federal tax law for years; it is cited in the business expense regulations[89] and the intermediate sanctions regulations[90] in this way: Reasonable compensation is that amount as would ordinarily be paid for like services by like enterprises under like circumstances. This alchemy—what the intermediate sanctions rules refer to as an accumulation and assessment of data as to comparability[91]—yields the conclusion as to whether a particular item of compensation or a compensation package is *reasonable* or is *excessive*.[92]

Traditionally, case law has dictated the criteria to be used in ascertaining the reasonableness of compensation. This approach has come to be known as utilization of the *multifactor test*. The elements—factors—to be utilized in a particular case can vary, depending on the court. (Even though the reasonableness of compensation is a matter of fact, the selection and application of the appropriate factors is a matter of law.) Much of the law in this field is based on case law concerning payments by for-profit corporations to their chief executive. This is because a payment of compensation, to be deductible as a business expense,[93] must be an *ordinary and necessary* outlay; the concepts of *reasonableness* and ordinary and

---

[85] E.g., Priv. Ltr. Rul. 9539016 (where the IRS discussed the coverage provided by a split-dollar life insurance plan as compensation).

[86] See § 3.8(d).

[87] E.g., Harding Hospital, Inc. v. United States, 505 F.2d 1068 (6th Cir. 1974); Birmingham Business College, Inc. v. Comm'r, 276 F.2d 476 (5th Cir. 1960); Mabee Petroleum Corp. v. United States, 203 F.2d 872 (5th Cir. 1953); Texas Trade School v. Comm'r, 30 T.C. 642 (1958), aff'd, 272 F.2d 168 (5th Cir. 1959); Northern Illinois College of Optometry v. Comm'r, 2 T.C.M. 664 (1943).

[88] E.g., Jones Brothers Bakery, Inc. v. United States, 411 F.2d 1282 (Ct. Cl. 1969); Home Oil Mill v. Willingham, 68 F. Supp. 525 (N.D. Ala. 1945), aff'd, 181 F.2d 9 (5th Cir. 1950), cert. den., 340 U.S. 852 (1950).

[89] Reg. § 1.162-7(b)(3).

[90] Reg. § 53.4958-4 (b)(1)(ii)(A). See § 3.8(d), text accompanied by note 314.

[91] Reg. § 53.4958-6(c)(2). See § 3.8(e), text accompanied by note 348.

[92] The process of determining reasonable compensation may include obtaining a report from an independent consultant and/or a ruling from the IRS. Nonetheless, these arrangements are, by definition, reviewed from the standpoint of hindsight, which may obviate the effectiveness of these documents. An excellent illustration of this process appeared in Priv. Ltr. Rul. 200020060, concerning the valuation of a compensation package paid to the executive of a tax-exempt charitable organization.

[93] IRC § 162(a).

necessary are essentially identical.[94] Also, as will be discussed, the advent of the intermediate sanctions rules has greatly informed this aspect of the law of tax-exempt organizations.

The factors commonly applied in the private inurement setting (and similar settings) to ascertain the reasonableness of compensation are:

- The levels of compensation paid by similar organizations (tax-exempt and taxable) for functionally comparable positions, with emphasis on comparable entities in the same community or region
- The need of the organization for the services of the individual whose compensation is being evaluated
- The individual's background, education, training, experience, and responsibilities
- Whether the compensation resulted from arm's-length bargaining, such as whether it was approved by an independent board of directors
- The size and complexity of the organization, in terms of elements such as assets, income, and number of employees
- The individual's prior compensation arrangement
- The individual's performance
- The relationship of the individual's compensation to that paid to other employees of the same organization
- Whether there has been a sharp increase in the individual's compensation (a spike) from one year to the next
- The amount of time the individual devotes to the position[95]

If the issue is litigated, the individual whose compensation is being challenged and the IRS are likely to have expert witnesses, who produce reports and testimony incorporating some or all of these factors. The judge in the case is called on to determine whether there has been payment of excessive compensation. Most of these cases originate in the U.S. Tax Court. A federal court of appeals observed (articulating a fact that, until then, no court had ventured to mention), however, that the "judges of the Tax Court are not equipped by training or experience to determine the salaries of corporate officers; no judges are."[96]

This appellate court excoriated the multifactor test, characterizing it as "redundant, incomplete, and unclear."[97] The test was found to "not provide adequate guidance to a rational decision."[98] Rather, wrote the court, the test to be applied when determining the reasonableness of an individual's compensation

---

[94] If the IRS or a court finds that a portion of a payment by a for-profit corporation constitutes excessive compensation, that amount is treated as a dividend and thus is not deductible by the payor corporation (e.g., Rapco, Inc. v. Comm'r, 85 F.3d 950 (2d Cir. 1996); Leonard Pipeline Contractors, Ltd. v. Comm'r, 72 T.C.M. 83 (1996), *rev'd and rem'd*, 142 F.3d 1133 (9th Cir. 1998)).

[95] E.g., Miller & Son Drywall, Inc. v. Comm'r, 89 T.C. 1279 (2005).

[96] Exacto Spring Corp. v. Comm'r, 196 F.3d 833, 835 (7th Cir. 1999).

[97] *Id.*

[98] *Id.*

package paid by a for-profit business is the *independent investor test*.[99] This test establishes a presumption that an executive's compensation is reasonable if the investors in the company (actual or hypothetical) believe that the return on their investment is reasonable, with the investment return percentage determined by an expert witness. This court proclaimed that, when these investors are obtaining a "far higher return than they had any reason to expect," the executive's salary is "presumptively reasonable," even if the compensation may otherwise be considered "exorbitant."[100] Under this approach, the presumption can be rebutted if the government shows that, although the executive's salary was reasonable, the company "did not in fact intend to pay him [or her] that amount as salary, that his [or her] salary really did include a concealed dividend though it need not have."[101] Also, according to this court, if the executive's salary is approved by the other owners of the corporation, who are independent of the executive—that is, who lacked an incentive to disguise a dividend as a salary—that approval "goes far" to rebut any evidence of "bad faith."[102]

It initially appeared that a federal court of appeals would use either the multifactor test or the independent investor test in determining the reasonableness of executive compensation. For example, a federal appellate court, considering this issue for the first time, elected to utilize the multifactor test.[103] In one instance, a court used the independent investor test to find an executive's compensation reasonable, portraying the individual as the "locomotive" of the company.[104] Yet, however, another federal court of appeals, in one of these cases, applied a multifactor test, then used the independent investor test to interpret one of the factors.[105] On another occasion, a court used the independent investor test to establish the presumption that an individual's compensation was reasonable, then applied the multifactor test to rebut the presumption and determine that the compensation was unreasonable.[106] The independent investor test will not be applied in determining the reasonableness of the compensation of executives of tax-exempt organizations[107]; rather, ongoing application of that test will provide additional illustrations of use of the multifactor test.

A large salary paid by a tax-exempt organization can be considered private inurement, particularly where the employee is concurrently receiving other forms of compensation from the organization (for example, fees, commissions,

---

[99] This approach was first advanced in Dexsil Corp. v. Comm'r, 147 F.3d 96 (2d Cir. 1998). This test subsequently has been characterized as the *hypothetical investor test* and the *hypothetical inactive independent investor test*.

[100] Exacto Spring Corp. v. Comm'r, 196 F.3d 833, 835, 838 (7th Cir. 1999).

[101] *Id.* at 839.

[102] *Id.* at 839.

[103] Haffner's Service Stations, Inc. v. Comm'r, 326 F.3d 1 (1st Cir. 2003).

[104] Beiner, Inc. v. Comm'r, 88 T.C.M. 297, 305 (2004). The court observed that this business would not have succeeded without this executive's "devotion, dedication, intelligence, foresight, and skill" (*id.*).

[105] LabelGraphics, Inc. v. Comm'r, 221 F.3d 1091 (9th Cir. 2000).

[106] Menard, Inc. v. Comm'r, 88 T.C.M. 229 (2004).

[107] Inexplicably, in an intermediate sanctions case, the IRS, in stating the factors it relied on in concluding that an individual's compensation, paid by a public charity, was excessive, invoked the independent investor test (writing, in the notice of deficiency, that "[i]t is not probable an outside investor would approve of such a compensation plan as reasonable") (Peters v. Comm'r, No. 8446-00 (U.S. Tax Court), docketed on August 3, 2000, and settled).

and/or royalties) and more than one member of the same family is compensated by the same organization.[108] Thus, where the control of an organization was in two ministers, whose contributions were its total receipts, all of which were paid to them as housing allowances, the exemption of the organization was revoked; the court said that the compensation was not "reasonable" although it may not be "excessive."[109] Yet large salaries and noncash benefits received by an exempt organization's employees can be reasonable, considering the nature of their services and skills, such as payments to physicians by a nonprofit entity that was an incorporated department of anesthesiology of a hospital.[110]

Another basis for finding private inurement is where the compensation paid annually is reasonable but the year-to-year increases of it are not justifiable. In one case, salary increases were found to be "abrupt," resulting in a "substantial" amount of compensation, leading the court to the conclusion that the salaries were "at least suggestive of a commercial rather than nonprofit operation."[111] Spikes in compensation amounts of this nature can also be seen in large bonuses.[112] Yet it is also possible to cast salary increases, abrupt or otherwise, as payments, in whole or in part, for prior years' compensation, where the executive was undercompensated in those years.[113]

Other forms of compensation are subject to the private inurement doctrine. For example, although a court held that an excessive parsonage allowance may constitute private inurement,[114] the same court subsequently ruled that another parsonage allowance was "not excessive as a matter of law."[115] The IRS revoked the tax-exempt status of a health care institution on the ground of several instances of private inurement, including various forms of compensation.[116]

---

[108] E.g., Founding Church of Scientology v. United States, 412 F.2d 1197 (Ct. Cl. 1969), *cert. den.*, 397 U.S. 1009 (1970); Bubbling Well Church of Universal Love, Inc. v. Comm'r, 74 T.C. 531 (1980), *aff'd*, 670 F.2d 104 (9th Cir. 1981); Unitary Mission Church of Long Island v. Comm'r, 74 T.C. 507 (1980), *aff'd*, 647 F.2d 163 (2d Cir. 1981).

[109] Church of the Transfiguring Spirit, Inc. v. Comm'r, 76 T.C. 1, 6 (1981). Cf. Universal Church of Scientific Truth, Inc. v. United States, 74-1 U.S.T.C. ¶ 9360 (N.D. Ala. 1973) (where the organization retained its tax exemption in part because its revenue was derived from fees for publications and its expenses included items other than the compensation of its ministers).

[110] B.H.W. Anesthesia Found., Inc. v. Comm'r, 72 T.C. 681 (1979). Also University of Massachusetts Medical School Group Practice v. Comm'r, 74 T.C. 1299 (1980).

[111] The Incorporated Trustees of the Gospel Worker Soc'y v. United States, 510 F. Supp. 374, 379 (D.D.C. 1981), *aff'd*, 672 F.2d 894 (D.C. Cir. 1981); *cert. den.*, 456 U.S. 944 (1982).

[112] E.g., Haffner's Service Stations, Inc. v. Comm'r, 326 F.3d 1 (1st Cir. 2003).

[113] E.g., Devine Brothers, Inc. v. Comm'r, 85 T.C.M. 768 (2003). In some circumstances, in the intermediate sanctions context (see § 3.8), a determination of the reasonableness of compensation for a year may take into account services performed by a disqualified person in prior years (Reg. § 53.4958-4(a)(1)).

[114] Hall v. Comm'r, 729 F.2d 632 (9th Cir. 1984).

[115] Carter v. United States, 973 F.2d 1479, 1487 (9th Cir. 1992).

[116] Tech. Adv. Mem. 9451001. Litigation ensued (LAC Facilities, Inc. v. United States (No. 94-604T, U.S. Ct. Fed. Cl.)); the case was settled. In general, Note, "What Is Reasonable Compensation for Deduction Purposes? Two Tests Exist But Neither Paints a Clear Picture, as Evidenced in *Devine Brothers v. Commissioner*, 57 *Tax Law.* (No. 3) 793 (2004); Peregrine & DeJong, "A General Counsel's Guide: Advising the Nonprofit Board on Executive Compensation Decisions," 40 *Exempt Org. Tax Rev.* (No. 1) 19 (April 2003); Note, "Determining the Deductibility of Executive Compensation: *Exacto Spring Corp. v. Commissioner*, 53 *Tax Law.*" (No. 4) 919 (2000); Griffith, "Compensation and Fraud Issues Trigger First Health Care Audit Revocation of the 1990s," 6 *J. Tax. Exempt Orgs.* (No. 6) 259 (May/June 1995).

(iii) Percentage-Based Compensation. Some compensation arrangements are not fixed payments based on a salary, wage, or (perhaps) bonus but, in whole or in part, on a percentage of the tax-exempt organization's revenue. (In the intermediate sanctions setting, these forms of compensation are often revenue-sharing arrangements.[117]) The law on this point is unclear and inconsistent. In one case, a court held that a percentage compensation arrangement involving an exempt organization amounted to private inurement, because there was no upper limit as to total allowable compensation.[118] This court subsequently restricted the import of this decision when it held that private inurement did not occur when an exempt organization paid its president a commission determined by a percentage of the contributions obtained by him. The court in the second of these cases held that the standard is whether the compensation is reasonable, rather than the manner in which it is ascertained. Fundraising commissions that are "directly contingent on success in procuring funds" were held by this court to be an "incentive well suited to the budget of a fledgling [charitable] organization."[119] In reaching this conclusion—and saying nothing about caps on compensation levels—the court reviewed states' charitable solicitation acts governing payments to professional solicitors, which the court characterized as "[s]anctioning such commissions and in many cases endors[ing] percentage commissions higher than" the percentage commission paid by the organization involved in the case.[120]

Another court subsequently introduced more confusion in this area when it ruled that "there is nothing insidious or evil about a commission-based compensation system" and thus that an arrangement, by which those who successfully secured contributions for a charitable organization were paid a percentage of the gift amounts, is "reasonable," despite the absence of any limit as to an absolute amount of compensation (and despite the fact that the law requires compensation to be reasonable, not the percentage by which it is determined).[121]

The IRS will likely closely scrutinize compensation programs of tax-exempt organizations that are predicated on an incentive feature by which compensation is a function of revenue received by the organization, is guaranteed, or is otherwise outside the boundaries of conventional compensation arrangements. These programs—sometimes termed *gainsharing arrangements*—have developed largely in the health care context. For example, the IRS concluded that the establishment of incentive compensation plans for the employees of an exempt hospital, with payments determined as a percentage of the excess of revenue over a budgeted level, will not constitute private inurement, where the plans are not devices to distribute profits to principals and are the result of arm's-length bargaining, and do not result in unreasonable compensation.[122] Employing similar reasoning, the agency approved guaranteed minimum annual salary contracts

---

[117] See § 3.8(d)(i), text accompanied by notes 325–330.
[118] People of God Community v. Comm'r, 75 T.C. 1053 (1989).
[119] World Family Corp. v. Comm'r, 81 T.C. 958, 970 (1983).
[120] *Id.* at 969. In general, see Hopkins, *The Law of Fundraising, Third Edition* (Hoboken, NJ: John Wiley & Sons, 2002) ("*Fundraising*"), § 5.13.
[121] Nat'l Found., Inc. v. United States, 87-2 U.S.T.C. ¶ 9602 (Ct. Cl. 1987).
[122] Gen. Couns. Mem. 39674. Also Lorain Avenue Clinic v. Comm'r, 31 T.C. 141 (1958); INFO 2002-0021.

pursuant to which physicians' compensation was subsidized so as to induce them to commence employment at a hospital.[123] The IRS promulgated guidance concerning the tax consequences of physician recruitment incentives.[124]

The agency has explored other forms of productivity incentive programs[125] and contingent compensation plans.[126] Outside the health care field, the IRS concluded that a package of compensation arrangements for the benefit of coaches of sports for schools, colleges, and universities, including deferred compensation plans, payment of life insurance premiums, bonuses, and moving expense reimbursements, did not constitute private inurement.[127] In one instance, the IRS approved of a "sharable income policy" by which a tax-exempt scientific research organization provided one-third of the revenue derived from patents, copyrights, processes, or formulae to the inventors and 15 percent of the revenue received from the licensing or other transfer of the organization's technology to valuable employees.[128]

Hospital audit guidelines issued by the IRS contain a substantive review of the law concerning unreasonable compensation.[129] Although these guidelines address private inurement transactions between hospitals and their physicians and senior executives, they apply to any category of tax-exempt organization where the private inurement rules are applicable. These guidelines reflect the fact that contemporary concerns at the IRS in this regard embrace incentive compensation plans, recruitment and retention incentives, purchases of physicians' practices, open-ended employment contracts, and compensation based on a percentage of the institutions' net revenue. IRS examiners were urged to review compensation contracts to determine whether they were negotiated at arm's length; where that is not the case (such as where a physician is also a member of the hospital's board of trustees or is a department head), the contracts were said to warrant "closer scrutiny."[130]

(iv) Multiple Payors. An individual may receive compensation (including fringe benefits) and/or other payments from more than one organization, whether tax-exempt or not. A determination as to the reasonableness of this compensation or other payments must be made in the aggregate. Thus, for example, in the college and university examination guidelines developed by the IRS, examining agents were advised that "[i]f an employee is compensated by several entities, even if the entities have independent boards or representatives, examine the total compensation paid to such person by all entities over which the institution has significant

---

[123] Gen. Couns. Mem. 39498.

[124] Rev. Rul. 97-21, 1997-1 C.B. 121. In general, see Hyatt & Hopkins, *The Law of Tax-Exempt Healthcare Organizations, Second Edition* (Hoboken, NJ: John Wiley & Sons, 2001), Chapter 25.

[125] E.g., Gen. Couns. Mem. 36918.

[126] E.g., Gen. Couns. Mem. 32453.

[127] Gen. Couns. Mem. 39670. Cf. Copperweld Steel Co.'s Warren Employees' Trust v. Comm'r, 61 T.C.M. 1642 (1991) (where an organization was denied tax-exempt status on the basis of IRC § 501(c)(3) because its primary purpose was the provision of compensatory fringe benefits).

[128] Priv. Ltr. Rul. 9316052.

[129] IRS Audit Guidelines for Hospitals, Manual Transmittal 7(10) 69-38 for Exempt Organizations Examinations Guidelines Handbook (March 27, 1992) ("Hospital Audit Guidelines") §§ 333.2, 333.3.

[130] *Id.* § 333.2(2).

control or influence."[131] The annual information return filed by most tax-exempt organizations[132] requires reporting of arrangements where a trustee, director, officer, or key employee of an organization received aggregate compensation of more than $100,000 from the organization and all related organizations, of which more than $10,000 was provided by the related organization.[133]

(v) Role of the Board. The law surrounding the private inurement doctrine does not mandate any particular conduct by the governing board of a tax-exempt organization. The contemporary trend, however, is imposition by regulators of corporate governance principles that include involvement by these boards in transactions and arrangements that may have private inurement implications. For example, the IRS prefers that a board of directors or trustees of an exempt organization, particularly a charitable one, be involved in deciding the compensation amounts of at least an organization's key employees. The IRS also is actively encouraging the boards of exempt organizations to adopt conflict-of-interest policies, in part to help bring relationships that have the potential for private inurement to the fore.

(vi) Tax-Exempt Organizations Checklist. In an attempt to avoid transgression of the private inurement doctrine, a tax-exempt organization that is subject to the doctrine should be prepared to answer these questions in connection with the compensation of those who are insiders with respect to it[134]:

1. What are the components of each individual's compensation?

2. How did the organization establish the amount of each individual's compensation?

3. What are the duties and responsibilities of each individual that performed services for the organization?

4. Does the amount of each individual's compensation represent the total economic benefits received from the exempt organization? If not, identify and value these additional benefits.

5. Does the exempt organization have documentation supporting the reasonableness of each individual's compensation? If so, identify it.

6. Did the organization's governing body approve the amount of each individual's compensation? If so, identify the manner of this approval.

7. Does the organization have an employment contract or other compensatory agreement with any individual? If so, provide a copy of the document.

8. Does the amount of each person's compensation agree with the amount reported on that individual's Form W-2 or Form 1099? If not, describe the difference.

---

[131] Examination Guidelines for Colleges and Universities, Internal Revenue Manual, Exempt Organization Handbook 7 (10)(69) § 342.

[132] See § 10.1.

[133] Form 990, Part V, line 75.

[134] For organizations that are subject to the private benefit doctrine (see § 3.6), these questions are pertinent to an exempt organization's payees even if they are not insiders.

9. Did any of these individuals use any property that the exempt organization owned or leased (such as an automobile, aircraft, real estate, credit card, laptop or other computer, or cell phone) for a purpose other than fulfillment of the organization's tax-exempt purposes? If so, was the value of this use included in compensation; was the value of this use included in the individual's Form W-2 or Form 1099?[135]

(vii) Board Member Compensation. The private inurement doctrine, to date, tends to focus on the compensation of board members of a tax-exempt organization for rendering services in an additional capacity, such as an officer or key employee. As the duties and responsibilities (and potential for liability) of exempt organization board members increases (due to the above-mentioned emerging corporate governance principles), so too does the propensity of board members to consider compensation for their services as board members. This practice is contrary to the culture of most charitable and many other types of exempt organizations; thus, there is little experience or documentation of compensation amounts in this context. From the standpoint of the private inurement doctrine, the test again is whether such compensation is reasonable; nonetheless, inasmuch as this type of board member compensation is so uncommon, it is nearly impossible to gauge the reasonableness of this compensation by means of the multifactor test, which stresses comparables.[136]

(viii) Actuality of Services Rendered. Aside from the reasonableness of compensation, it is axiomatic that a tax-exempt organization subject to the private inurement doctrine may not, without transgressing the doctrine, pay compensation where services are not actually rendered. For example, an organization was denied exempt status because it advanced funds to telephone solicitors, to be offset against earned commissions, where some of the solicitors resigned and kept the funds before earning commissions equal to or exceeding their advances.[137]

(b) Other Forms of Private Inurement

There are forms of private inurement other than excessive compensation. The principal ones are rental arrangements, lending arrangements, sales of assets, equity distributions, assumptions of liability, provision of employee benefits, a variety of tax avoidance schemes, the rendering of services, the provision of goods or refreshments, and certain retained interests, but not embezzlement.

---

[135] These questions are being posed by the IRS in connection with its Tax Exempt Compensation Enforcement Project, by which the agency is reviewing the compensation practices of public charities and private foundations, looking at how compensation amounts are determined and types of compensation transactions. During the federal government's fiscal year 2005, the IRS mailed approximately 1,250 compliance check letters; field examinations are under way. This initiative was launched in mid-2004 (IR-2004-106).

[136] See § 3.4(a)(ii). E.g., E.J. Harrison & Sons, Inc. v. Comm'r, 2005-2 U.S.T.C. ¶ 50,493 (9th Cir. 2005).

[137] Senior Citizens of Missouri, Inc. v. Comm'r, 56 T.C.M. 479 (1988). In general, Broeck, "Preventing Private Inurement by Measuring the Reasonableness of Compensation for Executives," 6 *J. Tax Exempt Orgs.* (No. 1) 21 (July/Aug. 1994); Steinberg, "Profits and Incentive Compensation in Nonprofit Firms," 1 *Nonprofit Management & Leadership* (No. 2) 137 (1990).

(i) Rental Arrangements. A tax-exempt organization subject to the doctrine of private inurement generally may lease property and make rental payments for the use of property, in a transaction involving an insider.[138] The rent payments, and other terms and conditions of the arrangement, must, however, be reasonable; it should be beneficial for the exempt organization. That is, an inflated rent amount favoring the insider is private inurement.[139]

The hospital audit guidelines pointed out that one form of private inurement is "payment of excessive rent" and stated that "[a]reas of concern" include "below market leases."[140] The guidelines observed that examining agents should be alert to the existence of "rent subsidies," noting that "[o]ffice space in the [tax-exempt] hospital/medical office building for use in the physician's private practice generally must be provided at a reasonable rental rate gauged by market data and by actual rental charges to other tenants in the same facility."[141] These guidelines stated that it is permissible for a physician to use an exempt organization's facility for both hospital duties and private practice, as long as the "time/use of [the] office [is] apportioned between hospital activities and private practice activities and a reasonable rent [is] charged for the private practice activities."[142]

The factors to be considered in determining reasonableness in the rental arrangement context include the duration of the lease and the amount and frequency of the rent payments, with all elements of the relationship evaluated in relation to comparable situations in the community.

(ii) Lending Arrangements. A loan involving the assets of a tax-exempt organization subject to the doctrine of private inurement, made to an insider, is likely to be closely scrutinized by the IRS.[143] As the IRS has noted, the "very existence of a private source of loan credit from an [exempt] organization's earnings may itself amount to inurement of benefit."[144]

Like rental arrangements, the terms of this type of loan should be reasonable, that is, financially advantageous to the exempt organization (or at least not be disadvantageous) and should be commensurate with the organization's purposes (including investment policies).[145] The factors to be considered when assessing reasonableness in this setting include the duration of the indebtedness, the rate of interest paid, the security underlying the loan, and the amount involved—all evaluated in relation to similar circumstances in the commercial

---

[138] A rental arrangement between a private foundation and a disqualified person with respect to it is likely, however, to constitute an act of self-dealing (IRC § 4941(d)(1)(A)).

[139] E.g., Founding Church of Scientology v. United States, 412 F.2d 1197 (Ct. Cl. 1969), *cert. den.*, 397 U.S. 1009 (1970); Texas Trade School v. Comm'r, 30 T.C. 642 (1958), *aff'd*, 272 F.2d 168 (5th Cir. 1959).

[140] Hospital Audit Guidelines §§ 333.2(1), 333.3(1).

[141] *Id.* at § 333.3(7)(b).

[142] *Id.*

[143] A loan by a private foundation to a disqualified person with respect to it is likely to constitute an act of self-dealing (IRC § 4941(d)(1)(B)). See *Private Foundations*, Chapter 5.

[144] Founding Church of Scientology v. United States, 412 F.2d 1197, 1202 (Ct. Cl. 1969), *cert. den.*, 397 U.S. 1009 (1970). Also Unitary Mission Church of Long Island v. Comm'r, 74 T.C. 507 (1980), *aff'd*, 647 F.2d 163 (2d Cir. 1981); Western Catholic Church v. Comm'r, 73 T.C. 196 (1979), *aff'd*, 631 F.2d 736 (7th Cir. 1980), *cert. den.*, 450 U.S. 981 (1981); Church in Boston v. Comm'r, 71 T.C. 102 (1978).

[145] Griswold v. Comm'r, 39 T.C. 620 (1962).

setting. If such a loan is not repaid on a timely basis, questions as to private inurement may well be raised.[146] Thus, for example, the tax exemption of a school was revoked, in part because two of its officers were provided by the school with interest-free, unsecured loans that subjected the school to uncompensated risks for no business purpose.[147]

A court found private inurement resulting from a loan where a nonprofit organization, formed to assume the operations of a school conducted up to that point by a for-profit corporation, required parents of its students to make interest-free loans to the corporation. Private inurement was detected in the fact that the property to be improved using the loan proceeds would revert to the for-profit corporation after a 15-year term; the interest-free feature of the loans was held to be an unwarranted benefit to individuals in their private capacity.[148]

This court earlier found private inurement in a case involving a tax-exempt hospital and its founder, who was a physician who operated a clinic located in the hospital building.[149] The hospital and the clinic shared supplies and services; most of the hospital's patients were also patients of the founding physician and his partner. The hospital made a substantial number of unsecured loans to a nursing home owned by the physician and a trust for his children at below-market interest rates. The court held that there was private benefit to the physician because this use of the hospital's funds reduced his personal financial risk in and lowered the interest costs for the nursing home. The court also found inurement in the fact that the hospital was the principal source of financing for the nursing home, since an equivalent risk incurred for a similar duration could be expected to produce higher earnings elsewhere. In general, the court observed, "[w]here a doctor or group of doctors dominate the affairs of a corporate hospital otherwise exempt from tax, the courts have closely scrutinized the underlying relationship to insure that the arrangements permit a conclusion that the corporate hospital is organized and operated *exclusively* for charitable purposes without any private inurement."[150]

The hospital audit guidelines state that a form of private inurement is "inadequately secured loans"[151] and that a loan used as a recruiting subsidy is appropriate (assuming the requisite need for the physician in the first instance) as long as the recruitment contract "require[s] full repayment (at prevailing interest rates)."[152] These guidelines provided three factors that the IRS considers in determining whether a loan made by a tax-exempt organization to an insider is reasonable: (1) generally, the loan agreement should specify a reasonable rate of interest (the prime rate plus 1 or 2 percent) and provide for adequate security, (2) the loan decision should be reviewed by the board of directors of the exempt organization and should include consideration of the history of payment of prior loans by the insider, and (3) even if determined reasonable, any variance in

---

[146] Best Lock Corp. v. Comm'r, 31 T.C. 1217 (1959); Rev. Rul. 67-5, 1967-1 C.B. 123.
[147] John Marshall Law School v. United States, 81-2 U.S.T.C. ¶ 9514 (Ct. Cl. 1981).
[148] Hancock Academy of Savannah, Inc. v. Comm'r, 69 T.C. 488 (1977).
[149] Lowry Hospital Ass'n v. Comm'r, 66 T.C. 850 (1976).
[150] *Id.* at 859 (emphasis in the original).
[151] Hospital Audit Guidelines § 333.2(1).
[152] *Id.* § 333.3(4).

the terms of the loan from what the borrower could obtain from a typical lending institution must be treated, and appropriately reported, as compensation.[153]

(iii) Sales of Assets. Another application of the private inurement doctrine involves the sale of assets of tax-exempt organizations to those who are insiders with respect to them. A charitable or other exempt organization may, for example, decide to sell assets relating to a program activity, because the organization no longer wishes to engage in that activity. Sometimes, for a variety of reasons, these assets are sold to one or more individuals who are insiders (usually directors or officers). As with other manifestations of these transactions, they are not prohibited; the requirement is that their terms and conditions be reasonable.

A case illustrates some of the difficulties and complexities that can arise in this context. The matter concerned the sale of the assets of an exempt hospital to an entity controlled by insiders with respect to the hospital. The court concluded that the transaction gave rise to private inurement because the sale was not at arm's length, which caused the assets to be sold for less than their fair market value.

An appraiser determined that the fair market value of the hospital in 1981 was between $3.5 and $4.3 million. The IRS issued a private letter ruling in 1982, holding that the sale would be on an arm's-length basis and would not jeopardize the organization's tax-exempt status.[154] The sale closed in 1983 with a purchase price (as ultimately determined by the court) of $6.6 million. The hospital expanded over the ensuing months and obtained a certificate of need for additional beds. The operating assets were sold in 1985 for $29.6 million to a large health care provider. In 1990 the hospital was sold for $4.3 million.

The court found that the lawyers who negotiated the sale in 1983, "as far as the legal as distinguished from the financial aspects of the sale were concerned, acted independently and in good faith and sought to protect the interests" of their clients.[155] The court continued, however, to state that "there are serious questions as to the extent to which the negotiations adequately took into account certain financial aspects of the transaction which may cause the negotiations and the resulting sale price to be categorized as not being at arm's length and therefore giving rise to inurement."[156]

The court noted an array of elements that were either not taken into account or were inadequately taken into account in arriving at the price, including various changes in the value of assets between 1981 and 1983, valuations of adjacent properties that were transferred as part of the deal, the value of a certificate of need, the impact of changes in Medicare reimbursement policy, and the sales of the hospital in 1985 and 1990. Factoring in these elements, the court concluded that the fair market value of the assets transferred in 1983 was $7.8 million.

This court was not unmindful of the subsequent sales, particularly the one in 1985. It wrote that "evidence as to [a] latter category of events may be admitted because of its potential relevance even though it may ultimately be determined

---

[153] *Id.* § 333.3(10).
[154] See Priv. Ltr. Rul. 8234084.
[155] Anclote Psychiatric Center, Inc. v. Comm'r, 76 T.C.M. 175, 182 (1998). Also Priv. Ltr. Rul. 9130002.
[156] Anclote Psychiatric Center, Inc. v. Comm'r, 76 T.C.M. 175, 183 (1998).

that such evidence does not have an impact on the determination of fair market value."[157] As to this case, the court cryptically wrote that "other evidence could provide a basis for concluding that the elements which impacted the 1985 sale may have been sufficiently known or anticipated at the time of the 1983 sale."[158]

The difference between $7.8 million and $6.6 million was found to be "substantial."[159] The value of $7.8 million was found to "fall outside the upper limit of any reasonable range of fair market values."[160] The negotiations between the lawyers were found to be "fatally flawed because of their apparent failure to take into account the obvious and substantial" increases in asset values over the period 1981–1983.[161] The court rejected reliance on the appraisal, in that, by the time of closing, it was more than 18 months old.

This opinion, being neither a model of clarity nor consistency,[162] nonetheless offers several lessons: (1) the fair market value of property sold by an exempt organization to one or more insiders should be established by an independent appraiser, whose appraisal should not be stale; (2) an IRS favorable ruling is not necessarily protection in relation to subsequent turns of events; (3) lawyers or others negotiating this type of transaction may not blindly rely on an appraisal but must independently assure themselves that all relevant items are valued; and (4) the IRS and the courts are permitted to take into account, in assessing value, events and actions that occur *after* the sale. Apparently, it is not enough to value items that are *known* at the time; consideration must somehow be accorded those that may be *anticipated*.

This opinion is not, however, completely adverse to the interests of tax-exempt organizations. The court rejected the claim of the IRS that it is necessary to determine a "precise amount" representing the fair market value of property in a private inurement case.[163] All that is required is an amount that is "sufficiently close to the fair market value of the property at the time of the sale."[164] The court wrote that, when the amount is within a "reasonable range" of what could be considered fair market value, there cannot be private inurement.[165]

An open issue is whether, in assigning a value to an item of property for private inurement purposes, a single valuation will suffice.[166] Moreover, there is no mandated valuation method. The IRS wrote that "no single valuation method is necessarily the best indicator of value in a given case."[167] Yet the agency has signaled its

---

[157] *Id.*

[158] *Id.*

[159] *Id.* at 186.

[160] *Id.*

[161] *Id.* at 187.

[162] This opinion opened with the court stating that the issue of revocation "turns on the question [of] whether petitioner's sale of its hospital in May 1983 was for less than fair market value" (at 176). Yet, a few pages later, the court wrote that "fair market value plays an important role but is not determinative herein" (at 182).

[163] *Id.* at 182.

[164] *Id.*

[165] *Id.* A similar case unfolded in the intermediate sanctions setting (Caracci v. Comm'r, 118 T.C. 379 (2002)); see, e.g., § 3.8(d)(i), text accompanied by note 321.

[166] In the charitable giving setting, where an appraisal of property is required, only a single appraisal is called for; see Hopkins, *The Tax Law of Charitable Giving, Third Edition* (Hoboken, NJ: John Wiley & Sons, 2005; 2006 supplement) ("*Charitable Giving*"), § 21.2.

[167] Priv. Ltr. Rul. 9130002.

preference for various appraisal methodologies in valuing property, observing in one instance that "it would be logical to assume that an appraisal that has considered and applied a variety of approaches in reaching its 'bottom line' is more likely to result in an accurate valuation than an appraisal that focused on a single valuation method."[168]

(iv) Equity Distributions. With the emphasis of the federal tax law, in the private inurement area, on *net earnings* and the reference to *private shareholders*, the most literal and obvious form of private inurement is the parceling out of an exempt organization's net income to those akin to shareholders, such as members of its board of directors. It is rare, however, that private inurement is this blatant.

In one instance, nonetheless, this type of private inurement was identified. In this case, the assets of a tax-exempt hospital relating to a pharmacy were sold to an organization, which then sold pharmaceuticals to the hospital at higher prices. A court held that that practice amounted to the "siphoning off" of the hospital's income for the benefit of its stockholders.[169] Thereafter, apparently according to a preconceived plan, the corporation was dissolved and the sales proceeds distributed to its shareholders. While the reasoning is far from clear, the court observed that "[i]t is doubtful, too, whether an organization's operation can be 'exclusively' for charitable purposes . . . when its income is being accumulated to increase directly the value of the interests of the stockholders which they expect, eventually, to receive beneficially."[170] This separation of the pharmacy from the hospital resulted in the retroactive revocation of the exempt status of the hospital.[171]

In nearly all of the states, nonprofit corporations may not be organized as entities with the ability to issue stock. Even in the few instances where tax-exempt organizations may have stockholders, the organizations may not pay dividends. In one instance, memberships in a tax-exempt hospital were found to not entitle the members to a beneficial interest in the capital or earnings of the hospital because the law of the state prohibited the corporation from paying any part of its income to members and required transfer of the assets upon dissolution for charitable purposes.[172]

(v) Assumptions of Liability. Generally, a tax-exempt organization can incur debt to purchase an asset at its fair market value, thereafter retire the debt with its receipts, and not thereby violate the private inurement proscription.[173] As is the case with the sale of an asset, however, if the purchase price for an asset acquired

---

[168] *Id.*

[169] Maynard Hospital, Inc. v. Comm'r, 52 T.C. 1006, 1027, 1032 (1969).

[170] *Id.* at 1031.

[171] An organization once classified as a charitable one had its tax exemption retroactively revoked because revenue was diverted to two of its officers for their personal use, including payments for school tuition, insurance, car repairs, and home landscaping (Tech. Adv. Mem. 9851001).

[172] Estate of Grace M. Scharf v. Comm'r, 316 F.2d 625 (7th Cir. 1963), *aff'g* 38 T.C. 15 (1962).

[173] E.g., Shiffman v. Comm'r, 32 T.C. 1073 (1959); Estate of Howes v. Comm'r, 30 T.C. 909 (1958), *aff'd sub nom.*, Comm'r v. Johnson, 267 F.2d 382 (1st Cir. 1959); Ohio Furnace Co., Inc. v. Comm'r, 25 T.C. 179 (1955), *app. dis.* (6th Cir. 1956). The acquisition of property by means of debt-financing may, however, generate unrelated business income (IRC § 514) (see § 5.10).

from an insider is in excess of the property's fair market value (debt-financed or not), private inurement may result.[174]

In one instance, a nonprofit corporation was formed to take over the operation of a school conducted up to that time by a for-profit corporation. The organization assumed a liability for goodwill, which a court determined was an excessive amount. The court ruled that this assumption of liability was a violation of the prohibition on private inurement because it benefited the private interests of the owners of the for-profit corporation.[175] This court strongly suggested that any payment by a tax-exempt organization to an insider for goodwill constitutes private inurement, inasmuch as goodwill generally is a measure of the profit advantage in an established business and the profit motive is, by definition, not supposed to be a factor in the operation of an exempt organization.[176] This is a quaint and probably, in the modern era, inaccurate understanding of nonprofit organization law; no other court has expanded on the point.

(vi) Employee Benefits. A tax-exempt organization can provide reasonable compensation, including standard benefits, to its employees.[177] For example, a court found that payments for medical insurance are "ordinary and necessary" expenses of a tax-exempt employer.[178] An organization may not be able to qualify as an exempt charitable one, however, where the provision of employee benefits is its purpose. For example, a trust created by an employer to pay pensions to retired employees failed to qualify as a charitable entity.[179] This would be the result where the recipients are still employees providing services, in part because they do not constitute a charitable class.[180] Thus, a foundation lost its tax-exempt status because it devoted its funds to the payment of the expenses of young performers employed by the foundation's founder, who was in show business.[181] Organizations such as these may, however, qualify for tax exemption under other provisions of the federal tax law.[182]

A school's tax exemption was revoked because, for one or more of its officers, it provided interest-free, unsecured loans, paid for household items and furnishings used in their residences, made scholarship grants to their children, paid personal travel expenses, paid for their personal automobile expenses, paid the premiums on life and health insurance policies (where the premiums were not paid for other employees), and purchased season tickets for them to sports events.[183] Yet, in another instance, a court concluded that the payment by a church of medical expenses for its minister and family did not constitute private inurement.[184]

---

[174] E.g., Kolkey v. Comm'r, 27 T.C. 37 (1956), *aff'd*, 254 F.2d. 51 (7th Cir. 1958).

[175] Hancock Academy of Savannah, Inc. v. Comm'r, 69 T.C. 488 (1977).

[176] *Id.* at 494, note 6.

[177] See § 11.9.

[178] Carter v. United States, 973 F.2d 1479, 1487 (9th Cir.1992).

[179] Rev. Rul. 56-138, 156-1 C.B. 202.

[180] Rev. Rul. 68-422, 1968-2 C.B. 207. Also Watson v. United States, 355 F.2d 269 (3d Cir. 1965).

[181] Horace Heidt Foundation v. United States, 170 F. Supp. 634 (Ct. Cl. 1959).

[182] E.g., IRC §§ 401, 501(c)(9), (c)(17).

[183] John Marshall Law School v. United States, 81-2 U.S.T.C. ¶ 9514 (Ct. Cl. 1981). Also Chase v. Comm'r, 19 T.C.M. 234 (1960).

[184] Brian Ruud International v. United States, 733 F. Supp. 396 (D.D.C. 1989).

The IRS came around to the view that charitable and other tax-exempt organizations may establish profit-sharing and similar compensation plans without causing private inurement,[185] having earlier taken the position that the establishment of qualified profit-sharing plans resulted in *per se* private inurement.[186] This shift in position was based on the reasoning that the principles of qualification of pension and profit-sharing plans[187] and the protections afforded by the Employee Retirement Income Security Act (enacted in 1974) are sufficient to ensure that operation of these plans would not jeopardize the tax-exempt status of the nonprofit organizations involved. Thereafter, legislation enacted in 1986 amended the employee plan rules to make it clear that tax-exempt organizations can, without jeopardy, maintain qualified profit-sharing plans[188] and extended deferred compensation rules[189] to make them applicable to tax-exempt organizations.

Tax-exempt organizations may maintain the qualified cash or deferral arrangements known as 401(k) plans.[190] A charitable organization may maintain a tax-sheltered annuity program for its employees.[191] In general, tax-exempt organizations may pay pensions, where the terms are reasonable, to their retired employees without adversely affecting their tax-exempt status.[192]

(vii) Tax Avoidance Schemes. Tax-exempt organizations can be used impermissibly as vehicles to avoid income taxation. The circumstance troubling the IRS in this context is the transfer by an individual, in a business or profession, of his or her business assets to a controlled nonprofit entity solely for the purpose of avoiding taxes, who then continues to operate the business or profession as an employee of the transferee organization. Transactions of this nature are seen as lacking in substance, with the nonprofit entity manipulated for private gain.

In one instance, a physician transferred his medical practice and other assets to a controlled organization, which hired him to conduct "research," which amounted to the ongoing examination and treatment of patients; tax exemption for this organization was denied.[193] In another case, an organization, ostensibly a church, was formed by a professional nurse, who was the organization's minister, director, and principal officer. It held assets and liabilities formerly owned and assumed by the nurse, and provided the nurse with a living allowance and use of the assets, including a house and automobile. The organization was found by the IRS to not qualify as a tax-exempt organization because it "serves as a vehicle for handling the nurse's personal financial transactions."[194] In another instance, a court found that "tax avoidance" was a "substantial nonexempt purpose" of an

---

[185] Gen. Couns. Mem. 39674.

[186] E.g., Gen. Couns. Mem. 35869.

[187] IRC § 401.

[188] IRC § 401(a)(27).

[189] IRC § 457.

[190] IRC § 401(k)(4)(B)(i).

[191] IRC § 403(b).

[192] Rev. Rul. 73-126, 1973-1 C.B. 220. See Chapter 16.

[193] Rev. Rul. 69-66, 1969-1 C.B. 151. Also Nittler v. Comm'r, 39 T.C.M. 422 (1979); Walker v. Comm'r, 37 T.C.M. 1851 (1978); Boyer v. Comm'r, 69 T.C. 521 (1977).

[194] Rev. Rul. 81-94, 1981-1 C.B. 330. Also Rev. Rul. 78-232, 1978-1 C.B. 69. These two rulings pertain to the *personal church* (see *Tax-Exempt Organizations* § 8.2(c)).

organization, as evidenced by its promotional literature and seminars, and for that reason revoked the organization's tax-exempt status.[195]

Another court, unwilling to recognize an organization as a church because most of the organization's support was derived from, and the organization paid the living expenses of, the founder, wrote that private "inurement is strongly suggested where an individual or small group is the principal contributor to an organization and the principal recipient of the distributions of the organization, and that individual or small group has exclusive control over the management of the organization's funds."[196] Another "church" failed to gain exemption because of the transfer to it of funds used to furnish a sports car to its donor and pastor.[197]

(viii) Services Rendered. An organization, the primary purpose of which is to render services to individuals in their private capacity, generally cannot qualify as a tax-exempt, charitable entity. There are exceptions to this general rule, of course, such as where the individuals benefited constitute members of a charitable class, the individual beneficiaries are considered merely instruments or means for advancement of a charitable objective, or the private benefit involved is incidental and/or unavoidable.

This type of private inurement takes many forms and involves judgments in specific cases that are difficult to quantify or generalize. For example, even though furtherance of the arts can be a charitable activity, a cooperative art gallery that exhibited and sold only its members' works was ruled to be serving their private ends—a "vehicle for advancing their careers and promoting the sale of their work"—and hence not tax-exempt, notwithstanding the fact that the exhibition and sale of works of art may sometimes be an exempt purpose.[198] Similarly, although the provision of housing assistance for low-income families may qualify as an exempt purpose, an organization that provided this form of assistance but gave preference for housing to employees of a farm proprietorship operated by the individual who controlled the organization was ruled to not qualify as a charitable organization.[199] Also, a school's tax exemption was revoked in part because it awarded scholarships to the children of two of its officers yet did not make scholarship grants to anyone else.[200]

The provision of services to individuals, as precluded by the private inurement proscription, takes several forms. For example, an organization created to provide bus transportation for school children to a tax-exempt private school was ruled to not be eligible for exemption.[201] The IRS said that the organization served a private rather than a public interest, in that it enabled the participating

---

[195] Freedom Church of Revelation v. United States, 588 F. Supp. 693 (D.D.C. 1984).

[196] The Church of Eternal Life & Liberty, Inc. v. Comm'r, 86 T.C. 916 (1986).

[197] McFall v. Comm'r, 58 T.C.M. 175 (1989). Also Good Friendship Temple v. Comm'r, 55 T.C.M. 1310 (1988); Church of Modern Enlightenment v. Comm'r, 55 T.C.M. 1304 (1988); Petersen v. Comm'r, 53 T.C.M. 235 (1987).

[198] Rev. Rul. 71-395, 1971-2 C.B. 228.

[199] Rev. Rul. 72-147, 1972-1 C.B. 147.

[200] John Marshall Law School v. United States, 8102 U.S.T.C. ¶ 9514 (Ct. Cl. 1981).

[201] Rev. Rul. 69-175, 1969-1 C.B. 149. Also Chattanooga Automobile Club v. Comm'r, 182 F.2d 551 (6th Cir. 1950).

parents to fulfill their individual responsibility of transporting children to school. The agency concluded: "When a group of individuals associate to provide a cooperative service for themselves, they are serving a private interest."[202] A testamentary trust established to make payments to charitable organizations and to use a fixed sum from its annual income for the perpetual care of the testator's burial lot was ruled to be serving a private interest and thus not qualify for tax exemption.[203] Further, an organization that operated a subscription "scholarship" plan, by which "scholarships" were paid to preselected, specifically named individuals designated by subscribers, was ruled to not be tax-exempt, since it was operated for the benefit of designated individuals.[204] Likewise, the furnishing of farm laborers for individual farmers, as part of the operation of a labor camp to house transient workers, was held to not be an agricultural purpose under the federal tax law but rather the provision of services to individual farmers that they would otherwise have to provide for themselves.[205] Also, a nonprofit corporation was deemed to be serving private purposes where it was formed to dredge a navigable waterway, little used by the general public, fronting the properties of its members.[206] Further, an organization that provided travel services, legal services, an insurance plan, an antitheft registration program, and discount programs to its members was held to be serving the interests of the members, thereby precluding the organization from qualifying as a tax-exempt educational organization.[207] Moreover, an organization was denied exempt status because a substantial portion of its funds was to be used to pay for the medical and rehabilitative care of an individual who was related to each of the trustees of the organization.[208]

Charitable organizations frequently provide services to individuals in their private capacity when they dispense financial planning advice in the context of designing major gifts. This type of personal service made available by tax-exempt organizations has never been regarded as jeopardizing the organization's tax exemption when undertaken by institutions such as churches, universities, colleges, and hospitals. The IRS, however, refused to accord tax exemption to an organization that engaged in financial counseling by providing tax planning services (including charitable giving considerations) to wealthy individuals referred to it by subscribing religious organizations. The court that subsequently heard the case upheld the agency's position, finding that tax planning is not an exempt activity (which, of course, it is not—outside of this context) and that the primary effect of the advice is to reduce individuals' liability for income taxes—a private benefit.[209] The court rejected the contention that the organization was

---

[202] Rev. Rul. 69-175, 1969-1 C.B. 149.

[203] Rev. Rul. 69-256, 1969-1 C.B. 150.

[204] Rev. Rul. 67-367, 1967-2 C.B. 188.

[205] Rev. Rul. 72-391, 1972-2 C.B. 249.

[206] Ginsburg v. Comm'r, 46 T.C. 47 (1966). Cf. Rev. Rul. 70-186, 1970-1 C.B. 128.

[207] U.S. C.B. Radio Ass'n, No. 1, Inc. v. Comm'r, 42 T.C.M. 1441 (1981).

[208] Wendy L. Parker Rehabilitation Found., Inc. v. Comm'r, 52 T.C.M. 51 (1986). This type of organization is, in any event, precluded from tax-exempt status pursuant to either IRC §§ 501(c)(3) or 501(c)(4) by reason of IRC § 501(m) (see *Tax-Exempt Organizations* § 22.1).

[209] Christian Stewardship Assistance, Inc. v. Comm'r, 70 T.C. 1037 (1978).

merely doing what the subscribing members can do for themselves without endangering their tax exemption: fundraising.

The private inurement proscription may apply not only to individuals in their private capacity but also to corporations, industries, professions, and the like. Thus, an organization primarily engaged in the testing of drugs for commercial pharmaceutical companies was ruled to not be engaged in scientific research or testing for public safety but to be serving the private interests of the manufacturers.[210] Similarly, an organization composed of members of a particular industry to develop new and improved uses for existing products of the industry was ruled to be operating primarily to serve the private interests of its creators and thus not be tax-exempt.[211] Further, an association of professional nurses that operated a nurses' registry was held to be affording greater employment opportunities for its members and thus to be substantially operating for private ends.[212]

On occasion, application of the rule that unwarranted services to members can cause denial or loss of an organization's tax-exempt status leads to bizarre circumstances. This limitation is, from time to time, stretched—bringing about adverse tax consequences for the organization involved—far beyond what Congress surely intended in legislating the proscription on private inurement.

A classic illustration of this expansionist reading of the rule against private inurement is the holding by a court that a genealogical society, the membership of which was composed of those interested in the migrations of individuals with a common name to and within the United States, failed to qualify as a charitable organization on the ground that its genealogical activities served the private interests of its members.[213] The society's activities included research of the "family's" development (primarily by collecting and abstracting historical data), preparation and dissemination of publications containing the research, promotion of scholarly writing, and instruction (by means of lectures and workshops) in the methodology of compiling and preserving historical, biographical, and genealogical research. The organization's underlying operational premise was that the growth and development of the continental United States can be understood by tracing the migratory patterns of a typical group of colonists and their descendants.

While the IRS and the court conceded that some of the society's activities were charitable and educational, they determined that the compilation and publication of the genealogical history of this "family" group was an activity that served the private interests of the organization's members. The court "note[d] specifically [the organization's] emphasis on compiling members' family lives and the [group's] family history" and held that any educational benefit "to the

---

[210] Rev. Rul. 68-373, 1968-2 C.B. 206. Also Rev. Rul. 65-1, 1965-1 C.B. 266.

[211] Rev. Rul. 69-632, 1969-2 C.B. 120.

[212] Rev. Rul. 61-170, 1961-2 C.B. 112.

[213] The Callaway Family Ass'n, Inc. v. Comm'r, 71 T.C. 340 (1978). This opinion presumably reinforces the IRS ruling that nonprofit genealogical societies in general qualify as tax-exempt social clubs (Rev. Rul. 67-8, 1967-1 C.B. 142) (see § 1.6(f)). In an opinion issued less than a month prior to the *Callaway Family Ass'n* case, the Tax Court recognized that a membership organization can qualify under IRC § 501(c)(3) where it provides information and services to both members and nonmembers (Nat'l Ass'n for the Legal Support of Alternative Schools v. Comm'r, 71 T.C. 118 (1978)).

public created by [the organization's] activities is incidental to this private purpose."[214] This conclusion ignored the discipline known as kinship studies, in which social history focuses extensively on families and family-related institutions, and strained to place a negative, private orientation on the term *family* when in fact the use of a family is merely a research technique by which the tracings of genealogy are undertaken pursuant to an objective standard.[215] This case presented a major threat to tax exemption for genealogical societies generally—but particularly *family associations*—because of the court's characterization of genealogical study as providing private inurement or other private benefit.[216]

Following this court's holding, the IRS acted to contain the reach of the decision. The agency ruled that a genealogical society may qualify as a tax-exempt educational organization by conducting lectures, sponsoring public displays and museum tours, providing written materials to instruct members of the general public on genealogical research, and compiling a geographical area's pioneer history.[217] This organization's membership, however, was open to all interested individuals in the area, rather than members of a "family," and the society did not conduct genealogical research for its members, although its members researched genealogies independently using the society's research materials. By contrast, the IRS also ruled that an organization cannot qualify as a charitable or educational entity where its membership is limited to descendants of a particular family, it compiled family genealogical research data for use by its members for reasons other than to conform to the religious precepts of the family's denomination, it presented the data to designated libraries, it published volumes of family history, and it promoted occasional social activities among family members.[218]

(ix) Provision of Goods or Refreshments. A tax-exempt organization subject to the private inurement doctrine cannot have as its primary purpose the provision of goods or refreshments (in the nature of social or recreational activities) to individuals in their private capacity. Of course, an organization of this nature may incidentally bear the expense of meals, refreshments, and the like (such as working luncheons and annual banquets) but, in general, "[r]efreshments, goods and services furnished to the members of an exempt corporation from the net profits of the business enterprise are benefits inuring to the individual members."[219] Thus, a discussion group that held closed meetings at which personally oriented speeches were given, followed by the serving of food and other refreshments, was ruled to not be tax-exempt, inasmuch as the public benefits were remote at

---

[214] *Id.* at 344.

[215] The Tax Court distinguished the general family association from the type of family association that engages in genealogical activities for religious purposes, usually one that is operated to collect and furnish information needed by the Mormon Church to advance its religious precepts (*id.* at 345). The IRS earlier ruled that these family associations are charitable entities because they advance religion (Rev. Rul. 71-580, 1971-2 C.B. 235). Yet the definition of the term *charitable* also includes the advancement of education. The private inurement restriction applies equally to all categories of charitable organizations.

[216] Also Manning Ass'n v. Comm'r, 93 T.C. 596 (1989); Benjamin Price Genealogical Ass'n v. Internal Revenue Service, 79-1 U.S.T.C. ¶ 9361 (D.D.C. 1979).

[217] Rev. Rul. 80-301, 1980-2 C.B. 180.

[218] Rev. Rul. 80-302, 1980-2 C.B. 182.

[219] Spokane Motorcycle Club v. United States, 222 F. Supp. 151, 153 (E.D. Wash. 1963).

best and the "functions of the organization are to a significant extent fraternal and designed to stimulate fellowship among the membership."[220]

(x) Retained Interests. A charitable organization may not be organized so that one or more individuals retains a reversionary interest, by which the principal would flow to an individual upon the entity's dissolution or liquidation; instead, in this event, net assets and income must be transferred to one or more other charitable or governmental entities.[221]

By contrast, a charitable organization may, in appropriate circumstances, accept an asset subject to a life estate or other income interest for one or more individuals; the fact that only a charitable remainder interest is acquired is not private inurement. Thus, there are bodies of law concerning permissible partial interest gifts to charitable organizations, of income and remainder interests.[222] Likewise, annuity payments made in exchange for a gift of property are not a form of private inurement to the annuitants, inasmuch as the payment of the annuity merely constitutes satisfaction of the charge on the transferred asset.[223]

(xi) Embezzlements. Private inurement does not occur when an insider steals money from a charitable or other tax-exempt organization. In a case where insiders stole proceeds from a charity's bingo games, private inurement was not found. The court wrote: "[W]e do not believe that the Congress intended that a charity must lose its exempt status merely because a president or a treasurer or an executive director of a charity has skimmed or embezzled or otherwise stolen from the charity, at least where the charity has a real-world existence apart from the thieving official."[224] It would be anomalous, indeed, for an exempt organization to suffer the loss and indignity of an embezzlement, and then be required to forfeit its tax-exempt status because it was the victim of the crime.[225]

§ 3.5 PRIVATE INUREMENT AND ASSOCIATIONS

The private inurement doctrine is, as noted, applicable with respect to tax-exempt business leagues. Therefore, an association or similar entity should know who its insiders are.[226] Directors and officers are, obviously, insiders, yet so too are key employees, members of the family of the foregoing individuals, and entities they control.

The doctrine is related to the proscription on unwarranted services to associations' members.[227] Thus, private inurement was deemed present with respect to an organization that used its funds to provide financial assistance and welfare

---

[220] Rev. Rul. 73-439, 1973-2 C.B. 176.

[221] Reg. § 1.501(c)(3)-1(c)(2); Rev. Rul. 66-259, 1966-2 C.B. 214.

[222] See *Charitable Giving*, Chapters 12 (charitable remainder trusts), 13 (pooled income funds), 15 (other gifts of remainder interests), and 16 (charitable lead trusts).

[223] Rev. Rul. 69-176, 1969-1 C.B. 150. See *Charitable* Giving, Chapter 14 (charitable gift annuities).

[224] Variety Club Tent No. 6 Charities, Inc. v. Comm'r, 74 T.C.M. 1485, 1494 (1997).

[225] In the intermediate sanctions setting, an economic benefit that a disqualified person obtains by theft or fraud cannot be treated as consideration for the performance of services (see § 3.8(d), note 317).

[226] See § 3.3.

[227] Reg. § 1.501(c)(6)-1. See § 2.10(c).

benefits to its members,[228] that paid its members for expenses incurred in malpractice litigation,[229] and that distributed royalties to its members.[230]

The doctrine can apply in the context of the level of members' dues in relation to an organization's receipt of nonmember income. Today this is an unrelated business issue,[231] although prior to the advent of those rules (in 1950) it had been held that a dues reduction subsidized by the earnings of a business constituted private inurement.[232] The IRS considered taking the position that a tiered dues structure of a tax-exempt association, with some members paying certain amounts and other members who were making payments to a related business league paying less dues, amounted to undue private benefit but elected to not get into that policy thicket.[233] Likewise, the IRS explored the matter of whether association members are being inappropriately subsidized when they pay less for publications, seminars, and the like than do nonmembers but chose to not pursue it.

A tax-exempt business league may receive income from nonmember sources without endangering its exemption where the income-producing activity is related to the exempt purposes of the association, such as a sports organization operating public championship tournaments,[234] a veterinarians' association operating a public rabies clinic,[235] an insurance agents association receiving commissions from handling insurance programs,[236] and a professional association conducting a training program for nonmembers.[237] Thus, an otherwise qualified exempt business league was able to derive its support primarily from the sale of television broadcasting rights to the tournaments it sponsored, without imperiling its exemption, because this sponsorship and sale of broadcasting rights by the organization "directly promotes the interests of those engaged in the sport and by enhancing awareness of the general public of the sport as a profession."[238]

Another private inurement issue of pertinence to tax-exempt associations concerns the tax consequences of cash rebates to exhibitors who participate in their trade shows.[239] As a general principle, a qualified business league may make cash distributions to its members without loss of exemption where the distributions represent no more than a reduction in dues or contributions previously paid to the organization in support of its activities.[240] The IRS extrapolated from this principle in ruling that an association may, without adversely affecting its exempt status, make cash rebates to member and nonmember exhibitors who participate in the association's annual trade show, where the rebates represent a

---

[228] Rev. Rul. 67-251, 1967-2 C.B. 196.
[229] Nat'l Chiropractor Ass'n v. Birmingham, 96 F. Supp. 874 (N.D. Iowa 1951).
[230] Wholesale Grocers Exchange v. Comm'r, 3 T.C.M. 699 (1944).
[231] See Chapter 5.
[232] Nat'l Automobile Dealers Ass'n v. Comm'r, 2 T.C.M. 291 (1943).
[233] Priv. Ltr. Rul. 9448036.
[234] Rev. Rul. 58-502, 1958-2 C.B. 271.
[235] Rev. Rul. 66-222, 1966-2 C.B. 223.
[236] Rev. Rul. 56-152, 1956-1 C.B. 56.
[237] Rev. Rul. 67-296, 1967-2 C.B. 22.
[238] Rev. Rul. 80-294, 1980-2 C.B. 187, 188.
[239] See § 5.9(n).
[240] E.g., King County Insurance Ass'n v. Comm'r, 37 B.T.A. 288 (1938).

portion of an advance floor deposit paid by each exhibitor to insure the show against financial loss, are made to all exhibitors on the same basis, and may not exceed the amount of the deposit.[241] Because the "effect of refunding a portion of the floor deposits is to reduce the exhibitors' cost of participating in the trade show," the IRS concluded that the return of funds would not constitute private inurement.[242] If, however, an exempt business league sponsoring an industry trade show, involving both member and nonmember exhibitors who are charged identical rates, makes space rental rebates only to its member exhibitors, the rebates are considered proscribed inurement of income.[243]

§ 3.6 PRIVATE BENEFIT DOCTRINE

An organization cannot qualify as a tax-exempt charitable entity if it has transgressed the *private benefit doctrine*. The tax regulations state that an organization is not organized or operated exclusively for one or more charitable purposes "unless it serves a public rather than a private interest."[244] As discussed, it apparently is an open question as to whether the doctrine is applicable outside the charitable area.[245] The concept of private benefit is a derivative of the operational test[246]; as one court put the matter, the private benefit proscription "inheres in the requirement that [a charitable] organization operate exclusively for exempt purposes."[247] The private benefit doctrine is separate from the private inurement doctrine, yet is broader than and thus subsumes that doctrine.[248]

(a) General Rules

The private benefit doctrine differs from private inurement doctrine in two significant respects. One is that the law recognizes the concept of *incidental* private benefit—that is, types of private benefit that will not cause loss or denial of tax-exempt status.[249] The other is that the private benefit doctrine can be applied in the absence of undue benefit to insiders.[250] As to the latter, a court noted that the private benefit doctrine embraces benefits provided to "disinterested persons."[251] Subsequently, this court wrote that impermissible private benefit can be conferred on "unrelated" persons.[252]

One of the few cases fully explicating the private benefit doctrine concerned an otherwise tax-exempt school that trained individuals for careers as political campaign professionals.[253] Nearly all of the school's graduates became employed

---

[241] Rev. Rul. 77-206, 1977-1 C.B. 149. Also Rev. Rul. 81-60, 1981-1 C.B. 335.

[242] Rev. Rul. 77-206, 1977-1 C.B. 149.

[243] Michigan Mobile Home & Recreational Vehicle Inst. v. Comm'r, 66 T.C. 770 (1976).

[244] Reg. § 1.501(c)(3)-1(d)(1)(ii).

[245] See text accompanied by *supra* notes 12–13.

[246] See *Tax-Exempt Organizations* § 4.5.

[247] Redlands Surgical Services v. Comm'r, 113 T.C. 47, 74 (1999), *aff'd*, 242 F.3d 904 (9th Cir. 2001).

[248] E.g., Church of Ethereal Joy v. Comm'r, 83 T.C. 20 (1984); Canada v. Comm'r, 82 T.C. 973 (1984); Goldsboro Art League, Inc. v. Comm'r, 75 T.C. 337 (1980); Aid to Artisans, Inc. v. Comm'r, 71 T.C. 202 (1978).

[249] E.g., Priv. Ltr. Rul. 200103083. Cf. *Tax-Exempt Organizations* § 19.9.

[250] Cf. § 3.3.

[251] American Campaign Academy v. Comm'r, 92 T.C.1053, 1069 (1989).

[252] Redlands Surgical Services v. Comm'r, 113 T.C. 47, 74 (1999), *aff'd*, 242 F.3d 904 (9th Cir. 2001).

[253] American Campaign Academy v. Comm'r, 92 T.C. 1053 (1989).

by or consultants to Republican Party organizations or candidates. A court concluded that the school did not primarily engage in activities that accomplished educational purposes, in that it benefited private interests to more than an insubstantial extent. That is, the school was found to be substantially benefiting the private interests of Republican Party entities and candidates.[254]

The heart of this opinion is the analysis of the concept—not previously or subsequently articulated—of *primary* private benefit and *secondary* private benefit. In this setting, the beneficiaries of primary private benefit were the students; the beneficiaries of secondary private benefit were the employers of the graduates. It was the existence of this secondary private benefit that caused this school to fail to acquire tax-exempt status. The court accepted the IRS's argument that "where the training of individuals is focused on furthering a particular targeted private interest, the conferred secondary benefit ceases to be incidental to the providing organization's exempt purposes."[255] The beneficiaries, at the secondary level, were found to be a "select group."[256]

The school unsuccessfully presented as precedent several IRS rulings holding tax-exempt, as educational organizations, entities that provide training to individuals in a particular industry or profession.[257] The court accepted the IRS's characterization of these rulings, which was that the "secondary benefit provided in each ruling was broadly spread among members of an industry . . . , as opposed to being earmarked for a particular organization or person."[258] The court said that the secondary benefit in each of these rulings was, because of the spread, "incidental to the providing organization's exempt purpose."[259]

The IRS has been advancing the private benefit doctrine as well. The most striking recent example of this was application of the doctrine, for the first time, in the private foundation setting. An individual requested access to an archive of materials, held by a foundation, concerning a distant and famous relative who had recently died, for the purpose of writing a book about the decedent. The book project was to be a commercial one; the foundation was not to be compensated for the author's use of the collection. The IRS ruled that, although provision of the materials to the author would not constitute self-dealing,[260] because the individual was not a disqualified person,[261] it would amount to substantial private benefit, which could endanger the tax-exempt status of the private foundation.[262]

Although tax-exempt charitable organizations may provide benefits to persons in their private capacity, benefits of this nature must—to avoid jeopardizing

---

[254] The court, in some portions of its opinion, seemed to be less concerned about private benefit and more troubled about assistance to a political party. For example, it wrote that the school "conducted its educational activities with [a] partisan objective" (at 1070) and operated to "advance Republican interests" (at 1072).

[255] *Id.* at 1074.

[256] *Id.* at 1076.

[257] E.g., Rev. Rul. 75-196, 1975-1 C.B. 155; Rev. Rul. 72-101, 1972-1 C.B. 144; Rev. Rul. 68-504, 1968-2 C.B. 211; Rev. Rul. 67-72, 1967-1 C.B. 125.

[258] American Campaign Academy v. Comm'r, 92 T.C. 1053, 1074 (1989).

[259] *Id.*

[260] IRC § 4941. See *Private Foundations*, Chapter 5.

[261] IRC § 4941. That is, this individual was not a member of the family of the decedent (IRC § 4946(a)(1)(D)). See *Private Foundations* § 4.4.

[262] Priv. Ltr. Rul. 200114040.

exempt status—be incidental both quantitatively and qualitatively in relation to the furthering of exempt purposes. To be quantitatively incidental, the private benefit must be insubstantial, measured in the context of the overall tax-exempt benefit conferred by the activity.[263] To be qualitatively incidental, private benefit must be a necessary concomitant of the exempt activity, in that the exempt objectives cannot be achieved without necessarily benefiting certain individuals privately.[264]

As an illustration, a nonprofit organization was formed to generate community interest in retaining classical music programming on a commercial radio station, by seeking sponsors for the programs, urging listeners to patronize the sponsors, and soliciting listener subscriptions to promote the programs; the IRS ruled that the organization could not qualify for tax exemption because these activities increased the station's revenues and thus benefited it in more than an insubstantial manner.[265] By contrast, a charitable organization that allocated Medicaid patients to physicians in private practice was held to provide qualitative and quantitatively incidental private benefits to the physicians, including some on the organization's board of directors, inasmuch as it would be "impossible" for the organization to accomplish its exempt purposes without providing some measure of benefit to the physicians.[266]

(b) Import of Joint Venture Law

The private benefit doctrine has been repeatedly invoked in a line of cases concerning the involvement of tax-exempt charitable organizations in partnerships and other joint ventures.[267] The IRS has an ongoing concern that some of these ventures may constitute a means for conferring unwarranted private benefit on nonexempt participants. The agency initially lost these cases, but recently its victories have propelled the private benefit doctrine into one of the major elements of the law of tax-exempt organizations.[268]

Overall, today, a tax-exempt charitable organization can participate as a general partner in a limited partnership, without endangering its exempt status, if the organization is serving a charitable purpose by means of the partnership, the organization is insulated from the day-to-day responsibilities as general partner, and the limited partners are not receiving an undue economic benefit from the partnership.[269]

(c) Perspective

The IRS is making much of the private benefit doctrine. Two examples illustrate this. The agency is of the view that private benefit is present when the founders of an otherwise tax-exempt school also are directors of a for-profit company that

---

[263] E.g., Ginsburg v. Comm'r, 46 T.C. 47 (1966); Rev. Rul. 75-286, 1975-2 C.B. 210; Rev. Rul. 68-14, 1968-1 C.B. 243.

[264] E.g., Rev. Rul. 70-186, 1970-1 C.B. 128.

[265] Rev. Rul. 77-206, 1977-1 C.B. 149.

[266] Priv. Ltr. Rul. 9615030.

[267] See Chapter 7.

[268] See § 7.2(a).

[269] E.g., Gen. Couns. Mem. 39862, 39732, 39546, 39444, 39005, 37789. See § 7.1.

manages the school; the nature of the benefit is largely financial, and the IRS asserted that the educational activities of the school could be undertaken without conferring the benefit (such as by use of employees or volunteers).[270] It also believes that certain scholarship-granting foundations are ineligible for tax exemption, by reason of the private benefit doctrine, because the recipients are individuals who are participants in beauty pageants operated by tax-exempt social welfare organizations; private benefit is thought to be bestowed on the social welfare organizations because the grant programs serve to attract contestants to enter the pageants and on the for-profit entities that are corporate sponsors of the pageants.[271]

Traditionally, then, the private benefit doctrine has been applied largely in cases concerning relationships between public charities and individuals. The application of this doctrine, however, is being expanded to encompass arrangements between charitable organizations and for-profit entities and charitable organizations and other categories of tax-exempt organizations.[272]

The IRS, from time to time, issues rulings denying recognition of, or revoking, tax exemption on the basis of the private benefit doctrine.[273]

§ 3.7 PRIVATE BENEFIT AND ASSOCIATIONS

The courts have applied the private benefit doctrine only to situations involving charitable organizations. Over the decades, the IRS has done the same. In 2004, however, the IRS suggested that the private benefit doctrine is applicable with respect to tax-exempt status for social welfare organizations.[274] Therefore, the agency could take the position that this doctrine is applicable with respect to exempt business leagues and similar organizations.

A decision from the U.S. Tax Court, issued in 2000, is of considerable interest (and should be of immense concern) to the association community, in that it invoked the private benefit doctrine in connection with a "foundation," seeking recognition of exemption, that was related to a tax-exempt business league.[275] This opinion is of sufficient import to warrant a full examination of it.

---

[270] "Private Benefit Under IRC 501(c)(3)," Topic H in the IRS Exempt Organizations Continuing Professional Education Technical Instruction Program textbook for fiscal year 2001.

[271] "Beauty Pageants: Private Benefit Worth Watching," Topic B in the IRS Exempt Organizations Continuing Professional Education Technical Instruction Program textbook for fiscal year 2002.

[272] The court of appeals that reversed the Tax Court in United Cancer Council, Inc. v. Comm'r, 165 F.3d 1173 (7th Cir. 1999), also remanded the case for consideration in light of the private benefit doctrine. Inasmuch as an act of private inurement is also an act of private benefit (see § 3.6, text accompanied by supra note 248), the *United Cancer Council* case was shaping up to be a significant private benefit case. The case, however, was settled before the Tax Court could rule on the private benefit law aspects. In general, Raby and Raby, "Private Inurement, Private Benefit, *UCC*, and Intermediate Sanctions," 24 *Exempt Org. Tax. Rev.* (No. 2) 315 (May 1999).

[273] E.g., Priv. Ltr. Rul. 200447050.

[274] Ex. Den. and Rev. Ltr. 20044008E. The organization involved in this matter was found by the IRS to be partisan in nature; the authority relied on by the IRS was American Campaign Academy v. Comm'r, 92 T.C. 1053 (1989). Inasmuch as the private benefit doctrine is a derivative of the operational test applicable only with respect to IRC § 501(c)(3) entities (see *Tax-Exempt Organizations* § 4.5), this reasoning by the agency seems incorrect.

[275] Quality Auditing Co. v. Comm'r, 114 T.C. 498 (2000).

The court held that a nonprofit organization that audits structural steel fabricators in conjunction with a quality certification program conducted by a related trade association does not constitute a charitable organization that lessens the burdens of government, and yields private benefit to the association and to the fabricators who are inspected. This is the first court case in which the private benefit doctrine was applied with respect to a benefit conferred on a tax-exempt, noncharitable organization.

(a) Summary of Facts

Developments and concerns within the structural steel fabrication industry, and particularly the response to them by the American Institute of Steel Construction, Inc. (AISC), led to the formation of the Quality Auditing Company (QAC). QAC was organized as a nonprofit charitable and educational entity. AISC, a tax-exempt business league, has been engaged primarily in the creation of standardized engineering codes and specifications for use in the fabrication and construction of steel-framed buildings and bridges.

During the 1960s, a number of governmental agencies and private industrial owners and developers approached AISC and requested that it develop a certification program for structural steel fabricators. Technological advances had increased both the predominance and the complexity of steel's role in commercial and residential structures; a growing concern over potential differences in quality had arisen among entities attempting to select contractors for this component of a building project. Yet few owners and developers had sufficient expertise, time, or funds to adequately investigate the fabricators submitting project bids. AISC undertook to create a program that would afford the requested quality assurances.

Working in collaboration with engineers, architects, contractors, and other industry participants (including government agencies), AISC developed and trademarked the AISC Quality Certification Program. The program incorporates codes, standards, and specifications for particular aspects of the fabricating process. It is designed to verify that fabricators have in place a quality control system that will ensure compliance with construction standards and contract requirements. Ongoing revision and upgrading of the program track changes and advancements within the industry.

Fabricators desiring certification, often because the owner or developer of a project conditioned bid awards on that requirement, submit an application and appropriate fee to AISC. The fees are determined in accordance with a schedule set by AISC and are based on the fabricator's status as a member or nonmember of AISC, the type of certification being sought, and the number of employees at the facility. The program is open to all fabricators, regardless of AISC membership.

AISC then contracts with and pays for an independent entity to perform the actual audit investigation of the fabricator's facility. The auditor evaluates the fabricator's quality control procedures to determine whether the procedures adequately test for and ensure compliance with the industry specifications incorporated in the program. No particular structure, project, or product is certified; the construction process itself is examined.

Following the audit, the auditor communicates the findings to the fabricator and recommends to AISC whether certification should be awarded. On receipt of a positive recommendation from the auditor, AISC forwards to the fabricator documentation reflecting AISC-certified status. If the auditor does not believe certification is warranted, the fabricator may choose to be reevaluated after corrective actions have been implemented. The specific report pertaining to a particular audit is not disseminated to the public, although AISC publishes the names of the certified companies.

In administering the program, AISC initially contracted with a for-profit company to conduct the facility audits. This approach was not successful, however, in that (in the words of the court) a "profit-driven enterprise was unwilling to reinvest a sufficient portion of the fees charged to achieve the level of auditor training and audit consistency necessary for a uniform, reliable certification program."[276]

Consequently, AISC provided the start-up capital to establish QAC as a nonprofit corporation. QAC's purpose is to conduct quality certification and inspection programs that meet the requirements of private and public standards-setting bodies and governmental agencies. No other organization presently provides this service. The boards of directors of AISC and QAC are overlapping.

QAC hires and trains independent contractors to inspect and audit the facilities of fabricators applying to AISC for certification. It pays royalties to AISC for use of its trademarked certification program. QAC's income is derived solely from the fees charged AISC for conducting the quality audits. Fees are set at a level that approximates actual costs.

The AISC certification program is increasingly becoming recognized as furthering structural integrity and quality within the steel fabrication industry. Numerous private and public owners, developers, and contractors (including the Army Corps of Engineers and as many as 40 state highway departments) require AISC certification for bridges and other metal work. To promote the program, AISC solicits owners and developers to require certification of fabricators submitting bids.

The IRS ruled that AISC was not entitled to recognition of tax-exempt status as a charitable entity.

(b) Summary of Opinion

QAC asserted that its purpose and activities are charitable in that quality auditing of steel fabrication firms lessens the burdens of government and encourages the safe construction of buildings and bridges for the benefit of the general public.

The IRS's view was that QAC's inspection activity does not lessen the burdens of any government and does not confer upon the public any benefit that is not merely incidental to QAC's furthering of the private interests of AISC and firms within the steel industry.

---

[276] *Id.* at 501.

Lessening the burdens of government is one way for a nonprofit organization to be charitable for federal income tax exemption purposes.[277] Generally, however, two criteria must be satisfied. One is that the activities engaged in by the organization must be those that a governmental unit considers to be its burden. The other is that the organization's performance of the activities must actually lessen the burdens of a government.

QAC failed the first of these tests. The court observed that there is no indication in the record that governmental units consider it their burden to inspect or certify the quality control procedures in place in the facilities of private fabricators. It was noted that governmental agencies were among those that initially requested that AISC develop a certification program and that have since made use of the program in awarding bids. But, wrote the court, these facts "fall short of demonstrating that governmental units view a program for auditing steel fabricators as a Government responsibility and recognize [QAC] as acting on their behalf."[278]

The court added that to the extent QAC facilitates government in selecting qualified fabricators, an equivalent benefit is conferred on private owners and developers. Private entities joined with public ones in requesting the AISC program and likewise utilize the program in awarding bids. The court concluded that if QAC is operated to lessen the burdens of government, it also operates to lessen the burdens on private parties.

The court wrote that "furthering public safety is indeed a charitable objective."[279] It agreed that the certification program and QAC's audit activities promote increased structural integrity and safety in steel buildings and bridges. Nonetheless, it concluded that QAC's activities also further private interests to a degree that is more than insubstantial.

The court reiterated that QAC performs quality audits at the request of AISC, which in turn acts at the request of steel fabricators applying for certification. The association and the fabricators are not, however, *public* entities.

It was written that the "development and administration of a quality certification program, at the request of and for the structural steel industry, would appear to be consistent with AISC's mission" as a business league.[280] The court added that the "focus thus seems to be on aiding industry participants, with any benefit to the general public being merely secondary."[281]

The court consequently perceived more than insubstantial private benefit in two contexts. One was the extent to which QAC serves AISC's interests in carrying out its role of industry betterment. QAC's efforts prevent problems in the industry that could flow from hiring fabricators with inadequate quality control, such as increased nonconformities, delays, project cost overruns, reduced structure longevity, and frequent repair expenditures. The court noted that safety is never mentioned in the solicitations of owners and developers.

---

[277] See *Tax-Exempt Organizations* § 6.4.
[278] Quality Auditing Co. v. Comm'r, 114 T.C. 498, 501 (2000).
[279] *Id.* at 509.
[280] *Id.* at 510.
[281] *Id.*

The other type of private benefit is that accruing to the steel fabricators that request audits and whose facilities are inspected by QAC. These are commercial entities, and the court was "constrained to assume" that they largely apply for certification when to do so furthers their primary objective of making a profit.[282] The fabricators "likely wish to pursue revenues from a contract requiring certification, or they see the certification process as a vehicle to increased work through an improved control process and reputation for quality."[283]

Both types of private benefit were found to be *substantial*, notwithstanding some "benefit reaped by the general public."[284]

(c) Commentary

This case amplifies and illuminates a body of law that is emerging as a major component of the law of tax-exempt organizations: the *private benefit doctrine*. This opinion illustrates the basic points that, unlike the *private inurement rule* (or the *intermediate sanctions rules*), there is no requirement that a party that privately benefits be an *insider*, and the law tolerates an *insubstantial* amount of private benefit.

This case also illustrates the perils of placing certification programs in charitable organizations. (This is true irrespective of whether the certification is of individuals or programs. Certification of organizations is termed *accreditation*; that usually is an exempt function.) The law is that although there is some public benefit to be gained from certification, the primary beneficiaries are those who are certified.[285]

From a larger perspective, the case further serves as a reminder that charitable organizations (often termed *foundations*) affiliated with business leagues need to be careful. The association and its members usually are *private* parties. Unwarranted programmatic relationships between the two entities can lead to denial or revocation of tax exemption for the related charitable foundation. (The association alone is likely to be an *insider* and/or *disqualified person* as well.)

Then there is this matter of definition of the term *charitable* for federal tax purposes. This is a concept that the courts are free to embellish. The Internal Revenue Code provides that *testing for public safety* is a charitable purpose—in the tax exemption setting (but not the charitable deduction setting). The Tax Court expanded the scope of the exemption somewhat by proclaiming that *furthering public safety* is a charitable objective.[286]

---

[282] *Id.*

[283] *Id.* at 510–511.

[284] *Id.* at 511.

[285] See §§ 1.3(c), 2.4(c).

[286] Congress expressly endorsed this type of in-tandem operating relationship involving tax-exempt organizations (see § 8.7). The supporting organizations rules permit an exempt business league (such as the AISC) to utilize a related charitable organization (such as the QAC). The court failed to acknowledge even the existence, let alone applicability, of this law. It is an anomaly that Congress would authorize such a relationship, only to have a court nullify it by application of the private benefit doctrine.

§ 3.8   EXCESS BENEFIT TRANSACTIONS

One of the newest, yet one of the most important, augmentations to the law of tax-exempt organizations is the set of rules pertaining to *excess benefit transactions*. These rules, which in many ways parallel and overlap the private inurement doctrine, were enacted in 1996 and took effect in 1995[287]; the final regulations to accompany these rules were issued in early 2002. The tax penalties that underlay these rules are termed *intermediate sanctions*.

(a) Introduction to Intermediate Sanctions

The intermediate sanctions rules emphasize the taxation of persons who engaged in impermissible private transactions with certain types of tax-exempt organizations, rather than revocation of the tax-exempt status of these entities. With this approach, tax law sanctions—structured as penalty excise taxes—may be imposed on those persons who improperly benefited from the transaction and on certain managers of the organization who participated in the transaction knowing that it was improper.

   This body of law[288] represents the most dramatic and important package of federal statutory tax law rules concerning tax-exempt organizations created since enactment of the basic statutory structure of the exempt organizations field in 1969.[289] The law as to excess benefit transactions is refocusing and reshaping application of the private inurement and private benefit doctrines, and is impacting the composition and functioning of many boards of directors of exempt organizations.

(b) Tax-Exempt Organizations Involved

The law as to excess benefit transactions applies with respect to tax-exempt public charities[290] and exempt social welfare organizations.[291] These entities are collectively

---

[287] The effective date of these rules is September 14, 1995 (Reg. § 53.4958-1(f)(1)). In the first of the reported intermediate sanctions cases, the effective date of the transactions was October 1, 1995 (Caracci v. Comm'r, 118 T.C. 379 (2002), on appeal to the U.S. Court of Appeals for the Second Circuit). In the second of the reported intermediate sanctions cases, the effective date of one of the contracts involved was January 12, 1995; the court held that transactions that took place during the term of this contract were "preempted from [these] excess benefit taxes" (Dzina v. United States, 2004-2 U.S.T.C. ¶ 50,133 (N.D. Ohio 2004)).

   The intermediate sanctions do not apply to any benefit that arose out of a transaction pursuant to a written contract that was binding on September 14, 1995, and continued in force through the time of the transaction, and the terms of which have not materially changed (Reg. § 53.4958-1(f)(2)).

[288] The excess benefit transactions rules are the subject of IRC § 4958. The report of the House Committee on Ways and Means, dated March 28, 1996 (H. Rep. 104-506, 104th Cong., 2d Sess. (1996)), constitutes the totality of the legislative history of these rules. The IRS provided a brief summary of the intermediate sanctions rules in Notice 96-46, 1996-2 C.B. 212. In general, see *Intermediate Sanctions*.

[289] A substantial portion of the Tax Reform Act of 1969 concerned enactment of law defining *public charities* (see § 8.1) and imposing stringent rules of operations of *private foundations* (IRC §§ 4940–4948). Much of the motivation for creation of the foundation rules, particularly those pertaining to self-dealing (IRC § 4941)—fear of considerable abuses—is mirrored in the reason for adoption of the excess benefit transactions rules. See *Private Foundations*, Chapter 5.

[290] A *public charity* is an organization that is tax-exempt for federal income tax purposes (IRC § 501(a)) because it is a charitable, educational, scientific, and /or like organization (that is, it is described in IRC § 501(c)(3)); this type of charitable organization is not (by reason of IRC § 509(a)) a private foundation (see § 8.1). The excess benefit transactions rules do not apply to private foundations because of application to them of the self-dealing rules (IRC § 4941).

[291] See § 1.6(a).

termed, for this purpose, *applicable tax-exempt organizations*.[292] Organizations of this nature include any organization described in either of these two categories of exempt organizations at any time during the five-year period ending on the date of the transaction.[293]

There are no exemptions from these rules.[294] That is, all tax-exempt public charities and all exempt social welfare organizations are applicable tax-exempt organizations. A foreign organization that receives substantially all of its support from sources outside the United States, however, is not an applicable tax-exempt organization.[295]

A social welfare organization is embraced by these rules if it has received recognition of tax exemption from the IRS, has filed an application for recognition of exemption, has filed an information return with the IRS as a social welfare organization, or has otherwise held itself out as an exempt social welfare organization.[296]

(c) Disqualified Persons

For these purposes,[297] the term *disqualified person* means (1) any person who was, at any time during the five-year period ending on the date of the transaction involved, in a position to exercise substantial influence over the affairs of the organization (whether by virtue of being an organization manager or otherwise),[298] (2) a member of the family of an individual described in the preceding category,[299] and (3) an entity in which individuals described in the preceding two categories own more than a 35 percent interest.[300]

A person is in a position to exercise substantial influence over the affairs of an applicable tax-exempt organization if that person is a voting member of the organization's governing body or is (or has the powers or responsibilities of) the organization's president, chief executive officer, chief operating officer, or chief financial officer.[301] Certain facts and circumstances tend to show this substantial influence, such as being the organization's founder, being a substantial contributor to it, having managerial control over a discrete segment of the organization, or serving as a key adviser to a person who has managerial authority.[302] Certain facts and circumstances tend to show a lack of substantial influence, such as

---

[292] IRC § 4958(e)(1); Reg. § 53.4958-2(a)(1).

[293] IRC § 4958(e)(2); Reg. § 53.4958-2(b)(1).

[294] In other areas of the law of tax-exempt organizations, by contrast, there are exemptions from the rules for entities such as, for example, small organizations and religious organizations (e.g., *Tax-Exempt Organizations* §§ 23.3(b), 24.3(b)).

[295] Reg. § 53.4958-2(b)(2).

[296] Reg. § 53.4958-2(a)(3). These distinctions are required because, unlike nearly all public charities, an entity can be a tax-exempt social welfare organization without applying for recognition of exemption (see § 2.2).

[297] The definition of the term *disqualified person* for purposes of the private foundation rules is the subject of IRC § 4946. See *Private Foundations*, Chapter 4.

[298] IRC § 4958(f)(1)(A); Reg. § 53.4958-3(a)(1).

[299] IRC § 4958(f)(1)(B); Reg. § 53.4958-3(b)(1).

[300] IRC § 4958(f)(1)(C); Reg. § 53.4958-3(b)(2).

[301] Reg. § 53.4958-3(c). The legislative history, however, states that an individual having the title of "trustee," "director," or "officer" is not automatically considered a disqualified person (H. Rep. 104-506 (104th Cong., 2d Sess. 58 (1996))).

[302] Reg. § 53.4958-3(e)(2).

service as an independent contractor (for example, as a lawyer, accountant, or investment adviser).[303] Certain persons are deemed not to have the requisite substantial influence, such as an employee who receives economic benefits that are less than the compensation referenced for a highly compensated employee[304] and public charities.[305]

An *organization manager* is a trustee, director, or officer of the applicable tax-exempt organization as well as an individual having powers or responsibilities similar to those of trustees, directors, or officers of the organization.[306]

The term *member of the family* is defined as being (1) spouses, ancestors, children, grandchildren, great-grandchildren, and the spouses of children, grandchildren, and great-grandchildren—namely, those individuals so classified under the private foundation rules,[307] and (2) the brothers and sisters (whether by whole- or half-blood) of the individual and their spouses.[308]

The entities that are disqualified persons because one or more disqualified persons owns more than a 35 percent interest in them are termed *35 percent controlled entities*. These are (1) corporations in which one or more disqualified persons own more than 35 percent of the total combined voting power, (2) partnerships in which one or more disqualified persons own more than 35 percent of the profits interest, and (3) trusts or estates in which one or more disqualified persons own more than 35 percent of the beneficial interest.[309] The term *voting power* includes voting power represented by holdings of voting stock, actual or constructive, but does not include voting rights held only as a director or trustee.[310] In general, constructive ownership rules apply for purposes of determining whether an entity is a 35 percent controlled entity.[311]

(d) Transactions Involved

This tax law regime has as its heart the excess benefit transaction. In an instance of an excess benefit transaction, tax sanctions are imposed on the disqualified person or persons who improperly benefited from the transaction and perhaps on any organization manager or managers who participated in the transaction knowing that it was improper.

(i) General Rules. An *excess benefit transaction* is any transaction in which an economic benefit is provided by an applicable tax-exempt organization directly or indirectly to or for the use of any disqualified person, if the value of the economic

---

[303] Reg. § 53.4958-3(e)(3).

[304] IRC § 414(q)(1)(B)(i). An individual is a highly compensated employee in 2006 if he or she earned more than $95,000 in 2005. This annual dollar limit is indexed for inflation; it increased to $100,000 in 2006 for determining highly compensated employees in 2007.

[305] Reg. § 53.4958-3(d). As to this last point, other types of tax-exempt organizations can be disqualified persons in this context. See § 3.9.

[306] IRC § 4958(f)(2); Reg. § 53.4958-1(d)(2)(i).

[307] IRC § 4946(d).

[308] IRC § 4958(f)(4); Reg. § 53.4958-3(b)(1).

[309] IRC § 4958(f)(3)(A); Reg. § 53. 4958-3(b)(2)(i).

[310] Reg. § 53.4958-3(b)(2)(ii).

[311] IRC § 4958(f)(3)(B); Reg. § 53.4958-3(b)(2)(iii).

benefit provided by the exempt organization exceeds the value of the consideration (including the performance of services) received for providing the benefit.[312] This type of benefit is known as an *excess benefit*.[313]

Payment of compensation that is not reasonable to a disqualified person is a type of excess benefit transaction. Compensation for the performance of services is reasonable if it is only such "amount that would ordinarily be paid for like services by like enterprises under like circumstances."[314] Generally, the circumstances to be taken into consideration are those existing at the date when the contract for services was made. When reasonableness cannot be determined on that basis, the determination is made based on all facts and circumstances, up to and including circumstances as of the date of payment. The IRS may not consider "circumstances existing at the date when the payment is questioned" in making a determination of the reasonableness of compensation.[315]

Compensation for these purposes means all items of compensation provided by an applicable tax-exempt organization in exchange for the performance of services. This includes (1) forms of cash and noncash compensation, such as salary, fees, bonuses, and severance payments; (2) forms of deferred compensation that are earned and vested, whether funded or not and whether the plan is a qualified one or not; (3) the amount of premiums paid for insurance coverage (including liability), as well as payment or reimbursement by the organization of charges, expenses, fees, or taxes not ultimately covered by the insurance coverage; and (4) other benefits, whether included in income for tax purposes or not, including payments to welfare benefit plans on behalf of the individuals being compensated, such as plans providing medical, dental, life insurance, severance pay, and disability benefits, and taxable and nontaxable fringe benefits,[316] including expense allowances or reimbursements or forgone interest on loans that the recipient must report as income for tax purposes.[317]

The criteria for determining the reasonableness of compensation and fair market value of property are not stated in the intermediate sanctions regulations. Preexisting law standards apply in determining reasonableness of this

---

[312] IRC § 4958(c)(1)(A); Reg. § 53.4958-4(a)(1). The IRS ruled that an annual monetary award presented by a public charity was an exempt activity and did not involve an excess benefit transaction (Priv. Ltr. Rul. 9802045).

[313] IRC § 4958(c)(1)(B). Thus, the definition of *excess benefit transaction* encompasses not only transactions where a benefit is provided *to* a disqualified person but also where a benefit is provided to a person who is not disqualified yet there nonetheless is a benefit provided *for the use of* a disqualified person. This latter element is sometimes overlooked (and, if applied, may change the ultimate outcome); an illustration is an IRS ruling finding certain grants to not be excess benefit transactions, without taking into consideration the *for the use of* aspect (Priv. Ltr. Rul. 200335037). See *Private Foundations* § 5.8.

[314] Reg. § 53.4958-4(b)(1)(ii)(A).

[315] Reg. § 53.4958-4(b)(2)(i). By contrast, the U.S. Tax Court is of the view that, in the private inurement setting, circumstances occurring after the transaction in question can be considered in determining reasonableness (e.g., Anclote Psychiatric Center, Inc. v. Comm'r, 76 T.C.M. 175 (1998)).

[316] This item, however, does not include working condition fringe benefits (IRC § 132(d)) or *de minimis* fringe benefits (IRC § 132(e)) (Reg. § 53.4958-4(a)(4)(ii)).

[317] Reg. § 53.4958-4(b)(1)(ii)(B). It is the view of the IRS that amounts embezzled by a disqualified person from an applicable tax-exempt organization are to be treated as amounts transferred by means of an excess benefit transaction—they cannot be rationalized as consideration for the performance of services (Reg. § 53.4958-4(c)(1)).

nature.[318] An individual need not necessarily accept reduced compensation merely because he or she renders services to a tax-exempt, as opposed to a taxable, organization.[319]

Excess benefit transactions can also include a rental arrangement,[320] borrowing arrangement, and sales of assets between an applicable tax-exempt organization and a disqualified person. Thus, a court held that the transfers of assets by public charities to disqualified persons, where the value of the assets "far exceeded" the consideration paid for them, were excess benefit transactions.[321]

The phraseology *directly or indirectly* means the provision of an economic benefit directly by the tax-exempt organization or indirectly by means of a controlled entity. Thus, an applicable tax-exempt organization cannot avoid involvement in an excess benefit transaction by causing a controlled entity to engage in the transaction.[322] An economic benefit may also be provided by an applicable tax-exempt organization indirectly to a disqualified person through an intermediary entity.[323] All consideration and benefits exchanged between a disqualified person and an applicable tax-exempt organization, and all entities the organization controls, are taken into account to determine whether an excess benefit transaction has occurred.

These economic benefits are disregarded for these purposes: (1) the payment of reasonable expenses for members of the governing body of an organization to attend board meetings; (2) an economic benefit received by a disqualified person solely as a member of (if the membership fee does not exceed $75) or volunteer for the organization; and (3) an economic benefit provided to a disqualified person solely as a member of a charitable class.[324]

Also, to the extent to be provided in tax regulations, the term *excess benefit transaction* includes any transaction in which the amount of any economic benefit provided to or for the use of a disqualified person is determined in whole or in part by the revenues generated by one or more activities of the organization, but only if the transaction results in private inurement.[325] In this context, the excess benefit is the amount of the private inurement.[326] This type of arrangement is known as a *revenue-sharing arrangement*. The Department of the Treasury

---

[318] H. Rep. 104-506, 104th Cong., 2d Sess. 56 (1996). See § 3.4. Where two or more disqualified persons perform services as a team, in determining whether they received any excess benefit in a year, each person is treated separately, so that the total value of each person's services provided to an exempt organization in a year must be compared with the value of the benefits received by the person for that year (Priv. Ltr. Rul. 200244028).

[319] H. Rep. 104-506, 104th Cong., 2d Sess. 56, note 5 (1996).

[320] The IRS held that an office-sharing arrangement involving public charities and other persons was not an excess benefit transaction (Priv. Ltr. Rul. 200421010).

[321] Caracci v. Comm'r, 118 T.C. 379, 415 (2002).

[322] *Id.* at 56, note 3.

[323] Reg. § 53.4958-4(a)(2).

[324] Reg. § 53.4958-4(a)(4). In application of the third of these elements, the IRS ruled that a health care organization, which will provide a bus service as an exempt function, will not confer unwarranted benefits on disqualified persons (namely, the physicians treating patients served by this means of transportation) (Priv. Ltr. Rul. 200247055). The IRS also ruled, in applying this charitable class exception, that a statewide scholarship program administered by a public charity and local community foundations did not cause any excess benefit transactions merely because some scholarship recipients may be related to members of a community foundation's directors or officers, or to members of a nominating committee (Priv. Ltr. Rul. 200332018).

[325] IRC § 4958(c)(2).

[326] *Id.*

was instructed to promptly issue guidance providing examples of revenue-sharing arrangements that violate the private inurement prohibition.[327] The tax regulations that were issued in 2002 are silent on the subject.[328]

Under the law in existence before enactment of the intermediate sanctions rules, certain revenue-sharing arrangements have been determined by the IRS to not constitute private inurement.[329] It is to continue to be the case that not all revenue-sharing arrangements are private inurement transactions. The legislative history of the intermediate sanctions rules, however, states that the IRS is not bound by any of its prior rulings in this area.[330]

The IRS ruled that economic benefits provided to disqualified persons that are "incidental and tenuous" are not violative of the excess benefit transactions rules.[331]

(ii) Automatic Excess Benefit Transactions. An economic benefit may not be treated as consideration for the performance of services unless the organization providing the benefit clearly indicates its intent to treat the benefit as compensation when the benefit is paid.[332] In determining whether payments or transactions of this nature are in fact forms of compensation, the relevant factors include whether (1) the appropriate decision-making body approved the transfer as compensation in accordance with established procedures or (2) the organization provided written substantiation (such as treatment of the payment as compensation on an IRS return or other form) that is contemporaneous with the transfer of the economic benefit at issue.[333] If an organization fails to provide this documentation, any services provided by the disqualified person will not be treated as provided in consideration for the economic benefit for purposes of determining the reasonableness of the transaction.[334] These transactions are thus known as *automatic excess benefit transactions*. These rules do not apply to nontaxable fringe benefits[335] and certain other types of nontaxable transfers (such as employer-provided health benefits and contributions to qualified pension plans).[336]

A transaction can be an automatic excess benefit transaction even though its terms and conditions show that it is, in fact, reasonable. Transactions of this nature include the provision by an applicable tax-exempt organization to a disqualified person of, for personal purposes, residential real property, use of a

---

[327] H. Rep. 104-506, 104th Cong., 2d Sess. 56 (1996).

[328] A section in the regulations has been reserved for these rules (Reg. § 53.4958-5).

[329] E.g., Gen. Couns. Mem. 39674, 38905, and 38283. See H. Rep. 104-506, 104th Cong., 2d Sess. 56, note 4 (1996).

[330] H. Rep. 104-506, 104th Cong., 2d Sess. 56, note 4 (1996).

[331] Priv. Ltr. Rul. 200335037.

[332] IRC § 4958(c)(1)(A); Reg. § 53.4958-4(c)(1).

[333] Reg. § 53.4958-4(c)(1). These returns or forms include the organization's annual information return filed with the IRS (usually Form 990), the information return provided by the organization to the recipient (Form W-2 or Form 1099), and the individual's income tax return (Form 1040) (H. Rep. 104-506, 104th Cong., 2d Sess. 57 (1996)); Reg. § 53.4958-4(c)(3)(i)(A)(1).

[334] Reg. § 53.4958-4(c)(1). An economic benefit that a disqualified person obtains by theft or fraud cannot be treated as consideration for the performance of services (*id.*).

[335] IRC § 132.

[336] The first intermediate sanctions case concerning the issue of excessive compensation was filed in the U.S. Tax Court on August 3, 2000 (Peters v. Comm'r, No. 8446-00; the case was settled).

vehicle, access to exempt organization charge accounts, use of a cellular telephone, and use of a computer.[337]

(iii) Initial Contract Exception. The intermediate sanctions rules do not apply to any fixed payment made to a person pursuant to an initial contract.[338] A *fixed payment* is an amount of money or other property specified in the contract, or determined by a fixed formula specified in the contract, which is to be paid or transferred in exchange for the provision of specified services or property.[339] An *initial contract* is a binding written contract between an applicable tax-exempt organization and a person who was not a disqualified person immediately prior to entering into the contract.[340] A compensation package can be partially sheltered by this initial contract exception; for example, an individual can have a base salary that is a fixed payment pursuant to an initial contract and also have an annual performance-based bonus that is subject to excess benefit transaction analysis.[341]

(e) Rebuttable Presumption of Reasonableness

This body of law includes a *rebuttable presumption of reasonableness* with respect to compensation arrangements and other transactions between an applicable tax-exempt organization and a disqualified person.[342] This presumption arises where the transaction was approved by a board of directors or trustees (or a committee of the board) of an applicable tax-exempt organization that was composed entirely of individuals who were unrelated to and not subject to the control of the disqualified person or persons involved in the transaction, obtained and relied on appropriate data as to comparability, and adequately documented the basis for its determination.[343]

The first of these criteria essentially requires an independent board. The standard as to independence, for governing bodies and committees, is based on the concept of an absence of a *conflict of interest*.[344] An individual is not regarded as a member of a governing body or committee when it is reviewing a transaction if that individual meets with the members only to answer questions, otherwise recuses himself or herself from the meeting, and is not present during debate and voting on the transaction.[345] A committee of a governing body may be composed of any individuals permitted under state law to serve on

---

[337] E.g., Tech. Adv. Mem. 200435018. Failure to properly account for or reimburse spousal travel can also constitute an automatic excess benefit transaction.

[338] Reg. § 53.4958-4(a)(3)(i).

[339] Reg. § 53.4958-4(a)(3)(ii).

[340] Reg. § 53.4958-4(a)(3)(iii).

[341] The *initial contract exception* is informally known as the *first bite rule*. In general, Jones, "'First Bite' and the Private Benefit Doctrine: A Comment on Temporary and Proposed Regulation 53-4958-4T(a)(3)," 62 *U. Pitt. L. Rev.* 715 (Summer 2001).

[342] This rebuttable presumption is not provided for in the Internal Revenue Code; it was created by the legislative history (H. Rep. 104-506, 104th Cong., 2d Sess. 56–57 (1996)), and is reflected in and amplified by the regulations (Reg. § 58.4958-6).

[343] Reg. § 53.4958-6(a).

[344] Reg. § 53.4958-6(c)(1)(iii).

[345] Reg. § 53.4958-6(c)(1)(ii).

the committee and may act on behalf of the governing body to the extent permitted by state law.[346]

As to the second of these criteria, an authorized body has appropriate data as to comparability if, given the knowledge and expertise of its members, it has information sufficient to determine whether the compensation arrangement in its entirety is reasonable or the property transfer is at fair market value.[347] In the case of compensation, appropriate data includes compensation levels paid by similarly situated organizations, both tax-exempt and taxable, for functionally comparable positions; the location of the organization, including the availability of similar services in the geographic area; independent compensation surveys by nationally recognized independent firms; and written offers from similar institutions competing for the services of the disqualified person.[348] In the case of property, relevant information includes current independent appraisals of the value of the property to be transferred and offers received as part of an open and competitive bidding process.[349]

In the case of an organization with annual gross receipts of less than $1 million, when reviewing compensation arrangements, the governing body or committee is considered to have appropriate data as to comparability if it has data on compensation paid by three comparable organizations in the same or similar communities for similar services.[350]

As to the third of these criteria, adequate documentation includes an evaluation of the individual whose compensation level and terms were being established, and the basis for the determination that the individual's compensation was reasonable in light of that evaluation and data.[351] The fact that a state or local legislative or agency body may have authorized or approved a particular compensation package paid to a disqualified person is not determinative of the reasonableness of the compensation paid.[352]

For a decision to be documented adequately, the written or electronic records of the governing body or committee must note the terms of the transaction that was approved, the date it was approved, the members of the governing body or committee who were present during debate on the transaction or arrangement that was approved and those who voted on it, the comparability data obtained and relied on by the governing body or committee and how it was obtained, and the actions taken with respect to consideration of the transaction by anyone who was otherwise a member of the governing body or committee but who had a conflict of interest with respect to the transaction or arrangement.[353] If the governing body or committee determines that reasonable compensation for a specific

---

[346] Reg. § 53.4958-6(c)(1)(i)(B).

[347] Reg. § 53.4958-6(c)(2)(i).

[348] House Report at 57; Reg. § 53.4958-6(c)(2)(i).

[349] Reg. § 53.4958(c)(2)(i). The IRS concluded that a process established for setting the coupon rate for the bonds of a tax-exempt hospital constituted an offer received as part of an open competitive bidding procedure (Priv. Ltr. Rul. 200413014).

[350] Reg. § 53.4958-6(c)(2)(ii).

[351] H. Rep. 104-506, 104th Cong., 2d Sess. 57 (1996).

[352] Id., note 7. Likewise, this type of authorization or approval is not determinative of whether a revenue-sharing arrangement violates the private inurement proscription (id.).

[353] Reg. § 53.4958-6(c)(3)(i).

arrangement or fair market value in a specific transaction is higher or lower than the range of comparable data received, the governing body or committee must record the basis for that determination.[354]

The documentation must be made concurrently with the determination.[355] This means that records must be prepared by the next meeting of the governing body or committee occurring after the final action or actions of the body or committee are taken. Records must be reviewed and approved by the governing body or committee as reasonable, accurate, and complete within a reasonable time thereafter.[356]

If these three criteria are satisfied, penalty excise taxes can be imposed only if the IRS develops sufficient contrary evidence to rebut the probative value of the comparability data relied on by the authorized governing body.[357] For example, the IRS could establish that the compensation data relied on by the parties was not for functionally comparable positions or that the disqualified person in fact did not substantially perform the responsibilities of the position.[358]

(f) Tax Structure

A disqualified person who benefited from an excess benefit transaction is subject to and must pay an excise tax—termed the *initial tax*—equal to 25 percent of the amount of the excess benefit.[359]

An organization manager who participated in an excess benefit transaction, knowing that it was such a transaction, is subject to and must pay an excise tax of 10 percent of the excess benefit (subject to a maximum amount of tax as to a transaction of $10,000[360]), where an initial tax is imposed on a disqualified person and if there was no correction of the excess benefit transaction within the taxable period.[361] This tax is not imposed, however, where the participation in the transaction was not willful and was due to reasonable cause.[362]

Another tax—the *additional tax*—may be imposed on a disqualified person where the initial tax was imposed and if there was no correction of the excess benefit within a specified period. This period is the *taxable period*, which means—with

---

[354] Reg. § 53.4958-6(c)(3)(ii).

[355] *Id.*

[356] *Id.* If reasonableness of compensation cannot be determined based on circumstances existing as of the date when a contract for services was made, this rebuttable presumption cannot arise until circumstances exist so that reasonableness of compensation can be determined, and the three requirements for the presumption are satisfied (Reg. § 53.4958-6(d)(1)).

The fact that a transaction between an applicable tax-exempt organization and a disqualified person does not qualify for this presumption does not create an inference that the transaction is an excess benefit transaction (Reg. § 53.4958-6(e)). (An instance of nonqualification for this presumption is in Priv. Ltr. Rul. 200244028.) The fact that a transaction qualifies for the presumption does not exempt or relieve any person from compliance with any federal or state law imposing any obligation, duty, responsibility, or other standard of conduct with respect to the operation or administration of any applicable tax-exempt organization (*id.*).

[357] Reg. § 53.4958-6(b).

[358] H. Rep. 104-506, 104th Cong., 2d Sess. 57 (1996).

[359] IRC § 4958(a)(1); Reg. § 53.4958-1(a), (c)(1).

[360] IRC § 4958(d)(2); Reg. § 53.4958-1(d)(7).

[361] IRC § 4958(a)(2); Reg. § 53.4958-1(d)(1). The concepts of *participation* and *knowing* are the subject of Reg. § 53.4958-1(d)(3), (4).

[362] IRC § 4958(a)(2); Reg. § 53.4958-1(d)(1). The concepts of *willful* and *reasonable cause* are the subject of Reg. § 53.4958-1(d)(5), (6).

respect to an excess benefit transaction—the period beginning with the date on which the transaction occurred and ending on the earliest of (1) the date of mailing of a notice of deficiency[363] as to the initial tax or (2) the date on which the initial tax is assessed.[364] In this situation, the disqualified person is subject to and must pay a tax equal to 200 percent of the excess benefit involved.[365]

The term *correction* means undoing the excess benefit transaction to the extent possible and taking any additional measures necessary to place the applicable tax-exempt organization in a financial position that is not worse than that in which it would be if the disqualified person were dealing under the highest fiduciary standards.[366] The correction amount with respect to an excess benefit transaction is the sum of the excess benefit and interest (at a rate that at least equals the applicable federal rate, compounded annually) on that benefit; generally, the correction must be made using cash or cash equivalents.[367] The IRS is of the view that a proper correction also requires a change in the policies or practices of the organization involved, to accord the agency some assurance that the infraction or infractions will not be repeated. If more than one organization manager or other disqualified person is liable for an excise tax, then all such persons are jointly and severally liable for the tax.[368]

The IRS has the authority to abate an intermediate sanctions excise tax penalty if it is established that the violation was due to reasonable cause and not due to willful neglect, and the transaction was corrected within the appropriate taxable period.[369]

(g) Reimbursements and Insurance

Any reimbursement by an applicable tax-exempt organization of excise tax liability is treated as an excess benefit transaction itself, unless it is included in the disqualified person's compensation for the year in which the reimbursement is made.[370] The total compensation package, including the amount of any reimbursement, must be reasonable. Similarly, the payment by an applicable tax-exempt organization of premiums for an insurance policy providing liability insurance to a disqualified person for excess benefit taxes is an excess benefit transaction itself, unless the amounts of the premiums are treated as part of the compensation paid to the disqualified person and the total compensation, including the premiums, is reasonable.[371]

(h) Return for Payment of Excise Taxes

Under the law in existence prior to enactment of the excess benefit transactions rules, charitable organizations and other persons liable for certain excise taxes

---

[363] IRC § 6212.

[364] IRC § 4958(f)(5); Reg. § 53.4958-1(c)(2)(ii).

[365] IRC § 4958(b); Reg. § 53.4958-1(c)(2)(i).

[366] IRC § 4958(f)(6); Reg. § 53.4958-7. The lawyers for the IRS wrote that the primary purpose of the intermediate sanctions rules is to "require insiders who are receiving excess benefits to make their exempt organizations whole, with the goal of keeping them operating for the benefit of the public" (Chief Counsel Adv. Mem. 200431023).

[367] Reg. § 53.4958-7(c).

[368] IRC § 4958(d)(1); Reg. § 4958-1(c)(1), (d)(8).

[369] IRC § 4962; Reg. § 53.4958-1(c)(2)(iii).

[370] H. Rep. 104-506, 104th Cong., 2d Sess. 58 (1996).

[371] *Id.*

are required to file returns—Form 4720—by which the taxes due are calculated and reported. These taxes are those imposed on public charities for excessive lobbying expenditures[372] and for political campaign expenditures,[373] and on private foundations and/or other persons for a range of impermissible activities.[374]

Disqualified persons and organization managers liable for payment of an intermediate sanctions excise tax are required to file Form 4720 as the return by which these taxes are paid.[375] In general, returns on Form 4720 for a disqualified person or organization manager liable for an excess benefit transaction tax are required to be filed on or before the 15th day of the fifth month following the close of the tax year of that person.[376]

(i) Statute of Limitations

In general, the statute of limitations for assessing an intermediate sanctions excise tax is three years.[377] This statute begins to run on the later of the date the applicable tax-exempt organization filed its annual information return[378] or the due date for the return.[379] A six-year statute of limitations applies if the exempt organization's return omits more than 25 percent of the excess taxes reported on the return; this statute, however, does not apply to tax omitted that has been adequately disclosed in the return.[380]

The IRS, when investigating the possibility of an excess benefit transaction, may send a summons to the applicable tax-exempt organization involved; this third-party summons may be sent after the three-year statute of limitations pertaining to the exempt organization expired. A court held that an IRS summons is valid, even when sent after expiration of a statute of limitations, as long as the investigation is being conducted for a legitimate purpose, the inquiry is relevant to that purpose, the information sought is not already within the IRS's possession, and the administrative steps required by the federal tax law are being followed.[381]

(j) Scope of the Sanctions

The intermediate sanctions penalties may be imposed by the IRS in lieu of or in addition to revocation of the tax-exempt status of an applicable tax-exempt organization.[382] In general, these sanctions are to be the sole penalty imposed in cases in which the excess benefit does not rise to such a level as to call into question

---

[372] IRC § 4911 or 4912. See *Tax-Exempt Organizations* §§ 20.3, 20.6.

[373] IRC § 4955. See *Tax-Exempt Organizations* § 21.2.

[374] IRC §§ 4940–4948.

[375] Reg. § 53.6011-1(b).

[376] Reg. § 53.6071-1(f)(1).

[377] IRC § 6501(a); Reg. § 53.4958-1(e)(3).

[378] See Chapter 10.

[379] IRC § 6501(b)(1), (4).

[380] IRC § 6501(e)(3).

[381] Lintzenich v. United States, 371 F. Supp. 2d 972 (S.D. Ind. 2005). These criteria are from United States v. Powell, 379 U.S. 48 (1964).

[382] H. Rep. 104-506, 104th Cong., 2d Sess. 59 (1996).

whether, on the whole, the organization functions as an exempt charitable or social welfare organization.[383]

Revocation of tax-exempt status, with or without the imposition of intermediate sanctions taxes, is to occur only when the applicable tax-exempt organization no longer operates as an exempt charitable or social welfare organization.[384] Existing law principles apply in determining whether an applicable tax-exempt organization no longer operates as an exempt organization. For example, the loss of tax-exempt status would occur in a year, or as of a year, the entity was involved in a transaction constituting a substantial amount of private inurement.

Proposed regulations issued by the IRS[385] provide that, in determining whether to continue to recognize the tax exemption of a charitable entity that engages in an excess benefit transaction that violates the private inurement doctrine, the IRS will consider all relevant facts and circumstances, including (1) the size and scope of the organization's regular and ongoing activities that further exempt purposes before and after one or more excess benefit transactions occurred, (2) the size and scope of one or more, excess benefit transactions in relation to the size and scope of the organization's regular and ongoing exempt functions, (3) whether the organization has been involved in repeated excess benefit transactions, (4) whether the organization has implemented safeguards that are reasonably calculated to prevent future violations, and (5) whether the excess benefit transaction has been corrected or the organization has made good faith efforts to seek correction from the disqualified person or persons who benefited from the excess benefit transaction.[386]

The fourth and fifth of these factors "weigh more strongly" in favor of continuing exemption where the organization has discovered the excess benefit transaction and takes corrective action before the IRS learns of the matter. Correction of an excess benefit transaction after the IRS discovers it by itself is, according to the proposal, never a sufficient basis for continuing recognition of exemption.[387]

An example concerns a newly created art museum (public charity) that, in its first two years, engaged in fundraising and preparation of its facilities. In its third year, a new board of trustees, consisting of local art dealers, was elected. Thereafter, the organization uses almost all of its funds to purchase art from its trustees at excessive prices. This organization exhibits and offers for sale all of the purchased art. The purchasing of art from its trustees was not disclosed in the organization's application for recognition of exemption. These transactions violate the private inurement doctrine and are excess benefit transactions. The preceding factors dictate that this museum is no longer tax-exempt, effective as of the third year.[388]

---

[383] The tax regulations state the matter this way: The intermediate sanctions law does not affect the substantive standards for tax exemption for applicable tax-exempt organizations; these entities qualify for exemption only if no part of their net earnings inures to the benefit of insiders (Reg. § 53.4958-8(a)).

[384] H. Rep. 104-506, 104th Cong., 2d Sess. 59, note 15 (1996).

[385] REG-111257-05.

[386] Prop. Reg. § 1.501(c)(3)-1(g)(2)(ii).

[387] Prop. Reg. § 1.501(c)(3)-1(g)(2)(iii).

[388] Prop. Reg. § 1.501(c)(3)-1(g)(2)(iv), Example 1.

Continuing with this illustration, in the fourth year, the entire museum board resigns and is replaced by members of the community who have experience operating educational institutions. The museum discontinues the selling of exhibited art, ceases to purchase art from its trustees, adopts a conflict-of-interest policy, adopts art valuation guidelines, retains the services of a lawyer to recover the excess payments to the former trustees, and implements a program of educational activities. Even though the payments were excess benefit transactions and private inurement, this implementation of safeguards and efforts to pursue correction enables the museum to remain exempt.[389]

As another example, a public charity conducts educational programs for the benefit of the public. In its fifth year, the organization's chief executive officer (CEO) begins causing the entity to divert substantial funds to the executive for personal use. The organization's board of directors did not authorize this practice, although some board members were aware of these diversions. The CEO claimed, despite a lack of documentation and no repayment amounts, that the diverted funds were loans. These diversions of funds were excess benefit transactions and private inurement. By application of the factors, this organization's tax exemption was lost in its fifth year.[390]

In a third example, the CEO of a public charity contracts with a for-profit company to construct an addition to the organization's building; this is a significant undertaking for the entity. The company, owned by the CEO, is paid an excessive amount for its work. At the time, the organization's board did not perform due diligence that would have made it aware of the excess payments. Thereafter (and before the IRS examination), the board concludes that the payments were excessive, fires the CEO, adopts a conflict-of-interest policy, adopts contract review procedures, and hires a lawyer to recover the excess payment amounts. Even though the payment to the company was private inurement and an excess benefit transaction, this organization continues to be tax-exempt.[391]

Another example concerns a large public charity that, during a year, paid $2,500 of the personal expenses of its chief financial officer. These payments constitute an automatic excess benefit transaction and private inurement. Inasmuch as only a *de minimis* portion of the organization's revenues were so diverted, this organization's tax exemption is not disturbed.[392]

§ 3.9 ASSOCIATIONS AND INTERMEDIATE SANCTIONS

Most tax-exempt associations—that is, those that are exempt business leagues[393]—are not applicable tax-exempt organizations.[394] Therefore, these entities are not entangled in the intermediate sanctions rules for that reason. By contrast,

---

[389] *Id.*, Example 2.

[390] *Id.*, Example 3.

[391] *Id.*, Example 4.

[392] *Id.*, Example 5. In general, Green, "Effective Corporate Governance Requires Building an Effective Intermediate Sanctions Compliance Process," 41 *Exempt Org. Tax Rev.* (No. 1) 41 (July 2003).

[393] That is, organizations that are exempt from federal income tax pursuant to IRC § 501(a) by reason of description in IRC § 501(c)(6).

[394] See § 3.8(b). Of course, associations that are exempt from federal income tax pursuant to IRC § 501(a) by reason of description in IRC § 501(c)(3) or (4) are applicable tax-exempt organizations.

associations that are tax-exempt charitable entities or exempt social welfare organizations are applicable tax-exempt organizations. Also, association-related foundations[395] are applicable tax-exempt organizations.

A tax-exempt business league can, however, become caught up in this body of law by being a disqualified person with respect to an applicable tax-exempt organization.[396] For example, an association with a related foundation is such a disqualified person because the association exercises substantial influence over the affairs of the foundation.[397]

The intermediate sanctions rules are of significance for tax-exempt associations in another respect. As noted, the law as to excess benefit transactions is refocusing and reshaping application of the private inurement doctrine (and the private benefit doctrine). Consequently, a finding that a transaction or other arrangement constitutes an excess benefit transaction yields the conclusion that it also amounts to a private inurement transaction.

---

[395] See Chapter 8.
[396] See § 3.8(c).
[397] See § 8.8(b).

CHAPTER FOUR

Lobbying and Political Activities

Of the wide range of services provided by tax-exempt business leagues to their members,[1] among the most prominent are attempts to influence legislation. Also, exempt business leagues are likely to be involved in political activities, usually by means of related political organizations.

§ 4.1 ASSOCIATIONS AND LOBBYING

It is common for a tax-exempt business league to engage in efforts to influence legislation—generically known as *lobbying*—that is of direct interest to the policies, practices, and objectives of its members. In some instances, furthermore, the lobbying is in connection with a proposal of concern to the business league itself.

The IRS recognized attempts to influence legislation as a valid function of a tax-exempt business league. The agency, on that occasion, put the matter this way: "There is no requirement, by statute or regulations, that a business league, chamber of commerce, etc., in order to be considered exempt as such, must

---

[1] See § 1.3(g).

refrain from carrying on propaganda or influencing legislation."[2] The organization involved, composed of business groups and individuals representing diverse lines of endeavor and geographic areas, had a membership united for the purpose of promoting a common business interest and improving their business conditions by working for the enactment of legislation designed to improve their competitive standing in the various lines of business in which they were engaged. The objectives sought by this organization could be attained only through legislation; the IRS held that these legislative activities were germane to the attainment of the entity's goals and that it could be exempt even where its sole activity is the advocacy of legislation.[3]

Thus, there is no restriction, from the standpoint of tax exemption for business leagues, on the amount of legislative activity these organizations may conduct, other than the obvious requirement that the lobbying, if it is more than incidental, must be in furtherance of the particular business league's exempt purposes.

§ 4.2 LOBBYING TAX LAW RULES

There are, however, federal tax law rules that stringently restrict the deductibility of business expenses for legislative activities.[4] These rules have meaningful consequences in this context, in that they can operate as an indirect constraint on lobbying activities by business leagues. Indeed, the inability to fully deduct membership dues may have an adverse impact on the extent of an association's membership.

(a) General Business Expense Deduction Disallowance Rules

Congress, in 1993, decided to essentially eliminate the business expense deduction for expenditures for lobbying activities.

(i) General Rules. Generally there is no business expense deduction[5] for any amount paid or incurred in connection with: influencing legislation; any attempt to influence the public, or segments of it, with respect to legislative matters or referendums; or any direct communication with a covered executive branch official in an attempt to influence the official actions or positions of the official.[6] This deduction disallowance rule, however, basically does not apply with respect to local legislation[7] or with respect to Indian tribal governments.[8]

---

[2] Rev. Rul. 61-177, 1961-2 C.B. 117.

[3] This revenue ruling modified Rev. Rul. 54-442, 1954-2 C.B. 131, to the extent it suggested that engaging in legislative activities, other than insubstantial ones, would preclude exemption as a business league. Indeed, that ruling stated that "[t]here is no prohibition in the statute or regulations relating to [business leagues] which disqualifies a corporation from exemption for legislative activities so long as such activities are only incidental." That statement was incorrect; there has never been such a rule.

[4] IRC § 162(e).

[5] IRC § 162(a).

[6] IRC § 162(e)(1)(A), (C), (D).

[7] IRC § 162(e)(2). The regulations developed under prior law (Reg. § 1.162-20) generally are pertinent to the costs of lobbying in connection with local legislation.

[8] IRC § 162(e)(7).

The first of these categories of lobbying includes what is generally termed *direct lobbying,* which is an attempt to influence legislation through communication with a member or employee of a legislative body.[9] In this context, the term also encompasses an attempt to influence legislation through communication with a government official or employee who may participate in the formulation of legislation.[10] The second of these categories of lobbying is known as *grass roots lobbying.* The term *legislation* includes action with respect to acts, bills, resolutions, or similar items by Congress, a state legislature, a local council, or similar governing body, or by the public in a referendum, initiative, constitutional amendment, or similar procedure.[11] The term *action* is limited to the introduction, amendment, enactment, defeat, or repeal of acts, bills, resolutions, or similar items.[12]

In this setting, *influencing legislation* means (1) any attempt to influence legislation through a lobbying communication and (2) all activities, such as research, preparation, planning, and coordination, including deciding whether to make a lobbying communication, even if not yet made.[13] A *lobbying communication* is any communication (other than one compelled by subpoena or otherwise compelled by federal or state law) with any member or employee of a legislative body or any other government official or employee who may participate in the formulation of the legislation that (1) refers to specific legislation and reflects a view on that legislation or (2) clarifies, amplifies, modifies, or provides support for views reflected in a prior lobbying communication.[14] The term *specific legislation* includes a specific legislative proposal that has not been introduced in a legislative body.[15]

The phrase *covered executive branch official* describes the President, the Vice President, any officer or employee of the White House Office of the Executive Office of the President, the two most senior-level officers of each of the other agencies within the Executive Office of the President, any individual serving in a position in level I of the Executive Schedule (for example, a member of the Cabinet),[16] any other individual designated by the President as having cabinet-level status, and an immediate deputy of an individual in the preceding two categories.[17]

(ii) Examples of Influencing Legislation.   An example of these rules concerns taxpayer P's employee, A, who is assigned to approach members of Congress to gain their support for a pending bill. A drafts and P prints a position letter on the proposal. P distributes the letter to members of Congress. Additionally, A personally contacts several members of Congress or their staffs to seek support for P's position on the bill. This letter and these contacts are lobbying communications; therefore, P is influencing legislation.[18]

---

[9] IRC § 162(e)(4)(A).
[10] *Id.*
[11] IRC §§ 162(e)(4)(B), 4911(e)(2); Reg. § 1.162-29(b)(4), (6).
[12] IRC § 4911(e)(3).
[13] Reg. § 1.162-29(b)(1).
[14] IRC § 162(e)(4)(A); Reg. § 1.162-29(b)(3).
[15] Reg. § 1.162-29(b)(5).
[16] 5 U.S.C. § 5312.
[17] IRC § 162(e)(6).
[18] Reg. § 1.162-29(b)(7), Example (1).

A second example involves taxpayer R who is invited to provide testimony at a congressional oversight hearing concerning the implementation of the Financial Institutions Reform, Recovery, and Enforcement Act of 1989. Specifically, the hearing concerns a proposed regulation increasing the threshold value of commercial and residential real estate transactions for which an appraisal by a state-licensed or state-certified appraiser is required. In testimony, R states that she supports the proposal. Because R does not refer to, or reflect a view on, any specific legislation, R has not made a lobbying communication. Therefore, R is not influencing legislation.[19]

In another example, State X enacts a statute that requires the licensing of daycare providers. Agency B in State X is charged with writing rules to implement the statute. After enactment of the statute, taxpayer S sends a letter to Agency B providing detailed proposed rules that S recommends Agency B adopt to implement this statute. Because the letter to Agency B neither refers to nor reflects a view on any specific legislation, it is not a lobbying communication. Therefore, S is not influencing legislation.[20]

As a fourth example, taxpayer T proposes to a state park authority that it purchase a particular tract of land for a new park. Even if T's proposal would require the authority eventually to seek appropriations to acquire the land and develop the new park, T has not made a lobbying communication because there has not been any reference to, nor any view reflected on, any specific legislation. Therefore, T's proposal does not constitute influencing legislation.[21]

In another illustration, taxpayer U prepares a paper asserting that lack of new capital is harming the economy of State X. The paper indicates that State X residents either should invest more in local businesses or increase their savings so that funds will be available to others interested in making investments. U forwards a summary of the unpublished paper to legislators in State X, with a cover letter that states: "You must take action to improve the availability of new capital in the state." Because neither the summary nor the cover letter refers to any specific legislative proposal and no other facts or circumstances indicate that they refer to an existing legislative proposal, forwarding the summary to the state legislators is not a lobbying communication. Therefore, U is not influencing legislation.[22]

In expansion of this example, Q, a member of the legislature of State X, calls U to request a copy of the paper. U forwards it with a cover letter that merely refers to the enclosed material. Because U's letter to Q and the unpublished paper do not refer to or reflect a view on any specific legislation, the letter is not a lobbying communication. Therefore, U is not influencing legislation.[23]

In another example, taxpayer V prepares a paper asserting that lack of new capital is harming the national economy. The paper indicates that lowering the capital gains rate would increase the availability of capital and increase tax receipts from the capital gains tax. V forwards the paper to his representative in Congress with a cover letter stating: "I urge you to support a reduction in the

---

[19] *Id.*, Example (2).
[20] *Id.*, Example (3).
[21] *Id.*, Example (4).
[22] *Id.*, Example (5)(i), (ii).
[23] *Id.*, Example (5)(iii).

capital gains tax rate." This communication is a lobbying communication because it refers to and reflects a view on a specific legislative proposal (namely, lowering the capital gains rate. Therefore, V is influencing legislation.[24]

As another example, taxpayer W, located in State A, notes in a letter to a legislator of State A that State X has passed a bill that accomplishes a stated purpose and then states that State A should pass a similar bill. Legislation of this nature has not been introduced in the State A legislature. The communication is a lobbying communication because it refers to and reflects a view on a specific legislative proposal. Therefore, W is influencing legislation.[25]

In another example, taxpayer Y represents citrus fruit growers. Y writes a letter to a U.S. senator discussing how pesticide O has benefited citrus fruit growers and disputing problems linked to its use. This letter references a bill pending in Congress and states: "This bill would prohibit the use of pesticide O. If citrus growers are unable to use this pesticide, their crop yields will be severely reduced, leading to higher prices for consumers and lower profits, even bankruptcy, for growers." Y's views on this bill are reflected in this statement. Thus, the communication is a lobbying communication and Y is influencing legislation.[26]

As another illustration, B, the president of taxpayer Z, an insurance company, meets with Q, who chairs the X state legislature's committee with jurisdiction over laws regulating insurance companies, to discuss the possibility of legislation to address current problems with surplus-line insurance. B recommends that legislation be introduced that would create minimum capital and surplus requirements for surplus-line companies and create clearer guidelines concerning the risks that surplus-line companies can insure. B's discussion with Q is a lobbying communication because B refers to and reflects a view on a specific legislative proposal. Therefore, Z is influencing legislation.[27]

In furtherance of this example, Q is not convinced that the market for surplus-line companies is sufficiently substantial to warrant this type of legislation, and thus requests that B provide information on the amount and types of risks covered by surplus-line companies. Following this meeting, B causes employees of Z to prepare estimates of the percentage of property and casualty insurance risks handled by surplus-line companies. B sends these estimates to Q with a cover letter that merely refers to the enclosed material. Although B's follow-up letter to Q does not refer to or reflect a view on specific legislation, B's letter supports the views reflected in his previous communication. Therefore, this letter is a lobbying communication and constitutes another instance where Z is influencing legislation.[28]

(iii) Lobbying and Nonlobbying Activities.   The purposes for engaging in an activity are determined on the basis of all the facts and circumstances, including whether:

- The activity and the lobbying communication are proximate in time
- The activity and the lobbying communication relate to similar subject matter

---

[24] *Id.*, Example (6).
[25] *Id.*, Example (7).
[26] *Id.*, Example (8).
[27] *Id.*, Example (9)(i).
[28] *Id.*, Example (9)(ii).

- The activity is performed at the request of, under the direction of, or on behalf of a person making the lobbying communication

- The results of the activity are also used for a nonlobbying purpose

- At the time the person engages in the activity, there is specific legislation to which the activity relates[29]

In instances of activities involving lobbying and nonlobbying purposes, costs must be allocated. This division of the activity must result in a reasonable allocation of costs to the influencing of legislation. A person's treatment of these multiple-purpose activities will, in general, not result in a reasonable allocation if it allocates to influencing legislation (1) only the incremental amount of costs that would not have been incurred but for the lobbying purpose or (2) an amount based solely on the number of purposes for engaging in the activity without regard to the relative importance of those purposes.[30]

Certain activities do not constitute lobbying. For example, there is no attempt to influence legislation if, before evidencing a purpose to influence any specific legislation, a person (1) determines the existence or procedural status of specific legislation, or the time, place, and subject of a hearing to be held by a legislative body with respect to specific legislation, or (2) prepares routine, brief summaries of the provisions of specific legislation. Also, it is not lobbying when a person (1) engages in an activity for purposes of complying with the requirements of a law (for example, satisfying state or federal securities law filing requirements), (2) reading a publication available to the public or viewing or listening to other mass media communications, or (3) attending a widely attended speech.[31]

For example, in 2005, agency F issues proposed regulations relating to the business of company W. There is no specific legislation during that year that is similar to the proposal. W undertakes a study of the impact of the proposed regulations on its business; it incorporates the results of that study in comments sent to agency F in 2005. In 2006, legislation is introduced in Congress that is similar to the regulatory proposal. Also, in 2006, W writes a letter to Senator P stating its opposition to the proposed legislation. W encloses with the letter a copy of the comments it sent to agency F. This letter is a lobbying communication, inasmuch as it refers to and reflects a view on specific legislation. Although W's study of the impact of the proposed regulations is proximate in time and similar in subject matter to its lobbying communication, W conducted the study and incorporated the results in comments sent to agency F at a time when legislation with a similar subject matter was not pending (a nonlobbying use). Thus, W engaged in this study solely for a nonlobbying purpose.[32]

As another example, the governor of state Q proposes a budget that includes a proposed sales tax on electricity. Using its records of electricity consumption, company Y estimates the additional costs that this proposal would impose on its

---

[29] Reg. § 1.162-29(c)(1).
[30] Reg. § 1.162-29(c)(2). See text accompanied by *infra* note 38.
[31] Reg. § 1.162-29(c)(3).
[32] Reg. § 1.162-29(c)(4), Example (1).

operations. In the same year, Y writes to members of the state's legislature in opposition to the proposed tax. With this letter, Y includes this estimate of the tax's costs. Y does not demonstrate any other use of its estimate. This letter is a lobbying communication, inasmuch as it refers to and reflects a view on specific legislation (the tax item in the proposed budget). Y's estimate of the additional costs that would be engendered by the proposal supports the lobbying communication, is proximate in time and similar in subject matter to a specific legislative proposal then in existence, and is not used for a nonlobbying purpose.[33]

In another illustration, a senator in the state Q legislature announces her intention to introduce legislation to require health insurers to cover a particular medical procedure in all policies sold in the state. Company X has different policies for two groups of employees, one covering and one not covering the procedure. After the bill is introduced, X's legislative affairs staff asks X's human resources staff to estimate the additional cost that would be entailed in covering the procedure for both groups of employees. This estimate is prepared; X's legislative staff then writes to members of the state's legislature, explaining that it opposes the proposed change in insurance coverage based on this study. X's legislative affairs staff thereafter forwards the study to its labor relations staff for use in negotiations with employees scheduled to begin later in the year. This letter is a lobbying communication, because it refers to and reflects a view on specific legislation. The activity of estimating X's additional costs under the proposed legislation relates to the same subject as the lobbying communication, occurs close in time to the lobbying communication, is conducted at the request of a person making a lobbying communication, and relates to specific legislation then in existence. Although X used the study in connection with its labor negotiations, the use for that purpose does not establish that X estimated its additional costs under the proposed legislation in part for a nonlobbying purpose. Thus, on the basis of all of the facts and circumstances, X estimated the additional costs it would incur under the proposal solely to make or support the lobbying communication.[34]

In another example, after several years of developmental work under various contracts, in 2005, company A contracts with the Department of Defense (DOD) to produce a prototype of a new generation military aircraft. A is aware that DOD will be able to fund the contract only if Congress appropriates an amount for that purpose in the upcoming appropriations process. In 2006, A conducts simulation tests of the aircraft and revises the specifications of the aircraft's expected performance capabilities, in compliance with the contract. A submits the results of these tests and the revised specifications to DOD. In 2007, Congress considers legislation to appropriate funds for this contract. A summarizes the results of the simulation tests and of the aircraft's expected performance capabilities and submits the summary to interested members of Congress with a cover letter that encourages them to support appropriations of funds for this contract. This letter is a lobbying communication; it refers to specific legislation (the appropriations bill) and requests its passage. The activities in 2005 to 2007 relate

---

[33] *Id.*, Example (2).
[34] *Id.*, Example (3).

to the same subject as the lobbying communication. The summary was prepared specifically for, and close in time to, that communication; it was prepared solely for a lobbying purpose. In contrast, A conducted the tests and revised the specifications to comply with its production contract with DOD. A conducted the test and revised the specifications solely for a nonlobbying purpose.[35]

As another example, C, the president of company W, travels to the state capital to attend a two-day conference on new manufacturing processes. C plans to spend a third day in the capital meeting with state legislators to explain why W opposes a pending bill that is unrelated to the subject of the conference. At the meetings with the legislators, C makes lobbying communications by referring to and reflecting a view on the pending bill. C's traveling expenses (transportation, meals, and lodging) are partially for the purpose of making or supporting the lobbying communications and partially for a nonlobbying purpose. As a result, W must reasonably allocate C's traveling expenses between these two purposes. Allocating to the influencing of legislation only C's incremental transportation expenses (such as the taxi fare to meet with the state legislators) would not result in a reasonable allocation of traveling expenses.[36]

In another example, on February 1, 2006, a bill is introduced in Congress that would affect company E. Employees in E's legislative affairs department, as is customary, prepare a brief summary of the bill and periodically confirm the procedural status of the bill through conversations with employees and members of Congress. On March 31, 2006, the head of E's legislative affairs department meets with E's president to request that B, a chemist, temporarily help the legislative affairs department analyze the bill. The president agrees, and suggests that B also be assigned to draft a position letter in opposition to the bill. Employees of this legislative affairs department continue to confirm periodically the procedural status of the bill. On October 31, 2006, B's position paper in opposition to the bill is delivered to members of Congress. B's letter is, of course, a lobbying communication because it refers to and reflects a view on specific legislation. The assignment of B to assist the legislative affairs department in analyzing the bill and in drafting the position letter in opposition to it evidences a purpose to influence legislation. Neither the activity of periodically confirming the procedural status of the bill nor the activity of preparing the routine, brief summary of the bill before March 31, 2006, constitutes the influencing of legislation. In contrast, periodically confirming the procedural status of the bill on or after March 31, 2006, relates to the same subject as, and is close in time to, the lobbying communication and is used for no nonlobbying purpose. Consequently, after March 31, 2006, E determined the procedural status of the bill for the purpose of supporting the lobbying communication by B.[37]

(iv) Research Expenditures. Any amount paid or incurred for research for, or preparation, planning, or coordination of, any lobbying activity subject to the general disallowance rule is treated as paid or incurred in connection with the

---

[35] *Id.*, Example (4).
[36] *Id.*, Example (5).
[37] *Id.*, Example (6).

lobbying activity.[38] The intent of this rule is to convert what might otherwise be a function constituting nonpartisan analysis, study, or research[39] into a lobbying undertaking where the research is subsequently used in an attempt to influence legislation. It is not clear how this rule is applied where the research is performed by one organization and the lobbying using that research is done by another organization, particularly where the two organizations are related.[40]

(v) In-House Expenditures. There is a *de minimis* exception for certain in-house expenditures where the organization's total amount of these expenditures for a tax year does not exceed $2,000 (computed without taking into account general overhead costs otherwise allocable to most forms of lobbying).[41] The term *in-house expenditures* means expenditures for lobbying (such as labor and materials costs) other than payments to a professional lobbyist to conduct lobbying for the organization and dues or other similar payments that are allocable to lobbying (such as association dues).[42]

(vi) Cost Allocation Rules. An organization, although able to use any reasonable[43] method of allocation of labor costs and general and administrative costs to lobbying activities, is authorized to use a *ratio method*, a *gross-up method*, or tax rules concerning allocation of service costs.[44] An organization may disregard time spent by an individual on lobbying activities if less than 5 percent of his or her time was expended for lobbying, although this *de minimis* test is not applicable with respect to *direct contact lobbying*, which is a meeting, telephone conversation, letter, or other similar means of communication with a federal or state legislator or a covered executive branch official and which otherwise qualifies as a lobbying activity.[45]

Other than a general exclusion for charitable organizations, there are no specific statutory exceptions to these rules. As noted, however, any communication

---

[38] IRC § 162(e)(5)(C).

[39] The phrase *nonpartisan analysis, study, or research* is taken from the lobbying rules pertaining to public charities. Pursuant to the substantial part test (see *Tax-Exempt Organizations* § 20.4(a)), a charitable organization may engage in nonpartisan analysis, study, and research, and publish the results, without being considered as engaged in lobbying, as long as it does not advocate the adoption of legislation to implement its findings (Reg. § 1.501(c)(3)-1(c)(3)(iv); Rev. Rul. 70-79, 1970-1 C.B. 127). That is, a charitable organization can permissibly evaluate a subject of proposed legislation or a pending item of legislation and present to the public an objective analysis of the subject or measure, as long as it does not participate in the presentation of one or more bills to a legislature and does not engage in any campaign to secure enactment of any proposals (Rev. Rul. 64-195, 1964-2 C.B. 138). This exception is also available in connection with the expenditure test (see *Tax-Exempt Organizations* § 20.4(b); it is a statutory rule in that context (IRC § 4911(d)(2)(A); Reg. § 56.4911-2(c)(1)).

[40] This rule may be contrasted with the one applicable to charitable organizations, pursuant to the expenditure test (see *Tax-Exempt Organizations* § 20.2(c)(i)), where the primary purpose of the organization in preparing materials was for use in lobbying and, in an instance of subsequent distribution of the materials by another organization, there is "clear and convincing" evidence of collusion between the organizations (Reg. § 56.4911-2(b)(2)(v)).

[41] IRC § 162(e)(5)(B)(i).

[42] IRC § 162(e)(5)(B)(ii).

[43] The concept of *reasonable* includes the requirement that the method be applied consistently (Reg. § 1.162-28(b)(1)).

[44] Reg. § 1.162-28(a)–(f). The third of these methods is the subject of IRC § 263A.

[45] Reg. § 1.162-28(g). In general, Pecarich & Primosch, "Final Lobbying Regs. Ease the Tracking of Expenses, but Some Definitions Remain Vague," 83 *J. Tax.* (No. 5) 261 (Nov. 1995).

compelled by subpoena, or otherwise compelled by federal or state law, does not constitute an attempt to influence legislation or an official's actions.[46]

(vii) Lobbying for Others. If a person engages in activities for a purpose of supporting a lobbying communication to be made by another person (or by a group of persons), the person's activities are treated as influencing legislation. For example, if a person or an employee of a person (as a volunteer or otherwise) engages in an activity to assist a trade association in preparing its lobbying communication, the person's activities constitute the influencing of legislation even if the lobbying communication is made by the association, rather than the person. If, however, a person's employee, acting outside the employee's scope of employment, volunteers to engage in those activities, the person is not considered to be influencing legislation.[47]

(viii) Anti-Cascading Rule. A cascading of the lobbying expense disallowance rule is prevented, to ensure that, when multiple parties are involved, the rule results in the denial of a deduction at only one level. Thus, in the case of an individual engaged in the business of providing lobbying services or an individual who is an employee and receives employer reimbursements for lobbying expenses, the disallowance rule does not apply to expenditures of the individual in conducting the activities directly on behalf of a client or employer. Instead, the lobbying payments made by the client or employer to the lobbyist or employee are nondeductible under the general disallowance rule.[48]

This anti-cascading rule applies where there is a direct, one-on-one relationship between the taxpayer and the entity conducting the lobbying activity, such as a client or employment relationship. It does not apply to dues or other payments to membership organizations that act to further the interests of all of their members rather than the interests of any one particular member. These organizations are themselves subject to the general disallowance rule, based on the amount of their lobbying expenditures.[49]

(ix) Anti-Avoidance Rule. An anti-avoidance rule is designed to prevent donors from using charitable organizations[50] as conduits to conduct lobbying activities, the costs of which would be nondeductible if conducted directly by the donor. Pursuant to this rule, there is no charitable contribution deduction (nor business expense deduction) for amounts contributed to a charitable organization if (1) the charitable organization's lobbying activities regard matters of direct financial interest to the donor's trade or business, and (2) a principal purpose of the contribution is to avoid the general disallowance rule that would apply if the contributor directly had conducted the lobbying activities.[51] The application of this anti-avoidance rule to a contributor would not adversely affect the tax-exempt status of the charitable organization as long as the activity qualified as nonpartisan

---

[46] See text accompanied by *supra* note 14. Also H. Rep. No. 213, 103d Cong., 1st Sess. 607 (1993).
[47] Reg. § 1.162-29(d).
[48] IRC § 162(e)(5)(A).
[49] H. Rep. No. 213, 103d Cong., 1st Sess. 610 (1993).
[50] That is, tax-exempt organizations described in IRC § 501(c)(3).
[51] IRC § 170(f)(9).

analysis, study, or research[52] or was not substantial under either the substantial part test or the expenditure test[53] of the rules limiting the legislative activities of charitable organizations.[54]

The determination regarding a *principal* purpose of the contribution is to be based on the facts and circumstances surrounding the contribution, including the existence of any formal or informal instructions relating to the charitable organization's use of the contribution for lobbying efforts (including nonpartisan analysis), the "temporal nexus" between the making of the contribution and the conduct of the lobbying activities, and any historical pattern of contributions by the donor to the charity.[55]

(b) Association Flow-Through and Proxy Tax Rules

A flow-through rule applicable with respect to membership associations disallows a business expense deduction for the portion of the membership dues (or voluntary payments or special assessments) paid to a tax-exempt organization that engages in lobbying activities.[56] Trade, business, and professional associations, and similar organizations, generally are required to provide annual information disclosure to their members, estimating the portion of their dues that is allocable to lobbying and thus nondeductible.

(i) Disclosure and Notice Requirements. The organization must disclose in its annual information return both the total amount of its lobbying expenditures and the total amount of dues (or similar payments) allocable to these expenditures.[57] For this purpose, an organization's lobbying expenditures for a tax year are allocated to the dues received during the tax year.[58] Any excess amount of lobbying expenditures is carried forward and allocated to dues received in the following tax year.[59]

The organization also is generally required to provide notice to each person paying dues (or similar payments), at the time of assessment or payment of the dues, of the portion of dues that the organization reasonably estimates will be allocable to the organization's lobbying expenditures during the year and that is, therefore, not deductible by the member.[60] This estimate must be reasonably

---

[52] See text accompanied by *supra* note 33.

[53] See *Tax-Exempt Organizations* §§ 20.1–20.6. There are exemptions for these four categories of organizations based on refinements of the 90-percent-of-dues test; organizations can avail themselves of this exemption by satisfying record-keeping and annual return filing requirements or by obtaining a private letter ruling from the IRS on the point. For example, social welfare organizations, and agricultural and horticultural organizations, are treated as satisfying the exemption requirements if either (1) more than 90 percent of all annual dues are received from persons who each pay less than $50 or (2) more than 90 percent of all annual dues are received from certain tax-exempt entities. (This $50 amount is indexed for inflation; for tax years beginning in 2006, the amount is $86 (Rev. Proc. 2005-70, 2005-47 I.R.B. 979).) The IRS occasionally issues rulings as to the availability of this exemption (e.g., Priv. Ltr. Rul. 9429016).

[54] H. Rep. No. 213, 103d Cong., 1st Sess. 610, note 70 (1993).

[55] *Id.* at 610. Special rules apply where a person engages in an activity for the purpose of making or supporting a lobbying communication but a lobbying communication does not ensue (Reg. § 1.162-29(e)).

[56] IRC § 162(e)(3).

[57] IRC § 6033(e)(1)(A)(i).

[58] IRC § 6033(e)(1)(C)(i).

[59] IRC § 6033(e)(1)(C)(ii).

[60] IRC § 6033(e)(1)(A)(ii).

calculated to provide organization members with adequate notice of the nondeductible amount. The notice must be provided in conspicuous and easily recognizable format.[61] These requirements of annual disclosure and notice to members are applicable to all tax-exempt organizations other than those that are charitable entities.[62]

(ii) Proxy Tax. If an organization's actual lobbying expenditures for a tax year exceed the estimated allocable amount of the expenditures (either because of higher-than-anticipated lobbying expenses or lower-than-projected dues receipts), the organization must pay a *proxy tax* on the excess amount[63] or seek permission from the IRS to adjust the following year's notice of estimated expenditures.[64] The proxy tax rate is equal to the highest corporate tax rate in effect for the taxable year[65]; the highest corporate tax rate is 35 percent.[66] If an organization does not provide its members with reasonable notice of anticipated lobbying expenditures allocable to dues, the organization is subject to the proxy tax on its aggregate lobbying expenditures for the year.

If an organization elects to pay the proxy tax rather than provide the requisite information disclosure to its members, no portion of any dues or other payments made by members of the organization is rendered nondeductible because of the organization's lobbying activities. That is, if the organization pays the tax, the dues payments are fully deductible by the members as business expenses (assuming they otherwise qualify).

This disclosure and notice element is not required, however, in the case of an organization that (1) incurs only *de minimis* amounts of in-house lobbying expenditures, (2) elects to pay the proxy tax on its lobbying expenditures incurred during the tax year,[67] or (3) establishes, pursuant to an IRS regulation or procedure, that substantially all of its dues monies are paid by members who are not entitled to deduct the dues in computing their taxable income. The concept of *de minimis* in-house expenditures in this setting is the same as that in the disallowance rules (including the $2,000 maximum).[68] Amounts paid to outside lobbyists, or as dues to another organization that lobbies, do not qualify for this exception.

Regarding this third component, if an organization establishes, to the satisfaction of the IRS, that substantially all of the dues monies it receives are paid by members who are not entitled to deduct their dues in any event (and obtains a waiver from the IRS), the organization is not subject to the disclosure and notice requirements (or the proxy tax).[69] In this context, the term *substantially all* means

---

[61] H. Rep. No. 213, 103d Cong., 1st Sess. 608, note 65 (1993). As to the standard of "conspicuous and easily recognizable," the IRC § 6113 rules are used (see *Tax-Exempt Organizations* § 22.2). The IRS promulgated rules concerning the format of the disclosure statement in instances of use of print media, telephone, television, and radio, which include guidance in the form of "safe harbor" provisions (Notice 88-120, 1988-2 C.B. 454).

[62] IRC § 6033(e)(1)(B).

[63] IRC § 6033(e)(2)(A)(ii).

[64] IRC § 6033(e)(2)(B).

[65] IRC § 6033(e)(2)(A).

[66] IRC § 11.

[67] IRC § 6033(e)(2)(A)(i).

[68] IRC § 6033(e)(1)(B)(ii). See text accompanied by *supra* note 35.

[69] IRC § 6033(e)(3).

at least 90 percent.[70] Examples of organizations of this nature are (1) an organization that receives at least 90 percent of its dues monies from members that are tax-exempt charitable organizations and (2) an organization that receives at least 90 percent of its dues monies from members who are individuals not entitled to deduct the dues payments because the payments are not ordinary and necessary business expenses.[71] Indeed, by IRS pronouncement,[72] there is a complete exemption from the reporting and notice requirements (and proxy tax) for all tax-exempt organizations, other than social welfare organizations[73] that are not veterans' organizations[74]; agricultural organizations[75]; horticultural organizations[76]; and trade, business, and professional associations, other business leagues, chambers of commerce, and boards of trade.[77]

If the amount of lobbying expenditures exceeds the amount of dues or other similar payments for the taxable year, the proxy tax is imposed on an amount equal to the dues and similar payments; any excess lobbying expenditures are carried forward to the next tax year.[78]

In general, if a person, alone or with others, structures its activities with a principal purpose of achieving results that are unreasonable in light of the purposes of the foregoing rules, the IRS can recast the person's activities for federal tax purposes as appropriate to achieve tax law results that are consistent with the intent of these rules.[79]

§ 4.3 ASSOCIATIONS AND POLITICAL CAMPAIGN ACTIVITIES

The federal tax law essentially is silent as to the extent to which tax-exempt business leagues can engage in political campaign activities and remain exempt; the little law there is on the point is inconsistent. Statutory law concerning political campaign activity by tax-exempt organizations is confined to two categories of entities: charitable organizations, as to which political campaign activity is prohibited,[80] and political organizations, as to which political activity is the exempt function.[81]

The federal tax regulations offer scant guidance on this subject. Although the regulations concerning tax-exempt business leagues do not address the point, the regulations pertaining to exempt social welfare organizations offer the

---

[70] H. Rep. No. 213, 103d Cong., 1st Sess. 609 (1993).

[71] E.g., Priv. Ltr. Rul. 9534021.

[72] Rev. Proc. 95-35, 1995-2 C.B. 391.

[73] See § 1.6(a).

[74] See § 1.6(m).

[75] See § 1.6(d).

[76] See § 1.6(c).

[77] See Chapter 2.

[78] H. Rep. No. 213, 103d Cong., 1st Sess. 608-609 (1993). In general, Cummings, Jr., "Tax Policy, Social Policy, and Politics: Amending Section 162(e)," 9 *Exempt Org. Tax Rev.* (No. 1) 137 (1994); Dillon, "Lobbying Provisions of H.R. 2264 for Tax-Exempt Membership Organizations," 8 *Exempt Org. Tax Rev.* (No. 5) 895 (1993).

[79] Reg. § 1.162-29(f).

[80] IRC § 501(c)(3). See *Tax-Exempt Organizations*, Chapter 21.

[81] IRC § 527. See § 4.7.

observation that the "promotion of social welfare does not include direct or indirect participation or intervention in political campaigns on behalf of or in opposition to any candidate for public office."[82] The concept thus is that political campaign activity is not inherently an exempt function for a social welfare organization. Presumably, political campaign activity is also not inherently an exempt function for business leagues.

These conclusions do not mean that social welfare organizations, business leagues, and many other types of tax-exempt organizations cannot engage in political campaign activity. They mean, instead, that political campaign activity cannot be the primary purpose or function of these entities. The IRS has issued pronouncements on this topic on two occasions.

The IRS observed, in 1981, that an organization "may carry on lawful political activities and remain exempt under section 501(c)(4) as long as it is primarily engaged in activities that promote social welfare."[83] As noted, presumably that principle is also applicable in connection with exempt business leagues. Inasmuch as *primarily* connotes a measure of activity in excess of 50 percent of total activities, probably in the range of 60 to 70 percent, this statement suggests that an exempt organization (other than a charitable one) may engage in political campaign activity to an extent of 30 to 40 percent of its functions and remain exempt. Yet, in 2003, the IRS issued guidance in which it stated that exempt business leagues may engage in "limited" political campaign activity.[84] This reference to *limited* political campaign activity, while undefined, seems considerably more restrictive than something less than *primary* activity.

§ 4.4 PUBLIC ADVOCACY ACTIVITIES

The IRS issued guidance for determining when expenditures by tax-exempt business leagues (and exempt social welfare organizations and unions) for certain public advocacy activities constitute outlays for political campaign activity.[85] The agency stated that business leagues "may, consistent with their exempt purpose, publicly advocate positions on public policy issues." The dilemma is that, while this type of advocacy may be attempts to influence legislation, it may also involve discussion of the position of public officials who are also candidates for public office, causing a public policy advocacy communication to be political activity. Among other outcomes, expenditures of this nature may be taxable pursuant to the political organizations tax rules.[86] These rules embrace all attempts to influence the selection, nomination, election, or appointment of individuals to a political position.

The IRS stated that all of the facts and circumstances must be considered to determine whether an expenditure for an advocacy communication relating to a public policy issue is for a political undertaking. Of course, if an advocacy

---

[82] Reg. § 1.501(c)(4)-1(a)(2)(ii).
[83] Rev. Rul. 81-95, 1981-1 C.B. 332.
[84] IR-2003-146.
[85] Rev. Rul. 2004-6, 2004-4 I.R.B. 328. In connection with an association that has its tax exemption based on IRC § 501(c)(3), treatment of an advocacy communication as a political one could adversely affect the exemption of the association.
[86] IRC § 527(f). See § 4.7.

communication explicitly advocates the election or defeat of an individual in connection with a public office, the communication is political activity. Thus, this facts-and-circumstances determination is made when an advocacy communication relating to a public policy issue is not so explicit. The factors that the IRS considers in this regard that tend to show that a communication is a political one include:

- The communication identifies a candidate for public office.
- The timing of the communication coincides with an electoral campaign.
- The communication targets voters in a particular election.
- The communication identifies that candidate's position on the public policy issue that is the subject of the communication.
- The position of the candidate on the public policy issue has been raised as distinguishing the candidate from others in the campaign, either in the communication or in other public communications.
- The communication is not part of an ongoing series of substantially similar advocacy communications by the organization on the same issue.

The factors that the IRS considers in this regard that tend to show that a communication is not a political one include:

- The absence of one or more of the foregoing six factors.
- The communication identifies specific legislation, or a specific event outside the control of the organization, that the organization hopes to influence.
- The timing of the communication coincides with a specific event outside the control of the organization that the organization hopes to influence, such as a legislative vote or other major legislative action (such as a hearing before a legislative committee on the issue that is the subject of the communication).
- The communication identifies the candidate solely as a government official who is in a position to act on the public policy issue in connection with the specific event (such as a legislator who is eligible to vote on the legislation).
- The communication identifies the candidate solely in the list of key or principal sponsors of the legislation that is the subject of the communication.

The IRS provided some illustrations of these rules. In all of the situations, the advocacy communication identifies a candidate in an election, appears shortly before that election, and targets the voters in that election. Nonetheless, the agency said, the other facts and circumstances need to be analyzed to determine if political campaign activity took place. Also, these examples assume that the payments are from the organization's general treasury (rather than from a separate segregated fund[87]), the organization would continue to be tax-exempt if the activity is determined to be political (because of the primary purpose rule[88]),

---

[87] See § 4.7, text accompanied by *infra* note 107.
[88] *Id.*, text accompanied by *infra* note 101.

and all of the advocacy communications include a solicitation of contributions to the organization.

As an illustration of application of these factors, a tax-exempt labor organization (LO) advocates for the betterment of conditions of law enforcement personnel. Senator A and Senator B represent state U in the U.S. Senate. In 2005, LO prepares and finances full-page newspaper advertisements supporting increased spending on law enforcement, which would require a legislative appropriation. These advertisements are published in several large-circulation newspapers in state U on a regular basis during 2005. One of these full-page advertisements is published shortly before an election in which Senator A, but not Senator B, is a candidate for reelection. The advertisement published shortly before the election stresses the importance of increased federal funding of local law enforcement and refers to numerous statistics indicating the high crime rate in state U. The advertisement does not mention Senator A's or Senator B's position on law enforcement issues. The advertisement ends with this statement: "Call or write Senators A and B to ask them to support increased federal funding for local law enforcement." Law enforcement has not been raised as an issue distinguishing Senator A from any opponent. At the time this advertisement is published, a legislative vote or other major legislative activity has not been scheduled in the Senate on increased federal funding for local law enforcement.

The advertisement in this example is not a political communication. Although the advertisement identifies Senator A, appears shortly before an election in which the senator is a candidate, and targets voters in that election, it is part of an ongoing series of substantially similar advocacy communications by LO on the same issue during 2005. The advertisement identifies both Senator A and Senator B, the latter not being a candidate at the time, as the representatives who would vote on this issue. Furthermore, LO's advertisement does not identify Senator A's position on the issue; law enforcement has not been raised as an issue distinguishing Senator A from any opponent. Therefore, there is nothing to indicate that Senator A's candidacy should be supported or opposed based on this issue. Based on these facts and circumstances, the amount expended by LO on this advertisement is not an expenditure for a political purpose.

In another example, a tax-exempt business league (BL) advocates for increased international trade. Senator C represents state V in the U.S. Senate. BL prepares and finances a full-page newspaper advertisement that is published in several large-circulation newspapers in state V shortly before an election in which Senator C is a candidate for nomination in a party primary. The advertisement states that increased international trade is important to a major industry in state V. The advertisement states that S. 25, a bill pending in the Senate, would provide manufacturing subsidies to certain industries to encourage export of their products. The advertisement also states that several manufacturers in the state would benefit from the subsidies and that Senator C has opposed similar measures supporting increased international trade. This advertisement closes with this statement: "Call or write Senator C to tell her to vote for S. 25." International trade concerns have not been raised as an issue distinguishing Senator C from any opponent. S. 25 is scheduled for a vote in the Senate before the election, soon after the date that the advertisement is published in the newspapers.

This advertisement is not a political communication. BL's advertisement identifies Senator C, appears shortly before an election in which Senator C is a candidate, and targets voters in that election. Although international trade issues have not been raised as an issue distinguishing Senator C from an opponent, the advertisement identifies Senator C's position on the issue as being contrary to BL's position. This advertisement, however, specifically identifies the legislation that BL is supporting and appears immediately before the Senate is scheduled to vote on that particular legislation. The candidate identified, Senator C, is a government official who is in a position to take action on the public policy issue in connection with the specific event. Based on these facts and circumstances, the amount expended by BL on the advertisement is not an expenditure for a political purpose.

As another example, a tax-exempt social welfare organization (SW1) advocates for better health care. Senator D represents state W in the U.S. Senate. SW1 prepares and finances a full-page newspaper advertisement that is published repeatedly in several large-circulation newspapers in state W beginning shortly before an election in which Senator D is a candidate for reelection. This advertisement is not part of an ongoing series of substantially similar advocacy communications by SW1 on the same issue. The advertisement states that a public hospital is needed in a major city in state W but that the public hospital cannot be built without federal financial assistance. The advertisement further states that Senator C has voted in the past year for two bills that would have provided the federal funding necessary for the hospital. The advertisement then concludes with this statement: "Let Senator D know that you agree about the need for federal funding for hospitals." Federal funding for hospitals has not been raised as an issue distinguishing Senator D from an opponent. At the time the advertisement is published, a bill providing federal funding for hospitals has been introduced in the Senate but a legislative vote or other major legislative activity on that bill has not been scheduled in the Senate.

Under the facts and circumstances of the preceding example, the advertisement is a political function. SW1's advertisement identifies Senator D, appears shortly before an election in which Senator D is a candidate, and targets voters in that election. Although federal funding of hospitals has not been raised as an issue distinguishing Senator D from an opponent, the advertisement identifies Senator D's position on the hospital funding issue as being in agreement with SW1's position and is not part of an ongoing series of substantially similar advocacy communications by SW1 on the same issue. Moreover, the advertisement does not identify any specific legislation and is not timed to coincide with a legislative vote or other major legislative action on the hospital funding issue. Based on these facts and circumstances, the amount expended by SW1 on the advertisement is an expenditure for a political end.

As another example, a tax-exempt social welfare organization (SW2) advocates for improved public education. Governor E is the chief executive of state X. SW2 prepares and finances a radio advertisement urging an increase in state funding for public education in state X, which requires a legislative appropriation. The radio advertisement is first broadcast on several radio stations in state X beginning shortly before an election in which Governor E is a candidate for reelection. The advertisement is not part of an ongoing series of substantially similar advocacy communications by SW2 on the same issue. The advertisement cites numerous statistics indicating that public education in state X is under-funded. While the advertisement does not say anything about Governor E's position on funding for public education, it ends with this statement: "Tell Governor E what you think about our underfunded schools." In public appearances and campaign literature, Governor E's opponent has made funding of public education an issue in the campaign by focusing on the governor's veto of an income tax increase the previous year to increase funding of public education. At the time the advertisement is broadcast, a legislative vote or other major legislative activity is not scheduled in the state's legislature on state funding of public education.

Under these facts and circumstances, this advertisement is for a political purpose. SW2's advertisement identifies Governor E, appears shortly before an election in which the governor is a candidate, and targets voters in that election. Although the advertisement does not explicitly identify Governor E's position on the funding of public schools issue, Governor E's opponent has raised that issue in the campaign. The advertisement does not identify any specific legislation, is not part of an ongoing series of substantially similar advocacy communications by SW2 on the same issue, and is not timed to coincide with a legislative vote or other major legislative action on that issue. Thus, the amount expended by SW2 on this advertisement was an expenditure for a political end.

In another example, a tax-exempt social welfare organization (SW3) advocates abolishment of the death penalty in state Y, of which F is the governor. SW3 regularly prepares and finances television advertisements opposing the death penalty. These advertisements appear on several television stations in state Y shortly before each scheduled execution by the state. One of these advertisements appears on state Y television stations shortly before the execution of G and shortly before an election in which Governor F is a candidate for reelection. The advertisement broadcast shortly before the election provides statistics regarding developed countries that have abolished the death penalty; it refers to studies indicating inequities related to the types of individuals executed in the United States. Like the advertisements appearing shortly before other scheduled executions in the state, this advertisement notes that Governor F has supported the death penalty and ends with this statement: "Call or write Governor F to demand that he stop the upcoming execution of G."

The advertisement in this example is not a political statement. SW3's advertisement identifies Governor F, appears shortly before an election in which the governor is a candidate, targets voters in that election, and identifies Governor F's position as contrary to SW3's position. This advertisement, however, is part of an ongoing series of substantially similar advocacy communications by SW3 on the same issue and the advertisement identifies an event outside the control of the organization (the scheduled execution) that the organization hopes to influence. Further, the timing of the advertisement coincides with this specific event that the organization hopes to influence. The candidate identified is a government official who is in a position to take action on the public policy issue in connection with the specific event. Based on these facts and circumstances, the amount expended by SW3 on the advertisements is not an expenditure for a political end.

As another example, a tax-exempt social welfare organization (SW4) advocates abolishment of the death penalty in state Z, of which H is the governor. Beginning shortly before an election in which Governor H is a candidate for reelection, SW4 prepares and finances a television advertisement broadcast on several television stations in the state. The advertisement is not part of an ongoing series of substantially similar advocacy communications by SW4 on the same issue. This advertisement provides statistics regarding developed countries that have abolished the death penalty; it refers to studies indicating inequities related to the types of individuals executed in the United States. The advertisement calls for abolishment of the death penalty; it notes that Governor H has supported the death penalty. The advertisement identifies several individuals previously executed in state Z, stating that Governor H could have saved their lives by stopping their execution. No executions are scheduled in the state in the near future. The advertisement concludes with this statement: "Call or write Governor H to demand a moratorium on the death penalty in state Z."

The advertisement in the preceding example is for a political end. SW4's advertisement identifies Governor H, appears shortly before an election in which Governor H is a candidate, targets the voters in that election, and identifies Governor H's position as being contrary to SW4's position. The advertisement is not part of an ongoing series of substantially similar advocacy communications by SW4 on the same issue. In addition, the advertisement does not identify and is not timed to coincide with a specific event outside the control of the organization that it hopes to influence. Based on these facts and circumstances, the amount expended by SW4 on the advertisement is an expenditure for a political objective.

§ 4.5 POLITICAL ACTIVITIES TAX LAW RULES

The rules concerning the impact of political campaign activity on the deductibility of members' dues are basically the same as those in the lobbying context.[89]

(a) General Business Expense Deduction Disallowance Rules

Generally there is no business expense deduction for any amount paid or incurred in connection with participation in, or intervention in, a political campaign on behalf of or in opposition to a candidate for public office; or any attempt to influence the public, or segments thereof, with respect to elections.[90] The above-referenced rules concerning a cascading of the expense disallowance rule,[91] the *de minimis* exception,[92] and the rules concerning research activities[93] are applicable in this setting.

---

[89] See § 4.2.
[90] IRC § 162(e)(1)(B), (C).
[91] IRC § 162(e)(5)(A). See § 4.2(a)(viii).
[92] IRC § 162(e)(5)(B). See § 4.2(a)(v).
[93] IRC § 162(e)(5)(C). See § 4.2(a)(iii).

(b) Association Flow-Through and Proxy Tax Rules

A flow-through rule applicable with respect to membership associations disallows a business expense deduction for the portion of the membership dues (or voluntary payments or special assessments) paid to a tax-exempt organization that engages in political campaign activities.[94] Trade, business, and professional associations, and similar organizations, generally are required to provide annual information disclosure tot their members, estimating the portion of their dues that is allocable to political campaign activity and thus is nondeductible.[95]

§ 4.6 CONSTITUTIONALITY OF STATUTORY SCHEME

The association community litigated the constitutionality of this body of law, contending that the enforcement provisions[96] impose financial penalties on tax-exempt business leagues and their members that engage in lobbying and that these penalties deter exempt organizations and their members from exercising their rights to freedom of expression and association and to petition the government. It was also asserted that the challenged provisions violate equal protection principles by favoring private individuals and for-profit corporations over tax-exempt associations. The courts rejected these arguments.

Prior to congressional action in 1993, the federal tax law allowed businesses to deduct direct lobbying expenses as business expenses. In that year, as noted, the foregoing statutory scheme was enacted. Observing that the Supreme Court stated that "[l]egislatures have especially broad latitude in creating classifications and distinctions in tax statutes,"[97] a federal district court concluded that the challenged provisions do not penalize business leagues and their members that engage in lobbying but merely enforce the decision made by Congress to repeal this tax subsidy for lobbying.[98] The court also rejected the proposition that the challenged provisions unconstitutionally hinder speech about legislation, in that such speech "encompasses the entire spectrum of possible viewpoints and is, therefore, viewpoint neutral."[99] These provisions were held to be rationally related to Congress's intent to eliminate this subsidy for lobbying. This reasoning also led to the conclusion that the provisions do not amount to a deprivation of a fundamental right and thus that there was no valid equal protection issue.

---

[94] IRC § 162(e)(3).

[95] See § 4.2(b).

[96] These provisions are IRC §§ 162(e)(3) (see § 4.2(b), text accompanied by *supra* note 56); 162(e)(5)(C) (see § 4.2(a)(iii), text accompanied by *supra* note 38); and 6033(e) (see § 4.2(b)(i)).

[97] Regan v. Taxation With Representation, 461 U.S. 540, 547 (1983).

[98] American Society of Ass'n Executives v. United States, 23 F. Supp. 2d 64 (D.D.C. 1998). In an earlier decision, this court wrote that this matter is "less an instance of penalizing the exercise of a fundamental right than a case of Congress deciding not to subsidize the exercise of that right" and that the U.S. government "is not obligated to subsidize any person's lobbying." American Society of Ass'n Executives v. Bentsen, 848 F. Supp. 245, 249 (D.D.C. 1994).

[99] American Society of Ass'n Executives v. United States, 23 F. Supp. 2d 64, 70 (D.D.C. 1998).

§ 4.7 ASSOCIATIONS' USE OF POLITICAL ORGANIZATIONS

A tax-exempt business league that wishes to make an expenditure for political purposes can do so either from its general treasury or from a separate segregated fund. Such a fund is, from a federal tax law standpoint, a *political organization*.

(a) Political Organizations in General

Political organizations that collect and expend monies for political purposes are exempt from federal income tax except as to their investment and other nonpolitical activity income.[100] For political organizations, their political undertakings are known as *exempt functions*.

A political organization is a party, committee, association, fund, or other organization (whether incorporated or not), organized and operated primarily for the purpose of accepting contributions or making expenditures, or both, for an exempt function.[101] The term *exempt function* means the function of influencing or attempting to influence the selection, nomination, election, or appointment of an individual to a federal, state, or local public office or office in a political organization, or the election of presidential or vice-presidential electors, whether the individual or electors are selected, nominated, elected, or appointed or not.[102] By its terms, as noted, the concept of an exempt function includes all activities that are directly related to and support the process of influencing or attempting to influence the selection, nomination, election, or appointment of an individual to public office or office in a political organization.[103] Whether an expenditure is for an exempt function is dependent on all of the facts and circumstances.[104]

A tax-exempt organization[105] is subject to tax on any amount expended for an exempt function at the highest rate of tax for corporations.[106] This tax is imposed on the lesser of the net investment income of the organization for the year involved or the amount expended on an exempt function during the year. An exempt organization is taxed under this rule only if the expenditure is from its general treasury rather than from a separate segregated fund. If a tax-exempt organization sets up a separate segregated fund that segregates monies for exempt function purposes, the fund will be treated as, and subject to tax as, a separate political organization.[107]

To be tax-exempt, a political organization is required to give notice to the IRS that it is a political organization, unless an exception is available.[108] An exempt organization that does not establish a separate segregated fund, but makes

---

[100] IRC § 527(b), (c).
[101] IRC § 527(e)(1).
[102] IRC § 527(e)(2).
[103] Reg. § 1.527-2(c)(1).
[104] Cf. § 4.4
[105] That is, an organization described in IRC § 501(c) and exempt from federal income tax under IRC § 501(a). This definition thus encompasses exempt business leagues.
[106] IRC § 527(f)(1).
[107] IRC § 527(f)(3).
[108] IRC § 527(i). This notice is provided by filing Form 8871.

exempt function expenditures itself (which are subject to tax), is not subject to this notice requirement.[109]

Unless exempt, a tax-exempt political organization that has given notice that it is a political committee and does not timely make periodic reports of contributions and expenditures, or that fails to include the information required, must pay an amount calculated by multiplying the amount of contributions and expenditures that are not disclosed by the highest corporate tax rate. Again, an exempt organization that does not set up a separate segregated fund but makes exempt function expenditures itself (which are subject to tax) is not subject to this reporting requirement.[110]

A tax-exempt organization may, if it is consistent with its exempt status, establish and maintain a separate segregated fund to receive contributions and make expenditures in a political campaign.[111]

(b) Associations and Political Organizations

Tax-exempt business leagues, when they engage in political activities, usually do so by means of related political organizations. This use of a separate segregated fund, rather than the making of expenditures from a league's general treasury, enables the league to avoid the federal tax imposed on amounts expended for a political objective.[112] This use of a separate segregated fund also facilitates compliance with the federal election laws.[113]

---

[109] IRC § 527(i)(5)(A).

[110] This reporting requirement includes filing of Form 8872. The reporting and disclosure requirements for political organizations are summarized in Rev. Rul. 2003-49, 2003-20 I.R.B. 903.

[111] Reg. § 1.527-6(f).

[112] See § 4.7(a), text accompanied by *supra* note 107.

[113] See § 11.5.

CHAPTER FIVE

Unrelated Business Rules

The federal tax law generally categorizes the activities of tax-exempt associations (and nearly all other exempt organizations) as being one of two types: those that are substantially related to the performance of exempt functions and those that are not. The former are *related trades or businesses*; the latter are *unrelated trades or businesses*. The net revenue occasioned by an unrelated business—absent application of a modification or an exception[1]—is subject to federal income tax. The judgments that go into the assignment of activities into these two categories are at the heart of some of the greatest tax law controversies facing exempt organizations.

The fundamentals of the unrelated business rules entail a determination as to whether a particular activity amounts to a business, whether the activity is regularly carried on, whether the activity is substantially in furtherance of the purposes of the tax-exempt organization involved, and (if needed) whether an exception is available. The balance of the basics is essentially refinements of these four determinations.

§ 5.1 ANALYTIC FRAMEWORK

An analysis of a tax-exempt business league's potential unrelated trade or business factual situation may involve as many as eight steps. They are:

1. Ascertainment of whether the activity involved constitutes a *business*.[2]

2. Determination of whether the business is *regularly carried on*.[3]

3. Determination of whether the regularly carried on business is *related* to the purposes of the business league.[4]

4. Determination of whether the regularly carried on business is *substantially* related to the purposes of the business league.[5]

5. Determination of whether one or more modifications or exceptions for types of *income* may be available.[6]

6. Determination of whether one or more modifications or exceptions for types of *activities* may be available.[7]

7. Marshalling of available expenses that can be deducted in computing *unrelated business taxable income*.[8]

8. Determination of whether the unrelated activity, or combination of unrelated activities, poses a threat to the business league's tax-exempt status.[9]

---

[1] See § 5.9.
[2] See § 5.2.
[3] See § 5.5.
[4] See § 5.6.
[5] See § 5.7.
[6] See § 5.9.
[7] *Id.*
[8] See § 5.12.
[9] See § 2.4. Occasionally, the IRS will assume a different stance toward the tax consequences of one or more unrelated businesses when the issue is qualification for exemption. That is, the agency may conclude that a business is unrelated to an organization's exempt purpose and thus is subject to the unrelated business income tax but the IRS may also agree that the purpose of the unrelated business is such that the activity furthers the organization's exempt functions (by generating funds for exempt programs), even if the unrelated business activity is more than one-half of total operations (e.g., Tech. Adv. Mem. 200021056). In this circumstance, then, the exempt organization can be in the anomalous position of having a considerable amount of taxable business activity—and nonetheless be tax-exempt.

§ 5.2 DEFINITION OF *TRADE OR BUSINESS*

As noted, some or all of the gross income of a tax-exempt business league may be includable in the computation of unrelated business income where it constitutes income derived from a *trade or business*.

(a) General Rules

The statutory definition of the term *trade or business*, used for unrelated business law purposes, states that it includes "any activity which is carried on for the production of income from the sale of goods or the performance of services."[10] This sweeping definition encompasses nearly every activity that a tax-exempt organization may undertake. Indeed, the federal tax law views an exempt organization as a cluster of businesses, with each discrete activity susceptible to evaluation independently from the others.[11]

The definition of the term *trade or business*, however, also embraces an activity that otherwise possesses the characteristics of a business as that term is defined by the federal income tax law in the business expense deduction setting.[12] This definition, then, is even more expansive than the statutory one, being informed by the considerable body of law as to the meaning of the word *business* that has accreted in the federal tax law generally.

Consequently, in general, any activity of a tax-exempt business league that is carried on for the production of income and that otherwise possesses the characteristics required to constitute a trade or business (within the meaning of the business expense deduction rules)—and that is not substantially related to the performance of exempt functions—presents sufficient likelihood of unfair competition[13] to be within the policy of the unrelated business income tax. Thus, for purposes of the unrelated business rules, the term *trade or business* has the same meaning that it has in the business expense deduction rules context and thus generally includes any activity carried on for the production of income from the sale of goods or the performance of services. The term *trade or business* is not, therefore, limited to integrated aggregates of assets, activities, and good will that comprise *businesses* for other federal tax law purposes.[14]

A third element to consider in this regard stems from the view that, to constitute a business, an income-producing activity of a tax-exempt organization must have the general characteristics of a trade or business. Some federal courts of appeals have recognized that an exempt organization must carry out extensive business activities over a substantial period of time to be considered engaged in a trade or business.[15] In one case, a court held that the proceeds derived by an exempt organization from fundraising operations were not taxable as unrelated business income, inasmuch as the organization's functions in

---

[10] IRC § 513(c).

[11] See the discussion of the *fragmentation rule* (§ 5.3).

[12] Reg. § 1.513-1(b). The business expense deduction is the subject of IRC § 162.

[13] See § 5.2(b).

[14] Reg. § 1.513-1(b).

[15] E.g., in the tax-exempt organizations context, Professional Insurance Agents of Michigan v. Comm'r, 726 F.2d 1097 (6th Cir. 1984). E.g., in the business expense deduction context, Zell v. Comm'r, 763 F.2d 1139 (10th Cir. 1985); McDowell v. Ribicoff, 292 F.2d 174 (3d Cir. 1961), *cert. den.*, 368 U.S. 919 (1961).

this regard were considered insufficiently "extensive" to warrant treatment as a business.[16] In another instance, the receipt of payments by an exempt association pursuant to involvement in insurance plans was ruled to not constitute a business because the association's role was not extensive and did not possess the general characteristics of a trade or business.[17] This aspect of the analysis, however, is close to a separate test altogether, which is whether the business activities are regularly carried on.[18]

Where an activity carried on for profit constitutes an unrelated business, no part of the business may be excluded from classification as a business merely because it does not result in profit.[19]

Traditionally, the IRS has almost always prevailed on the argument that an activity of a tax-exempt organization constitutes a trade or business. In recent years, however, courts have been more willing to conclude that an exempt organization's financial undertaking does not rise to the level of a business.[20]

(b) Commerciality

Where there is competition, a court may conclude that the activity of a tax-exempt organization is being conducted in a commercial manner[21] and thus is an unrelated business. For example, the operation of a television station by an exempt university was held to be an unrelated business because it was operated in a commercial manner; the station was an affiliate of a national television broadcasting company.[22]

Historically, the IRS (like the courts) has used the commerciality doctrine in assessing an organization's qualification for tax-exempt status; the doctrine was not used to ascertain the presence of an unrelated business. This appears to be changing, however, with the IRS employing the doctrine in rationalizing that a business is an unrelated one.[23]

To date, the courts have applied the commerciality doctrine only with respect to public charities.[24] The IRS suggested, however, that the commerciality doctrine applies to tax-exempt social welfare organizations.[25] The commerciality doctrine has never been applied to exempt business leagues.[26]

(c) Charging of Fees

Tax-exempt business leagues charge dues and other fees for the services they provide; where the business generating this revenue is a related one, the receipts

---

[16] Vigilant Hose Co. of Emmitsburg v. United States, 2001-2 U.S.T.C. ¶ 50,458 (D. Md. 2001).

[17] American Academy of Family Physicians v. United States, 91 F.3d 1155 (8th Cir. 1996).

[18] See § 5.5.

[19] IRC § 513(c).

[20] E.g., Laborer's Int'l Union of North America v. Comm'r, 82 T.C.M. 158 (2001).

[21] See *Tax-Exempt Organizations*, Chapter 25.

[22] Iowa State Univ. of Science & Technology v. United States, 500 F.2d 508 (Ct. Cl. 1974).

[23] E.g., Tech. Adv. Mem. 200021056.

[24] E.g., Living Faith, Inc. v. Comm'r, 950 F.2d 365 (7th Cir. 1991); Airlie Found. v. Internal Revenue Service, 283 F. Supp. 2d 58 (D.D.C. 2003). Public charities are the subject of § 8.1.

[25] Priv. Ltr. Rul. 200501020. Social welfare organizations are the subject of § 1.6(c).

[26] In general, see Hopkins, *The Tax Law of Unrelated Business for Nonprofit Organizations* (Hoboken, NJ: John Wiley & Sons, 2006) ("*Unrelated Business*"), Chapter 7.

are characterized as *exempt function revenue*.[27] This is common throughout the realm of exempt organizations in general: Universities, colleges, hospitals, museums, planetariums, orchestras, and like exempt institutions generate exempt function revenue, without adverse impact as to their exempt status.[28] Exempt organizations such as medical clinics, homes for the aged, and blood banks impose charges for their services and are not subject to unrelated business income taxation (or deprived of exemption) as a result.[29] Indeed, the IRS, in a ruling discussing the tax status of homes for the aged as charitable organizations, observed that the "operating funds [of these homes] are derived principally from fees charged for residence in the home."[30] Similarly, the agency ruled that a nonprofit theater may charge admission for its performances and nonetheless qualify as an exempt charitable organization.[31] Other fee-based exempt charitable entities include hospices,[32] organizations providing specially designed housing for the elderly,[33] and organizations providing housing for the disabled.[34] Moreover, for some types of publicly supported charities, exempt function revenue is regarded as support enhancing public charity status.[35] In addition to associations, several categories of exempt organizations, such as unions,[36] social clubs,[37] fraternal groups,[38] and veterans' organizations[39] are dues-based entities.

Consequently, as a general principle, gross income derived from charges for the performance of exempt functions does not constitute gross income from the conduct of unrelated trade or business.[40] For example, a tax-exempt school trains children in the performing arts, such as acting, singing, and dancing; it presents performances by its students and derives gross income from admission charges for the performances. The students' participation in performances before audiences is an essential part of their education and training. Since the income realized from the performances derives from activities that contribute importantly to the accomplishment of the school's exempt purposes, it does not constitute gross income from unrelated business.[41]

As another example, a tax-exempt union, to improve the skills of its members, conducts refresher training courses and supplies handbooks and technical manuals. The union receives payments from its members for these services and materials. The development and improvement of the skills of its members is one

---

[27] See, e.g., § 10.5(b).
[28] IRC § 170(b)(1)(A)(ii), (iii); Reg. § 1.170A-9(e)(1)(ii); Reg. § 1.501(c)(3)-1(d)(3)(ii), Example (4).
[29] E.g., Rev. Rul. 72-124, 1972-1 C.B. 145; Rev. Rul. 78-145, 1978-1 C.B. 169, *modifying* Rev. Rul. 66-323, 1966-2 C.B. 216.
[30] Rev. Rul. 72-124, 1972-1 C.B. 145.
[31] Rev. Rul. 73-45, 1973-1 C.B. 220.
[32] Rev. Rul. 79-17, 1979-1 C.B. 193.
[33] Rev. Rul. 79-18, 1979-1 C.B. 194.
[34] Rev. Rul. 79-19, 1979-1 C.B. 195.
[35] IRC § 509(a)(2). See § 8.4.
[36] See § 1.6(c).
[37] See § 1.6(f).
[38] See § 1.6(g).
[39] See § 1.6(m).
[40] Reg. § 1.513-1(d)(4)(i).
[41] *Id.*, Example (1).

of the exempt purposes of this union; these activities contribute importantly to that purpose. Therefore, the income derived from these activities is not unrelated business gross income.[42]

In a third illustration, a tax-exempt industry trade association presents a trade show in which members of an industry join in an exhibition of industry products. The association derives income from charges made to exhibitors for exhibit space and admission fees charged patrons or viewers of the show. The show is not a sales facility for individual exhibitors[43]; its purpose is the promotion and stimulation of interest in and demand for the industry's products in general, and it is conducted in a manner reasonably calculated to achieve that purpose. The stimulation of demand for the industry's products in general is one of the purposes for which the association was granted tax exemption. Consequently, the activities productive of the association's gross income from the show—that is, the promotion, organization, and conduct of the exhibition—contribute importantly to the achievement of an exempt purpose, and the income does not constitute gross income from unrelated business.[44]

Yet the receipt of fee-for-service revenue occasionally is regarded in some quarters as evidence of the conduct of an unrelated business. For example, the contention is made from time to time that an organization, to be charitable in nature, must provide its services and/or sell its goods without charge. In fact, the test is, for charitable and other exempt organizations, how the fees received are expended; the rendering of services without charge is not a prerequisite to tax-exempt status.

In one instance, the IRS opposed tax exemption for nonprofit consumer credit counseling agencies. The agencies asserted that their services, provided to individuals and families, as well as facilitating speakers and disseminating publications, were educational in nature as being forms of instruction of the public on subjects (such as budgeting) useful to the individual and beneficial to the community.[45] They also contended that their activities were charitable because they advance education and promote social welfare.[46] The IRS sought to deny these agencies exempt status on the ground that they charge a fee for certain services, even though the fee was nominal and waived in instances of economic hardship. This effort was rebuffed in court.[47] Thereafter, the IRS's Office of Chief Counsel advised that if the "activity [of consumer credit counseling] may be deemed to benefit the community as a whole, the fact that fees are charged for the organization's services will not detract from the exempt nature of the activity" and that the "presence of a fee is relevant only if it inhibits accomplishment of the desired result."[48] (Earlier, the chief counsel's office wrote that the fact that a charitable organization charges a fee for a good or service "will be relevant in very few cases," that the "only inquiry" should be whether the charges "significantly detract from the organization's charitable purposes," and that the cost issue is

[42] *Id.*, Example (2).
[43] Cf. § 5.9(n).
[44] Reg. § 1.513-1(d)(4)(i), Example (3).
[45] Reg. § 1.501(c)(3)-1(d)(3) (i) (b). See *Tax-Exempt Organizations* § 7.4.
[46] Reg. § 1.501(c)(3)-1(d)(2). See *Tax-Exempt Organizations* § 6.6.
[47] Consumer Credit Counseling Service of Ala., Inc. v. United States, 78-2 U.S.T.C. ¶ 9660 (D.D.C. 1978).
[48] Gen. Couns. Mem. 38459.

pertinent only where the activities involved are commercial in nature.[49]) At about the same time, the IRS ruled that an organization that is operated to provide legal services to indigents may charge, for each hour of legal assistance provided, a "nominal hourly fee determined by reference to the client's own hourly income."[50]

There have been instances where the IRS determined that an organization is charitable in nature, and thus tax-exempt, because it provides services that are free to the recipients. This is, however, an independent basis for finding a charitable activity, usually invoked where the services, assistance, or benefits provided are not inherently charitable in nature. This distinction may be seen in the treatment by the IRS of cooperative service organizations established by tax-exempt colleges and universities. In one instance, a computer services sharing organization was ruled to be an exempt charitable organization because the IRS concluded that the services provided to the participating institutions of higher education were charitable as advancing education; no requirement was imposed that the services be provided without charge.[51] In another instance, a similar organization was found to be charitable even though the services it rendered to the participating education institutions were regarded as nonexempt functions (being "administrative"); the distinguishing feature was that the organization received less than 15 percent of its financial support from the colleges and universities that received the services.[52] Thus, the recipient entities were receiving the services for, at most, a nominal charge. Had this latter organization been providing only an insubstantial extent of administrative services and a substantial amount of exempt services, its exemption would have been predicated on the bases that it was engaging in inherently exempt activities; the 15 percent rule was employed only as an alternative rationale for exemption as a charitable entity.[53]

On occasion, the issue will be whether there is an unrelated business, not so much because fees are being charged but because the charges result in a *profit* (excess of revenue over expenses). Profit-making is not an automatic indicator of unrelated trade or business; indeed, a profit motive may be a requirement for a finding of business activity.[54] In its regulations concerning travel tours and similar opportunities,[55] the IRS stipulated that, in the case of both related and unrelated activities, the travel tours were priced to produce a profit for the exempt organization.[56]

Consequently, the law does not require, as a condition of tax exemption or avoidance of unrelated business income, that the organization provide services without charge.[57] Likewise, the fact that an exempt organization charges a fee for the provision of goods or services, while perhaps an indicator that the underlying

---

[49] Gen. Couns. Mem. 37257.

[50] Rev. Rul. 78-428, 1978-2 C.B. 177.

[51] Rev. Rul. 74-614, 1974-2 C.B. 164, *amp. by* Rev. Rul. 81-29, 1981-1 C.B. 329.

[52] Rev. Rul. 71-529, 1971-2 C.B. 234.

[53] In general, see *Tax-Exempt Organizations* § 10.5.

[54] See § 5.4.

[55] See *Tax-Exempt Organizations* § 26.5(h).

[56] Reg. § 1.513-7(b).

[57] The "position that the test of a charitable institution is the extent of free services rendered, is difficult of application and unsound in theory" (Southern Methodist Hosp. & Sanatorium of Tucson v. Wilson, 77 P.2d 458, 462 (Ariz. 1943)).

activity is a *business*, should not lead to an automatic conclusion that the business is an unrelated one.

(d) Nonbusiness Activities

Not every activity of a tax-exempt organization that generates a financial return is a trade or business for purposes of the unrelated business rules. As the Supreme Court observed, the "narrow category of trade or business" is a "concept which falls far short of reaching every income or profit making activity."[58] Specifically in the exempt organizations' context, an appellate court wrote that "there are instances where some activities by some exempt organizations to earn income in a noncommercial manner will not amount to the conduct of a trade or business."[59]

The most obvious of the types of nonbusiness activities is the management by a tax-exempt organization of its own investment properties. Under the general rules, concerning the business expense deduction, defining *business activity*, the management of an investment portfolio composed wholly of the manager's own securities does not constitute the carrying on of a trade or business. The Supreme Court held that the mere derivation of income from securities and keeping of records is not the operation of a business.[60] On that occasion, the Court sustained the IRS's position that "mere personal investment activities never constitute carrying on a trade or business."[61] Subsequently, the Court stated that "investing is not a trade or business."[62] Likewise, a court of appeals observed that the "mere management of investments . . . is insufficient to constitute the carrying on of a trade or business."[63]

This principle of law is applicable in the tax-exempt organizations context. For example, the IRS ruled that the receipt of income by an exempt employees' trust from installment notes purchased from the employer-settlor was not income from the operation of a business, noting that the trust "merely keeps the records and receives the periodic payments of principal and interest collected for it by the employer."[64] Likewise, the agency held that a reversion of funds from a qualified plan to a charitable organization did not "possess the characteristics" required for an activity to qualify as a business.[65] For a time, there was controversy over whether the practice, engaged in by some tax-exempt organizations, of lending securities to brokerage houses for compensation was an unrelated business; the IRS ultimately arrived at the view that securities lending is a form

---

[58] Whipple v. Comm'r, 373 U.S. 193, 197, 201 (1963).

[59] Steamship Trade Ass'n of Baltimore, Inc. v. Comm'r, 757 F.2d 1494, 1497 (4th Cir. 1985). Also Adirondack League Club v. Comm'r, 458 F.2d 506 (2d Cir. 1972); Blake Construction Co., Inc. v. United States, 572 F.2d 820 (Ct. Cl. 1978); Monfore v. United States, 77-2 U.S.T.C. ¶ 9528 (Ct. C. 1977); Oklahoma Cattlemen's Ass'n, Inc. v. United States, 310 F. Supp. 320 (W.D. Okla. 1969); McDowell v. Ribicoff, 292 F.2d 174 (3d Cir. 1961), *cert. den.*, 368 U.S. 919 (1961).

[60] Higgins v. Comm'r, 312 U.S. 212 (1941).

[61] *Id.* at 215.

[62] Whipple v. Comm'r, 373 U.S. 193, 202 (1963).

[63] Continental Trading, Inc. v. Comm'r, 265 F.2d 40, 43 (9th Cir. 1959) *cert. den.*, 361 U.S. 827 (1959). Also VanWart v. Comm'r, 295 U.S. 112 (1935); Deputy v. duPont, 308 U.S. 488 (1940) (concurring opinion); Moller v. United States, 721 F.2d 810 (Fed. Cir. 1983); Comm'r v. Burnett, 118 F.2d 659 (5th Cir. 1941); Rev. Rul. 56-511, 1956-2 C.B. 170.

[64] Rev. Rul. 69-574, 1969-2 C.B. 130, 131.

[65] Priv. Ltr. Rul. 200131034.

of "ordinary or routine investment activities" and thus is not a business.[66] A court held that certain investment activities conducted by a charitable organization were not businesses.[67]

Other similar activities do not rise to the level of a business. In one instance, a tax-exempt association of physicians was held to not be taxable on certain payments it annually received by reason of its sponsorship of group insurance plans that were available to its members and their employees, with the court writing that the payments "were neither brokerage fees nor other compensation for commercial services, but were the way the parties decided to acknowledge the . . . [association's] eventual claim to the excess reserves while . . . [the insurance company involved] was still holding and using the reserves."[68] In another case, an exempt dental society that sponsored a payment plan to finance dental care was held to not be taxable on refunds for income taxes and interest on amounts paid as excess reserve funds from a bank and as collections on defaulted notes.[69] A comparable position was taken by a court in concluding that an exempt organization did not engage in an unrelated business by making health insurance available to its members, in that the organization did not control the financial result of the insurance activities.[70]

In still another case, a court held that the proceeds derived by a tax-exempt organization from fundraising operations were not taxable as unrelated business income, in that the economic activity did not constitute a business.[71] The operations involved the use of "tip jars," with the exempt organization's role confined to applying for gambling permits and purchasing the tip-jar tickets; the significant and substantial portion of the activities was the sale of the tickets at participating taverns. The exempt organization's functions in this regard were considered insufficiently "extensive" to warrant treatment as a business.[72]

(e) Real Estate Activities

A tax-exempt organization may acquire real property under a variety of circumstances and for a variety of reasons. The acquisition may be by purchase or by contribution. Often this acquisition activity is undertaken to advance exempt purposes or to make an investment. When an exempt organization decides to dispose of the property, the activity may be, or may be seen as being, a dealing in property in the ordinary course of a business. When exempt functions are not involved, the dichotomy becomes whether the exempt organization is a passive

---

[66] Rev. Rul. 78-88, 1978-1 C.B. 163. This issue was subsequently further resolved by statute (see § 5.9(d)).

[67] The Marion Found. v. Comm'r, 19 T.C.M. 99 (1960).

[68] American Academy of Family Physicians v. United States, 91 F.3d 1155, 1159 (8th Cir. 1996). Nonetheless, the IRS remains of the view that these types of oversight and like activities with respect to insurance programs constitute unrelated business (e.g., Tech. Adv. Mem. 9612003 (concerning a charitable organization, fostering competition in a sport (see *Tax-Exempt Organizations* § 10.2), that provided certain administrative services in connection with an insurance program covering its members for practices and other sports activities)).

[69] San Antonio Dist. Dental Soc'y v. United States, 340 F. Supp. 11 (W.D. Tex. 1972).

[70] Carolinas Farm & Power Equip. Dealers Ass'n, Inc. v. United States, 541 F. Supp. 86 (E.D. N. Car. 1982), aff'd, 699 F.2d 167 (4th Cir. 1983).

[71] Vigilant Hose Co. of Emmitsburg v. United States, 2001-2 U.S.T.C. ¶ 50,458 (D. Md. 2001).

[72] On occasion, as an alternative argument, the IRS will assert that the tax-exempt organization is involved in a joint venture with one or more for-profit entities and attempt to tax net revenues received by the exempt organization on that basis (see § 7.3).

investor or is a dealer in the property. Often the issue arises when the property, or portions of it, is being sold; the exempt organization may be liquidating an investment attempting to maximize the value of the property or selling property to customers in the ordinary course of business.

The IRS applies these factors in determining whether property being or to be sold has been held primarily for investment or for sale to customers in the ordinary course of business (in the latter case the resulting revenue is ordinary income rather than capital gain): the purpose for which the property was acquired; its cost; the length of time the property was held; the activities of the owner in the improvement and disposition of the property; the extent of improvements made to the property; the proximity of the sale to the purchase; the purpose for which the property was held; prevailing market conditions; and the frequency, continuity, and size of the sales.[73]

The factors are derived from case law. In one of the principal cases on the point, it was held that the frequency of the sales and the level of development and selling activities are the most important criteria; the court wrote that "although a taxpayer may have acquired property without intending to enter the real estate business, what was once an investment or what may start out as a liquidation of an investment, may become something else"; thus, "where sales are continuous the nature and purpose of a taxpayer's acquisition of property is significant only where sales activity results from unanticipated, externally introduced factors which make impossible the continued pre-existing use of the realty."[74]

Other court opinions provide a similar list of factors.[75] In one case, the court relied primarily on the frequency-of-sales factor.[76] A corporation that did not engage in any development or subdivision activity, and did not engage in any solicitation or marketing efforts, with respect to about 200 sales of lots over a 33-year period was found to be a dealer inasmuch as the sales activity was substantial and continuous.[77] A person was found to be a dealer with 107 sales over a 10-year period,[78] while another person who sold 25 lots in one year was held to not be a dealer.[79] The only aspect of this matter that is clear is that there is no fixed formula or other rule of thumb for determining whether property sold by a person was held by that person primarily[80] for sale to customers in business or for investment.[81]

---

[73] E.g., Priv. Ltr. Rul. 9619069.

[74] Houston Endowment v. United States, 606 F.2d 77, 82 (5th Cir. 1979) (internal quotations omitted) (where the court added that "[o]riginal investment intent is pertinent, for example, when a taxpayer is coerced to sell its property by acts of God, new and unfavorable zoning regulations or other uncontrollable forces" (at 82).

[75] E.g., Byram v. Comm'r, 705 F.2d 1418 (5th Cir. 1983); Winthrop v. Comm'r, 417 F.2d 905 (5th Cir. 1969); Heller Trust v. Comm'r, 382 F.2d 675 (9th Cir. 1967); Barrios Estate v. Comm'r, 265 F.2d 517 (5th Cir. 1959); Kaltreider v. Comm'r, 255 F.2d 833 (3d Cir. 1958), aff'g 28 T.C. 121 (1957); Brown v. Comm'r, 143 F.2d 468 (5th Cir. 1944); Buono v. Comm'r, 74 T.C. 187 (1980); Adam v. Comm'r, 60 T.C. 996 (1973); also Rev. Rul. 59-91, 1959-1 C.B. 15.

[76] Biedenharn Realty Co. v. United States, 526 F.2d 409 (5th Cir. 1976), cert. den., 429 U.S. 819 (1976).

[77] Suburban Realty v. United States, 615 F.2d 171 (5th Cir. 1980), cert. den., 449 U.S. 920 (1980).

[78] Wineberg v. Comm'r, 326 F.2d 157 (9th Cir. 1963).

[79] Farley v. Comm'r, 7 T.C. 198 (1946).

[80] The word primarily in this setting means "of first importance" or "principally" (Malat v. Riddell, 383 U.S. 569, 572 (1966)). By this standard, the IRS ruled, ordinary income would not result unless a "sales purpose" is "dominant" (Priv. Ltr. Rul. 9316032).

[81] Mauldin v. Comm'r, 195 F.2d 714 (10th Cir. 1952).

As examples of the IRS's decision making in this context, the agency ruled that the gain from the sale by tax-exempt organizations of leased fee interests in condominium apartments to lessees was not taxable because of the exclusion for capital gain.[82] Likewise, the IRS ruled that the sale by a charitable organization of its entire interest in an apartment building, to be converted to a condominium, would generate excludable capital gain, with the agency emphasizing that the organization did not play any role in the subsequent marketing or sale of the condominium units.[83] Further, a tax-exempt university was found to be engaged in a property disposition that was "passive" and "patient," following a land use plan that envisioned sale of the property in up to nine tracts to different developers over a period of time so as to maximize the institution's return from the disposition; the capital gain exclusion was ruled to be available.[84] Conversely, the improvement and frequent sale of land by an exempt organization was held by the agency to be an unrelated business.[85]

In a typical instance, the IRS reviewed a proposed sale of certain real estate interests held by a public charity. In the case, substantially all of the property was received by bequest and had been held for a significant period of time. The decision was made to sell the property (liquidate the investment) due to the enactment of legislation adverse to the investment, so as to receive fair market value. Availability of the property for sale was not advertised to the public. Applying the primary purpose test, the IRS concluded that the proposed sales did not involve property held primarily for sale to customers in the ordinary course of business.[86]

In another instance, a tax-exempt charitable organization presented four alternatives to the IRS for development of its real property. The first alternative was to continue a leasing arrangement with annual rental income of approximately $100,000. The second choice was sale of the property as is for about $4 million. The third alternative was completion of some preliminary development work (such as obtaining various permits) and selling the property in large tracts to a few developers, resulting in about $6 million. The fourth alternative was further development of the property, including design and construction of streets, curbs, gutters, sidewalks, lighting, and utilities, with sales of individual lots to the general public. The agency ruled that the organization would escape unrelated business income taxation if it adhered to any of the first three alternatives but would be subject to tax if it opted for the fourth choice.[87]

By contrast, a tax-exempt charitable organization purchased real estate, divided it into lots, and improved the lots. The project evolved into the equivalent of a municipality. Lots were sold to the general public pursuant to a marketing

---

[82] Priv. Ltr. Rul. 9629030.

[83] Priv. Ltr. Rul. 200246032.

[84] Priv. Ltr. Rul. 200510029.

[85] Priv. Ltr. Rul. 200119061.

[86] *Id.*

[87] Priv. Ltr. Rul. 8950072. Thus, obviously, an exempt organization in this position, in seeking to maximize value from the disposition of property (particularly real property), in adherence to principles of fiduciary responsibility, must balance the amount of projected revenue against the projected income tax consequences; an attempt at full maximization of value may cause the entity to be classified, for federal tax purposes, as a dealer in the property.

plan involving real estate companies. The IRS concluded that the subdivision, development, and sale of the lots was a business that was regularly carried on, "in a manner that is similar to a for-profit residential land development company." The organization advanced the argument that the land development and sales were done in furtherance of exempt purposes, by attracting members who participate in its educational programs.[88] But the IRS concluded that the relationship between the sales of lots for single-family homes and the organization's goal of increasing program attendance was "somewhat tenuous." Therefore, the agency held that the resulting sales income was unrelated business income.[89]

An IRS private letter ruling illustrated how fine these distinctions can be.[90] A tax-exempt school owned land underlying a residential condominium project, which had been developed and marketed before the school received the property by devise. Sale of the land to the condominium association failed, in part because of enactment of law that could enable the association to acquire the land as the result of a condemnation proceeding. The school decided to offer the land directly to the owners of the condominium units, process that would encompass several months. The IRS took into account the "political climate" in which the school was operating and placed emphasis on the fact that the availability of the property was not to be advertised, the fact that the property was obtained by gift, and the considerable length of time the school owned the land. These facts led the agency to observe that the proposed sales process was "completely contrary to the short turn around period experienced by a typical buyer and seller of real property."

In another of these circumstances, a tax-exempt vocational school sold 8,500 acres of property over a 25-year period, yet was found by the IRS to not be selling property in the ordinary course of business.[91] The original reason for acquisition of the property was to support the school's mission, which was to prepare students for life in an agrarian society. The school's farming operations eventually ceased and it desired to sell the farmland; its position was that the land must be sold over a lengthy period of time in an attempt to realize the fair market value of the property. The IRS, emphasizing that the school held the property for over 50 years, agreed, writing the sales of the property was a "liquidation of investment assets or a sale incident to the school's exempt property."[92]

The exception in the law for capital gain,[93] which interrelates with these rules, is not available when the property is sold in circumstances in which the tax-exempt organization is a dealer in the property. When dealer status exists or is imposed, the property is considered to be property sold in the ordinary course of business, giving rise to ordinary income.

---

[88] An argument of this nature was accepted in *Junaluska Assembly Housing, Inc. v. Comm'r*, 86 T.C. 1114 (1986).

[89] Tech. Adv. Mem. 200047049.

[90] Priv. Ltr. Rul. 9505020.

[91] Priv. Ltr. Rul. 9619069.

[92] In general, Nugent, "Possible Approaches for Avoiding UBIT on Real Estate Investment," 37 *Exempt Org. Tax Rev.* (No. 2) 285 (Aug. 2002).

[93] See § 3.10.

Even if the primary purpose underlying the acquisition and holding of real property is advancement of exempt purposes, the IRS may apply the fragmentation rule[94] in search of unrelated business. As the agency stated the matter in one instance, a charitable organization "engaged in substantial regularly carried on unrelated trade [or] business as a component of its substantially related land purchase activity."[95] In the matter, the IRS looked to substantial and frequent sales of surplus land that was not intended for exempt use, and found that those sales were unrelated businesses. The same factors were used to reach that conclusion as are used in the general context, such as the sale of land shortly after its purchase and the extent of improvements.

(f) Efficiencies of Operation

On occasion, a court will focus on the fact that a tax-exempt organization is operating in a fashion that is considered "efficient," "effectively managed," "run like a business," and the like.[96] This can lead to a finding that the organization, or an activity of it, is—for that reason alone—a business undertaking.[97]

(g) Occasional Sales

Another illustration of a transaction involving a tax-exempt organization that is not a business undertaking is the occasional sale of an item of property. For example, the IRS held that a sale of property by an exempt entity was not under circumstances where the property was held primarily for sale to customers in the ordinary course of business.[98] By contrast, as noted, the subdivision, development, and sale of real estate parcels by an exempt organization was held by the agency to be a business carried on in a manner similar to the activities of for-profit residential land development companies.[99]

The IRS reviewed a situation involving a group insurance trust, affiliated with a tax-exempt membership association, that experienced a substantial increase in its net worth and reserve balance due to the demutualization of an insurance company that provided insurance products to the association's members through the trust. The association decided to transfer all of the trust's assets to a related supporting organization. This transfer of assets was cast by the IRS as a one-time transfer, triggered by the unforeseen occurrence of demutualization; and the agency held that the transfer would not cause unrelated business income taxation.[100]

This aspect of the law, however, is closely analogous to the *regularly carried on* test.[101]

---

[94] See § 5.3.

[95] Priv. Ltr. Rul. 200119061.

[96] See *Unrelated Business*, Chapter 7.

[97] E.g., The Incorporated Trustees of the Gospel Worker Soc'y v. United States, 510 F. Supp. 374 (D.D.C. 1981), *aff'd*, 672 F.2d 894 (D.C. Cir. 1981), *cert. den.*, 456 U.S. 944 (1981); Presbyterian & Reformed Publishing Co. v. Comm'r, 79 T.C. 1070 (1983).

[98] Priv. Ltr. Rul. 9316032.

[99] Tech. Adv. Mem. 200047049. See § 5.2(e).

[100] Priv. Ltr. Rul. 200328042.

[101] See § 5.5.

§ 5.3 FRAGMENTATION RULE

The IRS has the authority to tax net income from an activity as unrelated business taxable income, where the activity is an integral part of a cluster of activities that is in furtherance of a tax-exempt purpose. To ferret out unrelated business, the agency regards an exempt organization as a bundle of activities and evaluates each of the activities in isolation to determine if one or more of them constitutes a trade or business. This assessment process is known as *fragmentation*.

The *fragmentation rule* states that an "activity does not lose identity as trade or business merely because it is carried on within a larger aggregate of similar activities or within a larger complex of other endeavors which may, or may not, be related to the exempt purpose of the organization."[102] Thus, as noted, the IRS is empowered to fragment the operations of a tax-exempt organization, operated as an integrated whole, into its component parts in search of one or more unrelated businesses. For example, the regular sale of pharmaceutical supplies to the general public by an exempt hospital pharmacy does not lose identity as trade or business merely because the pharmacy also furnishes supplies to the hospital and patients of the hospital in accordance with its exempt purposes or in compliance with the requirements of the convenience doctrine.[103] Similarly, activities of soliciting, selling, and publishing commercial advertising do not lose identity as trade or business even though the advertising is published in an exempt organization periodical that contains editorial matter related to the exempt purposes of the organization.[104]

The fragmentation rule was fashioned to tax the net income derived by a tax-exempt organization from the soliciting, selling, and publishing of commercial advertising, even where the advertising is published in a publication of an exempt organization that contains editorial matter related to the exempt purposes of the organization.[105] That is, the advertising functions constitute an unrelated business even tough the overall set of publishing activities amounts to one or more related businesses; the advertising is an integral part of the larger publication activity.[106]

There are no stated limits as to the level of detail the IRS may pursue in application of the fragmentation rule. A tax-exempt university may find the agency's examiners probing its campus bookstore operations, evaluating goods for sale on nearly an item-by-item basis. An exempt association may watch as the IRS slices up its various services to members into numerous businesses. An exempt charitable organization may be surprised to see the IRS carve its fundraising program into a range of business activities. The agency evaluated the status of a tax-exempt charitable organization and analyzed nine discrete businesses of the entity.[107]

---

[102] IRC § 513(c); Reg. § 1.513-1(b).
[103] Reg. § 1.513-1(b). The convenience doctrine is the subject of *Unrelated Business* § 4.1.
[104] Reg. § 1.513-1(b).
[105] The caption of IRC § 513(c), which also contains the basic definition of the term *business* (see § 5.2), is "Advertising, etc." (The rules by which advertising revenue is cast as unrelated business income are the subject of § 5.8.)
[106] Reg. § 1.512(a)-1(f).
[107] Priv. Ltr. Rul. 200512025.

A tax-exempt blood bank that sold blood plasma to commercial laboratories was found by the IRS to not be engaging in unrelated business when it sold by-product plasma and salvage plasma, because these plasmas were produced in the conduct of related businesses, but was ruled to be engaged in unrelated business when it sold plasmapheresed plasma and plasma it purchased from other blood banks.[108] An exempt organization, the primary purpose of which was to retain and stimulate commerce in the downtown area of a city where parking facilities were inadequate, was ruled to be engaged in related businesses when it operated a fringe parking lot and shuttle service to the downtown shops and an unrelated business by conducting a park-and-shop plan.[109]

The use of a tax-exempt university's golf course by its students and employees was ruled to not be unrelated businesses, while use of the course by alumni of the university and major donors to it were found to be unrelated businesses.[110] The fragmentation rule was applied to differentiate between related and unrelated travel tours conducted by an educational and religious organization.[111] An exempt charitable organization was held to be a dealer in certain parcels of real property and thus engaged in unrelated business with respect to those properties, even though the principal impetus for the acquisition and sale of real property by the organization was achievement of exempt purposes.[112] An exempt monastery, the members of which made and sold caskets, was ruled to be engaged in a related business as long as the caskets were used in funeral services conducted by churches that are part of the religious denomination supporting the monastery but was held to be conducting an unrelated business where the caskets were used in services conducted by other churches.[113] An exempt organization established to benefit deserving women, in part by enabling them to sell foodstuffs and handicrafts, was held to operate a consignment shop as a related business, but a retail gift shop and a small restaurant were found to be unrelated businesses.[114] If a fitness center operates as part of a larger charitable organization, the IRS uses the fragmentation rule to determine whether the center is a related or unrelated business.[115]

Where an activity carried on for the production of income constitutes an unrelated trade or business, no part of the trade or business may be excluded from classification as an unrelated trade or business merely because it does not result in profit.[116]

§ 5.4 PROFIT MOTIVE REQUIREMENT

The most important element in the federal tax law as to whether an activity is a trade or business, for purposes of the business expense deduction (aside from

---

[108] Rev. Rul. 78-145, 1978-1 C.B. 169.
[109] Rev. Rul. 79-31, 1979-1 C.B. 206.
[110] Tech. Adv. Mem. 9645004.
[111] Tech. Adv. Mem. 9702004.
[112] Priv. Ltr. Rul. 200119061.
[113] Priv. Ltr. Rul. 200033049.
[114] Tech. Adv. Mem. 200021056.
[115] INFO 2005-0002.
[116] IRC § 513(c); Reg. § 1.513-1(b).

the underlying statutory definition), is the presence of a *profit motive*. The courts have exported the profit objective standard into the unrelated business rules applicable to tax-exempt organizations.

The U.S. Supreme Court held that the principal test in this regard is that the "taxpayer's primary purpose for engaging in the activity must be for income or profit."[117] In the tax-exempt organizations' context, the Court said that the inquiry should be whether the activity "was entered into with the dominant hope and intent of realizing a profit."[118] An appellate court stated that the "existence of a genuine profit motive is the most important criterion for . . . a trade or business."[119]

Various federal courts of appeal have applied the profit motive element to ascertain whether an activity of a tax-exempt organization is a business for purposes of the unrelated business rules. For example, an appellate court employed an *objective profit motivation test* to ascertain whether an exempt organization's activity is a business. This court wrote that "there is no better objective measure of an organization's motive for conducting an activity than the ends it achieves."[120] Subsequently, this court held that an activity of an exempt organization was a business because it "received considerable financial benefits" from performance of the activity, which was found to be "persuasive evidence" of a business endeavor.[121] On this latter occasion, the court defined as a *business* the situation where a "non-profit entity performs comprehensive and essential business services in return for a fixed fee."[122] Thereafter, this appellate court wrote simply that for an activity of an exempt organization to be a business, it must be conducted with a "profit objective."[123] Another appellate court observed that an insurance company's payments to an exempt association were not taxable, in that "it does not matter whether the payments were brokerage fees, gratuities, to promote goodwill, or interest," since the association was not engaging in business activity for a profit.[124] Other courts of appeals have adopted this profit motive test.[125]

A court concluded, in the case of a tax-exempt labor union[126] that collected per capita taxes from unions affiliated with it, that, other than the services the union provides its members and affiliated unions in furtherance of its exempt purposes, the union "provide[d] no goods or services for a profit and therefore cannot be a trade or business."[127]

---

[117] Comm'r v. Groetzinger, 480 U.S. 23, 35 (1987).

[118] United States v. American Bar Endowment, 477 U.S. 105, 110, note 1 (1986). The Court cited for this proposition the appellate court opinion styled Brannen v. Comm'r, 722 F.2d 695 (11th Cir. 1984).

[119] Professional Insurance Agents of Michigan v. Comm'r, 726 F.2d 1097, 1102 (6th Cir. 1984).

[120] Carolinas Farm & Power Equipment Dealers Ass'n, Inc. v. United States, 699 F.2d 167, 170 (4th Cir. 1983).

[121] Steamship Trade Ass'n of Baltimore, Inc. v. Comm'r, 757 F.2d 1494, 1497 (4th Cir. 1985).

[122] *Id.* This latter statement, however, is a mischaracterization of the law. There is no requirement, for an activity to be a business, that the endeavor be *comprehensive,* nor is there a requirement that the activity be *essential.* Also, the mode of payment is irrelevant; whether the payment is by fixed fee, commission, or some other standard has no bearing on whether the income-producing activity is a business.

[123] West Va. State Medical Ass'n v. Comm'r, 882 F.2d 123, 125 (4th Cir. 1989), *cert. den.*, 493 U.S. 1044 (1990).

[124] American Academy of Family Physicians v. United States, 91 F.3d 1155, 1159-1160 (8th Cir. 1996).

[125] E.g., Louisiana Credit Union League v. United States, 693 F.2d 525 (5th Cir. 1982); Professional Ins. Agents of Michigan v. Comm'r, 726 F.2d 1097 (6th Cir. 1984).

[126] See *Tax-Exempt Organizations* § 15.1.

[127] Laborer's Int'l Union of North America v. Comm'r, 82 T.C.M. 158, 160 (2001).

The IRS applies the profit motive test. In one example, a tax-exempt health-care provider sold a building to another provider organization; it was used to operate a skilled nursing and personal care home. The selling entity provided food service to the patients for about seven months, at a net loss; the agency characterized the food service operation as merely an "accommodation" to the purchasing entity.[128] Finding the activity to not be conducted in a manner characteristic of a commercial enterprise—that is, an operation motivated by profit—the IRS looked to these factors: There was no evidence, such as a business plan, that a food service business was being started; the organization did not take any steps to expand the food service to other unrelated organizations; the organization did not actively solicit additional clientele for a meal (or food catering) business; the organization did not take any steps to increase the per-meal charge, which was substantially below cost; and the service relationship between the organizations was not evidenced by a contract. On another occasion, the IRS concluded that, although the development of a housing project and sales of parcels of land was an unrelated business of an exempt planned community, the provision of water, sewer, and garbage services in conjunction with the project lacked a profit motive, so that the income received for the services was not taxable as unrelated business income.[129]

A tax-exempt organization may have more than one activity that it considers a business. An activity of this nature may generate net income, or it may generate a net loss. When calculating net taxable unrelated business income, an exempt organization may offset the loss from one business against the gain from another business in determining taxable income.[130] If the loss activity, however, consistently (year in and year out) produces losses, the IRS may take the position that the activity is not a business, because of absence of a profit motive, and disallow the loss deduction. Occasional losses, however, do not lead to this result.

§ 5.5 *REGULARLY CARRIED ON* RULE

As noted, gross income of a tax-exempt business league may be includable in the computation of unrelated business income where the trade or business that produced the income is *regularly carried on* by the organization.

(a) General Rules

In determining whether a trade or business from which an amount of gross income is derived by a tax-exempt organization is *regularly carried on,*[131] regard must be paid to the frequency and continuity with which the activities productive of the income are conducted and the manner in which they are pursued. This requirement is applied in light of the purpose of the unrelated business income rules, which is to place exempt organization business activities on the

---

[128] Tech. Adv. Mem. 9719002.

[129] Tech. Adv. Mem. 200047049.

[130] The IRS had the occasion to observe that, where a tax-exempt organization carries on two or more unrelated businesses, its "unrelated business net income" is its gross income from all of the businesses, less the allowed deductions (Rev. Rul. 68-536, 1968-2 C.B. 244).

[131] IRC § 512.

same tax basis as the nonexempt business endeavors with which they compete.[132] Thus, for example, specific business activities of an exempt organization will ordinarily be deemed to be *regularly carried on* if they manifest a frequency and continuity and are pursued in a manner generally similar to comparable commercial activities of nonexempt organizations.[133]

An illustration of this body of law is the case of a tax-exempt organization that published a yearbook for its membership. The publication contained advertising; the organization contracted on an annual basis with a commercial firm for solicitation of advertising sales, printing, and collection of advertising charges. Although the editorial materials were prepared by the staff of the organization, the organization, by means of its contract with the commercial firm, was ruled by the IRS to be "engaging in an extensive campaign of advertising solicitation" and thus to be "conducting competitive and promotional efforts typical of commercial endeavors."[134] Therefore, the income derived by this organization from the sale of advertising in its yearbook was deemed to be unrelated business income.

By contrast, a one-time sale of property (as opposed to an ongoing income-producing program) by a tax-exempt organization is not an activity that is regularly carried on and thus does not give rise to unrelated business income.[135] For example, an exempt organization that was formed to deliver diagnostic and medical healthcare and that developed a series of computer programs concerning management and administrative matters, such as patient admissions and billings, payroll, purchases, inventory, and medical records, sold some or all of the programs to another exempt organization comprising three teaching hospitals affiliated with a university; the income derived from the sale was held to be from a "one-time only operation" and thus not taxable as unrelated business income.[136] Likewise, the transfer of investment assets from a public charity to its supporting organization[137] is exempt from unrelated business taxation under this rule,[138] as is the infrequent sale by an exempt organization of parcels of real estate.[139]

(b) Determining Regularity

Where income-producing activities are of a kind normally conducted by nonexempt commercial organizations on a year-round basis, the conduct of the activities by a tax-exempt organization over a period of only a few weeks does not constitute the regular carrying on of a business.[140] For example, the operation of

---

[132] See *Unrelated Business* § 1.6. This is one of only two aspects of the unrelated business rules where the commerciality doctrine (see *Unrelated Business*, Chapter 7) is expressly taken into account in the statute or tax regulations. The other aspect are the commercial-type insurance rules (see *Unrelated Business* § 7.3).

[133] Reg. § 1.513-1(c)(1).

[134] Rev. Rul. 73-424, 1973-2 C.B. 190, 191.

[135] See § 5.2(e).

[136] Priv. Ltr. Rul. 7905129.

[137] See *Tax-Exempt Organizations* § 11.3(c).

[138] E.g., Priv. Ltr. Rul. 9425030.

[139] The gain from transactions of this nature may be protected from taxation by the exclusion for capital gain (see § 5.9(h)).

[140] Reg. § 1.513-1(c)(2)(i).

a sandwich stand by an exempt hospital auxiliary organization for two weeks at a state fair is not the regular conduct of a business.[141] The conduct of year-round business activities for one day each week, such as the operation of a commercial parking lot once a week, however, constitutes the regular carrying on of a business.[142]

If income-producing activities are of a kind normally undertaken by nonexempt commercial organizations only on a seasonal basis, the conduct of the activities by a tax-exempt organization during a significant portion of the season ordinarily constitutes the regular conduct of a business.[143] For example, the operation of a track for horse racing for several weeks in a year is the regular conduct of a business where it is usual to carry on the business only during a particular season.[144] Likewise, where a distribution of greeting cards celebrating a holiday was deemed to be an unrelated business, the IRS measured regularity in terms of that holiday's season.[145]

In determining whether intermittently conducted activities are regularly carried on, the manner of conduct of the activities must, as noted, be compared with the manner in which commercial activities are normally pursued by nonexempt organizations.[146] In general, tax-exempt organization business activities that are engaged in only discontinuously or periodically will not be considered regularly carried on if they are conducted without the competitive and promotional efforts typical of commercial endeavors.[147] As an illustration, the publication of advertising in programs for sports events or music or drama performances will not ordinarily be deemed to be the regular carrying on of business.[148] Likewise, where an exempt organization sells certain types of goods or services to a particular class of individuals in pursuit of its exempt functions or primarily for the convenience of these individuals[149] (as, for example, the sale of books by an exempt college bookstore to students or the sale of pharmaceutical supplies by a hospital pharmacy to patients of the hospital), casual sales in the context of this activity that do not qualify as related to the exempt function involved or are not sheltered by the convenience doctrine are not treated as regular.[150]

Conversely, where the nonqualifying sales are not merely casual but are systematically and consistently promoted and carried on by an exempt organization, they meet the requirement of regularity.[151] Thus, a leasing arrangement that was "one-time, completely fortuitous" was held to involve a business not regularly

---

[141] *Id.*

[142] S. Rep. No. 2375, 81st Cong., 2d Sess. 106–107 (1950).

[143] *Id.*

[144] Reg. § 1.513-1(c)(2)(i). Applying this rule, the IRS held that the conduct of horse racing by a county fair association was a business that was regularly carried on, even though the racing meet occupied only two weeks each year (Rev. Rul. 68-505, 1968-2 C.B. 248); this application of the law was changed by statute (see § 5.9(n)).

[145] Priv. Ltr. Rul. 8203134.

[146] Reg. § 1.513-1(c)(1), (2)(ii).

[147] Reg. § 1.513-1(c)(2)(ii).

[148] *Id.*

[149] See *Unrelated Business* § 4.1.

[150] Reg. § 1.513-1(c)(2)(ii).

[151] *Id.*

carried on,[152] whereas a lease of extended duration can constitute a business that is regularly carried on.[153]

In determining whether a business is regularly carried on, the functions of a service provider with which a tax-exempt organization has contracted may be attributed to the exempt organization for these purposes. This is likely to be the case where the contract denominates the service provider as an agent of the exempt organization, inasmuch as the activities of an agent are attributed to and deemed to be the acts of the principal for law analysis purposes. In such a circumstance, the time expended by the service provider is attributed to the exempt organization for purposes of determining regularity.[154]

Noncompetition under a covenant not to compete, characterized as a "one-time agreement not to engage in certain activities," is not a taxable business inasmuch as the "activity" is not "continuous and regular."[155]

(c) Fundraising and Similar Activities

Fundraising activities, by charitable and other tax-exempt organizations,[156] can constitute unrelated business activities.[157] Inasmuch as these activities rarely are inherently exempt functions, the rules as to *regularity* are often the only basis on which the income from these activities is not taxed as unrelated business income.

Certain intermittent income-producing activities occur so infrequently that neither their recurrence nor the manner of their conduct causes them to be regarded as trades or businesses that are regularly carried on. For example, fundraising activities lasting only a short period of time are not ordinarily treated as being regularly carried on if they recur only occasionally or sporadically. Furthermore, activities will not be regarded as regularly carried on merely because they are conducted on an annual basis.[158] It is for this reason that many special event fundraising activities, such as dances, auctions, tournaments, car washes, and bake sales, do not give rise to unrelated business income.[159] In one instance, a court concluded that a vaudeville show conducted one weekend per year was an intermittent fundraising activity and thus not regularly carried on.[160]

(d) Preparatory Time

An issue of some controversy is whether the time expended by a tax-exempt organization in preparing for a business undertaking should be taken into account in

---

[152] Museum of Flight Found. v. United States, 63 F. Supp. 2d 1257, 1259 (W.D. Wash. 1999).

[153] Cooper Tire & Rubber Co. Employees' Retirement Fund v. Comm'r, 306 F.2d 20 (6th Cir. 1962).

[154] Nat'l Collegiate Athletic Ass'n v. Comm'r, 92 T.C. 456 (1989), aff'd, 914 F.2d 1417 (10th Cir. 1990).

[155] Ohio Farm Bureau Fed., Inc. v. Comm'r, 106 T.C. 222, 234 (1996). This opinion caused the IRS to issue Gen. Couns. Mem. 39891, revoking Gen. Couns. Mem. 39865 (which held that refraining from competition in this context was a business activity).

[156] See Chapter 9.

[157] See *Unrelated Business* § 9.6; *Fundraising* § 5.7.

[158] Reg. § 1.513-1(c)(2)(iii). "[I]ncome derived from the conduct of an annual dance or similar fund raising event for charity would not be income from trade or business regularly carried on" (*id.*).

[159] E.g., Orange County Builders Ass'n, Inc. v. United States, 65-2 U.S.T.C. ¶ 9679 (S.D. Cal. 1965); Priv. Ltr. Rul. 200128059.

[160] Suffolk County Patrolmen's Benevolent Ass'n, Inc. v. Comm'r, 77 T.C. 1314 (1981).

assessing whether the activity is regularly carried on. The IRS asserts that this preparatory time should be considered, even where the event itself occupies only one or two days each year.[161] This preparatory time argument, however, has been rejected on the occasions it was considered by a court.[162] In the principal case, a federal court of appeals held that the preparatory time argument is inconsistent with the tax regulations, which do not mention the concept. The court referenced the example concerning operation of the sandwich stand at a state fair,[163] denigrating the notion that preparatory time should be taken into account in this way: "The regulations do not mention time spent in planning the activity, building the stand, or purchasing the alfalfa sprouts for the sandwiches."[164]

Nonetheless, the IRS is in disagreement with these holdings,[165] and writes private letter rulings and technical advice memoranda that are openly contrary to these cases. One of these instances concerned a tax-exempt labor organization that sponsored a concert series open to the public, occupying two weekends each year, one in the spring and one in the fall. The preparation and ticket solicitation for each of the concerts usually occupied up to six months. Taking into account the preparatory time involved, the IRS concluded that the concerts were unrelated business activities that were regularly carried on.[166]

§ 5.6 *RELATED BUSINESS* RULE

Gross income derives from *unrelated trade or business* if the conduct of the trade or business that produces the income is not substantially related (other than through the production of funds) to the purposes for which exemption is granted. This fundamental rule of law necessitates an examination of the relationship between the business activities of a tax-exempt organization that generate the particular income in question—the activities, that is, of producing or distributing the goods or performing the services involved—and the accomplishment of the organization's exempt purposes.[167]

A trade or business is *related* to the tax-exempt purposes of an exempt organization where the conduct of the business has a *causal relationship* to the achievement of one or more exempt purposes (other than through the production of income). Whether activities productive of gross income contribute to the accomplishment of an organization's exempt purpose depends in each case on the facts and circumstances involved.[168]

For example, a tax-exempt charitable organization had as its purpose enabling needy and worthy women to support themselves. To this end, it operated three businesses, each of equal size: a consignment shop, a retail gift shop,

---

[161] E.g., Tech. Adv. Mem. 9147007.
[162] National Collegiate Athletic Ass'n v. Comm'r, 92 T.C. 456 (1989), *aff'd* 914 F.2d 1417 (10th Cir. 1990); Suffolk County Patrolmen's Benevolent Ass'n, Inc. v. Comm'r, 77 T.C. 1314 (1981).
[163] See § 5.5(b), text accompanied by *supra* note 141.
[164] National Collegiate Athletic Ass'n v. Comm'r, 914 F.2d 1417, 1423 (10th Cir. 1990).
[165] AOD No. 1991-015.
[166] Tech. Adv. Mem. 9712001. The IRS acquiesced in the *Suffolk County Patrolmen's Ass'n* case (*supra* note 160) (AOD 1249 (1984)). That acquiescence had no bearing in this instance, the IRS said, inasmuch as the preparatory time in that case was "much shorter."
[167] Reg. § 1.513-1(d)(1).
[168] Reg. § 1.513-1(d)(2).

and a tearoom. The IRS concluded that the consignment shop was a business that was substantially related to the achievement of the organization's exempt purpose.[169] As to the gift shop, the organization contended that it was a related business on the ground that the existence of the shop enhanced the likelihood of purchases of items in the consignment shop because the gift shop attracted upscale consumers who were unlikely to patronize only the consignment shop. The IRS agreed that there was a causal relationship between the organization's exempt purposes and the operation of the gift shop, recognizing that the gift shop items were purchased by the organization "with the intent of imbuing the consignment items with an aura of sophistication and tastefulness." The agency concluded, however, that this relationship was not substantial.[170]

§ 5.7 *SUBSTANTIALLY RELATED BUSINESS* RULE

As noted, gross income of a tax-exempt organization may be includable in the computation of unrelated business income where it is income from a trade or business that is regularly carried on and that is not *substantially related* to the exempt purposes of the organization.[171] (The fact that the organization needs or uses the funds in advancement of an exempt purpose does not make the underlying activity a related business.[172]) Thus, it is necessary to examine the *substantiality* of the relationship between the business activity that generates the income in question—the activity, that is, of producing or distributing the goods or performing the services involved—and the accomplishment of the organization's exempt purposes.[173]

To determine whether the conduct of an activity by a tax-exempt organization is substantially related to its exempt purposes, it is necessary to ascertain the organization's *primary* purpose or purposes and then ascertain the organization's primary purpose in conducting the activity. Where the primary purpose underlying the conduct of the activity is to further an exempt purpose, the activity meets the substantially related test. According to the IRS, this exercise entails examination of the "nature, scope and motivation" for conducting the activity.[174] As an example, the agency concluded that the construction and operation of a regulation-size 18-hole golf course, replete with warm-up area, snack bar, and pro shop, was substantially related to the purposes of an exempt school operated to rehabilitate court-referred juveniles, inasmuch as the course was utilized primarily as part of the school's vocational education and career development department.[175]

(a) General Rules

A trade or business is *substantially related* only if the causal relationship is a substantial one. Thus, for the conduct of a business from which a particular amount of gross income is derived to be substantially related to exempt purposes, the production or distribution of the goods or the performance of the services from

---

[169] See § 5.7.
[170] Tech. Adv. Mem. 200021056.
[171] IRC § 513(a); Reg. § 1.513-1(a).
[172] Cf. *supra* note 9.
[173] Reg. § 1.513-1(d)(2).
[174] Priv. Ltr. Rul. 200151061.
[175] *Id.*

which the gross income is derived must contribute importantly to the accomplishment of these purposes. Where the production or distribution of the goods or the performance of services does not contribute importantly to the accomplishment of the exempt purposes of an organization, the income from the sale of the goods or the performance of the services does not derive from the conduct of related business.[176] A court wrote that resolution of the substantial relationship test requires an examination of the "relationship between the business activities which generate the particular income in question . . . and the accomplishment of the organization's exempt purposes."[177]

Certainly, gross income derived from charges for the performance of a tax-exempt function does not constitute gross income from the conduct of an unrelated business.[178] Thus, as noted, income is not taxed when it is generated by functions such as performances by students enrolled in an exempt school for training children in the performing arts, the conduct of refresher courses to improve the trade skills of members of a union, and the presentation of a trade show for exhibiting industry products by a trade association to stimulate demand for the products.[179] Also, dues paid by bona fide members of an exempt organization are forms of related income.[180]

Whether activities productive of gross income contribute importantly to the accomplishment of an organization's exempt purpose depends in each case on the facts and circumstances involved.[181] A court observed that each of these instances requires a case-by-case identification of the exempt purpose involved and an analysis of how the activity contributed to the advancement of that purpose.[182] By reason of court opinions and IRS rulings, there have been many determinations over the years as to whether particular activities are substantially related businesses[183] or unrelated businesses.[184]

One of these determinations—the one concerning the organization functioning for the benefit of needy and deserving women[185]—is particularly illustrative of these points of law. As noted, the IRS concluded that the consignment shop was a substantially related business and that the gift shop was a related, but not substantially related, business. The tearoom was found to be an unrelated business.[186]

(b) Size and Extent Test

In determining whether an activity contributes importantly to the accomplishment of a tax-exempt purpose, the *size and extent* of the activity must be considered

---

[176] Reg. § 1.513-1(d)(2).
[177] Louisiana Credit Union League v. United States, 693 F.2d 525, 534 (5th Cir. 1982).
[178] Reg. § 1.513-1(d)(4)(i).
[179] *Id.*
[180] E.g., Rev. Rul. 67-109, 1967-1 C.B. 136. Certain forms of associate member dues, however, are taxable as unrelated business income (see § 5.9(p)).
[181] Reg. § 1.513-1(d)(2).
[182] Hi-Plains Hosp. v. United States, 670 F.2d 528 (5th Cir. 1982). Also Huron Clinic Found. v. United States, 212 F. Supp. 847 (D.S.D. 1962).
[183] See, e.g., *Unrelated Business* § 9.12.
[184] See, e.g., *id.* § 9.13.
[185] See § 5.6, text accompanied by *supra* note 169-170.
[186] Tech. Adv. Mem. 200021056.

in relation to the nature and extent of the exempt function that it purportedly serves.[187] Thus, where income is realized by an exempt organization from an activity that is generally related to the performance of its exempt functions, but the activity is conducted on a scale that is larger than reasonably necessary for performance of the functions, the gross income attributable to the portion of the activity that is in excess of the needs associated with exempt functions constitutes gross income from the conduct of an unrelated business.[188] This type of income is not derived from the production or distribution of goods or the performance of services that contribute importantly to the accomplishment of any exempt purpose of the organization.[189]

For example, one of the activities of a tax-exempt trade association, which had a membership of businesses in a particular state, was to supply companies (members and nonmembers) with job injury histories on prospective employees. Despite the association's contention that this service contributed to the accomplishment of its exempt purposes, the IRS ruled that the operation was an unrelated business, in that the activity went "well beyond" any mere development and promotion of efficient business practices.[190] The IRS adopted a similar position in ruling that a retail grocery store operation, formed to sell food in a poverty area at below-market prices and to provide job training for unemployed residents in the area, could not qualify for tax exemption because the operation was conducted on a "much larger scale than reasonably necessary" for the training program.[191] Similarly, the IRS ruled that the provision of private duty nurses to unrelated exempt organizations, by an exempt healthcare organization that provided temporary nurses and private duty nurses to patients of related organizations as related businesses, was an activity performed on a scale "much larger" than necessary for the achievement of exempt functions.[192]

By contrast, a tax-exempt organization formed to provide a therapeutic program for emotionally disturbed adolescents was the subject of a ruling from the IRS that a retail grocery store operation, almost fully staffed by adolescents to secure their emotional rehabilitation, was not an unrelated business because it was operated on a scale no larger than reasonably necessary for its training and rehabilitation program.[193] A like finding was made in relation to the manufacture and marketing of toys, which was the means by which an exempt organization accomplished its charitable purpose of training unemployed and underemployed individuals.[194]

---

[187] Reg. § 1.513-1(d)(3). One court discussed the point that, in a search for unrelated activity, there should be an examination of the scale on which the activity is conducted (Hi-Plains Hosp. v. United States, 670 F.2d 528 (5th Cir. 1982)).

[188] Reg. § 1.513-1(d)(3).

[189] *Id.* In essence, the size and extent test is an application of the fragmentation rule (see § 5.3).

[190] Rev. Rul. 73-386, 1973-2 C.B. 191, 192.

[191] Rev. Rul. 73-127, 1973-1 C.B. 221, 222. Under similar facts, a nonprofit organization that operated restaurants and health food stores in accordance with the tenets of a church was denied tax-exempt status as a charitable entity on the ground that it was operated for substantially commercial purposes (Living Faith, Inc. v. Comm'r, 60 T.C.M. 710 (1990), *aff'd*, 950 F.2d 365 (7th Cir. 1991)). See *Unrelated Business*, Chapter 7.

[192] Priv. Ltr. Rul. 9535023.

[193] Rev. Rul. 76-94, 1976-1 C.B. 171.

[194] Rev. Rul. 73-128, 1973-1 C.B. 222.

(c) Same State Rule

Ordinarily, gross income from the sale of products that result from the performance of tax-exempt functions does not constitute gross income from the conduct of an unrelated business if the item is sold in substantially the *same state* it is
in on completion of the exempt functions. Thus, in the case of an exempt charitable organization engaged in a program of rehabilitation of disabled individuals,
income from the sale of articles made by them as part of their rehabilitation
training is not gross income from the conduct of an unrelated business. The
income in this instance is from the sale of products, the production of which contributed importantly to the accomplishment of the organization's exempt purposes, namely, rehabilitation of the disabled. Conversely, if an item resulting
from an exempt function is utilized or exploited in further business endeavors
beyond that reasonably appropriate or necessary for disposition in the state it is
in on completion of exempt functions, the gross income derived from these
endeavors is from the conduct of unrelated business.[195]

As an illustration, in the case of an experimental dairy herd maintained for
scientific purposes by a tax-exempt research organization, income from the sale
of milk and cream produced in the ordinary course of operation of the project is
not gross income from the conduct of unrelated business. If, however, the organization utilized the milk and cream in the further manufacture of food items,
such as ice cream and pastries, the gross income from the sale of these products
would be from the conduct of unrelated business—unless the manufacturing
activities themselves contributed importantly to the accomplishment of an
exempt purpose of the organization.[196] Similarly, a charitable organization that
operated a salmon research facility as an exempt function was able to sell a portion of its harvested salmon stock in an unprocessed condition to fish processors
in an untaxed business. By contrast, when this organization converted the fish
into salmon nuggets (fish that was seasoned, formed into nugget shape, and
breaded), the sale of the fish in that state was an unrelated business.[197] Further,
an organization that educates individuals and conducts scientific research on
gardening was ruled to be able to sell, without tax, produce grown on-site to vis-
itors and to the general public.[198]

(d) Dual Use Rule

An asset or facility of a tax-exempt organization that is necessary to the conduct
of exempt functions may also be utilized for nonexempt purposes. In these *dual
use* instances, the mere fact of the use of the asset or facility in an exempt function does not, by itself, make the income from the nonexempt endeavor gross
income from a related business. Rather, the test is whether the activities productive of the income in question contribute importantly to the accomplishment of
exempt purposes.[199] For example, an exempt museum may have an auditorium

---

[195] Reg. § 1.513-1(d)(4)(ii).
[196] *Id.*
[197] Priv. Ltr. Rul. 9320042.
[198] Priv. Ltr. Rul. 200512025 (the sale of produce grown off-site, however, was not protected by this exception).
[199] Reg. § 1.513-1(d)(4)(iii).

that is designed and equipped for showing educational films in connection with its program of public education in the arts and sciences. The theater is a principal feature of the museum and is in continuous operation during the hours the museum is open to the public. If the museum were to operate the theater as a motion picture theater for public entertainment during the evening hours when the museum is otherwise closed, however, gross income from that operation would be gross income from the conduct of an unrelated business.[200] Similarly, a mailing service operated by an exempt organization was ruled to be an unrelated trade or business even though the mailing equipment was also used for exempt purposes.[201]

Another illustration of application of this rule concerns the athletic facilities of a tax-exempt college or university, which, while used primarily for educational purposes, may also be made available for members of the faculty, other employees of the institution, and members of the general public. Income derived from the use of the facilities by those who are not students or employees of the institution is likely to be unrelated business income.[202] For example, the IRS ruled that the operation by an exempt school of a ski facility for the general public was the conduct of an unrelated business, while use of the facility by the students of the school for recreational purposes and in its physical education program were related activities.[203] Likewise, an exempt college that made available its facilities and personnel to an individual not associated with the institution for the conduct of a summer tennis camp was ruled to be engaged in the conduct of an unrelated business.[204]

The provision of athletic or other activities by a tax-exempt educational institution to outsiders may be an exempt function, inasmuch as the instruction of individuals on the subject of a sport can be an educational activity.[205] As illustrations, the IRS held that these were exempt educational activities: the conduct of a summer hockey camp for youths by a college,[206] the conduct of four summer sports camps by a university,[207] and the operation of a summer sports camp by a university-affiliated athletic association.[208] Similarly, the agency determined that a college may operate a professional repertory theater on its campus that is open to the general public[209] and that a college may make its facilities available to outside organizations for the conduct of conferences[210]—both activities being in furtherance of exempt purposes.

This area of the law intertwines with the exclusion from unrelated income taxation for rent received by tax-exempt organizations.[211] For example, an

---

[200] *Id.*

[201] Rev. Rul. 68-550, 1968-2 C.B. 249.

[202] E.g., Tech. Adv. Mem. 9645004 (concerning dual use of a university's golf course).

[203] Rev. Rul. 78-98, 1978-1 C.B. 167.

[204] Rev. Rul. 76-402, 1976-2 C.B. 177.

[205] E.g., Rev. Rul. 77-365, 1977-2 C.B. 192. See *Tax-Exempt Organizations* § 10.2.

[206] Priv. Ltr. Rul. 8024001.

[207] Priv. Ltr. Rul. 7908009.

[208] Priv. Ltr. Rul. 7826003.

[209] Priv. Ltr. Rul. 7840072.

[210] Priv. Ltr. Rul. 8020010.

[211] See § 5.9(g).

exempt college may lease its facilities to a professional sports team for the conduct of a summer camp and receive nontaxable lease income, as long as the college does not provide food or cleaning services to the team.[212] By contrast, where the institution provided services, such as cleaning, food, laundry, security, and ground maintenance, the exclusion for rent is defeated.[213]

This dichotomy is reflected in the treatment the IRS accorded a tax-exempt school that used its tennis facilities, which were utilized during the academic year in the institution's educational program, in the summer as a public tennis club operated by employees of the school's athletic department. Because the school not only furnished its facilities, but operated the tennis club through its own employees who rendered substantial services for the participants in the club, the IRS held that the operation of the club was an unrelated business and that the income derived from the club's operation was not sheltered by the exclusion for rental income.[214] The agency also observed that, however, if the school had furnished its tennis facilities to an unrelated individual without the provision of services (leaving it to the lessee to hire the club's administrators) and for a fixed fee not dependent on the income or profits derived from the leased property, the rental income exclusion would have been available.[215] In a comparable ruling, the IRS determined that, when a university that leased its stadium to a professional sports team for several months of the year and provided the utilities, grounds maintenance, and dressing room, linen, and stadium security services, it was engaged in an unrelated business and was not entitled to the rental income exclusion.[216]

(e) Exploitation Rule

Activities carried on by a tax-exempt organization in the performance of exempt functions may generate goodwill or other intangibles that are capable of being exploited in commercial endeavors. Where an exempt organization exploits this type of intangible in commercial activities, the fact that the resultant income was dependent in part on the conduct of an exempt function of the organization does not make it gross income from a related business. In these cases, unless the activities contribute importantly to the accomplishment of an exempt purpose, the income that they produce is gross income from the conduct of an unrelated business.[217]

For example, a tax-exempt scientific organization enjoys an excellent reputation in the field of biological research. It exploits this reputation regularly by selling endorsements of various items of laboratory equipment to manufacturers. The endorsing of laboratory equipment does not contribute importantly to the accomplishment of any purpose for which exemption was granted to the

---

[212] Priv. Ltr. Rul. 8024001.

[213] Priv. Ltr. Rul. 7840072.

[214] Rev. Rul. 80-297, 1980-2 C.B. 196.

[215] *Id.*

[216] Rev. Rul. 80-298, 1980-2 C.B. 197. The dual use rule is, in some respects, an application of the fragmentation rule (see § 5.3).

[217] Reg. § 1.513-1(d)(4)(iv).

organization. Accordingly, the income derived from the sale of these endorsements is gross income from unrelated trade or business.[218]

As another example, during the school year, a tax-exempt university (thus having a regular faculty and a regularly enrolled student body) sponsors the appearance of professional theater companies and symphony orchestras that present drama and musical performances for the students and faculty members. Members of the general public are also admitted. The university advertises these performances and supervises advance ticket sales at various places, including such university facilities as the cafeteria and university bookstore. The university derives gross income from the conduct of the performances. Although the presentation of the performances makes use of an intangible generated by the institution's exempt educational functions—the presence of the student body and faculty—the presentation of these drama and music events contributes importantly to the overall educational and cultural function of the university. Therefore, the income that the university receives does not constitute gross income from the conduct of unrelated trade or business.[219]

A third example concerns a tax-exempt business league with a large membership. Pursuant to an arrangement with an advertising agency, the association regularly mails brochures, pamphlets, and other commercial advertising materials to its members, for which service the association charges the agency an agreed amount per enclosure. The distribution of the advertising materials does not contribute importantly to the accomplishment of any exempt purpose of the association. Accordingly, the payments made to this business league by the advertising agency constitute gross income from unrelated trade or business.[220]

A fourth example involves a tax-exempt organization that advances public interest in classical music, and owns and operates a radio station in a manner that contributes importantly to the accomplishment of the organization's exempt purposes. In the course of the operation of the station, however, the organization derives gross income from the regular sale of advertising time and services to commercial advertisers in the manner of a commercial station. Neither the sale of this time nor the performance of these services contributes importantly to the accomplishment of any of the organization's exempt purposes. Notwithstanding the fact that the production of the advertising income depends on the existence of the listening audience resulting from performance of exempt functions, the income is gross income from unrelated business.[221]

A fifth illustration involves a tax-exempt university that provides facilities, instruction, and faculty supervision for a campus newsletter operated by its students. In addition to news items and editorial commentary, the newspaper publishes paid advertising. The solicitation, sale, and publication of the advertising are conducted by students, pursuant to the supervision and instruction of the university. Although the services rendered to advertisers are of a commercial character, the advertising business contributes importantly to the university's

---

[218] *Id.*, Example (1).
[219] *Id.*, Example (2).
[220] *Id.*, Example (3). This type of financial arrangement may, however, be structured as an excludable royalty (see § 5.9(f)).
[221] *Id.*, Example (4).

educational program through the training of the students involved. Therefore, none of the income derived from publication of the newspaper constitutes gross income from the conduct of unrelated business. The same result would occur if the newspaper is published by a separately incorporated charitable organization, qualified under the university's rules for recognition of student activities, and even though the organization utilizes its own facilities and is independent of faculty supervision, but carries out its educational purposes by means of student instruction of other students in the editorial and advertising activities and student participation in those activities.[222]

Another illustration involves a tax-exempt association, formed to advance the interests of a profession and drawing its membership from members of the profession. The organization publishes a monthly journal containing articles and other editorial material that contribute importantly to the accomplishment of the association's exempt purposes. Income from the sale of subscriptions to members and others in accordance with the organization's exempt purposes, therefore, does not constitute gross income from unrelated trade or business. In connection with the publication of this journal, the association also derives income from the regular sale of space and services for general consumer advertising, including advertising of products such as soft drinks, automobiles, articles of apparel, and home appliances. Neither the publication of these advertisements nor the performance of services for these consumer advertisers contributes importantly to the accomplishment of the organization's exempt purposes. Therefore, notwithstanding the fact that the production of income from advertising utilizes the circulation developed and maintained in performance of exempt functions, this income is gross income from unrelated trade or business.[223]

As a final illustration of this point, assume the facts in the previous example, except that the advertising in the association's journal promotes only products that are within the general area of professional interests of its members. Following a practice common among for-profit magazines that publish advertising, the association requires its advertising to comply with certain general standards of taste, fairness, and accuracy; within these limits, the form, content, and manner of presentation of the advertising messages are governed by the basic objective of the advertisers to promote the sale of the advertised products. While the advertisements contain certain information, the informational function of the advertising is incidental to the controlling aim of stimulating demand for the advertised products and differs in no essential respect from the informational function of any commercial advertising. Like taxable publishers of advertising, this association accepts advertising only from those who are willing to pay its prescribed rates. Although continuing education of its members in matters pertaining to their profession is one of the association's exempt purposes, the publication of advertising designed and selected in the manner of ordinary commercial advertising is not an educational activity of the kind contemplated by the concept of tax exemption; it differs fundamentally from such

---

[222] *Id.*, Example (5).
[223] *Id.*, Example (6).

an activity both in its governing objective and in its method. Accordingly, this association's publication of advertising does not contribute importantly to the accomplishment of its exempt purposes; the income that it derives from advertising constitutes gross income from unrelated trade or business.[224]

Thus, the rules with respect to taxation of advertising revenue received by tax-exempt organizations treat advertising as an exploitation of exempt publication activity.[225] As another illustration of this *exploitation rule*, where access to athletic facilities of an educational institution by students is covered by a general student fee, outside use may trigger the exploitation rule; if separate charges for use of the facilities are imposed on students, faculty, and outsiders, any unrelated income is a product of the dual use rule.[226]

§ 5.8 ADVERTISING ACTIVITIES

Generally, the net income derived by a tax-exempt organization from the sale of advertising is taxable as unrelated business income.[227] Despite the extensive body of regulatory and case law in this area concerning when and how advertising revenue may be taxed, however, there is little law on the question as to what constitutes *advertising*. In one instance, a court considered the publication of "business listings," consisting of "slogans, logos, trademarks, and other information which is similar, if not identical in content, composition and message to the listings found in other professional journals, newspapers, and the 'yellow pages' of telephone directories," and found them to qualify as advertising.[228] The IRS ruled that the sale by an exempt organization of periodical and banner advertising on its Web site constituted an unrelated business.[229]

Under the rules defining what is a *trade or business*,[230] income from the sale of advertising in publications of tax-exempt organizations (even where the publications are related to the exempt purpose of the organization) generally constitutes unrelated business income, taxable to the extent it exceeds the expenses directly related to the advertising. If, however, the editorial aspect of the publication is carried on at a loss, the editorial loss may be offset against the advertising income from the publication. Thus, there will be no taxable unrelated trade or business income because of advertising where the publication as a whole is published at a loss. This rule embodies a preexisting regulation[231] that was promulgated in an effort to carve out (and tax) income from advertising and other

---

[224] *Id.*, Example (7).

[225] See § 5.8.

[226] E.g., Priv. Ltr. Rul. 7823062.

[227] IRC § 513(c). In one instance, the IRS concluded that an association did not receive any unrelated business income from a newspaper advertising program because the association did not conduct the activity and there was no basis for attribution of the advertising activities of its members (Tech. Adv. Mem. 200101036).

[228] Fraternal Order of Police, Illinois State Troopers Lodge No. 41 v. Comm'r, 87 T.C. 747, 754 (1986), *aff'd*, 833 F.2d 717 (7th Cir. 1987).

[229] Priv. Ltr. Rul. 200303062.

[230] See § 5.2.

[231] Reg. § 1.513-1(b). This regulation became effective on December 13, 1967. IRC § 513(c) became effective on December 31, 1969. With respect to tax years beginning between these dates, the regulation is of no effect, inasmuch as it is an impermissible administrative enlargement of the scope of the statutory unrelated business income law (Massachusetts Medical Soc'y v. United States, 514 F.2d 153 (1st Cir. 1975); American College of Physicians v. United States, 530 F.2d 930 (Ct. Cl. 1976)).

activities in competition with taxpaying business, even though the advertising may appear in a periodical related to the educational or other tax-exempt purpose of the organization.

These rules are not intended to encompass the publication of a magazine with little or no advertising, which is distributed free or at a nominal charge not intended to cover costs. This type of publication would likely be published basically as a source of public information and not for the production of income. For a publication to be considered an activity carried on for the production of income, it must be contemplated that the revenues from advertising in the publication or the revenues from sales of the publication, or both, will result in net income (although not necessarily in a particular year). Nonetheless, for the tax on unrelated business income to apply, the advertising activity must also constitute a trade or business that is regularly carried on. Further, the tax is inapplicable where the advertising activity is a tax-exempt function.[232]

As an example, a tax-exempt association of law enforcement officials published a monthly journal containing conventional advertising featuring the products or services of a commercial enterprise. The IRS ruled that the regular sale of space in the journal for the advertising was carried on for the production of income and constituted the conduct of trade or business, which was not substantially related to the organization's exempt functions.[233] The "controlling factor in this case," said the IRS, was that the "activities giving rise to the income in question constitute the sale and performance of a valuable service on the part of the publisher, and the purchaser of that service on the part of the other part to the transaction."[234]

In a similar situation, the IRS ruled that income derived by a tax-exempt membership organization from the sale of advertising in its annual yearbook was unrelated business income.[235] Preparation of the editorial materials in the yearbook was largely done by the organization's staff, which also distributed it. An independent commercial firm was used, under a full year contract, to conduct an intensive advertising solicitation campaign in the organization's name and the firm was paid a percentage of the gross advertising receipts for selling the advertising, collecting from advertisers, and printing the yearbook. The IRS stated that by "engaging in an extensive campaign of advertising solicitation, the organization is conducting competitive and promotional efforts typical of commercial endeavors."[236]

Initially, it appeared that the courts were willing to accede to this approach by the IRS. In the principal case, a tax-exempt medical organization was found to be engaging in an unrelated business by selling advertising in its scholarly journal. The court rejected the contention that the purpose of the advertising was to educate physicians, holding instead that its primary purpose was to raise revenue. In reaching this conclusion, the court reviewed the content, format, and

---

[232] E.g., Priv. Ltr. Rul. 7948113 (holding that proceeds from the sale of advertising in the program published in promotion of postseason all-star college football game are not unrelated income).

[233] Rev. Rul. 74-38, 1974-1 C.B. 144, *clar. by* Rev. Rul. 76-93, 1976-1 C.B. 170.

[234] Rev. Rul. 74-38, 1974-1 C.B. 144, 145.

[235] Rev. Rul. 73-424, 1973-2 C.B. 190.

[236] *Id.* at 191.

positioning of the advertisements, and concluded they were principally commercial in nature. The court, however, set forth some standards as to when journal advertising might be an exempt function, such as advertising that comprehensively surveys a particular field or otherwise makes a systematic presentation on an appropriate subject.[237]

These findings of the court were reversed, with the appellate court holding that the content of the advertisements was substantially related to the organization's educational purpose.[238] The court noted that the advertisements only appeared in bunches, at the beginning and end of the publications; were screened with respect to subject matter, with the contents controlled; and were indexed by advertiser. Also, only advertisements directly relevant to the practice of internal medicine were published. This decision, then, established the principle that advertising is like any other trade or business, in that it is not automatically an unrelated activity, in that it can be an information dissemination (educational) function.

This dispute as to the tax treatment of advertising revenue in the unrelated income context, specifically whether the IRS is correct in asserting that all net income from advertising in tax-exempt publications is always taxable, was resolved by the U.S. Supreme Court, in 1986, when it held, after reviewing the history of the regulations promulgated in 1967[239] and of the statutory revisions authored in 1969,[240] that it is possible to have related advertising.[241] The Court said that the standard is whether the conduct of the exempt organization in selling and publishing the advertising is demonstrative of a related function, rather than a determination as to whether the advertising is inherently educational.

The Supreme Court observed that in ascertaining relatedness, it is not sufficient merely to cluster the advertising in the front and back of the tax-exempt publication. Other facts that tended to mitigate against relatedness were that all advertising was paid, the advertising was for established products or services, advertising was repeated from one month to another, or the advertising concerned matters having "no conceivable relationship" to the exempt purpose of the sponsoring exempt organization.[242] The test, said the Court, quoting from the trial court's opinion, is whether the organization uses the advertising to "provide its readers a comprehensive or systematic presentation of any aspect of the goods or services publicized"; as the Court wrote, an exempt organization can "control its publication of advertisements in such a way as to reflect an intention to contribute importantly to its . . . [exempt] functions."[243] This can be

---

[237] The American College of Physicians v. United States, 83-2 U.S.T.C. ¶ 9652 (Ct. Cl. 1983).

[238] The American College of Physicians v. United States, 743 F.2d 1570 (Fed. Cir. 1984).

[239] See *supra* note 230.

[240] IRC § 513(c).

[241] United States v. American College of Physicians, 475 U.S. 834 (1986). A court found the advertising of a tax-exempt trade association to be taxable because it was not substantially related to the organization's exempt purposes and there was "[n]o systematic effort" made "to advertise products that relate to the editorial content of the magazine, and no effort . . . made . . . to limit the advertisements to new products" (Florida Trucking Ass'n, Inc. v. Comm'r, 87 T.C. 1039 (1986)). Display and listings in a yearbook published by a tax-exempt labor organization (see § 15.1) were found to be the result of unrelated business (State Police Ass'n of Massachusetts v. Comm'r, 97-2 U.S.T.C. ¶ 50, 627 (1st Cir. 1997)).

[242] United States v. American College of Physicians, 475 U.S. 834, 849 (1986).

[243] *Id.*

done, said the Court, by "coordinating the content of the advertisements with the editorial content of the issue, or by publishing only advertisements reflecting new developments."[244]

The foregoing may be contrasted with the situation involving a charitable organization that raised funds for a tax-exempt symphony orchestra. As part of this effort, the organization published an annual concert book that was distributed at the orchestra's annual charity ball. The IRS ruled that the solicitation and sale of advertising by volunteers of the organization was not an unrelated taxable activity because the activity was not regularly carried on and because it was conducted as an integral part of the process of fundraising for charity.[245] Thus, part of a successful contention that the unrelated income tax should not apply in the advertising context would seem to be a showing that the advertising over a four-month period by its paid employees, for publication in concert programs distributed free at symphony performances over an eight-month period, was found by the IRS to be carrying on an unrelated business.[246] In that ruling, the IRS observed:

> It is a matter of common knowledge that many non-exempt organizations make a regular practice of publishing and distributing a seasonal series of special interest publications covering only a portion of each year with a format that includes substantial amounts of advertising matter. It would not be unusual for such an organization to concentrate its efforts to sell the advertising space thus made available during similar periods of intensive activity that would frequently last for no more than three or four months of each year. Since it is likewise further apparent that the activities giving rise to the advertising income here in question do not otherwise substantially differ from the comparable commercial activities of nonexempt organizations, those activities of the subject organization are regularly carried on within the meaning of section 512 of the Code.[247]

Similarly, a tax-exempt business league that sold a membership directory, but only to its members, was held to not be engaged in an unrelated trade or business.[248] The directory was considered to contribute importantly to the achievement of the organization's exempt purposes by facilitating communication among its members and encouraging the exchange of ideas and expertise, resulting in greater awareness of collective and individual activities of the membership. The principal aspect governing the outcome of this matter, however, was the fact that the sale of the directory, done in a noncommercial manner, did not confer any private benefit on the organization's members.

Income attributable to a publication of a tax-exempt organization basically is regarded as either *circulation income* or (if any) *gross advertising income*.[249] Circulation income is the income attributable to the production, distribution, or circulation

---

[244] *Id.*, at 849–850. Subsequently, a court found that a tax-exempt organization's advertising did not contribute importantly to the carrying out of any of its tax-exempt purposes, although it was willing to explore the argument to the contrary and found that the subject matter of some of the advertising was related to the organization's exempt purpose (Minnesota Holstein-Friesian Breeders Ass'n v. Comm'r, 64 T.C.M. 1319 (1992)). The court concluded that the primary purposes underlying the advertising were commercial: stimulating demand for the advertised products and raising revenue for the tax-exempt organization.

[245] Rev. Rul. 75-201, 1975-1 C.B. 164.

[246] Rev. Rul. 75-200, 1975-1 C.B. 163.

[247] *Id.* at 164.

[248] Rev. Rul. 79-370, 1979-2 C.B. 238.

[249] Reg. § 1.512(a)-1(f)(3).

of a publication (other than gross advertising income), including amounts realized from the sale of the readership content of the publication. Gross advertising income is the amount derived from the unrelated advertising activities of an exempt organization publication.

Likewise, the costs attributable to a tax-exempt organization publication are characterized as *readership costs* and *direct advertising costs*.[250] A reasonable allocation may be made as between cost items attributable both to an exempt organization publication and to its other activities (such as salaries, occupancy costs, and depreciation).[251] Readership costs are, therefore, the cost items directly connected with the production and distribution of the readership content of the publication, other than the items properly allocable to direct advertising costs. Direct advertising costs include items that are directly connected with the sale and publication of advertising (such as agency commission and other selling costs, artwork, and copy preparation), the portion of mechanical and distribution costs attributable to advertising lineage, and any other element of readership costs properly allocable to the advertising activity.

As noted, a tax-exempt organization (assuming it is subject to the unrelated business income rules in the first instance) is not taxable on its advertising income where its direct advertising costs equal such (gross) income. Even if gross advertising income exceeds direct advertising costs, costs attributable to the readership content of the publication qualify as costs deductible in computing (unrelated) income from the advertising activity, to the extent that the costs exceed the income attributable to the readership content.[252] There are limitations on this rule, however, including the conditions that its application may not be used to realize a loss from the advertising activity nor to give rise to a cost deductible in computing taxable income attributable to any other unrelated activity. If the circulation income of the publication exceeds its readership costs, any unrelated business taxable income attributable to the publication is the excess of gross advertising income over direct advertising costs.

Another set of rules requires an allocation of membership dues to circulation income where the right to receive the publication is associated with membership status in the tax-exempt organization for which dues, fees, or other charges are received.[253] There are three ways of determining the portion of membership dues that constitute a part of circulation income (*allocable membership receipts*):

1. If 20 percent or more of the total circulation of the publication consists of sales to nonmembers, the subscription price charged to the nonmembers

---

[250] Reg. § 1.512(a)-1(f)(6).

[251] Once a reasonable method of allocation is adopted, it must be used consistently (Reg. § 1.512(a)-1(f)(6)(i)). One court held that the application of a ratio used in previous years for this purpose is not a "method"; it is the output of a method that cannot be automatically applied each year (National Ass'n of Life Underwriters, Inc. v. Comm'r, 94-2 U.S.T.C. ¶ 50,412 (D.C. Cir. 1994), *rev'g* 64 T.C.M. 379 (1992)).

[252] Reg. § 1.512(a)-1(f)(2)(ii), (d)(2).

[253] Reg. § 1.512(a)-1(f)(4). The IRS initially took the position that the requirement that membership receipts must be allocated on a pro rata basis to circulation income of a tax-exempt organization's periodical (Reg. § 1.512(a)-1(f)(4)(iii)) requires that the "cost of other exempt activities of the organization" must be offset by the income produced by the activities (the "net cost" rule) (Gen. Couns. Mem. 38104), but subsequently concluded that the gross cost of the other tax-exempt activities must be used in computing the denominator of the formula (Gen. Couns. Mem. 38205, 38168).

is the amount allocated from each member's dues to circulation income. It was held that the term *total circulation* means paid circulation, that is, it does not include distribution of a publication without charge to a tax-exempt organization's nonmembers.[254] It has also been held that this term means the actual number of copies of the publication distributed for compensation without regard to how the copies were purchased; in the case, members of an exempt association paid for subscriptions, by means of dues, and they designated nonmember recipients of the publication, who were considered part of the total circulation base.[255]

2. If rule (1) is inapplicable and if the membership dues from 20 percent or more of the members of the organization are less than the dues received from the remaining members because the former category of members does not receive the publication, the amount of the dues reduction is the amount used in allocating membership dues to circulation income.

3. Otherwise, the portion of membership receipts allocated to the publication is an amount equal to the total amount of the receipts multiplied by a fraction, the numerator of which is the total costs of the publication and the denominator of which is these costs plus the costs of the other exempt activities of the organization.[256]

These rules become more intricate where a tax-exempt organization publishes more than one publication for the production of income. (A publication is published for the production of income if the organization generally receives gross advertising income from the publication equal to at least 25 percent of its readership costs and the publication activity is engaged in for profit.) In this case, the organization may treat the gross income from all (but not just some) of the publications and the deductible items directly connected with the publications on a consolidated basis in determining the amount of unrelated business taxable income derived from the sale of advertising. (Thus, an organization cannot consolidate the losses of a publication not published for the production of income with the profit of other publications that are so published.) This treatment must be followed consistently and, once adopted, is binding, unless the

---

[254] American Hosp. Ass'n v. United States, 654 F. Supp. 1152 (N.D. Ill. 1987).

[255] North Carolina Citizens for Business and Indus. v. United States, 89-2 U.S.T.C. ¶ 9507 (Cl. Ct. 1989).

[256] The reference to the "costs of the other exempt activities" means the total costs or expenses incurred by an organization in connection with its other tax-exempt activities, not offset by any income earned by the organization from the activities (Rev. Rul. 81-101, 1981-1 C.B. 352).

An organization, including a business league, may have within it an integral fund that is a charitable organization, and the costs of the fund can be included in the formula used to calculate the business league's net unrelated business taxable income derived from advertising, thereby reducing the tax liability of the business league (American Bar Ass'n v. United States, 84-1 U.S.T.C. ¶ 9179 (N.D. Ill. 1984)).

These regulations, particularly the third pro rata allocation method rule, were challenged in court on substantive and procedural grounds; while the challenge was initially successful, it essentially failed on appeal (American Medical Ass'n v. United States, 887 F.2d 760 (7th Cir. 1989), *aff'g and rev'g* 608 F. Supp. 1085 (N.D. Ill. 1987), 668 F. Supp. 1101 (N.D. Ill. 1987), 668 F. Supp. 358 (N.D. Ill. 1988), 691 F. Supp. 1170 (N.D. Ill. 1988)). The basic assertion, which was ultimately rejected, was that a tax-exempt organization can deduct, as direct advertising costs, the readership content costs of periodicals distributed for the purpose of generating advertising revenue.

organization obtains the requisite permission from the IRS to change the method.[257]

It is the position of the IRS, as supported by the U.S. Tax Court, that the specific rules concerning the computation of net unrelated income derived from advertising are inapplicable in a case where the "issue of whether the . . . [organization's] publication of the readership content of the magazines is an exempt activity has not been decided, stipulated to, or presented for decision" and where the IRS "has not sought to apply such regulations, maintaining that they cannot be applied due to the . . . [organization's] failure to produce credible evidence of its advertising and publishing expenses."[258]

§ 5.9 EXCEPTIONS TO RULES

Pursuant to the general rules, an activity may constitute an unrelated business that is regularly carried on,[259] yet the income generated by the activity may escape federal taxation as unrelated business income pursuant to one or more statutory exceptions. There are also statutory exceptions for certain forms of income. There are two basic categories of these exceptions. Some of them appear in the federal tax law concerning a variety of modifications. Others are formally denominated as exceptions.

The facts and circumstances of each case determine whether a particular item of income falls within any of these modifications. For example, a payment may be termed *rent* by the parties but in fact amount to a return of profits by a person operating the property for the benefit of a tax-exempt organization or constitute a share of the profits retained by the organization as a partner or a joint venturer.[260]

The exceptions most likely to be applicable with respect to tax-exempt business leagues and/or entities related to them are discussed next.

(a) Passive Income in General

The unrelated business rules were enacted principally to ameliorate the effects of competition between tax-exempt organizations and for-profit (taxable) organizations by generally taxing the net income of exempt organizations from unrelated business activities.[261] The principle underlying this statutory scheme is that the business endeavors must be *active* ones for competitive activity to result. Correspondingly, income derived by a tax-exempt organization in a *passive* manner generally is income that is not acquired as the result of competitive activity; consequently, most forms of passive income paid to exempt organizations are

---

[257] IRC § 446(e); Reg. § 1.446-1(e).

[258] CORE Special Purpose Fund v. Comm'r, 49 T.C.M. 626, 630 (1985). Notwithstanding the differences in the manner in which tax-exempt social clubs are treated for purposes of unrelated taxation, the rules concerning the taxation of advertising revenue are applicable to them (Chicago Metropolitan Ski Council v. Comm'r, 104 T.C. 341 (1995)). In general, *Unrelated Business* § 6.5.

[259] See §§ 5.2, 5.5, 5.7.

[260] Reg. § 1.512(b)-1, first paragraph.

[261] See *Unrelated Business* § 1.6.

not taxed as unrelated business income.[262] Therefore, passive income is generally excluded from unrelated business taxable income, taking into account deductions that are directly connected to this type of income.[263]

The legislative history of these provisions indicates that Congress believed that passive income should not be taxed under these rules "where it is used for exempt purposes because investments producing incomes of these types have long been recognized as proper for educational and charitable organizations."[264]

Thus, for example, a tax-exempt organization can capitalize a for-profit corporation without endangering the tax exemption of the organization, an exempt organization can own all of the stock of a for-profit corporation without endangering its tax exemption,[265] the for-profit corporation can pay dividends to the exempt organization without jeopardizing the tax exemption of the exempt entity, and the dividend income received by the exempt entity will not be taxable as unrelated income.[266]

There may be forms of passive income incurred by tax-exempt organizations that may not be strictly within the technical meaning of one of the specific terms referenced in the passive income rules, yet which are nonetheless outside the framework of unrelated business income taxation. Occasionally, however, the IRS takes the position that the only items of income that can be regarded as passive income are those that are specifically referenced in the statutory modification rules. This has led to conflict, with the matter usually resolved in favor of tax-exempt organizations by Congress, such as in the instances of the writing of options[267] and the lending of securities.[268]

The legislative history of the unrelated business income tax provisions is clear on the point that Congress, in enacting these rules, did not intend and did not authorize taxation of the passive income of tax-exempt organizations, and that a technical satisfaction of the definitional requirements of the terms used in the passive income rules is not required. Thus, for example, the Senate Finance Committee observed in 1950 that the unrelated business income tax was to apply to "so much of . . . [exempt organizations'] income as rises from active business enterprises which are unrelated to the tax exempt purposes of the organizations."[269] This committee added: "The problem at which the tax on unrelated business income is directed is primarily that of unfair competition."[270] Speaking of the exclusion for passive sources of income, the committee stated:

> Dividends, interest, royalties, most rents, capital gains and losses and *similar items* are excluded from the base of the tax on unrelated income because your

---

[262] Two significant exceptions to this rule concern income from unrelated debt-financed property (see § 5.10) and income from controlled subsidiaries (see § 5.11).

[263] IRC §§ 512(b)(1)–(3), (5); Reg. § 1.512(b)-1(a)–(d). In Louis W. Hill Family Found. v. United States, 347 F. Supp. 1225 (D. Minn. 1972), the court concluded that "conducting a trade or business requires some business activity beyond the mere receipt of profits" (at 1229).

[264] H. Rep. No. 2319, 81st Cong., 2d Sess. 38 (1950). Also S. Rep. No. 2375, 81st Cong., 2d Sess. 30–31 (1950).

[265] There are, however, special rules for private foundations in this regard (see *Private Foundations*, Chapter 7).

[266] E.g., Priv. Ltr. Rul. 8244114.

[267] See *Unrelated Business* § 3.11.

[268] See § 5.9(d).

[269] S. Rep. No. 2375, 81st Cong., 2d Sess. 27 (1950) (emphasis supplied).

[270] *Id.* at 28.

committee believes that they are "passive" in character and are not likely to result in serious competition for taxable businesses having similar income. Moreover, investment-producing incomes of these types have long been recognized as a proper source of revenue for educational and charitable organizations and trusts.[271]

Therefore, it is unmistakable that passive income, regardless of type, is generally excluded from unrelated business income taxation.[272]

Illustrations of the IRS acceptance of this viewpoint is the development of regulations[273] concerning the exclusion of income derived from certain notional principal contracts[274] and other forms of a tax-exempt organization's ordinary and routine investments.[275] This concept is also embedded in the evolution of the rules concerning securities lending.[276]

The preceding analysis notwithstanding, there is a component of this law that rejects the premise that, for an item of income to be excluded from unrelated business income taxation (absent a specific statutory exclusion), it must be passive in nature. That is, there is a view that an item of income—once classified as a royalty or other similar item—is excludable from unrelated income taxation irrespective of whether it is passively derived.

Only the U.S. Tax Court has expressed this view, which arose in the course of consideration of whether payments for the use of mailing lists and payments from the operation of an affinity card program constitute excludable *royalties*. This court held that, if the arrangement is properly structured, mailing lists payments are royalties and thus they are excludable from unrelated business income taxation even if they are not forms of passive income.[277] The court also so held in the case of affinity card program payments.[278] The essence of this view is that, although Congress *believed* these types of income to be passive,[279] that does not necessarily mean that they always must be passive.[280] Stated in the reverse, this view holds that a statutorily classified item of excludable income remains excludable from unrelated business income taxation irrespective of whether the income is passive or is derived from the active conduct of a trade or business. The validity of this view was, however, substantially eroded by a subsequent appellate court opinion.[281]

(b) Dividends

Dividends paid to a tax-exempt organization generally are not taxable as unrelated business income.[282] Basically, a *dividend* is a share allotted to each of one or

---

[271] *Id.* at 30–31 (emphasis supplied).

[272] Also H. Rep. No. 2319, 81st Cong., 2d Sess. 36–38 (1950).

[273] Reg. § 1.512(b)-1(a)(2).

[274] Reg. § 1.512(b)-1(a)(1).

[275] *Id.*

[276] See § 5.9(d).

[277] Sierra Club, Inc. v. Comm'r, 65 T.C.M. 2582 (1993); Disabled American Veterans v. Comm'r, 94 T.C. 60 (1990), *rev'd on other grounds*, 942 F.2d 309 (6th Cir. 1991).

[278] Sierra Club, Inc. v. Comm'r, 103 T.C. 307 (1994).

[279] See text accompanied by *supra* note 264.

[280] This view is based on additional language in the committee reports indicating that the exception for dividends, interest, annuities, royalties, and the like "applies not only to investment income [a concept broader than passive income], but also to such items as business interest on overdue open accounts receivable" (S. Rep. No. 2375, 81st Cong., 2d Sess. 108 (1950); H. Rep. No. 2319, 81st Cong., 2d Sess. 110 (1950)).

[281] See § 5.9(f), text accompanied by *infra* notes 332-334.

[282] IRC § 512(b)(1); Reg. § 1.512(b)-1(a)(1).

more persons who are entitled to share in the net profits generated by a business undertaking, usually a corporation; it is a payment out of the payor's net profits.

There are some exceptions to this exclusion, principally dividends that are unrelated debt-financed income[283] and those that are from controlled foreign offshore insurance captives.[284] Generally, however, dividends paid to tax-exempt organizations from controlled corporations are not taxable.[285]

(c) Interest

Interest paid to a tax-exempt organization generally is not taxable as unrelated business income.[286] Basically, the term *interest* is defined as compensation that one person (debtor) pays to another person (creditor) for the use or forbearance of money.[287] Similarly, *interest* is defined in the income tax regulations for personal holding company income purposes as amounts received for the use of money loaned.[288]

The IRS set forth criteria for use in determining whether a debtor-creditor relationship exists for the purpose of treating as *interest* certain loan processing fees (commonly known as points) paid by a mortgagor-borrower as compensation to a lender solely for the use or forbearance of money. The agency held that, where the taxpayer is able to establish that the fee is paid as compensation to the lender solely for the use or forbearance of money, the fee is considered to be interest. It was not necessary that the parties to the transaction label a payment made for the use of money as interest for it to be treated as interest. In order for these fees to be treated as interest, however, the fees must not be paid for any specific services that have been performed or will be performed in connection with the loan. For example, interest would not include separate charges made for investigating the prospective borrower and the borrower's security, closing costs of the loan, and papers prepared in connection with the transaction, or fees paid to a third party for servicing and collecting the loan.[289] Also, even where service charges are not stated separately on a borrower's account, interest cannot include amounts attributable to these services.[290] The IRS applied these principles of law in ruling that services fees received by a tax-exempt organization from mortgage loans do not constitute interest for purpose of the unrelated business income tax exclusion for interest income.[291]

There are some exceptions to this exclusion, principally interest that is unrelated debt-financed income[292] and that is paid by a controlled corporation.[293]

---

[283] IRC § 512(b)(4); Reg. § 1.512(b)-1(a)(2); Reg. § 1.512(b)-1(k).
[284] See *Unrelated Business* § 3.15.
[285] See § 5.11.
[286] IRC § 512(b)(1); Reg. § 1.512(b)-1(a)(1).
[287] Deputy v. du Pont, 308 U.S. 488, 498 (1940).
[288] Reg. § 1.543-1(b)(2).
[289] Rev. Rul. 69-188, 1969-1 C.B. 54.
[290] Rev. Rul. 67-297, 1967-2 C.B. 87.
[291] Rev. Rul. 79-349, 1979-2 C.B. 233.
[292] IRC § 512(b)(4); Reg. §§ 1.512(b)-1(a)(2), 1.512(b)-1(k). See § 5.10.
[293] Reg. § 1.512(b)-1(a)(2). See § 5.11.

The IRS issues private letter rulings as to what constitutes excludable interest in this context.[294]

(d) Securities Lending Transactions

Qualified payments with respect to loans of securities are generally excluded from unrelated business income taxation.[295] These amounts are not excluded from this tax, however, if they constitute unrelated debt-financed income.[296]

This exclusion is available for the lending of securities to a broker and the return of identical securities. For this nontaxation treatment to apply, the security loans must be fully collateralized and must be terminable on five business days' notice by the lending organization. Additionally, an agreement between the parties must provide for reasonable procedures to implement the obligation of the borrower to furnish collateral to the lender with a fair market value on each business day the loan is outstanding in an amount at least equal to the fair market value of the security at the close of business on the preceding day.[297]

In the typical securities lending transaction involving a tax-exempt organization, the exempt organization lends securities (stocks and bonds) from its investment portfolio to a brokerage house, to enable the broker to effect delivery of the securities to cover either a short sale or a failure to receive equivalent securities. In this type of transaction, the broker receiving the certificates posts cash collateral with the lending institution in an amount equal to or exceeding the then–fair market value of the particular securities. This collateral may be available to the lending organization in the interim for the purpose of short-term investment as it deems appropriate.

Under this arrangement, either the lending tax-exempt organization or the broker can terminate the lending relationship by giving notice. In this instance, the broker becomes obligated to return the identical securities to the exempt organization, which has retained beneficial ownership of them, and the organization becomes obligated to return the collateral to the broker. In the event of default on the part of the broker, the organization is required to use the collateral to purchase replacement securities and has a claim against the borrowing broker for any deficiency. Any excess funds derived in the process of securing replacement securities must be returned to the broker. Thus, the concept is that the exempt organization's portfolio position should not be improved by virtue of any default by a broker-borrower. An amount equivalent to any dividend or interest that comes due during the course of the lending period must be paid by the broker to the organization whether or not the broker holds the securities. The brokerage house also pays the lending organization compensation for entering into the arrangement, either as a predetermined premium computed as a percentage of the value of the loaned securities or, as noted, by allowing the organization to invest the collateral and retain the income.[298]

---

[294] E.g., Priv. Ltr. Rul. 9108021.

[295] IRC § 512(b)(1); Reg. § 1.512(b)-1(a)(1).

[296] Reg. § 1.512(b)-1(a)(2).

[297] IRC § 512(a)(5).

[298] An IRS private letter ruling illustrated a qualified securities lending program involving a private foundation (Priv. Ltr. Rul. 200501017).

A threshold issue in the federal tax context was whether this type of a securities-lending arrangement constituted a *business*.[299] The management of an investment portfolio comprised wholly of the manager's own securities does not constitute the conduct of a trade or business. For example, the U.S. Supreme Court held that the mere keeping of records and collection of interest and dividends from securities, through managerial attention to the investments, is not the operation of a business.[300] On that occasion, the Court sustained the *government's* position that "mere personal investment activities never constitute carrying on a trade or business."[301] Subsequently, the Court stated that "investing is not a trade or business."[302] Likewise, a federal court of appeals observed that the "mere management of investments . . . is insufficient to constitute the carrying on of a trade or business."[303] Investment activities by a tax-exempt organization for its own benefit thus do not constitute business undertakings in the unrelated business context.[304] It is thus settled that mere record keeping and income collection for an exempt organization's own investments are not activities that are regarded as the carrying on of a business.[305]

Until late in 1977, when an IRS private letter ruling was issued to a tax-exempt college, it was not clear whether the agency would regard the practice of securities lending as a trade or business. The initial position of the IRS was that the activity was an unrelated business.[306] When it became clear to the agency that the matter was going to be resolved in favor of the tax-exempt organizations' community by legislation, the IRS attempted to preclude the legislation by issuing a ruling in 1978 that securities lending by exempt organizations is a form of "ordinary or routine investment activities" and thus not a business.[307] This ploy failed, with Congress adopting the legislation[308] notwithstanding the promulgation of the favorable ruling.

It seems clear, nonetheless, based on the state of the law before 1978, that the interest earned by the lending organization on the collateral and the interim dividend and interest payments were excludable from treatment as unrelated business income.[309] The accepted rule is that the amounts received through independent investment are characterized in accordance with the nature of the investment. Therefore, the income derived from an investment of this collateral by an exempt organization in bank certificates of deposit or a form of short-term investment was without question excludable interest. Similarly, an investment of

---

[299] See § 5.2.

[300] Higgins v. Comm'r, 312 U.S. 212 (1941).

[301] *Id.* at 215. The issue in this context was whether the activity was a business for purposes of the business expense deduction rules (IRC § 162).

[302] Whipple v. Comm'r, 373 U.S. 193, 202 (1963).

[303] Continental Trading, Inc. v. Comm'r, 265 F.2d 40, 43 (9th Cir. 1959), *cert. den.,* 361 U.S. 827 (1959).

[304] See § 5.2(d).

[305] E.g., Moller v. United States, 721 F.2d 810 (Fed. Cir. 1983) (holding that investment activities in a home office do not constitute a business).

[306] See Stern & Sullivan, "Exempt Organizations Which Lend Securities Risk Imposition of Unrelated Business Tax," 45 *J. Tax.* 240 (1976).

[307] Rev. Rul. 78-88, 1978-1 C.B. 163.

[308] See *supra* note 297.

[309] See §§ 5.9(b), 5.9(c).

the collateral by the organization in stocks or bonds unquestionably produced excludable dividends or interest.

The amounts paid by the brokers to a lending tax-exempt organization in reflection of any dividends or interest earned in respect of the securities on loan were excludable from unrelated business income. Certainly the dividends or interest, if paid to the exempt organization while it was in physical possession of the certificates or comparable investment vehicle, were excluded from unrelated business income taxation by virtue of these rules. It would have exalted form over substance to treat the pass-through payments from the broker for dividends and interest any differently. The essence of the transaction should have prevailed[310]—and ultimately it did.

As noted, the term *interest* generally is defined as compensation paid for the use or forbearance of money.[311] In the securities-lending transaction, the income received by the organization derives from an arrangement involving the use of property. Courts have, however, utilized another definition of *interest*, that being an amount paid that is contingent on having some relationship to an indebtedness.[312] The term *indebtedness* has been defined as something owed in money that a person is unconditionally obligated to repay, the payment of which is enforceable.[313] Therefore, these amounts paid by the brokers to an exempt organization constitute interest, inasmuch as they are amounts paid in conjunction with an enforceable indebtedness, namely, the obligation of the broker to return the securities or in lieu thereof work a forfeiture of the collateral.

Even if these payments were not regarded as interest as such, they nonetheless retained their character as dividends, interest, or other form of passive income for purposes of the exclusion. In the securities-lending transaction, the income paid to the lending organization by brokers need not lose its character as dividends or interest. For example, the IRS in a ruling distinguished between *sale and purchase transactions* and *loan transactions*. The facts underlying this ruling were that bank customers "sold" securities to a bank in return for loans from the bank, agreeing to "repurchase" the identical securities at the close of the loan period. The agency ruled that this transaction did not amount, in law, to a sale or exchange but instead was a loan of money upon collateral security (that is, the securities).[314]

The pertinence of this ruling is enhanced by the fact that the securities in question were state or municipal bonds, the interest of which is exempt from federal income taxation.[315] At issue was the appropriate party to have the benefit of this exclusion: the lender-customer or the borrower-bank. Concurrent with its finding that the transaction was a loan and not a sale, the IRS ruled that the tax-exempt interest is the income of the customer who tendered the securities to the

---

[310] McBride v. Comm'r, 44 B.T.A. 273 (1941); Kell v. Comm'r, 31 B.T.A. 212 (1934); Peck v. Comm'r, 31 B.T.A. 87 (1934), *aff'd*, 77 F.2d 857 (2d Cir. 1935), *cert. den.*, 296 U.S. 625 (1935).

[311] See § 5.9(c), text accompanied by supra note 287.

[312] Comm'r v. Wilson, 163 F.2d 680 (9th Cir. 1947), *aff'g* 5 T.C.M. 647 (1946), *cert. den.*, 332 U.S. 842 (1947); Comm'r v. Park, 113 F.2d 352 (3d Cir. 1940), *aff'g* 38 B.T.A. 1118 (1938).

[313] Gilman v. Comm'r, 53 F.2d 47 (8th Cir. 1931).

[314] Rev. Rul. 74-27, 1974-1 C.B. 24.

[315] IRC § 103.

bank for collateral and that the bank was not entitled to treat the interest paid by the customers as exempt from tax.[316]

The analogy between the facts of this ruling and the securities-lending transaction is unmistakable. Just as the bank in that ruling was unable to treat customer-paid interest as tax-exempt income, having to associate that tax feature with its customers' holdings, so too are the broker-paid amounts to exempt organizations properly treated as dividends or interest (as the case may be) to them, rather than as dividends or interest paid to the broker. This parallel in the transactions was underscored by the characterization by the IRS of the transaction as a loan rather than a sale or exchange, which is the correct portrayal to be given the organization's transactions with brokers. It is the exempt organization, not the broker, that retains the debt or equity position in the issuer-corporation.

The courts have recognized the concept of *equivalency payments*, with the result that the payments are regarded as dividends, interest, or the like even though the technical elements of the definitions of those terms may not be wholly satisfied. As an illustration, a federal court of appeals, in characterizing oil and gas lease bonus payments for personal holding company purposes as passive income, concluded that the payments were a "hybrid category of income not expressly provided for in the statute, which, as a matter of semantics, is not clearly either rent or royalty" and decided that, "[b]ecause it seems to us that the type of lease bonus here under consideration is precisely the sort of passive investment income with which the statute is concerned . . . we have no doubt that the lease bonus falls within one category or another."[317] Similarly, the income received by exempt organizations from brokers in securities-lending transactions, reflecting dividends or interest paid by the issuer, is properly regarded as dividends or interest for these purposes—even if it is treated as a hybrid category of income that does not fully meet all of the semantic definitional requirements.

It was not necessary, however, for unrelated business law purposes, to resolve the question as to whether a pass-through theory was pertinent. This is because, irrespective of whether the payments are to be considered dividends or interest by virtue of an equivalency approach, they should nonetheless have been so characterized for purposes of the unrelated business income rules. That is, regardless of the availability of a pass-through rationale, the payments by brokers to exempt lending organizations are still appropriately characterized as coming within the exclusion for passive income.

The monies paid by the brokers to exempt organizations perhaps may not satisfy the precise doctrinal requirements of the terms used in these rules, such as interest or dividends. Nonetheless, these monies clearly constitute passive income to the organization and accordingly warrant treatment as being within the scope of the intentions underlying the exclusions. It may be technically advanced, as noted, that payments by borrowing brokers to a tax-exempt organization cannot

---

[316] Reliance for the IRS's position in this regard was placed on First American Nat'l Bank of Nashville v. United States, 467 F.2d 1098 (6th Cir. 1972), and American Nat'l Bank of Austin v. United States, 421 F.2d 442 (5th Cir. 1970), *cert. den.*, 400 U.S. 819 (1970).

[317] Bayou Verret Land Co. v. Comm'r, 450 F.2d 840, 855, 854 (5th Cir. 1971), *rev'g and rem'g* 52 T.C. 971 (1970).

qualify as interest inasmuch as the payments are made for the use of securities, which are property, not money. These payments may technically not constitute *rent* because the securities recovered by an exempt organization are different from those that were borrowed, the right to sell the property become vested in the borrower, and the borrower has the authority to sell the securities—features of a transaction usually antithetical to the typical lease arrangement.[318] Nonetheless, the strict definitional classifications of the types of passive income are not dispositive of the question as to their treatment in relation to the unrelated business rules. Rather, "[w]hether a particular item of income falls within any of the modifications . . . shall be determined by all of the facts and circumstances of each case."[319]

In this factual setting, the income generated by the typical securities-lending transaction is clearly passive in nature, thereby warranting treatment as being encompassed by the modifications. That is, from the standpoint of the tax-exempt lending organization, there is no additional activity necessitated to procure the income (the only *activity* is the investment effort in entering into the contracts with brokers) and the amount of income is essentially the same (albeit from a different source).

The validity of the foregoing analysis is borne out by the line of law that holds that payments made by a broker-borrower in a securities-lending transaction are the functional equivalent of interest paid in connection with a business loan and therefore are deductible by the broker as an ordinary and necessary business expense. Thus, it was held that a taxpayer, engaged in extensive short sales transactions, properly deducted the payments to the lender, which were amounts equal to dividends declared during the period the seller is short, as business expenses.[320] Similarly, on like facts, a court first noted that *interest* is an amount having some relationship to an indebtedness, in turn defined as "something owed in money which one is unconditionally obligated or bound to pay, the payment of which is enforceable."[321] Realizing that the securities transaction under examination necessarily involves a borrower and a lender, the court concluded that the "payment of the dividend here represents a sum of money unconditionally owed by the borrower to the lender of stock; it arises out of the relationship of debtor and creditor and is a customary expense in a 'short' sale incident to obtaining and using the stock" and is "ordinary and necessary in this type of transaction."[322]

The acceptance by the IRS of this rationale was memorialized in a ruling involving an investor who paid loan premiums and amounts equal to cash dividends to the lenders of securities to the investor. The dividend equivalency and other payments were ruled by the agency to be deductible under these rules.[323]

Therefore, the correct conclusion in this regard—even if securities lending is regarded as a trade or business and even if this matter had not been rectified by statute—would be treatment of the brokers' payments to the lending tax-exempt

---

[318] See § 5.9(g).
[319] Reg. § 1.512(b)-1. See § 5.9(a), text accompanied by supra note 271.
[320] Comm'r v. Wiesler, 161 F.2d 997 (6th Cir. 1947), *aff'g* 6 T.C. 1148 (1946), *cert. den.*, 322 U.S. 842 (1947).
[321] Comm'r v. Wilson, 163 F.2d 680, 682 (9th Cir. 1947).
[322] *Id.*
[323] Rev. Rul. 72-521, 1972-2 C.B. 178.

organization as dividends or interest, excludable from unrelated business income taxation by operation of the rules encompassing passive income or as income items so functionally equivalent to interest and dividends by virtue of their nature as passive income as to be similarly excludable.

(e) Annuities

Income received by a tax-exempt organization as an annuity generally is not taxable as unrelated business income.[324] Basically, an *annuity* is an amount of money, fixed by contract between the annuitor and the annuitant, that is paid annually, either in one sum or in installments (such as semiannually or quarterly).

This exclusion is not available where the income is unrelated debt-financed income[325] or is from a controlled corporation.[326]

(f) Royalties

Generally, a royalty, including an overriding royalty,[327] paid to a tax-exempt organization is excludable from unrelated income taxation.[328]

Basically, a *royalty* is a payment for the use of a valuable intangible right, such as a trademark, trade name, service mark, logo, or copyright, regardless of whether the property represented by the right is used; royalties also include the right to a share of production reserved to the owner of property for permitting another to work mines and quarries or to drill for oil or gas.[329] Royalties have also been characterized as payments that constitute passive income, such as the compensation paid by a licensee to the licensor for the use of the licensor's patented invention.[330]

It was the stance of the U.S. Tax Court that a royalty, excludable from unrelated business income taxation, is a payment for the use of valuable intangible property rights, irrespective of whether the income was passive.[331] A federal appellate court, however, is of the view that the Tax Court's definition of the term *royalty* is overly broad, in that a royalty "cannot include compensation for services rendered by the owner of the property."[332] This position, then, is a compromise between the approach of the Tax Court and that of the IRS on the point. Thus, the appellate court wrote that, to the extent the IRS "claims that a tax-exempt organization can do nothing to acquire such fees [to have the income regarded as an excludable royalty]," the agency is "incorrect."[333] Yet, the court continued, "to the extent that . . . [the exempt organization involved] appears to argue that a 'royalty' is any payment for the use of a property

---

[324] IRC § 512(b)(1); Reg. § 1.512(b)-1(a)(1).

[325] IRC § 512(b)(4); Reg. § 1.512(b)-1(a)(1). See § 5.10.

[326] Reg. § 1.512(b)-1(a)(2); Reg. § 1.512(b)-1(k). See § 5.11.

[327] A discussion of the addition of this term is in J.E. & L.E. Mabee Found., Inc. v. United States, 533 F.2d 521 (10th Cir. 1976), *aff'g* 389 F. Supp. 673 (N.D. Okla. 1975).

[328] IRC § 512(b)(2); Reg. § 1.512(b)-1(b).

[329] E.g., Fraternal Order of Police Ill. State Troopers Lodge No. 41 v. Comm'r, 833 F.2d 717, 723 (7th Cir. 1987).

[330] Disabled Am. Veterans v. United States, 650 F.2d 1178, 1189 (Ct. Cl. 1981).

[331] Sierra Club, Inc. v. Comm'r, 103 T.C. 307, 337 (1994); Sierra Club, Inc. v. Comm'r, 65 T.C.M. 2582, 2586–2588 (1993); Disabled Am. Veterans v. Comm'r, 94 T.C. 60, 70 (1990).

[332] Sierra Club, Inc. v. Comm'r, 86 F.3d 1526, 1532 (9th Cir. 1996).

[333] *Id.* at 1535.

right—such as a copyright—regardless of any additional services that are performed in addition to the owner simply permitting another to use the right at issue, we disagree."[334]

Thus, despite the exclusion for royalty income, it is the position of the IRS that monies will be taxed, even if they are characterized by the parties as royalties, when the tax-exempt organization is actively involved in the enterprise that generates the revenue, such as through the provision of services.[335] Frequently, the IRS will view the relationship between the parties as that of partners or joint venturers.[336] A common instance of this treatment is the insistence by the agency that the funds an exempt organization receives for an endorsement are taxable, while the organization asserts that the monies are royalties for the use of its name and logo.[337] An approach to resolution of this issue is to make partial use of the royalty exclusion by means of two contracts: one for the taxable services and one for the royalty arrangement.[338]

Additional litigation has somewhat transformed the IRS's stance in this regard. This process began when an appellate court ruled that a tax-exempt organization could treat income as a royalty even when the organization provided some services.[339] It was furthered when the Tax Court held that revenue was royalty income under this new definition.[340] The IRS's position further eroded when the Tax Court subsequently held, in two decisions, that mailing list rental payments qualified as royalties.[341] The denouement of the government's stance probably came when two other appellate court opinions on the subject of royalty income went against it.[342]

By the close of 1999, the IRS realized that this series of defeats was insurmountable—that the courts were not going to accept its interpretation of the scope of the tax-excludable royalty. The IRS National Office, late that year, communicated with its exempt organizations specialists in the field, essentially capitulating on the point; a memorandum distributed to them stated bluntly that cases should be resolved "in a manner consistent with the existing court cases."[343] This memorandum added that "it is now clear that courts will continue

---

[334] *Id.*

[335] E.g., Nat'l Water Well Ass'n, Inc. v. Comm'r, 92 T.C. 75 (1989).

[336] E.g., Tech. Adv. Mem. 9509002.

[337] E.g., Priv. Ltr. Rul. 9450028.

[338] There is support for this approach in Texas Farm Bureau, Inc. v. United States, 53 F.3d 120 (5th Cir. 1995), in which the contracts involved did not expressly cast the revenues at issue as royalties.

[339] See text accompanied by *supra* notes 332–334.

[340] Sierra Club, Inc. v. Comm'r, 77 T.C.M. 1569 (1999). This case was heard on remand; the first decision is at 103 T.C. 307 (1994). In general, Tsilas, "Sierra Club, Inc. v. Commissioner: Why Is the IRS Continuing to Fight a Losing Battle?" 24 *Exempt Org. Tax Rev.* (No. 3) 487 (June 1999); Lauber & Mayer, "Tax Court Rules (Again) on Sierra Club Affinity Card Income," 24 *Exempt Org. Tax Rev.* (No. 2) 311 (May 1999).

[341] Common Cause v. Comm'r, 112 T.C. 332 (1999); Planned Parenthood Fed'n of America, Inc. v. Comm'r, 77 T.C.M. 2227 (1999). Also Mississippi State Univ. Alumni, Inc. v. Comm'r, 74 T.C.M. 458 (1999).

[342] Oregon State Univ. Alumni Ass'n, Inc. v. Comm'r; Alumni Ass'n of Univ. of Ore., Inc. v. Comm'r, 193 F.3d 1098 (9th Cir. 1999), *aff'g* 71 T.C.M. 1935 (1996), 71 T.C.M. 2093 (1996).

[343] Memorandum from Jay H. Rotz, IRS Exempt Organizations Division, National Office, dated December 16, 1999. This is not to say that the government loses every case on this point. When the tax-exempt organization participates in and maintains control over significant aspects of the activities that generate the income, the courts will reject the contention that the revenue is an excludable royalty (e.g., Arkansas State Police Ass'n, Inc. v. Comm'r, 81 T.C.M. 1172 (2001), *aff'd*, 282 F.3d 556 (8th Cir. 2002)).

to find the income [generated by activities such as mailing list rentals and affinity card programs] to be excluded royalty income unless the factual record clearly reflects more than unsubstantial services being provided." Two factors were highlighted by the agency as establishing nontaxable royalty income: where the involvement of the exempt organization is "relatively minimal" and where the exempt organization "hired outside contractors to perform most services associated with the exploitation of the use of intangible property."[344]

Earlier, the U.S. Tax Court held that a tax-exempt organization that received income from the rental of mailing lists was not taxable on that income because it was properly characterized as royalties, notwithstanding the extent of activities the organization engaged in to preserve and enhance the list.[345] The court seemed to state that it was irrelevant in this setting as to whether the royalty income was passive or not. It appears, nonetheless, that the active endeavors of the organization that the court acknowledged were activities to preserve and enhance the asset (maintain the list) rather than the provision of services to others in connection with rental activities. On appeal, however, it was held that the organization was collaterally estopped from bringing the case in the first instance, in that the same issue was litigated previously.[346]

Mineral royalties, whether measured by production or by gross or taxable income from the mineral property, are excludable by a tax-exempt organization in computing unrelated business taxable income. Where, however, an exempt organization owns a working interest in a mineral property, and is not relieved of its share of the development costs by the terms of any agreement with an operator, income received from the interest is not excludable from unrelated business income taxation.[347] The holder of a mineral interest is not liable for the expenses of development (or operations) for these purposes where the holder's interest is a net profit interest not subject to expenses that exceed gross profits. Thus, an exempt university was ruled to have excludable royalty interests, where the interests it held in various oil and gas producing properties were based on the gross profits from the properties reduced by all expenses of development and operations.[348] The foregoing reference to development costs is for purposes of illustration; the concept also extends to operating costs because, to be an excludable royalty interest, income received from a mineral lease by an exempt organization must be free of both types of cost.[349]

The IRS ruled that patent development and management service fees deducted from royalties collected from licensees by a tax-exempt charitable organization for distribution to the beneficial owners of the patents were not within this exception for royalties; the agency said that "although the amounts paid to the [exempt] organization are derived from royalties, they do not retain

---

[344] An issue under consideration at the IRS is whether there should be an allocation of a single payment between compensation for the use of intangible property and compensation for more than insubstantial services.

[345] Disabled Am. Veterans v. Comm'r, 94 T.C. 60 (1990).

[346] Disabled Am. Veterans v. Comm'r, 942 F.2d 309 (6th Cir. 1991). This previous litigation is reflected in Disabled Am. Veterans v. United States, 650 F.2d 1178 (Ct. Cl. 1981), aff'd and rem'd, 704 F.2d 1570 (Fed. Cir. 1983).

[347] Reg. § 1.512(b)-1(b).

[348] Priv. Ltr. Rul. 7741004.

[349] Rev. Rul. 69-179, 1969-1 C.B. 158.

the character of royalties in the organization's hands" for these purposes.[350] Similarly, the IRS decided that income derived by an exempt organization from the sale of advertising in publications produced by an independent firm was properly characterized as royalty income.[351] By contrast, the agency determined that amounts received from licensees by an exempt organization, which was the legal and beneficial owner of patents assigned to it by inventors for specified percentages of future royalties, constituted excludable royalty income.[352] A federal court of appeals held that income consisting of 100 percent of the net profits in certain oil properties, received by an exempt organization from two corporations controlled by it, constituted income from overriding royalties and thus was excluded from unrelated business income taxation.[353]

A matter of concern to the IRS was the proper tax treatment of payments to a tax-exempt organization, the principal purpose of which is the development of a U.S. team for international amateur sports competition, in return for the right to commercially use the organization's name and logo. The organization entered into licensing agreements that, in consideration of the annual payment of a stated sum, authorized use of the organization's name and logo in connection with the sale of products. The initial position of the IRS was that payments must be measured according to the use made of a valuable right to be characterized as a royalty and thus be excludable from unrelated income taxation. The agency became sufficiently persuaded, on the basis of case law precedent,[354] however, that fixed-sum payments for the right to use an asset qualify as excludable royalties, although it continues to adhere to the position that absent the statutory exclusion, the income would be taxable as being from an unrelated trade or business.[355]

Subsequently, the IRS ruled that certain payments a labor organization received from various business enterprises for the use of its trademark and similar properties were excludable royalties.[356] This conclusion was reached notwithstanding the fact that the organization retained the right to approve the quality or style of the licensed products and services, and the payments sometimes were set as flat annual payments.[357]

Of all of the exclusions from unrelated business income taxation that are available by reason of the modifications, the exclusion for royalties is the most versatile from a planning standpoint. There is not much flexibility in the terms

---

[350] Rev. Rul. 73-193, 1973-1 C.B. 262, 263.

[351] Priv. Ltr. Rul. 7926003.

[352] Rev. Rul. 76-297, 1976-2 C.B. 178.

[353] United States v. The Robert A. Welch Found., 334 F.2d 774 (5th Cir. 1964), aff'g 228 F. Supp. 881 (S.D. Tex. 1963). The IRS refused to follow this decision (Rev. Rul. 69-162, 1969-1 C.B. 158).

[354] Comm'r v. Affiliated Enterprises., Inc., 123 F.2d 665 (10th Cir. 1941), cert. den., 315 U.S. 812 (1942). Also Comm'r v. Wodehouse, 337 U.S. 369 (1949); Rohmer v. Comm'r, 153 F.2d 61 (2d Cir. 1946), cert. den., 328 U.S. 862 (1946); Sabatini v. Comm'r, 98 F.2d 758 (2d Cir. 1938).

[355] Priv. Ltr. Rul. 8006005.

[356] Rev. Rul. 81-178, 1981-2 C.B. 135. By contrast, other payments were held to not be royalties because the personal services of the organization's members were required.

[357] The IRS cited the following authority for its conclusion: Uhlaender v. Henrickson, 316 F. Supp. 1277 (D. Minn. 1970); Cepeda v. Swift & Co., 415 F.2d 1205 (8th Cir. 1969); Comm'r v. Wodehouse, 337 U.S. 369 (1949); Rohmer v. Comm'r, 153 F.2d 61 (2d Cir. 1946); Comm'r v. Affiliated Enterprises, Inc., 123 F.2d 665 (10th Cir. 1941); Sabatini v. Comm'r, 98 F.2d 758 (2d Cir. 1938).

dividend, interest, and *annuity,* yet the term *royalty* is sufficiently supple to often enable an exempt organization to convert what would otherwise be unrelated business income into excludable royalties. For example, instead of publishing and selling a book in a commercial manner directly (an unrelated business that is regularly carried on), an exempt organization can transfer the processes to a publishing company and receive nontaxable royalties.[358]

The IRS issues private letter rulings as to what constitutes excludable royalties in this context.[359]

Unrelated debt-financed income is not subject to this exclusion,[360] nor is royalty income from a controlled corporation.[361]

(g) Rent

An exclusion from unrelated business income taxation is available with respect to certain rents.[362] The principal exclusion is for rents from real property.[363]

(i) General Rules. *Rent* is a form of income that is paid for the occupation or other use of property. In general, this exclusion is available for rental income where the tax-exempt organization is not actively involved in the enterprise that generates the revenue, such as through the provision of services for the convenience of tenants. Payments for the use or occupancy of entire private residences or living quarters in duplex or multiple housing units, of offices in any office building, and the like are generally considered as excludable rent.[364]

The exclusion from unrelated business taxable income for rents is sometimes misunderstood, inasmuch as not all income labeled *rent* qualifies for the exclusion. Where a tax-exempt organization carries on activities that constitute an activity carried on for trade or business, even though the activities involve the leasing of real estate, the exclusion will not be available.[365] Thus, payments for the use or occupancy of rooms and other space where services are also rendered to the occupant, such as for the use or occupancy of rooms or other quarters in hotels, boardinghouses, or apartment houses furnishing hotel services, or in tourist camps or tourist homes, motor courts, or motels, or for the use or occupancy in parking lots, warehouses, or storage garages, does not constitute excludable rent. Generally, services are considered *rendered to the occupant* if they are primarily for that person's convenience and are other than those usually or customarily rendered in connection with the rental of rooms or other space for occupancy only. The supplying of maid service, for example, constitutes such service. By contrast, an exempt organization may perform normal maintenance services, such as the furnishing of heat, air conditioning, and light; the cleaning

---

[358] Rev. Rul. 69-430, 1969-2 C.B. 129.

[359] E.g., Priv. Ltr. Rul. 8708031.

[360] IRC § 512(b)(4); Reg. § 1.512(b)-1(b); Reg. § 1.512(b)-1(k) . See § 5.10.

[361] Reg. § 1.512(b)-1(b). See § 5.11.

[362] IRC § 512(b)(3); Reg. § 1.512(b)-1(c)(2).

[363] IRC § 512(b)(3)(A)(i).

[364] Reg. § 1.512(b)-1(c)(5).

[365] In general, the rental of real estate constitutes the carrying on of a trade or business (e.g., Hazard v. Comm'r, 7 T.C. 372 (1946)).

of public entrances, exits, stairways, and lobbies; and the collection of trash, and the like, and retain the benefit of the exclusion. Thus, where, an exempt organization undertakes functions beyond these maintenance services, the payments will not be considered as being from a passive source but instead from an unrelated trade or business (assuming that the activity is regularly carried on and is not substantially related to the organization's tax-exempt purposes).[366]

Thus, for example, a tax-exempt organization that allowed use of its hall for a fee, where only utilities and janitorial services were provided, was held able to utilize this exclusion because the services were minimal, causing the receipts to be rental income from real property.[367] Conversely, where an exempt organization operating to foster public interest in the arts leased studio apartments to artists, providing telephone switchboard and maid services, and operated a dining hall for the tenants, payments pursuant to the leases were not sheltered by the rental exclusion because substantial services were rendered to the tenants and the leasing activity was not an exempt function.[368]

The contractual relationship between the parties, from which the ostensible rental income is derived, must be that as reflected in a *lease*, rather than a *license*, for the exclusion for rental income to be available. A lease "confers upon a tenant exclusive possession of the subject premises as against all the world, including the owner."[369] The difference is the conferring of a privilege to occupy the owner's property for a particular use, rather than general possession of the premises. Thus, a tax-exempt organization that conferred to an advertising agency the permission to maintain signs and other advertisements on the wall space in the exempt organization's premises was held to receive income from a license arrangement, rather than a rental one, so that the exclusion for rental income was unavailable.[370]

For example, a tax-exempt organization held title to a pipeline system consisting of right-of-way interests in land, pipelines buried in the ground, pumping stations, equipment, and other appurtenant property. The organization leased the system. In concluding that the resultant income constituted *rent* for purposes of this exclusion, the IRS observed that the basic component of the pipeline system, an easement giving the right-of-way interests, amounted to real property.[371] Thus, income passively received from the rental of real property, such as that from a valid landlord-tenant relationship where the landlord receives nothing more than net rental payments, is not taxable; the analysis changes, however, if the arrangement is that of a management contract rather than a lease.[372]

---

[366] Reg. § 1.512(b)-1(c)(5).

[367] Rev. Rul. 69-178, 1969-1 C.B. 158. The facts that the use of the hall was for only short periods of time and that the agreement to use the facility was usually verbal did not destroy the character of these receipts as qualifying rental income.

[368] Rev. Rul. 69-69, 1969-1 C.B. 159.

[369] Union Travel Associates, Inc. v. Int'l Associates, Inc., 401 A.2d 105, 107 (D.C. Ct. App. 1976).

[370] Priv. Ltr. Rul. 9740032.

[371] Rev. Rul. 67-218, 1967-2 C.B. 213.

[372] State Nat'l Bank of El Paso v. United States, 509 F.2d 832 (5th Cir. 1975), *rev'g and rem'g* 75-2 U.S.T.C. ¶ 9868 (W.D. Tex. 1975).

As a general rule, the exclusion for rent is not applicable where the relationship between the parties is a partnership[373] or a joint venture.[374] Where the requisite profit motive is absent, even if the arrangement is a partnership or joint venture in the broad sense of ownership of property and sharing of net rents, there presumably is no partnership or joint venture for federal tax purposes because of the lack of an intent of a return of profits and because the relationship does not involve a working interest or operational control of the "business."[375] Thus, where the income is truly rent and where the relationship is a passive one (of investor only), the exclusion for rental income is available.[376]

The rents that are excluded from unrelated business income taxation are all rents from real property[377] and certain rents from personal property[378] leased with real property.[379] The exclusion from unrelated business income for rents of personal property leased with real property is limited to instances where the rents attributable to the personalty are an incidental amount of the total rents received or accrued under the lease (that is, no more than 10 percent of total rental income).[380] This determination is made at the time the personal property is first placed in service by the lessee.[381] Thus, for example, if rents attributable to personal property leased are $3,000 annually and the total rents from all property leased are $10,000 annually, the $3,000 amount cannot be excluded from the computation of unrelated business income, inasmuch as that amount is not an incidental portion of the total rents.[382]

Moreover, this exclusion is not available, however, if more than 50 percent of the total rent received or accrued pursuant to the lease is attributable to the personalty leased (determined at the time the personal property is first placed in service by the lessee).[383] Thus, where the rent attributable to personalty is between 10 percent and 50 percent of the total, only the exclusion with respect to personalty is lost.[384]

As an illustration, a tax-exempt organization owns a printing facility consisting of a building housing two printing presses and other printing equipment. On January 1, 2006, the exempt organization rents the building and the printing

---

[373] See *Tax-Exempt Organizations* §§ 32.1, 32.2.

[374] *Id.* § 32.3.

[375] E.g., Rev. Rul. 58-482, 1958-2 C.B. 273 (where an exempt organization leased real property pursuant to the terms of a lease under which the organization was not a partner or other joint venturer).

[376] United States v. Myra Found., 382 F.2d 107 (8th Cir. 1967), where it was held that a private foundation that was a lessor of farmland and received a portion of the crops produced by the tenant as rent was not subject to the unrelated business income tax on the rent.

[377] IRC § 512(b)(3)(A)(i). The term *real property* means all real property, including property described in IRC §§ 1245(a)(3)(C) and 1250(c) (Reg. § 1.512(b)-1(c)(3)(i)).

[378] The term *personal property* means all personal property, including property described in IRC § 1245(a)(3)(B) (Reg. § 1.512(b)-1(c)(3)(ii)).

[379] If separate leases are entered into with respect to real and personal property, and the properties have an integrated use (for example, one or more leases for real property and another lease or leases for personal property to be used on the real property), all of the leases are treated as one lease (Reg. § 1.512(b)-1(c)(3)(iii)).

[380] IRC § 512(b)(3)(A)(ii); Reg. § 1.512(b)-1(c)(2)(ii).

[381] Property is *placed in service* by the lessee when it is first subject to its use in accordance with the terms of the lease (Reg. § 1.512(b)-1(c)(3)(iv)).

[382] Reg. § 1.512(b)-1(c)(2)(ii).

[383] IRC § 512(b)(3)(B)(i); Reg. § 1.512(b)-1(c)(2)(iii).

[384] Reg. § 1.512(b)-1(c)(2).

equipment to a person for $100,000 annually. The lease states that $90,000 of the rent is for the building and $10,000 is for the printing equipment. It is determined, however, that, the terms of the lease notwithstanding, $40,000 of the rent is in fact attributable to the printing equipment. During 2006, this exempt organization has $30,000 of deductions, all of which are properly allocable to the land and building. The exempt organization need not take into account, in computing its unrelated business taxable income, the $60,000 of rent attributable to the building and the $30,000 of deductions directly connected with that rent. By contrast, the $40,000 of rent attributable to the printing equipment is not excluded from the computation of the exempt organization's unrelated business taxable income inasmuch as that rent represents more than an incidental portion of the total rents (being 40 percent of the total).[385]

As another example, on January 1, 2006, a tax-exempt organization executed two leases with a person. One lease is for the rental of a computer system, with a stated annual rent of $7,500. The other lease is for the rental of office space in which to use the computer, at a stated annual rental of $72,500. At the time the computer system is first placed in service, taking both leases into consideration, it is determined that, the terms of the leases notwithstanding, $30,000 of the rent is in fact attributable to the computer system. Therefore, for 2006, only $50,000 of the total of $80,000 rent attributable to rental of the office space is excludable from the computation of this exempt organization's unrelated business taxable income (37.5 percent of this rent is attributable to the personal property).[386]

If (1) by reason of the placing of additional or substitute personal property in service, there is an increase of 100 percent or more in the rent attributable to all of the personal property leased, or (2) there is a modification of the lease by which there is a change in the rent charged (whether there is a change in the amount of personal property rented or not), the rent attributable to personal property must be recomputed to determine whether the exclusion, or the exception from it, applies. Any change in the treatment of rents, attributable to a recomputation under this rule, is effective only with respect to rents for the period beginning with the event which occasioned the recomputation.[387]

Another example embellishes on the facts of the previous one. The leases to which the computer system and office space are subject provide that the rent may be increased or decreased, depending on the prevailing rental value for similar systems and office space. On January 1, 2007, the total annual rent is increased in the computer system lease to $20,000 and in the office space lease to $90,000. For 2007, it is determined that, notwithstanding the terms of the leases, $60,000 of the total rent (54.5 percent of the total) is in fact attributable to the computer system as of that time. Even though the rent attributable to personal property now exceeds 50 percent of the total rent, the rent attributable to real property will continue to be excluded, since there was no modification of the terms of the leases and since the increase in the rent was not attributable to the placement of new personal property in service. Thus, for 2007, the $50,000 of

---

[385] Reg. § 1.512(b)-1(c)(2)(iv).
[386] Reg. § 1.512(b)-1(c)(4), Example (1).
[387] Reg. § 1.512(b)-1(c)(3)(v).

rent attributable to the office space continues to be excluded from the computation of the exempt organization's unrelated business taxable income.[388]

Another example is based on the example provided before the previous one. On January 1, 2008, the lessee rents additional computer equipment from the exempt organization, which is placed in service on that date. The total rent is increased to $20,000 for the computer system lease and to $100,000 for the office space lease. It is determined at the time the additional computer equipment is first placed in service that, notwithstanding the terms of the leases, $70,000 of the rent is in fact attributable to all of the computer equipment. Inasmuch as the rent attributable to personal property has increased by more than 100 percent (the increase is 133 percent), a redetermination must be made. As a result, 58.3 percent of the total rent is determined to be attributable to personal property. Accordingly, since more than 50 percent of the total rent the exempt organization receives is attributable to the personal property leased, none of the rents is excludable in computing the organization's unrelated business taxable income.[389]

This example is based on the facts of the previous one, except that on June 30, 2010, the lease is modified. The total rent for the computer system is reduced to $15,000 and the total rent for the office space lease is reduced to $75,000. A redetermination is made as of June 30, 2010; as of this modification date, it is determined that, notwithstanding the terms of the leases, the rent in fact attributable to the computer system is $40,000 (44.4 percent of the total rent). Since less than 50 percent of the total rent is now attributable to personal property, the rent attributable to real property ($50,000), for periods after June 30, 2010, is excluded from the computation of the exempt organization's unrelated business taxable income. The rent attributable to personal property ($40,000), however, is not excluded from unrelated business taxable income for the periods, since it represents more than an incidental portion of the total rent.[390]

Consequently, where all of the rental income involved in a fact situation is derived from personal property, the exclusion is not available. For example, a tax-exempt employees' trust that owned railroad tank cars leased them to an industrial company. The IRS ruled that this leasing activity was a regularly carried on business of a kind ordinarily carried on for profit, and thus was an unrelated business conducted by the trust. The exclusion for rental income was not available because the rental income was generated solely from the leasing of personal property.[391]

The IRS issues private letter rulings as to what constitutes excludable rent in this context.[392]

Unrelated debt-financed income is not subject to this exclusion,[393] however, nor is royalty income from a controlled corporation.[394]

---

[388] Reg. § 1.512(b)-1(c)(4), Example (2).

[389] *Id.*, Example (3).

[390] *Id.*, Example (4).

[391] Rev. Rul. 60-206, 1960-1 C.B. 201.

[392] E.g., Priv. Ltr. Rul. 9246032.

[393] IRC § 512(b)(4); Reg. §§ 1.512(b)-1(c)(2)(i), 1.512(b)-1(k). See § 5.10.

[394] Reg. § 1.512(b)-1(c)(2)(i). See § 5.11.

(ii) Profits-Based Income.   Notwithstanding these general rules, the exclusion for rent does not apply if the determination of the amount of the rent depends in whole or in part on the income or profits derived by any person from the property leased, other than an amount based on a fixed percentage or percentages of receipts of sales.[395]

An amount is excluded from consideration as rents from real property if, considering the lease and all of the surrounding circumstances, the arrangement does not conform with normal business practice and is in reality a means of basing the rent on income or profits.[396] This rule is intended to prevent avoidance of the unrelated business income tax where a profit-sharing arrangement would, in effect, make the lessor an active participant in the operation of the property.

As noted, an exception is provided for amounts based on a fixed percentage or percentages of sales. These amounts are customary in rental contracts and are generally considered to be different from the profit or loss of the lessee. Generally, rents received from real property are not disqualified from the exclusion solely by reason of the fact that the rent is based on a fixed percentage of total receipts or sales of the lessee. The fact that a lease is based on a percentage of total receipts, however, would not necessarily qualify the amount received or accrued as rent from real property. For example, an amount would not qualify as rent from real property if the lease provided for an amount measured by varying percentages of receipts and the arrangement did not conform with normal business practices but was used as a means of basing the rent on income or profits.[397]

This rule can be applied, for example, in determining whether income from share-crop leasing is excludable rent or taxable rental income.[398] In one of these instances, the IRS argued that, even if there was a landlord-tenant relationship, the rents were nonetheless taxable as unrelated business income because they were not in conformance with the passive rent test.[399] The agency contended that, because of the splitting of the expenditures by the tax-exempt organization/landlord, its involvement in the farming operation, and its receipt of a percentage of production as rents rather than a percentage of receipts, the exempt organization violated the passive rent test; the court disagreed. The exempt organization's rental fee was based solely on a fixed percentage of the crops. The organization shared the costs of some of the expenses related to farming; the tenant, however, bore the entire cost of damages, claims, interest, and other liabilities. The share-crop lease explicitly exonerated the exempt organization from any liability, claim, and/or damages. Thus, the court held that the crop shares to the exempt organization were excludable rental income based on a percentage of the receipts of the harvest. This, wrote the court, is the "equivalent of the tenant's reducing the crops to cash and then giving . . . [the exempt organization] its

---

[395] IRC § 512(b)(3)(B)(ii); Reg. § 1.512(b)-1(c)(2)(iii)(b).

[396] Reg. §§ 1.512(b)-1(c)(2)(iii)(b), 1.856-4(b)(3), 1.856-4(b)(6) (other than (b)(6)(ii)). The latter set of regulations is part of the rules pertaining to real estate investment trusts.

[397] Reg. § 1.856-4(b)(3).

[398] The law concerning share-crop leases in the unrelated business income tax context is the subject of *Unrelated Business* § 9.9.

[399] Trust U/W Emily Oblinger v. Comm'r, 100 T.C. 114 (1993).

share of the total receipts collected."[400] "It is not," the court continued, a "percentage of profits or net income."[401]

(iii) Rental Activity as Related Business. On occasion, rental income is derived by a tax-exempt organization from the operation of a related business, with the revenue is nontaxable for that reason. As an illustration, an exempt museum, having acquired by gift a historically significant and important aircraft, was asked to lease it back to the manufacturer of the airplane for research purposes. The aircraft was returned to the museum, repainted and with the engine-test equipment, which enhanced its value as a historical and educational artifact. A court found that this lease "significantly advanced the [m]useum's mission to restore and display historic aircraft" and made the airplane "more conducive to public display" because it was returned to the museum facility rather than a field where it was originally displayed, so that there was the requisite substantial causal relationship between the leasing activity and the advancement of exempt purposes,[402] leading to the conclusion that the rental income was exempt function revenue.[403]

In one instance, a public charity with a training program shared office space with a tax-exempt business league that owned the building, in part because the tenants of the league provided volunteer teaching faculty to the charitable organization; the charity accorded the business league the right to allow the tenants use of its research equipment in exchange for maintenance of the equipment; the IRS held that the value of the maintenance services was phantom rent that was not taxable.[404] Similarly, the IRS ruled that an exempt hospital may lease facilities to another exempt hospital, with the leasing activity constituting an exempt function, because of the direct physical connection and close professional affiliation of the institutions.[405] Likewise, the IRS ruled that an exempt charitable organization owning and operating nursing homes could lease, as a related business, a skilled nursing facility to another exempt charitable organization that owned and operated nursing homes.[406]

(h) Capital Gains

Excluded from unrelated business income taxation generally are gains from the sale, exchange, or other disposition of capital gain property.[407]

(i) General Rules. This exclusion for capital gains does not extend to dispositions of inventory or property held primarily for sale to customers in the ordinary

---

[400] *Id.* at 123.

[401] *Id.* Also Harlan E. Moore Charitable Trust v. United States, 812 F. Supp. 130 (C.D. Ill. 1993), *aff'd*, 9 F.3d 623 (7th Cir. 1993).

[402] See § 3.8(c).

[403] Museum of Flight Found. v. United States, 63 F. Supp. 2d 1257, 1260 (W.D. Wash. 1999). The court was satisfied that "failing to tax this income will not result in a rush of air and space museums clamoring to lease their historic planes" (at 1260).

[404] Priv. Ltr. Rul. 9615045.

[405] Priv. Ltr. Rul. 200314031.

[406] Priv. Ltr. Rul. 200404057.

[407] IRC § 512(b)(5); Reg. § 1.512(b)-1(d)(1). This exclusion applies with respect to "gains and losses from involuntary conversions, casualties, etc." (Reg. § 1.512(b)-(d)(1)).

course of a business; these transactions cause the seller to be regarded as a *dealer* in the property, which results in ordinary income.[408]

The IRS applies these factors in determining whether property being or to be sold has been held primarily for investment or for sale to customers in the ordinary course of business (in the latter case the resulting revenue is ordinary income rather than capital gain): the purpose for which the property was acquired; the cost of it; the activities of the owner in the improvement and disposition of the property; the extent of improvements made to the property; the proximity of the sale to the purchase; the purpose for which the property was held; prevailing market conditions; and the frequency, continuity, and size of the sales.[409]

The general exclusion for capital gains does not apply with respect to the cutting of timber, which is considered[410] as a sale or exchange of the timber.[411] The exclusion also does not apply to gain derived from the sale or other disposition of debt-financed property.[412]

The IRS issues private letter rulings as to what constitutes excludable capital gains in this context.[413]

(ii) Exception. Nonetheless, there is an exception from this second limitation[414] that excludes gains and losses from the sale, exchange, or other disposition of certain real property and mortgages acquired from financial institutions that are in conservatorship or receivership.[415] Only real property and mortgages owned by a financial institution (or held by the financial institution as security for a loan) at the time when the institution entered conservatorship or receivership are eligible for the exception.

This exclusion is limited to properties designed as *foreclosure property* within nine months of acquisition and disposed of within two and a half years of acquisition.[416] The 2.5-year disposition period may be extended by the IRS if the extension is necessary for the orderly liquidation of the property. No more than one-half by value of properties acquired in a single transaction may be designated as disposal property. This exception is not available for properties that are improved or developed to the extent that the aggregate expenditures on development do not exceed 20 percent of the net selling price of the property.[417]

(i) Research Income

Income derived from research for the United States or any of its agencies or instrumentalities or a state or political subdivision of a state, and all deductions

---

[408] IRC § 512(b)(5)(A), (B); Reg. § 1.512(b)-1(d)(1).
[409] E.g., Priv. Ltr. Rul. 9619069. See § 5.2(e).
[410] By application of IRC § 631(a).
[411] Reg. § 1.512(b)-1(d)(1).
[412] IRC § 512(b)(4); Reg. § 1.512(b)-1(d)(1); Reg. § 1.512(b)-1(k). See § 5.10.
[413] E.g., Priv. Ltr. Rul. 9247038.
[414] IRC § 512(b)(5)(B).
[415] IRC § 512(b)(16).
[416] IRC §§ 512(b)(16)(B), 514(c)(9)(H)(v).
[417] IRC § 512(b)(16)(A).

directly connected with this type of income, is excluded in computing unrelated business income.[418]

Also excluded from unrelated business income taxation is income derived from research performed for anyone, and all deductions directly connected with the income, when conducted by a tax-exempt college, university, or hospital.[419]

In the case of an organization operated primarily for the purpose of carrying on fundamental research (as distinguished from applied research) the results of which are freely available to the general public, all income derived from research performed for anyone and all deductions directly connected with the income is excluded in computing unrelated business income.[420]

According to the legislative history, the term *research* includes "not only fundamental research but also applied research such as testing and experimental construction and production."[421] With respect to the separate exemption for college, university, or hospital research, "funds received for research by other institutions [do not] necessarily represent unrelated business income," such as a grant by a corporation to a foundation to finance scientific research if the results of the research are to be made freely available to the public.[422] Without defining the term *research*, the IRS was content to find applicability of this rule because the studies involved were not "merely quality control programs or ordinary testing for certification purposes, as a final procedural step before marketing."[423]

In employing the term *research* in this context, the IRS generally looks to the body of law defining the term in relation to what is considered tax-exempt scientific research.[424] Thus, the issue is usually whether the activity is being carried on as an incident to commercial or industrial operations, such as the ordinary testing or inspection of materials or products or the designing or construction of equipment, buildings, and the like.[425] If it is, it will almost assuredly be regarded as an unrelated trade or business.[426] In one instance, the IRS found applicability of the exclusion for research because the studies undertaken by an exempt medical college in the testing of pharmaceutical products under contracts with the manufacturers were held to be more than "mere quality control programs or ordinary testing for certification purposes, as a final procedural step before marketing."[427] In another instance, the exclusion for research income was held to be applicable to contract work done by an exempt educational institution for the federal government in the field of rocketry.[428]

---

[418] IRC § 512(b)(7); Reg. § 1.512(b)-1(f)(1).

[419] IRC § 512(b)(8); Reg. § 1.512(b)-1(f)(2). Also Rev. Rul. 54-73, 1954-1 C.B. 160; IIT Research Inst. v. United States, 9 Cl. Ct. 13 (1985).

[420] IRC § 512(b)(9); Reg. § 1.512(b)-1(f)(3).

[421] H. Rep. No. 2319, 81st Cong., 2d Sess. 37 (1950).

[422] S. Rep. No. 2375, 81st Cong., 2d Sess. 30 (1950).

[423] Priv. Ltr. Rul. 7936006.

[424] Rev. Rul. 76-296, 1976-2 C.B. 141. Cf. IRC § 41 (which provides a tax credit for certain research). In general, *Tax-Exempt Organizations* § 9.2.

[425] Reg. § 1.512(b)-1(f)(4).

[426] Rev. Rul. 68-373, 1968-2 C.B. 206.

[427] Priv. Ltr. Rul. 7936006.

[428] Priv. Ltr. Rul. 7924009.

College and university audit guidelines issued by the IRS[429] included a section on research activities by these institutions. The auditing agent was directed to determine whether "purported research is actually the conduct of an activity incident to a commercial enterprise (e.g., testing, sampling or certifying of items to a known standard)"[430]; determine whether the research is conducted by the institution or by a separate entity[431]; review the institution's safeguards for managing and reporting conflicts of interest and any requirements imposed by any federal agency sponsoring research[432]; review the institution's policy regarding ownership of intellectual property[433]; review research arrangements with government sponsors and joint venture or royalty-sharing arrangements with industry sponsors[434]; determine who holds the patent or right to license technology derived from the research[435]; determine whether the institution is investing in licensee firms, either directly or through venture capital funds[436]; obtain a list of all publications that discuss the institution's research activities[437]; if the institution conducts government-funded research, review copies of audit reports from the funding agency[438]; and review sample closed research projects.[439]

The term *fundamental research* does not include research carried on for the primary purpose of commercial or industrial application.[440]

(j) Charitable Deductions

Tax-exempt organizations[441] are allowed, in computing their unrelated business taxable income (if any), a federal income tax charitable contribution deduction.[442] This deduction is allowable irrespective of whether the contribution is directly connected with the carrying on of the trade or business or not. This deduction may not exceed 10 percent of the organization's unrelated business taxable income computed without regard to the deduction.[443]

Trusts[444] are allowed a charitable contribution deduction[445]; the amount that is deductible is basically the same as that allowable pursuant to the rules applicable

---

[429] See *Tax-Exempt Organizations* § 24.8(d).
[430] College and University Audit Guidelines § 342 (10)(3).
[431] *Id.* § 342 (10)(2).
[432] *Id.* § 342 (10)(4).
[433] *Id.* § 342 (10)(5).
[434] *Id.* § 342 (10)(6)(a).
[435] *Id.* § 342 (10)(6)(b).
[436] *Id.* § 342 (10)(7).
[437] *Id.* § 342 (10)(8).
[438] *Id.* § 342 (10)(9).
[439] IRC § 512(b)(1)-(3).
[440] Reg. § 1.512(b)-1(f)(4).
[441] That is, entities described in IRC § 511(a).
[442] IRC § 512(b)(10); Reg. § 1.512(b)-1(g)(1). This deduction is provided by IRC § 170. See *Charitable Giving*, Chapter 3.
[443] IRC § 512(b)(10); Reg. § 1.512(b)-1(g)(1) (which has not been revised to reflect the increase in this percentage limitation, in 1982, from 5 to 10 percent). E.g., Independent Ins. Agents of Huntsville, Inc. v. Comm'r, 63 T.C.M. 2468 (1992), *aff'd*, 998 F.2d 898 (11th Cir. 1993) (where the percentage limitation was applied with respect to the unrelated business income of a business league).
[444] That is, trusts described in IRC § 511(b)(2).
[445] IRC § 512(b)(11); Reg. § 1.512(b)-1(g)(2).

to charitable gifts by individuals.[446] Again, a deductible charitable gift from a trust need not be directly connected to the conduct of an unrelated business.

Qualification for either of these charitable contribution deductions requires that the payments be made to another organization, rather than use of the funds by the organization in administration of its own charitable programs. For example, a tax-exempt university that operates an unrelated business is allowed this charitable deduction for contributions to another exempt university for educational purposes, but is not allowed the deduction for amounts expended in administering its own educational program.[447]

(k) Specific Deduction

In computing unrelated business taxable income, a specific deduction of $1,000 is available.[448] This deduction, however, is not allowed in computing net operating losses.[449] In the case of a diocese, province of a religious order, or a convention or association of churches, there is allowed, with respect to each parish, individual church, district, or other local unit, a specific deduction equal to the lower of $1,000 or the gross income derived from an unrelated business regularly carried on by such an entity.[450] This deduction is intended to eliminate imposition of the unrelated income tax in cases where the exaction of it would involve excessive costs of collection in relation any payments received by the government.[451]

(l) Net Operating Losses

The net operating loss deduction[452] is allowed in computing unrelated business taxable income.[453] The net operating loss carryback or carryover (from a tax year for which the exempt organization is subject to the unrelated business income tax) is determined under the net operating loss deduction rules without taking into account any amount of income or deduction that is not included under the unrelated business income tax rules in computing unrelated business taxable income. For example, a loss attributable to an unrelated trade or business is not to be diminished by reason of the receipt of dividend income.[454]

For the purpose of computing the net operating loss deduction, any prior tax year for which a tax-exempt organization was not subject to the unrelated business income tax may not be taken into account. Thus, if the organization was not subject to this tax for a preceding tax year, the net operating loss is not a carryback

---

[446] In applying the percentage limitations, the contribution base is determined by reference to the organization's unrelated business taxable income (computed with the charitable deduction), rather than by reference to adjusted gross income. See *Charitable Giving* § 7.2.

[447] Reg. § 1.512(b)-1(g)(3).

[448] IRC § 512(b)(12); Reg. § 1.512(b)-1(h)(1). The IRS rejected the proposition that, when a tax-exempt organization is engaged in two or more unrelated businesses, there is a specific deduction with respect to each business (Rev. Rul. 68-536, 1968-2 C.B. 244).

[449] *Id.* See § 5.9(l).

[450] IRC § 512(b)(12); Reg. § 1.512(b)-1(h)(2).

[451] H. Rep. No. 2319, 81st Cong., 2d Sess. 37 (1950); S. Rep. No. 2375, 81st Cong., 2d Sess. 30 (1950).

[452] IRC § 172.

[453] IRC § 512(b)(6); Reg. § 1.512(b)-1(e)(1).

[454] Reg. § 1.512(b)-1(e)(1).

to such preceding tax year, and the net operating loss carryover to succeeding tax years is not reduced by the taxable income for such preceding tax year.[455]

A net operating loss carryback or carryover is allowed only from a tax year for which the exempt organization is subject to the unrelated business income tax rules.[456] In determining the span of years for which a net operating loss may be carried for purposes of the net operating loss deduction rules, tax years in which an exempt organization was not subject to the unrelated business income tax regime may be taken into account. For example, if an exempt organization is subject to the unrelated business income tax rules for the tax year 2001 and has a net operating loss for that year, the last tax year to which any part thereof may be carried over is the tax year 2006, irrespective of whether the organization was subject to the unrelated business income tax rules in any of the intervening tax years.[457]

(m) Businesses Conducted by Volunteers

Exempt from the scope of unrelated trade or business is an endeavor in which substantially all of the work in carrying on the business is performed for the tax-exempt organization without compensation.[458] An example of applicability of this exception is an exempt orphanage operating a secondhand clothing store and selling to the general public, where substantially all of the work in operating the store is performed for the organization by volunteers.[459] Another illustration of this rule is the production and sale of phonograph records by a medical society, where the services of the performers were provided without compensation.[460] Still another illustration of this exception concerned a trade association that sold advertising in a commercial, unrelated manner, but avoided unrelated income taxation of the activity because the work involved was provided solely by volunteers.[461] Further, when an advisory council to an exempt insurance board serving a municipal board of education received brokerage commissions, which were required to be deposited in a special fund for public purposes, the income was not taxable to the board as unrelated business income inasmuch as all of the work of the council members was performed without compensation.[462]

As to the scope of this exception, Congress apparently intended to provide an exclusion from the definition of unrelated trade or business only for those unrelated business activities in which the performance of services is a material income-producing factor in carrying on the business and substantially all of the services are performed without compensation.[463] Relying on the legislative history underlying this rule, the IRS ruled that the rental of heavy machinery under long-term lease agreements requiring the lessees to provide insurance, pay the

---

[455] Reg. § 1.512(b)-1(e)(2).
[456] Reg. § 1.512(b)-1(e)(3).
[457] Reg. § 1.512(b)-1(e)(4).
[458] IRC § 513(a)(1); Reg. § 1.513-1(e)(1).
[459] Reg. § 1.513-1(e); S. Rep. No. 2375, 81st Cong., 2d Sess. 108 (1950).
[460] Greene County Med. Soc'y Found. v. United States, 345 F. Supp. 900 (W.D. Mo. 1972).
[461] Priv. Ltr. Rul. 9302023.
[462] Rev. Rul. 56-152, 1956-1 C.B. 56.
[463] H. Rep. No. 2319, 81st Cong., 2d Sess. 37 (1950); S. Rep. No. 2375, 81st Cong. 2d Sess. 107–108 (1950).

applicable taxes, and make and pay for most repairs, with the functions of securing leases and processing rental payments performed without compensation, was not an unrelated trade or business excluded under this exception since there was "no significant amount of labor regularly required or involved in the kind of business carried on by the organization," and thus the performance of services in connection with the leasing activity was not a material income-producing factor in the business.[464]

A membership entity of a tax-exempt art museum published and sold a book containing recipes, all of which were contributed. Inasmuch as substantially all of the work in preparing and selling the cookbook was performed by volunteers, the IRS ruled that the activity was not an unrelated business, by reason of this exception.[465]

A court ruled that this exception was defeated in part because free drinks provided to the collectors and cashiers in connection with the conduct of a bingo game by a tax-exempt organization were considered "liquid compensation."[466] This position was, however, rejected on appeal.[467] This court subsequently held that this exception was not available, in the case of an exempt organization that regularly carried on gambling activities, because the dealers and other individuals received tips from patrons of the games.[468] In another case, this court found that an exempt religious order that operated a farm was not taxable on the income derived from the farming operations because the farm was maintained by the uncompensated labor of the members of the order.[469]

For an activity to be eligible for this exception, it must be carried on by the tax-exempt organization. This dichotomy can arise when an exempt organization outsources one or more functions.[470]

The matter of *substantiality* does not arise, of course, where all of the work in conducting the business is performed without compensation.[471] Where there are one or more compensated persons (whether as employees or independent contractors), substantiality is generally assessed in terms of time expended. Although the term *substantially all* is not defined in this setting, it is defined in other contexts to mean at least 85 percent; the IRS follows that rule when applying the volunteer exception.[472]

The volunteer exception was held by a court to be unavailable where 77 percent of the services were provided to a tax-exempt organization without compensation.[473] By contrast, another court ruled that the exception was available where the volunteer services amounted to 94 percent of total hours worked.[474]

---

[464] Rev. Rul. 78-144, 1978-1 C.B. 168.

[465] Tech. Adv. Mem. 8211002.

[466] Waco Lodge No. 166, Benevolent & Protective Order of Elks v. Comm'r, 42 T.C.M. 1202 (1981).

[467] 696 F.2d 372 (5th Cir. 1983).

[468] Executive Network Club, Inc. v. Comm'r, 69 T.C.M. 1680 (1995).

[469] St. Joseph Farms of Ind. Bros. of the Congregation of Holy Cross, Southwest Province, Inc. v. Comm'r, 85 T.C. 9 (1985), *app. dis.* (7th Cir. 1986).

[470] E.g., Tech. Adv. Mem. 8041007.

[471] E.g., Rev. Rul. 74-361, 1974-2 C.B. 159.

[472] E.g., Tech. Adv. Mem. 8433010.

[473] Waco Lodge No. 166, Benevolent & Protective Order of Elks v. Comm'r, 696 F.2d 372 (5th Cir. 1983).

[474] St. Joseph Farms of Ind. Bros. of the Congregation of Holy Cross, Southwest Province, Inc. v. Comm'r, 85 T.C. 9 (1985).

The IRS ruled that the exception is available where the percentage of volunteer labor was 87 percent,[475] 91 percent,[476] and 97 percent.[477]

This exception references receipt of *compensation*. Thus, individuals who do not receive any economic benefits in exchange for their services to a tax-exempt organization are uncompensated workers (volunteers).[478] Mere reimbursement of expenses incurred by volunteers is not compensation.[479] Economic benefits, however, can be considered compensation, even if not formally cast as a salary or fee-for-service,[480] unless they are incidental.[481] In some circumstances, non-monetary benefits can constitute compensation.[482]

(n) Trade Shows

(i) General Rules. Activities that promote demand for industry products and services, such as advertising and other promotional activities, generally constitute unrelated businesses if carried on for the production of income. The federal tax law provides what the IRS termed a "narrow exception" in this context,[483] for certain tax-exempt organizations that conduct industry-promotion activities in connection with a convention, annual meeting, or trade show. This exception with respect to trade show activities[484] is available for qualifying organizations, namely, exempt labor, agricultural, and horticultural organizations, business leagues,[485] and charitable and social welfare organizations[486] that regularly conduct, as a substantial exempt purpose, shows that stimulate interest in and demand for the products of a particular industry or segment of industry or that educate persons in attendance regarding new developments or products or services related to the exempt activities of the organization.[487] This provision overruled contrary IRS determinations.[488]

Under these rules, the term *unrelated trade or business* does not include qualified convention and trade show activities of an eligible organization.[489] The

---

[475] Priv. Ltr. Rul. 7806039.

[476] Priv. Ltr. Rul. 9544029.

[477] Tech. Adv. Mem. 8040014.

[478] E.g., Tech. Adv. Mem. 8211002.

[479] E.g., Greene County Med. Soc'y Found. v. United States, 345 F. Supp. 900 (W.D. Mo. 1972).

[480] E.g., Executive Network Club, Inc. v. Comm'r, 69 T.C.M. 1680 (1995).

[481] E.g., Waco Lodge No. 166, Benevolent & Protective Order of Elks v. Comm'r, 696 F.2d 372, 375 (5th Cir. 1983) (free drinks were considered a "trifling inducement").

[482] Occasionally, the availability of this exception goes to the matter of an organization's tax-exempt status (e.g., South Community Ass'n v. Comm'r, 90 T.C.M. 568 (2005), where an organization had its exempt status revoked when it was discovered that individuals involved in gaming activities, which were regularly carried on (see § 5.5), were surreptitiously compensated).

[483] Rev. Rul. 2004-112, 2004-51 I.R.B. 985.

[484] IRC § 513(d)(1), (3); Reg. § 1.513-3(a)(1), (b).

[485] IRC § 501(c)(5), (6). See § 1.6(c)-(e).

[486] IRC § 501(c)(3), (4). See (as to social welfare organizations) § 1.6(a).

[487] IRC § 513(d)(3)(C).

[488] Rev. Ruls. 75-516–75-520, 1975-2 C.B. 220-226 (holding, *inter alia*, that income received by an exempt business league at its convention or trade show from renting display space may constitute unrelated business income if selling by exhibitors is permitted at the show). Also Rev. Rul. 67-219, 1967-1 C.B. 210; Rev. Rul. 58-224, 1958-1 C.B. 242. Subsequently, these rulings were revoked or rendered obsolete by the IRS (Rev. Rul. 85-123, 1985-2 C.B. 168).

[489] IRC § 513(d)(1).

phrase *convention, annual meeting, or trade show* is defined to mean any "activity of a kind traditionally conducted at conventions, annual meetings, or trade shows, including but not limited to, any activity one of the purposes of which is to attract persons in an industry generally (without regard to membership in the sponsoring organization) as well as members of the public to the show for the purpose of displaying industry products or services, or to educate persons engaged in the industry in the development of new products and services or new rules and regulations affecting the industry."[490] This term thus refers to a "specific event at which individuals representing a particular industry and members of the general public gather in person at one location during a certain period of time."[491]

A *qualified convention and trade show activity* is a convention and trade show activity that is (1) carried on by a qualifying organization; (2) conducted in conjunction with an international, national, state, regional, or local convention, annual meeting, or show; (3) sponsored by a qualifying organization that has as one of its purposes in sponsoring the activity the promotion and stimulation of interest in and demand for the products and services of the industry involved in general or the education of persons in attendance regarding new developments or products and services related to the exempt activities of the organization; and (4) designed to achieve this purpose through the character of the exhibits and the extent of the industry products displayed.[492] It is the nature of the activities and their connection to a specific convention, annual meeting, and trade show that distinguishes qualified convention and trade show activity from other types of advertising and promotional activities conducted for the benefit of an industry.[493] Thus, as an example of such qualified activity, an exempt business league conducted semiannual trade shows at an exhibition facility, with each of the shows occurring over a period of 10 consecutive days.[494]

The income that is excluded from taxation by these rules is derived from the rental of display space to exhibitors. This is the case even though the exhibitors who rent the space are permitted to sell or solicit orders, as long as the show is a qualified trade show or a qualified convention and trade show.[495] This exclusion is also available with respect to a supplier's exhibit[496] that is conducted by a qualifying organization in conjunction with a qualified convention or trade show.

As an illustration, an exempt business league, formed to promote the construction industry, had as its membership manufacturers of heavy construction machinery, many of whom own, rent, or lease one or more digital computers produced by various computer manufacturers. This organization was a qualifying one that regularly holds an annual meeting. At this meeting, a national

---

[490] IRC § 513(d)(3)(A); Reg. § 1.513-3(c)(4).
[491] Rev. Rul. 2004-112, 2004-51 I.R.B. 985.
[492] IRC § 513(d)(3)(B); Reg. § 1.513-3(c)(2).
[493] Rev. Rul. 2004-112, 2004-51 I.R.B. 985.
[494] *Id.*
[495] Reg. § 1.513-3(d)(1).
[496] A *suppliers' exhibit* is one in which the exhibitors display goods or services that are supplied to, rather than by, the members of the qualifying organization in the conduct of the members' own trades or businesses (Reg. § 1.513-3(d)(2)).

industry sales campaign and methods of consumer financing for heavy construction machinery were discussed. Also, new construction machinery developed for use in the industry was on display, with representatives of the various manufacturers present to promote their machinery. Both members and nonmembers attended this portion of the conference. In addition, manufacturers of computers were present to educate the organization's members. While this aspect of the conference was a supplier's exhibit, the income earned from this activity did not constitute unrelated business income to the business league because the activity was conducted as part of a qualified trade show.[497]

Another illustration is based on the facts in the preceding one, except that the only goods or services displayed are those of suppliers, namely, the computer manufacturers. Order-taking and selling was permitted. Member exhibits were not maintained. Taken alone, this supplier's exhibit would have constituted a supplier show and not a qualified convention or trade show. In this situation, however, the rental of exhibition space to suppliers was not an unrelated business. It was conducted by a qualifying organization in conjunction with a qualified convention or trade show. The show (the annual meeting) was a qualified convention or trade show because one of its purposes was the promotion and stimulation of interest in and demand for the products or services of the industry through the character of the annual meeting.[498]

In another example, an exempt business league conducted an annual show at which its members exhibit their products and services in order to promote public interest in the line of business. Potential customers are invited to the show; order-taking and sales were permitted. The organization secured the exhibition facility, undertook the planning and direction of the show, and maintained exhibits designed to promote the line of business in general. The show was a qualified convention or trade show; the provision of exhibit space to individual members was a qualified trade show activity, and not an unrelated business.[499]

Another illustration concerned an exempt business league that sponsored an annual show. As the sole activity of the show, suppliers to the members of the organization exhibited their products and services for the purpose of stimulating the sale of these products and services. Order-taking and selling were permitted. This show was a supplier's show and did not meet the definition of a qualified convention show in that it did not satisfy any of the three alternative bases for qualification.

1. The show did not stimulate interest in the members' products through the character of product exhibits inasmuch as the only products exhibited were those of suppliers, not members.

2. The show did not stimulate interest in members' products through conferences or seminars as these activities were not conducted at the show.

---

[497] Reg. § 1.513-3(e), Example (1).
[498] *Id.*, Example (2).
[499] *Id.*, Example (3).

3. The show did not meet the definition of a qualified show on the basis of educational activities as the exhibition of suppliers' products was designed primarily to stimulate interest in and the sale of suppliers' products.

Thus, the organization's provision of exhibition space was not a qualified convention or trade show activity; income derived from the rentals of exhibition space to suppliers was unrelated business income.[500] Nonetheless, income from a suppliers' show is not unrelated business income where the displays are educational in nature and are displays at which soliciting and selling are prohibited.[501]

An aspect of this matter may resolve the tax issue for many tax-exempt organizations not expressly covered by these rules. This aspect relates to the fact that an unrelated business must be *regularly carried on* before the revenue from the business can be regarded as unrelated business income.[502] Thus, the net income derived by an exempt organization (irrespective of the statutory basis for its tax exemption) from the conduct of a trade show cannot be taxable as unrelated business income if the trade show is not regularly carried on. A court opinion provides support for the premise that the conduct of a typical trade show is not an activity that is regularly carried on.[503] This court held that an exempt organization that annually sponsored a vaudeville show did not generate any unrelated business income from the activity because the show was not regularly carried on—rather, it was an "intermittent activity."[504] Consequently, to the extent that an annual trade or similar show of an exempt organization can be regarded as an intermittent activity, it would not give rise to unrelated business income, irrespective of the exempt status of the organization and without regard to invocation of these special rules. It must be noted, however, that in measuring regularity, the IRS sometimes looks not only to the time expended in conducting the activity itself but also to the time expended in preparing for the activity and any time expended after, yet related to, the activity.[505]

A tax-exempt organization may sponsor and perform educational and supporting services for a trade show (such as use of its name, promotion of attendance, planning of exhibits and demonstrations, and provision of lectures for the exhibits and demonstrations) without having the compensation for its efforts taxed as unrelated business income, as long as the trade show is not a sales facility.[506] The IRS ruled that this type of activity both stimulates interest in and demand for services of the profession involved (the organization being an exempt business league) and educates the members on matters of professional interest.

---

[500] *Id.*, Example (4). The legislative history of these statutory rules suggests, however, that the exclusion is applicable with respect to shows that are suppliers' shows in their entirety (S. Rep. No. 94-938, 94th Cong., 2d Sess. 601-603 (1976)).

[501] Rev. Rul. 75-516, 1975-2 C.B. 220. In general, Fones, "Taxation of Trade Shows and Public Entertainment Activities," 64 *A.B.A.J.* 913 (1978).

[502] See § 5.5.

[503] Suffolk County Patrolmen's Benevolent Ass'n, Inc. v. Comm'r, 77 T.C. 1314 (1982).

[504] *Id.* at 1321, 1322.

[505] See § 5.5(d).

[506] Rev. Rul. 78-240, 1978-1 C.B. 170.

(ii) Virtual Trade Shows. The IRS issued guidance as to when Internet activities conducted by qualifying organizations (or at least tax-exempt business leagues) fall within this exception for qualified convention and trade-show activity. The agency held that activities conducted on the premises of exempt business league's trade shows, and on a special section of the organization's Web site that allows members and the interested public to access the same information available at the show, constituted qualified convention and trade-show activity. Each show occurred over a consecutive 10-day period, and the special section of the Web site was available online during that period as well as during a three-day period prior to the show and a three-day period following the show. The IRS cast these Web site sections, each of which thus lasted 16 days, as an "alternative medium," and characterized these online activities as being carried out in conjunction with, ancillary to, and as an extension of each show. If, however, this type of Internet activity does not overlap or coincide with an exempt organization's international, national, regional, state, or local convention, annual meeting, or trade show, or augment or enhance such a show—such as a Web site posting trade show–type information available to the general public 24 hours a day, seven days a week, for a two-week period—the Internet activity will be ineligible for the trade show–activity exception. Moreover, this type of site itself is not a convention, annual meeting, or trade show, because it is not a "specific event" at which an exempt organization's members, suppliers, and potential customers gather in person at a physical location during a certain period of time and have face-to-face interaction.[507]

(o) Gambling Activities

In general, gambling activities by tax-exempt organizations constitute unrelated business. Bingo game income realized by most exempt organizations, however, is not subject to unrelated business income taxation.[508] This exclusion applies only where the bingo game is not conducted on a commercial basis and where the game does not violate state or local laws.[509]

More specifically, this exception is not available with respect to a bingo game conducted in a jurisdiction in which bingo games are ordinarily carried out on a commercial basis. Bingo games are "ordinarily carried out on a commercial basis" within a jurisdiction if they are regularly carried on[510] by for-profit organizations in any part of that jurisdiction. Normally, the entire state will constitute the appropriate jurisdiction for determining whether bingo games are ordinarily carried out on a commercial basis. If, however, state law permits local jurisdictions to determine whether bingo games may be conducted by for-profit organizations or if state law limits or confines the conduct

---

[507] Rev. Rul. 2004-112, 2004-2 C.B. 985. Because this type of Web site activity usually is conducted over what this ruling referred to as a "relatively short period of time," it is likely to avoid unrelated business taxation because it is not regularly carried on (see § 5.5).

[508] IRC § 513(f); Reg. § 1.513-5(a). The rules pertaining to this exception are inapplicable with respect to a bingo game otherwise excluded from consideration as an unrelated business because substantially all of the work is performed without compensation (Reg. § 1.513-5(b)).

[509] Reg. § 1.513-5(c); H. Rep. No. 95-1608, 95th Cong. 2d Sess. 7-8 (1978).

[510] See § 5.5.

by for-profit organizations to specific local jurisdictions, then the local jurisdiction will constitute the appropriate jurisdiction for determining whether bingo games are ordinarily carried out on a commercial basis.[511]

For example, this exception was held to be unavailable because the bingo game in question was illegal under state law as being a lottery.[512] Absent this exception, then, bingo game operations of exempt organizations would be treated as the conduct of unrelated business.[513] Indeed, the argument that the operation of bingo games does not amount to the conduct of business was rejected by a court.[514]

A *bingo game* is a game of chance played with cards that are generally printed with five rows of five squares each. Participants place markers over randomly called numbers on the cards in an attempt to form a preselected pattern, such as a horizontal, vertical, or diagonal line, or all four corners. The first participant to form the preselected pattern is the winner of the game. The term *bingo game* means any game of bingo in which all wagers are placed, all winners are determined, and all prizes or other property are distributed in the presence of all persons placing wagers in that game.[515] Consequently, the term does not refer to any other game of chance, such as keno games, dice games, card games, and lotteries[516]; the conduct of a "pull-tab operation" is not embraced by the exception.[517] This view as to the scope of the definition of the term was reflected in a court opinion holding that proceeds attributable to an organization's "instant bingo" activities were not protected by the exception inasmuch as individuals could play and win in isolation.[518]

The reach of this exception is illustrated by this illustration.[519] A tax-exempt church conducted weekly bingo games in a state where state and local laws provide that bingo games may be conducted by exempt organizations. For-profit businesses do not conduct bingo games in the state. Inasmuch as the church's bingo games are not conducted in violation of state or local law and are not the type of activity ordinarily carried out on a commercial basis in the state, these bingo games are not regarded as unrelated business.[520]

As another illustration, an exempt rescue squad conducts weekly bingo games in a state that has a statute prohibiting all forms of gambling, including bingo games. This law, however, is not generally enforced by state officials against local charitable organizations, such as the rescue squad, that conduct bingo games to raise funds. Nonetheless, since bingo games are illegal under

---

[511] Reg. § 1.513-5(c)(2).

[512] Waco Lodge No. 166, Benevolent & Protective Order of Elks v. Comm'r, 42 T.C.M. 1202 (1981).

[513] E.g., Clarence LaBelle Post No. 217, Veterans of Foreign Wars of the United States v. United States, 580 F.2d 270 (8th Cir. 1978).

[514] Smith-Dodd Businessman's Ass'n, Inc. v. Comm'r, 65 T.C. 620 (1975).

[515] Reg. § 1.513-5(d).

[516] *Id.*

[517] Tech. Adv. Mem. 8602001.

[518] Julius M. Israel Lodge of B'nai B'rith No. 2113 v. Comm'r, 70 T.C.M. 673 (1995), *aff'd*, 98 F.3d 190 (5th Cir. 1996).

[519] This example and the two that follow assume that the bingo games referred to are operated by individuals who are compensated for their services (see § 5.9(m)).

[520] Reg. § 1.513-5(c)(3), Example (1).

this state's law, these bingo games constitute unrelated business, irrespective of the degree to which this state law is enforced.[521]

In another example, two exempt veterans' organizations operate in a state the statutes of which permit the conduct of bingo games by tax-exempt organizations. This state's law also permits bingo games to be conducted by for-profit organizations in a particular city, which is a resort community. Several for-profit organizations conduct nightly bingo games in this city. One of these veterans' organizations also conducts weekly bingo games in this city. The other veterans' organization conducts weekly bingo games in the county in which this city is located. Since state law confines the conduct of bingo games by for-profit organizations to this city and since bingo games are regularly carried on there by these organizations, the bingo games conducted by the veterans' organization in that city constitute unrelated business. By contrast, the bingo games conducted by the other veterans' organization in the county, and outside of this city, are not regarded as unrelated business.[522]

The term *unrelated trade or business* does not include any trade or business that consists of the conduct of games of chance, conducted after June 30, 1981, which, under state law (in effect as of October 5, 1983), can be conducted only by nonprofit organizations.[523] This exception, however, is applicable only with respect to the law of the state of North Dakota.[524]

(p) Associate Member Dues

An issue for tax-exempt associations can be the tax treatment of dues derived from associate members (or affiliate or patron members), although the intensity of activity in this area has declined in recent years. In some instances, these dues are treated as forms of unrelated business income, on the ground that the associate member is paying for a specific service or to gain access to the regular membership for purposes of selling products or services. Thus, in one instance, the agency's lawyers recommended taxation of associate members' dues, where the associates allegedly joined solely to obtain coverage under the association's automobile, health, dental, and farm owners' insurance programs.[525] In another instance, IRS legal counsel recommended taxation as advertising income of the dues paid by associate members for listings in a variety of publications, allegedly to make them accessible to the regular members; the IRS creatively recast the dues as *access fees*.[526] Taxation of dues is more likely where the associate

---

[521] *Id.*, Example (2).

[522] *Id.*, Example (3).

[523] Tax Reform Act of 1984 § 311.

[524] Tax Reform Act of 1986 § 1834. This clarification in 1986 would have caused retroactive taxation of this type of revenue derived by tax-exempt organizations in states other than North Dakota. The Technical Corrections and Miscellaneous Revenue Act of 1988 (§ 6201), however, made the 1986 clarification effective for games of chance conducted after October 22, 1986 (the date of enactment of the 1986 technical correction), so that revenue derived by exempt organizations from games of chance conducted prior to the 1986 effective date in any state is governed by the rules enacted in 1984. The IRS issued an explanation of the law on this point (Ann. 89-138, 1989-45 I.R.B. 41).

[525] Tech. Adv. Mem. 9416002.

[526] Tech. Adv. Mem. 9345004.

members do not receive exempt function benefits, cannot serve as directors or officers, may not vote on association matters, or otherwise lack any meaningful right or opportunity to participate in the affairs of the organization.

The first court opinion on the point held that dues collected by a tax-exempt labor organization from persons who were not regular active members of the organization, who became members so as to be able to participate in a health insurance plan sponsored by the organization, constituted unrelated business income.[527] The court concluded that this special class of members was created to generate revenue and not to contribute importantly to an exempt purpose. The fact that the organization generated substantial net revenues through the sale of these memberships was considered evidence that revenue-raising was the principal intent underlying the establishment of the membership category.

The IRS stated that, in the case of tax-exempt labor, agricultural, and horticultural organizations,[528] dues payments from associate members will not be regarded as unrelated business income unless, for the relevant period, the membership category was formed or availed of for the principal purpose of producing unrelated income.[529] This aspect of the law was subsequently altered by statute, however, in that certain dues payments to exempt agricultural or horticultural organizations are exempt from unrelated business income taxation.[530] Specifically, if a tax-exempt agricultural or horticultural organization[531] requires annual dues not exceeding $100 (indexed for inflation[532]) to be paid in order to be a member of the organization, no portion of the dues may be considered unrelated business income because of any benefits or privileges to which these members are entitled.[533]

The term *dues* is defined for this purpose as any "payment required to be made in order to be recognized by the organization as a member of the organization."[534] If a person makes a single payment that entitles the person to be recognized as a member of the organization for more than 12 months, the payment can be prorated for purposes of applying the $100 cap.[535]

Nonetheless, this IRS position continues to be its view with respect to labor organizations (and to agricultural and horticultural entities that do not qualify

---

[527] Nat'l League of Postmasters v. Comm'r, 69 T.C.M. 2569 (1995), aff'd, 86 F.3d 59 (4th Cir. 1996).

[528] See § 1.6(c)–(e).

[529] Rev. Proc. 95-21, 1995-1 C.B. 686.

[530] See *Unrelated Business* § 9.4(c).

[531] See *Tax-Exempt Organizations* §§ 15.2, 15.3.

[532] IRC § 512(d)(2). For years beginning in 1998, this threshold was $109 (Rev. Proc. 97-57, 1997-2 C.B. 584); for years beginning in 1999, this threshold was $110 (Rev. Proc. 98-61, 1998-2 C.B. 811); for years beginning in 2000, this threshold was $112 (Rev. Proc. 99-42, 1999-2 C.B. 568); for years beginning in 2001, this threshold was $116 (Rev. Proc. 2001-13, 2001-1 C.B. 337); for years beginning in 2002, this threshold was $120 (Rev. Proc. 2001-59, 2001-2 C.B. 623); for years beginning in 2003, this threshold was $122 (Rev. Proc. 2002-70, 2002-2 C.B. 845); for years beginning in 2004, this threshold was $124 (Rev. Proc. 2003-85, 203-49 I.R.B. 1184); for years beginning in 2005, this threshold is $127 (Rev. Proc. 2004-71, 2004-71 I.R.B. 970); and for years beginning in 2006, this threshold is $131 (Rev. Proc. 2005-70, 2005-47 I.R.B. 979).

[533] IRC § 512(d)(1).

[534] IRC § 512(d)(3).

[535] H. Rep. No. 104-737, 104th Cong., 2d Sess. 14 (1996).

for the exception); moreover, the agency indicated that it will follow this approach with respect to associations generally.[536]

(q) Low-Cost Articles

Another exception from classification as unrelated business is available only to tax-exempt organizations eligible to receive tax-deductible charitable contributions,[537] for activities relating to certain distributions of low-cost articles incidental to the solicitation of charitable contributions.[538] While this statutory provision is generally reflective of a similar rule stated in the income tax regulations,[539] there is one important refinement, which is that the term *low-cost article* is defined as any article (or aggregate of articles distributed to a single distributee in a year) that has a cost not in excess of $5 (adjusted for inflation[540]) to the organization that distributes the item or on behalf of which the item is distributed.[541] These rules also require that the distribution of the items be unsolicited and be accompanied by a statement that the distributee may retain the low-cost article irrespective of whether a charitable contribution is made.[542]

(r) Mailing Lists

Another exception from unrelated business income taxation available to the category of tax-exempt organizations eligible for the low-cost articles exception[543] is applicable to the exchanging or renting of membership or donor mailing lists with or to others of these exempt organizations.[544]

Absent this exception, however, the rental or exchange of a mailing list by a tax-exempt organization, when regularly carried on, is considered by the IRS to

---

[536] Rev. Proc. 97-12, 1997-1 C.B. 631, *mod.* Rev. Proc. 95-21, 1995-1 C.B. 686. Associate member dues received by an exempt association were found to not be taxable because the associate member category was not formed or availed of for the principal purpose of producing unrelated business income; voting rights were held to not be the sole criterion in this evaluation (Tech. Adv. Mem. 9742001). Associate member dues received by an exempt union were, however, held taxable as unrelated business income because the membership category was availed of for the principal purpose of producing this type of income (Tech. Adv. Mem. 9751001).

[537] That is, an organization described in IRC § 501, where it qualifies as a charitable donee under IRC § 170(c)(2) or § 170(c)(3) (namely, as a charitable or veterans' organization).

[538] IRC § 513(h)(1)(A).

[539] Reg. § 1.513-1(b).

[540] IRC § 513(h)(2)(C). The IRS calculated that the low-cost article cost threshold was $5.71 for years beginning in 1991 and $6.01 for years beginning in 1992 (Rev. Proc. 92-58, 1992-2 C.B. 410); was $6.20 for years beginning in 1993 (Rev. Proc. 92-102, 1992-2 C.B. 579); was $6.40 for years beginning in 1994 (Rev. Proc. 93-49, 1993-2 C.B. 581); was $6.60 for years beginning in 1995 (Rev. Proc. 94-72, 1994-2 C.B. 811); was $6.70 for years beginning in 1996 (Rev. Proc. 95-53, 1995-2 C.B. 445); was $6.90 for years beginning in 1997 (Rev. Proc. 96-59, 1996-2 C.B. 390); was $7.10 for years beginning in 1998 (Rev. Proc. 97-57, 1997-2 C.B. 584); was $7.20 for years beginning in 1999 (Rev. Proc. 98-61, 1998-2 C.B. 811); was $7.40 for years beginning in 2000 (Rev. Proc. 99-42, 1999-2 C.B. 568); was $7.60 for years beginning in 2001 (Rev. Proc. 2001-13, 2001-1 C.B. 337); was $7.90 for years beginning in 2002 (Rev. Proc. 2001-59, 2001-2 C.B. 623); was $8.00 for years beginning in 2003 (Rev. Proc. 2002-70, 2002-2 C.B. 845); was $8.20 for years beginning in 2004 (Rev. Proc. 2003-85, 2003-49 I.R.B. 1184); was $8.30 for years beginning in 2005 (Rev. Proc. 2004-71, 2004-50 I.R.B. 970); and is $8.60 for years beginning in 2006 (Rev. Proc. 2005-70, 2005-47 I.R.B. 979).

[541] IRC § 513(h)(2).

[542] IRC § 513(h)(3).

[543] See § 5.9(q).

[544] IRC § 513(h)(1)(B). The purpose of this provision is to nullify the decision in Disabled Am. Veterans v. United States, 650 F.2d 1178 (Ct. Cl. 1981). Also Disabled Am. Veterans v. Comm'r, 68 T.C. 95 (1994).

be an unrelated business. This is not a major problem from an economic stand-point when the activity involves a list rental,[545] in that taxes can be paid from the resulting income. When the activity is a list exchange, however, there is no income from the transaction available to pay the tax; it is nonetheless the view of the agency that these exchanges are unrelated businesses.[546] In calculating the amount of "income" of this nature, the IRS advised that the method to use should be in accordance with the rules concerning facilities used for related and unrelated purposes; thus, expenses and deductions are to be allocated between the two uses on a reasonable basis.[547] According to the agency, the "actual calcu-lating of the costs and expenses associated with or allocable to the rental or exchange activities and the income they generate is a factual determination."[548]

If properly structured, however, a mailing list rental or exchange program involving a noncharitable tax-exempt organization can avoid unrelated business treatment by utilization of the exception for royalties.[549]

(s) S Corporation Holdings and Sales

Nearly all types of tax-exempt organizations are barred by the federal tax law from holding interests in small business corporations, also known as an *S corpo-rations*. There is, however, an exception in this regard for exempt charitable orga-nizations; these entities are allowed to be shareholders in these corporations.[550] The authorization to own this type of a security is a revision of prior law.[551]

This type of interest is considered an interest in an unrelated business.[552] Items of income, loss, or deduction of an S corporation flow through to these exempt organizations as unrelated business income, irrespective of the source or nature of the income.[553] Thus, for example, unlike the partnership rules,[554] pas-sive income of a small business corporation automatically flows to an exempt charitable organization as unrelated business income.

If a charitable organization has acquired by purchase stock in a small busi-ness corporation (whether the stock was acquired when the corporation was a regular corporation—known as a C corporation—or an S corporation) and

---

[545] Rev. Rul. 72-431, 1972-2 C.B. 281.

[546] Tech. Adv. Mem. 9502009.

[547] See *Unrelated Business* § 11.2.

[548] In Tech. Adv. Mem. 9502009, the IRS ruled that these exchanges are not a disposition of property causing the realization of gain or loss for tax purposes (IRC § 1001), in that capital assets (IRC § 1222) are not involved; this holding precluded application of the exception from income taxation for capital gains (see § 5.9(h)). The agency also held that the nontaxation rules concerning like-kind exchanges (IRC § 1031) are inapplicable, be-cause the title to the lists does not pass and the rights to the properties acquired by the parties are not perpetual (Koch v. Comm'r, 37 T.C.M. 1167 (1978); Rev. Rul. 55-749, 1955-2 C.B. 295). An earlier technical advice memorandum, concluding that exchanges of mailing lists between tax-exempt organizations did not give rise to unrelated business income (Tech. Adv. Mem. 8128004), was thereafter revoked by the IRS on a prospective basis (Tech. Adv. Mem. 9635001).

[549] E.g., Sierra Club, Inc. v. Comm'r, 86 F.3d 1526 (9th Cir. 1996). Also American Academy of Ophthalmology, Inc. v. Comm'r (Tax Ct. No. 21657-94) (where the IRS abandoned its mailing list revenue taxation stance in the aftermath of the *Sierra Club* holding).

[550] This exception is also available for employee benefit entities described in IRC § 401(a).

[551] IRC § 1361(c)(6).

[552] IRC § 512(e)(1)(A).

[553] IRC § 512(e)(1)(B)(i).

[554] See 7.1.

receives a dividend distributions with respect to the stock, the shareholder generally must reduce its basis in the stock by the amount of the dividend.[555] Any gain that may be received on the disposition of stock in an S corporation also automatically results in unrelated business income.

§ 5.10 UNRELATED DEBT-FINANCED INCOME RULES

Income-producing property held by a tax-exempt organization is considered to be unrelated debt-financed property (making income from it, less deductions, taxable) only where there is an acquisition indebtedness attributable to it. *Acquisition indebtedness*, with respect to debt-financed property, means the unpaid amount of the indebtedness incurred by the exempt organization in acquiring or improving the property, the indebtedness incurred before any acquisition or improvement of the property if the indebtedness would not have been incurred but for the acquisition or improvement, and the indebtedness incurred after the acquisition or improvement of the property if the indebtedness would not have been incurred but for the acquisition or improvement and the incurring of the indebtedness was reasonably foreseeable at the time of the acquisition or improvement.[556]

If property is acquired by a tax-exempt organization subject to a mortgage or other similar lien, the indebtedness thereby secured is considered an acquisition indebtedness incurred by the organization when the property is acquired, even though the organization did not assume or agree to pay the indebtedness.[557] Some relief is provided, however, with respect to mortgaged property acquired as a result of a bequest or devise. That is, the indebtedness secured by this type of mortgage is not treated as acquisition indebtedness during the 10-year period following the date of acquisition. A similar rule applies to mortgaged property received by gift, where the mortgage was placed on the property more than five years before the gift and the property was held by the donor more than five years before the gift.[558]

A tax-exempt charitable organization acquired an undivided interest in income-producing rental property subject to a mortgage; the property was leased for purposes unrelated to the organization's exempt purposes. To liquidate its share of the mortgage, the organization prepaid its proportionate share of the mortgage indebtedness, thereby receiving releases of liability from the mortgagee and the co-owners. The lien securing payment of the mortgage nonetheless extended to the entire rental property; the mortgagee was not to release the lien until the co-owners paid the entire principal of the mortgage. The IRS ruled that the organization, by satisfying the full amount of its indebtedness under the mortgage, did not have any acquisition indebtedness.[559]

By contrast, a charitable organization purchased mineral production payments with borrowed funds to obtain income for its grant-making program, receiving from each payment the difference between the aggregate amount

---

[555] IRC § 512(e)(2).
[556] IRC § 514(c)(1).
[557] IRC § 514(c)(2)(A).
[558] IRC § 514(c)(2)(B).
[559] Rev. Rul. 76-95, 1976-1 C.B. 172.

payable to the lender of the borrowed funds and the total amount of the production payment, with the difference generally amounting to 1/16 of 1 percent of each payment purchased. The IRS held that the indebtedness incurred to purchase the production payment was an acquisition indebtedness and that, accordingly, the payments were debt-financed property.[560]

The regulations accompanying the statutory unrelated debt-financed income rules provide, in effect, a special rule for debts for the payment of taxes, stating that "in the case where State law provides that a tax lien attaches to property prior to the time, when such lien becomes due and payable, such lien shall not be treated as similar to a mortgage until after it has become due and payable and the organization has had an opportunity to pay such lien in accordance with State law."[561] Prior to enactment of the Tax Reform Act of 1976, however, the IRS took the position that a lien arising from a special assessment imposed by a state or local government on land for the purpose of making improvements on the land, with the improvements financed by the sale of bonds secured by the lien, constituted acquisition indebtedness, even though (like the property tax lien) the installment payments were due in future periods. In 1976, Congress took action to reverse this position so that, as respects tax years that began after December 31, 1969, where state law provides that a lien for taxes or for assessments made by the state or a political subdivision of the state attaches to property prior to the time when the taxes or assessments become due and payable, the indebtedness does not become acquisition indebtedness (that is, the lien is not regarded as similar to a mortgage[562]) until and to the extent that the taxes or assessments become due and payable and the organization has had an opportunity to pay the taxes or assessments in accordance with state law.[563] The Senate Finance Committee noted that "it is not intended that this provision apply to special assessments for improvements which are not of a type normally made by a State or local governmental unit or instrumentality in circumstances in which the use of the special assessment is essentially a device for financing improvements of the sort that normally would be financed privately rather than through a government."[564]

Other exemptions from the scope of acquisition indebtedness follow.

1.   The term does not include indebtedness that was necessarily incurred in the performance or exercise of an organization's tax-exempt purpose or function, such as the indebtedness incurred by an exempt credit union[565] in accepting deposits from its members.[566] It has been held, however, that the purchase of securities on margin and with borrowed funds is not inherent in (meaning essential to) the performance or exercise of a credit union's exempt purposes or function, so that a portion of the resulting income is taxable as debt-financed income.[567]

---

[560] Rev. Rul. 76-354, 1976-2 C.B. 179.
[561] Reg. § 1.514(c)-1(b)(2).
[562] IRC § 514(c)(2)(A).
[563] IRC § 514(c)(2)(C).
[564] S. Rep. No. 94-938 (Part 2), 94th Cong., 2d Sess. 86 (1976).
[565] See *Tax-Exempt Organizations* § 18.7.
[566] IRC § 514(c)(4).
[567] Alabama Central Credit Union v. United States, 646 F. Supp. 1199 (N.D. Ala. 1986).

2. The term does not include an obligation to pay an annuity that (a) is the sole consideration issued in exchange for property if, at the time of the exchange, the value of the annuity is less than 90 percent of the value of the property received in the exchange; (b) is payable over the life of one individual who is living at the time the annuity is issued, or over the lives of two individuals living at that time; and (c) is payable under a contract that does not guarantee a minimum amount of payments or specify a maximum amount of payments and does not provide for any adjustment of the amount of the annuity payments by reference to the income received from the transferred property or any other property.[568]

3. The term does not include an obligation to finance the purchase, rehabilitation, or construction of housing for low and moderate income persons to the extent that it is insured by the Federal Housing Administration.[569]

4. The term does not include a tax-exempt organization's obligation to return collateral security pursuant to a securities lending arrangement, thereby making it clear that, in ordinary circumstances, payments on securities loans are not debt-financed income.[570]

The IRS ruled that a tax-exempt employees' trust (which was, in general, subject to tax on unrelated business taxable income[571]), which was a partner in a partnership that was organized to make investments in securities, could experience unrelated debt-financed income.[572] The partnership borrowed money to invest in securities and became primarily liable for repayment of the debt and for payment of interest on the debt, with the partners secondarily liable on a pro rata basis. The IRS held that the indebtedness was an acquisition indebtedness because it was incurred to acquire property for investment purposes, the incurring of the debt was not inherent in the performance of the trust's exempt function (namely, to receive employer and employee contributions and to use them and increments on them to provide retirement benefits to the plan participants[573]), and the investment property was not substantially related to the exercise of the trust's exempt purposes. Thus, whether the trust's investment activity can result in unrelated business taxable income under these rules is determined by whether its share of any partnership income was derived from or on account of debt-financed property.[574] Subsequently, a court held that the income from securities purchased on margin by a qualified profit-sharing plan was unrelated debt-financed income, in that this type of indebtedness was not inherent in the exercise of the trust's exempt function.[575] Similarly, another court concluded that, when an exempt organization withdrew the accumulated cash values in life

---

[568] IRC § 514(c)(5).
[569] IRC § 514(c)(6). In general, Reg. § 1.514(c)-1.
[570] IRC § 514(c)(8).
[571] Rev. Rul. 71-311, 1971-2 C.B. 184.
[572] Rev. Rul. 74-197, 1974-1 C.B. 143.
[573] Reg. § 1.401-1(a)(2)(i).
[574] Reg. § 1.702-1(a).
[575] Elliot Knitwear Profit Sharing Plan v. Comm'r, 71 T.C. 765 (1979), *aff'd*, 614 F.2d 347 (3d Cir. 1980). Also Ocean Cove Corp. Retirement Plan & Trust v. United States, 657 F. Supp. 776 (S.D. Fla. 1987); Alabama Central Credit Union v. United States, 646 F. Supp. 1199 (N.D. Ala. 1986).

insurance policies and reinvested the proceeds in income-paying investments, it created an acquisition indebtedness and thus unrelated debt-financed income, even though the organization did not have an obligation to repay the funds.[576] Likewise, a court held that the interest earned on certificates of deposit obtained by an exempt organization was taxable as debt-financed income because the certificates were acquired using the proceeds of a loan that was collateralized with other certificates of deposit previously purchased by the organization.[577]

By contrast, the IRS examined similar practices engaged in by a trust forming part of a leveraged employee stock ownership plan (ESOP).[578] (An ESOP is a technique of corporate finance designed to build beneficial equity ownership of shares in an employer corporate into its employees substantially in proportion to their relative income without requiring any cash outlay on their part, any reduction in pay or other employee benefits, or the surrender of any rights on the part of the employees.[579]) This type of trust generally acquires stock of the employer with the proceeds of a loan made to it by a financial institution. Consequently, the IRS concluded that a leveraged ESOP's capital growth and stock ownership objectives were part of its tax-exempt function[580] and "borrowing to purchase employer securities is an integral part of accomplishing these objectives."[581] Thus, the borrowing was not an acquisition indebtedness and the securities thereby purchased were not debt-financed property. But the IRS cautioned that these circumstances are "distinguishable from a situation in which a person or profit sharing plan that satisfies the requirements of [IRC] section 401(a) borrows money to purchase securities of the employer; in the latter situation the exempt trusts borrowing to purchase employer securities could result in unrelated business income within the meaning of [IRC] section 512."[582]

For these purposes, the term *acquisition indebtedness* generally does not include indebtedness incurred by a qualified organization in acquiring or improving any real property.[583] A *qualified organization* is an operating educational institution,[584] an affiliated support organization,[585] and a tax-exempt multiparent title-holding organization,[586] as well as any trust that constitutes a pension trust.[587] Nonetheless, in computing the unrelated income of a shareholder or beneficiary of a disqualified holder (namely, a multiparent title-holding organization[588]) of an interest in a multiparent title-holding entity attributable to

---

[576] Mose & Garrison Siskin Memorial Found., Inc. v. United States, 603 F. Supp. 91 (E.D. Tenn. 1985), *aff'd*, 790 F.2d 480 (6th Cir. 1986).

[577] Kern County Elec. Pension Fund v. Comm'r, 96 T.C. 845 (1991), *aff'd in unpub. opinion* (9th Cir. 1993).

[578] IRC § 4975(e)(7).

[579] S. Rep. No. 94-938, 94th Cong., 2d Sess. (1976).

[580] IRC § 401(a).

[581] Rev. Rul. 79-122, 1979-1 C.B. 204, 206.

[582] *Id.* Cf. Rev. Rul. 79-349, 1979-2 C.B. 233.

[583] IRC § 514(c)(9)(A).

[584] That is, one described in IRC § 170(b)(1)(A)(ii). See § 8.2(b).

[585] That is, one described in IRC § 509(a)(3). See § 8.6.

[586] That is, one described in IRC § 501(c)(25). See *Tax-Exempt Organizations* § 18.2(b).

[587] That is, one described in IRC § 401. The definition of *qualified organization* is the subject of IRC § 514(c)(9)(C).

[588] IRC § 514(c)(9)(F)(iii). An entity that is this type of shareholder or beneficiary, however, is not a disqualified holder if it otherwise constitutes a qualified organization by reason of being an educational institution, a supporting organization of an educational institution, or a pension trust (*id.*).

the interest, the holder's pro rata share of the items of income that are treated as gross income derived from an unrelated business (without regard to the exception for debt-financed property) is taken into account as gross income of the disqualified holder derived from an unrelated business; the holder's pro rata share of deductions is likewise taken into account.[589]

Thus, under this exception, income from investments in real property is not treated as income from debt-financed property and therefore as unrelated business income. Mortgages are not considered real property for purposes of this exception.[590]

This exception for real property in the debt-financed income rules is available for investments only if these six restrictions are satisfied:

1. Where the purchase price for an acquisition or improvement of real property is a fixed amount determined as of the date of the acquisition or completion of the improvement (the *fixed prove restriction*)[591]

2. Where the amount of the indebtedness, any amount payable with respect to the indebtedness, or the time for making any payment of that amount is not dependent (in whole or in part) on revenues, income, or profits derived from the property (the *participating loan restriction*)[592]

3. Where the property is not, at any time after the acquisition, leased by the qualified organization to the seller or to a person related[593] to the seller (the *leaseback restriction*)[594]

4. In the case of a pension trust, where the seller or lessee of the property is not a disqualified person[595] (the *disqualified person restriction*)[596]

5. Where the seller or a person related to the seller (or a person related to the plan with respect to which a pension trust was formed) is not providing financing in connection with the acquisition of the property (the *seller-financing restriction*)[597]

6. If the investment in the property is held through a partnership, where certain additional requirements are satisfied by the partnership, namely: (a) the partnership satisfies the rules in the foregoing five circumstances, and (b)(i) all of the partners are qualified organizations,[598] (ii) each allocation to a partner of the partnership is a qualified allocation,[599] or

---

[589] IRC § 514(c)(9)(F)(i), (ii). The purpose of this rule is to prevent the benefits of this exception from flowing through the title-holding company to its shareholders or beneficiaries (unless those organizations themselves are qualified organizations) (see *supra* note 586).

[590] IRC § 514(c)(9)(B), last sentence.

[591] IRC § 514(c)(9)(B)(i).

[592] IRC § 514(c)(9)(B)(ii).

[593] As described in IRC § 267(b) or 707(b).

[594] IRC § 514(c)(9)(B)(iii).

[595] As described in IRC § 4975(e)(2)(C), (E), (H).

[596] IRC § 514(c)(9)(B)(iv).

[597] IRC § 514(c)(9)(B)(v).

[598] For this purpose, an organization cannot be treated as a qualified organization if any income of the organization is unrelated business income (IRC § 514(c)(9)(B), penultimate sentence).

[599] A *qualified allocation* is one described in IRC § 168(h)(6).

(iii) the partnership meets the rules of a special exception (the *partnership restrictions*)[600]

Nonetheless, the leaseback restriction and the disqualified person restriction are related to permit a limited leaseback of debt-financed real property to the seller (or a person related to the seller) or to a disqualified person[601]; and the fixed price restriction and the participating loan restriction are relaxed for certain sales of real property foreclosed on by financial institutions.[602]

An example of the flexibility of the potential application of the unrelated debt-financed income rules was the suggestion that this type of income is realized by tax-exempt organizations in the lending of securities transaction.[603] This conclusion was arrived at by way of the contention that the exempt institution is not actually lending the securities but is "borrowing" the collateral, thereby making—so the argument goes—the entire interest (and perhaps the dividend or interest equivalent) taxable.

This matter was clarified, however, by enactment of a special rule[604] and earlier by an IRS ruling that the income from the investment of the collateral posted by the broker is not unrelated debt-financed income, since the organization did not incur the indebtedness "for the purpose of making additional investments."[605]

The intent of these rules is to treat an otherwise tax-exempt organization in the same manner as an ordinary business enterprise to the extent that the exempt organization purchases property through the use of borrowed funds.[606]

---

[600] IRC § 514(c)(9)(B)(vi). This special exception is the subject of IRC § 514(c)(9)(E). Rules similar to those of this situation also apply in the case of any pass-thru entity other than a partnership and in the case of tiered partnerships and other entities (IRC § 514(c)(9)(D)).

[601] This exception applies only where (1) no more than 25 percent of the leasable floor space in a building (or complex of buildings) is leased back to the seller (or related party) or to the disqualified person and (2) the lease is on commercially reasonable terms, independent of the sale and other transactions (IRC § 514(c)(9)(G)). A leaseback to a disqualified person remains subject to the prohibited transaction rules (IRC § 4975).

The fixed price restriction and the participating loan restriction are not subject to this refinement. Thus, for example, income from real property acquired with seller financing, where the timing or amount of payment is based on revenue, income, or profits from the property, generally continues to be treated as income from debt-financed property, unless another exception applies.

[602] For this purpose, the term *financial institutions* includes financial institutions in conservatorship or receivership, certain affiliates of financial institutions, and government corporations that succeed to the rights and interests of a receiver or conservator (IRC § 514(c)(9)(H)(iv)).

This exception is limited to instances where (1) a qualified organization obtained real property from a financial institution that acquired the property by foreclosure (or after an actual or imminent default), or the property was held by the selling financial institution when it entered into conservatorship or receivership; (2) any gain recognized by the financial institution with respect to the property is ordinary income; (3) the stated principal amount of the seller financing does not exceed the financial institution's outstanding indebtedness (including accrued but unpaid interest) with respect to the property at the time of foreclosure or default; and (4) the present value of the maximum amount payable to pursuant to any participation feature cannot exceed 30 percent of the total purchase price of the property (including contingent payments) (IRC § 514(c)(9)(H)(i)–(iii), (v)).

In general, Ferguson & Brown, "More Investment Options Are Available for Tax-Exempt Organizations," 4 *J. Tax. Exempt Orgs.* (No. 4) 22 (Jan./Feb. 1993); McDowell, "Taxing Leveraged Investments of Charitable Organizations: What Is the Rationale?" 39 *Case W. Res. L. Rev.* (No. 3) 705 (1988–1989).

[603] See § 5.9(d).

[604] IRC § 514(c)(8) (see text accompanied by *supra* note 569).

[605] Rev. Rul. 78-88, 1978-1 C.B. 163–164.

[606] H. Rep. No. 91-413, 91st Cong., 1st Sess. 46 (1969).

The IRS recalled this intent in passing on the tax status of indebtedness owed to an exempt labor union by its wholly owned subsidiary title-holding company resulting from a loan to pay debts incurred to acquire two income-producing office buildings. The IRS ruled that this *interorganizational indebtedness* was not an acquisition indebtedness because the "very nature of the title-holding company as well as the parent-subsidiary relationship show this indebtedness to be merely a matter of accounting between the organizations rather than an indebtedness as contemplated by" these rules.[607]

The income of a tax-exempt organization that is attributable to a short sale of publicly traded stock through a broker is not unrelated debt-financed income and thus is not taxable as unrelated business income.[608] This is because, although a short sale creates an obligation, it does not create an indebtedness for tax purposes,[609] and thus there is no acquisition indebtedness. This position of the IRS is not intended to cause any inference with respect to a borrowing of property other than publicly trade stock sold short through a broker. Securities purchased on margin by a tax-exempt organization constitute debt-financed property, which generates unrelated business income.[610]

---

[607] Rev. Rul. 77-72, 1977-1 C.B. 157, 158. His rationale was also applied to avoid the prospect of unrelated business income taxation resulting from use of joint operating agreements in the health care context (see § 26.5(j)).

[608] Rev. Rul. 95-8, 1995-1 C.B. 107.

[609] Deputy v. du Pont, 308 U.S. 488 (1940).

[610] E.g., Henry E. & Nancy Horton Bartels Trust for the Benefit of the University of New Haven v. United States, 209 F.3d 147 (2d Cir. 2000).

The unrelated business income tax treatment of revenue from a controlled entity is the subject of § 6.7. The rules concerning the reporting of and payment of tax on unrelated business income is the subject of § 10.7.

CHAPTER SIX

For-Profit Subsidiaries and Limited Liability Companies

It is common, if not sometimes essential, for a tax-exempt organization, including an exempt association, to utilize a for-profit subsidiary, usually to house one or more unrelated business activities[1] that are too extensive to be operated within the organization, without jeopardizing or losing the parent entity's exempt status. This is the prevalent if not the sole reason for the establishment and operation of a for-profit subsidiary by an exempt organization.

There are at least five other reasons for use of this technique: situations where the management of a tax-exempt organization (a) does not want to report the receipt of unrelated business income and so shifts the generation of it to a separate subsidiary, (b) wants to insulate the assets of the parent exempt organization

---

[1] See Chapter 5.

from potential liability, (c) desires expansion of the sources of revenue or capital, (d) wishes to use a subsidiary in a partnership, and/or (e) simply is enamored with the idea of utilization of a for-profit subsidiary.[2] For example, in illustration of the third of these five reasons, a tax-exempt educational organization licensed to and otherwise utilized a for-profit subsidiary to maximize, for membership and business purposes, the operation of its Web site[3]; a scientific research institution developed an IRS-approved arrangement to further technology transfer by means of a supporting organization and a for-profit subsidiary[4]; and an organization that operated a multiservice geriatric center was allowed by the IRS to market its software, developed for tracking services to the elderly, by means of a taxable subsidiary.[5]

An unrelated business may be operated as an activity within a tax-exempt organization, as long as the primary purpose of the organization is the carrying out of one or more exempt functions or the commensurate test is satisfied.[6] With one exception, there is no fixed percentage of unrelated activity that may be engaged in by an exempt organization.[7]

Therefore, if a tax-exempt organization engages in one or more unrelated activities where the activities are substantial in relation to exempt activities, the use of a for-profit subsidiary is necessary, if exemption is to be retained.[8] Indeed, tax exemption cannot be maintained as a matter of law if there is a substantial nonexempt activity or set of activities.[9] An organization can lose its exempt status for a period of time, because of extensive unrelated activities, before transfer of unrelated operations to a for-profit subsidiary.[10]

§ 6.1 FUNDAMENTALS OF FOR-PROFIT SUBSIDIARIES

Several matters concerning structure should be taken into account when contemplating the use by a tax-exempt organization, including a business league, of a for-profit subsidiary. They include choice of form and the control mechanism.

(a) Establishing For-Profit Subsidiary

Essentially, the factors to be considered in determining whether a particular activity should be contained within a tax-exempt organization or a related for-profit organization are the same as those that should be weighed when there is

---

[2] In general, Sanders, *Joint Ventures Involving Tax-Exempt Organizations, Second Edition* (Hoboken, NJ: John Wiley & Sons, 2000) § 4.6(a).

[3] Priv. Ltr. Rul. 200225046.

[4] Priv. Ltr. Rul. 200326035.

[5] Priv. Ltr. Rul. 200425050, reissued as Priv. Ltr. Rul. 200444044.

[6] Reg. § 1.501(c)(3)-1(e)(1). Also Reg. § 1.501(c)(3)-1(c)(1). The commensurate test is the subject of *Tax-Exempt Organizations* § 4.7.

[7] The one exception is a 10 percent limit on the unrelated business activities of title-holding companies (see *Tax-Exempt Organizations* § 28.3).

[8] In Orange County Agric. Soc'y, Inc. v. Comm'r, 893 F.2d 529 (2d Cir. 1990), the court discussed the fact that the operation of a substantial unrelated business by a tax-exempt organization is likely to result in loss of the organization's exemption.

[9] Better Business Bur. of Washington, D.C. v. United States, 326 U.S. 279 (1945).

[10] Tech. Adv. Mem. 200203069.

contemplation of the commencement of a business that potentially may be conducted in either an exempt or a for-profit form. These factors are the value of or need for tax exemption, the motives of those involved in the enterprise (for example, a profit motive), the desirability of creating an asset (such as stock that may appreciate in value and/or serve as the means for transfer of ownership) for equity owners of the enterprise (usually shareholders), and the compensatory arrangements contemplated for the employees.

The law is clear that a tax-exempt organization can have one or more exempt (or at least nonprofit) subsidiaries and/or one or more for-profit subsidiaries.[11] Thus, the IRS observed that an exempt organization can "organize, capitalize and own, provide services and assets (real and personal, tangible and intangible) to a taxable entity without violating the requirements for [tax] exemption, regardless of whether the taxable entity is wholly or partially owned."[12] Indeed, the agency acknowledged that the "number of subsidiaries or related entities an exempt organization can create for the purpose of conducting business activities is not set."[13] With respect to for-profit subsidiaries, the exempt parent organization can own some or all of the equity (usually stock) of the for-profit subsidiary (unless the parent is a private foundation, in which case special rules apply[14]).[15] For example, a public charity created a for-profit management corporation, to provide services to it and two other exempt organizations, and provided it operating funds in exchange for 100 percent of the subsidiary's stock.[16]

The IRS from time to time issues private determinations concerning the use of for-profit subsidiaries by tax-exempt organizations.[17]

(b) Choice of Form

Just as in forming a tax-exempt organization,[18] when establishing a for-profit subsidiary, consideration should be given to choice of organizational form. Most will be corporations, inasmuch as a corporation is the most common of the business forms, provides a shield against liability for management and the exempt parent, and enables the exempt parent to own the subsidiary by holding all or at least a majority of its stock.[19]

Some taxable businesses are organized as sole proprietorships; however, this approach is of no avail in the tax-exempt organization context since the business

---

[11] E.g., Priv. Ltr. Rul. 9016072 (where a tax-exempt organization owned a for-profit subsidiary and that subsidiary in turn owned a network of for-profit subsidiaries).

[12] Priv. Ltr. Rul. 199938041.

[13] Priv. Ltr. Rul. 8304112.

[14] See *Tax-Exempt Organizations* § 11.4(c).

[15] The extent of stock ownership may determine whether income from a subsidiary to a tax-exempt parent is taxable (see § 6.7). A transfer without consideration from a taxable corporation to a charitable organization, which is its sole stockholder, is considered a dividend rather than a charitable contribution (Rev. Rul. 68-296, 1968-1 C.B. 105).

[16] Priv. Ltr. Rul. 9308047.

[17] E.g., Priv. Ltr. Rul. 8706012.

[18] See *Tax-Exempt Organizations* § 4.1.

[19] Charitable organizations may be shareholders in small business corporations (*S corporations*) (IRC § 1361(b)(1)(B), (c)(7)(B)). The applicability of the unrelated business income rules in this context is the subject of § 5.8(s).

activity conducted as a sole proprietorship is an undertaking conducted directly by the exempt organization and thus does not lead to the desired goal of having the related activity in a separate entity.

Some taxable businesses are structured as partnerships; however, the participation by a tax-exempt organization in a partnership can involve unique legal complications.[20] Another alternative is use of a limited liability company for this purpose.[21] This aspect of the law is evolving and offers interesting opportunities for tax-exempt organizations.[22]

Some states allow businesses to be conducted by means of "business trusts," so this approach may be available to a tax-exempt organization. Before this approach (or any other approach involving a vehicle other than a corporation) is used, however, it is imperative that those involved are certain that the corporate form is not the most beneficial. One important consideration must be that of stock ownership, as stock is an asset that can appreciate in value and can be sold in whole or in part.

In some instances, an activity of a tax-exempt organization can be placed in a taxable nonprofit organization.[23] This approach is a product of the distinction between a nonprofit organization and a tax-exempt organization.[24] The former is a state law concept; the latter essentially is a federal tax law concept. Assuming state law permits (in that an activity may be *unrelated* to the parent's exempt functions, yet still be a *nonprofit* one), a business activity may be placed in a nonprofit, albeit taxable, corporation.[25] There may be some advantage (such as public relations) to this approach.

(c) Control Element

Presumably, a tax-exempt organization will, when forming a taxable subsidiary, intend to maintain control over the subsidiary. Certainly, after capitalizing the enterprise,[26] nurturing its growth and success, and desiring to enjoy some profits from the business, the prudent exempt organization parent usually would not want to place the activity in a vehicle over which it cannot exercise ongoing control.

Where the taxable subsidiary is structured as a business corporation, the tax-exempt organization parent can own the entity and ultimately control it simply by owning the stock (received in exchange for the capital contributed). The exempt organization parent as the stockholder can thereafter select the board of directors of the subsidiary corporation and, if desired, its officers.

---

[20] See Chapter 7.

[21] E.g., Priv. Ltr. Rul. 9637050.

[22] See § 6.10.

[23] Still another approach is use of a tax-exempt subsidiary, such as a supporting organization (see § 8.6), a title-holding company (see *Tax-Exempt Organizations* § 18.2), a lobbying arm of a charitable organization (see, e.g., *Tax-Exempt Organizations* § 20.7), a political organization (see § 4.7), and fundraising vehicles for foreign charitable organizations (see *Tax-Exempt Organizations* § 30.2(d)).

[24] See *Tax-Exempt Organizations* §§ 1.1(a), 1.2.

[25] Of course, in this situation, the subsidiary, then, is not a for-profit one.

[26] See § 6.3(a).

If the taxable subsidiary is structured as a nonprofit corporation, three choices are available.

1. The tax-exempt organization parent can control the subsidiary by means of interlocking directorates.

2. The subsidiary can be a membership corporation, with the parent entity the sole member.

3. In this, the least utilized, approach, the entity can be structured as a nonprofit organization that can issue stock, in which instance the exempt organization parent would control the subsidiary by holding its stock.

If the latter course is chosen and if the nonprofit subsidiary is to be headquartered in a (foreign) state where stock-based nonprofit organizations are not authorized, the subsidiary can be incorporated in a state that allows nonprofit organizations to issue stock and thereafter be qualified to do business in the home (domestic) state.

§ 6.2 POTENTIAL OF ATTRIBUTION TO PARENT

For federal income tax purposes, a parent corporation and its subsidiary are respected as separate entities as long as the purposes for which the subsidiary is formed are reflected in authentic business activities.[27] That is, where an organization is established with the bona fide intention that it will have some real and substantial business function, its existence generally will not be disregarded for tax purposes.[28]

By contrast, where the parent organization so controls the affairs of the subsidiary that it is merely an extension of the parent, the subsidiary may not be regarded as a separate entity.[29] In an extreme situation (such as where the parent is directly involved in the day-to-day management of the subsidiary), the establishment and operation of an ostensibly separate subsidiary may be regarded as a sham perpetrated by the parent and thus ignored for tax purposes; with this outcome, the tax consequences are the same as if the two entities were one.[30]

The position of the IRS on this subject can be traced through three pronouncements from its Office of Chief Counsel. In 1968, the agency was advised by its lawyers that an attempt to attribute the activities of a subsidiary to its parent "should be made only where the evidence clearly shows that the subsidiary

---

[27] E.g., Comm'r v. Bollinger, 485 U.S. 340 (1988); Nat'l Carbide Corp. v. Comm'r, 336 U.S. 422 (1949); Moline Properties, Inc. v. Comm'r, 319 U.S. 436 (1943); Britt v. United States, 431 F.2d 227 (5th Cir. 1970). Also Sly v. Comm'r, 56 T.C.M. 209 (1988), Universal Church of Jesus Christ, Inc. v. Comm'r, 55 T.C.M. 143 (1988).

[28] Britt v. United States, 431 F.2d 227 (5th Cir. 1970).

[29] E.g., Krivo Industrial Supply Co. v. Nat'l Distillers & Chemical Corp., 483 F.2d 1098 (5th Cir. 1973); Orange County Agric. Soc'y, Inc. v. Comm'r, 55 T.C.M. 1602 (1988), aff'd, 893 F.2d 529 (2d Cir. 1990).

[30] Gen. Couns. Mem. 39598. In a similar set of circumstances, courts are finding nonprofit organizations to be the alter ego of the debtor, with the result that the assets of the organization are made available to IRS levies (see the cases collected in *Tax-Exempt Organizations* § 4.1, note 22).

In the reverse situation, where a for-profit entity controls a tax-exempt organization (such as by day-to-day management of it), the exemption of the controlled entity may be jeopardized (see, e.g., United Cancer Council, Inc. v. Comm'r, 109 T.C. 326 (1997), *rev'd and rem'd*, 165 F.3d 1173 (7th Cir. 1999); see *Tax-Exempt Organizations* §§ 19.4, 33.3). Nonetheless, management of an exempt organization by a for-profit company generally does not raise these concerns (e.g., Priv. Ltr. Rul. 9715031).

is merely a guise enabling the parent to carry out its . . . [disqualifying] activity or where it can be proven that the subsidiary is an arm, agent, or integral part of the parent."[31] In 1974, the IRS chief counsel advised that to "disregard the corporate entity requires a finding that the corporation or transaction involved was a sham or fraud any valid business purpose, or the finding of a true agency or trust relationship between the entities."[32] In 1984, the IRS's lawyers reviewed a situation where a separate for-profit corporation provided management and operations services to several tax-exempt hospitals. Although the IRS rulings division was inclined otherwise, its lawyers advised that, where a subsidiary is organized for a bona fide business purpose and the exempt parent is not involved in the day-to-day management of the subsidiary, the activities of the subsidiary cannot be attributed to the parent for purposes of determining the parent's exempt status.[33] In the third of these instances, this was the outcome irrespective of the fact that the parent exempt organization owned all of the stock of the subsidiary corporation.

Thus, the contemporary posture of the IRS in this regard can be distilled to two tests, which are that, for the legitimacy of a for-profit subsidiary to be respected, it must engage in an independent, bona fide function and not be a mere instrumentality of the tax-exempt parent. As to the former, the IRS's lawyers wrote that

> the first aspect [in determining the authenticity of a for-profit subsidiary] is the requirement that the subsidiary be organized for some bona fide purpose of its own and not be a mere sham or instrumentality of the [exempt] parent. We do not believe that this requirement that the subsidiary have a bona fide business purpose should be considered to require that the subsidiary have an inherently commercial or for-profit activity. The term "business" . . . is not synonymous with "trade or business" in the sense of requiring a profit motive.[34]

As to the latter, the IRS's lawyers observed that

> the second aspect of the test is the requirement that the parent not be so involved in, or in control of, the day-to-day operations of the subsidiary that the relationship between parent and subsidiary assumes the characteristics of the relationship of principal and agent, i.e., that the parent not be so in control of the affairs of the subsidiary that it is merely an instrumentality of the parent.[35]

At one point, the IRS demonstrated a proclivity to treat two organizations in this situation as one where the entities' directors and officers are the same. For example, the agency ruled that the activities of a for-profit subsidiary are to be attributed to its tax-exempt parent, for purposes of determining the ongoing tax exemption of the parent, where the officers and directors of the two organizations are identical.[36]

The rationale underlying this ruling rests on the premise that, when the tax-exempt parent is involved in the day-to-day management of the subsidiary, the

---

[31] Gen. Couns. Mem. 33912.
[32] Gen. Couns. Mem. 35719.
[33] Gen. Couns. Mem. 39326.
[34] Gen. Couns. Mem. 39598.
[35] *Id.*
[36] Priv. Ltr. Rul. 8606056.

activities of the subsidiary are imputed to the parent. In this ruling, the IRS stated that an exempt parent is "necessarily" involved in the day-to-day management of the subsidiary simply because the officers and directors of the parent serve as the officers and directors of the subsidiary. Thus, because of this structural overlap, the IRS attributed the activities of the subsidiary to the parent. Once this attribution occurs, the impact of the attribution must be ascertained to determine whether the parent will remain exempt.

In the case, the attribution to the tax-exempt parent of the activities of the for-profit subsidiary was not fatal to the parent because the involvement was deemed to be insubstantial. (The exempt parent was a scientific research organization; the subsidiary developed and manufactured products that were derived from patentable technology generated out of the parent's research activities. The parent's average annual income was $50 million; the subsidiary's was $10,000 to $70,000.) The for-profit subsidiary was capitalized by the parent (for between $10,000 and $100,000). The parent maintained a controlling interest in the subsidiary. There was an overlapping of employees as between the parent and subsidiary. Likewise, there was a sharing of facilities and equipment. These relationships were evidenced by employment contracts and lease agreements. Separate books and records of the two entities were maintained.

The principles of law do not, however, support the conclusion of the IRS in this ruling, which is that overlapping directors and officers of two organizations automatically results in an attribution of the subsidiary's activities to the parent. The case law is instructive in that this can be the consequence where the facts show that the arrangement is a sham; however, this cannot be a mechanical and inexorable outcome. Indeed, in subsequent rulings, the IRS's rulings division has been guided by this advice from its lawyers:

> Control through ownership of stock, or power to appoint the board of directors, of the subsidiary will not cause the attribution of the subsidiary's activities to the parent. We do not believe that [a prior general counsel memorandum] should be read to suggest, by negative inference, that when the board of directors of a wholly owned subsidiary is made up entirely of board members, officers, or employees of the parent there must be attribution of the activities of the subsidiary to the parent.[37]

Contemporary rulings from the IRS evidence an abandonment of this earlier approach.[38]

Indeed, the IRS subsequently distilled the law on the point in this way: "The activities of a separately incorporated subsidiary cannot ordinarily be attributed to its parent organization unless the facts provide clear and convincing evidence that the subsidiary is in reality an arm, agent or integral part of the parent."[39] In that instance, the IRS offered a most munificent application of this aspect of the law, concluding that the activities of a for-profit subsidiary were not to be attributed to the tax-exempt organization that was its parent, notwithstanding extensive and ongoing in-tandem administrative and programmatic functions. That is, the agency observed that the two entities will "maintain a close working relationship,"

---

[37] Gen. Couns. Mem. 39598.
[38] E.g., Priv. Ltr. Rul. 9245031 (the "activities of [the] subsidiary cannot be attributed to [the] [p]arent").
[39] Priv. Ltr. Rul. 200132040.

they will be "sharing investment leads," they will coinvest in companies, the subsidiary will rent office space from the exempt parent, the subsidiary will purchase administrative and professional services from the parent, and the subsidiary will reimburse its parent for the services of some of the parent's employees. The IRS subsequently ruled that payments to its subsidiary by a tax-exempt organization for services rendered did not cause attribution[40] and reiterated that an employee-leasing arrangement between a tax-exempt parent and its subsidiary will not trigger attribution.[41]

There was somewhat of an aberration in these regards, in a situation involving a law issue concerning tax-exempt cooperatives. These entities must, to be exempt, receive at least 85 percent of their income from amounts collected from members for the sole purpose of meeting losses and expenses.[42] The IRS initially ruled that the gross receipts of a wholly owned subsidiary of such a cooperative must be aggregated with the receipts of the subsidiary for purposes of calculating the 85 percent member-income test.[43] The rationale for this approach was based on cooperative principles, where a subsidiary must be created to perform a function that the parent cooperative might engage in as an integral part of its operations without adversely affecting its exempt status.[44] This ruling was met with stiff opposition from the industry and members of Congress; the IRS subsequently ruled, using conventional analysis, that the income of a subsidiary is not included for purposes of determining whether the parent cooperative satisfied the member-income test.[45] In this latter ruling, the IRS reiterated the point that a corporation is a separate taxable entity for federal income tax purposes if the corporation is formed for valid business purposes, and is not a sham, agency, or instrumentality.[46]

Thus, the IRS is highly unlikely to attribute the activities of a for-profit subsidiary of a tax-exempt organization to the parent entity, by reason of the foregoing elements of law. The use of for-profit subsidiaries in the contemporary exempt organizations setting has become too customary for this form of attribution to occur, absent the most egregious of facts.[47]

§ 6.3 FINANCIAL CONSIDERATIONS

Financial considerations relating to the establishment and maintenance of a for-profit subsidiary by a tax-exempt organization include the capitalization of the subsidiary, the compensation of employees of either or both entities, and the sharing of resources.

---

[40] Priv. Ltr. Rul. 200149043.

[41] Priv. Ltr. Rul. 200405016.

[42] See *Tax-Exempt Organizations* § 18.5, text accompanied by note 109.

[43] Priv. Ltr. Rul. 9722006.

[44] E.g., Rev. Rul. 69-575, 1969-2 C.B. 134.

[45] Rev. Rul. 2002-55, 2002-37 I.R.B. 529.

[46] For this proposition, the IRS cited Comm'r v. Bollinger, 485 U.S. 340 (1988); Moline Properties, Inc. v. Comm'r, 319 U.S. 436 (1943).

[47] This does not mean that revenue from a for-profit subsidiary to an exempt parent is not taxable; in fact, just the opposite is often the case (see § 6.7).

(a) Capitalization

Assets of a tax-exempt organization that are currently being used in an unrelated business activity may, with little (if any) legal constraint, be spun off into an affiliated for-profit organization. The extent to which a for-profit corporation can be capitalized using exempt organization assets (particularly charitable ones), however, is a matter involving far more strict confines.

A tax-exempt organization can, as noted, invest a portion of its assets and engage in a certain amount of unrelated activities. At the same time, the governing board of an exempt organization must act in conformity with basic fiduciary responsibilities, and the organization cannot (without jeopardizing its exemption) contravene the prohibitions on private inurement and private benefit.[48]

IRS private letter rulings suggest that only a small percentage of tax-exempt organization's resources ought to be transferred to controlled for-profit subsidiaries.[49] These percentages approved by the IRS are usually low and, in any event, probably pertain only to cash. (Many IRS rulings in this area do not state the amount of capital involved.[50]) In some cases, a specific asset may—indeed, perhaps must—be best utilized in an unrelated activity, even though its value represents a meaningful portion of the organization's total resources.[51] Also, the exempt parent may want to make subsequent advances or loans to the subsidiary.

The best guiding standard in this regard is that of the prudent investor. In capitalizing a subsidiary, a tax-exempt organization should only part with an amount of resources that is reasonable under the circumstances and that can be rationalized in relation to amounts devoted to programs and invested in other fashions. Relevant to all of this is the projected return on the investment, in terms of income and capital appreciation. If a contribution to a subsidiary's capital seems unwise, the putative parent should consider a loan (albeit one bearing a fair rate of interest and accompanied by adequate security).[52]

In all instances, it is preferable that the operation of the subsidiary furthers (if only by providing funds for) the exempt purposes of the parent.[53] Certainly, circumstances where exempt purposes are thwarted by reason of operation of a for-profit subsidiary are to be avoided.

(b) Compensation

The structure of a tax-exempt parent and a taxable subsidiary may generate questions and issues as to compensation of employees.

---

[48] See Chapter 3.

[49] E.g., Priv. Ltr. Rul. 8505044.

[50] E.g., Priv. Ltr. Rul. 9305026.

[51] In one instance, the IRS characterized the amount of capital transferred as "substantial"; the exempt parent was not a charitable entity but rather a tax-exempt social welfare organization (see § 1.6(a)) (Priv. Ltr. Rul. 9245031).

[52] Payments by a tax-exempt organization to its subsidiary for services provided, with the payments from revenues generated by the services, are likely to be considered by the IRS to be compensation for services rather than contributions to capital (Priv. Ltr. Rul. 200227007).

[53] E.g., Priv. Ltr. Rul. 8709051.

The compensation of the employees of the taxable subsidiary is subject to an overarching requirement that the amount paid may not exceed a reasonable salary or wage.[54] The compensation of the employees of the parent tax-exempt organization is subject to a like limitation, by reason of the private inurement, private benefit, and/or excess benefit transaction doctrines.[55] An individual may be an employee of both the parent and subsidiary organizations; in that circumstance, a reasonable allocation of compensation as between the entities is required.[56] Also, if an officer, director, trustee, or key employee received aggregate compensation of more than $100,000 from an exempt organization and one or more of its related organizations, of which more than $10,000 was provided by a related organization, that fact must be reported to the IRS, with an explanation.[57] The employees of a for-profit subsidiary of a parent exempt organization may be included in one or more employee benefit plans of the parent, without endangering the exempt status of the parent, as long as the costs of the plan are allocated among the two employees on a per-capita basis.[58]

The employees of the tax-exempt parent could participate in deferred compensation plans[59] or perhaps tax-sheltered annuity programs.[60] Deferred salary plans may also be used by the subsidiary, as may qualified pension plans. Both the parent and the subsidiary may utilize 401(k) plans.[61]

Use of a taxable subsidiary may facilitate the offering of stock options to employees, to enable them to share in the growth of the corporation. The subsidiary similarly may offer an employee stock ownership plan, which is a plan that invests in the stock of the sponsoring company.[62] The subsidiary may issue unqualified options to buy stock or qualified incentive stock options.[63]

(c) Sharing of Resources

Generally, a tax-exempt organization and its for-profit subsidiary may share resources without adverse consequences, as a matter of the law of tax-exempt organizations, to the exempt entity. That is, the two organizations may share office facilities, equipment, supplies, and the like. Particularly where the exempt entity is a charitable one, however, all relevant costs must be allocated on the basis of actual use, and each organization must pay fair market value for the resources used.[64]

It is generally preferable for the tax-exempt organization to reimburse the for-profit entity for the exempt organization's use of resources, to avoid even a

---

[54] IRC § 162.

[55] See Chapter 3.

[56] One of the burgeoning issues in this regard is potential misuses of for-profit subsidiaries, such as by unduly shifting expenses to them, excess and/or additional compensation paid by them, and lack of disclosure of the relationship; sometimes there are also conflict-of-interest issues.

[57] Form 990, Part V. In general, see § 10.1.

[58] E.g., Priv. Ltr. Rul. 9242039.

[59] IRC § 457.

[60] IRC § 403(b).

[61] See *Tax-Exempt Organizations* § 16.1(d)(ii), text accompanied by note 13.

[62] IRC § 4975(e)(7).

[63] E.g., Priv. Ltr. Rul. 9242038.

[64] E.g., Priv. Ltr. Rul. 9308047.

perception that the funds of an exempt organization are being used to subsidize a for-profit organization. Nonetheless, this approach often is impractical where the exempt organization is the parent entity.

§ 6.4 ASSET ACCUMULATIONS

The IRS, in 2004, evidenced concern about the undue accumulation of assets in a for-profit subsidiary of a tax-exempt organization. The issue is whether such an accumulation is evidence of a substantial nonexempt purpose.[65]

The agency's lawyers wrote that, in cases involving exempt organizations, entities "bear a very heavy burden" to demonstrate, by "contemporaneous and clear evidence," that they have plans to use the substantial assets in a subsidiary for exempt purposes.[66] In the case, the exempt organization invested in a for-profit subsidiary, which grew rapidly. "This growth presents a continuing obligation," the IRS wrote, on the organization to "translate this valuable asset into funds," and use these funds for the expansion" of its exempt activities. The IRS suggested that some of the subsidiary's assets be sold or a portion of the subsidiary's stock be sold, with the proceeds used to fund programs. The IRS's lawyers said that the organization "cannot be allowed to focus its energies on expanding its subsidiary's commercial business and assets, and neglect to translate that financial success into specific, definite and feasible plans for the expansion of its" tax-exempt activities.

The IRS on this occasion concluded that the "fact that the assets are being accumulated in a for-profit company under the formal legal control of [a tax-exempt organization] does not excuse [the exempt organization] from using such assets" for exempt purposes. This aspect of the analysis ended with this sweeping pronouncement: "Excess accumulations maintained in a subsidiary entity under legal control of the exempt organization, but under the de facto control of the founder, are deemed to be for the founder's personal purposes if no exempt purpose is documented or implemented."

As the foregoing indicates, the IRS is particularly concerned about asset accumulations in a subsidiary when the tax-exempt organization is a closely controlled entity.[67] The IRS admonished the bar: "[C]ounsel to closely held [that is, controlled] organizations should take care to ensure that for-profit subsidiaries are not being used to divert exempt organization financial assets, resources, and income to the founding families and other insiders." The agency said that it "may examine ongoing activities to verify that there is a plan for using income and assets generated by subsidiaries for the organization's underlying exempt purposes." The IRS concluded: "De minimis levels of exempt activities, millions of dollars in unsecured loans to closely controlled affiliates, with or without formal repayment arrangements, and/or failures to create and implement documented plans for asset accumulations to be used for exempt purposes are likely to be subject to further—and detailed—IRS scrutiny."

---

[65] In general, see *Tax-Exempt Organizations* § 4.4.
[66] Tech. Adv. Mem. 200437040.
[67] See *Tax-Exempt Organizations* § 4.8.

§ 6.5 SUBSIDIARIES IN PARTNERSHIPS

There is a dimension to the use of a taxable subsidiary by a tax-exempt organization parent that is alluded to in the discussion of exempt organizations in partnerships.[68] This is the attempt by a charitable organization to avoid endangering its exempt status because of involvement in a partnership as a general partner by causing a taxable subsidiary to be the general partner in its stead.[69]

This can be an effective stratagem as long as all of the requirements of the law as to the bona fides of the subsidiary are satisfied, including the requirement that the subsidiary be an authentic business entity. As discussed,[70] however, if the tax-exempt organization parent is intimately involved in the day-to-day management of the subsidiary, the IRS may impute the activities of the subsidiary to the parent, thereby endangering the exempt status of the parent by treating it as if it were directly involved as a general partner of the limited partnership.[71]

An illustration of this use of a partnership was presented in an IRS ruling.[72] A tax-exempt hospital wanted to expand its provision of medical rehabilitation services; a for-profit corporation that managed the rehabilitation program at the hospital was a subsidiary of the nation's largest independent provider of comprehensive rehabilitation services. The hospital, through this subsidiary, sought a joint venture with its for-profit parent to utilize its expertise and methodologies and to operate the rehabilitation facility as a venture so that the expansion would not jeopardize the institution's role as a community hospital. The joint venture was structured so that it was between the hospital and a system of which it was a component, and a wholly owned for-profit subsidiary of the for-profit parent entity and its subsidiary. The IRS ruled favorably in the case, concluding that the hospital's participation in the venture was consistent with its purposes of promoting health.[73]

§ 6.6 EFFECT OF FOR-PROFIT SUBSIDIARIES ON PUBLIC CHARITY STATUS

Just as it is possible for the operations of a for-profit subsidiary to have an adverse impact on the tax-exempt status of a parent organization (by an attribution of the activities for tax purposes[74]), so too is there potential that the functions of a for-profit subsidiary will have a pernicious effect on the public charity status of the exempt charitable parent organization.

---

[68] See § 7.1.

[69] E.g., Gen. Couns. Mem. 39598. One area of the federal tax law concerning tax-exempt organizations where the use of a for-profit subsidiary in a partnership, instead of an exempt organization, generally will not alter the tax outcome is the set of rules pertaining to tax-exempt entity leasing (see *Tax-Exempt Organizations* § 29.5(g)). On occasion, some or all of these results can be accomplished by the use of a tax-exempt subsidiary (e.g., Priv. Ltr. Rul. 8638131).

[70] See § 6.2.

[71] In one instance, the IRS, without explanation, expressly ignored a tax-exempt organization's use of a for-profit subsidiary as the general partner in a partnership, reviewing the facts as though the exempt organization were directly involved in the partnership (Tech. Adv. Mem. 8939002).

[72] Priv. Ltr. Rul. 9352030.

[73] In general, see *Tax-Exempt Organizations* § 6.3.

[74] See § 6.2.

(a) Publicly Supported Organizations

Any impact of a for-profit subsidiary organization on the status of a tax-exempt charitable organization that is its parent, where the parent is classified as a publicly supported organization, is derived from funding of the parent by the subsidiary. If the funding is in the form of a charitable contribution, it may be regarded for tax purposes as a dividend.[75]

Where a parent charitable organization has its nonprivate foundation status based on a classification as a donative type of publicly supported charity,[76] a transfer of money or property to it by a subsidiary will, if treated as a dividend, not qualify as public support.[77] Moreover, where the item or items transferred to the publicly supported donative parent are considered gifts, they do not constitute public support to the extent the amount exceeded the 2 percent limitation threshold.[78]

If the parent organization is not a private foundation by reason of categorization as a service provider type of publicly supported charity,[79] any amount paid to it by a subsidiary would not be public support if the amount was regarded as a dividend.[80] Moreover, a payment of this nature accorded dividend treatment would be investment income, as to which there is a one-third limitation with respect to receipt of this type of revenue.[81] If the item or items transferred to the publicly supported service provider parent are considered gifts, they would not constitute public support where the subsidiary is a disqualified person[82] with respect to the parent organization.[83]

(b) Supporting Organizations

Some tax-exempt charitable organizations are classified as public charities by virtue of the rules concerning supporting organizations.[84]

Because the public charity status of a supporting organization is not derived from the nature of its funding, the considerations pertaining to publicly supported organizations discussed previously are inapplicable (although a transfer from a for-profit subsidiary to a supporting organization may nonetheless be considered a dividend).

The public charity classification of a charitable organization that is a supporting organization rests on the rule that it must be operated exclusively to support or benefit one or more eligible public charitable organizations.[85] There was a school of thought that held that a supporting organization cannot have a for-profit subsidiary because to do so would be a violation of the exclusively requirement. There was some merit to this position, since the term *exclusively*

---

[75] See *supra* note 15.
[76] See § 8.3.
[77] Reg. §1.170A-9(e)(2).
[78] Reg. § 1.170A-9(e)(6)(i).
[79] See § 8.4.
[80] IRC § 509(a)(2)(A); Reg. § 1.509(a)-3(a)(2).
[81] IRC § 509(a)(2)(B); Reg. § 1.509(a)-3(a)(3)(i).
[82] See *Private Foundations*, Chapter 4.
[83] IRC § 509(a)(2)(A); Reg. § 1.509(a)-3(b)(2).
[84] See § 11.3(c).
[85] IRC § 509(a)(3)(A). See § 8.6.

means, in this setting, *solely*,[86] as opposed to its definition in the context of charitable organizations generally, where the term means *primarily*.[87]

Contentions to the contrary included the view that, where the reason for organizing and utilizing the subsidiary is to assist in the supporting or benefiting of one or more eligible public charities, there should not be a prohibition on the use of for-profit subsidiaries in this manner. This issue arose when the IRS ruled that, as long as a supporting organization does not actively participate in the day-to-day management of a for-profit subsidiary and both entities have a legitimate economic and business purpose and operations, the supporting organization can utilize a for-profit subsidiary without jeopardizing its tax-exempt status.[88] This ruling was silent on the matter of the impact of the use of the subsidiary on the organization's supporting organization classification. The IRS subsequently held, however, that a supporting organization can have a for-profit subsidiary and not disturb its status as a supporting entity.[89]

§ 6.7 TREATMENT OF REVENUE FROM SUBSIDIARY

Most tax-exempt organizations assume that an unrelated business will serve as a source of revenue. Thus, the development within, or shifting of the unrelated business to, a taxable subsidiary should be done in such a way as to not preclude or inhibit the flow of income from the subsidiary to the parent.

(a) Income Flows to Parent

The staff and other resources of an affiliated business are usually those of the tax-exempt organization parent. Thus, the headquarters of the taxable subsidiary are likely to be the same as its parent. This means that the taxable subsidiary may have to reimburse the exempt organization parent for the subsidiary's occupancy costs, share of employees' time, and use of the parent's equipment and supplies. Therefore, one way for money to flow from the subsidiary to the parent is as this form of reimbursement, which may include an element of rent.

Another type of relationship between a tax-exempt organization parent and a taxable subsidiary is that of lender and borrower. That is, in addition to funding its subsidiary by means of one or more capital contributions (resulting in a holding of equity by the parent), the parent may find it appropriate to lend money to its subsidiary. Inasmuch as a no-interest loan to a for-profit subsidiary by a tax-exempt organization parent may endanger the exempt status of the parent, and trigger problems under the below-market interest rules,[90] it would be prudent for this type of loan to bear a fair market rate of interest. Therefore, another way for money to flow from the subsidiary to the parent is in the form of interest.

The business activities of a for-profit subsidiary may be to market and sell a product of service. When done in conformity with its tax-exempt status, the parent

---

[86] Reg. § 1.509(a)-4(e)(1).

[87] See *Tax-Exempt Organizations* § 4.6.

[88] Priv. Ltr. Rul. 9305026.

[89] Priv. Ltr. Rul. 9637051. The IRS ruled as to the tax consequences of a liquidation of a for-profit subsidiary into a supporting organization (Priv. Ltr. Rul. 9645017) (in general, see § 6.8).

[90] IRC § 7872.

can license the use of its name, logo, acronym, and/or some other feature that would enhance the sale of the product or service provided by the subsidiary. For this license, the subsidiary would pay to the parent a royalty—another way of transferring money from a for-profit subsidiary to a tax-exempt parent.

A conventional way of transferring money from a corporation to its stockholders is for the corporation to distribute its earnings and profits to them. These distributions are dividends and represent yet another way in which a taxable subsidiary can transfer money to its tax-exempt parent.

(b)   Taxable Income from Subsidiary

Certain types of income are exempted from taxation as unrelated income—principally the various forms of passive income.[91] Were it not for a special rule of federal tax law, a tax-exempt organization could have it both ways: avoid taxation of the exempt organization on unrelated income by housing the activity in a subsidiary and thereafter receive passive, nontaxable income from the subsidiary.

Congress, however, was mindful of this potential double benefit and thus legislated a rule that is an exception to the general body of law that exempts passive income from taxation: Otherwise passive nontaxable income that is derived from a controlled taxable subsidiary is generally taxed as unrelated income. Thus, when a tax-exempt organization parent receives interest, annuities, royalties, and/or rent from a controlled taxable subsidiary, those revenues will generally be taxable to the parent as unrelated business income.[92]

There is no tax deduction, however, for the payment of dividends. Consequently, when a for-profit subsidiary pays a dividend to its tax-exempt organization parent, the dividend payments are not deductible by the subsidiary. Therefore, Congress determined that it would not be appropriate to tax revenue to an exempt organization parent where it is not deductible by the taxable subsidiary.

Thus, payments of interest, annuities, royalties, and/or rents (but not dividends) by a controlled organization to a tax-exempt, controlling organization can be taxable as unrelated income, notwithstanding the fact that these forms of income are generally otherwise nontaxable as passive income.[93] The purpose of this provision is to prevent an exempt organization from housing an unrelated activity in a separate but controlled organization and receiving nontaxable income by reason of the passive income rules (for example, by renting unrelated income property to a subsidiary).[94]

Under these rules, the percentage threshold for determining control is a more than 50 percent standard. Thus, in the case of a corporation, *control* means

---

[91] See, e.g., § 5.8(a).

[92] IRC § 512(b)(13).

[93] IRC § 512(b)(13); Reg. § 1.512(b)-1(1). Also J.E. & L.E. Mabee Found., Inc. v. United States, 533 F.2d 521 (10th Cir. 1976); United States v. The Robert A. Welch Found., 334 F.2d 774 (5th Cir. 1964); Campbell v. Carter Found. Prod. Co., 322 F.2d 827 (5th Cir. 1963), *aff'g in part* 61-2 U.S.T.C. ¶ 9630 (N.D. Tex. 1961).

[94] S. Rep. No. 91-552, 91st Cong., 1st Sess. 73 (1969). In general, Crosby Valve & Gage Co. v. Comm'r, 380 F.2d 146 (1st Cir. 1967); Bird, "Exempt Organizations and Taxable Subsidiaries," 4 *Prac. Tax Law.* (No. 2) 53 (1990); Heinlen, "Commercial Activities of Exempt Organizations—Joint Ventures and Taxable Subsidiaries," *N. Ky. L. Rev.* (No. 2) 285 (1989); Nagel, "The Use of For-Profit Subsidiaries by Non-Profit Corporations," 17 *Col. Law.* (No. 7) 1293 (1998).

ownership by vote or value of more than 50 percent of the stock in the corporation.[95] In the case of a partnership, control is ownership of more than 50 percent of the profits interest or capital interests in the partnership.[96] In an instance of a trust or any other case, control is measured in terms of more than 50 percent of the beneficial interests in the entity.[97]

Preexisting constructive ownership rules have been engrafted onto this area for purposes of determining ownership of stock in a corporation.[98] Similar principles apply for purposes of determining ownership of interests in any other entity.[99] For example, if 50 percent or more in value of the stock in a corporation is owned, directly or indirectly, by or for the corporation, in the proportion that the value of the stock the person so owns bears to the value of all of the stock in the corporation.[100] Likewise, if 50 percent or more in value of the stock in a corporation is owned, directly or indirectly, by or for any person, the corporation is considered as owning the stock owned, directly or indirectly, by or for that person.[101] There are attribution rules that apply with respect to stock owned by members of a family, partnerships, estates, and trusts.[102] Thus, when a controlling organization receives, directly or indirectly, a specified payment from a controlled entity (whether tax-exempt or not), the controlling entity may have to treat that payment as income from an unrelated business.[103] The term *specified payment* means interest, annuity, royalties, or rent.[104] A specified payment must be treated as unrelated business income to the extent the payment reduced the net unrelated income of the controlled entity or increased any net unrelated loss of the controlled entity.[105] The controlling organization may deduct expenses that are directly connected with amounts that are treated as unrelated business income under this rule.[106]

In the case of a controlled entity that is not tax-exempt, the term *net unrelated income* means the portion of the entity's taxable income that would be unrelated business taxable income if the entity were exempt and had the same exempt purposes as the controlling organization.[107] When the controlled entity is exempt, *net unrelated income* means the amount of the unrelated business taxable income of the controlled entity.[108] The term *net unrelated loss* means the net operating loss adjusted under rules similar to those pertaining to net unrelated income.[109]

---

[95] IRC § 512(b)(13)(D)(i)(I).
[96] IRC § 512(b)(13)(D)(i)(II).
[97] IRC § 512(b)(13)(D)(i)(III).
[98] IRC § 512(b)(13)(D)(ii), 318.
[99] IRC § 512(b)(13)(D)(ii).
[100] IRC § 318(a)(2)(C).
[101] IRC § 318(a)(3)(C).
[102] IRC § 318(a)(1), (2)(A), (B), and (3)(A), (B).
[103] IRC § 512(b)(13)(A). Examples of indirect payments appear in J.E. & L.E. Mabee Found., Inc. v. United States, 533 F.2d 521 (10th Cir. 1976), and Gen. Couns. Mem. 38878.
[104] IRC § 512(b)(13)(C). The term does not include capital gain, enabling a controlling organization to sell appreciated property to a controlled entity without generating unrelated business income. Cf. IRC § 4040(c).
[105] IRC § 512(b)(13)(A).
[106] *Id.*
[107] IRC § 512(b)(13)(B)(i)(I). E.g., Priv. Ltr. Rul. 200602039.
[108] IRC § 512(b)(13)(B)(i)(II).
[109] IRC § 512(b)(13)(B)(ii).

§ 6.8 LIQUIDATIONS

The federal tax law causes recognition of gain or loss by a for-profit corporation in an instance of a liquidating distribution of its assets (as if the corporation had sold the assets to the distributee at fair market value) and in the event of liquidating sales. There is an exception for liquidating transfers within an affiliated group (which is regarded as a single economic unit), so that the basis in the property is carried over from the distributor to the distributee in lieu of recognition of gain or loss.

This nonrecognition exception is modified for eligible liquidations in which an 80 percent corporate shareholder receives property with a carryover basis, to provide for nonrecognition of gain or loss with respect to any property actually distributed to that shareholder. Nonetheless, this nonrecognition rule under the exception for 80 percent corporate shareholders is generally not available where the shareholder is a tax-exempt organization. That is, any gain or loss generally must be recognized by the subsidiary on the distribution of its assets in liquidation as if the assets were sold to the exempt parent at their fair market value.[110] (Gain or loss is not recognized by the parent entity on its receipt of the subsidiary's assets pursuant to the liquidation.[111]) This nonrecognition treatment is available in the exempt organizations context, however, where the property distributed is used by the exempt organization in an unrelated business immediately after the distribution. If the property subsequently ceases to be used in an unrelated business, the exempt organization will be taxed on the gain at that time.[112]

In one instance, a tax-exempt home health and hospice agency formed a wholly owned for-profit subsidiary to provide home companion services and operate an assisted living facility. Years later, the parent organization expanded its programs and facilities, and determined that the activities conducted by the subsidiary could be undertaken by the parent without adversely affecting the parent's exempt status. The parent organization proceeded to liquidate the subsidiary and transfer to it all of the assets, which had appreciated in value, in the subsidiary. The IRS ruled that the gain attributable to the distribution of the subsidiary's assets to the parent organization on liquidation would be excludable from taxation as unrelated business income by reason of the exclusion from taxation of capital gains.[113] This ruling was silent on the tax consequences of transfer of the appreciated assets by the subsidiary.[114]

---

[110] IRC § 337(b)(2)(A).

[111] IRC § 332(a).

[112] IRC § 337(b)(2)(B)(ii). Cf. Centre for Int'l Understanding v. Comm'r, 62 T.C.M. 629 (1991) (applying the liquidation rules of IRC § 337(c)(2)(A)). Regulations were issued in final form, under authority of IRC § 337(d), concerning the liquidation of for-profit entities into tax-exempt organizations, when the relationship is not that of parent and subsidiary. The rules in this regard are essentially the same as those that apply to liquidations of subsidiaries, although they also apply when a for-profit corporation converts to an exempt entity (see *Tax-Exempt Organizations* §§ 33.4(b), (c), 33.5).

[113] Priv. Ltr. Rul. 9438029.

[114] In general, this ruling did not utilize the liquidation rules of IRC §§ 332 and 337. It is not clear from this ruling whether the assets in the subsidiary were to be used in related or unrelated activities by the exempt parent after the liquidation. If the assets were to be used in related activities, the gain should have been recognized and taxable to the subsidiary (IRC § 337(b)(2)(A)).

In another instance, one of the functions of a tax-exempt charitable entity was the publication and circulation of religious materials. This organization had a for-profit subsidiary that engaged in both exempt and commercial printing activities. Once it decided to discontinue the commercial printing operations, the exempt parent proposed to liquidate the subsidiary and distribute its assets to the parent organization. The IRS ruled that any gain or loss must be recognized by the subsidiary on the distribution of its assets in liquidation (as if they were sold to the exempt parent at fair market value) to the extent the assets are to be used in related business activities.[115]

These rules as to liquidations may be contrasted with the rules as to tax-free distributions of securities (spin-offs) of controlled operations,[116] where one of the requirements is that the transaction not be used principally as a device for distribution of the earnings and profits of the distributing corporation and/or the controlled corporation.[117] In one instance, a for-profit corporation, wholly owned by a supporting organization, distributed all of the stock of nine subsidiaries (an affiliated group) to the supporting organization, which subsequently transferred the stock to another supporting organization; both supporting organizations operated to benefit the same supported organization. The reason for this transfer was to enhance the success of the various for-profit businesses by eliminating control and management inefficiencies caused by the prior structure; the IRS ruled[118] that no gain or loss was recognized when the stock was distributed.[119]

§ 6.9 ASSOCIATIONS AND FOR-PROFIT SUBSIDIARIES

It is common, as noted, for a tax-exempt business league to utilize a for-profit subsidiary, usually to accommodate unrelated business activities so as to preserve the ongoing exempt status of the business league. This is also true in instances of associations with other exempt statuses, such as charitable entities[120] and social welfare organizations.[121]

As is the case with other types of tax-exempt organizations, the biggest problem facing a tax-exempt business league in this regard is attribution to it of the operations and finances of the for-profit subsidiary. Although rulings from the IRS on this topic have been amply generous from the exempt organizations law standpoint, an exempt business league nonetheless should proceed cautiously in this context. Board overlap between the two entities is not likely to cause attribution, nor is operation of the two entities at the same location. Integration of officers and/or employees, or common or overlapping investments or other endeavors, could place an exempt business league in a position of participating in a sham arrangement.

---

[115] Priv. Ltr. Rul. 9645017. This ruling expressly addressed the point that, to the extent the assets were to be used by the parent in unrelated activities, any gain would not be recognized during the pendency of that type of use (IRC § 337(b)(2)(B)(ii)).

[116] IRC § 355.

[117] IRC § 355(a)(1)(B).

[118] Priv. Ltr. Rul. 200435005.

[119] IRC § 355(c).

[120] See § 1.4, text accompanied by note 40.

[121] See § 1.6(a).

The other already discussed considerations certainly apply in the tax-exempt business league context. These matters include capitalization of the subsidiary, compensation practices as between parent and subsidiary, assets accumulations, involvement in partnerships, tax treatment of revenue from the subsidiary, and liquidations. If the association is a public charity, and/or if an association-related foundation[122] is the parent of a for-profit subsidiary, the effect of such a subsidiary on the parent's public charity status should also be taken into account.

§ 6.10 LIMITED LIABILITY COMPANIES

The limited liability company (LLC) is a form of entity recognized under federal and state law. Created as a type of business organization, it quickly became a staple in the tax-exempt organizations context, in large part because of its general feature of being exempt from federal income taxation. There are two general types of LLCs: the multi-member LLC (frequently utilized in the joint venture context[123]) and the single-member LLC (generally, an entity disregarded for federal tax purposes).

(a) Entity Classification Fundamentals

In general, the classification of an entity as a particular type of organization can have significant federal tax consequences. Although this is an issue principally for for-profit entities, there are some ramifications in this area for tax-exempt organizations.

(i) General Rules. In the for-profit context, classification of this nature can be problematic for unincorporated business organizations (that is, this issue does not pertain to entities that are formed as corporations). Under old law, an unincorporated entity was classified as a trust or an association, depending on certain characteristics. If an entity was determined to be an association, it was then classified as a corporation or partnership for tax purposes, according to criteria as to limited liability, centralized management, continuity of life, and free transferability of member interests.[124]

The IRS decided to simplify the entity classification process and did so by means of regulations that generally took effect in 1997; these rules are known as the *check-the-box* regulations.[125] Basically, under these rules, an organization is either a trust[126] or a *business entity*.[127] A business entity with two or more members is classified for federal tax purposes as a corporation or a partnership. A business entity with only one owner either is classified as a corporation or is

---

[122] See Chapter 8.

[123] See, e.g., §§ 7.4, 7.5.

[124] Prior Reg. § 301.7701-2.

[125] This name is derived from the simple way in which the entity classification is made: by checking the appropriate box on Form 8832 (Reg. § 301.7701-3(c)(1)).

[126] A *trust* essentially is a nonbusiness entity; it is an arrangement created by a will or lifetime instrument by which trustees take title to property for the purpose of protecting or conserving it for designated beneficiaries (Reg. § 301.7701-4(a)).

[127] Reg. § 301.7701-2(a).

disregarded. When an entity is disregarded, its activities are treated as those of the owner, in the manner of a sole proprietorship.[128] A *corporation* includes a business entity organized under a federal or state statute, an *association*, or a business entity owned by a state or political subdivision of a state.[129]

A business entity that is not classified as a corporation is an *eligible entity*. An eligible entity with at least two members can elect to be classified as either an association (and thus a corporation[130]) or a partnership. An eligible entity with a single owner can elect to be classified as an association or to be disregarded as an entity separate from its owner.[131] If there is no election, an eligible entity with two or more members is a partnership and an eligible entity with a single member is disregarded as an entity separate from its owner.[132] Thus, an eligible entity is required to act affirmatively only when it desires classification as a corporation.[133]

(ii) Tax-Exempt Organization Rules. There is a *deemed election* in the tax-exempt organization's context. That is, an eligible entity that has been determined to be, or claims to be, exempt from federal income taxation[134] is treated as having made the election to be classified as an association.[135] As noted, this in turn causes the exempt entity to be regarded as a corporation.[136]

Some organizations are tax-exempt because of a relationship to a state or a political subdivision of a state.[137] When a state or political subdivision conducts an enterprise through a separate entity, the entity may be exempt from federal income tax,[138] or its income may be excluded from federal income tax.[139] Generally, if income is earned by an enterprise that is an integral part of a state or political subdivision of a state, that income is not taxable. In determining whether an enterprise is an integral part of a state, it is necessary to consider all the facts and circumstances, including the state's degree of control over the enterprise and the state's financial commitment to the enterprise.

These distinctions are reflected in the check-the-box regulations. A business entity can be recognized as a distinct entity when it is wholly owned by a state or a political subdivision of a state; it then is classified as a corporation.[140] Yet an entity formed under local law is not always recognized as a separate entity for

---

[128] *Id.* Also Reg. § 301.7701-2(c).

[129] Reg. § 301.7701-2(b). An organization wholly owned by a state is not recognized as a separate entity for these purposes if it is an integral part of a state (Reg. § 301.7701-1(a)(3)) (see § 1.6(t)).

[130] Reg. § 301.7701-2(b)(2).

[131] Reg. § 301.7701-3(a).

[132] Reg. § 301.7701-3(b)(1).

[133] In general, Pillow, Schmalz, & Starr, "Simplified Entity Classification Under the Final Check-the-Box Regulations," 86 *J. Tax.* (No. 4) 197 (April 1997). Rules as to the tax consequences associated with entity conversions by election were proposed, as amendments to the check-the-box regulations, on Oct. 27, 1997 (REG-105162-97). In general, Pillow, Schmalz, & Starr, "Changing an Entity's Classification by Election: The First Modifications to Check-the-Box," 88 *J. Tax.* (No. 3) 143 (March 1998).

[134] That is, exempt from tax by IRC § 501(a).

[135] Reg. § 301.7701-3(c)(1)(v)(A).

[136] See text accompanied by *supra* note 129.

[137] See, e.g., *Tax-Exempt Organizations* §§ 6.9, 18.17.

[138] That is, exempt from tax by reason of IRC § 501(a).

[139] IRC § 115.

[140] Reg. § 301.7701-2(b)(6). See *Tax-Exempt Organizations* § 18.17, text accompanied by note 416.

federal tax purposes. The regulations state that an "organization wholly owned by a State is not recognized as a separate entity for federal tax purposes if it is an integral part of the State."[141]

(b) Disregarded Entities

Another instance of an interrelationship between the law of tax-exempt organizations and the check-the-box regulations is the matter of formation by exempt organizations of single-member limited liability companies for various purposes. Under a default rule,[142] these LLCs are disregarded for federal income tax purposes; these entities are known as *disregarded LLCs*.[143]

The IRS contemplated whether a single-member LLC can qualify for tax-exempt status.[144] In the case of an LLC owned wholly by a charitable organization, the issue was whether the LLC, like its owner,[145] is obligated to file an application for recognition of tax-exempt status. The IRS decided that a disregarded LLC is regarded as a branch or division of its member owner.[146] Thus, separate recognition of tax exemption for these LLCs is not required (or available).[147] The IRS subsequently addressed the matter of the tax-exempt status of LLCs that have more than one exempt member.[148]

(c) Multi-Member Limited Liability Company

The multi-member limited liability company (MMLLC) is a form of joint venture.[149] Thus, it is a type of flow-through entity.[150] From the standpoint of the law of tax-exempt organizations, there are two categories of MMLLCs: the entity where some of the members are exempt organizations and the entity where all of the members are exempt organizations. Usually, the function carried out by this type of LLC is a related business in relation to the purposes of the exempt members.

(i) General Rules.   Not surprisingly, the initial use of the MMLLC in this context was in the health care field.[151] Illustrations of this use include formation of an

---

[141] Reg. § 301.7701-1(a)(3). See *Tax-Exempt Organizations* § 18.17, text accompanied by notes 414 and 417.

[142] See text accompanied by *supra* note 132.

[143] Many interesting IRS rulings concerning the use of disregarded LLCs by charitable organizations are emerging. As an illustration, the IRS ruled that a charitable organization may transfer parcels of contributed real property to separate LLCs—for the purpose of sheltering other properties from legal liability that may be caused by the gifted property—yet report the gift properties on its annual information return as if it owned them directly (Priv. Ltr. Rul. 200134025).

[144] An LLC is not taxable; that is, it is treated, for federal income tax purposes, as a partnership (IRC § 701). The issue, however, is whether an LLC can qualify for tax-exempt status under IRC § 50l; in some instances, it can (see *Tax-Exempt Organizations* § 4.3(d)).

[145] See § 2.2.

[146] Ann. 99-102, 1999-43 I.R.B. 545.

[147] E.g., Priv. Ltr. Rul. 200134025. The IRS has before it the issue of whether a contribution of money or property directly to a single-member LLC, where the member is a charitable (IRC § 501(c)(3)) organization, is deductible as a charitable contribution.

[148] See § 6.9(c).

[149] See § 7.3.

[150] See § 7.1.

[151] See, e.g., § 7.4.

LLC by exempt health care providers for the purpose of providing neonatal intensive care services[152]; creation of an LLC by exempt health care providers to provide rehabilitation services in a community[153]; formation of an LLC by a tax-exempt community-based health care system and a group of physicians for the purpose of owning and operating an ambulatory surgical center[154]; and creation of an LLC by an exempt hospital and physicians for the purpose of operating a cardiac catheterization laboratory.[155]

In another example of this approach, a public charity (a fundraising vehicle for a tax-exempt hospital and for medical research), two exempt educational institutions (that operated medical schools and engaged in scientific research), and a state university (that managed an entity that facilitated technology transfer and the general growth of advanced technology companies) formed a charitable organization that served as a center of research, technology, and entrepreneurial expertise; to facilitate the acquisition of land for this center, the organizations (other than the center organization) created an LLC.[156]

(ii) Association Case Study. An MMLLC can be used in the business league context. In one instance, three tax-exempt trade associations, for a considerable period of time, each conducted a trade show. These associations had comparable exempt purposes and members with similar interests. Presumably under pressure from the members, the associations decided to organize and operate a single trade show. This approach was designed to facilitate a significant reduction in the administrative costs of the shows.

Because the purposes and membership of these associations were not identical, the organizations did not want to merge and produce one show. There was also concern about legal liabilities (tort claims) associated with the combined trade show. The solution was operation of the trade show in an LLC. Income from the three trade shows represented a significant portion of the annual revenue of these associations. The LLC elected to be taxed for federal income tax purposes as a partnership.[157]

One association acquired a 50 percent interest in the LLC; the other two associations each obtained a 25 percent interest. The LLC's operating agreement provided that it is organized and operated to plan, market, implement, and host trade shows. The members of this LLC join with investment intent.

The IRS ruled that the income to be derived by these three associations from the trade show conducted by the LLC will be protected from unrelated business income taxation by virtue of the exception for convention and trade show activity.[158] The tax consequences to the associations thus were the same regardless of whether the trade show activity was conducted directly by them or indirectly by means of the LLC.

---

[152] Priv. Ltr. Rul. 200044040.
[153] Priv. Ltr. Rul. 200102052.
[154] Priv. Ltr. Rul. 200118054.
[155] Priv. Ltr. Rul. 200304041.
[156] Priv. Ltr. Rul. 200411044.
[157] See § 6.10(a).
[158] Priv. Ltr. Rul. 200333031. The exception is the subject of § 5.9(n).

(d) Single-Member Limited Liability Company

The advent of the LLC has brought use of the single-member LLC and the multi-member LLC into the tax-exempt organizations context. Initially the focus was on the LLC in which an exempt organization was not the only member. In these instances, there may be a mix of exempt and nonexempt members, or all of the members may be exempt organizations.[159]

More recently, use of the single-member LLC (SMLLC), where the member is a tax-exempt organization,[160] is emerging. The SMLLC can be a form of exempt subsidiary organization, in that the LLC is a separate legal entity, it is exempt from federal income taxes,[161] it is wholly owned by the exempt member, and it can perform exempt functions.

Generally, as noted, SMLLCs are disregarded for federal income tax purposes. A disregarded LLC is regarded as a branch or a division of its member owner. (Thus, although an SMLLC is a separate legal entity for most purposes, it is treated as a component of its owner for federal income tax purposes, and in that sense is not literally a subsidiary of the member.) In one instance, the IRS wrote that, when the sole member of an LLC is a tax-exempt organization, the function of the LLC is treated as an "activity" of the exempt organization.[162]

A disregarded (single-member) LLC is not required to file an application for recognition of tax exemption.[163] The exempt owner of an SMLLC treats the operations and finances of the LLC as its own for purposes of the annual information return filing requirements.[164] The interplay of the law of exempt organizations and the rules as to SMLLCs also are being manifested in other contexts.[165]

Creative uses of the SMLLC by tax-exempt organizations abound. One of them pertains to the acceptance by charitable organizations of gifts of property that may carry with them exposure of the donee to legal liability (such as environmental or premises tort liability). Previously, a charitable organization could attempt to shield its other assets from liability by placing the gift property in a separate exempt entity, such as a supporting organization[166] or a title-holding company.[167] Among the difficulties with this approach is the need or desire to file an application for recognition of tax exemption for the new entity and/or file annual information returns on its behalf. As an alternative, however, a charitable organization can utilize an SMLLC as a vehicle to receive and hold each contribution of property separately, thus presumably obtaining the desired liability protection.[168]

---

[159] See § 6.10(c).

[160] To date, the tax-exempt organizations utilizing an SMLLC have been confined to charitable (IRC § 501(c)(3)) entities, but that may soon change.

[161] An LLC with two or more tax-exempt charitable members can itself qualify as a charitable organization (see *Tax-Exempt Organizations* § 4.3(e)).

[162] Priv. Ltr. Rul. 200134025.

[163] In general, see § 2.3.

[164] In general, see *Tax-Exempt Organizations* § 24.3(c).

[165] E.g., *id.* § 29.3, note 61.

[166] See § 8.6.

[167] See *Tax-Exempt Organizations* § 18.2.

[168] E.g., Priv. Ltr. Rul. 200134025.

The SMLLC can also be used to facilitate program activities. As an illustration, a tax-exempt charitable organization owned and operated a downtown parking facility in an SMLLC; the IRS ruled that the operation of the facility was lessening the burdens of government.[169] Similarly, an exempt museum, organized as a private operating foundation,[170] owned and operated a racetrack and a campground, with these activities in an SMLLC; the IRS ruled[171] that these activities were functionally related businesses.[172] In another instance involving a private operating foundation, the IRS ruled that a foundation can retain its operating foundation status notwithstanding expansion of its activities to include control over and management of, by means of an SMLLC, a school or tax-exempt university.[173] Likewise, a public charity, with the objective of constructing, owning, and leasing student housing for the benefit of a tax-exempt college, developed and operated the project through an SMLLC; in this fashion it issued taxable and tax-exempt bonds, and provided temporary construction jobs and permanent employment opportunities in the community.[174] Also, a charitable organization that provided educational opportunities to low-income and other students, including housing, provided facilities for various colleges, with ownership and operation of each facility in a separate SMLLC.[175] Further, a tax-exempt hospital participated in a joint venture, by use of an SMLLC, in furtherance of its health care purposes.[176]

In the unrelated business setting, a supporting organization[177] affiliated with an operating educational institution[178] was the sole member of an LLC; the IRS ruled that when the SMLLC receives real property encumbered by debt, it and the supporting organization will be afforded an exemption from the rules concerning acquisition indebtedness[179] for purposes of determining debt-financed income.[180]

In another context, a tax-exempt health care system that wholly owned a business housed in an SMLLC was able to extend participation in its 403(b) plan[181] (which must be confined to employees of employers that are charitable entities or public schools) to employees of the business; because the SMLLC is disregarded for federal tax purposes, the IRS ruled that the employees of the business may be treated as employees of the system for this purpose.[182]

---

[169] Priv. Ltr. Rul. 200124033. Lessening the burdens of a government is an exempt charitable function (see *Tax-Exempt Organizations* § 6.4).

[170] See *Private Foundations* § 3.1.

[171] Priv. Ltr. Rul. 200202077.

[172] See *Private Foundations* § 7.3.

[173] Priv. Ltr. Rul. 200431018.

[174] Priv. Ltr. Rul. 200249014.

[175] Priv. Ltr. Rul. 200304036

[176] Priv. Ltr. Rul. 200436022.

[177] See § 8.6.

[178] See § 8.2(b).

[179] See § 5.10.

[180] Priv. Ltr. Rul. 200134025.

[181] See § 11.9.

[182] Priv. Ltr. Rul. 200341023.

CHAPTER SEVEN

Associations, Partnerships, and Joint Ventures

One of the most important developments involving business leagues and other tax-exempt organizations in the modern era is the use of separate but related organizations. This phenomenon is reflected, for example, in the frequent utilization of subsidiaries and limited liability companies by exempt organizations.[1] What is striking, nonetheless, is the contemporary willingness—and, in some instances, necessity—of many exempt organizations to simultaneously use different forms of related entities, be they for-profit or nonprofit, trust or corporation, taxable or nontaxable. This includes participation by exempt business leagues in partnerships or other forms of joint venture.

§ 7.1 PARTNERSHIPS FUNDAMENTALS

A partnership is a form of business entity, recognized in the law as a separate legal entity, as is a corporation or trust. It is usually evidenced by a partnership agreement, executed between persons who are the partners; the persons may be individuals, corporations, and/or other partnerships. Each partner owns one or more interests, called units, in the partnership.

The term *partnership* is defined in the federal tax law to include a "syndicate, group, pool, joint venture, or other unincorporated organization, through or by means of which any business, financial operation, or venture is carried on, and which is not . . . a trust or estate or a corporation."[2] This term is broadly applied. For example, co-owners of income-producing real estate who operate

---

[1] See Chapter 6.
[2] IRC § 7701(a)(2).

the property (either directly or through an agent of one or more of them) for their joint profit are considered to be operating by means of a partnership.[3]

A partnership usually entails a profit motive. Thus, a court defined a partnership as a "contract of two or more persons to place their money, efforts, labor, and a skill, or some or all of them, in lawful commerce or business, and to divide the profit and bear the loss in definite proportions."[4]

Partners are of two types: general and limited. The types are delineated principally by their role in the venture (active or passive) and the extent of the partners' liability for the acts of the partnership. Generally, liability for the consequences of a partnership's operations rests with the general partner or partners, while the exposure to liability for the functions of the partnership for the limited partners is confined to the amount of the limited partner's contribution to the partnership. A general partner is liable for satisfaction of the ongoing obligations of the partnership and can be called on to make additional contributions of capital to it. Every partnership must have at least one general partner. Sometimes where there is more than one general partner, one of them is designated the managing general partner.

Many partnerships have only general partners, who contribute cash, property, and/or services. This type of partnership is termed a *general partnership*. The economic interests of the general partners may or may not be equal. In this type of partnership, which is essentially akin to a joint venture,[5] generally all of the partners are equally liable for satisfaction of the obligations of the partnership and can be called on to make additional capital contributions to the entity.

Some partnerships, however, need or want to attract capital from sources other than the general partners. This capital can come from investors, who are termed *limited partners*. Their interest in the partnership is, as noted, limited in the sense that their liability is limited. The liability of a limited partner is confined to the amount of the capital contribution—the investment. The limited partners are in the venture to obtain a return on their investment and perhaps to procure some tax advantages. A partnership with both general and limited partners is called a *limited partnership*.

The partnership is the entity that acquires the property, develops it (if necessary), and sometimes continues to operate and maintain the property. Where a tax-exempt organization is the general partner, it is not the owner of the property (the partnership is), but nonetheless it can have many of the incidents of ownership, such as participation in the cash flow generated by the property, a preferential leasing arrangement, and/or the general perception by the outside world that the property is owned by the exempt organization. The exempt organization may lease space in property owned by the partnership. The exempt entity may have an option to purchase from the partnership after the passage of a stated period of time.

Partnerships do not pay taxes—and, in this sense, are themselves tax-exempt organizations.[6] They are conduits—technically, flow-through entities—of net revenue to the partners, who bear the responsibility for paying tax on their

---

[3] Rev. Rul. 54-369, 1954-2 C.B. 364; Rev. Rul. 54-170, 1954-1 C.B. 213.
[4] Whiteford v. United States, 61-1 U.S.T.C. ¶ 9301, at 79, 762 (D. Kan. 1960).
[5] See § 7.3.
[6] See *Tax-Exempt Organizations* § 1.2.

net income. Partnerships are also conduits of the tax advantages of the ownership of property and thus can pass through preference items, such as depreciation and interest deductions.

If an entity fails to qualify under the federal tax laws as a partnership, it will be treated as an *association*, which means taxed as a corporation. When that happens, as a general rule the entity will have to pay taxes, and the ability to pass through tax advantages to the equity owners is unavailable.[7]

In most instances, it is clear that the parties in an arrangement intend to create and operate a partnership. Nonetheless, however, the law will treat an arrangement as a general partnership (or other joint venture) for tax purposes, even though the parties involved intended (or insist they intended) that their relationship is something else (such as landlord and tenant or payor and payee of royalties). The issue often arises in the unrelated business context, where a tax-exempt organization is asserting that certain income is passive in nature (most frequently, rent or royalty income) and the IRS is contending that the income was derived from active participation in a partnership (or joint venture).[8]

Federal tax law is inconsistent in stating the criteria for ascertaining whether a partnership is to be found as a matter of law. The U.S. Supreme Court stated that "[w]hen the existence of an alleged partnership arrangement is challenged by outsiders, the question arises whether the partners really and truly intended to join together for the purpose of carrying on business and sharing in the profits or losses or both."[9] The Court added that the parties' "intention is a question of fact, to be determined from testimony disclosed by their 'agreement considered as a whole, and by their conduct in execution of its provisions.'"[10] In one instance, a court examined state law and concluded that the most important element in determining whether a landlord-tenant relationship or joint venture agreement exists is the intention of the parties. This court also held that the burden of proving the existence of a partnership is on the party who claims that that type of relationship exists (which can include the IRS).[11]

Conversely, another court declared that it is "well settled that neither local law nor the expressed intent of the parties is conclusive as to the existence or nonexistence of a partnership or joint venture for federal tax purposes."[12] The court stated that the standard to follow is "whether, considering all the facts—the agreement, the conduct of the parties in execution of its provisions, their statements, the testimony of disinterested persons, the relationship of the parties,

---

[7] Moreover, the partnership must have effective ownership of the property for these deductions to be available, rather than have the ownership be by the exempt organization/general partner (e.g., Smith v. Comm'r, 50 T.C.M. 1444 (1985)).

[8] See, e.g., § 5.9.

[9] Comm'r v. Tower, 327 U.S. 280, 286–287 (1946).

[10] *Id.* at 287 (citations omitted). These principles are equally applicable in determining the existence of a joint venture (e.g., Estate of Smith v. Comm'r, 313 F.2d 724 (8th Cir. 1963), *aff'g in part, rev'g in part, and remanding* 33 T.C. 465 (1959); Luna v. Comm'r, 42 T.C. 1067 (1964); Beck Chemical Equip. Corp. v. Comm'r, 27 T.C. 840 (1957)).

[11] Harlan E. Moore Charitable Trust v. United States, 812 F. Supp. 130, 132 (C.D. Ill. 1993), *aff'd,* 9 F.3d 623 (7th Cir. 1993).

[12] Trust U/W Emily Oblinger v. Comm'r, 100 T.C. 114 (1993). The court cited a number of court opinions as authority for this proposition, relying principally on Haley v. Comm'r, 203 F.2d 815 (5th Cir. 1953), *rev'g and rem'g* 16 T.C. 1509 (1951).

their respective abilities and capital contributions, the actual control of income and the purposes for which it is used, and any other facts throwing light on their trust intent—the parties in good faith and acting with a business purposes intended to join together in the present conduct of the enterprise."[13]

This court wrote that the "realities of the taxpayer's economic interest rather than the niceties of the conveyancer's art should determine the power to tax."[14] The court added: "Among the critical elements involved in this determination are the existence of controls over the venture and a risk of loss in the taxpayer."[15] This court further observed that it is not bound by the "nomenclature used by the parties," so that a document titled, for example, a lease may as a matter of law be a partnership agreement.[16]

This dichotomy was illustrated by a case involving a tax-exempt charitable organization and its tenant farmer; the issue was whether the relationship was landlord-tenant, partnership, or other joint venture.[17] The question before the court was whether the rent, equaling 50 percent of the crops and produce grown on the farm, constituted rent that was excludable from taxation as unrelated business income.[18] The court looked to state law to ascertain the meaning to be given the term *rent*. It observed that the written contracts at issue contained provisions usually found in leases, the tenant furnished all of the machinery and labor in the production of crops, and the tenant generally made decisions with a farm manager as to the day-to-day operation of the farm. The court concluded that the contracts as a whole clearly reflected the intention of the parties to create a landlord-tenant relationship rather than a partnership.

The IRS unsuccessfully contended that this charitable organization, by furnishing the seed and one-half of the cost of fertilizer, weed spray, and combining, engaged in farming as a partner or joint venturer. The court observed that these types of arrangements were not uncommon in share-crop leases, and noted that the furnishing of these items ordinarily increased the crop yield and the net return of both the landlord and tenant substantially more than the amount invested by each for the items. The court also analyzed the effect on the landlord-tenant relationship of the hiring by the charitable organization of the farm manager for the supervision of the tenant farmer. The manager advised the tenant on topics such as crops, seed, weed spray, and fertilizer; decisions were made by the mutual agreement of the tenant and the manager. The court concluded that the utilization of the farm manager did not adversely affect the landlord-tenant relationship and found that the arrangement was not that of a partnership (or other joint venture).[19]

---

[13] Trust U/W Emily Oblinger v. Comm'r, 100 T.C. 114, 118 (1993), citing Comm'r v. Culbertson, 337 U.S. 733, 742 (1949).

[14] Trust U/W Emily Oblinger v. Comm'r, 100 T.C. 114 (1993).

[15] *Id.* at 118–119.

[16] *Id.* at 119.

[17] United States v. Myra Found., 382 F.2d 107 (8th Cir. 1967).

[18] See § 5.9(g). This case was decided before enactment of the *passive rent rules*.

[19] The foregoing is, by necessity, an overview of the law of partnerships. For a comprehensive analysis of these entities (from a tax-exempt organizations perspective), see Sanders, *Joint Ventures Involving Tax-Exempt Organizations, Second Edition* (Hoboken, NJ: John Wiley & Sons, Inc., 2000) ("*Joint Ventures*"), particularly Chapters 1, 3, and 4.

§ 7.2 TAX EXEMPTION ISSUE

The IRS has long been concerned about the participation of tax-exempt organizations—particularly charitable ones—in partnerships, other than as limited partners in a prudent investment vehicle.[20] Exempt organizations, nonetheless, often view the use of partnerships as a useful and beneficial way to acquire, finance, own, and/or operate property. This controversy has centered on exempt charitable organizations in partnerships, although some or all of the principles of law being developed could apply to other types of exempt organizations, including business leagues.

The concern of the IRS is that substantial benefits may be provided to the for-profit participants in a partnership (usually the limited partners) with a tax-exempt organization where the exempt organization is a or the general partner. This uneasiness in the agency has its origins in arrangements involving exempt hospitals and physicians, such as a limited partnership formed to build and manage a medical office building, with a hospital as the general partner and investing physicians as limited partners.[21] Where these substantial benefits are present, the IRS usually will not be hesitant to deploy the doctrines of private inurement, excess benefit transaction, and/or private benefit.[22] Yet the law, in general, is now clear that an exempt charitable or other organization may participate as a general partner in a partnership without adversely affecting its exempt status.[23]

It is the position of the IRS that a tax-exempt charitable organization will lose or be denied exemption if it participates as the, or a, general partner in a limited partnership, unless the principal purpose of the partnership is to further exempt purposes.[24] Even where the partnership can so qualify, exemption is not available if the charitable organization/general partner is not adequately insulated from day-to-day management responsibilities of the partnership and/or if the limited partners are to receive an undue economic return. The IRS recognizes that a charitable organization can be operated exclusively for exempt purposes, and simultaneously be a general partner and satisfy its fiduciary responsibilities with respect to the other partners.[25]

---

[20] E.g., Gordanier, Jr., "Structuring Securities Partnerships for Tax-Exempt and Foreign Investors," 7 *J. Partnership Tax.* (No. 2) 24 (1990); Menna, "Leveraged Real Estate Investments by Tax-Exempt and Taxable Investors: Comparing the Forms of Investment," 17 *J. Real Estate Tax.* (No. 3) 231 (1990); Williamson & Blum, "Tax Planning for Real Estate Ownership and Investment by Tax-Exempt Entities," 16 *J. Real Estate Tax.* (No. 2) 139 (1989).

[21] The history of the position of the IRS in these regards is detailed in *Joint Ventures*, at § 4.2.

[22] The IRS is not averse to using its authority in this context. For example, the agency created the private inurement *per se* doctrine in the healthcare context as a basis for revocation of hospitals' tax-exempt status using a joint venture theory (see *Tax-Exempt Organizations* § 19.8). The IRS revoked the exemption of hospitals for engaging in private inurement transactions (e.g., Priv. Ltr. Rul. 9130002). In general, Hyatt & Hopkins, *The Law of Tax-Exempt Healthcare Organizations, Second Edition* (Hoboken, NJ: John Wiley & Sons, 2001), particularly Chapters 4, 22.

[23] On one occasion, the IRS ruled that the tax-exempt status of a charitable organization should not be revoked; the issue was its participation as a general partner in seven limited partnerships (Priv. Ltr. Rul. 8938001). On another occasion, the IRS held that a hospital organization continued to qualify as an exempt charitable entity, notwithstanding its function as the sole partner of a limited partnership, where some of the limited partnership interests were held by related individuals (Tech. Adv. Mem. 200151045).

[24] Gen. Couns. Mem. 39005.

[25] Gen. Couns. Mem. 39546.

Confusion as to the ability of tax-exempt charitable organizations to partici-pate as general partners in limited partnerships was added when a court held, without recognition, let alone discussion, of the considerable body of law devel-oped on the point, that an organization did not qualify as an exempt entity where it was a co-general partner in limited partnerships, where the other gen-eral partner was a for-profit corporation and the limited partners were individu-als, and where the purpose of the partnerships was to operate low-income housing projects. The court said that the organization's participation violated the operational test[26] in that the operation of the partnerships would cause fed-eral and state tax benefits to flow to the nonexempt partners.[27] By reason of the organization's involvement in the partnerships, the underlying properties would receive property tax reductions. The partnership would be eligible, under federal tax law, for general business credits and low-income housing credits; pursuant to management agreements, the organization had the responsibility for ensuring that the partnership complied with the business tax credit require-ments. The organization received, as compensation, percentages of state tax sav-ings. The court concluded that the "keystone of . . . [this] entire plan is of course to lend [the organization's] exempt status to achieving the objective of property tax reduction."[28] The organization also was deprived of exempt status by reason of the private inurement doctrine[29] because its "activities here serve the commer-cial purposes of the for-profit partners in the limited partnerships of which . . . [the organization] is a general partner."[30]

Prior to a review of the law concerning charitable organizations in partner-ships, it is appropriate to trace the evolution of this body of law.

(a) Evolution of Law

Originally the IRS was of the view that involvement by a tax-exempt charitable organization as a general partner in a limited partnership would automatically lead to revocation of its exempt status, irrespective of the organization's purpose for joining the venture. This *per se* rule surfaced when the IRS ruled that partici-pation by a charitable organization in a partnership, where the organization would be the general partner and private investors would be limited partners, is inconsistent with eligibility for exempt status in that undue economic benefit would flow to the limited partners. The agency wrote that, if the charity "entered [into] the proposed partnership, [it] would be a direct participant in an arrangement for sharing the net profits of an income producing venture with private individuals and organizations of a noncharitable nature." By serving as the general partner in the project, the IRS said, the charity would be furthering the "private financial interests" of the limited partners, which would "create a conflict of interest that is legally incompatible with [the charity] being operated

---

[26] See *Tax-Exempt Organizations* § 4.5.

[27] Housing Pioneers, Inc. v. Comm'r, 65 T.C.M. 2191 (1993).

[28] *Id.* at 2195.

[29] See Chapter 3.

[30] Housing Pioneers, Inc. v. Comm'r, 65 T.C.M. 2191, 2196 (1993). This opinion was affirmed but on the grounds that the organization failed to show that it was a qualified nonprofit organization for purposes of the low-income housing tax credit (IRC § 42(h)(5)(B)) (95-1 U.S.T.C. ¶ 50,126 (9th Cir. 1995)).

exclusively for charitable purposes."[31] This was the position of the IRS, even though the purpose of the partnership was to advance a charitable objective—the development and operation of a low-income housing project.

The *per se* rule was followed again the next year, when the IRS issued an adverse ruling to a charitable organization that was the general partner in a limited partnership, also created for the purpose of maintaining a low-income housing development. As before, the agency declared that the organization was a "direct participant in an arrangement for sharing the net profits of an income producing venture" with private individuals, so that the organization was "further[ing] the private financial interest of the [limited] partners."[32] The organization took the matter to court but the case was settled.[33]

Another IRS ruling, concerning whether certain fees derived by a tax-exempt lawyer referral service were items of unrelated business income,[34] reflected this IRS position. The agency ruled that, while flat counseling fees paid by clients and registration fees paid by lawyers were not taxable, the fees paid by lawyers to the organization based on a percentage of the fees received by the lawyers for providing legal services to clients referred to them constituted unrelated business income. The reason: The subsequently established lawyer-client relationship was a commercial undertaking, and the ongoing fee arrangement with the percentage feature placed the exempt organization in the position of being in a joint venture in furtherance of these commercial objectives.[35]

The first of the court decisions, concerning a charitable organization in a joint venture, sanctioned the involvement of a charitable organization as a general partner in a limited partnership. The case concerned an arts organization that, to generate funds to pay its share of the capital required to produce a play with a tax-exempt theater, sold a portion of its rights in the play to outside investors, utilizing the limited partnership. The arts organization was the general partner, with two individuals and a for-profit corporation as limited partners. Only the limited partners were required to contribute the capital; they collectively received a share of the profits or losses resulting from the production. In disagreeing with the IRS's position that the organization, solely because of its involvement in the joint venture should lose its tax-exempt status, the courts in the case emphasized the facts that the sale of the interest in the play was for a reasonable price, the transaction was at arm's length, the organization was not obligated for the return of any capital contributions made by the limited partners, the limited partners lacked control over the organization's operations, and none of the limited partners nor any officer or director of the for-profit corporation was an officer or director of the arts organization.[36]

Around that same time, the IRS approved an undertaking between a tax-exempt blood plasma fractionation facility and a commercial laboratory, by

---

[31] Priv. Ltr. Rul. 7820058.

[32] Unnumbered private letter ruling dated Feb. 6, 1979.

[33] Strawbridge Square, Inc. v. United States (Ct. Cl. No. 471-79T).

[34] See Chapter 5.

[35] Priv. Ltr. Rul. 7952002.

[36] Plumstead Theatre Soc'y, Inc. v. Comm'r, 74 T.C. 1324 (1980). Cf. Broadway Theatre League of Lynchburg, Va., Inc. v. United States, 293 F. Supp. 346 (W.D. Va. 1968).

which the parties acquired a building and constructed a blood fractionation facility. This arrangement enabled the facility to become self-sufficient in its production of blood fractions, to reduce the cost of fractioning blood, and thus to be able to more effectively carry out its charitable blood program. Each party had an equal ownership of, and shared equally in the production capacity of, the facility. The IRS concluded that the exempt organization's participation in this venture was substantially related to its exempt purposes and that there was no private benefit.[37]

The first manifestation of a relaxation of the stance of the IRS in these regards appeared in 1983 in the form of an IRS general counsel memorandum.[38] On that occasion, the IRS chief counsel's office opined that it was possible for a charitable organization to participate as a general partner in a limited partnership without jeopardizing its tax exemption. The IRS's lawyers advised that two aspects of the matter should be reviewed: (1) whether the participation may be in conflict with the goals and purposes of the charitable organization, and (2) whether the terms of the partnership agreement contain provisions that "insulate" the charitable organization from certain of the obligations imposed on a general partner. In this instance, the limited partnership (another low-income housing venture) was found to further the organization's charitable purposes, and several specific provisions of the partnership agreement were deemed to provide the requisite insulation for the charitable organization/general partner. Thus, the organization was permitted to serve as the partnership's general partner and simultaneously retain its exemption.

This position of the IRS chief counsel opened the way for many favorable private letter rulings concerning charitable organizations in partnerships. Each of these partnerships was held to be in furtherance of charitable objectives, such as the construction and operation of a medical office building on the grounds of a hospital, the purchase and operation of a CAT scan at a hospital, and low-income housing projects.

The sweeping rule of law in this regard was articulated, in one of the two most radical of these cases, by a federal court of appeals, which wrote that the "critical inquiry is not whether particular contractual payments to a related for-profit organization are reasonable or excessive, but instead whether the entire enterprise is carried on in such a manner that the for-profit organization benefits substantially from the operation of" the tax-exempt organization.[39] This, to date, represents the outer reaches of the ambit of the private benefit doctrine: the thought that there can be unwarranted private benefit, conferred on a noninsider, even if the terms and conditions of the arrangement are reasonable and substantial exempt functions are occurring.

In the other of these cases, two for-profit organizations that did not have any formal structural control over the nonprofit entity, the tax exemption of which was at issue, nevertheless were found to have exerted "considerable control" over its activities.[40] The for-profit entities set fees that the nonprofit organization

---

[37] Priv. Ltr. Rul. 7921018.
[38] Gen. Couns. Mem. 39005.
[39] Church by Mail, Inc. v. Comm'r, 765 F.2d 1387, 1392 (9th Cir. 1985).
[40] est of Hawaii v. Comm'r, 71 T.C. 1067, 1080 (1979), aff'd, 647 F.2d 170 (9th Cir. 1981).

charged for training sessions, required the nonprofit organization to carry on certain types of educational activities, and provided management personnel paid for and responsible to one of the for-profit organizations. Pursuant to a licensing agreement with the for-profit organizations, the nonprofit entity was allowed to use certain intellectual property for 10 years; at the end of the license period, all copyrighted material, including new material developed by the nonprofit organization, was required to be turned over to the for-profit organizations.[41] The nonprofit organization was required to use its excess funds for the development of its program activities or related research. The for-profit organizations also required that trainers and local organizations sign an agreement to not compete with these activities for two years after terminating their relationship with the organizations involved.

The trial court, in this case, concluded that the nonprofit organization was "part of a franchise system which is operated for private benefit and . . . its affiliation with this system taints it with a substantial commercial purpose."[42] The nonprofit organization was "simply the instrument to subsidize the for-profit corporations and not vice versa."[43] The nonprofit organization was held to not be operating exclusively for charitable purposes.

These two cases have framed this analysis. Even without formal control over the ostensible tax-exempt organization by one or more for-profit entities, the ostensible exempt organization can be viewed as merely the instrument by which a for-profit organization is subsidized (benefited). The nonprofit organization's "affiliation" with a for-profit entity or a "system" involving one or more for-profit entities can taint the nonprofit organization, actually or seemingly imbuing it with a substantial commercial purpose. The result is likely to be a finding of private benefit (or, if an insider is involved,[44] private inurement[45]), causing the nonprofit organization to lose or be denied tax-exempt status.

Matters worsen in this context when there is actual control. This is the principal message of the decision concerning whole entity joint ventures. In that case, a tax-exempt subsidiary of a public charity (hospital) became a co-general partner with a for-profit organization in a partnership that owned and operated a surgery center. A for-profit management company affiliated with the for-profit co-general partner managed the arrangement. The subsidiary's sole activity was participation in the partnership. The court termed this relationship "passive participation [by the charitable subsidiary] in a for-profit health-service enterprise."[46] The court concluded that it was "patently clear" that the partnership was not being operated in an exclusively charitable manner. The income-producing activity of the partnership was characterized as "indivisible" as between the nonprofit and for-profit organizations. No "discrete part" of these activities was

---

[41] See *Tax-Exempt Organizations* § 19.8.

[42] est of Hawaii v. Comm'r, 71 T.C. 1067, 1080 (1979), *aff'd*, 647 F.2d 170 (9th Cir. 1981).

[43] *Id.*, 71 T.C. at 1082.

[44] See § 3.3.

[45] The private inurement doctrine was invoked in a case concerning a charitable organization in a partnership in Housing Pioneers, Inc. v. Comm'r, 65 T.C.M. 2191 (1993).

[46] Redlands Surgical Services v. Comm'r, 113 T.C. 47, 77 (1999), *aff'd*, 242 F.3d 904 (9th Cir. 2001).

"severable from those activities that produce income to be applied to the other partner's profit."[47]

The heart of the whole entity joint venture decision is this: To the extent a public charity "cedes control over its sole activity to for-profit parties [by, in this case, entering into the joint venture] having an independent economic interest in the same activity and having no obligation to put charitable purposes ahead of profit-making objectives," the charity cannot be assured that the partnership will in fact be operated in furtherance of charitable purposes.[48] The consequence is the conferring on the for-profit party in the venture "significant private benefits."[49]

(b) Current State of Law

To date, the IRS has yet to issue a private letter ruling denying a charitable organization tax-exempt status because of its involvement as a general partner in a limited partnership.[50] Indeed, the IRS frequently concludes that an exempt charitable organization can participate as a general partner in a limited partnership without endangering its exempt status.[51] Also, on occasion, a charitable organization can achieve exempt purposes by involvement in a partnership as a limited partner.[52]

(i) General Rules. The current position of the IRS as to whether a charitable organization will have its tax-exempt status revoked (or recognition of exemption denied) if it functions as a general partner in a limited partnership is the subject of a three-part test,[53] which is the successor to the *per se* rule.[54]

Under this three-part test, the IRS first looks to determine whether the charitable organization/general partner is serving a charitable purpose by means of the partnership. If the partnership is advancing a charitable purpose, the IRS applies the remainder of the test. Should the partnership fail to adhere to the charitability standard, however, the charitable organization/general partner will be deprived of its tax-exempt status.

The balance of the test is designed to ascertain whether the charity's role as general partner inhibits its charitable purposes. Here the IRS looks to means by which the organization may, under the particular facts and circumstances, be insulated from the day-to-day responsibilities as general partner and whether the limited partners are receiving an undue economic benefit from the partnership or

---

[47] *Id.*, 113 T.C. at 77.

[48] *Id.* at 78.

[49] *Id.* This opinion was a major victory for the IRS, which earlier staked out, in Rev. Rul. 98-15, 1998-1 C.B. 718, the position adopted by the court. In general, Jones, "Private Benefit and the Unanswered Questions from Redlands," 89 *Tax Notes* 121 (2000).

[50] This observation is made with the understanding that the facts in some of these rulings are altered at the request of the IRS and that some ruling requests in this area are withdrawn in anticipation of the issuance of an adverse ruling.

[51] E.g., Priv. Ltr. Rul. 8338127.

[52] E.g., Priv. Ltr. Rul. 9608039.

[53] This was articulated in Gen. Couns. Mem. 39005 (see text accompanying *supra* note 38).

[54] In general, Hopkins, "Tax Consequences of a Charity's Participation as a General Partner in a Limited Partnership Venture: A Commentary on the McGovern Analysis," 30 *Tax Notes* (No. 4) 361 (1986), written in response to McGovern, "The Tax Consequences of a Charity's Participation as a General Partner in a Limited Partnership Venture," 29 *Tax Notes* 1261 (1985).

not. It remains the view of the IRS that there is an inherent tension between the ability of a charitable organization to function exclusively in furtherance of its exempt functions and the obligation of a general partner to operate the partnership for the ecnomic benefit of the limited partners. This tension is the same perceived phenomenon that the IRS, when applying its *per se* rule, chose to characterize as a "conflict of interest."

An instance of application of this test appeared in an IRS private letter ruling made public in 1985.[55] In that case, a charitable organization became a general partner in a real estate limited partnership that leased all of the space in the property to the organization and a related charitable organization. The IRS applied the first part of the test and found that the partnership was serving exempt ends because both of the tenants were charitable organizations. (The IRS general counsel memorandum underlying this ruling[56] noted that, if the lessee organization that was not the general partner had not been a charitable entity, the general partner would have forfeited its tax exemption.) On application of the rest of the test, the IRS found that the general partner was adequately insulated from the day-to-day management responsibilities of the partnership and that the limited partners' economic return was reasonable.

In this ruling, the IRS offered this guidance in explication of the second and third elements of the test:

> If a private interest is served [by a limited partnership in which a charitable organization is the general partner], it must be incidental in both a qualitative and quantitative sense. In order to be incidental in a qualitative sense, it must be a necessary concomitant of the activity which benefits the public at large. In other words, the activity can be accomplished only by benefiting certain private individuals. To be incidental in a quantitative sense, the private benefit must not be substantial after considering the overall public benefit conferred by the activity.

The IRS added that if the charitable organization in the partnership is "serving a private interest, other than incidentally, then its participation in a limited partnership [as general partner] will [adversely] affect its exempt status." As discussed next, however, considerable clarity has been subsequently provided in this area of the federal tax law as the IRS formulated its policies concerning the involvement of hospitals and other health care institutions in partnerships where physicians practicing at the hospitals are limited partners in these partnerships.

A commentator identified 11 favorable factors or categories that the IRS looks to in evaluating a tax-exempt charitable organization's involvement as a general partner in a limited partnership: (1) limited contractual liability of the tax-exempt partner; (2) limited rate of return on the capital invested by the limited partners (a stated ceiling that is, under the circumstances, reasonable); (3) an exempt organization's right of first refusal on the sale of partnership assets; (4) the presence of additional general partners obligated to protect the interest of the limited partners; (5) lack of control over the venture or the exempt organization by the for-profit limited partners (that is, there is no limited partner serving as a

---

[55] Priv. Ltr. Rul. 8541108.
[56] Gen. Couns. Mem. 39444.

director or officer of the exempt organization) except during the initial start-up period; (6) absence of any obligation to return the limited partners' capital from the exempt organization's funds; (7) absence of profit as a primary motivation for entering into the arrangement; (8) all transactions with partners are at arm's length; (9) management contract terminable for cause by the venture, with a limited term, renewal subject to approval of the venture, and preferably with an independent entity; (10) effective control in the exempt organization over major decisions as to the venture; and (11) written commitment in the joint venture governing document to the fulfillment of charitable purposes in the event of a conflict with a duty to maximize profit.[57]

Conversely, unfavorable factors include (1) disproportionate allocation of profits and/or losses in favor of the limited partners; (2) commercially unreasonable loans by the exempt organization to the partnership; (3) inadequate compensation received by the tax-exempt organization in exchange for services it receives; (4) control of the exempt organization by the limited partners or lack of sufficient control by the exempt organization to ensure that it is able to carry out its charitable activities; (5) abnormal or insufficient capital contributions by the limited partners; (6) profit motivation by the exempt partner; and (7) guarantee of the limited partner's projected tax credits or return on investment to the detriment of the exempt general partner.[58]

Until mid-1994, the IRS position with respect to charitable organizations in partnerships was presented solely by the three-part test. At this time, however, a private letter ruling appeared that added requirements to the basic test.[59] The IRS observed that the organization was "governed by an independent board of directors" composed of church and community leaders and that it had no other relationship with any of the commercial companies involved in the project. The IRS added that no information indicated that the organization was controlled by or "otherwise unduly influenced" by the limited partners or any company involved in the development or management of the project.

(ii) Health Care Institutions. Nearly all of the federal tax law in this setting has developed as the result of the innovative financing techniques, including partnerships, by or for the benefit of hospitals and other health care organizations, institutions, and systems.

One of the manifestations of this phenomenon was the IRS's position with respect to the sale of a hospital department's net revenue stream to a limited partnership (or joint venture) involving the hospital and physicians practicing in the department. The IRS held that this use of hospital assets was private inurement *per se* (that is, the amount of the funds flowing to the physicians was not evaluated against a standard or reasonableness), causing the hospital to lose its

---

[57] *Joint Ventures* § 4.2(h)(i). If the tax-exempt organization/general partner is shielded too much, however, the partnership may lose its tax status as a partnership (that is, a nontaxable flow-through entity). Should that occur, the entity may become an association taxable as a corporation (IRC § 7701(a)(3)) (see text accompanied by *supra* note 2). The IRS's office of Chief Counsel raised this issue for the benefit of the agency's reviewers (Gen. Couns. Mem 39546).

[58] *Joint Ventures* § 4.2(h)(ii).

[59] Priv. Ltr. Rul. 9438030.

tax exemption. In formulating its position in this regard, the chief counsel's office of the IRS used the occasion (in late 1991) to restate and update the analysis the agency uses in evaluating the participation of hospitals in a partnership arrangement.

The IRS's lawyers emphasized that the participant by a tax-exempt hospital as a general partner in a limited partnership is not inconsistent with exemption on a *per se* basis.[60] In each partnership situation, the IRS determines the presence or absence of private inurement or more than incidental private benefit[61] by evaluating all of the facts and circumstances, applying a standard of review termed "careful scrutiny." This three-step analysis asks:

1. Does the partnership further a charitable purpose?

2. If so, does the partnership agreement reflect an arrangement that permits the exempt organization to act primarily in furtherance of its exempt (charitable) purposes?

3. If so, does the arrangement cause the exempt organization to provide an impermissible private benefit to the limited partners?[62]

The third criterion requires a finding, if the hospital is to continue to be tax-exempt, that the benefits received by the limited partners are incidental to the exempt purposes advanced by the partnership. Thus, according to this analytical approach, a hospital's participation in a partnership or joint venture is inconsistent with its exemption if it does not further a charitable purpose or if there is either inadequate protection against financial loss by the hospital or inappropriate or excessive financial gain flowing to the limited partners (investors/physicians).

The IRS, in evaluating these situations, looks to see "what the hospital gets in return for the benefit conferred on the physician-investors." The agency is least likely to find a basis for revocation of tax exemption because of hospital partnerships where a "new health care provider or resource was made available to the community."[63] Of importance also is whether the partnership itself became a "property owner or service provider, subject to all the attendant risks, responsibilities, and potential rewards." By contrast, in the net revenue stream partnerships, the IRS saw insufficient community benefit; the partnership was viewed as a "shell type of arrangement where the hospital continues to own and operate the facilities in question and the joint venture invests only in a profits interest." The arrangement was perceived as only incidentally promoting health; the IRS believed that the hospitals "engaged in these ventures largely as a means to retain and reward members of their medical staffs; to attract their admissions and referrals; and to preempt the physicians from investing in or creating a competing provider."

---

[60] Gen. Couns. Mem. 39862. The IRS bluntly stated that it "no longer contends that participation [by a charitable organization] as a general partner in a partnership is *per se* inconsistent with [tax] exemption."

[61] E.g., Gen. Couns. Mem. 37789.

[62] In stating these factors, the IRS reaffirmed the ongoing validity of Gen. Couns. Mem. 39005 (see *supra* note 38), 39444 (see *supra* note 56), and 39546 (see *supra* note 25).

[63] E.g., Gen. Couns. Mem. 39732.

Another feature the IRS deplores is the situation where the general partner (such as a hospital or a taxable subsidiary of the hospital) is liable for partnership losses and is required to maintain a loss reserve, while the limited partners are not burdened with much risk. The net revenue stream arrangement did not, the IRS wrote, result in "improved patient convenience, greater accessibility of physicians, or any other direct benefit to the community."

The IRS has identified these legitimate purposes (absent private inurement *per se*) for involvement of a hospital in a partnership (or joint venture): the raising of needed capital, the bringing of new services or a new provider to the community, the sharing of a risk inherent in a new exempt activity, and/or the pooling of diverse areas of expertise. Prior pronouncements from the IRS reflect the factors favored by the agency: a limited contractual investment by the limited partners, a limited (reasonable) rate of return on the investment by the limited partners, a right in the exempt organization of first refusal on the disposition of an asset of the partnership, the involvement of other general partners obligated to protect the interests of the limited partners, and the absence of any obligation to return the limited partners' capital from the resources of the exempt general partner. For example, the IRS held that a charitable organization, created by 10 unrelated exempt hospitals, could remain exempt, even though it, as its only function, became a sole general partner in a limited partnership, including individuals as limited partners, because the purpose of the partnership was furtherance of exempt purposes (operation of a lithotripsy center) and because the benefit to nonexempt limited partners (including physicians) was incidental.[64]

The IRS's audit guidelines for the examination of tax-exempt hospitals[65] summarize the fact situations that may cause private inurement to arise: where participation in the venture imposes on the exempt organization obligations that conflict with its exempt purposes; where there is a disproportionate allocation of profits and losses to the nonexempt (usually, limited) partners; where the exempt partner makes loan to the partnership that are commercially unreasonable (that is, they have a low interest rate or inadequate security); where the exempt partner provides property or services to the partnership at less than fair market value; and/or where a nonexempt partner receives more than reasonable compensation for the sale of property or services to the joint venture.[66]

The IRS is likely to pursue a private inurement rationale where there is a "complete lack of symmetry in upside opportunities and downside risks for the physician-investors." At the same time, the position struck by the IRS in the context of hospitals and physicians in partnerships should not "be read to imply that a typical joint venture that involves true shared ownership, risks, responsibilities, and rewards and that demonstrably furthers a charitable purpose should be met automatically with suspicion or disapproved merely because physician-investors haven an ownership interest."

---

[64] Tech. Adv. Mem. 200151045.

[65] IRS Audit Guidelines for Hospitals, Manual Transmittal 7(10)69-38 for Exempt Organizations Examinations Guidelines Handbook (March 27, 1992).

[66] *Id.* § 342.

On occasion, a tax-exempt hospital or hospital system will create a taxable subsidiary and cause that entity to be a (or the) general partner in a limited partnership.[67]

These pronouncements by the IRS in the health care context have added considerable clarity to the dimensions of the federal tax law concerning the permissible and impermissible participation, in general, of tax-exempt charitable organizations in partnerships.

§ 7.3 JOINT VENTURES FUNDAMENTALS

A tax-exempt organization may enter into a joint venture with a for-profit organization, without adversely affecting its exempt status, as long as doing so furthers exempt purposes and the joint venture agreement does not present it from acting exclusively to further those purposes. A joint venture does not present the private inurement problems that the IRS associates with participation by charitable organizations as general partners in limited partnerships. By contrast, an involvement in a joint venture by an exempt organization would lead to a loss (or denial) of exemption if the primary purpose of the exempt organization is to participate in the venture and if the function of the venture is unrelated to the exempt purposes of the exempt organization.

A court defined a *joint venture* as an association of two or more persons with intent to carry out a single business venture for joint profit, for which purpose they combine their efforts, property, money, skill, and knowledge, but they do so without creating a formal partnership, trust, or corporation.[68] Thus, two or more entities (including tax-exempt organizations) may operate a business enterprise as a joint venture.[69]

Generally, when a tax-exempt organization acquires an interest in a joint venture (such as by transfer of funds), the event is not a taxable one, because the action is a one-time activity and thus is not a business that is regularly carried on.[70] That is, the exempt organization is not likely to be characterized as being in the business of establishing or investing in partnerships.[71]

Where the purpose of the joint venture is investment, the joint venture will be looked through to determine the nature of the revenue being received by the tax-exempt organization. It is rare that the investment income will be exempt function revenue. Usually the income is passive investment income and thus is not taxed.[72] But if the participation in the joint venture is the principal activity of the exempt organization and the purpose of the venture is not an exempt one for the organization, it will, as observed, lose (or be denied) exempt status by reason of participation in the venture.

A tax-exempt organization may become involved in joint venture with a for-profit organization in advancement of an exempt purpose. Again, the look-through principle applies, with the revenue derived by the exempt organization

---

[67] See § 6.5.
[68] Whiteford v. United States, 61-1 U.S.T.C. ¶ 9301, at 79,762 (D. Kan. 1960).
[69] Stevens Bros. Found., Inc. v. Comm'r, 324 F.2d 633 (8th Cir. 1963).
[70] See § 5.6.
[71] E.g., Priv. Ltr. Rul. 8818008.
[72] See § 5.1.

from the venture characterized as related revenue. For example, an exempt charitable organization participating as a general partner in a venture, with a for-profit entity, to own and operate an ambulatory surgical center was determined by the IRS to be engaging in a related activity.[73] Likewise, the IRS ruled that a joint venture between a charitable organization and a for-profit one, for the purpose of organizing and operating a free-standing alcoholism/substance abuse treatment center, would not jeopardize the exempt status of the charitable organization.[74] Still another illustration is an IRS ruling that an exempt hospital may, without endangering its exempt status, participate with a for-profit organization for the purpose of providing magnetic resonance imaging services in an under-served community.[75] Other IRS private letter rulings provide examples of joint ventures that did not adversely affect the exempt status of the exempt organization involved.[76]

A joint venture of this nature may be structured as a limited liability company.[77]

The IRS is concerned, nonetheless, about situations where the involvement of a tax-exempt organization in a joint venture gives rise, or may give rise, to private inurement.[78] For example, it is the view of the IRS, as noted, that an exempt hospital endangers its exemption because of its involvement in a joint venture the net revenue stream of a hospital department for a stated period of time.[79] In this situation and others that are similar, the application of the private inurement doctrine is triggered by the inherent structure of the joint venture and not by whether the compensation is reasonable.

In some instances, the IRS will characterize an arrangement between parties as a joint venture for tax purposes. That is, the agency may attempt to overlay the joint venture structure on a set of facts, irrespective of the intent of the participants. This can occur, for example, as an alternative to an assertion that a tax-exempt organization is directly engaged in an unrelated business.[80] As an illustration, in a case in which a court held that an exempt labor union[81] was not engaged in an unrelated business when it collected per capita taxes from its affiliated unions, the IRS retorted with the (unsuccessful) contention that the revenue should nonetheless be taxed because the unions were involved in a "joint enterprise."[82] Another example of this point was provided when, having lost the argument that a form of gambling—"tip jars" placed by an exempt organization in taverns so that the patrons could purchase tip-jar tickets to provide revenue to the organization—was not an unrelated business, the IRS's (unsuccessful) riposte was that the exempt organization and the taverns were engaged in a joint

---

[73] Priv. Ltr. Rul. 8817039.

[74] Priv. Ltr. Rul. 8521055.

[75] Priv. Ltr. Rul. 8833038.

[76] E.g., Priv. Ltr. Rul. 8621059.

[77] E.g., Priv. Ltr. Rul. 9637050. A limited liability company is an entity formed under state law; it has the attributes of a corporation for purposes of limiting liability, yet it can, under the *check-the-box* regulations (see § 6.10(a)), be treated as a partnership for federal income tax purposes (e.g., Priv. Ltr. Rul. 9839039).

[78] See Chapter 3.

[79] Gen. Couns. Mem. 39862.

[80] See Chapter 5.

[81] See § 1.6(c).

[82] Laborer's Int'l Union of North America v. Comm'r, 82 T.C.M. 158, 160 (2001).

venture, with the activities of the employees of the taverns imputed to the exempt organization.[83]

A tax-exempt organization may also enter into a joint venture with another exempt organization, in furtherance of the exempt purposes of both of them.[84] For example, two public charities organized to develop, construct, own, and operate a medical center formed a limited liability company to develop, construct, own, and operate an outpatient ambulatory surgery center; the IRS ruled that the charities will continue to engage in the promotion of health[85] directly and through the operation of the joint venture.[86]

§ 7.4 WHOLE-ENTITY JOINT VENTURES

Developments brewing in the health care field are generating significant implications for all public charities and other types of tax-exempt organization that are in, or are contemplating participation in, a joint venture. This matter concerns the *whole-hospital joint venture* or what is generically known as the *whole-entity joint venture*.

(a) Overview of the Law

As discussed, a tax-exempt health care organization, as well as nearly any other type of exempt organization, can participate in a joint venture with a for-profit entity and not adversely affect the organization's exempt status, as long as the purpose of involvement of the exempt organization in the joint venture is furtherance of exempt purposes.[87] In this type of joint venture, the exempt entity utilizes its assets (usually only some of them) in furtherance of an exempt purpose.

The whole-entity joint venture is much different from a conventional joint venture. With this approach, the tax-exempt entity transfers the entirety of its assets to the joint venture, with the for-profit organization perhaps assuming control over the assets and managing the day-to-day operations of the venture. For example, ownership of one or more hospitals might be transferred. The exempt health care organization does not directly engage in health care activities; it receives income and other distributions attributable to its ownership interest in the venture. There usually is a board of directors of this joint venture. Technically, the venture is a partnership[88] or a limited liability company.[89]

A whole-entity joint venture can lead to access to managed care contracts, greater efficiency of operations, and additional funding of charitable programs. From the standpoint of the for-profit entity, the venture provides a means to "acquire" a hospital without having to engage in an outright purchase of the institution.

Thus, the fundamental distinction between joint ventures in general and whole entity joint ventures—one that may determine whether the tax-exempt

---

[83] Vigilant Hose Co. of Emmitsburg v. United States, 2001-2 U.S.T.C. ¶ 50,458 (D. Md. 2001).
[84] E.g., Priv. Ltr. Rul. 9249026.
[85] See *Tax-Exempt Organizations* § 6.3.
[86] Priv. Ltr. Rul. 200117043.
[87] See § 7.3.
[88] See § 7.1.
[89] See § 7.3, text accompanied by note 77.

organization is able to obtain or maintain exemption—is that, in instances of the former, the exempt entity continues to engage in health care functions while, in the latter case, the entity is an owner of the venture that itself controls the assets and operates the programs underlying the health care activity. This raises the question, unresolved at this time, as to whether participation in a whole-hospital joint venture would cause the hospital or other health care organization to lose or be denied exempt status. Other issues are the possibility of private inurement or private benefit to the for-profit entity in the venture,[90] imposition of the intermediate sanctions penalties,[91] and/or the likelihood that income from the venture is unrelated business income to the exempt hospital.[92] Further complicating this area of the law is the impact of any new rules on entities outside the health care field, such as on tax-exempt organizations that are managed by for-profit companies,[93] as well as nuances concerning the future viability of these ventures.[94]

(b) IRS Guidance

The IRS stated its position with respect to whole entity joint ventures in 1998.[95] Two situations were sketched in which involvement by a tax-exempt hospital in one of these ventures does or does not jeopardize the hospital's exempt status.

(i) Fact Situation 1. The first of these situations concerned a nonprofit corporation that owned and operated an acute care charitable hospital (H1), which concluded that it could better serve its community if it obtained additional funding. A for-profit corporation (FP1) that owned and operated a number of hospitals was interested in providing financing for the hospital if it could earn a reasonable rate of return. These two entities formed a limited liability company (LLC1).

H1 contributed all of its operating assets, including the hospital, to LLC1. FP1 also contributed assets to LLC1. In return, H1 and FP1 received ownership interests in LLC1 proportional and equal in value to their respective contributions.

LLC1's governing instruments provided that it is to be managed by a governing board consisting of three individuals selected by H1 and two individuals selected by FP1. H1 intended to appoint community leaders who have experience with hospital matters but who were not on the hospital staff and did not otherwise engage in business transactions with the hospital. These documents

---

[90] See Chapter 3.

[91] See § 3.8.

[92] See Chapter 5.

[93] Under current law, this utilization of management companies is quite common and appropriate (see, e.g., Priv. Ltr. Rul. 9715031). Cf. Priv. Ltr. Rul. 9709014.

[94] In general, Boisture & Varley, "Emphasis on Control by Exempt General Partners May Indicate Restrictive Rules on Joint Ventures," 9 *J. Tax. Exempt Orgs.* (No. 3) 109 (Nov./Dec. 1997); Sullivan, "Whole-Hospital Joint Ventures," 19 *Exempt Org. Tax. Rev.* (No. 1) 45 (Jan. 1998); Tsilas, "Whole Hospital Joint Ventures— Do Exempt Organizations Really Know What They're Getting Themselves Into?" 17 *Exempt Org. Tax. Rev.* (No. 2) 273 (Aug. 1997); Fondo & Jedrey, "States Move to Limit Joint Ventures with For-Profit Health Care Providers," 9 *J. Tax Exempt Orgs.* (No. 1) 3 (July/Aug. 1997); Greenwalt & Legget, "Whole-Hospital Joint Ventures with Taxable Entities Raise Tax Questions for Exempts," 6 *J. Tax Exempt Orgs.* (No. 4) 163 (Jan./ Feb. 1995).

[95] Rev. Rul. 98-15, 1998-1 C.B. 718. In general, *Joint Ventures* § 4.2(e).

also provided that the governing instruments may be amended only by the approval of both owners and that a majority of three board members must approve certain major decisions relating to the operation of LLC1 (such as the budget, distributions of earnings, and selection of key executives).

These governing documents further required that any LLC1-owned hospital be operated in a manner that advances charitable purposes by promoting health for a broad cross-section of its community. They stated that the board members' duty to adhere to this requirement overrides any obligation they may have to operate LLC1 for the financial benefit of its owners. Thus, the community benefit standard took precedence over the considerations of maximizing profitability.

The governing documents provided that all returns of capital and distributions earnings made to the owners of LLC1 must be proportional to their ownership interests in the venture. The terms of these instruments were legal, binding, and enforceable under state law.

LLC1 entered into an agreement with a management company (MC1) for the purpose of providing day-to-day management services to LLC1. MC1 was not related to H1 or FP1. This contract was for a five-year term and was renewable for additional five-year periods by mutual consent. MC1 was paid a management fee based on the gross revenues of LLC1. The terms and conditions of the contract were reasonable and comparable to what other management firms receive for comparable services for similarly situated hospitals. LLC1 may terminate this agreement for cause.

None of the directors, officers, or key employees of H1 involved in the decision to form LLC1 was promised employment or any other inducement by FP1 or LLC1 and their related entities if the transaction were approved. None of these individuals had any interest, directly or indirectly, in FP1 or any of its related entities.

H1 intended to use any distributions it received from LLC1 to fund grants to support activities that promote the health of H1's community and to help the indigent obtain health care. Substantially, all of H1's grant-making will be funded by distributions by LLC1. H1's projected grant-making program and its participation as an owner of LLC1 constituted H1's only activities.

(ii) **Fact Situation 2.** The second of these situations concerned a nonprofit corporation that owned and operated an acute care charitable hospital (H2), which concluded that it could better serve its community if it obtained additional funding. A for-profit corporation (FP2) that owned and operated a number of hospitals and provided management services to several other hospitals was interested in providing financing for the hospital if it could earn a reasonable rate of return. These two entities formed a limited liability company (LLC2).

H2 contributed all of its operating assets, including the hospital, to LLC2. FP2 also contributed assets to LLC2. In return, H2 and FP2 received ownership interests in LLC2 proportional and equal in value to their respective contributions.

LLC2's governing instruments provided that it is managed by a governing board consisting of three individuals selected by H2 and three individuals selected by FP2. H2 intended to appoint community leaders with experience in hospital matters but not on the hospital staff and not engaging in business transactions with the hospital. These documents also provided that the governing instruments may be amended only by the approval of both owners and that a majority of board members must approve certain major decisions relating to the operation of LLC2 (such as the budget, distributions of earnings, and selection of key executives).

These governing documents further provided that LLC2's purpose was to construct, develop, own, manage, operate, and take other action in connection with operating the health care facilities it owned and to engage in other healthcare-related activities. The documents also provided that all returns of capital and distributions of earnings made to LLC2's owners must be proportional to their ownership interests in LLC2.

LLC2 entered into an agreement with a management company (MC2) for the purpose of providing day-to-day management services to LLC2. MC2 was a wholly owned subsidiary of FP2. This contract was for a five-year term and was renewal for additional five-year periods at the discretion of MC2. MC2 was to be paid a management fee based on the gross revenues of LLC2. The terms and conditions of the contract, other than its renewal terms, were reasonable and comparable to what other management firms receive for comparable services for similarly situated hospitals. LLC2 may terminate this agreement only for cause.

As part of the agreement to form LLC2, H2 agreed to approve the selection of two individuals to serve as MC2's chief executive officer and chief financial officer. These individuals previously worked for FP2 in hospital management and had business expertise. They worked with MC2 to oversee the day-to-day management of LLC2. Their compensation was comparable to what like executives are paid at similarly situated hospitals.

H2 intended to use any distributions it received from LLC2 to fund grants to support activities that promote the health of H2's community and to help the indigent obtain health care. Substantially all of H2's grant-making was funded by distributions from LLC2. H2's projected grant-making program and its participation as an owner of LLC2 constituted H2's only activities.

(iii) Summary of Guidance. In this guidance, the IRS articulated five precepts of law never before publicly stated by the agency:

1. The rule that activities of a partnership are often considered to be the activities of a tax-exempt partner is termed the *aggregate principle*. This principle applies for purposes of the operational test.[96]

2. The activities of a limited liability company are considered the activities of a nonprofit organization that is an owner of the company when evaluating whether the nonprofit entity is operated primarily for charitable purposes.[97]

3. A charitable organization may form and participate in a partnership, including a limited liability company, and meet the operational test if

---

[96] See *Tax-Exempt Organizations* § 4.5(c).
[97] *Id.* § 4.4.

participation in the partnership furthers a charitable purpose, the partnership arrangement permits the exempt organization to act primarily in furtherance of tax-exempt purposes, and there is only incidental benefit to the for-profit partners.[98]

Two more of these rules are central to the findings by the IRS in this guidance:

4. A tax-exempt charitable organization may enter into a management contract with a private party, according that party authority to conduct activities on behalf of the organization and direct use of the organization's assets, as long as the charity retains ultimate authority over the assets and activities being managed, and the terms and conditions of the contract (including compensation and the term) are reasonable.

5. If a private party is allowed to control the nonprofit organization's activities or use its assets for the benefit of the private party, and the benefit is not merely incidental, the organization will not qualify for tax exemption.

In application of these principles, H1's tax exemption was preserved. H1's exempt functions consisted of the health care services it will provide through LLC1, and its grant-making activities are to be funded with income distributed by LLC1. H1's capital interest in LLC1 is equal in value to the assets it contributed to the venture. The returns from LLC1 to its owners will be proportional to their investments. The governing instruments of LLC1 clearly reflect exempt functions and purposes. The appointees of H1 will control the board of LLC1. The renewal feature of the contract is favorable to H1.

Under these facts, H1 can ensure that the assets it owns and the activities it conducts through LLC1 are used primarily to further tax-exempt purposes. Thus, H1 can ensure that the benefit to FP1 and other private parties, such as MC1, will be incidental to the accomplishment of charitable ends.

It was stipulated that the terms and conditions of the management contract were reasonable and that the grants by H1 were intended to support education and research, and assist the indigent.

The IRS acknowledged that when H2 and FP2 formed LLC2, and H2 contributed its assets to LLC2, H2 will—like H1—be engaged in activities that consist of the health care services to be provided through LLC2 and the grant-making activities it conducted using income distributed by LLC2. The IRS said, however, that H2 will fail the primary purpose test, because there was no binding obligation in LLC2's governing instruments for it to serve charitable purposes or otherwise benefit the community. Thus, LLC2 had the ability to deny care to segments of the community, such as the indigent.

The control element was significant in the second set of facts. H2 shared control of LLC2 with FP2. This means that H2 cannot initiate programs within LLC2 to serve new health needs in the community without consent of at least one board member appointed by FP2. Inasmuch as FP2 is a for-profit entity, the IRS stated that it "will not necessarily give priority to the health needs of the community over the consequences of [FP's] profits."

---

[98] These principles are the essence of the law as summarized *supra* (§ 7.4(b)(i)), but this was the first time that the IRS stated them in a precedential document.

MC2 had "broad discretion" over LLC2's activities and assets that may not always be under the supervision of LLC2's board. For example, MC2 could enter into all but "unusually large" contracts without board approval. Also, MC2 could unilaterally renew the management agreement.

The consequence of all of this for H2 is that FP2 was receiving benefits resulting from the conduct of LLC2 that were private in nature and not incidental. H2 failed the operational test when it participated in the formation of LLC2, contributed its operating assets to H2, and then served as an owner of LLC2.[99]

(iv) Subsequent Case Law. The IRS's position with respect to whole-hospital joint ventures was basically adopted wholesale when the issue was first litigated.[100] The court concluded that the tax-exempt health care entity involved in the venture (a surgical center) "ceded effective control" over its sole activity to for-profit parties that had an independent economic interest in the same property.[101] The documents made it clear that the partnership lacked any obligation to place charitable purposes ahead of profit-making objectives. Significant private benefits were found to be conferred by the charitable entity on private parties, to the extent that the organization was no longer exempt because it failed the primary purpose test and the operational test.

In this case, the structure of the management of the venture was fatal to the charitable participant. The trial court observed that it could exert influence by blocking actions proposed to be taken by the managing directors, but it could not initiate action without the consent of at least one of the appointees of the for-profit co-venturer. The nonprofit organization was perceived as lacking sufficient control unilaterally to cause the venture to respond to community needs for new health services, modify the delivery or cost structure of its present health services to better serve the community, or terminate the management company involved if it was determined to be managing the venture in a manner inconsistent with charitable objectives. Indeed, the management contract, an arrangement like the one posited on the IRS's guidance, was portrayed by the court as a "salient indicator" of the charity's surrender of effective control over the operations of the venture.

In the other case on the point, the government lost.[102] This court concluded that there were "exceptional protections" in place to preclude the venture from being operated to serve private interests. For example, the venture agreement required that hospitals owned by the venture operate in accord with the community benefit standard, with the tax-exempt entity unilaterally able to dissolve the venture if that is not done. Other facts, such as enabling the charity entity to

---

[99] In general, Louthian, III, "Revenue Ruling Brings New Life to Joint Ventures but Kills Off a GCM," 10 *J. Tax Exempt Orgs.* (No. 1) 3 (July/Aug. 1998); Mancino, "New Ruling Provides Guidance, Raises Questions for Joint Ventures Involving Exempt Organizations," 88 *J. Tax* (No. 5) 294 (May 1998); Griffith, "Revenue Ruling 98-15: Dimming the Future of All Nonprofit Joint Ventures?" 20 *Exempt Org. Tax. Rev.* (No. 3) 405 (1998); Peregrine & Sullivan, "Rev. Rul. 98-15 Confirms Traditional Tax Planning Approach for 'Typical' Joint Venture," 20 *Exempt Org. Tax. Rev.* (No. 2) 220 (1998).

[100] Redlands Surgical Servs. v. Comm'r, 113 T.C. 47 (1999), aff'd 242 F.3d 904 (9th Cir. 2001). In general, *Joint Ventures* § 4.2(f).

[101] Redlands Surgical Servs. v. Comm'r, 113 T.C. 47 (1999), aff'd, 242 F.3d 904 (9th Cir. 2001).

[102] St. David's Health Care System, Inc. v. United States, 2002-1 U.S.T.C. ¶ 50,452 (W.D. Tex. 2002).

appoint the chair of the venture's governing board and unilaterally remove its chief executive officer, led the court to conclude that "these provisions clearly protect the non-profit, charitable pursuits [of the exempt organization] as well as any community board could."[103]

This court wrote that "not all joint ventures between non-profit and for-profit organizations are either *per se* exempt or *per se* non-exempt."[104] It said that it was following the statement of the law laid down in the previous case, "without deciding whether it is in fact the governing standard."[105] The court said that it is "difficult to imagine a corporate structure more protective of an organization's charitable purpose than the one at issue in this case."[106] Language in the venture agreement led the court to the conclusion that the exempt partner had "substantially more control" than the for-profit partner (even though each entity appointed 50 percent of the governing board).[107] Although this court did not expressly articulate the points, it held that the exempt organizations did not cede control of its resources to the for-profit partner, that charitable objectives were ahead of profit-making ones in the case, and that there was no unwarranted private benefit.[108]

This summary judgment decision, however, was vacated by a federal court of appeals and remanded to the district court for trial.[109] The appellate court adhered to the principles of the law established in the previous case, observing that the case before it "illustrates why, when a non-profit organization forms a partnership with a for-profit entity, courts should be concerned about the relinquishment of control."[110] The court reviewed the joint venture documents and pronounced itself "uncertain" as to whether the hospital ceded control of its resources and operations to the for-profit corporation.[111] Although the court of appeals found facts to show that control by the hospital was not lost, it also concluded that "there are reasons to doubt that the partnership documents provide [the hospital] with sufficient control."[112] The court observed that the exempt hospital did not control a majority of the venture's board of governors, the company managing the venture was a for-profit subsidiary of the for-profit co-venturer, the board of governors was not empowered to deal with the day-to-day operation of the venture, there was uncertainty as to the extent of the hospital's control over the chief executive officer of the venture, and the likelihood that the hospital would threaten dissolution of the partnership because of concerns as to impact of the arrangement on its exempt status was questionable.

---

[103] *Id.* at 84,253.

[104] *Id.*

[105] *Id.* at 84,254.

[106] *Id.*

[107] *Id.*

[108] In general, Griffith, "St. David's TAM: Goliath's Hidden Slingshot," 38 *Exempt Org. Tax Rev.* (No. 2) 195 (Nov. 2002); Griffith, "Redefining Joint Venture Control Requirements: St. David's vs. Goliath?" 37 *Exempt Org. Tax. Rev.* (No. 2) 255 (Aug. 2002).

[109] St. David's Health Care System, Inc. v. United States, 349 F.3d 232 (5th Cir. 2003).

[110] *Id.* at 239.

[111] *Id.* at 240.

[112] *Id.* at 241.

§ 7.5 ANCILLARY JOINT VENTURES

The law as to tax-exempt organizations and joint ventures has evolved to the point where there are essentially three types of these joint ventures. In one, the entirety of the exempt organization is in the venture.[113] In another, the primary operations of the exempt organization are in the venture. In the third approach, concerning the *ancillary joint venture*, something less than primary operations of the exempt organization is in the venture.

The aggregate principle and the control test presumably are applicable in connection with the first two types of these ventures. Certainly the operational test[114] is. In the ancillary joint venture setting, however, the context is different. The IRS is of the view, which seems to be correct, that the aggregate principle applies when determining if there is unrelated business.[115] When the involvement in a venture is a small portion of the exempt organization's overall activities, however, the operational test is not implicated (assuming the organization continues to be operated primarily for exempt purposes[116]).

Assuming that the tax-exempt organization must—to remain exempt—retain control of its assets in connection with entire and primary involvement in a joint venture, the question remains as to whether control is needed in the ancillary joint venture setting. In its first ruling on the point, the IRS took the position that control was necessary in that context for a charitable organization to retain its exempt status.[117] Similarly, the IRS ruled that a public charity could enter into an ancillary joint venture with for-profit corporations for the purpose of financing small businesses for the benefit of low-income individuals without jeopardizing its tax-exempt status or incurring unrelated business income.[118] The agency observed that the venture (structured as a limited liability company) would be operated in conformity with its whole-entity joint venture principles.

The IRS, in 2004, issued formal guidance as to the tax consequences of public charities' involvement in ancillary joint ventures, ruling that a public charity in this type of arrangement with a for-profit entity will not lose its tax-exempt status if the involvement is an insubstantial part of its total operations, and that it will not be subject to unrelated business income taxation if the charity retains control over the partnership arrangement and operations that constitute one or more related businesses.[119]

This guidance concerned a tax-exempt university that offered, as part of its educational programs, summer seminars to enhance the skill level of elementary and secondary school teachers. To expand the reach of these seminars, the

---

[113] See § 7.4.

[114] See *Tax-Exempt Organizations* § 4.5.

[115] Priv. Ltr. Rul. 200118054.

[116] See *Tax-Exempt Organizations* § 4.4.

[117] Priv. Ltr. Rul. 200118054 (concerning a venture to operate an ambulatory surgery center, involving a public charity and a group of physicians). This ruling is confusing, in part because the facts indicate that the "primary business" of the charity is a set of unidentified activities, so the involvement of the charity in the venture (which utilized a limited liability company) must be less than primary, yet the law analysis speaks of a "nonprofit organization whose principal activity is the ownership of a membership interest in a limited liability company."

[118] Priv. Ltr. Rul. 200351033.

[119] Rev. Rul. 2004-51, 2004-22 I.R.B. 974.

university, along with a for-profit company, formed a limited liability company (LLC), classified as a partnership for federal tax purposes. The for-profit company specialized in the conduct of interactive video training programs. The sole purpose of the LLC, as stated in its governing instruments, was to offer teacher training seminars at locations off the university's campus using interactive video technology.

The university and the for-profit company each held a 50 percent interest in the LLC, which was proportionate to the value of their respective capital contributions to the LLC. The governing documents of the LLC provided that all returns of capital, allocations, and distributions were to be made in proportion to the members' respective ownership interests. The university's participation in the LLC was an insubstantial part of its activities.

Its governing documents provided that the LLC was to be managed by a governing board comprised of three directors selected by the university and three directors selected by the for-profit company. The LLC arranged and conducted all aspects of the video teacher training seminars, including advertising, enrolling participants, arranging for the necessary facilities, distributing the course materials, and broadcasting the seminars to various locations. The LLC's teacher training seminars covered the same content that was covered in the seminars that the university conducted on its campus. Schoolteachers participated through an interactive video link at various locations, rather than in person.

The LLC's governing documents granted the university the exclusive right to approve the curriculum, training materials, and instructors and to determine the standards for successful completion of the seminars. The for-profit company was granted the exclusive right to select the locations where participants could receive a video link to the seminars and to approve other personnel (such as camera operators) necessary to conduct the video seminars. All other actions required the mutual consent of the university and the for-profit company.

The governing documents required that the terms of all contracts and transactions entered into by the LLC, with the university, the for-profit company, or any other party, be at arm's length and that all contract and transaction prices be at fair market value determined by reference to the prices for comparable goods or services. These documents limited the LLC's activities to the conduct of the teacher training seminars and required that the LLC not engage in any activities that would jeopardize the tax-exempt status of the university. The LLC operated, in all respects, in accordance with its governing documents.

The IRS ruled that the university's activities conducted through the LLC constituted a business that was substantially related to the exercise and performance of the university's purposes and functions. Even though the LLC arranged and conducted all aspects of the teacher training seminars, the university alone approved the curriculum, training materials, and instructors, and determined the standards for successful completion of the seminars. The fact that the for-profit entity selected the seminar locations and approved the other personnel was held not to change the conclusion that the seminars were a related business.

The seminars were conducted using interactive video technology and embraced the same content as the seminars conducted by the university on its campus. The LLC's activities expanded the reach of the university's teacher training seminars. Therefore, the IRS concluded that the manner in which the LLC conducted the seminars contributed importantly to the accomplishment of the university's educational purposes; the activities of the LLC were substantially related to the university's educational purposes. Thus, the university was not required to pay any unrelated business income tax on its distributive share of the LLC's income.

This ruling did not resolve all of the federal tax issues as to public charities in ancillary joint ventures. It did demonstrate that the IRS agrees that an exempt organization in a joint venture can retain control over venture activities in ways other than by means of the composition of the joint venture vehicle. Inasmuch as the involvement of the university in the LLC was insubstantial, there could not be an issue as to the presence of undue private benefit. Likewise, because the activities of the LLC were deemed to be inherently educational, the income flowing to the university could not, under the general flow-through rules, be unrelated business income.

The question remains, therefore, as to the tax consequences when the primary operations of the exempt organization are in the venture (the second type of joint venture referenced above). Even if the activity in the venture is related, it would seem that, if the public charity ceded its authority to the for-profit co-venturer, exempt status would be an issue because of application of the private benefit doctrine. Also, the IRS seemed to say that if the public charity ceded control over the venture to the for-profit company, the business in the venture would be converted to an unrelated business, even if the business remained inherently related. Further developments in this area must be awaited as the tax policy regarding these types of ventures is shaped.[120]

§ 7.6 INFORMATION REPORTING

If a partnership in which a tax-exempt organization is a partner regularly carries on a trade or business that would constitute an unrelated trade or business if directly carried on by the exempt organization, the organization generally must include its share of the partnership's income and deductions from the business in determining its unrelated income tax liability.[121]

A partnership generally must furnish to each partner a statement reflecting the information about the partnership required to be shown on the partner's tax return or information return.[122] The statement must set forth the partner's distributive share of the partnership income, gain, loss, deduction, or credit required to be shown on the partner's return, along with any additional information as provided by IRS forms or instructions that may be required to apply particular provisions of the federal tax law to the partner with respect to items related to the partnership.[123]

---

[120] The IRS ruled that a tax-exempt hospital may participate in a joint venture in furtherance of its healthcare purposes and thus without loss of exemption, because the partnership and management agreements involved provided that charitable purposes overrode other purposes (Priv. Ltr. Rul. 200436022).

[121] See *Tax-Exempt Organizations* § 28.4.

[122] IRC § 6031(b).

[123] Temp. Reg. § 1.6031(b)-1T.

The instructions accompanying the statement for partners (Schedule K-1, Form 1065) require the partnership to identify whether the partner is a tax-exempt organization. Also, the partnership must attach a statement furnishing any other information needed by the partner to file its return that is not shown elsewhere on the schedule.

The federal tax statutory law provides that, in the case of any partnership regularly carrying on a trade or business, it must furnish to the partners the information necessary to enable each tax-exempt partner to compute its distributive share of partnership income or loss from the business.[124] The conference report underlying this rule stated that it "emphasize[d] that the IRS should monitor and enforce the present-law reporting requirements and, where appropriate, should provide further guidance to partnerships through regulations or instructions as to how such information must be furnished" and that "information that must be furnished to tax-exempt partners under this provision is to be reflected by such organization on Form 990 or Form 990-T in the manner prescribed by Treasury regulations or by the IRS instructions for such Forms."[125]

Partnerships of tax-exempt organizations, including those comprised wholly of exempt organizations, must annually file federal information returns.[126]

§ 7.7 ALTERNATIVES TO PARTNERSHIPS

As the foregoing indicates, tax-exempt charitable organizations should avoid substantive participation in partnerships as general partner where the purpose of the partnership is not itself advancement of charitable objectives.

One way for a charitable organization to avoid the dilemma is to establish a wholly owned organization, usually a for-profit corporation, that would serve as the general partner in the partnership. This approach has been upheld by the IRS in private letter rulings.[127] The tax-exempt entity leasing rules, however, makes this approach somewhat less attractive.[128]

Rather than utilize a corporation in this setting, a tax-exempt organization may utilize a single-member limited liability company.[129]

Another approach is for tax-exempt organizations to avoid partnerships altogether and utilize a leasing arrangement. This works best in situations such as where an exempt organization acquires unimproved land and subsequently desires to have it improved, perhaps for its offices. The organization can acquire the land and enter into a long-term ground lease with a developer or development group. The developer would construct the building, perhaps giving it the organization's name and otherwise providing all external appearances of the

---

[124] IRC § 6031(d). This reporting requirement applies without regard to the modifications of IRC §§ 512(b)(8)–(15) (see *Tax-Exempt Organizations* § 27.1(l)–(n), (q)).

[125] H. Rep. 100-1104, 100th Cong., 2d Sess. 13 (1988). As to these reporting requirements, see Chapter 10.

[126] IRC § 6031. This return is Form 1065. E.g., Priv. Ltr. Rul. 8925092. In determining the tax year (the current year) of a partnership (IRC § 706(b)), a partner that is tax-exempt (IRC § 501(a)) is disregarded if the partner was not subject to tax on any income attributable to its investment in the partnership during the partnership's tax year immediately preceding the current year (Reg. § 1.706-1(b)(5)).

[127] E.g., Priv. Ltr. Rul. 7820057. In general, Rev. Rul. 68-296, 1968-1 C.B. 105.

[128] See *Tax-Exempt Organizations* § 29.5(g).

[129] E.g., Priv. Ltr. Rul. 200436022. See § 6.10.

structure being the organization's own building. This leaves the developer or development group in the position of fully utilizing all of the tax advantages. The exempt organization can lease space in the building, perhaps pursuant to a "sweetheart" lease, and may be accorded an option to purchase the building after the passage of years.[130] In this way, the organization fixes its headquarters expenses and seemingly owns the building from the outset, while avoiding jeopardizing its tax exemption and allocating the tax benefits to those who can utilize them.[131]

Another alternative to a partnership is the limited liability company.[132] A limited liability company often is the vehicle utilized to structure and operate a joint venture.[133] The principal attribute of a limited liability company, from the standpoint of tax-exempt organizations, is that it is treated as a partnership for federal tax purposes, which means that the entity itself does not pay taxes.[134] One or more exempt organizations can own interests in a limited liability company, and a limited liability company can engage wholly in exempt activities. Thus, an exempt organization can utilize a limited liability company for the performance of exempt functions; these functions are in a separate entity, that entity does not pay federal income taxes, and any income that flows from the limited liability company to the exempt organization shareholder is not taxable, by reason of the partnership look-through rule.[135]

In some instances, a pooled income fund can be employed as an alternative to a limited partnership.[136] Where the facts cause the relationship between the pooled income fund and the tax-exempt charitable organization that is the remainder interest beneficiary of the pooled income fund to be manifested in a lease, however, the tax-exempt entity leasing rules make the fund, as an investment vehicle, somewhat unattractive.[137]

---

[130] E.g., Priv. Ltr. Rul. 8715055.

[131] In general, Bean, "Tax Exempt Organizations' Investment in Leveraged Real Estate," 5 *Prac. Tax Law.* (No. 2) 67 (1991); Brenman, "A Lesson in Fractions: How to Attract Capital from Tax-Exempt Investors," 8 *J. Part. Tax.* (No. 1) 70 (1991); Kirchick & Cavell, "Tax-Exempt Organizations in Real Estate Transactions: A General Survey," 41 *U.S.C. Inst. on Fed. Tax.* 24 (1989).

[132] See § 6.10.

[133] See, e.g., § 7.4.

[134] See § 7.1.

[135] *Id.* An illustration of these points was the use by a group of healthcare organizations in the United States of a limited liability company to partner with public hospitals in a foreign country to establish and operate a charitable hospital in that country; the hospital itself was operated by the limited liability company (Priv. Ltr. Rul. 9839039).

[136] See § 9.2(c).

[137] The depreciation deduction (and perhaps other tax benefits) can flow through a pooled income fund to the income beneficiaries of the fund in determining their federal income tax liability (e.g., Priv. Ltr. Rul. 8347010). This feature can provide useful tax incentives to donors to charity by means of a pooled income fund, when coupled with the income tax charitable deduction that is occasioned by reason of the transfer of cash or property to the fund. As a general rule, the depreciation deduction available to the income beneficiaries is not computed by applying the tax-exempt entity leasing rules. Where, however, the property that is the (or a) medium of investment of the pooled income fund is located on the premises of the tax-exempt charitable organization that maintains the fund or is otherwise available to those who are served by that charity, the tax-exempt entity leasing rules are likely to be applicable. This is because of the provision of these rules that includes within the definition of a *lease* the grant of the *right to use* property, thereby causing the grant of a right to use property to be a *disqualified lease* (Reg. § 1.168(j)-1T, Q-5, A-5).

CHAPTER EIGHT

Association-Related Foundations

Tax-exempt business leagues, not being charitable organizations, are not concerned with public charity/private foundation status for themselves. By contrast, this distinction is important to associations that are charitable entities and/or that have related charitable, educational, and/or scientific foundations. Charitable associations and association-related foundations should always be public charities; that is, there is no valid reason why any of them should be classified as private foundations.

§ 8.1 DISTINCTIONS BETWEEN PUBLIC AND PRIVATE CHARITIES

The significance of *public charity* status for organizations that are tax-exempt charitable organizations[1] is multifaceted and is of utmost importance to both private and public exempt organizations. The substance of the four parts of a pertinent section of the Internal Revenue Code[2] is the key to understanding public charities. All charitable organizations, other than those referenced in the four subsections that follow, are private foundations and are subject to the operational constraints and charitable giving limitations imposed on and in connection with these foundations.[3] The five categories of public charities are:

§ 509(a)(1)—Institutions, such as colleges, universities, and hospitals

§ 509(a)(1)—Organizations supported by gifts and grants from the general public

§ 509(a)(2)—Organizations supported by gifts, grants, and/or fee-for-service revenue

§ 509(a)(3)—Supporting organizations

§ 509(a)(4)—Organizations that test for public safety

Private foundations must comply with a variety of special rules (some of which are onerous) and sanctions; these constraints are not applicable to public charities. Therefore, it is prudent, when possible, to obtain and maintain public charity status.[4] The important distinctions between private foundations and public charities are:

- The charitable giving rules differ as to public charities and private foundations.[5] The federal income tax annual percentage limitation on deductions for charitable contributions by individuals to private foundations is 30 percent of adjusted gross income for gifts of money and 20 percent for gifts of appreciated property. Up to 50 percent of an individual's income can be deducted for cash gifts and 30 percent for gifts of appreciated

---

[1] That is, organizations that are described in IRC § 501(c)(3) and tax-exempt by reason of IRC § 501(a).

[2] IRC § 509.

[3] See IRC §§ 4940–4948; *Private Foundations*, Chapters 4–10.

[4] Despite the fact that these rules have been in existence more than 35 years, there still is confusion surrounding them. This phenomenon was reflected in a decision by a federal court of appeals, which twice misstated the law as to private foundations and public charities, yet nonetheless managed to reach the correct conclusion (Stanbury Law Firm, P.A. v. Internal Revenue Service, 221 F.3d 1059 (8th Cir. 2000)).

[5] See Chapter 9.

property to public charities. To illustrate, assume that an individual with an income of $1 million wants to give $500,000 in cash annually for charitable pursuits. If the money is given to a private foundation, $300,000 of the annual gift would be deductible for the year of the gift. The full $500,000 is deductible for the gift year if it is given to one or more public charities.

- Appreciated property generally is not fully deductible when given to a private foundation; only the basis of real estate, closely held stock, or most other types of property is deductible.[6] The fair market value of shares of qualified appreciated stock contributed to a private foundation may, however, be fully deductible.[7] A full deduction for the market value of the property is potentially available for a gift of this type of property to a public charity.[8]

- An excise tax of 2 percent must be paid on a private foundation's investment income.[9] There is no tax on investment income for a public charity unless the unrelated business income tax applies.[10]

- A private foundation cannot buy or sell property, nor enter into most self-dealing transactions with its directors, officers, contributors, their family members, or other disqualified persons.[11] Public charities can have business dealings with their insiders, within limits.[12]

- Annual information returns are required to be filed by private foundations regardless of revenue levels and value of assets. These returns tend to be more complex for private foundations. A return is not required for certain public organizations, and a short form is available for many others.[13]

- Fundraising between private foundations is constrained by expenditure responsibility requirements, which essentially prohibit a private foundation from making a grant to another private foundation without contractual agreements and follow-up procedures.[14] No such policing of grant monies is required by law in the case of public charities.

- Lobbying activity by private foundations is generally not permitted,[15] while a limited amount of lobbying is allowed by public charities.[16] Political campaign activity by either public or private charities is a contravention of the rules underlying their tax exemption.[17]

---

[6] IRC § 170(e)(1)(B)(ii).
[7] IRC § 170(e)(5).
[8] Reg. § 1.170A-1(c)(1).
[9] IRC § 4940.
[10] See Chapter 5.
[11] IRC § 4941.
[12] IRC § 4958. See § 3.8.
[13] See Chapter 10.
[14] IRC § 4945(d)(4)(B), (h).
[15] IRC § 4945(d)(1), (e).
[16] IRC § 501(c)(3). See Chapter 4.
[17] Id.

- A private foundation's annual spending for grants to other organizations and charitable projects must meet minimum distribution requirements.[18] A public charity rarely has any specific spending mandate.

- Holding more than 20 percent of a business enterprise, including shares owned by board members and contributors, is generally prohibited for private foundations,[19] as are jeopardizing investments.[20] Limits of this nature are not placed on public charities.

§ 8.2 ORGANIZATIONS WITH INHERENTLY PUBLIC ACTIVITY

Churches, schools, colleges, universities, hospitals, medical research organizations, and governmental units qualify as public charities by reason of the inherently exempt nature of their program activities. These include many of the *institutions* found in the charitable sector.[21] The institutions that are public charities in this category are those that satisfy the requirements of at least one category of public institution.

Organizations in other categories of nonprivate foundation status may also have the attributes of institutions (such as museums and libraries), but they must qualify, if they can, under one or more other categories of public charity. Thus, these public institutions are not private foundations by reason of the nature of their programmatic activities (rather than by reason of how they are funded[22] or their relationship with one or more other tax-exempt organizations[23]).

(a) Churches

A church or a convention or association of churches is a public charity.[24] To qualify as a church, a religious organization must, at a minimum, have a body of believers or communicants who assemble regularly in order to worship. The IRS uses a 14-element test to determine whether an organization constitutes a church.[25]

(b) Educational Institutions

An "educational organization which normally maintains a regular faculty and curriculum and normally has a regularly enrolled body of pupils or students in attendance at the place where its educational activities are regularly carried on" is a public charity.[26] This type of institution is essentially a school[27]; thus, an organization that has as its primary function the presentation of formal instruction, has courses that are interrelated and given in a regular and continuous

---

[18] IRC § 4942.
[19] IRC § 4943.
[20] IRC § 4944.
[21] IRC § 509(a)(1).
[22] See §§ 8.3, 8.4.
[23] See § 8.5.
[24] IRC § 170(b)(1)(A)(i); Reg. § 1.170A-9(a).
[25] See *Tax-Exempt Organizations* § 8.3.
[26] IRC § 170(b)(1)(A)(ii).
[27] Reg. § 1.170A-9(b).

manner (thereby constituting a regular curriculum), normally maintains a regular faculty, and has a regularly enrolled student body in attendance at the place where its educational activities are regularly carried on qualifies as a public educational institution.[28]

Educational institutions qualifying for public charity status include primary, secondary, preparatory, and high schools, and colleges and universities. For purposes of the charitable contribution deduction and nonprivate foundation status, these organizations also encompass federal, state, and other publicly supported schools that otherwise qualify, although their tax exemption may be a function of their status as governmental units. An organization may not achieve public charity status as an operating educational institution where it is engaged in both operating educational and nonoperating educational activities (for example, an organization functioning as both a school and a museum), unless the latter activities are merely incidental to the former.[29] Thus, the IRS denied public charity status to an organization the primary function of which was not the presentation of formal instruction but the maintenance and operation of a museum.[30]

An organization may be regarded as presenting formal instruction even through it lacks a formal course program or formal classroom instruction. Thus, a tax-exempt organization that provided elementary education on a full-time basis to children at a facility maintained exclusively for that purpose, with a faculty and enrolled student body, was held to be a public charity despite the absence of a formal course program.[31] Similarly, an exempt organization that conducted a survival course was granted public charity classification, even though its course periods were only 26 days and it used outdoor facilities more than classrooms, since it had a regular curriculum, faculty, and student body.[32] By contrast, an exempt organization, the primary activity of which was provision of specialized instruction by correspondence and a 5- to 10-day seminar program of personal instruction for students who had completed the correspondence course, was ruled not to be an operating educational organization "since the organization's primary activity consist[ed] of providing instruction by correspondence."[33] In another instance, tutoring on a one-to-one basis in its students' homes was ruled insufficient to make an exempt tutoring organization an operating educational entity.[34]

The fact that an otherwise qualifying organization offers a variety of lectures, workshops, and short courses concerning a general subject area, open to the general public and to its members, is not sufficient for it to acquire nonprivate foundation status as an educational institution.[35] This is because such an "optional, heterogeneous collection of courses is not formal instruction" and

---

[28] Rev. Rul. 78-309, 1978-2 C.R. 123.
[29] Reg. § 1.170A-9(b).
[30] Rev. Rul. 76-167, 1976-1 C.B. 329.
[31] Rev. Rul. 72-430, 1972-2 C.B. 105.
[32] Rev. Rul. 73-434, 1973-2 C.B. 71.
[33] Rev. Rul. 75-492, 1975-2 C.B. 80.
[34] Rev. Rul. 76-384, 1976-2 C.B. 57.
[35] Rev. Rul. 78-82, 1978-1 C.B. 70.

does not constitute a curriculum.[36] Where the attendees are members of the general public and can attend the functions on an optional basis, there is no "regularly enrolled body of pupils or students."[37] Further, where the functions are led by various invited authorities and personalities in the field, there is no "regular faculty."[38]

Even if an organization qualifies as a school or other type of "formal" educational institution, it will not be able to achieve tax-exempt status if it maintains racially discriminatory admissions policies[39] or if it benefits private interests to more than an insubstantial extent.[40] As an illustration of the latter point, an otherwise qualifying school, which trained individuals for careers as political campaign professionals, was denied exempt status because of the secondary benefit accruing to entities of a national political party and its candidates, since nearly all of the school's graduates become employed by or consultants to these entities or candidates.[41]

(c) Hospitals and Other Medical Organizations

An "organization the principal purpose or functions of which are the providing of medical or hospital care or medical education or medical research, if the organization is *a hospital*," is a public charity.[42]

For public charity classification purposes, the term *hospital* includes federal government hospitals, state, county, and municipal hospitals that are instrumentalities of governmental units, rehabilitation institutions, outpatient clinics, extended care facilities, or community mental health or drug treatment centers, and cooperative hospital service organizations,[43] if they otherwise qualify. The term does not include, however, convalescent homes, homes for children or the aged, or institutions the principal purpose or function of which is to train disabled individuals to pursue a vocation,[44] nor does it include free clinics for animals.[45] For these purposes, the term *medical care* includes the treatment of any physical or mental disability or condition, whether on an inpatient or outpatient basis, as long as the cost of the treatment is deductible[46] by the person treated.[47]

Medical research organizations directly engaged in the continuous active conduct of medical research in conjunction with a hospital can qualify as a public charity. The term *medical research* means the conduct of investigations, experiments, and studies to discover, develop, or verify knowledge relating to the causes, diagnosis, treatment, prevention, or control of physical or mental diseases and impairments of human beings. To qualify, an organization must have

---

[36] Rev. Rul. 62-23, 1962-1 C.B. 200.

[37] Rev. Rul. 64-128, 1964-1 (Part I) C.B. 191.

[38] Rev. Rul. 78-82, 1978-1 C.B. 70.

[39] Bob Jones University v. United States, 461 U.S. 574 (1983).

[40] Reg. § 1.501(c)(3)-1(c)(1).

[41] American Campaign Academy v. Comm'r, 92 T.C. 1053 (1989). In general, *Tax-Exempt Organizations* § 7.3.

[42] IRC § 170(b)(1)(A)(iii).

[43] Cf. Rev. Rul. 76-452, 1976-2 C.B. 60.

[44] Reg. § 1.170A-9(c)(1).

[45] Rev. Rul. 74-572, 1974-2 C.B. 82.

[46] IRC § 213.

[47] Reg. § 1.170A-9(c)(1).

the appropriate equipment and professional personnel necessary to carry out its principal function.[48] Medical research encompasses the associated disciplines spanning the biological, social, and behavioral sciences.

An organization, to be a public charity under these rules, must have the conduct of medical research as its principal purpose or function[49] and be primarily engaged in the continuous active conduct of medical research in conjunction with a hospital, which itself is a public charity.[50]

(d) Governmental Units

The United States, District of Columbia, states, possessions of the United States, and their political subdivisions are classified as governmental units.[51] Such a unit qualifies as a public charity without regard to its sources of support, partly because, by its nature, it is responsive to all citizens.[52] A *governmental unit* presumably encompasses not only political subdivisions of states and the like, but also government instrumentalities, agencies, and entities referenced by similar terms.[53]

§ 8.3 PUBLICLY SUPPORTED ORGANIZATIONS—DONATIVE ENTITIES

One way for a tax-exempt charitable organization to avoid private foundation status is to receive its financial support from a sufficient number of sources. A publicly supported charity is the antithesis of a private foundation, in that the latter customarily derives its financial support from one source, while a publicly supported organization is primarily supported by the public. The law in this area principally concerns the process for determining *public* support.

There are essentially two ways by which a charitable organization can be publicly supported for federal tax law purposes. One way is to be an organization the revenues of which are derived in the form of gifts and grants—a *donative* charitable entity.[54] The other way is to be an organization that is primarily supported by an appropriate combination of fee-for-service (exempt function) revenue, gifts, and grants—a *service provider* charitable entity.[55] The rules concerning the donative type of organization were enacted in 1964; the rules concerning the service provider type of organization were introduced in 1969. Thus, Congress has provided two definitions of the same type of organization (in a generic sense); although there are substantive differences between the two sets of rules, many charitable organizations are able to satisfy the requirements of both.[56]

---

[48] Reg. § 1.170A-9(c)(2)(iii).

[49] Reg. § 1.170A-9(c)(2)(iv).

[50] In general, *Tax-Exempt Organizations* § 7.3.

[51] IRC § 170(c)(1).

[52] IRC § 170(b)(1)(A)(v); Reg. § 1.170A-9(d).

[53] In general, see *Tax-Exempt Organizations* § 18.17.

[54] IRC §§ 170(b)(1)(A)(vi), 509 (a)(1).

[55] IRC § 509(a)(2). See § 8.4.

[56] The donative type of publicly supported organization is generally perceived as the preferred category of the two. For example, only a charitable organization that satisfies the requirements of the donative organization rules (or the rules pertaining to public institutions (see § 8.2)) is able to maintain a pooled income fund (IRC § 642(c)(5)(A)). See *Charitable Giving*, Chapter 13.

(a) General Rules

An organization is a publicly supported organization, as a donative charitable organization, if it is a charitable entity that "normally receives a substantial part of its support" (other than income from the performance of an exempt function) from a governmental unit[57] or from direct or indirect contributions from the general public.[58]

The principal way for an organization to be a publicly supported organization under these rules is for it to normally derive at least one-third of its support from qualifying contributions and grants.[59] Thus, an organization classified as a publicly supported entity under these rules must maintain a support fraction, the denominator of which is total eligible support received during the computation period and the numerator of which is the amount of support from eligible public and/or governmental sources for the period. The cash basis method of accounting must be utilized in determining the nature of an organization's support under these rules.[60]

A 2 percent ceiling is used to determine the donations that may be included as public support. Only this minimal amount of a particular contributor's gift or gifts made during a four-year measuring period is counted as public support, whether that contributor is an individual, corporation, trust, private foundation, or other type of entity (taking into account amounts given by related parties).

Consider, for example, an organization receiving total support of $1 million during the four-year test period. In such a case, all contributions and grants of up to $20,000 could be counted as public support. If one person gave a total of $80,000, or $20,000 each year, only $20,000 is counted. The $1 million organization must receive at least $333,333 in public donations of $20,000 or less each. It could receive $666,666 from one source and the $10,000 from 33 sources, or $20,000 from 17 sources, for example.

Therefore, the total amount of support by a donor or grantor is included in full in the denominator of the support fraction, and the amount determined by application of the 2 percent limitation is included in the numerator of the support fraction. The latter amount is the amount of support in the form of direct contributions and/or grants from the general public. Donors or grantors who stand in a defined relationship to one another (such as spouses) must be considered as one source for purposes of computing the 2 percent limitation amount. Support that is received from governmental units and/or other donative publicly supported organizations is considered to be a form of indirect contributions from the general public (in that these grantors are considered conduits of direct public support).

For these purposes, the legal nature of the donors or grantors is not relevant. That is, in addition to individuals, public support can be derived from for-profit entities (including corporations and partnerships) and nonprofit entities (including various forms of tax-exempt organizations). For example, the IRS ruled that

---

[57] IRC § 170(c)(1).
[58] IRC § 170(b)(1)(A)(vi).
[59] Reg. § 1.170A-9(e)(2).
[60] E.g., Gen. Couns. Mem. 39109.

contributions made by a business league to a charitable organization seeking designation as a donative publicly supported entity are subject to this 2 percent limitation.[61] (It frequently happens, therefore, that private foundations are sources of public support, albeit subject to the 2 percent inclusion limit.) The fact that contributions are restricted or earmarked does not detract from their being qualified as public support.[62]

The 2 percent limitation does not generally apply to support received from other donative publicly supported organizations nor to support from governmental units[63]—that is, this type of support is, in its entirety, public support.[64] Organizations classified as other than private foundations because of their inherently public activities may also meet the requirements of a donative publicly supported organization.[65] The 2 percent limitation, therefore, does not apply with respect to grants from these organizations. Assistance from a foreign government may be considered allowable support in determining an organization's qualifications as a donative publicly supported entity.[66] By contrast, the 2 percent limitation is applicable to amounts received from a supporting organization.

Nonetheless, the 2 percent limitation applies with respect to support received from a donative publicly supported charitable organization or governmental unit if the support represents an amount that was expressly or impliedly earmarked by a donor or grantor to the publicly supported organization or unit of government as being for or for the benefit of the organization asserting status as a publicly supported charitable organization.[67] Earmarked contributions constitute support of the intermediary organization under these rules to the extent that they are treated as contributions to the organization under the law concerning the charitable deduction, except where the intermediary organization receives the contributions as the agent for the donor for delivery to the ultimate recipient.[68]

(b) Support Test

A matter that can be of considerable significance in enabling a charitable organization to qualify as a donative publicly supported organization is the meaning of the term *support*. For this purpose, *support* means amounts received as gifts, grants, contributions, net income from unrelated business activities, gross investment income,[69] tax revenues levied for the benefit of the organization and either paid to or expended on behalf of the organization, and the value of services or facilities (exclusive of services or facilities generally furnished to the public

---

[61] Rev. Rul. 77-255, 1977-2 C.B. 74.

[62] Priv. Ltr. Rul. 8822096.

[63] IRC § 170(c)(1).

[64] Reg. § 1.170A-9(e)(6)(i).

[65] Rev. Rul. 76-416, 1976-2 C.B. 57.

[66] Rev. Rul. 75-435, 1975-2 C.B. 215.

[67] Reg. § 1.170A-9(e)(6)(v); Reg. § 1.509(a)-3(j)(3).

[68] Gen. Couns. Mem. 39748. This conclusion is based on the fact that the extent of the deductibility of gifts to private foundations is not dependent on any earmarking (e.g., IRC § 170(b)(1)(E)(ii)) and, thus, that gifts to nonprivate foundations should not be treated any differently.

[69] IRC § 509(e).

without charge) furnished by a governmental unit to the organization without charge.[70] All of these items are amounts that, if received by the organization, comprise the denominator of the support fraction. *Support* does not include any gain from the disposition of property that would be considered as gain from the sale or exchange of a capital asset, or the value of exemption from any federal, state, or local tax or any similar benefit.[71] Also, funding in the form of a loan does not constitute this type of support.[72]

Sponsorship payments that are acknowledged by the tax-exempt organization without quantitative and qualitative information so as to avoid classification as advertising revenue[73] can be treated as contributions for public support purposes.[74]

In constructing the support fraction, an organization must exclude from both the numerator and the denominator amounts received from the exercise or performance of its exempt purpose or function and contributions of services for which a deduction is not allowable.[75] An organization will not be treated as meeting this support test, however, if it receives almost all of its support from gross receipts from related activities and an insignificant amount of its support from governmental units and the general public.[76] Moreover, the organization may exclude from both the numerator and the denominator of the support fraction an amount equal to one or more qualifying unusual grants.[77]

In computing the support fraction, the organization's support *normally* received must be reviewed. This means that the organization must meet the one-third support test for a period encompassing the four tax years immediately preceding the year involved, on an aggregate basis. Where this is done, the organization is considered as meeting the one-third support test for its current tax year and for the tax year immediately succeeding its current tax year.[78] For example, if an organization's current tax year is calendar year 2006, the computation period is calendar years 2002 to 2005; if the support fraction is satisfied on the basis of the support received over this four-year period, the organization satisfies the support test for 2006 and 2007. (A five-year period for meeting this support test is available for organizations during the initial five years of their existence.)

Several issues can arise in computing the public support component (the numerator) of the support fraction for donative publicly supported organizations, including:

- Whether a contribution or grant is from a qualifying publicly supported charity[79]

---

[70] IRC § 509(d); Reg. 1.170A-9(e)(7)(i).
[71] IRC § 509(d).
[72] E.g., Priv. Ltr. Rul. 9608039.
[73] Reg. § 513-4(c)(2)(iv).
[74] Reg. § 1.170A-9(e)(6).
[75] Reg. § 1.170A-9(e)(7)(i).
[76] Reg. § 1.170A-9(e)(7)(ii).
[77] Reg. § 1.170A-9(e)(6)(ii), (iii).
[78] Reg. § 1.170A-9(e)(4)(i).
[79] IRC § 170(b)(1)(A)(vi) (donative organization).

- Whether a contribution or grant from a qualifying publicly supported charity or governmental unit is a pass-through transfer from another donor or grantor[80]

- Whether a membership fee constitutes a donation rather than a payment for services[81]

- Whether a payment pursuant to a government contract is support from a governmental unit (a grant) rather than revenue from a related activity (exempt function revenue)[82]

- Whether an organization is primarily dependent on gross receipts from related activities[83]

In making these computations, care must be taken in a situation where the organization being evaluated under these rules previously had to make changes in its operations to qualify as a charitable entity. The position of the IRS is that the rules that require, as discussed, a determination of the extent of broad public financial support in prior years "presuppose" that the organization was organized and operated exclusively for charitable purposes and otherwise qualified as a charitable entity during those years. Consequently, support received by an organization in these circumstances in one or more years in which it failed to meet the requirements for a charitable entity cannot be considered in ascertaining its status as a publicly supported charitable organization.[84]

(c) Facts-and-Circumstances Test

One of the defects of the donative organization support rules is that organizations that are not private foundations in a generic sense, because they have many of the attributes of a public organization, may be classified as private foundations because they cannot meet the mechanical one-third test. Organizations in this position include museums and libraries that rely principally on their endowments for financial support and thus have little or no need for contributions and grants. Although the statutory law is silent on the point, the tax regulations offer some relief in this regard, by means of the *facts-and-circumstances test.*

The history of the organization's fundraising efforts and other factors can be considered as an alternative method to the mathematical formula for qualifying for public support under the general donative charitable entity rules. (This test is not available in connection with the service provider entity rules.) Several factors must be present to meet this test[85]:

- Public support must be at least 10 percent of the total support; a higher percentage is preferable.

---

[80] See § 8.3(a), fifth paragraph, last sentence.
[81] Reg. § 1.170A-9(e)(7)(iii).
[82] Reg. § 1.170A-9(e)(8).
[83] Reg. § 1.170A-9(e)(7)(ii).
[84] Rev. Rul. 77-116, 1977-1 C.B. 155.
[85] Reg. § 1.170A-9(e)(3).

- The organization must have an active "continuous and bona fide" fundraising program designed to attract new and additional public and governmental support. Consideration will be given to the fact that, in its early years of existence, the charitable organization may limit the scope of its solicitations to those persons deemed most likely to provide seed money in an amount sufficient to enable it to commence its charitable activities and to expand its solicitation program.

- Other favorable factors must be present, such as:

    1. The composition of the board is representative of broad public interests.

    2. Support comes from governmental and other sources representative of the general public.

    3. Facilities and programs are made available to the general public, such as those of a museum or symphony society.

    4. Programs appeal to a broad-based public.[86]

The higher the percentage of support from public or governmental sources, the less is the burden of establishing the publicly supported nature of the organization through the other factors—and the converse is also true.

Concerning the governing board factor, the organization's nonprivate foundation status will be enhanced where it has a governing body that represents the interests of the public, rather than the personal or private interests of a limited number of donors. This can be accomplished by the election of the board members by a broad-based membership or by having the board composed of public officials, persons having particular expertise in the field or discipline involved, community leaders, and the like.

As noted, one of the important elements of the facts-and-circumstances test is the availability of public facilities or services. Examples of entities meeting this requirement are a museum that holds its building open to the public, a symphony orchestra that gives public performances, a conservation organization that provides educational services to the public through the distribution of educational materials, and an old age home that provides domiciliary or nursing services for members of the general public.

§ 8.4 PUBLICLY SUPPORTED ORGANIZATIONS—SERVICE PROVIDER ENTITIES

A tax-exempt charitable organization can be a publicly supported organization by being financially supported as a *service provider* entity. Qualification for the service provider category of public charities is measured by sources of revenue, but there are significant differences in relation to the donative entity rules.[87] Public support for this purpose includes *exempt function income*, and thus this

---

[86] Reg. § 1.170A-9(e)(3).

[87] The Supreme Court referred to organizations of this nature as "nonprofit service provider[s]" (Camps Newfound/Owatonna, Inc. v. Town of Harrison, Maine, 520 U.S. 564, 572 (1997)).

category usually includes organizations receiving a major portion of their support from fees and charges for program activities.

A two-part support test must be met to qualify under this category:

1. Investment income cannot exceed one-third of total support. *Total support* basically means the organization's gross revenue except for capital gains or the value of exemptions from local, state, or federal taxes.

2. More than one-third of the organization's total support must be received from a combination of:

   o Gifts, grants, contributions, and membership dues received from non-disqualified persons

   o Admissions to exempt function facilities or performances, such as theater or ballet performance tickets, museum or historical site admission fees, movie or video tickets, seminar or lecture fees, and athletic event charges

   o Fees for performance of services, such as school tuition, day care fees, hospital room and laboratory charges, psychiatric counseling fees, testing fees, scientific laboratory fees, library fines, animal neutering charges, and athletic facility fees

   o Merchandise sales of goods related to the organization's activities, including books and educational literature, pharmaceuticals and medical devices, handicrafts, reproductions and copies of original works of art, by-products of a blood bank, and goods produced by disabled workers

Exempt function revenues received from one source are not counted if they exceed $5,000 or 1 percent of the support of the organization, whichever is higher.

Subject to certain limitations,[88] the support must come from *permitted sources*. Thus, an organization seeking to qualify under this one-third support test must construct a *support fraction*, with the amount of support received from permitted sources constituting the numerator of the fraction and the total amount of support received being the denominator.[89]

Permitted sources are governmental units,[90] certain public and publicly supported organizations,[91] and persons other than disqualified persons[92] with respect to the organization. Thus, with these limitations,[93] support (other than from disqualified persons) from another service provider publicly supported entity, a supporting organization,[94] any other tax-exempt organizations (other than governmental units, public institutions, and donative publicly supported

---

[88] See § 8.4(d).

[89] IRC § 509(a)(2)(A); Reg. § 1.509(a)-3(a)(2).

[90] IRC § 170(c)(1).

[91] These are the organizations described in IRC § 509(a)(1) (*public* and *donative*) entities described in §§ 8.2 and 8.3.

[92] See *Private Foundations*, Chapter 4.

[93] See § 8.4(d).

[94] See § 8.6.

organizations), a for-profit organization, or an individual constitutes public support for the service provider publicly supported organization, albeit confined by these limitations. The cash basis method of accounting is utilized to determine the nature of an organization's support under these rules.[95]

The term *support*[96] means (in addition to the categories of public support just referenced) (1) net income from unrelated business activities,[97] (2) gross investment income,[98] (3) tax revenues levied for the benefit of the organization and either paid to expended on behalf of the organization, and (4) the value of services (exclusive of services or facilities generally furnished to the public without charge) furnished by a governmental unit to the organization without charge. The term does not include any gain from the disposition of property that would be considered as gain from the sale or exchange of a capital asset or the value of exemption from any federal, state, or local tax or any similar benefit.[99] Also, funding in the form of a loan does not constitute this type of support.[100] These items of support are combined to constitute the denominator of the *support fraction.*

Sponsorship payments that are acknowledged by the tax-exempt organization without quantitative and qualitative information so as to avoid classification as advertising revenue[101] can be treated as contributions for public support purposes.[102] This parallels rules applicable in the donative publicly supported charity context.[103]

(a) Investment Income Test

An organization, to avoid private foundation classification by being a *service provider* publicly supported entity, also must normally receive not more than one-third of its support from the sum of (1) gross investment income,[104] including interest, dividends, payments with respect to securities loans, rents, and royalties, and (2) any excess of the amount of unrelated business taxable income over the amount of the tax on that income.[105] To qualify under this test, an organization must construct a *gross investment fraction*, with the amount of gross investment income and any unrelated income (less the tax paid on it) received constituting the numerator of the fraction and the total amount of support received being the denominator.[106] In certain instances it may be necessary to distinguish between *gross receipts* and *gross investment income.*[107]

---

[95] E.g., Gen. Couns. Mem. 39109.
[96] IRC § 509(d).
[97] See Chapter 5.
[98] IRC § 509(e).
[99] IRC § 509(d).
[100] E.g., Priv. Ltr. Rul. 9608039.
[101] Reg. § 513-4(c)(2)(iv).
[102] Reg. § 1.509(a)-3(f)(1).
[103] See § 8.3.
[104] IRC § 509(e).
[105] IRC § 509(a)(2)(B).
[106] Reg. § 1.509(a)-3(a)(3).
[107] Reg. § 1.509(a)-3(m).

For these purposes, amounts received by a putative service provider publicly supported organization from (1) an organization seeking classification as a supporting organization[108] by reason of its support of the would-be publicly supported organization or from (2) a charitable trust, corporation, fund, or association or a split-interest trust,[109] which is required by its governing instrument or otherwise to distribute, or which normally does distribute at least 25 percent of its adjusted net income to the putative publicly supported organization, and where the distribution normally comprises at least 5 percent of the would-be publicly supported organization's adjusted net income, retain their character as gross investment income (that is, are not treated as gifts or contributions) to the extent that the amounts are characterized as gross investment income in the possession of the distributing organization. Where an organization, as described here, makes distributions to more than one putative service provider publicly supported organization, the amount of gross investment income deemed distributed is prorated among the distributees.[110] Further, where this type of an organization expends funds to provide goods, services, or facilities for the direct benefit of a putative service provider publicly supported organization, the amounts are treated as gross investment income to the beneficiary organization to the extent that the amounts are so characterized in the possession of the organization distributing the funds.[111]

(b) Concept of *Normally*

These support and investment income tests are computed on the basis of the nature of an organization's *normal* sources of support. An organization is considered as *normally* receiving one-third of its support from permitted sources and not more than one-third of its support from gross investment income for its current tax year and immediately succeeding tax year if, for the four tax years immediately preceding its current tax year, the aggregate amount of support received over the four-year period from permitted sources is more than one-third of its total support and the aggregate amount of support over the four-year period from gross investment income is not more than one-third of its total support.[112] For example, if an organization's current tax year is calendar year 2006, the computation period is calendar years 2002 to 2005; if the two support fractions are satisfied on the basis of the support received over this four-year period, the organization satisfies the support tests for 2006 and 2007. (A five-year period for meeting this support test is available for organizations during the initial five years of their existence.)

If, in an organization's current tax year, there are substantial and material changes in its sources of support (for example, an unusually large contribution or bequest), other than changes arising from unusual grants, the computation

---

[108] See § 8.6.
[109] IRC § 4947(a)(2).
[110] Reg. § 1.509(a)-5(a)(1).
[111] Reg. § 1.509(a)-5(a)(2).
[112] Reg. § 1.509(a)-3(c)(1)(i).

period becomes the tax year of the substantial and material changes and the four immediately preceding tax years.[113]

A *substantial and material change* in an organization's support may cause it to no longer meet either the public support test or the investment income test of these rules and thus no longer qualify as a service provider publicly supported charity. Nonetheless, its status as a publicly supported charity under these rules, with respect to a grantor or contributor, will not be affected until notice of a change of status is communicated by the IRS to the public. If the grantor or contributor was either aware of or responsible for the substantial and material change, or acquired knowledge that the agency had given notice to the organization that it had lost its designation as a service provider publicly supported charitable organization, however, then the status would be affected.[114] The foregoing rule does not apply if, under appropriate circumstances, the grantor or contributor acted in reliance on a written statement by the grantee organization that the grant or contribution would not cause the organization to lose its nonprivate foundation classification.[115] This statement must be signed by a responsible officer of the organization and must set forth sufficient information to assure a reasonably prudent person that the grant or contribution will not cause loss of the organization's classification as a publicly supported entity.

(c) Unusual Grants

Under the *unusual grant* rule, a contribution may be excluded from the numerator of the one-third support fraction and from the denominator of both the one-third support and one-third gross investment income fractions. When inclusion of this type of a gift would cause loss of public charity status, the exception is important. A grant is unusual if it is an unexpected and substantial gift attracted by the public nature of the organization *and* received from a disinterested party.[116] A number of factors are taken into account and no single factor is determinative. The eight positive factors are shown in the next list, along with their opposites, or negative factors, in parentheses.[117]

1. The contribution is received from a party with no connection to the organization. (The gift is received from a person who created the organization, is a substantial contributor, a board member, a manager, or related to such a person.)[118]

2. The gift is in the form of cash, marketable securities, or property that furthers the organization's exempt purposes. (The property is illiquid, difficult to dispose of, and not pertinent to the organization's activities.) A gift

---

[113] Reg. § 1.509(a)-3(c)(1)(ii).

[114] Reg. § 1.509(a)-3(c)(1)(iii)(a).

[115] Reg. § 1.509(a)-3(c)(1)(iii)(b).

[116] Thus, the term *unusual grant* is somewhat of a misnomer; a better term would have been *unexpected grant*, and the term should also reflect the fact that it also applies with respect to contributions.

[117] Reg. § 1.509(a)-3(c)(3). Similar rules for IRC § 170(b)(1)(A)(vi) organizations ("donative" publicly supported organizations—see § 8.3) are stated in Reg. § 1.170A-9(e)(6)(ii), (iii).

[118] See *Private Foundations*, Chapter 4.

of a painting to a museum or a gift of wetlands to a nature preservation society would be useful and appropriate property for this purpose.

3. No material restrictions or conditions are placed on the transfer.

4. The organization attracts a significant amount of support to pay its operating expenses on a regular basis, and the gift adds to an endowment or pays for capital items. (The gift pays for operating expenses for several years and is not added to an endowment.)

5. The gift is a bequest. (The gift is an inter vivos transfer.)

6. An active fundraising program exists and attracts significant public support. (Fund solicitation programs are limited or unsuccessful.)

7. A representative and broad-based governing body controls the organization. (Related parties control the organization.)

8. Prior to the receipt of the unusual grant, the organization qualified as a publicly supported entity. (The unusual grant exclusion was relied on in the past to satisfy the test.)

The IRS provided an illustration of the unusual grant rule in the case of a tax-exempt organization that received a large inter vivos gift of undeveloped land from a disinterested party, with the condition that the land be used in perpetuity to further its tax-exempt purpose of preserving the natural resources of a particular town. The agency ruled that the gift constituted an unusual grant and, thus, that the organization's nonprivate foundation status was not adversely affected, even through all of the aforementioned factors were not satisfied and the organization had previously received an unusual grant ruling. The IRS cited these facts as being of "particular importance": the donor was a disinterested party, the organization's operating expenses were paid for primarily through public support, the gift of the land furthered the exempt purpose of the organization, and the contribution was in the nature of new endowment funds because the organization was relatively new.[119]

A potential grantee organization may request an advance ruling from the IRS as to whether an unusually large grant may be excluded under this exception.[120] The agency promulgated "safe haven" criteria that, if satisfied, automatically cause a contribution or grant to be considered *unusual*, if the gift or grant, by reason of its size, would otherwise adversely affect the recipient organization's public status. If the first four factors in the preceding list are present, unusual grant status can be claimed automatically and relied on. As to item 4, the terms of the grant cannot provide for more than one year's operating expense.[121] If the grant is payable over a period of years, it can be excluded each year,[122] but any income earned on the sums would be included.[123]

---

[119] Rev. Rul. 76-440, 1976-2 C.B. 58.

[120] Reg. § 1.509(a)-3(c)(5)(ii).

[121] Rev. Proc. 81-7, 1981-1 C.B. 621.

[122] Reg. § 1.170A-9(e)(6)(ii)(c).

[123] These rules do not preclude a potential donee or grantee organization from requesting a ruling from the IRS as to whether a proposed gift or grant will constitute an unusual gift or grant.

These rules may be illustrated in this way:

During the calendar years 2002–2005, A, a publicly supported organization,[124] received total support of $350,000. Of this amount, $105,000 was received from grants, contributions, and receipts from admission that constituted qualifying public support.[125] Of this amount, $150,000 was received in the form of grants and contributions from persons who were disqualified persons because they were substantial contributors. The remaining $95,000 was gross investment income.[126] Among the contributions was a gift of $50,000 from X, who was not a substantial contributor to A prior to the making of this gift. All of the other requirements of the guidelines were met with respect to X's contribution. If X's contribution is excluded from A's support as an unusual grant, A will have received, for the years 2002–2005, $105,000 from public sources, $100,000 in grants and contributions from disqualified persons, and $95,000 in gross investment income. Therefore, if X's contribution is excluded from A's support, A meets the requirements for being a service provider publicly supported organization for the year 2006, because more than one-third of its support is from "public" sources and no more than one-third of its support is gross investment income. Thus, X's contribution would adversely affect the publicly supported status of A and, since the guidelines are met, the contribution is excludable as an unusual grant. X will not be considered responsible for a "substantial and material" change in A's support.

The computations to show the effect of excluding X's contribution from A's support are:

Total support for A during 2002–2005	$350,000	
Less: Contribution from X	50,000	
Total support of A less X's contribution	$300,000	
Gross investment income received by A	$ 95,000	
as a percentage of A's total support (less X's contribution)	$300,000	= 31.67%
Public support received by A as a percentage of A's total support (less X's contribution)	$105,000	= 35%

Under the same facts, except that for the years 2002 to 2005 A received $100,000 in grants and contributions from disqualified persons, the result would be different. In this case, if X's contribution is excluded as a unusual grant, A will have received $105,000 from public sources, $50,000 in grants and contributions from disqualified persons, and $95,000 in gross investment income. If X's contribution is excluded from A's support, A will have received more than one-third of its support from gross investment income and thus not meet all of the requirements of the support test for 2006. Consequently, even though the guidelines are satisfied, X's contribution is not excludable as an unusual grant because it would not adversely affect the status of A as a publicly supported organization.

---

[124] In this example, the organization is a service provider public charity.
[125] IRC § 509(a)(2)(A)(i) and (ii).
[126] IRC § 509(e).

The computations to show the effect of excluding X's contribution from A's support are:

Total support for A during 2002–2005	$300,000	
Less: Contribution from X	50,000	
Total support of A less X's contribution	$250,000	
Gross investment income received by A as a percentage of A's total support (less X's contribution)	$\dfrac{\$\ 95,000}{\$250,000}$	= 38%

(d) Limitations on Support

The support taken into account in determining the numerator of the support fraction under these rules concerning gifts, grants, contributions, and membership fees must come from permitted sources. Thus, transfers from disqualified persons cannot qualify as public support under the service provider organization's rules. In computing the amount of support received from gross receipts that is allowable toward the one-third support requirement, however, gross receipts from related activities (other than from membership fees) received from any person or from any bureau or similar agency of a governmental unit are includible in any tax year to the extent that these receipts do not exceed the greater of $5,000 or 1 percent of the organization's support for the year.[127] Thus, it is frequently significant to determine precisely the persons who are the actual payors (rather than a single entity/payor). The fact that contributions are restricted or earmarked does not detract from their qualification as public support.[128]

The phrase *government bureau or similar agency*[129] means a specialized operating (rather than policymaking or administrative) unit of the executive, judicial, or legislative branch of government, usually a subdivision of a department of government. Therefore, an organization receiving gross receipts from both a policymaking or administrative unit (for example, the Agency for International Development [AID]) and an operational unit of a department (for example, the Bureau for Latin America, an operating unit within AID) is treated as receiving gross receipts from two agencies, with the amount from each separately subject to the $5,000 or 1 percent limitation.

A somewhat comparable *permitted sources* limitation excludes support from a disqualified person, including a *substantial contributor*.[130] A *substantial contributor* is a person who contributes or bequeaths an aggregate amount of more than $5,000 to a charitable organization, where that amount is more than 2 percent of the total contributions and bequests received by the organization before the close of its tax year in which the contribution or bequest from the person is

---

[127] Reg. § 1.509(a)-3(b)(1). The term *person*, as used in IRC § 509(a)(2)(A)(ii), includes IRC § 509(a)(1) organizations, so that, for example, rent paid to a tax-exempt medical center by related hospitals constitutes support subject to the $5,000/1 percent limitation (Gen. Couns. Mem. 39104).

[128] Priv. Ltr. Rul. 8822096.

[129] Reg. §. 1.509(a)-3(i).

[130] See *Private Foundations*, Chapter 4.

received.[131] Thus, transfers from a substantial contributor (or any other type of disqualified person) cannot qualify as public support under the service provider organizations rules.[132] Grants from governmental units and certain public and publicly supported organizations[133] are not subject to this limitation.[134]

The income tax regulations define the various forms of support referenced in the service provider organization rules: *gift, contribution,* or *gross receipts*[135]; *grant* or *gross receipts*[136]; *membership fees*[137]; *gross receipts* or *gross investment income*[138]; and *grant* or *indirect contribution.*[139] For example, the term *gross receipts* means amounts received from a related activity where a specific service, facility, or product is provided to serve the direct and immediate needs of the payor, while a *grant* is an amount paid to confer a direct benefit on the general public. Any payment of money or transfer of property without adequate consideration is generally considered a gift or contribution. The furnishing of facilities for a rental fee or the making of loans as part of an exempt purpose will likely give rise to gross receipts rather than gross investment income. The fact that a membership organization provides services, facilities, and the like to its members as part of its overall activities will not result in the fees received from members being treated as gross receipts rather than membership fees.

§ 8.5 COMPARATIVE ANALYSIS OF CATEGORIES OF PUBLICLY SUPPORTED CHARITIES

The principle underlying the two discrete categories of publicly supported organizations—the donative and the service provider organizations—is much the same, in that both types of entities generally must, to qualify, receive at least one-third of their support from public sources. The principal difference is the manner in which public support is determined. Conceptually, the donative organization is one that is principally funded with contributions and grants, while the service provider organization is one that is principally funded with exempt function revenue (such as revenue generated from the sale of publications, admission to programs, and student tuition).

(a) Definition of *Support*

The items of gross income included in the requisite *support* are different for each category and do not equal total revenue in an accounting sense under either class. *Support* forms the basis of public status for both categories, and the calculations

---

[131] IRC § 507(d)(2)(A).

[132] Since the concept of *disqualified person* is inapplicable in the context of the donative publicly supported charity (see § 8.3), however, a contribution from a person who would be a disqualified person under the service provider organization rules may be, in whole or in part, public support under the donative organization rules.

[133] See §§ 8.2 and 8.3.

[134] See *supra* notes 90, 91.

[135] Reg. § 1.509(a)-3(f).

[136] Reg. § 1.509(a)-3(g).

[137] Reg. § 1.509(a)-3(h).

[138] Reg. § 1.509(a)-3(m).

[139] Reg. § 1.509(a)-3(j).

are made on a four-year moving average basis using the cash method of accounting.[140] For purposes of the donative publicly supported organizations rules, certain revenues are not counted as support and are not included in the numerator or the denominator[141]:

- Exempt function revenue, or that amount earned through charges for the exercise or performance of exempt activities, such as admission tickets and patient fees
- Capital gains or losses
- Unusual grants

For purposes of the service provider publicly supported organizations rules, total revenue less capital gains or losses and unusual grants equals total support.

(b) Major Gifts and Grants

Contributions and grants received are counted as public support differently for each category. For planning purposes, these rules are important to consider. Under the donative publicly supported organizations category, a particular giver's donations or grantor's grants are counted only up to an amount equal to 2 percent of the total support for the four-year period. Gifts and grants from other public charities and governmental entities are not subject to this 2 percent floor.

For purposes of the service provider publicly supported organizations rules, all gifts, grants, and contributions are counted as public support, except those received from disqualified persons. Such a person may be a substantial contributor, or one who gives over $5,000 if such amount is more than 2 percent of the organization's aggregate contributions for its life, or a relative of such a person. For purposes of the service provider publicly supported organizations rules, gifts from these insiders are not counted in the numerator at all. Subject to the 2 percent ceiling, their gifts are counted for purposes of donative publicly supported organizations. Significantly, only donative publicly supported organizations can qualify under the *facts-and-circumstances test*, meaning the amount of public support can be as low as 10 percent. *Unusual grants* are excluded from gross revenue in calculating total support for both types.[142]

(c) Types of Support

Not all revenue is counted as support. The basic definition of *support* excludes capital gains from the sale or exchange of capital assets. Some types of gross revenue are counted differently under differing circumstances.

Membership fees for both classes may represent donations or charges for services rendered. In some cases a combined gift and payment for services may be

---

[140] Reg. § 1.509(a)-3(k); Gen. Couns. Mem. 39109.
[141] Reg. § 1.170A-9(e)(7).
[142] See § 8.4(c).

present, and the facts in each circumstance must be examined to properly classify the revenue. A membership fee is a donation if it is paid by members to support the goals and interests they have in common with the organization, rather than to purchase admission, merchandise, services, or the use of facilities. When services are provided to members as part of overall activity, the payment may still be classified as member dues (donations).[143] If instead the organization solicits membership fees as a means to sell goods and services to the general public, the so-called membership fees are treated as gross receipts. Particularly for purposes of the donative publicly supported organizations rules, this distinction is very important, because exempt function fees are not included in the public support calculation.

Grants for services to be rendered for the granting organization are treated under both categories as exempt function income rather than contributions or grants. A grant normally is made to encourage the grantee organization to carry on certain programs or activities in furtherance of its own exempt purposes; no economic or physical benefit accrues to the grant-maker.[144] *Gross receipts*, however, result whenever the recipient organization performs a service or provides a facility or product to serve the needs of the grantor.

Under both categories, this distinction is important to determine amounts qualifying as contributions. For status as a service provider publicly supported organization, the distinction has yet another dimension. Only the first $5,000 of fees for these services received from a particular person or organization are includable in public support.[145]

Investment income is subject to a specific no-more-than-one-third test under the service provider publicly supported organizations rules, while donative publicly supported organizations can receive up to two-thirds of their total support from investment income.

Another distinction between these two types of organizations is that supporting organization payments to a service provider publicly supported organization retain their character as investment income (where applicable),[146] while the same payments to a donative publicly supported organization can be considered as grants[147] (although likely subject to the 2 percent limitation).[148]

As discussed earlier in connection with the rules pertaining to the donative publicly supported charitable organization,[149] care must be taken in making these computations in relation to an organization that failed to qualify as a charitable entity during one or more years, since the IRS asserts that support received by an organization during the period of its disqualification cannot be taken into account in determining its foundation/public charity status.[150]

---

[143] Reg. § 509(a)-3(h).

[144] Reg. § 1.509(a)-3(g).

[145] IRC § 509(a)(2)(A)(ii).

[146] See § 8.4(a).

[147] Reg. § 1.509(a)-3(j).

[148] Gen. Couns. Mem. 39748 was issued in 1988 to clarify this subject and was later withdrawn by Gen. Couns. Mem. 39875.

[149] See § 8.3.

[150] Rev. Rul. 77-116, 1977-1 C.B. 155.

§ 8.6 SUPPORTING ORGANIZATIONS

Another category of tax-exempt charitable organization that is deemed to not be a private foundation is the *supporting organization*.[151]

Charitable supporting organizations usually are those entities that are not themselves publicly supported or qualified public institutions, but are instead sufficiently related to one or more organizations that are publicly supported or are otherwise public entities so that the requisite degree of public control and involvement is considered present. Thus, the supported or benefited organization is usually a public charity,[152] while the organization that is not a private foundation by virtue of these rules is termed a supporting organization. The supported organization may be a foreign organization as long as it otherwise qualifies as a public or publicly supported entity.[153]

A supporting organization must be organized, and at all times thereafter operated, exclusively for the benefit of, to perform the functions of, or to carry out the purposes of one or more public institutions or publicly supported organizations.[154]

Thus, the relationship between a supporting organization and a supported organization must be one of three types:

1. "Operated, supervised, or controlled by"
2. "Supervised or controlled in connection with"
3. "Operated in connection with"[155]

A supporting organization must not be controlled directly or indirectly by one or more disqualified persons (other than foundation managers or eligible public charitable organizations).[156]

A supporting organization may evolve out of a public or publicly supported charity.[157] To qualify as a supporting organization, a charitable organization must meet both an organizational test and an operational test.[158]

(a) Organizational Test

A supporting organization must be organized exclusively to support or benefit one or more specified public institutions or publicly supported charitable organizations.[159] Its articles of organization[160] must limit its purposes to one or more of the purposes that are permissible for a supporting organization,[161] may not expressly empower the organization to engage in activities that are not in furtherance of these purposes, must state the specified public institution or publicly

---

[151] IRC § 509(a)(3).

[152] See §§ 8.2–8.4.

[153] Rev. Rul. 74-229, 1974-1 C.B. 142.

[154] IRC § 509(a)(3)(A); Reg. § 1.509(a)-4(a)(2).

[155] IRC § 509(a)(3)(B); Reg. §§ 1.509(a)-4(a)(3), 1.509(a)-4(f)(2). These supporting organizations are known informally as Type I, Type II, or Type III, respectively.

[156] IRC § 509(a)(3)(C); Reg. § 1.509(a)-4(a)(4).

[157] E.g., Priv. Ltr. Rul. 8825116.

[158] Reg. § 1.509(a)-4(b).

[159] IRC § 509(a)(3)(A).

[160] Reg. § 1.501(c)(3)-1(b)(2).

[161] IRC § 509(a)(3)(A).

supported organization (or institutions and/or organizations) on behalf of which it is to be operated, and may not expressly empower the organization to operate to support or benefit any other organizations.[162]

To qualify as a supporting organization, an organization's stated purposes may be as broad as, or more specific than, the purposes that are permissible for a supporting organization. Thus, an organization formed "for the benefit of" one or more public institutions and/or publicly supported organizations will meet this organizational test, assuming the other requirements are satisfied. An organization that is "operated, supervised, or controlled by" or "supervised or controlled in connection with" one or more public institutions and/or publicly supported organizations to carry out their purposes will satisfy these requirements if the purposes as stated in its articles of organization are similar to, but no broader than, the purposes stated in the articles of the supported public organization or organizations.[163]

An organization will not meet this organizational test if its articles of organization expressly permit it to operate to support or benefit any organization other than its specified supported organization or organizations. The fact that the actual operations of the organization have been exclusively for the benefit of one or more specified public institutions or publicly supported organizations is not sufficient to permit it to satisfy this organizational test.[164]

(b) Operational Test

A supporting organization generally must be operated exclusively to support or benefit one or more public charitable organizations.[165] Unlike the definition of the term *exclusively*, as applied in the context of charitable organizations generally, which means *primarily*,[166] the term *exclusively* in this context means *solely*.[167]

The supporting organization must engage solely in activities that support or benefit one or more eligible supported organizations.[168] These activities may include making payments to or for the use of, or providing services or facilities for, individual members of the charitable class benefited by the specified public or publicly supported organization. A supporting organization may make a payment indirectly through an unrelated organization to a member of a charitable class benefited by a specified public or publicly supported organization, but only where the payment constitutes a grant to an individual rather than a grant to an organization.[169]

---

[162] Reg. § 1.509(a)-4(c)(1). The U.S. Tax Court applied these regulations in concluding that an organization was not a supporting organization because the organizational documents of the entity expressly empowered it to benefit organizations other than specified publicly supported organizations (Trust Under the Will of Bella Mabury v. Comm'r, 80 T.C. 718 (1983)).

[163] Reg. § 1.509(a)-4(c)(2).

[164] Reg. § 1.509(a)-4(c)(3).

[165] IRC § 509(a)(3)(A).

[166] See *Tax-Exempt Organizations* § 4.4.

[167] Reg. § 1.509(a)-4(e)(1).

[168] Reg. § 1.509(a)-4(e)(1), (2).

[169] The criteria used to distinguish grants to individuals from grants to organizations are the same as those used in the private foundation taxable expenditures context (Reg. § 53.4945-4(a)(4); see *Private Foundations*, Chapter 9).

An organization is regarded as operated exclusively to support or benefit one or more public charitable organizations even if it supports or benefits a charitable organization, other than a private foundation, that is operated, supervised, or controlled directly by or in connection with the public charitable organizations.[170] Consequently, it is possible for a supporting organization to ultimately support or benefit a public charitable organization by supporting or benefiting another supporting organization, although it is the view of the IRS chief counsel that this possibility was not intended and that perhaps the regulations should be revised to preclude that possibility.[171] An organization generally will not be regarded as operated exclusively, however, if any part of its activities is in furtherance of a purpose other than supporting or benefiting one or more public charitable organizations.[172]

The concept of the supporting organization includes, but is not confined to, one that pays more than a suitable amount of its income to one or more eligible supported organizations. A supporting organization may carry on a discrete program or activity that supports or benefits one or more supported organizations. For example, a supporting organization, supportive of the academic endeavors of the medical school at a university, was used to operate a faculty practice plan in furtherance of the teaching, research, and service programs of the school.[173] As another illustration, a supporting organization to an entity that provided residential placement for mentally and physically disabled adults had as its supportive programs the construction and operation of a facility to provide employment suitable to disabled persons and to establish an information center about the conditions of disabled individuals.[174] A supporting organization may also engage in fundraising activities, such as solicitations of contributions and grants, special events, and unrelated trade or business activities, to raise funds for one or more supported organizations or for other permissible beneficiaries.[175]

A supporting organization has many characteristics of a private foundation, such as, as noted, the absence of any requirement to be publicly supported.[176] Thus, like a private foundation, a supporting organization can be funded entirely by means of investment income; it can satisfy the operational test by engaging in investment activities (assuming charitable ends are being served).[177]

(c) Specified Public Charities

As noted, generally a supporting organization must be organized and operated to support or benefit one or more *specified* public charitable organizations.[178] This

---

[170] Reg. § 1.509(a)-4(e)(1).

[171] Gen. Couns. Mem. 39508.

[172] Reg. § 1.509(a)-4(e)(1).

[173] Priv. Ltr. Rul. 9434041, superseded by Priv. Ltr. Rul. 9442025.

[174] Priv. Ltr. Rul. 9438013.

[175] Reg. § 1.509(a)-4(e)(2).

[176] See § 8.6, second paragraph.

[177] This point is illustrated by the case styled Henry E. & Nancy Horton Bartels Trust for the Benefit of the University of New Haven v. United States, 209 F.3d 147 (2d Cir. 2000). This aspect of the law does not, however, cause the investment activity to be an exempt function to the extent that the unrelated debt-financed income rules (see § 5.10) become inapplicable.

[178] IRC § 509(a)(3)(A).

specification must be in the supporting organization's articles of organization, although the manner of the specification depends on which of the three types of relationships with one or more eligible supported organizations is involved.[179]

Generally, it is expected that the articles of organization of the supporting organization will designate (that is, *specify*) each of the specified public charities by name.[180] If the relationship is one of *operated, supervised, or controlled by* or *supervised or controlled in connection with,* however, designation by name is not required as long as the articles of organization of the supporting organization require that it be operated to support or benefit one or more beneficiary organizations that are designated by class or purpose and that include one or more public institutions or publicly supported charities, as to which there is one of the foregoing two relationships (without designating the organizations by name), or public charitable organizations that are closely related in purpose or function to public or publicly supported charities, as to which there is one of the two relationships (again, without designating the organizations by name).[181] Therefore, if the relationship is one of *operated in connection with,* generally the supporting organization must designate the specified public charitable organizations by name.[182]

Where the relationship is other than *operated in connection with,* the articles of organization of a supporting organization may permit the substitution of one eligible organization within a designated class for another eligible organization either in the same or a different class designated in the articles of organization, permit the supporting organization to operate for the benefit of new or additional eligible organizations of the same or a different class designated in the articles of organization, or permit the supporting organization to vary the amount of its support among different eligible supported organizations within the class or classes of organizations designated by the articles of organization.[183]

These rules were illustrated in the reasoning followed by the IRS in according supporting organization classification to a tax-exempt community trust.[184] The community trust was created by a publicly supported community chest to hold endowment funds and to distribute the income from the endowment to support public or publicly supported charities in a particular geographic area. The governing body of the community chest appointed a majority of the trustees of the community trust. The trust was required by the terms of its governing instrument to distribute its income to public or publicly supported charities in a particular area, so that, the IRS held, even though the public or publicly supported charities were not specified by name, the trust qualified as a supporting organization because the community chest was specified by the requisite class or

---

[179] Reg. § 1.509(a)-4(c)(1).

[180] Reg. § 1.509(a)-4(d)(2)(i).

[181] Reg. § 1.509(a)-4(d)(2). The IRS denied an organization supporting organization/public charity classification where, after payment of a certain amount to qualified supported organizations, the supporting requirements would not be met (Rev. Rul. 79-197, 1979-2 C.B. 204).

[182] Reg. § 1.509(a)-4(d)(4). In one case, the U.S. Tax Court generally ignored these regulations and found compliance with the specificity requirement of IRC § 509(a)(3)(A) merely by reading the statutory provision in light of the facts of the case (Warren M. Goodspeed Scholarship Fund v. Comm'r, 70 T.C. 515 (1978)).

[183] Reg. § 1.509(a)-4(d)(3).

[184] Reg. § 1.170A-9(e)(11).

purpose, in that the trust was organized and operated exclusively for the benefit of this class of organizations. Inasmuch as the community chest appointed a majority of the trust's trustees, the trust was ruled to be *operated, supervised, or controlled by* the community chest, so that the *specification* requirement was met.[185]

An organization that is *operated in connection with* one or more eligible supported organizations can satisfy the specification requirement even if its articles of organization permit an eligible supported organization that is designated by class or purpose (public or publicly supported charities rather than by name) to be substituted for the supported organizations designated by name in its articles, but "only if such substitution is conditioned upon the occurrence of an event which is beyond the control of the supporting organization."[186] This type of event is stated as being one such as loss of tax exemption, substantial failure or abandonment of operations, or dissolution of the eligible supported organization or organizations designated in the articles of organization.[187] In one case, the trustee of a charitable entity had the authority to substitute other charitable beneficiaries for those named in its articles whenever, in the trustee's judgment, the charitable uses had become "unnecessary, undesirable, impracticable, impossible or no longer adapted to the needs of the public." A court held that the organization failed the organizational test, and thus was a private foundation, because the events that could trigger the substitution of beneficiaries were "within the trustee's control for all practical purposes" since the standard "require[d] the trustee to make a judgment as to what is desirable and what are the needs of the public."[188] The court stated that this organizational test is essential to qualification of organizations as supporting entities because the "public scrutiny [necessary to obviate the need for governmental regulation as a private foundation] derives from the publicly supported beneficiaries, which, in turn, oversee the activities of the supporting organization" and "this oversight function is substantially weakened if the trustee has broad authority to substitute beneficiaries and, thus, it is essential that such authority be strictly limited."[189]

A supporting organization that has one or more public institutions and/or publicly supported charities designated by name in its articles of organization may have in the articles a provision that permits it to operate for the benefit of a beneficiary organization that is not a public or publicly supported charity, but only if the supporting organization is currently operating for the benefit of a publicly or publicly supported charity and the possibility of its operating for the benefit of an organization other than a public or publicly supported charity is a "remote contingency."[190] Should that contingency occur, however, the supporting organization would then fail to meet this operational test.[191] Moreover, under these circumstances, the articles of organization of a supporting organization can

---

[185] Rev. Rul. 81-43, 1981-1 C.B. 350.

[186] Reg. § 1.509(a)-4(d)(4)(i)(a).

[187] *Id.*

[188] William F., Mable E., & Margaret K. Quarrie Charitable Fund v. Comm'r, 70 T.C. 182, 187 (1978), *aff'd*, 603 F.2d 1274 (7th Cir. 1979).

[189] *Id.*, 70 T.C. at 190.

[190] Reg. § 1.509(a)-4(d)(4)(i)(b).

[191] Reg. § 1.509(a)-4(d)(4)(ii).

permit it to vary the amount of its support between different designated organizations as long as it meets the requirements of the integral part test[192] with respect to at least one beneficiary organization.[193]

A supporting organization will be deemed to meet the specification requirement even though its articles of organization do not designate each supported organization by name—despite the nature of the relationship—if there has been a historical and continuing relationship between the supporting organization and the supported organizations and, by reason of the relationship, there has developed a substantial identity of interests between the organizations.[194]

(d) Required Relationships

As noted, to meet these requirements, an organization generally must be operated, supervised, or controlled by or in connection with one or more public charitable organizations. Thus, if an organization does not stand in at least one of the three required relationships to one or more eligible supported organizations, it cannot qualify as a supporting organization.[195] Regardless of the applicable relationship, it must be ensured that the supporting organization will be *responsive* to the needs or demands of one or more eligible supported organizations and that the supporting organization will constitute an *integral part* of or maintain a *significant involvement* in the operations of one or more public charitable organizations.[196]

(e) Operated, Supervised, or Controlled By

The distinguishing feature of the relationship between a supporting organization and one or more public institutions or publicly supported charities encompassed by the phrase *operated, supervised, or controlled by* is the presence of a substantial degree of direction by one or more public or publicly supported charities in regard to the policies, programs, and activities of the supporting organization—a relationship comparable to that of a subsidiary and a parent.[197]

This relationship is established by the fact that a majority of the officers, directors, or trustees of the supporting organization are either composed of representatives of the supported organizations or at least appointed or elected by the governing body, officers acting in their official capacity, or the membership of the supported organizations.[198] This relationship will be considered to exist with respect to one or more public charitable organizations and the supporting organization considered to operate *for the benefit of* one or more different public charitable organizations only where it can be demonstrated that the purposes of the former organizations are carried out by benefiting the latter organizations.[199]

---

[192] See text accompanying *infra* notes 211–223.
[193] Reg. § 1.509(a)-4(d)(4)(i)(c).
[194] Reg. § 1.509(a)-4(d)(2)(iv). E.g., Cockerline Memorial Fund v. Comm'r, 86 T.C. 53 (1986).
[195] Reg. § 1.509(a)-4(f)(1).
[196] Reg. § 1.509(a)-4(f)(3).
[197] Reg. § 1.509(a)-4(f)(4), (g)(1)(i).
[198] Reg. § 1.509(a)-4(g)(1)(i).
[199] Reg. § 1.509(a)-4(g)(1)(ii).

(f) Supervised or Controlled in Connection With

The distinguishing feature of the relationship between a supporting organization and one or more public charitable organizations encompassed by the phrase *supervised or controlled in connection with* is the presence of common supervision or control by the persons supervising or controlling both the supporting organization and the supported organizations to ensure that the supporting organization will be responsive to the needs and requirements of the supported organizations.[200] Therefore, in order to meet this requirement, the control or management of the supporting organization must be vested in the same individuals who control or manage the public charitable organizations.[201]

A supporting organization will not be considered to be in this relationship with one or more eligible supported organizations if it merely makes payments (mandatory or discretionary) to one or more named public charitable organizations, regardless of whether the obligation to make payments to the named beneficiaries is enforceable under state law and the supporting organization's governing instrument contains the private foundation rules provisions.[202] This arrangement provides an insufficient connection between the payor organization and the needs and requirements of the public charitable organizations to constitute supervision or control in connection with these organizations.[203]

(g) Operated in Connection With

Qualification as a supporting organization by reason of the *operated in connection with* relationship entails the loosest of the relationships between a supporting organization and one or more supported organizations; this relationship usually is more of a programmatic one that a governance one. A court nicely observed that this category of supporting organization involves the "least intimate" of the three types of relationships.[204] The IRS believes that most of the abuses concerning supporting organizations involve this relationship and thus generally disfavors it. Often the agency views this relationship as the most tenuous one; it has referred to these entities as "razor edge" organizations.[205]

The distinguishing feature of the relationship between a supporting organization and one or more public institutions or publicly supported organizations encompassed by the phrase *operated in connection with* is that the supporting organization must be responsive to and significantly involved in the operations of the public charitable organization or organizations.[206] Generally, to satisfy the criteria of this relationship, a supporting organization must meet a *responsiveness test* and an *integral part test*.[207]

The responsiveness test is designed to ensure that the supporting organization is responsive to the needs of the supported organization by requiring that the

---

[200] Reg. §§ 1.509(a)-4(f)(4), 1.509(a)-4(h)(1).
[201] Reg. § 1.509(a)-4(h)(1).
[202] IRC § 508(e)(1)(A), (B).
[203] Reg. § 1.509(a)-4(h)(2).
[204] Lapham Found., Inc. v. Comm'r, 84 T.C.M. 586, 593 (2003), *aff'd*, 389 F.3d 606 (6th Cir. 2004).
[205] IRS Exempt Organizations Continuing Professional Education Program textbook for fiscal year 2001, at 110.
[206] Reg. § 1.509(a)-4(f)(4).
[207] Reg. § 1.509(a)-4(i)(1)(i).

supported organization have the ability to influence the activities of the supporting organization. The integral part test seeks to ensure that the supporting organization maintains a significant involvement in the operations of one or more supported organizations and that the supported organization or organizations are dependent on the supporting organization for the type of support it provides.

A supporting organization meets the responsiveness test when it is responsive to the needs or demands of one or more public institutions or publicly supported organizations.[208] This test may be satisfied in either of two ways:

1. The supporting organization and the supported organization(s) are in *close operational conjunction*. This is manifested by a showing that (a) one or more officers, directors, or trustees of the supporting organization are elected or appointed by the officers, directors, trustees, or membership of the supported organization(s); (b) one or more members of the governing bodies of the supported organization(s) are also officers, directors, or trustees of, or hold other important offices in, the supporting organization; or (c) the officers, directors, or trustees of the supporting organization maintain a close and continuous working relationship with the officers, directors, or trustees of the supported organization(s). It must also be demonstrated that the officers, directors, or trustees of the supported organization(s) have a significant voice in the investment policies of the supporting organization, the timing of grants, the manner in which they are made, and the selection of recipients by the supporting organization, and in otherwise directing the use of the income or assets of the supporting organization.[209]

2. The supporting organization is a charitable trust under state law, each specified public institution or publicly supported organization is a named beneficiary under the charitable trust's governing instrument, and the beneficiary organization has the power to enforce the trust and compel an accounting under state law.[210]

A supporting organization meets the integral part test when it maintains a significant involvement in the operations of one or more public institutions or publicly supported charities and these supported organizations are in turn dependent on the supporting organization for the type of support that it provides.[211] This test may be satisfied in either of two ways:

1. The activities engaged in by the supporting organization for or on behalf of the supporting organization(s) are activities to perform the functions

---

[208] Reg. § 1.509(a)-4(i)(2)(i).

[209] Reg. § 1.509(a)-4(1)(2)(ii). E.g., Roe Foundation Charitable Trust v. Comm'r, 58 T.C.M. 402 (1989) (holding that the organization did not have the requisite relationship with a public charity to satisfy the *in connection with* test). An organization's governance and affairs were structured so that the requirements of the responsiveness test were satisfied in Lapham Found., Inc. v. Comm'r, 84 T.C.M. 586 (2003), *aff'd*, 389 F.3d 606 (6th Cir. 2004).

[210] Reg. § 1.509(a)-4(i)(2)(iii). An organization was able to satisfy the test because it was organized as a charitable trust (Christie E. Cuddeback & Lucille M. Cuddeback Memorial Fund v. Comm'r, 84 T.C.M. 623 (2003)).

[211] Reg. § 1.509(a)-4(i)(3)(i); also Reg. § 1.509(a)-4(i)(4). A special rule allows a supporting organization, under certain circumstances, to be considered as meeting the integral part test even though the test cannot be met for the current year (Reg. § 1.509(a)-4(i)(1)(iii)).

of, or to carry out the purposes of, the supported organization(s), and, but for the involvement of the supporting organization, would normally be engaged in by the supported organization(s) itself.[212]

2. The second way to meet the integral part test involves a set of requirements that are considerably more complex than those entailed in the first way to meet the test. This package of rules represents the farthest and least demanding reaches under which a charitable organization can avoid private foundation status, particularly where it has met the responsiveness test solely because it is a charitable trust.[213] The supporting organization must make payments of substantially all of its income to or for the use of one or more supported organizations. The amount of support provided must be sufficient to ensure the attentiveness of the supported organization to the operations of the supporting organization,[214] and a substantial amount of the support provided by the supporting organization goes to the supported organization that meets the attentiveness requirement.

The IRS ruled that the term *substantially all* means at least 85 percent because that was the meaning given to the same term in the rules concerning private operating foundations.[215] In that ruling, the agency decided that the integral part test was violated by a charitable trust that distributed 75 percent of its income annually to a church, accumulating the balance until the original corpus was doubled, at which time all of the organization's income was to be distributed to the church.[216] The IRS privately ruled that the term *income* for this purpose does not include short-term or long-term capital gain.[217]

In evaluating qualification for the attentiveness test, the portion of the supportee's overall support that is provided by the supporting organization is evaluated. Although there is no specific numerical test in the regulations, the amount of monetary support received by the supported organization must represent a sufficient part of its total support (spending) to represent attentiveness. In one situation, less than 10 percent was considered by the IRS to be unlikely, by itself, to ensure attentiveness.[218] As another example, the agency approved an organization that provided 2 to 6 percent of the support of each of four supported organizations. Although the percentage for each supportee would not normally be enough to meet the integral part test, the support when combined with other facts was considered satisfactory. The individual grants were substantial and had been paid for more than 20 years, and various financial and tax reports were provided to allow the supportees to exercise requisite attentiveness. In another

---

[212] Reg. §. 1.509(a)-4(i)(3)(ii). A court held that a charitable organization did not satisfy this aspect of the responsiveness test because it was structured as a donor-advised fund (see *Tax-Exempt Organizations* § 11.6) so that the ostensible supported organization was not bound by the ostensible supporting organization's recommendations (Lapham Found., Inc. v. Comm'r, 84 T.C.M. 586 (2003), *aff'd*, 389 F.3d 606 (6th Cir. 2004).

[213] Nellie Callahan Scholarship Fund v. Comm'r, 73 T.C. 626 (1980).

[214] Where the *attentiveness* component of this requirement is satisfied, it is not necessary that substantially all of the income of the supporting organization be distributed in the year in which it is earned, although there may not be an extended accumulation of income (Gen. Couns. Mem. 36523).

[215] IRC § 4942(j)(3)(A); Reg. § 53.4942(b)-1(c). See *Private Foundations* § 3.1.

[216] Rev. Rul. 76-208, 1976-1 C.B. 161.

[217] Priv. Ltr. Rul. 9021060.

[218] Gen. Couns. Mem. 36379; Reg. § 1.501-4(i)(3)(iii)(c).

example, attentiveness was achieved under the "all pertinent factors" test.[219] The facts indicated that the organization, a trust, was making grants to a zoo, a part of the city government, for the purpose of aiding the zoo in animal acquisition and housing. Among the factors indicating attentiveness was that the zoo was historically a component part of the city government and that the trust was only one of two nongovernmental organizations to support the zoo. When a supported organization is not dependent on the supporting organization for a sufficient amount of support, the integral part test is not met merely because the supported organization has enforceable rights under state law.

Even where the support is numerically insufficient to meet the integral part test, however, it may be demonstrated that, in order to avoid the interruption of the carrying on of a particular function or activity, the beneficiary organization will be sufficiently attentive to the operations of the supporting organization. This may be the case where either the supporting organization or the beneficiary organization earmarks the support received from the supporting organization for a particular program or activity, even if the program or activity is not the beneficiary organization's primary program or activity, so long as the program or activity is a substantial one.[220]

All pertinent factors, including the number of beneficiaries, the length and nature of the relationship between the beneficiary and the supporting organization, and the purpose to which the funds are put, will be considered in determining whether the amount of support received by a beneficiary organization is sufficient to ensure its attentiveness to the operations of the supporting organization. Inasmuch as, in the government's view, the attentiveness of a beneficiary organization is motivated by reason of the amounts received from the supporting organization, the more substantial the amount involved (in terms of a percentage of the supported organization's total support), the greater the likelihood that the required degree of attentiveness will be present. In satisfaction of this test, however, evidence of actual attentiveness by the beneficiary organization is of almost equal importance. An example of acceptable evidence in this regard is the imposition of a requirement that the supporting organization furnish reports at least annually to the beneficiary organization to assist the latter in ensuring that the former has invested its endowment in assets productive of a reasonable rate of return (taking appreciation into account) and has not engaged in any activity that would give rise to liability for any of the private foundation excise taxes if the supporting organization were a private foundation. The imposition of this requirement is, however, merely one of the factors used in determining whether a supporting organization is complying with the requirements of this test, and the absence of the requirement will not necessarily preclude an organization from classification as a supporting organization based on other factors.[221] Thus, the IRS ruled that reports, submitted by a trustee to each of the beneficiaries

---

[219] Gen. Couns. Mem. 36523.

[220] Reg. § 1.509(a)-4(i)(3)(iii)(b). A court ruled that an organization failed to meet this test, inasmuch as the requisite *earmarking* could not occur because the entity was structured as a donor-advised fund (see *Tax-Exempt Organizations* § 11.6) and the amount of proposed support was not *substantial* (Lapham Found., Inc. v. Comm'r, 84 T.C.M. 586 (2003), *aff'd*, 389 F.3d 606 (6th Cir. 2004).

[221] Reg. § 1.509(a)-4(i)(3)(iii)(d).

of a charitable trust, will not alone satisfy the attentiveness requirement of the integral part test.[222]

Where none of the beneficiary organizations is dependent on the supporting organization for a sufficient amount of the beneficiary organizations' support within the meaning of these requirements, however, this test will not be satisfied, even though the beneficiary organizations have enforceable rights against the supporting organization under state law.[223]

(h) Limitation on Control

A supporting organization may not be controlled directly or indirectly by one or more disqualified persons, other than foundation managers and one or more public institutions or publicly supported organizations.[224] An individual who is a disqualified person with respect to a supporting organization (for example, a substantial contributor) does not lose that status because a beneficiary public or publicly supported charity appoints or designates him or her to be a foundation manager of the supporting organization to serve as the representative of the public or publicly supported charity.[225]

A supporting organization is considered *controlled* if the disqualified persons, by aggregating their votes or positions of authority, may require the organization to perform any act that significantly affects its operations or may prevent the supporting organization from performing such an act. Generally, control exists if the voting power of these persons is 50 percent or more of the total voting power of the organization's governing body, or if one or more disqualified persons has the right to exercise veto power over the actions of the organization. All pertinent facts and circumstances, including the nature, diversity, and income yield of an organization's holdings; the length of time particular securities or other assets are retained; and its manner of exercising its voting rights with respect to securities in which members of its governing body also have some interest, will be taken into consideration in determining whether a disqualified person does in fact indirectly control an organization. Supporting organizations are permitted to establish, to the satisfaction of the IRS, that disqualified persons do not directly or indirectly control them.[226]

For example, this control element may be the difference between the qualification of an organization as a supporting organization and its qualification as a common fund private foundation. This is because the right of the donors to designate the recipients of the organization's gifts can constitute control of the organization by disqualified persons, namely, substantial contributors.[227]

---

[222] Rev. Rul. 76-32, 1976-1 C.B. 160.

[223] Reg. § 1.509(a)-4(i)(3)(iii)(e). An argument that the support of an ostensible supporting organization was such that loss of it would cause the ostensible supported organization to interrupt or discontinue a program failed in one case (Christie E. Cuddeback & Lucille M. Cuddeback Memorial Fund v. Comm'r, 84 T.C.M. 623 (2003)). Calling these regulations "fantastically intricate and detailed," a court concluded that a charitable organization failed both the responsiveness test and the integral part test (Windsor Found. v. United States, 77-2 U.S.T.C. ¶ 9709 (E.D. Va. 1977)).

[224] IRC § 509(a)(3)(C).

[225] Reg. § 1.509(a)-4(j)(1).

[226] Reg. § 1.509(a)-4(j)(2).

[227] Rev. Rul. 80-305, 1980-2 C.B. 71.

In one instance, the IRS found indirect control of a supporting organization by, in effect, "legislating" an expanded definition of the term *disqualified person.* The matter involved a charitable organization that made distributions to a university. The organization's board of directors was composed of a substantial contributor to the organization, two employees of a business corporation of which more than 35 percent of the voting power was owned by the substantial contributors, and one individual selected by the university. None of the directors had veto power over the organization's actions. Conceding that the organization was not directly controlled by disqualified persons, the IRS said that "one circumstance to be considered is whether a disqualified person is in a position to influence the decisions of members of the organization's governing body who are not themselves disqualified persons." Thus, the agency decided that the two directors who were employees of the disqualified person corporation should be considered disqualified persons for purposes of applying the 50 percent control rule. This position in turn led to the conclusion that the organization was indirectly controlled by disqualified persons and, therefore, could not be a nonprivate foundation by virtue of being a qualifying supporting organization.[228]

The operation of these rules is further illustrated by two IRS rulings. One instance concerned a charitable trust formed to grant scholarships to students graduating from a particular public high school. The sole trustee of the trust was the council of the city in which the school was located; the city's treasurer managed its funds. The school system was an integral part of the city's government. One of the purposes of the city, as outlined in its charter, was to provide for the education of its citizens. The IRS granted the trust classification as a supporting organization (and thereby determined it was not a private foundation),[229] using this rationale: (1) the city, being a governmental unit,[230] was a qualified supported entity[231]; (2) because of the involvement of the city council and treasurer, the trust satisfied the requirements of the *operated, supervised, or controlled by* relationship; (3) the organizational test was met because of the similarity of educational purpose between the trust and the city; (4) the *exclusive* operation requirement was deemed met because the trust benefited individual members of the charitable class aided by the city through its school system; and (5) the trust was not controlled by a disqualified person (other than a public charity).

By contrast, the IRS considered the public or publicly supported charity status of a charitable trust formed to grant scholarships to students graduating from high schools in a particular county. A committee composed of officials and representatives of the county selected the scholarship recipients.

The trustee of the trust was a bank. The IRS denied the trust classification as a supporting organization (and thereby determined that it was a private foundation),[232] using this rationale: (1) the high schools were qualified supported organizations[233]; (2) since the trustee was independent of the county, neither the

---

[228] Rev. Rul. 80-207, 1980-2 C.B. 193.

[229] Rev. Rul. 75-436, 1975-2 C.B. 217.

[230] IRC §§ 170(c)(1), 170(b)(1)(A)(v).

[231] IRC § 509(a)(1).

[232] Rev. Rul. 75-437, 1975-2 C.B. 218.

[233] IRC §§ 170(b)(1)(A)(ii) or (v); 509(a)(1).

operated, supervised, or controlled by nor the *supervised or controlled in connection with* relationship was present; (3) the integral part test of the *operated in connection with* relationship was not met because of the independence of the trustee, the county's lack of voice in the trust's investment and grant-making policies, and the absence of the necessary elements of significant involvement, dependence on support, and sufficient attentiveness; (4) the responsiveness test of the same relationship was not met because the beneficiary organizations were not named and lacked the power to enforce the trust and compel an accounting; and (5) the trust failed the organization test because its instrument lacked the requisite statement of purpose and did not *specify* the publicly supported organizations.

The U.S. Tax Court demonstrated a disposition to avoid this type of stringent reading of these requirements. In finding a scholarship-granting charitable trust to be a public charity pursuant to the operated in connection with requirements, the court ruled that it satisfied the responsiveness and integral part tests even though the school was not a named beneficiary of the trust and the funds were paid directly to the graduates rather than to the school or a school system.[234]

§ 8.7 NONCHARITABLE SUPPORTED ORGANIZATIONS

Federal tax law enables three categories of tax-exempt organizations that are not charitable entities to qualify as supported organizations; this means that the charitable organization that is supportive of one or more of these noncharitable entities is able to avoid classification as a private foundation on the ground that it is a supporting organization.[235] This result is accomplished by virtue of a cryptic passage in the Internal Revenue Code, which provides that, for purposes of the supporting organization rules, an organization "described in paragraph (2) [IRC § 509(a)(2)] shall be deemed to include an organization described in section 501(c)(4) [the exempt social welfare organization], (5) [the exempt labor, agricultural, or horticultural organization], or (6) [the exempt business league] which would be described in paragraph (2) if it were an organization described in section 501(c)(3)."[236]

Translated, this means that a tax-exempt charitable entity may be operated in conjunction with an exempt business league, and thus qualify as a supporting organization (and therefore a public charity), assuming that the supported business league meets the one-third support test of the rules concerning the service provider organization.[237] Business leagues almost always meet this support requirement inasmuch as they have a membership that pays dues; dues constitute public support.

Operations of this type of supporting organization often generate inherent tension: The supporting organization must be charitable in function to qualify for tax exemption yet be supportive of a business league to be a public charity.

---

[234] Nellie Callahan Scholarship Fund v. Comm'r, 73 T.C. 626 (1980).

[235] One of these categories of exempt organizations is the business league, with tax-exempt status predicated on IRC § 501(c)(6). These considerations to be discussed in this context also apply where the organization has its tax exemption based on IRC § 501(c)(4) (see § 1.6(a)) or IRC § 501(c)(5) (see § 1.6(c)).

[236] IRC § 509(a), last sentence.

[237] Reg. § 1.509(a)-4(k). See § 8.4. Also Rev. Rul. 76-401, 1976-2 C.B. 175.

§ 8.8 ASSOCIATION-RELATED FOUNDATIONS

Many tax-exempt business leagues and other types of exempt associations find it appropriate—if not essential—to utilize a *related foundation*.[238] This is the essence of the concept of *bifurcation*: the utilization of two organizations instead of one.[239] Bifurcation in this context is underlain with two motives: (1) transfer of and/or funding of programs that are inherently charitable, educational, and/or scientific, and/or (2) fundraising.

(a) Reasons for Association-Related Foundations

Bifurcation of an organization occurs because one or more important reasons dictate that there should be two entities rather than one. The division of an entity comes about usually for law and/or management reasons. This phenomenon is manifest in the realm of tax-exempt organizations, reflected in arrangements such as lobbying arms of charitable organizations,[240] political action committees of associations and unions,[241] and for-profit subsidiaries of exempt organizations.[242] Association-related foundations are among the most classic of bifurcation structures; establishment and utilization of them is based on both solid management and law reasons.[243]

The fundamental reason for use of a related foundation is to facilitate fundraising.[244] It may be safely stated that most individuals involved in the governance of tax-exempt organizations would prefer to avoid engaging in forms of fundraising. Conversely, many individuals who happen to enjoy raising money for charitable causes do not wish to be a board member or officer of a charitable organization with many programs to oversee. In the association setting, the association-related foundation resolves this dichotomy of management functions by enabling those who are primarily interested in program governance to serve on the association board and those who prefer to concentrate on fundraising to sit on the foundation board. As to the latter, they are trustees, directors, and/or officers of a charitable organization, to be sure, but they need not have any direct responsibility for the conduct of programs. Also, there usually is greater prestige associated with the position of board member (particularly when the term *trustee* is applied) than merely being a member of a committee.[245]

---

[238] It should be reiterated that, although the word *foundation* is used in this context, these entities are not *private foundations* (see § 8.1).

[239] In fact, this matter goes beyond bifurcation and into trifurcation and beyond: an exempt association with a related foundation, a political action committee (see § 4.7), a for-profit subsidiary (see Chapter 6), and perhaps more.

[240] See *Tax-Exempt Organizations*, § 30.3.

[241] *Id.*, Chapter 17.

[242] See Chapter 6.

[243] The use of this type of "foundation" is by no means confined to associations, however. It is common for tax-exempt colleges, universities, hospitals, churches, and many other types of tax-exempt organizations.

[244] See Chapter 9.

[245] Some charitable organizations place the fundraising function in a committee rather than a separate organization; this committee is usually named the development committee or the advancement committee. Likewise, an individual who is the director of development or vice-president for development for a nonbifurcated charitable organization is, in the case of a related foundation, the president or executive director of the foundation.

This is principally why charitable organizations establish related charitable foundations.

The principal law reason why associations utilize related foundations is found in the federal tax law: the charitable contribution deductions.[246] Where the association is tax-exempt on the basis of a status other than charitable,[247] contributions to the organization are not deductible for federal tax purposes as charitable gifts. Inasmuch as nearly all donors want the benefits of the charitable deduction(s), the use of an association-related foundation facilitates fundraising by bringing into the equation the factor of deductibility as a consequence of giving. This is the case irrespective of whether the association-related foundation has charitable, educational, and/or scientific programs or is wholly engaged in fundraising.

In sum, the main reasons for utilization of an association-related foundation are separation of the fundraising function from the association governance function (the management reason) and establishment of a means for assuring that gifts made in support of some or all association programs are deductible as charitable contributions (the law reason).

(b) Control Factor

Although there are no known statistics on the point, it is undoubtedly accurate to state that most—perhaps nearly all—foundations that operate for the benefit of a tax-exempt association are *controlled* by that association. There are several variations on this theme of control and the manner in which it is achieved; the common mechanisms, more than one of which may be used simultaneously, are:

- The governing board of the association selects all of the members of the board of the foundation.

- The governing board of the association selects a majority of the members of the board of the foundation (leaving the foundation board some flexibility to add to its number, such as individuals with a high potential for fundraising prowess and/or giving).

- Those who are the officers of the association are the members of the board of the foundation (ex officio positions).

- The association is the sole member of the foundation and, in that capacity, appoints some or all of the foundation's board.

- Those who serve on the association's board comprise the foundation's board (another variant of ex officio positions).[248]

In some instances, the members of the foundation's board are elected by the membership of the association (which presumably also elects the board of the association). This approach, however, is not likely to result in control of the foundation by the association in a legal sense.

---

[246] See Chapter 9.
[247] See, e.g., § 1.6.
[248] This approach, however, is inconsistent with the usual effort to differentiate the governance and fundraising functions.

There are some foundations functioning for the benefit of an association that are not controlled by that association. This approach is usually the product of the view that it is somehow unseemly or otherwise inappropriate for the foundation to be a controlled entity. On occasion, it is said that donors prefer that the foundation be "independent" of the association. These purist perspectives are based on an "ethic" that a philanthropic entity should not have its purposes and operations sullied by being controlled, particularly where the controlling organization is not a charitable one.

There is no rule of law that calls for control by a tax-exempt association of a foundation that was established and is being operated for the association's benefit. Nonetheless, it is usually imprudent for an association to allow another organization to raise money for the benefit of that association without control of that other organization by the association, the more so as the revenue and assets of the other organization increase. Organizations that are financially healthy present the prospect of inducement of the individuals who direct them to divert the organization's resources to ends other than the original ones. If an association has a foundation operating for its benefit, the preferable practice is for the foundation to be controlled by the association.

(c) Exempt Functions

To be tax-exempt, a supporting organization must engage in activities that are charitable, educational, scientific, and the like. To be a supporting organization, the entity must engage in functions that support or benefit the supported organization. Where the supported organization is a tax-exempt business league, there is potential for a clash of these two principles; thus, the exempt functions of the association-related foundation of this type should be carefully considered. In the realm of associations, there are many functions that qualify as charitable, educational, and/or scientific. They include conferences and seminars, publications, maintenance of a library, community service programs, scholarships, fellowships, awards, and research.

If these activities dominate, the association will undoubtedly qualify as an IRC § 501(c)(3) organization. More often than not, some or all of these activities will be conducted, yet other activities will be the principal ones (such as other membership services, including certification), with the result that the association will be an IRC § 501(c)(6) organization.

In this context, there are two problem areas for the association-related foundation. One concerns the creation, expansion, and maintenance of an endowment fund. Certainly an association-related foundation can create and operate such a fund. An IRC § 501(c)(3) organization cannot, however, maintain an endowment fund for the general support of an IRC § 501(c)(6) organization, although an IRC § 501(c)(3) entity can maintain an endowment fund for the general support of another IRC § 501(c)(3) entity and/or for programs it conducts. If a foundation related to a tax-exempt business league maintains an endowment fund, the foundation should be certain that the fund is used to support only those programs of the association (if that is its purpose) that are charitable, educational, and/or scientific. It is hoped that the point is not being belabored to observe that holding and granting from an endowment fund is an excellent reason for use of the supporting organization vehicle.

The second problem is the acquisition and use of real estate owned by the foundation, when the association supported by the foundation is a tax-exempt business league. An association-related foundation cannot make real property available without charge to an exempt business league[249] (although that can be done when both entities are IRC § 501(c)(3) organizations). There are two fundamental ways to resolve this dilemma. One approach is to cause the business league to pay rent, on a fair market value basis, to the related foundation for the business league's use of the building and/or other real estate. (These rental funds can thereafter be paid out by the foundation to the business league in support of charitable, educational, and/or scientific programs conducted by the business league.) The other approach is to transfer charitable, educational, and/or scientific programs from the business league to the association-related foundation and use the property for support and conduct of these programs.

There are other approaches with respect to the matter of real estate ownership and utilization. One obvious approach is to have the property acquisition and utilization by the business league—but this approach forgoes use of the charitable contribution deduction and thus is impractical. Still other approaches are co-ownership of the property or placement of the property in a joint venture (such as a limited liability company) where the association and foundation are members; the difficulty with this approach is that it is fraught with private inurement, private benefit, and nonexempt function problems.

An association-related foundation can play two fundamental roles in this regard; in some instances, the foundation's activities are a blend of these approaches. With the first approach, the activities of the association that are charitable, educational, and/or scientific are (to the extent feasible) transferred from the association to the foundation. Pursuant to the alternative approach, the charitable, educational, and/or scientific activities remain in the association but are funded by the foundation, by means of restricted grants. The selection of one of these approaches (or, as noted, a combination of them) is likely to be a political decision far more than a legal one.

(d) Fundraising

Almost assuredly, the principal or sole role of the association-related foundation is or will be engaging in fundraising. As discussed, the funds derived from fundraising will be expended in one of two basic ways: the money will be used to fund programs operated by the foundation or used to make grants to fund the charitable, educational, and/or charitable programs conducted by the association. If the latter approach is used, the sole functions of the association-related foundation will be fundraising and grant-making. Once again, it can be seen that the supporting organization structure is ideal for an association-related foundation. This is particularly the case where the association is an IRC § 501(c)(6) organization, but the supporting organization can be used effectively where both the

---

[249] This is because such an activity would be a nonexempt function.

supported organization and the supporting organization are IRC § 501(c)(3) organizations. Again, it may be noted that many individuals do not think of their membership association as a charity, creating the need—for that reason alone—to utilize an association-related foundation for tax purposes.

There are many types of fundraising techniques and practices; some are more appropriate for an association-related foundation than others. Although an association-related foundation should make at least one annual solicitation of the association's membership by letter (probably timed to take into consideration the propensity for year-end giving), the foundation is unlikely to send hundreds of thousands of fundraising pieces in the nature of direct-mail fundraising, unless the association is quite large. Some association-related foundations conduct a special event, usually in conjunction with the association's annual meeting, such as a dinner, dance, run, or golf tournament. An association-related foundation can undertake a capital campaign or an infrequent special campaign, which could also embrace fundraising for program and endowment, as distinct from the annual fundraising appeal. The association-related foundation can solicit gifts by means somewhat unique to associations, such as by having a booth as part of the association's trade show and/or by means of articles in the association's journal or newsletter. The association-related foundation can maintain a planned giving program.

(e) Planned Giving Program

As noted, there are several ways in which an association-related foundation can raise funds to support its association's programs. Of these various fundraising techniques, however, the one that is likely to be the most financially successful for the association-related foundation is the planned giving program. Yet many association-related foundations have an ineffectual planned giving program; some do not make the effort at all.

The absence of strong planned giving programs throughout the entirety of the association universe is surprising, if only because all of the ingredients for a solid planned giving program are present in the association context:

- There is a defined constituency containing many prospective contributors of planned gifts: the association's membership.

- An association's members, particularly those who are serving or have served as a director and/or officer, tend to have an intense affinity with their association.

- Association members, with emphasis on those who have been active in the organization for several years, tend to have higher incomes and more assets than others.

- With the appropriate approach, a member of an association can be induced to make a planned gift to the association-related foundation because of his or her interest in the present and future endeavors of the association.

Admittedly, planned giving programs are difficult to initiate. The association's board, officers, and/or staff may not be inclined to launch a planned giving program, perhaps because they are concentrating on other forms of fundraising that bring funds to the foundation on a current (as opposed to deferred) basis. Members of an association tend to not think of their association when considering charitable giving, particularly in the context of major financial and estate planning.

Nonetheless, these impediments to an effective planned giving program for the association-related foundation can be overcome. The steps to achieving this end are:

- An individual or group of individuals—whether board members, officers, and/or staff—becomes convinced that a planned giving program should be established for the benefit of the association.

- A relationship is established with a lawyer or other planned giving professional.

- The board of the foundation (and/or association) approves, ideally by passage of a corporate resolution, the implementation of a planned giving program.

- A brochure briefly describing the programs of the foundation and the planned giving techniques to be utilized is developed.

- Prototype instruments of various planned giving instruments are developed (particularly for the benefit of lawyers advising prospective donors to the foundation), particularly one or more charitable remainder trust and will codicil forms.

- Other marketing approaches are developed, such as articles in the association's journal or newsletter and/or a booth at the association's annual conference.

- A list of prospective planned giving donors is developed; this is a project that should be continued indefinitely. This effort should be undertaken in conjunction with other fundraising undertakings of the foundation.

- The first prospective donor of a planned gift to the foundation is identified. Often this individual is a member of the board of the association and/or foundation; alternatively, such a board member cultivated this individual. One or more staff members and/or one or more consultants meet with this prospective donor (and often with this individual's spouse and/or other family members) to design the appropriate planned gift (or gifts) that is appropriate under the circumstances. The factors to be considered in this regard are:

  o The means by which the gift is to be funded, which are likely to be appreciated property and/or money

  o The vehicle or vehicles to be used to accomplish the planned gift (or gifts)

  o Identification of any beneficiaries of the gift other than the foundation

  o The amount to be paid to any income beneficiaries

  o The mechanism by which that amount is to be determined

- The gift is made.

- This process is repeated with subsequent donors.

- A form of recognition of these donors is developed.

A staple of an association-related foundation's planned giving program is the bequest. The goal in this regard is to cause individuals to remember the foundation (or perhaps the association) in their will. Like many forms of planned giving, however, a disadvantage is that it may take considerable time for the gift funds to materialize.

Of the various other forms of planned giving, the one most suitable from the standpoint of the association-related foundation is likely to be the charitable remainder trust.[250] Also appropriate for an association-related foundation is an insurance giving program.[251] Other possibilities are the charitable gift annuity,[252] creation of a life estate in real property,[253] and use of a charitable lead trust.[254] Indeed, an outright gift of property (as contrasted with a gift of a remainder interest or an income interest) may be considered a *planned gift*, where the subject of the gift has considerable value and/or entails complexity, such as the transfer of a business, office building, or major work of art.

(f) Public Charity Status

As noted, there is no reason why the association-related foundation should be a private foundation. That is, this type of organization should always be able to qualify as a public charity. Public charity status will, among other attributes, attract charitable contributions that are deductible to the fullest extent.

The category of public charity status that will be used in a given circumstance will depend on these factors:

- Whether the foundation is to be controlled by the association; the leaders of some associations believe that it is inappropriate or unseemly for the foundation to be controlled by the association, while leaders in other cases believe that control (over funds and/or programs) in the foundation is essential (and a matter of fiduciary obligation)[255]

- The nature of the activity of the foundation, that is, whether it will house program activity, fund program activity in the association, or do both

- The nature of the funding of the foundation, including the extent of its investment income

- Political factors, such as board composition of the two organizations

In many instances, a foundation will qualify simultaneously as more than one type of public charity.

---

[250] See § 9.2(b).
[251] See *Charitable Giving*, Chapter 17.
[252] See § 9.2(e).
[253] See *Charitable Giving* § 15.2.
[254] See § 9.2(d).
[255] In the author's opinion, the latter view is the prudent one.

The association-related foundation usually will be a public charity because it is either a publicly supported organization or a supporting organization. Which type of publicly supported organization it will be (assuming that is the case) will depend in large part on whether the foundation is wholly or principally engaged in fundraising or whether program activity of any consequence is conducted by the foundation. If the former, the foundation will likely be a donative-type publicly supported charitable organization, because its funding will primarily be in the forms of gifts and grants.[256] If the latter, the foundation probably can qualify as a service provider publicly supported charitable organization, inasmuch as its funding will be a blend of gifts, grants, and exempt function revenue.[257] On occasion, the related organization may constitute a public charity on another basis, such as by being a school.[258]

(g) Focus on Supporting Organizations

The supporting organization can be the ideal vehicle for the association-related foundation. This type of related foundation can qualify as a public charity without having to be concerned with the ongoing calculation of public support. To reiterate: Public support is not a requirement for a supporting organization.

Qualification of the association-related foundation as a supporting organization may turn on whether the foundation is controlled by the association or not. The parent-subsidiary model[259] in this setting is commonplace. *Control* can be manifested in a number of ways; usually control is accomplished by use of interlocking directorates or by causing the association be the sole member of the foundation.

If the association itself is a public charity, supporting organization status is nearly a foregone conclusion if the parties involved want it. On occasion, an association is a public charity because it is a supporting organization, such as a state association related to a national association. In general, a supporting organization cannot support or benefit another supporting organization; this is permissible, however, where the supported entity is "described in" one of the other categories of public charity.

(h) Conversions

An association-related foundation that is not a supporting organization with respect to a tax-exempt business league may be converted to such a supporting organization. The principal reasons in law for doing this are to retain public charity status for the foundation where it is having difficulty satisfying (or is about to fail) one of the public support tests[260] or to eliminate the need for computing public support. Nearly every association-related foundation can be converted to this type of supporting organization.

---

[256] See § 8.3.
[257] See § 8.4.
[258] See § 8.2(b).
[259] See § 8.6(e).
[260] See §§ 8.3, 8.4.

A determination that the foundation qualifies as a supporting organization must be obtained from the IRS. There is no formal procedure for doing this; that is, there is no IRS form or other stated process in this regard.

The informal process consists of filing Schedule D to Form 1023 (the application for recognition of exemption filed by organizations that seek status as exempt charitable entities) with the IRS.[261] (There is no need to file another application because this process does not entail a reapplication for recognition of tax exemption.) This summary of the process assumes that the association controls or will control the foundation[262] (that is, that the foundation is to be converted to a Type I supporting organization[263]). The four steps to effect this type of conversion follow.

1. The foundation's articles of incorporation or other organizing instrument[264] should be amended to include the requisite supporting organization provisions.[265]

2. The foundation's bylaws should be amended in a comparable manner.

3. The Schedule D should be prepared:

    a. The name, address, and taxpayer identification number of the supported association is provided.[266]

    b. The fact that the supported organization is not a public charity is indicated.[267]

    c. The tax-exempt status of the supported organization is provided.[268]

    d. The requisite statement of revenues of the supported association is provided.[269]

    e. A list of revenues received by the supported association from disqualified persons is provided.[270]

    f. A list of revenues received by the supported association from persons who are not disqualified persons with respect to the association, where the payments were greater than the larger of (1) 1 percent of the association's annual revenue[271] or (2) $5,000 is provided.[272]

---

[261] See Appendix D.

[262] See 8.8(b).

[263] See 8.6, note 155.

[264] See *Tax-Exempt Organizations* § 4.3.

[265] See § 8.6(b).

[266] Schedule D, Section I, line 1.

[267] *Id.*, line 2.

[268] *Id.*, line 3.

[269] *Id.* This information is provided by submitting Form 1023, Part IX-A, lines 1–13. For this arrangement to qualify, the revenues of the supported organization must qualify under the rules concerning service provider publicly supported charities (see § 8.4).

[270] Schedule D, Section I, line 3. This information is provided as requested in Form 1023, Part X, line 6b(ii)(a). Support from disqualified persons cannot qualify as public support (see § 8.4).

[271] See Form 1023, Part IX-A, line 10.

[272] Schedule D, Section I, line 3. This information is provided as requested in Form 1023, Part X, line 6b(ii)(b). Support that exceeds these limitations cannot qualify as public support (see § 8.4).

g. A list of unusual grants received by the supported association is provided.[273]

h. An indication that the relationship between the supported association and the supporting foundation is that reflected in the Type I form of supporting organization.[274]

i. An indication that the supporting organization organizational test has been satisfied.[275]

j. An indication that the foundation is not controlled, directly or indirectly, by disqualified persons.[276]

4. The Schedule D, accompanied by copies of the amended governing instruments and statements providing factual information, should be filed with the IRS, along with an explanatory cover letter.

§ 8.9   PRIVATE BENEFIT DOCTRINE

There is a court opinion in this context that holds that the association-related foundation cannot qualify for tax exemption as a charitable, educational, or scientific entity because it confers unwarranted private benefit on the association and its members.[277] This decision was made with no reference to the statutory law authorizing noncharitable supported organizations.[278] It is anomalous to believe that Congress would create such an in-tandem arrangement, only to have its effect eliminated by the courts by application of the private benefit doctrine.

---

[273] Schedule D, Section I, line 3. This information is provided as requested in Form 1023, Part X, line 7.

[274] Schedule D, Section II, line 1; the "yes" box should be checked. The description of the process by which the foundation's governing board is selected can be made by reference to the appropriate article and/or section of the governing instruments. See § 8.6(e).

[275] Schedule D, Section III, line 1a; the "yes" box should be checked. See § 8.6(a).

[276] Schedule D, Section IV, lines 1a–1c; the three "no" boxes should be checked. See § 8.6(h).

[277] Quality Auditing Co. v. Comm'r, 114 T.C. 498 (2000). In the author's opinion, this case was wrongly decided. See § 3.7.

[278] See § 8.7.

CHAPTER NINE

Charitable Giving and Fundraising

The solicitation and generation of gifts and grants has become a major effort in the tax-exempt association realm. No longer solely reliant on dues revenue, exempt associations are turning to earned income undertakings and charitable support.

As to the latter, some associations are themselves charitable entities[1] and thus can directly engage in fundraising. The majority of associations, however, have exempt status rested on another basis[2] and thus utilize related foundations.[3]

The federal tax law rules pertaining to the making of and deductibility of gifts to charitable organizations are complex. Moreover, the federal and state laws concerning regulation of the fundraising process are intricate and often onerous.

§ 9.1 CHARITABLE GIVING RULES IN GENERAL

The basic concept of the federal income tax deduction for a charitable contribution is this: Individuals who itemize their deductions, and corporations, can annually deduct, within certain limits, an amount equivalent to the sum contributed (money) or to the value of a contribution (property) to a qualified donee. A *charitable contribution* for income tax purposes is a gift to or for the use of one or more qualified donees. Some states' and localities' tax laws also include a charitable deduction for income tax purposes.

Deductions for charitable gifts are also allowed under the federal gift tax and estate tax laws. Donors and the charitable organizations they support commonly expect gifts to be in the form of outright transfers of money or property. For both parties (donor and donee), a gift is usually a unilateral transaction, in a financial sense: The donor parts with the contributed item; the charity acquires it.

The advantages of charitable donation to the donor generally are the resulting charitable deduction and the gratification derived from the giving. Planned giving[4] provides additional financial and tax advantages to the donor. Overall, the economic advantages that can result from a charitable gift are (1) a federal, state, and/or local tax deduction; (2) avoidance of capital gains taxation (when property that has appreciated in value is contributed); (3) creation of or an increase in cash flow; (4) improved tax treatment of income; (5) free professional tax and investment management services; (6) opportunity to transfer property between the generations of a family; and (7) receipt of benefits from the charitable donee. Aside from these financial considerations, however, the prime motivator underlying charitable gifts is the donors' interest in furthering a charitable cause.

(a) Defining Charitable *Gift*

A fundamental requirement of the charitable contribution deduction law is that the cash or property transferred to a charitable organization must be transferred in the form of a *gift*. Just because money is paid or property is transferred to a charity does not necessarily mean that the payment or transfer is a gift. When a

---

[1] That is, organizations described in IRC § 501(c)(3).

[2] Usually the exempt association is a business league—an entity described in IRC § 501(c)(6) (see Chapter 2). Some associations have other exempt statuses, such as exemption by reason of IRC § 501(c)(4) (see § 1.6(a)).

[3] See Chapter 8.

[4] See §§ 8.8(e), 9.2.

tax-exempt university's tuition, an exempt hospital's health care fee, or an exempt association's dues are paid, there is no gift and thus there is no charitable deduction for the payment.

Basically, a gift has two elements: It involves a transfer that is *voluntary* and is motivated by something other than consideration (value received in return for a payment or transfer). Where payments are made to receive something in exchange (education, health care, and the like), the transaction is a purchase. The law places more emphasis on what is received by the payor than on the mere existence of a payment or transfer. The federal income tax regulations state that a transfer is not a contribution when it is made "with a reasonable expectation of financial return commensurate with the amount of the donation."[5] Instead, this type of a payment is a purchase of a product or a service. Thus, the IRS stated that a contribution is a "voluntary transfer of money or property that is made with no expectation of procuring financial benefit commensurate with the amount of the transfer."[6] A single transaction, however, can be partially a gift and partially a purchase[7]; when a charity is the payee, only the gift portion is deductible.

The U.S. Supreme Court observed that a gift is a transfer motivated by "detached or disinterested generosity."[8] The Court also characterized a gift as a transfer stimulated "out of affection, respect, admiration, charity, or like impulses."[9] Thus, the focus in this area for the most part has been an objective analysis, comparing what the "donee" parted with and what (if anything) the "donor" received net in exchange.

Another factor, that of donative intent, sometimes is taken into consideration. A set of federal tax regulations states that, for any part of a payment made in the context of a charity auction to be deductible as a charitable gift, the patron must have donative intent.[10] More broadly, a congressional committee report contains this statement:

> The term "contribution or gift" is not defined by statute, but generally is interpreted to mean a voluntary transfer of money or other property without receipt of adequate consideration and with donative intent. If a taxpayer receives or expects to receive a quid pro quo in exchange for a transfer to charity, the taxpayer may be able to deduct the excess of the amount transferred over the fair market value of any benefit received in return provided the excess payment is made with the intention of making a gift.[11]

A federal court of appeals described the matter as to what is a gift this way: It is a "particularly confused issue of federal taxation."[12] The statutory law on the subject, said this court, is "cryptic," and "neither Congress nor the courts have offered any very satisfactory definitions" of the terms *gift* and *contribution* (which are, for these purposes, basically synonymous).[13]

---

[5] Reg. § 1.162-15(b).

[6] Reg. § 1.170A-1(c)(5).

[7] E.g., § 9.5.

[8] Comm'r v. Duberstein, 363 U.S. 278, 285 (1960), quoting from Comm'r v. LoBue, 351 U.S. 243, 246 (1956).

[9] Robertson v. United States, 343 U.S. 711, 714 (1952).

[10] Reg. § 1.170A-1(h)(1).

[11] H. Rep. No. 106-478, 106th Cong., 1st Sess. 168 (1999).

[12] Miller v. Internal Revenue Service, 829 F.2d 500, 502 (4th Cir. 1987).

[13] *Id.* In general, see *Charitable Giving* § 3.1(a).

(b) Qualified Donees

Qualified donees are charitable organizations (including educational and scientific entities), certain fraternal organizations, certain cemetery companies, and most veterans' organizations.[14] Contributions to both private and public charities are deductible, but the law favors gifts to public charities.[15]

Federal, state, and local governmental bodies are charitable donees. State or local law, however, may preclude a governmental entity from accepting charitable gifts. In most jurisdictions, a charitable organization can be established to solicit deductible contributions for and make grants to governmental bodies. This is a common technique for public schools, colleges, universities, and hospitals.

An otherwise nonqualifying organization may be allowed to receive a deductible charitable gift in cases where the gift property is used for charitable purposes or received by an agent for a charitable organization. An example of the former is a gift to a trade association that is earmarked for a charitable fund within the association. Examples of an agent for a charity is a title-holding company that holds property for charitable purposes and a for-profit company that acquires and disposes of vehicles as part of a charity's used vehicle donation program.[16]

(c) Gifts of Property

Aside from the eligibility of the gift recipient, the other basic element in determining whether a charitable contribution is deductible is the nature of the property given. Basically, the distinctions are between outright giving and planned giving, and between gifts of cash and gifts of property. In many instances, the tax law differentiates between personal property and real property, and tangible property and intangible property (securities).

The federal income tax treatment of gifts of property is dependent on whether the property is *capital gain property*. The federal tax law makes a distinction between long-term capital gain and short-term capital gain. Property that is not capital gain property is termed *ordinary income property*. These three terms are based on the tax classification of the type of revenue that would be generated on sale of the property. Short-term capital gain property generally is treated as ordinary income property. Therefore, the actual distinction is between capital gain property (really, long-term capital gain property) and ordinary income property.

Capital gain property is a capital asset that, if it has appreciated in value and was sold, would give rise to long-term capital gain. To result in long-term capital gain, property must be held for at least 12 months. Most forms of capital gain property are securities and real estate.

The charitable deduction for capital gain property is often equal to its fair market value—or at least is computed using that value. Gifts of ordinary income property generally produce a deduction equivalent to the donor's cost basis in

---

[14] IRC § 170(c).

[15] For the distinction between public and private charitable organizations, see § 8.1.

[16] In general, see *Charitable Giving*, Chapter 4.

the property. The law provides exceptions to this basis-only rule; an example is a gift by a corporation out of its inventory.[17] A charitable deduction based on the full fair market value of an item of appreciated property (with no recognition of the built-in capital gain) is a critical feature of the federal tax law incentives for charitable giving.

(d) Limitations on Deductibility

The extent of charitable contributions that can be deducted for federal income tax purposes for a particular tax year is limited to a certain amount, which for individuals is a function of the donor's *contribution base*—essentially, an amount equal to the individual's adjusted gross income.[18] This level of allowable annual deductibility is determined by five percentage limitations. They are dependent on several factors, principally the nature of the charitable recipient and the type of property contributed. The examples used here assume an individual donor with an annual contribution base of $100,000.

The first three limitations apply to gifts to public charities and to private operating foundations.

First, there is a percentage limitation of 50 percent of the donor's contribution base for gifts of cash and ordinary income property. A donor with a $100,000 contribution base may, in a year, make deductible gifts of these items up to a total of $50,000. If an individual makes contributions that exceed the 50 percent limitation, the excess generally may be carried forward and deducted in one to five subsequent years. Thus, if this donor gave $60,000 in the form of money to one or more public charities in year 1 and made no other charitable gifts in that year, he or she would be entitled to a deduction of $50,000 in year 1, and the remaining $10,000 would be available for deductibility in year 2.

The second percentage limitation is 30 percent of the donor's contribution base for gifts of capital gain property. A donor thus may, in a year, contribute up to $30,000 of qualifying stocks, bonds, real estate, and like property, and receive a charitable deduction for that amount. Any excess (more than 30 percent) of the amount of these gifts is subject to the carryforward rule. If a donor gave $50,000 in capital gain property in year 1 and made no other charitable gifts that year, he or she would be entitled to a charitable contribution deduction of $30,000 in year 1 and the $20,000 would be available in year 2.

A donor who makes gifts of cash and capital gain property to public charities (and/or private operating foundations) in any one year generally is limited by a blend of these percentage limitations. For example, if the donor in year 1 gives $50,000 in cash and $30,000 in appreciated capital gain property to a public charity, his or her charitable deduction in year 1 is considered to be the $30,000 of capital gain property and $20,000 of the cash (to keep the deduction within the overall 50 percent ceiling); the other $30,000 of cash would be carried forward to year 2 (or to years 2 through 5, depending on the donor's financial circumstances).

---

[17] *Id.* § 9.3.
[18] IRC § 170(b).

The third percentage limitation allows a donor of capital gain property to use the 50 percent limitation, instead of the 30 percent limitation, where the amount of the contribution is reduced by all of the unrealized appreciation in the value of the property. This election usually is made by donors who want a larger deduction in the year of the gift for an item of property that has not appreciated in value to a great extent. Once made, this election is irrevocable.

The fourth and fifth percentage limitations apply to gifts to private foundations and certain other charitable donees (other than public charities and private operating foundations). These donees are generally veterans' and fraternal organizations.

Under the fourth percentage limitation, contributions of cash and ordinary income property to private foundations and other entities may not exceed 30 percent of the individual donor's contribution base. The carryover rules apply to this type of gift. If the donor gives $50,000 in cash to one or more private foundations in year 1, his or her charitable deduction for that year (assuming no other charitable gifts) is $30,000, with the balance of $20,000 carried forward into subsequent years (up to five).

The carryover rules blend with the first three percentage limitations. For example, if in year 1 a donor gave $65,000 to charity, of which $25,000 went to a public charity and $40,000 went to a private foundation, his or her charitable deduction for that year would be $50,000: $30,000 for the gift to the private foundation and $20,000 for the gift to the public charity. The remaining $10,000 of the gift to the foundation and the remaining $5,000 of the gift to the public charity would be carried forward into year 2.

The fifth percentage limitation pertaining to individuals is 20 percent of the contribution base for gifts of capital gain property to private foundations and other charitable donees. There is a carryforward for any excess deduction amount. For example, if a donor gives appreciated securities, having a value of $30,000, to a private foundation in year 1, his or her charitable deduction for year 1 (assuming no other charitable gifts) is $20,000; the remaining $10,000 may be carried forward.

Deductible charitable contributions by corporations in any tax year may not exceed 10 percent of pretax net income. Excess amounts may be carried forward and deducted in subsequent years (up to five). For gifts by corporations, the federal tax laws do not differentiate between gifts to public charities and gifts to private foundations. As an illustration, a corporation that grosses $1 million in a year and incurs $900,000 in expenses in that year (not including charitable gifts) may generally contribute to charity and deduct in that year an amount up to $10,000 (10 percent of $100,000); in computing its taxes, this corporation would report taxable income of $90,000. If the corporation contributed $20,000 in that year, the numbers would remain the same, except that the corporation would have a $10,000 charitable contribution carryforward.

A corporation on the accrual method of accounting can elect to treat a contribution as having been made in a tax year if it is actually donated during the first 2½ months of the following year. Corporate gifts of property are generally subject to the deduction reduction rules, discussed next.

A business organization that is a flow-through entity generates a different tax result when it comes to charitable deductions. (These organizations are partnerships, other joint ventures, small business (S) corporations, and limited liability companies.) Entities of this nature, even though they may make charitable gifts, do not claim charitable contribution deductions. Instead, the deduction is passed through to the partners, members, or other owners on an allocable basis, and they claim their share of the deduction on their tax return.[19]

(e) Deduction Reduction Rules

A donor (individual or corporation) who makes a gift of *ordinary income property* to a charitable organization (public or private) must confine the charitable deduction to an amount equal to the donor's cost basis in the property. The deduction is not an amount equal to fair market value of the property; it must be reduced by the amount that would have been gain (ordinary income) if the property had been sold. As an example, if a donor gave to a charity an item of ordinary income property having a value of $1,000, for which he or she paid $600, the resulting charitable deduction would be $600.

Any donor who makes a gift of capital gain property to a public charity generally can compute the charitable deduction using the property's fair market value at the time of the gift, regardless of the basis amount and with no taxation of the appreciation (the capital gain inherent in the property). Suppose, however, a donor makes a gift of capital gain tangible personal property (such as a work of art) to a public charity and the use of the gift property by the donee is unrelated to its tax-exempt purposes. The donor must reduce the deduction by an amount equal to all of the long-term capital gain that would have been recognized had the donor sold the property at its fair market value as of the date of the contribution.

Generally, a donor who makes a gift of capital gain property to a private foundation must reduce the amount of the otherwise allowable deduction by all of the appreciate elements (built-in capital gain) in the gift property. An individual, however, is allowed full fair market value for a contribution to a private foundation of certain publicly traded stock (known as *qualified appreciated stock*).[20]

(f) Twice-Basis Deductions

As a general rule, when a corporation makes a charitable gift of property from its inventory, the resulting charitable deduction cannot exceed an amount equal to the donor's cost basis in the donated property. In most instances, this basis amount is rather small, being equal to the cost of producing the property. Under certain circumstances, however, corporate donors can receive a greater charitable deduction for gifts out of their inventory. Where the tests are satisfied, the deduction can be equal to cost basis plus one-half of the appreciated value of the

---

[19] In general, see *Charitable Giving*, Chapter 7.
[20] *Id.*, Chapter 4.

property. The charitable deduction may not, in any event, exceed an amount equal to twice the property's cost basis.

Five requirements have to be met for this twice-basis charitable deduction to be available: (1) the donated property must be used by the charitable donee for a related use; (2) the donated property must be used solely for the care of the ill, the needy, or infants; (3) the property may not be transferred by the donee in exchange for money, other property, or services; (4) the donor must receive a written statement from the donee representing that the use and disposition of the donated property will be in conformance with these rules; and (5) where the donated property is subject to regulation under the U.S. Food, Drug, and Cosmetic Act, the property must fully satisfy the act's requirements on the date of transfer and for the previous 180 days.

For these rules to apply, the donee must be a public charity; that is, cannot be a private foundation or a private operating foundation. An S corporation—the tax status of many businesses—cannot utilize these rules.

Similarly computed charitable deductions are available for contributions of scientific property used for research and contributions of computer technology and equipment for educational purposes.[21]

(g) Contributions of Vehicles

Congress and the IRS have, in recent years, become greatly troubled over the matter of contributions to charity of vehicles. One of the principal issues in this regard is valuation of the gift property; the IRS has issued considerable guidance in this regard. Where a charitable organization uses the services of a for-profit company to receive and process the donated vehicles, a charitable contribution deduction is available where the company is designated the agent of the charity.[22] For unrelated business purposes, the charity is not taxable on the resulting income because of the *donated goods exception*.[23] The IRS warned that it will apply the private inurement doctrine, the private benefit doctrine, and the intermediate sanctions rules[24] in this setting. Also potentially applicable are penalties for aiding and abetting understatements of tax liability and for promoting abusive tax shelters.

Statutory rules enacted in 2004 entail deductibility and substantiation requirements in connection with contributions to charity of motor vehicles, boats, and airplanes—collectively termed *qualified vehicles*.[25] These requirements supplant the general gift substantiation rules[26] where the claimed value of the gifted property contributed exceeds $500.

Pursuant to these rules, a federal income tax charitable contribution deduction is not allowed unless the donor substantiates the contribution by a contemporaneous written acknowledgment of the contribution by the donee organization

---

[21] *Id.* §§ 9.3–9.5.
[22] See *Charitable Giving* § 10.2.
[23] See *Unrelated Business* § 4.3.
[24] See Chapter 3.
[25] IRC § 170(f)(12).
[26] See § 9.4.

and includes the acknowledgment with the donor's income tax return reflecting the deduction. This acknowledgment must contain the name and taxpayer identification number of the donor and the vehicle identification number or similar number. If the gift is of a qualified vehicle that was sold by the donee charitable organization without any "significant intervening use or material improvement," the acknowledgment must also contain a certification that the vehicle was sold in an arm's-length transaction between unrelated parties, a statement as to the gross proceeds derived from the sale, and a statement that the deductible amount may not exceed the amount of the gross proceeds. If there is such use or improvement, the acknowledgment must include a certification as to the intended use or material improvement of the vehicle and the intended duration of the use and a certification that the vehicle will not be transferred in exchange for money, other property, or services before completion of the use or improvement. An acknowledgment is *contemporaneous* if the donee organization provides it within 30 days of the sale of the qualified vehicle or, in an instance of an acknowledgment including the foregoing certifications, of the contribution of the vehicle.

The amount of the charitable deduction for a gift of a qualified vehicle is dependent on the nature of the use of the vehicle by the donee organization. If the charitable organization sells the vehicle without any significant intervening use or material improvement of the vehicle by the organization, the amount of the charitable deduction may not exceed the gross proceeds received from the sale. Where there is such a use or improvement, the charitable deduction is based on the fair market value of the vehicle.

The legislative history accompanying this law states that these two exceptions are to be strictly construed. To meet this *significant use* test, the organization must actually use the vehicle to substantially further the organization's regularly conducted activities and the use must be significant. The test is not satisfied if the use is incidental or not intended at the time of the contribution. Whether a use is *significant* also depends on the frequency and duration of use.

The legislative history of this legislation provided an example of a charitable organization that, as part of its regularly conducted activities, delivers meals to needy individuals. The use requirement would be satisfied if the organization used a donated vehicle to deliver food to the needy. Use of the vehicle to deliver meals substantially furthers a regularly conducted activity of the organization. The use also must be significant, which depends on the nature, extent, and frequency of the use. If the organization used the vehicle "only once or a few times" to deliver meals, the use would not be considered significant. If the organization used the vehicle to deliver meals every day for one year, the use would be considered significant. If the organization drove the vehicle 10,000 miles while delivering meals, such use likely would be considered significant. Use of a vehicle in such an activity for one week or for several hundreds of miles generally would not be considered a significant use.

This legislative history provides a second example concerning use by a charitable organization of a donated vehicle to transport its volunteers. The use would not be significant merely because a volunteer used the vehicle over a "brief period of time" to drive to or from the organization's premises. Conversely, if at the time the organization accepts the contribution of a qualified vehicle, the organization intends to use the vehicle as a "regular and ongoing" means of transport for volunteers of the organization, and the vehicle is so used, the significant use test would be met.

The legislative history provides a third example, concerning an individual who makes a charitable contribution of a used automobile in good running condition and that needs no immediate repairs to a charitable organization that operates an elder care facility. The organization provides the donor with a written acknowledgment that includes a certification that the donee intends to retain the vehicle for a year or longer to transport the facility's residents to community and social events and to deliver meals to the needy. A few days after receiving the vehicle, the donee organization commences to use the vehicle three times a week to transport some of its residents to various community events and twice a week to deliver food to needy individuals. The organization continues to use the vehicle for these purposes regularly for approximately one year and then sells the vehicle. The donee's use of this vehicle constitutes a significant intervening use prior to the sale by the organization.

A *material improvement* includes major repairs to a vehicle or other improvements to the vehicle that improve its condition in a manner that significantly increases the vehicle's value. Cleaning the vehicle, minor repairs, and routine maintenance do not constitute material improvements. This legislative history does not provide any examples pertaining to this exception. Presumably, this exception is available only when the donee charitable organization expresses its intent at the outset (at least in part by means of the certification) that the donee plans to materially improve the vehicle.

A donee organization that is required to provide an acknowledgment under these rules must also provide that information to the IRS. A penalty is imposed for the furnishing of a false or fraudulent acknowledgment, or an untimely or incomplete acknowledgment, by a charitable organization to a donor of a qualified vehicle.[27]

(h) Contributions of Intellectual Property

A person may contribute intellectual property, by means of transfer of a patent, a license to use a patent, or otherwise, to a charitable organization and obtain a charitable deduction. Where, however, a contribution to a charity of a license to use a patent involves retention by the person of a substantial right in the patent (such as the right to license the patent to others or the right to use the patent or license in certain geographical areas), the transaction constitutes a nondeductible transfer of a partial interest.[28] The IRS issued the guidance as to valuation of this type of property and rules by which the value for deduction purposes must be reduced because of consideration provided to the donor. The agency also announced that it may impose penalties on those claiming inappropriate charitable deductions for these gifts, as well as on promoters and appraisers involved in improper deductions.

---

[27] In general, *Charitable Giving* § 9.25 (2006 Supp.).
[28] *Id.* § 9.23.

Congress, in 2004, enacted legislation concerning charitable contributions of intellectual property. This legislation is predicated on the view that excessive charitable contribution deductions enabled by inflated valuations in this context is best addressed by confining the amount of the deduction for gifts of intellectual property to the donor's basis in the property, while allowing for additional charitable contribution deductions thereafter if the contributed property generates income for the charitable organization.

Contributions of certain types of intellectual property have been added to the list of gifts that give rise to a charitable contribution deduction that is confined to the donor's basis in the property, although, as discussed later, in instances of gifts of intellectual property there may be one or more subsequent charitable deductions. This property consists of patents, copyrights (with exceptions), trademarks, trade names, trade secrets, know-how, software (with exceptions), or similar property, or applications or registrations of such property. Collectively, these properties are termed *qualified intellectual property* (except in instances when contributed to standard private foundations).[29]

A person who makes this type of gift, denominated a *qualified intellectual property contribution*, is provided a charitable contribution deduction (subject to the annual percentage limitations[30]) equal to the donor's basis in the property in the year of the gift and, in that year and/or subsequent years, a charitable deduction equal to a percentage of net income that flows to the charitable donee as the consequence of the gift of the property. For a contribution to be a qualified intellectual property contribution, the donor must notify the donee at the time of the contribution that the donor intends to treat the contribution as a qualified intellectual property contribution for deduction and reporting purposes. The net income involved is termed *qualified donee income.*

Thus, a portion of qualified donee income is allocated to a tax year of the donor, although this income allocation process is inapplicable to income received by or accrued to the donee after 10 years from the date of the gift; the process is also inapplicable to donee income received by or accrued to the donee after the expiration of the legal life of the property.

The amount of qualified donee income that materializes into a charitable deduction, for one or more years, is ascertained by the *applicable percentage*, which is a sliding-scale percentage determined by this table, which appears in the Internal Revenue Code:

Donor's Tax Year	Applicable Percentage
1st	100
2nd	100
3rd	90
4th	80
5th	70
6th	60

[29] IRC § 170(m).
[30] See § 9.1(d).

Donor's Tax Year	Applicable Percentage
7th	50
8th	40
9th	30
10th	20
11th	10
12th	10

Thus, if, following a qualified intellectual property contribution, the charitable donee receives qualified donee income in the year of the gift, and/or in the subsequent tax year of the donor, that amount becomes, in full, a charitable contribution deduction for the donor (subject to the general limitations). If such income is received by the charitable donee eight years after the gift, for example, the donor receives a charitable deduction equal to 40 percent of the qualified donee income. As this table indicates, the opportunity for a qualified intellectual property deduction arising out of a qualified intellectual property contribution terminates after the 12th year of the donor ending after the date of the gift.

The IRS is authorized to issue anti-abuse rules that may be necessary to prevent avoidance of this body of law, including preventing (1) the circumvention of the reduction of the charitable deduction by embedding or bundling the patent or similar property as part of a charitable contribution of property that includes the patent or similar property; (2) the manipulation of the basis of the property to increase the amount of the initial charitable deduction through use of related persons, pass-through entities, or intermediaries, or through the use of any provision of statutory law or regulation (including the consolidated return regulations); and (3) a donor from changing the form of the patent or similar property to property of a form to which different deduction rules would apply.

The reporting requirements rules, concerning certain dispositions of contributed property, were amended in 2004 to encompass qualified intellectual property contributions.[31]

(i) Partial Interest Gifts

Most charitable gifts are of all ownership of a property: the donor parts with all right, title, and interest in and to the property. A gift of a *partial interest*, however, is also possible—a contribution of less than a donor's entire interest in the property.

As a general rule, charitable deductions for gifts of partial interests in property, including the right to use property, are not available. The exceptions, which are many, include (1) gifts made in trust form (using a *split-interest trust*); (2) gifts of an outright remainder interest in a personal residence or farm; (3) gifts of an undivided portion of the donor's entire interest in an item of property; (4) gifts of a lease on, option to purchase, or easement with respect to real property granted in perpetuity to a public charity exclusively for conservation purposes;

---

[31] In general, *Charitable Giving* § 9.26 (2006 Supp.).

and (5) a remainder interest in real property granted to a public charity exclusively for conservation purposes.

Contributions of income interests in property in trust are basically confined to the use of charitable lead trusts. Aside from a charitable gift annuity and gifts of remainder interests, there is no charitable deduction for a contribution of a remainder interest in property unless it is in trust and is one of three types: a charitable remainder annuity trust, a charitable remainder unitrust, or a pooled income fund.

Defective charitable split-interest trusts may be reformed to preserve the charitable deduction where certain requirements are satisfied.[32]

(j) Gifts of Insurance

Another type of charitable giving involves life insurance. To secure a federal income tax charitable deduction, the gift must include all rights of ownership in a life insurance policy. Thus, an individual can donate a fully paid-up life insurance policy to a charitable organization and deduct (for income-tax purposes) its value. Or an individual can acquire a life insurance policy, give it to a charity, pay the premiums, and receive a charitable deduction for each premium payment made.

For the donation of an insurance policy to be valid, the charitable organization must be able to demonstrate that it has an insurable interest in the life of the donor of the policy (unless state statutory law eliminates the requirement). From an income tax deduction standpoint, it is not enough for a donor simply to name a charitable organization as the or as a beneficiary of a life insurance policy. There is no income tax charitable contribution deduction for this philanthropic act. Although the life insurance proceeds become part of the donor's estate, however, there will be an offsetting estate tax charitable deduction.[33]

§ 9.2 PLANNED GIVING

Planned giving is the most sophisticated form of charitable giving. For the most part, planned gifts are partial interest gifts. In a broader sense, planned giving encompasses contributions made via decedents' estates and by use of life insurance.

(a) Introduction

There are two basic types of planned gifts. One type is a legacy: Under a will, a gift comes out of an estate (as a bequest or a devise). The other type is a gift made during a donor's lifetime, using a trust or other agreement.

These gifts once were termed *deferred gifts* because the actual receipt of the contribution amount by the charity is deferred until the happening of some event (usually the death of the donor or subsequent death of the donor's spouse). This term, however, has fallen out of favor. Some donors (to the chagrin

---

[32] *Id.*, Chapter 5.
[33] *Id.*, Chapter 17.

of the gift-seeking charities) gained the impression that it was their tax benefits that were being deferred.

A planned gift usually is a contribution of a donor's interest in money or an item of property rather than an outright gift of the money or property in its entirety. (The term *usually* is used because gifts involving life insurance do not neatly fit this definition and because an outright gift of property, in some instances, is treated as a planned gift.) Technically, this type of gift is a conveyance of a partial interest in property; planned giving is (usually) partial interest giving.

An item of property conceptually has within it two interests: an income interest and a remainder interest.

The *income interest* within an item of property is a function of the income generated by the property. A person may be entitled to all of the income from a property or to some portion of the income—for example, income equal to 6 percent of the fair market value of the property, even though the property is producing income at the rate of 9 percent. This person is said to have the (or an) income interest in the property. Two or more persons (such as spouses or siblings) may have income interests in the same property; these interests may be held concurrently or consecutively.

The *remainder interest* within an item of property is equal to the projected value of the property, or the property produced by reinvestments, at some future date. That is, the remainder interest in property is an amount equal to the present value of the property (or its offspring) when it is to be received at a subsequent point in time.

These interests are measured by the value of the property, the age of the donor(s), the period of time that the income interest(s) will exist, and the frequency and type of the income payout. The computation of these interests is made by means of actuarial tables, usually those promulgated by the Department of the Treasury.

An income interest or a remainder interest in property may be contributed to charity, but a deduction is almost never available for a charitable gift of an income interest in property. (This is more of an estate planning technique.) By contrast, the charitable contribution of a remainder interest in an item of property will—assuming all of the technical requirements are satisfied—give rise to a (frequently sizable) charitable deduction.

When a gift of a remainder interest in property is made to a charity, the charity will not acquire that interest until the income interest(s) in the property have expired. The donor receives the charitable contribution deduction for the tax year in which the recipient charity's remainder interest in the property is established. On the occasion of a gift of an income interest in property to a charity, the charity acquires that interest immediately and retains it until such time as the remainder interest commences.

Basically, under the federal tax law, a planned gift must be made by means of a trust if a charitable contribution deduction is to be available. The trust used to facilitate a planned gift is known as a *split-interest trust* because it is the mechanism for satisfying the requirements involving the income and remainder interests. In other words, this type of trust is the medium for—in use of a legal fiction—splitting the property into its two component categories of interests. Split-interest trusts are charitable remainder trusts, pooled income funds, and charitable lead trusts. There are some exceptions to the general requirements as to the use of a split-interest trust in the planned giving context. The principal exception is the charitable gift annuity, which entails a contract rather than a trust. Individuals may give a remainder interest in their personal residence or farm to charity and receive a charitable deduction without utilizing a trust.

A donor, although desirous of financially supporting a charity, may be unwilling or unable to fully part with property, either because of a present or perceived need for the income that the property generates and/or because of the capital gains taxes that would be experienced if the property were sold. The planned gift is likely to be the solution in this type of situation: The donor may satisfy his or her charitable desires and yet continue to receive income from the property (or property that results from reinvestment). The donor also receives a charitable deduction for the gift of the remainder interest, which will reduce or eliminate the tax on the income from the gift property. There is no tax imposed on the capital gain inherent in the property. If the gift property is not throwing off sufficient income, the trustee of the split-interest trust may dispose of the property and reinvest the proceeds in more productive property. The donor may then receive more income from the property in the trust than was received prior to the making of the gift.[34]

The various planned giving vehicles are explored next.

(b) Charitable Remainder Trusts

The most widespread form of planned giving involves a split-interest trust known as the charitable *remainder trust*. The term is nearly self-explanatory: The entity is a trust by which a remainder interest destined for charity has been created. Each charitable remainder trust is designed specifically for the particular circumstances of the donor(s), with the remainder interest in the gift property designated for one or more charities. (Occasionally, because of miscommunication with the donor(s), lack of skill in use of a word processor, or incompetence, a remainder trust will be drafted that is the wrong type. The IRS generously characterizes these trusts as the product of a *scrivener's error*, and will recognize the qualification of the corrected trust, which must be undertaken by court-supervised reformation.)

A qualified charitable remainder trust must provide for a specified distribution of income, at least annually, to or for the use of one or more beneficiaries (at least one of which is not a charity). This flow of income must be for life or for a term of no more than 20 years, with an irrevocable remainder interest to be held for the benefit of the charity or paid over to it. The income beneficiaries are those deriving income from the trust (those holding an income interest); the charity has the remainder interest.

How the income interests in a charitable remainder trust are ascertained depends on whether the trust is a charitable remainder annuity trust (income payments are in the form of a fixed amount, an annuity) or a charitable remainder

---

[34] *Id.* § 5.3.

unitrust (income payments are in the form of an amount equal to a percentage of the fair market value of the assets in the trust, determined annually). (Recently promulgated tax regulations have changed the concept of trust income, doing away with the traditional precepts of income and principal, with as yet-unknown consequences for some charitable remainder unitrusts.)

There are four types of charitable remainder unitrusts. The one just described is known as the *standard charitable remainder unitrust* or the *fixed percentage charitable remainder unitrust*. There are two types of unitrusts that are known as *income exception charitable remainder unitrusts*. One of these types enables income to be paid to the income interest beneficiary once there is any income generated in the trust; this is the *net income charitable remainder unitrust*. The other type of income-exception unitrust is akin to the previous one, but can make catch-up payments for prior years' deficiencies once income begins to flow; this is the *net income make-up charitable remainder unitrust*. The fourth type of unitrust is allowed to convert (flip) once from one of the income exception methods to the fixed percentage method for purposes of calculating the unitrust amount; this is the *flip charitable remainder unitrust*.

The income payout of both of these types of trusts is subject to a 5 percent minimum. That is, the annuity must be an amount equal to at least 5 percent of the value of the property initially placed in the trust. Likewise, the unitrust amount must be an amount equal to at least 5 percent of the value of the trust property, determined annually. These percentages may not be greater than 50 percent. Also, the value of the remainder interest in the property must be at least 10 percent of the value of the property contributed to the trust.

Nearly any kind of property can be contributed to a charitable remainder trust. Typical gift properties are cash, securities, and/or real estate. Yet a charitable remainder trust can accommodate gifts of artworks, collections, and just about any other forms of property. One of the considerations must be the ability of the property (or successor property, if sold) to generate sufficient income to satisfy the payout requirement with respect to the income interest beneficiary or beneficiaries.

All categories of charitable organizations—public charities and private foundations—are eligible to be remainder interest beneficiaries of as many charitable remainder trusts as they can muster. The amount of the charitable deduction will vary for contributions to different types of charitable organizations, however, because of the percentage limitations.[35]

Often a bank or other financial institution serves as the trustee of a charitable remainder trust. The financial institution should have the capacity to administer the trust, make appropriate investments, and timely adhere to all income distribution and reporting requirements. It is not unusual, however, for the charitable organization that is the remainder interest beneficiary to act as trustee. If the donor or a related person is named the trustee, the grantor trust rules may apply: The gain from the trust's sale of appreciated property is taxed to the donor.

---

[35] See § 9.1(d).

Conventionally, once the income interest expires, the assets in a charitable remainder trust are distributed to the charitable organization (or organizations) that is the remainder interest beneficiary. If the assets (or a portion of them) are retained in the trust, the trust will be classified as a private foundation, unless it can qualify as a public charity (most likely, a supporting organization).[36]

There have been some abuses in this area in recent years. One problem has been the use of short-term (such as a term of two years) charitable remainder trusts to manipulate the use of assets and payout arrangements for the tax benefit of the donors. Certain of these abuses were stymied by legislation creating some of the previously referenced percentage rules. The tax regulations were revised in an attempt to prevent transactions by which a charitable remainder trust is used to convert appreciated property into money while avoiding tax on the gain from the sale of the assets.

Inasmuch as charitable remainder trusts are split-interest trusts, they are subject to at least some of the prohibitions that are imposed in private foundations, most notably the rules concerning self-dealing and taxable expenditures. The IRS has an informal procedure (reflected only in private letter rulings) for the premature termination of a charitable remainder trust, where the termination does not give rise to self-dealing because the procedure devised for allocation of the trust's assets to beneficiaries is reasonable.

A qualified charitable remainder trust generally is exempt from federal income taxation. In any year, however, in which it has unrelated business taxable income,[37] the trust loses its tax-exempt status.[38]

(c) Pooled Income Funds

Another planned giving technique involves gifts to charity via a *pooled income fund*. Like a charitable remainder trust, a pooled income fund is a form of split-interest trust.

A donor to a qualified pooled income fund receives a charitable deduction for giving the remainder interest in the donated property to charity. The gift creates income interests in one or more noncharitable beneficiaries; the remainder interest in the gift property is designated for the charity that maintains the fund.

The pooled income fund's basic instrument (a trust agreement or a declaration of trust) is written to facilitate gifts from an unlimited number of donors, so the essential terms of the transactions must be established in advance for all participants. The terms of the transfer cannot be tailored to fit any one donor's particular circumstances (as is the case with the charitable remainder trust). The pooled income fund constitutes, literally, a pool of gifts.

Contributions to a pooled income fund may be considerably smaller than is practical for those to a charitable remainder trust. Gifts to pooled income funds generally are confined to cash and readily marketable securities (other than tax-exempt bonds).

---

[36] See §§ 8.3–8.6.
[37] See Chapter 5.
[38] In general, *Charitable Giving*, Chapter 12.

Each donor to a pooled income fund contributes an irrevocable remainder interest in the gift property to (or for the use of) an eligible charitable organization. Each donor creates an income interest for the life of one or more beneficiaries, who must be living at the time of the transfer. The properties transferred by the donors must be commingled in the fund (thereby creating the necessary pool of gifts).

Each income interest beneficiary must receive income at least once each year. The pool amount is determined by the rate of return earned by the fund for the year. Beneficiaries receive their proportionate share of the fund's income. The dollar amount of the income share is based on the number of units owned by the beneficiary; each unit must be based on the fair market value of the assets when transferred. Thus, a pooled income fund is essentially an investment vehicle whose funding is motivated by charitable intents.

A pooled income fund must be maintained by one or more charitable organizations. Usually a pooled income fund serves only one charity. The charity must exercise control over the fund; it does not have to be the trustee of the fund (although it can be), but it must have the power to remove and replace the trustee. A donor or an income beneficiary of the fund may not be a trustee. A donor may be a trustee or officer of the charitable organization that maintains the fund, however, as long as he or she does not have the general responsibilities with respect to the fund that are ordinarily exercised by a trustee.

Unlike other forms of planned giving, a pooled income fund is restricted to only certain categories of charitable organizations. Most types of public charities can maintain a pooled income fund; private foundations and some other charities cannot.

Pooled income funds are subject to at least some of the prohibitions that are imposed on private foundations, most particularly the rules concerning self-dealing and taxable expenditures.

A qualified pooled income fund is not treated as an association for tax purposes, nor does such a fund have to be a trust under local law. Generally, a pooled income fund is subject to federal income taxation. In actuality, however, a pooled income fund usually is not taxable, because it receives a deduction for amounts paid out to income interest beneficiaries and a set-aside deduction for the remainder interests reserved for the charitable beneficiary.

Pooled income funds currently are somewhat out of favor due to declines in interest rates and bond yields. This is causing a reduction in the investment return of these funds and, thus, a reduction in the amount of income paid to the income beneficiaries. Donors are avoiding pooled income funds, thereby increasing the costs to the charities of maintaining them. Some charities have terminated their pooled income fund(s), although many funds at the larger institutions continue to perform adequately.[39]

(d) Charitable Lead Trusts

Most forms of planned giving have a common element: The donor transfers to a charitable organization the remainder interest in an item of property, and one or

---

[39] *Id.*, Chapter 13.

more noncharitable beneficiaries retain or obtain the income interest. A reverse sequence may occur, however—and that is the essence of the *charitable lead trust.*

The property transferred to a charitable lead trust is apportioned into an income interest and a remainder interest. Like the charitable remainder trust and the pooled income fund, this is a split-interest trust. An income interest in property is contributed to a charitable organization, either for a term of years or for the life of one individual (or the lives of more than one individual). The remainder interest in the property is reserved to return, at the expiration of the income interest (the lead period), to the donor or pass to some other noncharitable beneficiary or beneficiaries. Often the property passes from one generation (the donor's) to another.

The tax regulations limit the types of individuals whose lives can be used as measuring lives for determining the period of time the charity will receive the income flow from a charitable lead trust. The only individuals whose lives can be used as measuring ones are those of the donor, the donor's spouse, and/or a lineal ancestor of all the remaining beneficiaries. These regulations are intended to eliminate the practice of using the lives of seriously ill individuals to move assets and income away from charitable beneficiaries prematurely and instead to private beneficiaries.

The charitable lead trust can be used to accelerate into one year a series of charitable contributions that would otherwise be made annually. There can be a corresponding single-year deduction for the "bunched" amount of charitable gifts.

In some circumstances, a charitable deduction is available for the transfer of an income interest in property to a charitable organization. There are stringent limitations, however, on the deductible amount of charitable contributions of these income interests.[40]

(e) Charitable Gift Annuities

Still another form of planned giving is the *charitable gift annuity*. It is not based on use of a split-interest trust; instead, the annuity is arranged in an agreement between the donor and the charitable donee. The donor agrees to make a gift and the donee agrees, in return, to provide the donor (and/or someone else) with an annuity.

With one payment, the donor is thus engaging in two transactions: the purchase of an annuity and the making of a charitable gift. The contribution gives rise to the charitable deduction. One sum is transferred; the money in excess of the amount necessary to purchase the annuity is the charitable gift portion. Because of the dual nature of the transaction, the charitable gift annuity transfer constitutes a bargain sale.

The annuity resulting from the creation of a charitable gift annuity arrangement (like an annuity generally) is a fixed amount paid at regular intervals. The exact amount paid depends on the age of the beneficiary, which is determined at the time the contribution is made. Frequently, the annuity payment period

---

[40] *Id.,* Chapter 16.

begins with the creation of the annuity payment obligation. The initiation of the payment period can, however, be postponed to a future date; this type of arrangement is termed the *deferred payment charitable gift annuity.*

A portion of the annuity paid is tax-free because it constitutes a return of capital. Where appreciated securities (or other capital gain property) are given, there will be capital gain on the appreciation that is attributable to the value of the annuity. If the donor is the annuitant, the capital gain can be reported ratably over the individual's life expectancy. The tax savings occasioned by the charitable contribution deduction may, however, shelter the capital gain (resulting from the creation of a charitable gift annuity) from taxation.

Inasmuch as the arrangement is by contract between the donor and donee, all of the assets of the charitable organization are subject to liability for the ongoing payment of the annuities. (With most planned giving techniques, the resources for payment of the income are confined to those in a split-interest trust.) That is why some states impose a requirement that charities must establish a reserve for the payment of gift annuities—and why many charitable organizations are reluctant to embark on a gift annuity program. Charities that are reluctant to commit to the ongoing payment of annuities can eliminate the risk by reinsuring them.[41]

§ 9.3 CORPORATE SPONSORSHIP RULES

The federal tax law includes rules pursuant to which, under certain circumstances, a payment from a corporate sponsor to a tax-exempt (usually charitable) organization is treated in essence as a contribution, rather than being considered unrelated business income.[42]

(a) Background

The IRS caused a substantial stir in 1991 by determining that a payment received by a college bowl association from a for-profit corporation sponsoring a bowl football game was taxable as unrelated business income, because the payment was for a package of "valuable" services rather than a gift. This IRS pronouncement was a technical advice memorandum passing on the federal tax consequences of *corporate sponsorships,* arrangements under which the sponsoring business has the corporate name included in the name of the event.[43] The associations involved contended that the payments were gifts, but the IRS held that the companies received a substantial *quid pro quo* for the payments. This determination raised the question, once again, of whether a payment is a "gift" when the "donor" is provided something of value in return.

Charitable organizations throughout the United States became concerned about this IRS initiative—and properly so, as it had implications far beyond college and university bowl games. The IRS bowl game technical advice memorandum

---

[41] *Id.,* Chapter 14.
[42] IRC § 513(i).
[43] Tech. Adv. Mem. 9147007.

raised the deeper question of when the extent of donor recognition renders a payment not a gift or only partially a gift.

The IRS promptly recognized this problem. Thus, it soon thereafter promulgated proposed guidelines for its auditing agents to use when conducting examinations of tax-exempt organizations.[44] The issuance of these guidelines was followed by hearings conducted by the IRS in mid-1992; in that connection, the IRS sought comment on other issues. As the IRS was endeavoring to finalize its guidelines in this area, Congress attempted to legislate in this area, only to have the measure vetoed (for other reasons). In early 1993, the IRS issued proposed regulations concerning the tax treatment, as gifts or items of unrelated income, of sponsorship payments received by tax-exempt organizations.

(b) Qualified Sponsorship Payments

These developments led to the enactment of legislation that added to the federal tax statutory law to the concept of the *qualified sponsorship payment*. These payments received by tax-exempt organizations and state colleges and universities are, pursuant to this safe-harbor provision, exempt from the unrelated business income tax. That is, the activity of soliciting and receiving these payments is not an unrelated business.[45]

From the standpoint of charitable giving, these rules differentiate between a qualified sponsorship payment, which is a deductible charitable contribution and as to which there is merely an acknowledgment, and a payment for services that are, or are in the nature of, advertising.

A *qualified sponsorship payment* is a payment made by a person engaged in a trade or business, with respect to which there is no arrangement or expectation that the person will receive any substantial return benefit other than the use or acknowledgment of the name or logo (or product lines) of the person's trade or business in connection with the organization's activities.[46] It is irrelevant whether the sponsored activity is related or unrelated to the organization's exempt purpose.[47]

This use or acknowledgment does not include advertising of the person's products or services, including messages containing qualitative or comparative language, price information or other indications of savings or value, an endorsement, or an inducement to purchase, sell, or use the products or services.[48] For example, if in return for receiving a sponsorship payment, an exempt organization promises to use the sponsor's name or logo in acknowledging the sponsor's support for an educational or fundraising event conducted by the organization, the payment is not taxable. If, however, if an organization provides advertising of a sponsor's products, the payment made to the organization by the sponsor in order to receive the advertising is subject to unrelated business income tax (assuming that the other requirements for taxation are satisfied).[49]

---

[44] Ann. 92-15, 1992-1 I.R.B. 51.

[45] IRC § 513(i)(1).

[46] IRC § 513(i)(2)(A).

[47] H. Rep. No. 105-220, 105th Cong., 1st Sess. 69 (1997).

[48] IRC § 513(i)(2)(A).

[49] H. Rep. No. 105-220, 105th Cong., 1st Sess. 68 (1997).

A qualified sponsorship payment does not include any payment arrangement whereby the amount of the payment is contingent on the level of attendance at one or more events, broadcast ratings, or other factors indicating the degree of public exposure to one or more events.[50] The fact that a sponsorship payment is contingent on an event actually taking place or being broadcast, in and of itself, does not, however, cause the payment to fail to qualify. Also, mere distribution or display of a sponsor's products by the sponsor or the exempt organization to the general public at a sponsored event, whether for free or for remuneration, is considered a "use or acknowledgment" of the sponsor's product lines—not advertising.[51]

This law does not apply to a payment that entitles the payor to the use or acknowledgment of the name or logo (or product line) of the payor's trade or business in a tax-exempt organization's periodical. A *periodical* is regularly scheduled and printed material published by or on behalf of the payee organization that is not related to and primarily distributed in connection with a specific event conducted by the payee organization.[52] Thus, the exclusion does not apply to payments that lead to acknowledgment in a program or brochure distributed at a sponsored event.[53] The term *qualified sponsorship payment* also does not include a payment made in connection with a qualified convention or trade show activity.[54]

To the extent that a portion of a payment would (if made as a separate payment) be a qualified sponsorship payment, that portion of the payment is treated as a separate payment.[55] Therefore, if a sponsorship payment made to a tax-exempt organization entitles the sponsor to product advertising and use or acknowledgment of the sponsor's name or logo by the organization, the unrelated business income tax does not apply to the amount of the payment that exceeds the fair market value of the product advertising provided by the sponsor.[56]

The provision of facilities, services, or other privileges by an exempt organization to a sponsor or the sponsor's designees (such as complimentary tickets, pro-am playing spots in golf tournaments, or receptions for major donors) in connection with a sponsorship payment does not affect the determination of whether the payment is a qualified one. Instead, the provision of the goods or services is evaluated as a separate transaction in determining whether the organization has unrelated business income from the event. In general, if the services or facilities do not constitute a substantial return benefit (or if the provision of the services or facilities is a related business activity), the payments attributable to them are not subject to the unrelated business income tax.[57]

Likewise, a sponsor's receipt of a license to use an intangible asset (such as a trademark, logo, or designation) of the tax-exempt organization is treated as

---

[50] IRC § 513(i)(2)(B)(i).
[51] H. Rep. No. 105-220, 105th Cong., 1st Sess. 69 (1997).
[52] IRC § 513(i)(2)(B)(ii)(I).
[53] H. Rep. No. 105-220, 105th Cong., 1st Sess. 69 (1997).
[54] IRC § 513(i)(2)(B)(ii)(II).
[55] IRC § 513(i)(3).
[56] H. Rep. No. 105-220, 105th Cong., 1st Sess. 69 (1997).
[57] *Id.*

separate from the qualified sponsorship transaction in determining whether the organization has unrelated business taxable income.[58]

The corporate sponsorship rules are, as noted, formulated as a safe-harbor body of law. Thus, if the terms and conditions of these rules cannot be satisfied, the opportunity nonetheless remains for application of other rules that may cause a corporate sponsorship payment not to be treated as unrelated business income. These other rules might include use of the exclusion for royalties,[59] or the exception for activities substantially all the work for which is performed by volunteers,[60] or the exception for activities not regularly carried on.[61]

§ 9.4 CONTRIBUTION SUBSTANTIATION RULES

As to contributions of at least $250, a set of substantiation rules imposed by statute applies. Under these rules, donors who make a separate charitable contribution of $250 or more in a year, for which they claim a charitable contribution deduction, must obtain written substantiation from the donee charitable organization.

More specifically, the charitable deduction is not allowed for a *separate contribution* of $250 or more unless the donor has written substantiation from the charitable donee of the contribution in the form of a *contemporaneous written acknowledgment*.[62] Thus, donors cannot rely solely on a cancelled check as substantiation for a gift of $250 or more.[63] (A cancelled check will suffice as substantiation for gifts of less than $250.[64])

An acknowledgment meets this requirement if it includes this information: (1) the amount of money and a description (but not value) of any property other than money that was contributed; (2) whether the donee organization provided any goods or services in consideration, in whole or in part, for any money or property contributed[65]; and (3) a description and good faith estimate of the value of any goods or services involved or, if the goods or services consist solely of intangible religious benefits, a statement to that effect.[66]

The phrase *intangible religious benefit* means "any intangible religious benefit which is provided by an organization organized exclusively for religious purposes and which generally is not sold in a commercial transaction outside the donative context."[67] An acknowledgment is considered to be *contemporaneous* if the contributor obtains the acknowledgment on or before the earlier of (1) the date on which the donor filed a tax return for the taxable year in which the contribution was made or (2) the due date (including extensions) for filing the

---

[58] *Id.*

[59] See § 5.9(f).

[60] See § 5.9(m).

[61] See § 5.6. In general, *Charitable Giving* § 23.3.

[62] IRC § 170(f)(8)(A); Reg. § 1.170A-13(f)(1).

[63] Likewise, a corporation was denied a charitable contribution deduction in part for this reason (Tech. Adv. Mem. 200003005).

[64] See *Charitable Giving* § 21.1(a).

[65] See *id.* § 22.2.

[66] IRC § 170(f)(8)(B); Reg. § 1.170A-13(f)(2).

[67] IRC § 170(f)(8)(B), last sentence.

return.[68] Even when no good or service is provided to a donor, a statement to that effect must appear in the acknowledgment.

As noted, this substantiation rule applies with respect to *separate payments*. Separate payments generally are treated as separate contributions and are not aggregated for the purpose of applying the $250 threshold. When contributions are paid by withholding from wages, the deduction from each paycheck is treated as a separate payment.[69]

The written acknowledgment of a separate gift is not required to take any particular form. Thus, acknowledgments may be made by letter, postcard, electronic mail,[70] or computer-generated form. A donee charitable organization may prepare a separate acknowledgment for each contribution or may provide donors with periodic (such as annual) acknowledgments that set forth the required information for each contribution of $250 or more made by the donor during the period.[71]

It is the donor's responsibility to obtain the substantiation documentation and maintain it in his or her records. (Again, the charitable contribution deduction depends on compliance with these rules.)

The substantiation rules do not impose on charitable organizations any requirement as to the reporting of gift information to the IRS. Charitable organizations potentially have the option to avoid these rules by filing an information return with the IRS, reporting information sufficient to substantiate the amount of the deductible contribution.[72]

This substantiation requirement is in addition to the rules that:

- Require the provision of certain information if the amount of the claimed charitable deduction for all noncash contributions exceeds $500,[73] and

---

[68] IRC § 170(f)(8)(C); Reg. § 1.170A-13(f)(3).

[69] H. Rep. No. 103-213, 103d Cong., 1st Sess. 565, note 29 (1993).

[70] The IRS first announced that charitable organizations can substantiate gifts electronically when it posted the advance text of *Charitable Contributions—Substantiation and Disclosure Requirements* (Publication 1771) on its Web site in March 2002. There the agency wrote that an organization "can provide either a paper copy of the acknowledgment to the donor, or an organization can provide the acknowledgment electronically, such as via e-mail addressed to the donor." Substantiation of charitable gifts by e-mail message was thereafter referenced in notice 2002-25, 2002-1 C.B. 743. Given the way the law is evolving, the IRS had no choice but to allow e-mail substantiation. See, e.g., Rio Properties, Inc. v. Rio Int'l Interlink, 284 F.3d 1007 (9th Cir. 2002), holding that a court, in certain circumstances, may order service of process on foreign business entities by e-mail.

The IRS first signaled that it would allow substantiation of charitable gifts by e-mail in 2000 (INFO 2000-0070). Subsequently, in a solicitation of public comment concerning application of the federal tax law, governing tax-exempt organizations, to activities they conduct on the Internet (Ann. 2000-84, 2000-42 I.R.B. 385), the agency posed a series of questions, including this: "Does a donor satisfy the requirement under [IRC §] 170(f)(8) for a written acknowledgment of a contribution of $250 or more with a printed webpage confirmation or copy of a confirmation e-mail from the donee organization?" As to the latter approach, the answer now is yes.

[71] H. Rep. No. 103-213, 103d Cong., 1st Sess. At 565 note 32 (1993). A charitable organization that knowingly provides a false written substantiation document to a donor may be subject to the penalty for aiding and abetting an understatement of tax liability (IRC § 6701; see *Charitable Giving* § 10.14).

[72] IRC § 170(f)(8)(D). This approach has not, however, been implemented by regulations and currently is not available. Earlier versions of this requirement would have caused donee charitable organizations to file information returns with the IRS reflecting contributions made to them.

[73] See *Charitable Giving* § 21.1(a), text accompanied by notes 22–27.

- Apply to noncash gifts exceeding $5,000 per item or group of similar items (other than certain publicly traded securities), under which the services of a qualified appraiser are required and the charitable donee must acknowledge receipt of the gift and provide certain other information.[74]

Tax regulations pertain to contributions made by means of withholding from individuals' wages and payment by individuals' employers to donee charitable organizations. (The problems in this setting include the fact that the donee charity often does not know the identities of the donors/employees, nor the amounts contributed by each.) These regulations state that fits of this nature may be substantiated by both:

- A pay receipt or other document (such as Form W-2) furnished by the donor's employer, setting forth the amount withheld by the employer for the purpose of payment to a donee charity

- A pledge card or other document prepared by or at the direction of the donee organization that includes a statement to the effect that the organization does not provide goods or services in whole or partial consideration for any contributions made to the organization by payroll deduction[75]

For purposes of the $250 threshold in relation to contributions made by payroll deduction, the amount withheld from each payment is treated as a separate contribution.[76] Thus, the substantiation requirement does not apply to contributions made by means of payroll deduction unless the employer deducts $250 or more from a single paycheck for the purposes of making a charitable gift. The preamble to these regulations contains a discussion of this question: Can a Form W-2 that reflects the total amount contributed by payroll deduction, but does not list each contribution of $250 or more, be used as evidence of the amount withheld from the employee's wages to be paid to the donee charitable organization? The IRS noted that the statute provides that an acknowledgment must reflect the amount of cash and a description of property other than cash contributed to a charitable organization. When a person makes multiple contributions to a charitable organization, the law does not require the acknowledgment to list each contribution separately. Consequently, an acknowledgment may substantiate multiple contributions with a statement of the total amount contributed by a person during the year, rather than an itemized list of separate contributions. Therefore, said the IRS, a Form W-2 reflecting an employee's total annual contribution, without separately listing the amount of each contribution, can be used as evidence of the amount withheld from the employee's wages. (The IRS determined that the regulations need not address this point.)

A charitable organization, or a Principal Combined Fund Organization for purposes of the Combined Federal Campaign and acting in that capacity, that receives a payment made as a contribution is treated as a donee organization for

---

[74] See *id.* § 21.2.
[75] Reg. § 1.170A-13(f)(11)(i).
[76] Reg. § 1.170A-13(f)(11)(ii).

purposes of the substantiation requirements, even if the organization (pursuant to the donor's instructions or otherwise) distributes the amount received to one or more charitable organizations.[77]

This preamble also contains a discussion of a problem, the IRS's answer to which was: Stop engaging in the practice. This concerns the making of lump-sum contributions by employees through their employers other than by payroll deduction. Employees may make contributions in the form of checks payable to their employer, which then deposits the checks in an employer account and sends the donee charity a single check drawn on the employer's account. When employees' payments are transferred to a donee organization in this manner, it is difficult for the charitable organization to identify the persons who made the contributions, and thus the employees may be unable to obtain the requisite substantiation. These difficulties, the IRS advised, can be eliminated if the employees' contribution checks are made payable to the donee organization and the employer forwards the employees' checks to the charitable organization. (In the context of political fundraising, this is known as *bundling*.) The donee organization then is in a position to provide the necessary substantiation as it otherwise would. (The regulations remain silent on the subject.) This rule is inapplicable, however, when the distribute organization provides goods or services as part of a transaction "structured with a view to avoid taking the goods or services into account in determining the amount of the [charitable] deduction."[78]

The regulations define a *good faith estimate* as meaning the donee charitable organization's estimate of the fair market value of any goods or services, "without regard to the manner in which the organization in fact made that estimate."[79]

These regulations also define the phrase *in consideration for*. A charitable organization is considered as providing goods or services in consideration for a person's payment if, at the time the person makes the payment, the person receives or expects to receive goods or services in exchange for the payment.[80] Goods or services a donee charity provides in consideration for a payment by a person would include goods or services provided in a year other than the year in which the payment is made.[81]

---

[77] Reg. § 1.170A-13(f)(12).

[78] *Id.*

[79] Reg. § 1.170A-13(f)(7). The phrase *goods or services* means money, property, services, benefits, and privileges. Reg. § 1.170A-13(f)(5).

[80] Reg. § 1.170A-13(f)(6).

[81] This rule relates to a subject that torments the fundraising professional: What should one do about the situation in which a charitable organization decides, months after contributions have been made, to honor a class or donors by providing them in a tangible benefit, such as a thank-you dinner? The event or other benefit may be provided in a subsequent year. Does the fair market value of this benefit have to be subtracted from the amount of the gift for deduction purposes? The answer generally is no. This is affirmed by these regulations, which require that the goods or services be provided "at the time" the payment is made, when the donor receives or expects to receive a benefit. In this instance, the donors did not receive or expect to receive a dinner or anything else at the time of their gifts. But suppose a charitable organization develops a regular pattern of providing these after-the-fact benefits. At what point do expectations arise? This is probably not something the regulations can address further; it may have to be left added to a facts-and-circumstances analysis. The regulations observe, however, that the benefit can arise in a year other than (usually subsequent to) the year of the gift.

Certain goods or services may be disregarded when applying these substantiation rules:

- Those that have an insubstantial value, in that the fair market value of all the benefits received is not more than 2 percent of the contribution or $50 (indexed for inflation), whichever is less.[82]

- Those that have an insubstantial value, in that the contribution is $25 or more (indexed for inflation) and the only benefits received by the donor in return have an aggregate cost of not more than a low-cost article, which generally is one with a cost not in excess of $5 (indexed for inflation).[83]

- Annual membership benefits offered to an individual for a payment of no more than $75 per year that consist of rights or privileges that the individual can exercise frequently during the membership period.[84] This exception is not available with respect to payments made in exchange for the opportunity to preferred seating at athletic events of educational institutions, for which there are special rules.[85] Examples of these rights and privileges include free or discounted admission to the organization's facilities or events, free or discounted parking, preferred access to goods or services, and discounts on the purchase of goods or services.

- Annual membership benefits offered to an individual for a payment of no more than $75 per year that consist of admission to events during the membership period that are open only to members of the donee organization.[86] For this rule to apply, the organization must reasonably project that the cost per person (excluding any allocable overhead) for each event is within the limits established for low-cost articles.[87] The projected cost to the donee organization is determined at the time the organization first offers its membership package for the year.

- Goods or services provided by a charitable organization to an entity's employees in return for a payment to the organization, to the extent the goods or services provided to each employee are the same as those covered by the previous two exceptions.[88] When one or more of these goods or services are provided to a donor, the contemporaneous written acknowledgment may indicate that no goods or services were provided in exchange for the donor's payment.

These regulations illustrate the rules pertaining to membership benefits, rights, and privileges. An example is offered concerning a charitable organization

---

[82] Reg. § 1.170A-13(f)(8)(i)(A).

[83] Reg. § 1.170A-13(f)(8)(i)(A).

[84] Reg. § 1.170A-13(f)(8)(i)(B)(1).

[85] IRC § 170(1); Reg. § 1.170A-13(f)(14).

[86] Reg. § 1.170A-13(f)(8)(i)(B)(2).

[87] IRC § 513(h)(2).

[88] Reg. § 1.170A-13(f)(9)(i). An acknowledgment in a program at a charity-sponsored event identifying a person as a donor to the charity also is an inconsequential benefit with no significant value; "[s]uch privileges as being associated with or being known as a benefactor of the [charitable] organization are not significant return benefits that have monetary value." Rev. Rul. 68-432, 1968-2 C.B. 104.

that operates a performing arts center.[89] In return for a payment of $75, the center offers a package of basic membership benefits, which includes the right to purchase tickets to performances one week before they go on sale to the general public; free parking in its garage during the evening and weekend performances; and a 10 percent discount on merchandise sold in its gift shop. In exchange for a $150 payment, the center offers a package of preferred membership benefits, which includes all of the benefits in the $75 package as well as a poster that is sold in the center's gift shop for $20. The basic membership and the preferred membership are each valid for 12 months, and there are approximately 50 performances of various productions at the center during a 12-month period. The gift shop is open for several hours each week and at performance times. An individual is solicited by the center to make a contribution, being offered the preferred membership option. This individual makes a payment of $300. This individual can satisfy the substantiation requirement by obtaining a contemporaneous written acknowledgment from the center that includes a description of the poster and a good faith estimate of its fair market value ($20), and disregards the remaining membership benefits.

Another example[90] concerning a charitable organization that operates a community theater organization that performs four plays every summer; each is performed twice. In return for a membership fee of $60, the organization offers its members free admission to any of its performances. Nonmembers may purchase tickets on a performance-by-performance basis for $15 a ticket. An individual, being solicited by the organization to make a contribution, is advised that the membership benefit will be provided for a payment of $60 or more. This individual chooses to make a payment of $350 to the organization and receives in exchange the membership benefit. This membership benefit does not qualify for the exclusion because it is not a privilege that can be exercised frequently (due to the limited number of performances offered). Therefore, to meet the substantiation requirements, a contemporaneous written acknowledgment of the $350 payment would have to include a description of the free admission benefit and a good faith estimate of its value. (The example does not continue to state that that value is $60 and the charitable deduction thus is $290.)

If a person makes a contribution of $250 or more to a charitable organization and, in return, the charity offers the person's employees goods or services (other than those that may be disregarded), the contemporaneous written acknowledgment of the person's contribution does not have to include a good faith estimate of the value of the goods or services, but must include a description of those goods or services.[91]

An individual who incurred unreimbursed expenditures incident to the rendition of services is treated as having obtained a contemporaneous written acknowledgment of the expenditures if the individual:

- Has adequate records to substantiate the amount of the expenditures, and

---

[89] Reg. § 1.170A-13(f)(8)(ii), Example 1.
[90] *Id.*, Example 3.
[91] Reg. § 1.170A-13(f)(9)(ii).

- Timely obtains a statement prepared by the donee charity containing (1) a description of the services provided; (2) a statement as to whether the donee provides any goods or services in consideration, in whole or in part, for the unreimbursed expenditures; and (3) the information summarized in the third and fourth of the items that must be reflected in the written acknowledgment.[92]

The substantiation rules do not apply to a transfer of property to a charitable remainder trust or a charitable lead trust.[93] They do, however, apply with respect to transfers by means of pooled income funds.[94] The reason for this distinction is grounded in the fact that the grantor of a remainder trust or lead trust is not required to designate a specific organization as the charitable beneficiary at the time property is transferred to the trust, so in these instances there is no designated charity available to provide a contemporaneous written acknowledgment to the donor. Also, even when a specific beneficiary is designated, the identification of the charity can be revocable. By contrast, a pooled income fund must be created and maintained by the charitable organization to which the remainder interests are contributed.

If a partnership or S corporation makes a charitable contribution of $250 or more, the partnership or corporation is treated as the taxpayer for gift substantiation purposes.[95] Therefore, the partnership or corporation must substantiate the contribution with a contemporaneous written acknowledgment from the donee charity before reporting the contribution on its information return or income tax return for the appropriate year, and must maintain the contemporaneous written acknowledgment in its records. A partner of a partnership or a shareholder of an S corporation is not required to obtain any additional substantiation for his or her share of the partnership's or S corporation's charitable contribution.

If a person's payment to a charitable organization is matched, in whole or in part, by another payor, and the person received goods or services in consideration for the payment and some or all of the matched payment, the goods or services are treated as provided in consideration for the person's payment and not in consideration for the matching payment.[96]

The required substantiation may be provided by a properly authorized agent of the charitable donee.[97] For example, when the contribution is of a used vehicle, a for-profit fundraising company or other entity licensed to sell vehicles may act as the charitable donee's agent.[98] The IRS approved of an arrangement whereby a charitable organization that engaged in the solicitation, processing,

---

[92] Reg. § 1.170A-13(f)(10).

[93] Reg. § 1.170A-13(f)(13). Charitable remainder trusts are the subject of § 9.2(b), and charitable lead trusts are the subject of § 9.2(d).

[94] Pooled income funds are the subject of § 9.2(c).

[95] Reg. § 1.170A-13(f)(15). If a person purchases an annuity from a charitable organization and claims a charitable contribution deduction of $250 or more for the excess of the amount paid over the value of the annuity, the contemporaneous written acknowledgment must state whether any goods or services in addition to the annuity were provided to the person. Reg. § 1.170A-13(f)(16). The contemporaneous written acknowledgment need not include a good faith estimate of the value of the annuity. *Id.*

[96] Reg. § 1.170A-13(f)(17).

[97] See *Charitable Giving* § 10.1(c).

[98] Rev. Rul. 2002-67, 2002-2 C.B. 873.

and sale of donated vehicles denominated a for-profit corporation that was in the business of buying, maintaining, dismantling, and selling used vehicles as the charity's agent for the acceptance of contributed vehicles.[99]

To reiterate, these rules apply with respect to the making of *contributions*; the donor's deduction is not available unless there is full compliance with the rules. By making the requisite acknowledgment, the charitable organization involved is acquiescing in or concurring with the donor's position that the payment is in fact a contribution. There may, however, be an issue as to whether the payment is a gift.[100] A charitable organization that certifies in this fashion that a payment is a gift, when the transaction is not in law a gift, may be subject to one or more tax penalties, such as for participating in an understatement of income tax or promotion of a tax shelter.[101]

§ 9.5 *QUID PRO QUO* CONTRIBUTION RULES

The federal tax law imposes certain disclosure requirements on charitable organizations that receive *quid pro quo* contributions. A *quid pro quo contribution* is a payment "made partly as a contribution and partly in consideration for goods or services provided to the payor by the donee organization."[102] The term does not include a payment made to an organization, operated exclusively for religious purposes, in return for which the donor receives solely an intangible religious benefit that generally is not sold in a commercial transaction outside the donative context.[103] Specifically, if a charitable organization (other than a state, a possession of the United States, and the District of Columbia[104]) receives a *quid pro quo* contribution in excess of $75, the organization must, in connection with the solicitation or receipt of the contribution, provide a written statement that: (1) informs the donor that the amount of the contribution that is deductible for federal income tax purposes is limited to the excess of the amount of any money and the value of any property other than money contributed by the donor over the value of the goods or services provided by the organization; and (2) provides the donor with a good faith estimate of the value of the goods or services.[105]

It is intended that this disclosure be made in a manner that is reasonably likely to come to the donor's attention. Therefore, immersing the disclosure in fine print in a larger document is inadequate.[106]

For purposes of the $75 threshold, separate payments made at different times of the year with respect to separate fundraising events generally will not be aggregated.

These rules do not apply when only *de minimis*, token goods or services (such as key chains and bumper stickers) are provided to the donor. In defining

---

[99] Priv. Ltr. Rul. 200230005.

[100] See *Charitable Giving* §§ 3.1, 9.15, 9.16(a).

[101] See *id.* § 10.14.

[102] IRC § 6115(b).

[103] *Id.*

[104] IRC §§ 6115(a), 170(c)(1).

[105] IRC § 6115(a).

[106] H. Rep. No. 103-213, 103d Cong., 1st Sess. 566, note 35 (1993).

these terms, prior IRS pronouncements are followed.[107] Also, these rules do not apply to transactions that do not have a donative element (such as the charging of tuition by a school, the charging of health care fees by a hospital, or the sale of items by a museum).[108]

A nearly identical disclosure provision was part of the Revenue Act of 1992, which was vetoed. The report of the Senate Finance Committee, which accompanied the proposal, contained this explanation of the need for these rules:

> Difficult problems of tax administration arise with respect to fundraising techniques in which an organization that is eligible to receive deductible contributions provides goods or services in consideration for payments from donors. Organizations that engage in such fundraising practices often do not inform their donors that all or a portion of the amount paid by the donor may not be deductible as a charitable contribution. Consequently, the [Senate Finance] [C]ommittee believes...[it] is appropriate that, in all cases where a charity receives a quid pro quo contribution...the charity should inform the donor that the [federal income tax charitable contribution] deduction...is limited to the amount by which the payment exceeds the value of goods or services furnished, and provide a good faith estimate of the value of such goods or services.[109]

There is a penalty for violation of these requirements.[110]

A charitable organization is able to use "any reasonable methodology in making a good faith estimate, provided it applies the methodology in good faith."[111] A good faith estimate of the value of goods or services that are not generally available in a commercial transaction may, under these regulations, be determined by reference to the fair market value of similar or comparable goods or services. Goods or services may be similar or comparable even though they do not have the "unique qualities of the goods or services that are being valued."[112]

An example concerns a charitable organization that operates a museum.[113] In return for a payment of $50,000 or more, the museum allows a donor to hold a private event in one of its rooms; in the room is a display of a unique collection of art. No other private events are permitted to be held in the museum. In the community, there are four hotels with ballrooms having the same capacity as the room in the museum. Two of these hotels have ballrooms that offer amenities

---

[107] See *Charitable Giving* § 22.1, text accompanied by notes 19–23.

[108] H. Rep. No. 103-213, 103d Cong., 1st Sess. 566 (1993). The IRS issued temporary regulations (T.D. 8544) and proposed regulations (IA-74-93) to accompany these rules. A hearing on them was held on November 10, 1995, at which time witnesses from the charitable sector expressed dismay at the prospect of having to value benefits, particularly intangible ones, provided in exchange for charitable contributions. A summary of this hearing is at 2 Fund-Raising Reg. Rep. (no. 1) 1 (Jan./Feb. 1995). There is little in the final regulations to assuage witness concerns.

[109] Technical Explanation of the Finance Committee Amendment (hereinafter Technical Explanation), at 586. The Technical Explanation was not formally printed; it is, however, reproduced in the Congressional Record. 138 Cong. Rec. (no. 112) S11246 (Aug. 3, 1992).

[110] IRC § 6714; see *Charitable Giving* § 10.14. This requirement is separate from the substantiality rules. See § 9.4. An organization may be able to meet both sets of requirements with the same written document. An organization in this position should, however, be careful to satisfy the *quid pro quo* contribution rules in a timely manner because of this penalty.

[111] Reg. § 1.6115-1(a)(1).

[112] Reg. § 1.6115-1(a)(2).

[113] Reg. § 1.6115-1(a)(3), Example 1.

and atmosphere that are similar to the amenities and atmosphere of the room in the museum; none of them has any art collections. Because the capacity, amenities, and atmosphere of the ballrooms in these two hotels are comparable to the capacity, amenities, and atmosphere of the room in the museum, a good faith estimate of the benefits received from the museum may be determined by reference to the cost of renting either of the two hotel ballrooms. The cost of renting one of these ballrooms is $2,500. Thus, a good faith estimate of the fair market value of the right to host a private event in the room in the museum is $2,500. Here, the ballrooms in the two hotels are considered similar and comparable facilities in relation to the museum's room for valuation purposes, notwithstanding the fact that the room in the museum displays a unique collection of art.

In another example, a charitable organization offers to provide a one-hour tennis lesson with a tennis professional in return for the first payment of $500 or more it receives.[114] The professional provides tennis lessons on a commercial basis at the rate of $100 per hour. An individual pays the charity $500 and in return receives the tennis lesson. A good faith estimate of the fair market value of the tennis lesson provided in exchange for the payment is $100.

In this context, the regulations somewhat address the matter of the involvement of celebrities. This is another of the problems plaguing the fundraising community, as was articulated so well at an IRS hearing in November 1994.[115] This subject is not addressed by a separate regulation but rather by an example.[116] A charity holds a promotion in which it states that, in return for the first payment of $1,000 or more it receives, it will provide a dinner for two followed by an evening tour of a museum conducted by an artist whose most recent works are on display there. The artist does not provide tours of the museum on a commercial basis. Typically, tours of the museum are free to the public. An individuals pays $1,000 to the charity and in exchange receives a dinner valued at $100 and the museum tour. Because the tours are typically free to the public, a good faith estimate of the value of the tour conducted by the artist is $0. The fact that the tour is conducted by the artist rather than one of the museum's regular tour guides does not render the tours dissimilar or incomparable for valuation purposes.[117]

Five types of goods or services are disregarded for purposes of the *quid pro quo* contribution rules.[118] A comparable rule as to goods or services provided to employees of donors is applicable in this context.[119]

No part of this type of a payment can be considered a deductible charitable gift unless two elements exist: (1) the patron makes a payment in an amount that

---

[114] Reg. § 1.6115-1(a)(3), Example 2.

[115] See *supra* note 108.

[116] Reg. § 1.6115-1(a)(3), Example 3.

[117] This rule as to celebrity presence is more important for what it does say than for what it actually says. Basically, the regulation states that if the celebrity does something different from what he or she is known for (for example, a painter conducting a tour), the fact that he or she is part of the event can be ignored for valuation purposes. The regulation suggests, however, that if the celebrity does what he or she is celebrated for (for example, a singer or a comedian who performs as such), the value of that performance—being a service available on a commercial basis—should be taken into account in valuing the event.

[118] See § 21.1(b), text accompanied by notes 51–60.

[119] *Id.*, text accompanied by note 57.

is in fact in excess of the fair market value of the goods or services received, and (2) the patron intends to make a payment in an amount that exceeds that fair market value.[120] This requirement of the element of *intent* may prove to be relatively harmless, as the patron is likely to know the charity's good faith estimate figure in advance of the payment and thus cannot help but have this intent. Still, proving intent is not always easy. This development is unfortunate, inasmuch as the law has been evolving to a more mechanical test (and thus is less reliant on subjective proof): Any payment to a charitable organization in excess of fair market value is regarded as a charitable gift.[121]

§ 9.6 DISCLOSURES BY NONCHARITABLE ORGANIZATIONS

Certain contribution disclosure rules are part of the federal tax law.[122] These rules are *not* applicable to charitable organizations.

These disclosure rules *are* applicable to all types of tax-exempt organizations (other than charitable ones) and are targeted principally at social welfare organizations.[123] They are designed to prevent these noncharitable organizations from engaging in gift-solicitation activities under circumstances in which donors will assume, or be led to assume, that the contributions are tax deductible, when in fact they are not. These rules do not, however, apply to an organization that has annual gross receipts that are normally no more than $100,000.[124] Also, when all of the parties being solicited are tax-exempt organizations, the solicitation does not have to include the disclosure statement (inasmuch as these grantors have no need of a charitable deduction).[125]

This law applies in general to any organization to which contributions are not deductible as charitable gifts and which:

- Is tax-exempt,[126]

- Is a political organization,[127]

- Was either type of organization at any time during the five-year period ending on the date of the solicitation, or

---

[120] Reg. § 1.170A-1(h)(1).

[121] See § 3.2(b). A payment made to a charitable organization in excess of the fair market value of an item is not necessarily the consequence of donative intent. In the case of an auction, for example, the patron (successful bidder) may just intensely want the item or be motivated by peer pressure or extensive access to an open bar; charity may be the furthest thing from the patron's mind.

[122] IRC § 6113. The IRS published rules to accompany this law (IRS Notice 88-120, 1988-2 C.B. 459).

[123] That is, organizations that are exempt under IRC § 501(a) by reason of being described in IRC § 501(c)(4). See § 1.6(a).

[124] IRC § 6113(b)(2)(A). In determining this threshold, the same principles that obtain in ascertaining the annual information return (Form 990) $25,000 filing threshold apply (see § 10.1(b)(ii)).

A local, regional, or state chapter of an organization with gross receipts under $100,000 must include the disclosure statement in its solicitations if at least 25 percent of the money solicited will go to the national, or other, unit of the organization that has annual gross receipts over $100,000, because the solicitation is considered as being in part on behalf of that unit. Also, if a trade association or labor union with more than $100,000 in annual gross receipts solicits funds that will pass through to a political action committee with less than $100,000 in annual gross receipts, the solicitation must include the required disclosure statement.

[125] Notice 88-120, 1988-2 C.B. 459.

[126] That is, is described in IRC § 501(a) and IRC § 501(c) (other than, as noted, charitable organizations described in IRC § 501(c)(3)).

[127] That is, is described in IRC § 527 (see § 4.7).

- Is a successor to one of these organizations at any time during this five-year period.[128]

The IRS is accorded the authority to treat any group of two or more organizations as one organization for these purposes when "necessary or appropriate" to prevent the avoidance of these rules through the use of multiple organizations.[129]

Under these rules, each fundraising solicitation by or on behalf of a tax-exempt noncharitable organization must contain an express statement, in a "conspicuous and easily recognizable format," that gifts to it are not deductible as charitable contributions for federal income tax purposes.[130] A *fundraising solicitation* is any solicitation of gifts made in written or printed form, by television, radio, or telephone (although there is an exclusion for letters or calls not part of a coordinated fundraising campaign soliciting more than 10 persons during a calendar year).[131] Despite the clear reference in the statute to "contributions and gifts," the IRS interprets this rule to mandate the disclosure when any tax-exempt organization (other than a charitable one) seeks funds, such as dues from members.

Failure to satisfy this disclosure requirement can result in imposition of penalties.[132] The penalty is $1,000 per day (maximum of $10,000 per year), albeit with a reasonable-cause exception. In an instance of "intentional disregard" of these rules, however, the penalty for the day on which the offense occurred is the greater of $1,000 or 50 percent of the aggregate cost of the solicitations that took place on that day, and the $10,000 limitation is inapplicable. For these purposes, the days involved are those on which the solicitation was telecast, broadcast, mailed, otherwise distributed, or telephoned.

The IRS promulgated rules in amplification of this law, particularly the requirement of a disclosure statement.[133] These rules, which include guidance in the form of "safe-harbor" provisions, address the format of the disclosure statement in instances of use of print media, telephone, television, and radio. They provide examples of acceptable disclosure language and methods (which, when followed, amount to the safe-harbor guidelines), and of included and excluded solicitations. They also contain guidelines for establishing the $100,000 threshold.[134]

The safe-harbor guideline for print media (including solicitations by mail and in newspapers) is fourfold:

1. The solicitation should include language like this: "Contributions or gifts to [name of organization] are not deductible as charitable contributions for federal income tax purposes."

2. The statement should be in at least the same type size as the primary message stated in the body of the letter, leaflet, or advertisement.

---

[128] IRC § 6113(b)(1). For this purpose, a fraternal organization (see § 1.6(g)) is treated as a charitable organization only with respect to solicitations for contributions that are to be used exclusively for purposes referred to in IRC § 170(c)(4) (IRC § 6113(b)(3)).

[129] IRC § 6113(b)(2)(B).

[130] IRC § 6113(a).

[131] IRC § 6113(c).

[132] IRC § 6710.

[133] IRS Notice 88-120, 1988-2 C.B. 459.

[134] See text accompanied by *supra* note 124.

3. The statement should be included on the message side of any card or tear-off section that the contributor returns with the contribution.

4. The statement should be either the first sentence in a paragraph or itself constitute a paragraph.

The safe-harbor guidelines for telephone solicitations are:

- The solicitation includes language like this: "Contributions or gifts to [name of organization] are not deductible as charitable contributions for federal income tax purposes."

- The statement must be made in close proximity to the request for contributions, during the same telephone call, by the same solicitor.

- Any written confirmation or billing sent to a person pledging to contribute during the telephone solicitation must be in compliance with the requirements for print media solicitations.

To conform to the guideline, solicitation by television must include a solicitation statement that complies with the first of the print medium requirements. Also, if the statement is spoken, it must be in close proximity to the request for contributions. If the statement appears on the television screen, it must be in large, easily readable type appearing on the screen for at least five seconds.

In the case of a solicitation by radio, the statement must, to meet the safe-harbor test, comply with the first of the print medium requirements. Also, the statement must be made in close proximity to the request for contributions during the same radio solicitation announcement.

When the soliciting organization is a membership entity, classified as a trade or business association or other form of business league, or a labor or agricultural organization,[135] this statement is in conformance with the safe-harbor guideline: "Contributions or gifts to [name of organization] are not tax deductible as charitable contributions. They may, however, be deductible as ordinary and necessary business expenses."

If an organization makes a solicitation to which these rules apply and the solicitation does not comply with the applicable safe-harbor guidelines, the IRS will evaluate all of the facts and circumstances to determine whether the solicitation meets the disclosure rule. A good faith effort to comply with these requirements is an important factor in the evaluation of the facts and circumstances. Nonetheless, disclosure statements made in "fine print" do not comply with the statutory requirement.

This disclosure requirement applies to solicitations for voluntary contributions as well as to solicitations for attendance at testimonials and similar fundraising events. The disclosure must be made in the case of solicitations for contributions to political action committees.

Exempt from this disclosure rule are the billing:

- Of those who advertise an organization's publications

- By social clubs for food and beverages

---

[135] See § 1.6(c)–(e).

- Of attendees of a conference
- For insurance premiums of an insurance program operated or sponsored by an organization
- Of members of a community association for mandatory payments for police and fire (and similar) protection
- For payments to a voluntary employees' beneficiary association,[136] as well as similar payments to a trust for pension and/or health benefits

General material discussing the benefits of membership in a tax-exempt organization, such as a trade association or labor union, does not have to include the required disclosure statement. The statement is required, however, when the material both requests payment and specifies the amount requested as membership dues. If a person responds to the general material discussing the benefits of membership, the follow-up material requesting the payment of a specific amount in membership dues (such as a union check-off card or a trade association billing statement for a new member) must include the disclosure statement. General material discussing a political candidacy and requesting persons to vote for the candidate or "support" the candidate need not include the disclosure statement, unless the material specifically requests either a financial contribution or a contribution of volunteer services in support of the candidate.

§ 9.7 STATE FUNDRAISING REGULATION

The solicitation of charitable contributions in the United States involves practices that are recognized as being forms of free speech protected by federal and state constitutional law. Thus, there are limitations on the extent to which fundraising for charitable, educational, scientific, religious, and like organizations can be regulated by government. Nevertheless, nonprofit organizations in the United States face considerable regulatory requirements at the federal, state, and local levels when they solicit contributions for charitable purposes. The purpose of this section is to summarize this body of law.[137]

The process of raising funds for charitable purposes is heavily regulated by the states. At this time, all but four states have some form of statutory structure by which the fundraising process is regulated.[138] Of these states, 39 have formal charitable solicitation acts.

(a) State Regulation in General

The various state charitable solicitation acts generally contain certain features, including:

- A process by which a charitable organization registers or otherwise secures a permit to raise funds for charitable purposes in the state

---

[136] That is, an organization that is tax-exempt under IRC § 501(a) by reason of description in IRC § 501(c)(9). See *Tax-Exempt Organizations* § 16.3.

[137] This body of law is summarized in greater detail in *Fundraising*, particularly Chapter 3.

[138] The states that have no statutory or other regulatory law in this regard are Alaska, Idaho, Montana, and Wyoming.

- Requirements for reporting information (usually annually) about an organization's fundraising program

- A series of organizations or activities that are exempt from some or all of the statutory requirements

- A process by which a professional fundraiser, professional solicitor, and/or commercial co-venturer registers with, and reports to, the state

- Record-keeping requirements, applicable to charitable organizations, professional fundraisers, professional solicitors, and/or commercial co-venturers

- Rules concerning the contents of contracts between a charitable organization and a professional fundraiser, professional solicitor, and/or a commercial co-venturer

- A series of prohibited acts

- Provision for reciprocal agreements among the states as to coordinated regulation in this field

- A summary of the powers of the governmental official having regulatory authority (usually the attorney general or secretary of state)

- A statement of the various sanctions that can be imposed for failure to comply with this law (such as injunctions, fines, and imprisonment)

These elements of the law are generally applicable to the fundraising charitable organization. Nevertheless, several provisions of law are directed at the fundraising professional or the professional solicitor, thus going beyond traditional fundraising regulation.

(b) Historical Perspective

Until the mid-1950s, the matter of fundraising practices was not addressed by state law. At that time, not much attention was paid to those practices from the legal perspective. Some counties had adopted fundraising regulation ordinances, but there was no state or federal law on the subject.

This began to change about 50 years ago as part of the disclosure and consumer protection movements. North Carolina was the first state to enact a fundraising regulation law. Others soon followed, however, generating a series of laws that came to be known as *charitable solicitation acts*. New York was the second state to enact one of these acts, and this law became the prototype for the many that were to follow.

The New York law and its progeny involved a statutory scheme based on registration and reporting. Charitable organizations are required to register in advance of solicitation and to annually report; bond requirements came later. Subsequently, forms of regulation involving professional fundraisers and professional solicitors were developed. Exceptions evolved, disclosure requirements expanded, and a variety of prohibited acts (see below) were identified.

Today's typical charitable solicitation statute is far more extensive than its forebears of decades ago. When charitable solicitation acts began to develop (as noted, beginning in the mid-1950s), the principal features were registration and annual reporting requirements. These laws were basically licensing statutes. They gave the states essential information about the fundraising to be conducted, so that they would have a basis for investigation and review should there be suspicion of some abuse.

During the ensuing years, some states decided to go beyond the concept of licensing and began to regulate charitable solicitations affirmatively. This was done in part because of citizen complaints; another part was political grandstanding. The regulation worked its way into the realm of attempting to prevent "less qualified" (including out-of-the-mainstream) charities from soliciting in the states.

Structurally, the typical charitable solicitation statute originally did not have much to do with actual regulation of the efforts of either the fundraising institution or the fundraising professional. Rather, the emphasis was on information gathering and disclosure of that information to ostensibly desirous donors. As noted, its requirements were based on the submission of written information (registration statements, reports, and the like) by charitable organizations and their fundraising advisers; the typical statute also contained bond requirements and granted enforcement authority to the attorneys general, secretaries of state, or other governmental officials charged with administering and enforcing the law.

Later, however, law requirements began to creep in that sounded more like ethical precepts. These requirements were more than just mechanics—they went beyond registration requirements, filing due dates, and accounting principles. They went beyond telling the charity and the professional fundraisers when to do something and entered the realm of telling them how they must conduct the solicitation and what they cannot do in that regard.

From the regulators' viewpoint, the apogee of this form of regulation came when the states could ban charitable organizations with "high" fundraising costs. (As noted later, this form of regulation ultimately was found to be unconstitutional.) This application of constitutional law rights to charitable solicitation acts left the state regulators without their principal weapon. In frustration, they turned to other forms of law, those based on the principle of "disclosure" (to be discussed).

In this aftermath, more state fundraising law developed. The registration and annual reports became more extensive. The states tried, with limited success, to force charities and solicitors into various forms of point-of-solicitation disclosure of various pieces of information. Some states dictated the contents of the scripts of telephone solicitors. This disclosure approach failed to satisfy the regulatory impulse. More frustration ensued.

The regulators turned to even more ways to have a role in the charitable fundraising process. They started to micromanage charitable fundraising and began to substitute their judgment for that of donors, charities, and professional fundraisers. Thus, they engendered laws that beefed up the record-keeping requirements, spelled out the contents of contracts between charities and fundraising consultants and solicitors, stepped into commercial co-ventures, and even injected themselves into matters such as the sale of tickets for charitable events and solicitations by fire and police personnel.

The regulatory appetite still remained unsatisfied. Having accomplished the imposition of just about all of the *law* they could think of, they turned to principles of ethics. For example, in one state, charities that solicit charitable gifts and their professional fundraisers and solicitors are "fiduciaries." This is a role historically confined to trustees of charitable trusts and more recently to directors of charitable corporations.

(c) States' Police Power

Prior to a fuller analysis of state law regulation in this field, it is necessary to reference briefly the underlying legal basis for this body of law: the *police power*. Each state (and local unit of government) inherently possesses the police power. This power enables a state or other political subdivision of government to regulate—within the bounds of constitutional law principles (to be discussed)—the conduct of its citizens and others, so as to protect the safety, health, and welfare of its citizens.

Generally, it is clear that a state can enact and enforce, in the exercise of its police power, a charitable solicitation act that requires a charity planning on fundraising in the jurisdiction first to register with (or secure a license or permit from) the appropriate regulatory authorities and subsequently to file periodic reports about the results of the solicitation. There is nothing inherently unlawful about this type of requirement. It may also mandate professional fundraisers and professional solicitors to register and report, or empower the regulatory authorities to investigate the activities of charitable organizations in the presence of reasonable cause to do so, and impose injunctive remedies, fines, and imprisonment for violation of the statute. It appears clear that a state can regulate charitable fundraising notwithstanding the fact that the solicitation utilizes the federal postal system, uses television and radio broadcasts, or otherwise occurs in interstate commerce. The rationale is that charitable solicitations may be reasonably regulated to protect the public from deceit, fraud, or the unscrupulous obtaining of money under a pretense that the money is being collected and expended for a charitable purpose.

Despite the inherent police power lodged in the states (and local jurisdictions) to regulate the charitable solicitation process, and the general scope of the power, principles of law operate to confine its reach. Most of these principles are based on constitutional law precepts, such as freedom of speech, procedural and substantive due process, and equal protection of the laws, as well as the standards usually imposed by statutory law, which bar the exercise of the police power in a manner that is arbitrary.

(d) Fundamental Definitions

State law regulation of this nature pertains to fundraising for charitable purposes. The use of the term *charitable* in this setting refers to a range of activities and organizations that is much broader than that embraced by the term as used in the federal tax context. That is, while the term includes organizations that are charitable, educational, scientific, and religious, as those terms are used for federal tax law purposes, it also includes (absent specific exemption) organizations that are civic, social welfare, recreational, and fraternal. Indeed, the general definition is so encompassing as to cause some of these statutes to expressly exclude fundraising by political action committees, labor organizations, and trade organizations.

Some of this regulation is applicable to a *professional fundraiser* (or similar term). The majority of the states define a *professional fundraiser* as one who, for a fixed fee under a written agreement, plans, conducts, advises, or acts as a consultant, whether directly or indirectly, in connection with soliciting contributions for, or on behalf of, a charitable organization. This definition usually excludes those who actually solicit contributions. Other terms used throughout the states include *professional fundraising counsel, professional fundraiser consultant,* and *independent fundraiser.*

Much of this regulation is applicable to those who are *professional solicitors.* Most of the states that use this term define this type of person as one who, for compensation, solicits contributions for or on behalf of a charitable organization, whether directly or through others, or a person involved in the fundraising process who does not qualify as a professional fundraiser. A minority of states define the term as a person who is employed or retained for compensation by a professional fundraiser to solicit contributions for charitable purposes.

There is considerable confusion in the law as to the appropriate line of demarcation between these two terms. Because the extent of regulation can be far more intense for a professional solicitor, it is often very important for an individual or company to be classified as a professional fundraiser rather than a professional solicitor.

Some states impose disclosure requirements with respect to the process known as *commercial co-venturing* or *charitable sales promotions.* This process occurs when a business announces to the general public that a portion (a specific amount or a specific percentage) of the purchase price of a product or service will, during a stated period, be paid to a charitable organization, the amount of which depends on consumer response to the promotion by, and positive publicity for, the business sponsor.

(e) Registration Requirements

A cornerstone of each state's charitable solicitation law is the requirement that a charitable organization (as defined in that law and not exempt from the obligation [described later]) that intends to solicit—by any means—contributions from persons in that state must first apply for and acquire permission to undertake the solicitation. This permission usually is characterized as a *registration*; some states denominate it a *license* or *permit*. If successful, the result is authorization to conduct the solicitation. These permits are usually valid for one year.

These state laws apply to fundraising within the borders of each state involved. Thus, a charitable or like organization soliciting in more than one state must register under (and otherwise comply with) not only the law of the state in which it is located, but also the law of each of the states in which it will be fundraising. Moreover, many counties, townships, cities, and similar jurisdictions throughout the United States have ordinances that attempt to regulate charitable fundraising within their borders.

As will be noted, most states' charitable solicitation acts require a soliciting charity (unless exempt) to file annually information with the appropriate governmental agency. This is done either by an annual updating of the registration or the like, or by the filing of a separate annual report.

In many states, professional fundraisers and professional solicitors are required to register with the state.

(f) Reporting Requirements

Many of the state charitable solicitation acts mandate annual reporting to the state by registered charitable organizations, professional fundraisers, and professional solicitors. This form of reporting can be extensive and may entail the provision of information concerning gifts received, funds expended for programs and fundraising, payments to service providers, and a battery of other information.

These reports are made on forms provided by the states. These forms, and the rules and instructions that accompany them, vary considerably in content. Underlying definitions and accounting principles can differ. There is little uniformity with respect to due dates for these reports. In recent years, however, there has been progress in the development of a uniform reporting form, although many states persist in adding differing reporting requirements to it.

In many states, professional fundraisers and professional solicitors are required to file annual reports with the state.

(g) Exemptions from Regulation

Many of the states exempt one or more categories of charitable organizations from the ambit of their charitable solicitation statutes. The basic rationale for these exemptions is that the exempted organizations are not part of the objective that the state is endeavoring to achieve through this type of regulation: the protection of the state's citizens from fundraising fraud and other abuse. (Other rationales are the constitutional law limitations involved in the case of churches and the ability of one or more categories of organization to persuade the legislature to exempt them.)

The most common exemption in this context is for churches and their closely related entities. These entities include conventions of churches and associations of churches. Some states broadly exempt religious organizations. These exemptions are rooted in constitutional law principles, barring government from regulating religious practices and beliefs. Some states have run into successful constitutional law challenges when they have attempted to define narrowly the concept of *religion* for this purpose.

Some states exempt at least certain types of educational institutions from the entirety of their charitable solicitation acts. Usually this exemption applies when the educational institution is accredited. The more common practice is to exempt educational institutions from only the registration or licensing, and reporting, requirements.

Some states, either as an alternative or in addition to the foregoing approach, exempt from the registration and reporting requirements educational institutions that confine their solicitations to their constituency. That is, this type of exemption extends to the solicitation of contributions by an educational institution to its student body, alumni, faculty, and trustees, and their families. Solicitations by educational institutions of their constituency are exempt from the entirety of their charitable solicitation laws in a few states.

Many educational institutions undertake some or all of their fundraising by means of related foundations. Some states expressly provide exemption, in tandem with whatever exemption their laws extend to educational institutions, to these supporting foundations. Alumni associations occasionally are exempted from the registration requirements.

The rationales for exempting educational institutions from coverage under these laws is that they generally do not solicit contributions from the public, there have not been any instances of abuses by these institutions of the fundraising process, these institutions already adequately report to state agencies, and the inclusion of these institutions under the charitable solicitation statute would impose an unnecessary burden on the regulatory process.

Some states exempt hospitals (and, in some instances, their related foundations) and other categories of health care entities. Again, the exemption can be from the entirety of the statute or from its registration and reporting requirements. Other exemptions for organizations may include veterans' organizations; police and firefighters' organizations; fraternal organizations; and, in a few states, organizations identified by name. Exemptions are also often available for membership organizations, small solicitations (ranging from $1,000 to $10,000) and solicitations for specified individuals.

Some of these exemptions are available as a matter of law. Others must be applied for, sometimes on an annual basis. Some exemptions are not available or are lost if the organization utilizes the services of a professional fundraiser or professional solicitor.

(h) Fundraising Cost Limitations

At one time, the chief weapon for state regulators regarding fundraising costs was laws that prohibited charitable organizations with "high" fundraising costs from soliciting in the states. Allegedly "high" fundraising expenses were defined in terms of percentages of gifts received. These laws proliferated, with percentage limitations extended to the compensation of professional fundraising consultants and professional solicitors. The issue found its way to the Supreme Court, where all of these percentage limitations were struck down as violating the charities' free speech rights. This application of the First and Fourteenth Amendments to the Constitution stands as the single most important bar to more stringent government regulation of the process of soliciting charitable contributions.

As noted, the states possess the police power to regulate the process of soliciting contributions for charitable purposes. The states cannot, however, exercise this power in a manner that unduly intrudes on the rights of free speech of the soliciting charitable organizations and their fundraising consultants and solicitors.

First, the Supreme Court held that a state cannot use the level of a charitable organization's fundraising costs as a basis for determining whether a charity may lawfully solicit funds in a jurisdiction.[139] Four years later, the Court held that the free speech principles apply, even though the state offers a charitable organization an opportunity to show that its fundraising costs are reasonable, despite the presumption that costs in excess of a specific ceiling are "excessive."[140] Another four years later, the Court held that these free speech principles applied when the limitation was not on a charity's fundraising costs but on the amount or extent of fees paid by a charitable organization to professional fundraisers or professional solicitors.[141] Subsequent litigation suggests that the courts are consistently reinforcing the legal principles so articulately promulgated by the Supreme Court during the 1980s.

(i) Prohibited Acts

Most states' charitable solicitation laws contain a list of one or more acts in which a charitable organization (and perhaps a professional fundraiser and/or professional solicitor) may not lawfully engage. These acts may be some or all of these:

- A person may not, for the purpose of soliciting contributions, use the name of another person (except that of an officer, director, or trustee of the charitable organization by or for which contributions are solicited) without the consent of that other person. This prohibition usually extends to the use of an individual's name on stationery or in an advertisement or brochure, or as one who has contributed to, sponsored, or endorsed the organization.

- A person may not for the purpose of soliciting contributions, use a name, symbol, or statement so closely related or similar to that used by another charitable organization or governmental agency that it would tend to confuse or mislead the public.

- A person may not use or exploit the fact of registration with the state so as to lead the public to believe that the registration in any manner constitutes an endorsement or approval by the state.

- A person may not represent to or mislead anyone, by any manner, means, practice, or device, to believe that the organization on behalf of which the solicitation is being conducted is a charitable organization or that the proceeds of the solicitation will be used for charitable purposes, when that is not the case.

- A person may not represent that the solicitation for charitable gifts is for or on behalf of a charitable organization or otherwise induce contributions from the public without proper authorization from the charitable organization.

---

[139] Village of Schaumberg v. Citizens for a Better Environment, 444 U.S. 620 (1980).
[140] Secretary of State of Maryland v. Joseph H. Munson Co., Inc., 467 U.S. 947 (1984).
[141] Riley v. National Fed'n of the Blind of North Carolina, Inc., 487 U.S. 781 (1981).

In one state, it is a prohibited act to represent that a charitable organization will receive a fixed or estimated percentage of the gross revenue from a solicitation in an amount greater than that identified to the donor. In another state, it is a prohibited act for an individual to solicit charitable contributions if the individual has been convicted of a crime involving the obtaining of money or property by false pretenses, unless the public is informed of the conviction in advance of the solicitation.

In still another state, prohibited acts for a charitable organization (or, in some instances, a person acting on its behalf) include:

- Misrepresenting the purpose of a solicitation
- Misrepresenting the purpose or nature of a charitable organization
- Engaging in a financial transaction that is not related to accomplishment of the charitable organization's exempt purpose
- Jeopardizing or interfering with the ability of a charitable organization to accomplish its charitable organization's exempt purpose
- Expending an "unreasonable amount of money" for fundraising or for management

Some states make violation of a separate law concerning "unfair or deceptive acts and practices" a violation of the charitable solicitation act as well.

(j) Contractual Requirements

Many of the state charitable solicitation acts require that the relationship between a charitable organization and a professional fundraiser, and/or between a charitable organization and a professional solicitor, be evidenced in a written agreement. This agreement is required to be filed with the state soon after the contract is executed. These types of requirements are clearly lawful and are not particularly unusual.

A few states, however, have enacted requirements—some of them rather patronizing—that dictate to the charitable organization the contents of the contract. For example, under one state's law, a contract between a charitable organization and a fundraising counsel must contain sufficient information "as will enable the department to identify the services the fundraising counsel is to provide and the manner of his compensation." Another provision of the same law mandates that the agreement "clearly state the respective obligations of the parties."

The law in another state requires a contract between a charitable organization and a fundraising counsel to contain provisions addressing the services to be provided, the number of persons to be involved in providing the services, the time period over which the services are to be provided, and the method and formula for compensation for the services.

Under another state's law, whenever a charitable organization contracts with a professional fundraiser or other type of fundraising consultant, the charitable organization has the right to cancel the contract, without cost or penalty, for a period of 15 days. Again, this type of law seems predicated on the assumption that charitable organizations are somehow not quite capable of developing their own contracts and tend to do so impetuously. It can be argued that these laws are forms of overreaching, in terms of scope and detail, on the part of government, and that charitable organizations ought to be mature enough to formulate their own contracts.

(k) Disclosure Requirements

Many of the states that were forced to abandon or forgo the use of the percentage mechanism as a basis for preventing fundraising for charity (as discussed earlier) utilize the percentage approach in a disclosure setting. Several states, for example, require charitable organizations to make an annual reporting, either to update a registration or as part of a separate report, to the authorities as to their fundraising activities in the prior year, including a statement of their fundraising expenses. Some states require a disclosure of a charity's fundraising costs, stated as a percentage, to donors at the time of the solicitation—although this requirement arguably is of dubious constitutionality. In a few states, solicitation literature used by a charitable organization must include a statement that, upon request, financial and other information about the soliciting charity may be obtained directly from the state.

Some states require a statement as to any percentage compensation in the contract between the charitable organization and the professional fundraiser and/or the professional solicitor. A few states require the compensation of a paid solicitor to be stated in the contract as a percentage of gross revenue; another state has a similar provision with respect to a professional fundraiser. One state wants a charitable organization's fundraising cost percentage to be stated in its registration statement.

An example of this type of law is a statute that imposed on the individual who raises funds for a charitable organization the responsibility to "deal with" the contributions in an "appropriate fiduciary manner." Thus, an individual in these circumstances owes a fiduciary duty to the public. These persons are subject to a surcharge for any funds wasted or not accounted for. A presumption exists in this law that funds not adequately documented and disclosed by records were not properly spent.

By direction of this law, all solicitations must "fully and accurately" identify the purposes of the charitable organization to prospective donors. Use of funds, to an extent of more than 50 percent, for "public education" must be disclosed under this law. The charitable organization's governing board must, under some of these laws, approve every contract with a professional fundraiser. Some of the provisions of this law probably are unconstitutional, such as the requirement that professional fundraisers or solicitors must disclose to those being solicited the percentage of their compensation in relation to gifts received.

Another example is some of the provisions of another state's law, which makes an "unlawful practice" the failure of a person soliciting funds to "truthfully" recite, on request, the percentage of funds raised to be paid to the solicitor. This state, like many other states, is using the concept of prohibited acts (discussed earlier) to impose a sort of code of ethics on all who seek to raise funds for charity.

Under one state's law, any person who solicits contributions for a charitable purpose and who receives compensation for the service must inform each person being solicited, in writing, that the solicitation is a "paid solicitation." In another state, when a solicitation is made by "direct personal contact," certain information must be "predominantly" disclosed in writing at the point of solicitation. In another state, the solicitation material and the "general promotional plan" for a solicitation may not be false, misleading, or deceptive, and must afford a "full and fair" disclosure.

In general, the typical state charitable solicitation act seems immune from successful constitutional law challenge. That is, the constitutional law attacks on these laws prevail only in relation to particularly egregious features of them. The same may be said of local fundraising regulation ordinances. The difficulty with the latter, however, is not so much their content as their number. A charitable organization involved in a multistate charitable solicitation may be expected to comply with hundreds, perhaps thousands, of these ordinances. To date, when responding to complaints by charities as to this burden of regulation, the courts review only the content of each local law, refusing to evaluate the difficulties they pose in the aggregate.

§ 9.8 ASSOCIATIONS AND CHARITABLE GIVING

As noted at the outset, charitable giving is assuming a greater role in the financing, directly and indirectly, of associations' programs. Increasingly, associations that are not themselves charitable entities are reaping the benefits of use of related foundations. Overall, associations are relying more heavily on contributions and grants as the basis for funding their charitable, educational, and scientific efforts; this form of funding frees up more dues and other fee-for-service revenue to enable associations to advance their noncharitable functions.

Notwithstanding this increase in solicitation and receipt of gifts and grants by associations, many of these organizations are struggling with the implementation of planned giving programs and the strange world of fundraising regulation. Even though associations have all of the inherent characteristics underlying successful planned giving programs,[142] many of them are finding it difficult to launch these initiatives. Associations relatively new to the realm of fundraising often are stunned to learn of the intense federal and state government regulation that encompasses and often constrains what initially seems to be a simple process: the asking for and making of charitable contributions.

---

[142] See § 9.2.

CHAPTER TEN

Annual Reporting and Disclosure Requirements

Federal tax law imposes annual reporting and disclosure requirements on tax-exempt business leagues and exempt organizations that are affiliated with them. Usually there are state law requirements as well.

§ 10.1 FEDERAL TAX LAW ANNUAL REPORTING REQUIREMENTS IN GENERAL

Nearly every organization that is exempt from federal income taxation must file an annual information return with the IRS.[1] This return generally is one of these types:

- Most tax-exempt organizations—Form 990[2]
- Small tax-exempt organizations[3]—Form 990-EZ
- Private foundations[4]—Form 990-PF
- Political organizations[5]—Form 1120-POL

The annual information return must state a tax-exempt organization's items of gross income, disbursements, and other information; an exempt organization must keep appropriate records, render statements under oath, make other returns, and comply with other requirements, as the tax regulations, return instructions, and the return itself prescribes.[6] The federal tax law imposes certain other record-keeping requirements.[7] Generally, an exempt organization must file an annual information return irrespective of whether it is chartered by, or affiliated or associated with, any central, parent, or other organization.[8]

(a) Contents of Annual Information Return

The annual information return filed with the IRS by most tax-exempt organizations—Form 990—is not merely akin to a tax return that principally requires the submission of financial information. A substantial amount of other factual information, communicated by sentences and paragraphs, also is required to be provided. This annual return is often the document that is used principally by government officials, prospective contributors, representatives of the media, and others to evaluate the finances, operations, programs, and overall merits of an exempt organization.[9]

(i) Form 990. The annual information return filed by most tax-exempt organizations must include these items: a summary of the types of gross revenue received for the year involved[10]; its expenses for the year[11]; its net assets as of the close of

---

[1] IRC § 6033(a)(1); Reg. § 1.6003-2(a)(1). This filing requirement applies to organizations that are tax-exempt by reason of IRC § 501(a) or 527. Thus, it is not applicable to entities that are exempt pursuant to IRC § 521 (see *Tax-Exempt Organizations* § 18.11), 526 (*id.* § 18.9), 528 (*id.* § 18.3), or 529 (*id.* § 18.16).

[2] Form 990 is also generally filed by nonexempt charitable trusts (IRC § 4947(a)(1)). The filing requirements for charitable trusts are the subject of Rev. Proc. 73-29, 1973-2 C.B. 474.

[3] See § 10.1(b)(ii).

[4] See § 8.1.

[5] See § 4.7.

[6] IRC § 6033(a)(1); Reg. § 1.6033-2. The contents of the return for charitable organizations (entities described in IRC § 501(c)(3) and tax-exempt by reason of IRC § 501(a)) are stated in IRC § 6033(b); Reg. § 1.6033-2(a)(2).

[7] IRC § 6006.

[8] Reg. § 1.6033-2(a)(1).

[9] In general, Dylewsky, "Form 990 Offers Opportunity for Exempts to Position Themselves Favorably," 6 *J. Tax. Exempt Orgs.* 120 (Nov./Dec. 1994).

[10] Form 990, Part I, lines 1–12.

[11] *Id.*, Part I, lines 13–17.

the year[12]; a statement of program service accomplishments[13]; a list of trustees, directors, officers, and key employees[14]; an analysis of income-producing activities[15]; and information concerning taxable subsidiaries and disregarded entities.[16] Expenses must be reported on a functional basis.[17] Information is required with respect to cost allocations where there are joint costs for educational and fundraising purposes.[18] An exempt organization must report aggregate compensation of directors and the like from the reporting organization and related organizations, where the aggregate compensation was more than $100,000, of which more than $10,000 was provided by a related organization.[19]

A tax-exempt organization is required to inventory its sources of revenue, such as program service revenues identified by discrete activities, membership dues, investment income, special fundraising events, and sales of inventory.[20] These items of revenue must be characterized as either taxable or nontaxable unrelated business income or related (exempt function) income.[21] Each type of related income must be accompanied by an explanation as to how the income-producing activities relate to the accomplishment of exempt purposes.[22] If revenue received by an exempt organization is excluded from unrelated business income taxation,[23] it must report the amount and identify an *exclusion code* corresponding with the section of the Internal Revenue Code that provides the exclusion.[24]

In determining whether an activity of a tax-exempt organization is a *business*, the IRS and the courts look to the presence or absence of a *profit motive* prompting the conduct of the activity.[25] An activity that is not conducted with this motive is not regarded as a *business*. (This means that any net loss from an activity of this nature cannot be offset against net gain from a business undertaking.[26]) To induce exempt organizations to disclose any activities that do not qualify as businesses for this purpose, the IRS utilizes a special business code.[27]

A tax-exempt organization is required to report certain other facts, including its Web site address, a statement as to any changes in operations, any changes made in governing documents, a liquidation or substantial contraction, relationship with another organization, political expenditures, receipt of nondeductible gifts, compliance with the requirement to disclose its application for recognition of exemption and recent annual information returns, deductibility of membership dues (in the case of social welfare, labor, agricultural, and horticultural

---

[12] *Id.*, Part I, lines 18–21; Part IV.

[13] *Id..*, Part III.

[14] *Id.*, Part V.

[15] *Id.*, Part VII.

[16] *Id.*, Part IX. See Chapter 6.

[17] *Id.*, Part II.

[18] *Id.*, Part II, last question.

[19] *Id.*, Part V, question 75.

[20] *Id.*, Part VII.

[21] *Id.*, Part VII, columns (B), (E).

[22] *Id.*, Part VIII.

[23] See § 5.8.

[24] Form 990, Part VII, columns (C), (D).

[25] See § 5.4.

[26] As reflected on Form 990-T, net income and net losses from unrelated businesses conducted in a year can be netted in determining any unrelated business income. See § 10.7; Appendix F.

[27] Form 990 instructions, exclusion code 41.

organizations, and business leagues), revenue items unique to social clubs, payment of taxes for excessive lobbying or political campaign activities (in the case of public charities), ownership of an interest in a taxable corporation or partnership, and information about any involvement in an excess benefit transaction (in the case of public charities and social welfare organizations).[28]

The accounting system used by a tax-exempt organization to maintain its books and records may be different from that reflected on the annual information return, particularly because of changes in generally accepted accounting principles.[29] A portion of the annual information return is used to reconcile these two approaches.[30]

(ii) Form 990, Schedule A. In addition to filing an annual information return, a tax-exempt charitable organization[31] must file an accompanying schedule (Schedule A) requiring other information.

This schedule is the means by which a charitable organization reports on the compensation of its five highest paid employees,[32] the compensation of the five highest paid independent contractors for professional services,[33] certain activities,[34] eligibility for nonprivate foundation status,[35] compliance by private schools with the antidiscrimination rules,[36] and information regarding transfers, transactions, and relationships with other organizations.[37]

Charitable organizations that elected the expenditure test with respect to their lobbying activities[38] must report their lobbying expenses, including those over the four-year averaging period.[39] Organizations that have not made this election, and thus remain subject to the substantial part test,[40] are subject to other reporting requirements.[41]

(iii) Form 990, Schedule B. Another schedule (Schedule B) must be attached to the annual information return filed by a tax-exempt organization, unless the organization certifies that it does not meet the filing requirement by checking the appropriate box in the heading of the return.

This schedule is the means by which filing tax-exempt organizations provide information concerning contributions made to them. Generally, the exempt organization must list (in Parts I and/or II) every contributor who, during the year, gave the organization, directly or indirectly, money, securities, or any other

---

[28] Form 990, Part VI, questions 76–77, 79, 80, 81 (see § 4.3), 82, 83, (see §§ 9.4, 9.5), 84 (see § 9.6), 85 (see §§ 4.2, 4.5), 86, 87, 88 (see Chapter 6), and 89 (see § 3.8).

[29] Financial Accounting Standards Boards Statements Nos. 116, 117.

[30] Form 990, Parts IV-A, IV-B.

[31] That is, an organization that is tax-exempt under IRC § 501(a) by reason of IRC § 501(c)(3).

[32] Schedule A, Part I.

[33] Schedule A, Part II.

[34] Schedule A, Part III.

[35] Schedule A, Part IV. See Chapter 8.

[36] Schedule A, Part V.

[37] Schedule A, Part VII.

[38] See *Tax-Exempt Organizations* § 20.3.

[39] Form 990, Schedule A, Part VI-A.

[40] See § 20.3.

[41] Form 990, Schedule A, Part VI-B.

type of property aggregating $5,000 or more for the year. The donors must be identified by name and address, and there must be reporting as to whether the contributions were made by payroll deduction or were noncash gifts. In an instance of the latter, the schedule must contain a description of the property given, the value or estimate of value of the property, and the date of receipt of the gift.

A tax-exempt charitable organization that meets the donative organization public support test[42] is required to list only the contributors whose contribution(s) of $5,000 or more is greater than 2 percent of the organization's total support for the measuring period. A social club, or fraternal beneficiary or domestic fraternal society, order, or association, that received contributions exclusively for charitable purposes must list those from contributors who gave more than $1,000 during the year (Parts I, II, and/or III). A social club or fraternal entity that did not receive a contribution of more than $1,000 during the year for charitable purposes is only required to report the total contributions it received during the year for charitable purposes.

(iv) Form 990-EZ. To alleviate the annual reporting burden for smaller tax-exempt organizations, the IRS promulgated a less extensive annual information return. This is the two-page Form 990-EZ.

This return may be used by tax-exempt organizations that have gross receipts that are less than $100,000 and total assets that are less than $250,000 in value at the end of the reporting year.[43]

An organization can use this annual information return in any year in which it meets the two criteria, even though it was, and/or is, required to file a Form 990 in other years. Private foundations are not permitted to file Form 990-EZ. A charitable organization filing a Form 990-EZ must also file a Schedules A and B (Form 990).[44]

(v) Due Dates. The annual information return (Form 990, Form 990-EZ, or Form 990-PF) and any unrelated business income tax return (Form 990-T) are due on or before the 15th day of the fifth month following the close of the tax-exempt organization's tax year.[45] Thus, the return for a calendar year exempt organization should be filed by May 15 of each year. One or more extensions may be obtained. These returns are filed with the IRS service center in Ogden, Utah.[46]

The filing date for an annual information return (Form 990, Form 990-EZ, or Form 990-PF) may fall due when the organization's application for recognition of tax-exempt status is pending with the IRS. In that instance, the organization should nonetheless file the information return (rather than a tax return) and indicate on it that the application is pending.[47]

---

[42] See § 8.3.

[43] This is not a statutory rule; it is a threshold established by the IRS.

[44] See § 10.1(a)(ii), (iii).

[45] IRC § 6072(e); Reg. § 1.6033-2(e). This due date is also applicable with respect to Form 4720 (the tax return by which certain excise taxes imposed on private foundations, public charities, and others are paid). See Appendix C.

[46] Ann. 96-63, 1996-29 I.R.B. 18.

[47] Reg. §. 1.6033-2(c).

(vi) Penalties. Failure to timely file the appropriate information return, or failure to include any information required to be shown on the return (or failure to show the correct information) absent reasonable cause, can give rise to a $20 per day penalty, payable by the organization, for each day the failure continues, with a maximum penalty for any one return not to exceed the lesser of $10,000 or 5 percent of the gross receipts of the organization for one year.[48] An additional penalty may be imposed at the same rate and maximum of $10,000 on the individual(s) responsible for the failure to file, absent reasonable cause, where the return remains unfiled following demand for the return by the IRS.[49] There is a much larger penalty on organizations having gross receipts in excess of $1 million for a year. In this circumstance, the per-day penalty is $100 and the maximum penalty is $50,000.[50] An addition to tax for failure to timely file a federal tax return, including a Form 990-T, may also be imposed.[51]

In one instance, an organization required to file a Form 990 submitted an incomplete return by omitting material information from the form, failed to supply the missing information after being requested to do so by the IRS, and did not establish a reasonable cause for its failure to file a complete return. Under these circumstances, the filing of the incomplete return was a failure to file the return for purposes of the penalty.[52] The IRS observed that the legislative history underlying the pertinent law "shows that Congressional concern was to ensure that information requested on exempt organization returns was provided timely and completely so that the Service would be provided with the information needed to enforce the tax laws."[53] The IRS added:

> Form 990 and accompanying instructions issued by the Service request information that is necessary in order for the Service to perform the duties and responsibilities placed upon it by Congress for proper administration of the revenue laws. These duties and responsibilities include making exempt organization returns available for public inspection as well as conducting audits of exempt organizations to determine their compliance with statutory provisions. When a return is submitted that has not been satisfactorily completed, the Service's ability to perform its duties is seriously hindered, and the public's right to obtain meaningful information is impaired. Thus, when material information is omitted, a return is not completed in the manner prescribed by the form and instructions and the organization has not met the filing requirements of section 6033(a)(1) of the Code.[54]

In the case of failure to file a return, the tax may be assessed, or a proceeding in court for the collection of the tax may be begun without assessment, at any time.[55] In the just-discussed situation, the organization was considered[56] to have

---

[48] IRC § 6652(c)(1)(A), (c)(3).

[49] IRC § 6652(c)(1)(B); Reg. § 301.6652-2. Two or more organizations exempt from taxation under IRC § 501, one or more of which is described in IRC § 501(c)(2) (see *Tax-Exempt Organizations* § 18.2(a)) and the other(s) of which derives income from IRC § 501(c)(2) organization(s), are eligible to file a consolidated return Form 990 (and/or Form 990-T) in lieu of separate return, (IRC § 1504(e)).

[50] IRC § 6652(c)(1)(A), last sentence.

[51] IRC § 6651(a)(1).

[52] Rev. Rul. 77-162, 1977-1 C.B. 4011.

[53] *Id.*, citing S. Rep. 552, 91st Cong., 1st Sess. 52 (1969).

[54] Rev. Rul. 77-162, 1977-1 C.B. 401.

[55] IRC § 6501(c)(3).

[56] IRC § 6652(c)(1)(A).

failed to file any return at all and, therefore, the period of limitations on assessment and collection of the tax[57] was ruled to have not commenced.[58]

It is the practice of the IRS to omit from its listing of organizations to which deductible gifts may be made[59] those organizations that fail to establish their nonfiling status with the IRS. The chief counsel of the IRS upheld this practice.[60] The continuing validity of this procedure was temporarily cast in doubt because of a court opinion,[61] although the lawyers at the IRS ultimately concluded that the opinion did not raise any concerns with respect to the practice.[62]

The IRS occasionally will revoke the tax-exempt status of an organization for failure to file annual information returns.[63]

(vii) Assessments. The IRS generally must assess any tax within three years of the due date of the return or the date on which the return involved is actually filed, whichever is later.[64] A six-year statute of limitations applies, however, if an excise tax return "omits an amount of such tax properly includible thereon which exceeds 25 percent of the amount of such tax reported thereon"; this extended period does not apply, in the case of the private foundation and certain other taxes, where there is adequate disclosure in the return to the IRS.[65] In one case, a private foundation timely filed its annual information return, reflecting certain salary payments to an officer; believing the payments to be reasonable, the foundation did not file a return showing any excise taxes due. A court held that, under these facts, only the annual information return was due, adequate disclosure was made on that return, and the six-year statute of limitations was inapplicable (thereby precluding the IRS from assessing the tax because the deficiency notice was mailed more than three years after the organization's returns were filed).[66]

(viii) Miscellaneous. The filing of an annual information return is also the opportunity for the changing of annual accounting periods by most tax-exempt organizations. An exempt organization desiring to change its annual accounting period may effect the change by timely filing its annual information return with the IRS for the short period for which the return is required, indicating in the return that a change of accounting period is being made. If an organization is not required to file an annual information return or a tax return reflecting unrelated

---

[57] IRC § 6501(c)(3).

[58] In general, reliance on the advice of a competent tax advisor can constitute reasonable cause for a failure to file a return, for purposes of the IRC § 6651(a)(1) addition to tax and the IRC § 6652(c)(1)(A) or § 6652(c)(1)(B) penalty (e.g., Waco Lodge No. 166, Benevolent & Protective Order of Elks v. Comm'r, 42 T.C.M. 1202 (1981), aff'd in part and rev'd in part, 696 F.2d 372 (5th Cir. 1983); Coldwater Seafood Corp. v. Comm'r, 69 T.C. 966 (1978); West Coast Ice Co. v. Comm'r, 49 T.C. 345 (1968)).

[59] Publication No. 78, "Cumulative List of Organizations Described in Section 170(c) of the Internal Revenue Code."

[60] Gen. Couns. Mem. 39389.

[61] Estate of Clopton v. Comm'r, 93 T.C. 275 (1989).

[62] Gen. Couns. Mem. 39809.

[63] E.g., Priv. Ltr. Rul. 200531024.

[64] IRC § 6501(a).

[65] IRC § 6501(e)(3).

[66] Cline v. Comm'r, 55 T.C.M. 540 (1988).

income, it is not necessary to otherwise notify the IRS that a change of accounting period is being made. If, however, an organization has previously changed its annual accounting period at any time within 10 calendar years ending with the calendar year that includes the beginning of the short period resulting from the change of an annual accounting period, and if the organization had a filing requirement at any time during the 10-year period, it must file an application for a change in accounting period with the IRS.[67]

Special rules apply with respect to filing of annual information returns by organizations under a group exemption.[68]

(b) Exceptions to Reporting Requirements

This requirement of filing an annual information return does not apply to several categories of tax-exempt organizations.

Some of these exceptions are mandatory[69]; others are at the discretion of the IRS.[70]

(i) Churches and Certain Other Religious Organizations. Churches (including an interchurch organization of local units of a church), their integrated auxiliaries, and conventions or associations of churches do not have to file annual information returns.[71] Also, the reporting requirements do not apply to the exclusively religious activities of any *religious order.*[72]

(ii) Small Organizations. The requirement of filing an annual information return is inapplicable to certain organizations (other than private foundations) the gross receipts[73] of which in each year are normally not more than $25,000.[74]

(iii) Other Organizations. Other organizations may be relieved from filing annual information returns where a filing of these returns by them is not necessary to the efficient administration of the internal revenue laws, as determined by the IRS.[75] This category of organizations[76] embraces:

- Religious organizations[77]
- Educational organizations[78]

---

[67] Rev. Proc. 85-58, 1985-2 C.B. 740, *supp. by* Rev. Proc. 76-9, 1985-1 C.B. 547, as *mod. by* Rev. Proc. 79-2, 1979-1 C.B. 482. This application is made by means of Form 3115.

    The IRS provided relief from the filing of an application for change in accounting method for tax-exempt organizations changing their method so as to comply with the Statement of Financial Accounting Standards No. 116 issued by the Financial Accounting Standards Board (Notice 96-30, 1996-1 C.B. 378).

[68] Reg. 1.6033-2(d). The group exemption rules are the subject of *Tax-Exempt Organizations* § 23.6.

[69] IRC § 6033(a)(2)(A).

[70] IRC § 6033(a)(2)(B).

[71] IRC § 6033(a)(2)(A)(i).

[72] IRC § 6033(a)(2)(A)(iii).

[73] The term *gross receipts* means total receipts without any reduction for costs or expenses, including costs of goods sold (Form 990, part 1, line 8).

[74] IRC § 6033(a)(2)(A)(ii). The statute references a $5,000 threshold; the IRS increased the threshold to $25,000 (see text accompanied by *infra* note 93).

[75] IRC § 6033(a)(2)(B); Reg. § 1.6033-2(g)(6).

[76] IRC § 6033(a)(2)(C).

[77] See *Tax-Exempt Organizations*, Chapter 8.

[78] IRC § 170(b)(1)(A)(ii). See *Tax-Exempt Organizations*, Chapter 7, § 11.3(a).

- Charitable organizations or organizations operated for the prevention of cruelty to children or animals,[79] if the organizations are supported by funds contributed by the federal or a state government or are primarily supported by contributions from the general public

- Organizations operated, supervised, or controlled by or in connection with a religious organization

- Certain fraternal beneficiary organizations[80]

- A corporation organized under an act of Congress if it is wholly owned by the United States or any agency or instrumentality of the United States or a wholly owned subsidiary of the United States[81]

In the exercise of this discretionary authority, the IRS announced that organizations, other than private foundations, with gross receipts not normally in excess of $25,000 do not have to file annual information returns.[82]

As noted, other organizations may be relieved from filing annual information returns where a filing of these returns by them is not necessary to the efficient administration of the internal revenue laws, as determined by the IRS.[83] The IRS has used this discretion to exempt from the filing requirement:

1. An educational organization (below college level) that is qualified as a school, has a program of a general academic nature, and is affiliated with a church or operated by a religious order[84]

2. Mission societies sponsored by or affiliated with one or more churches or church denominations, more than one-half of the activities of which are conducted in, or directed at persons in, foreign countries[85]

3. State institutions, the income of which is excluded from gross income on the ground that the income is accruing to the state[86]

4. A tax-exempt foreign organization (other than a private foundation) which normally does not receive more than $25,000 in gross receipts annual from sources from within the United States[87] and which does not have any significant activity (including lobbying or political activity) in the United States[88]

---

[79] IRC § 501(c)(3). See *Tax-Exempt Organizations* § 10.1.

[80] IRC § 501(c)(8). See *Tax-Exempt Organizations* § 18.4(a).

[81] IRC § 501(c)(1). See *Tax-Exempt Organizations* § 18.1.

[82] Ann. 82-88, 1982-25 I.R.B. 23. For purposes of the $25,000 rule, a tax-exempt organization is relieved from the requirement of filing an annual information return where (1) during its first year, it received (including pledges) gross receipts of $37,500 or less; (2) during a period of more than one year of its existence and less than three years, it received, as an average of gross receipts experienced in the first two tax years, gross receipts of $30,000 or less; and (3) during its existence of more than three years, it received, as an average of gross receipts, $25,000 or less (*id*).

[83] IRC § 6033(a)(2)(B).

[84] Reg. 1.6033-2(g)(1)(vii). See *Tax-Exempt Organizations* § 7.3.

[85] IRC § 115; Reg. § 1.6033-2(g)(1)(iv).

[86] Reg. § 1.6033-2(g)(1)(v).

[87] IRC §§ 861-865; Reg. § 53.4948-1(b).

[88] Rev. Proc. 94-17, 1994-1 C.B. 579.

5. A governmental unit[89]

6. An affiliate of a governmental unit[90]

7. A tax-exempt United States possession organization (other than a private foundation) that normally does not receive more than $25,000 in gross receipts annually from sources within the United States and that does not have any significant activity within the United States[91]

For purposes of the fifth of these items, an entity is a *governmental unit* if it is (1) a state or local governmental unit as defined in the rules providing an exclusion from gross income for interest earned on bonds issued by these units,[92] (2) entitled to receive deductible charitable contributions as a unit of government,[93] or (3) an Indian tribal government or a political subdivision of this type of government.[94]

For purposes of the sixth of these items, an entity is an *affiliate of a governmental unit* if it is a tax-exempt organization[95] and meets one of two sets of requirements. One of these sets of requirements is that it has a ruling or determination letter from the IRS that (1) its income, derived from activities constituting the basis for its exemption, is excluded from gross income under the rules for political subdivisions and the like[96]; (2) it is entitled to receive deductible charitable contributions[97] on the basis that contributions to it are for the use of governmental units; or (3) it is a wholly owned instrumentality of a state or political subdivision of a state for employment tax purposes.[98] The other set of requirements is available for an entity that does not have a ruling or determination letter from the IRS but (1) it is either operated, supervised, or controlled by governmental units, or by organizations that are affiliates of governmental units, or the members of the organization's governing body are elected by the public at large, pursuant to local statute or ordinance; (2) it possesses two or more of certain affiliation factors[99]; and (3) its filing of an annual information return is not otherwise necessary to the efficient administration of the internal revenue laws.[100] An organization can (but is not required to) request a ruling or determination letter from the IRS that is an affiliate of a governmental unit.[101]

---

[89] Rev. Proc. 95-48, 1995-2 C.B. 418, *supp'g* Rev. Proc. 83-23, 1983-1 C.B. 687.

[90] *Id.*

[91] Rev. Proc. 2003-21, 2003-6 I.R.B. 448.

[92] IRC § 103; Reg. 1.103-1(b). See *Tax-Exempt Organizations* § 6.9.

[93] IRC § 170(c)(1). See *Tax-Exempt Organizations* § 18.18.

[94] IRC §§ 7701(a)(40), 7871. This tripartite definition of *governmental unit* is in Rev. Proc. 95-48, 1995-2 C.B. 418 § 4.01.

[95] That is, as described in IRC § 501(c).

[96] IRC § 115. See *Tax-Exempt Organizations* § 18.17.

[97] IRC § 170(c)(1).

[98] IRC §§ 3121(b)(7), 3306(c)(7). This definition is provided by Rev. Proc. 95-48, 1995-2 C.B. 418 § 4.02(a).

[99] Rev. Proc. 95-48, 1995-2 C.B. 418 § 4.03.

[100] *Id.* § 4.02(b). Relevant facts and circumstances as to whether an annual return is necessary include those provided at *id.* § 4.04.

[101] *Id.* § 5.

(c) Limited Liability Companies

A tax-exempt organization can be the sole member of a limited liability company (LLC) or two or more exempt organizations can be members of an LLC.[102] In the case of the single-member LLC, it generally is a disregarded entity for federal tax purposes and thus its activities are treated as the activities of the member.[103] In this instance, then, the single-member LLC is not required to file annual information returns; rather, the activities of the LLC are reported as activities of the exempt member.[104] Where, however, there is a multi-member LLC, the members of which are exempt organizations, the LLC may be able to qualify as an exempt organization[105] and if so would be subject to the annual reporting requirements.

(d) Political Organization Reporting Requirements

(i) General Rules. A political organization,[106] other than those involved only in state or local electoral activities and subject to comparable state disclosure laws, that accepts a contribution or makes an expenditure for an exempt political function during a year must file quarterly reports with the IRS in the case of a year in which a federal election is held. Also, preelection and postelection reports may be required. Otherwise, generally, the reports are due semiannually. A political organization has the option of filing these reports monthly. Whatever the choice, the organization must file on the same schedule basis for the entire calendar year.[107]

This report must contain: the amount and date of each expenditure made to a person if the aggregate amount of expenditures to the person during the year is at least $200; the purpose of the contribution if it is at least $500; the name and address of the person (in the case of an individual, including the individual's occupation and employer); the name and address (including occupation and employer in the case of an individual) of all contributions which contributed an aggregate amount of at least $200 to the organization during the year; and the amount of such contribution.[108]

This set of rules does not apply to a person required to report under the Federal Election Campaign Act as a political committee; a state or local committee of a political party or political committee of a state or local candidate; an organization that reasonably anticipates that it will not have gross receipts of $25,000 or more for any year; another type of tax-exempt organization that is subject to the

---

[102] See § 6.10.

[103] In general, see *Tax-Exempt Organizations* § 30.7.

[104] E.g., Priv. Ltr. Rul. 200134025.

[105] See *Tax-Exempt Organizations* § 4.3(e).

[106] See § 4.7.

[107] IRC § 527(j)(2). This return is Form 8872. These rules are summarized in Rev. Rul. 2003-49, 2003-20 I.R.B. 903. These rules were first enacted in 2000 (P.L. 106-230, 106th Cong., 2d Sess. (2000); see *Tax-Exempt Organizations* § 23.6, note 168). The exception for state and local political organizations and certain other changes in this aspect of the law were enacted in 2002 (P.L. 107-276, 107th Cong., 2d Sess. (2002)), and made retroactive to 2000.

[108] IRC § 527(j)(3).

political campaign activities tax; or independent expenditures (as that term is defined in the Federal Election Campaign Act).[109]

There are penalties for failure to comply with this requirement (by filing late, insufficiently, or incorrectly). The penalty is 35 percent of the total amount of contributions and expenditures not properly reported.[110] Political organizations are also required to file income tax returns.[111]

(ii) Filing Dates.   Political organizations that choose to file monthly generally must file their reports by the 20th day after the end of the month; the reports must be complete as of the last day of the month. The year-end report, however, is due by January 31 of the following year.

If, however, the year is one in which a regularly scheduled election is to be held, the organization filing monthly does not file the reports regularly due on November and December (that is, the monthly reports for October and November). Instead, the organization must file a report 12 days before the general election (or 15 days before the general election if posted by registered or certified mail) that contains information through the 20th day before the general election. The organization must also file a report no more than 30 days after the general election that contains information through the day after the election. Rather than a December monthly report, the year-end report is due by January 31 of the following year.

As noted, political organizations that choose to not file on a monthly basis must file semiannual reports in nonelection years. These reports are due on July 31 for the first half of the year and, for the second half of the year, on January 31 of the following year.

In an election year, these political organizations must file quarterly reports, which are due on the 15th day after the last day of the quarter, except that the return for the final quarter is due on January 31 of the following year. These organizations must also file preelection reports with respect to any election for which they receive a contribution or make an expenditure. These reports are due 12 days before the election (15 days if posted by registered or certified mail) and must contain information through the 20th day before the election. These organizations must also file a post–general election report, due 30 days after the general election and containing information through the 20th day after the election.

(e) Electronic Filing

A tax-exempt organization has the option of filing its annual information returns electronically, although for some larger exempt organizations the electronic filing requirement became mandatory in 2006. The IRS's electronic filing system, named Modernized e-File (MeF), was developed and delivered through the IRS Business Systems Modernization program. MeF, initiated in February 2004,[112]

---

[109] IRC § 527(j)(5).
[110] IRC § 527(j)(1).
[111] IRC § 6012(a)(6). These returns are Form 1120-POL.
[112] IR-2004-43.

uses XML, rather than a proprietary data format, to process these returns.[113] This system enables exempt organizations to transmit return data using an Internet connection by means of IRS-approved software and IRS-approved submitter organizations. This return information is sent to the agency through a secure Internet site accessible only to registered users.

Electronically filed returns are processed on receipt, and, shortly thereafter, an IRS acknowledgment message is generated to inform filers or tax professionals that the return has been accepted or rejected. Error messages for rejected returns identify the reasons the return was rejected and make it easier for the filer or tax professional to correct the errors. MeF is intended to streamline electronic filing by eliminating the need for the mailing of paper documents to the IRS and enables filers to attach certain forms, schedules, and other documents and information to the return in electronic format. There has been controversy as to the costs and other burdens of electronic filing on exempt organizations, but the IRS has resisted efforts to postpone mandatory electronic filing and is of the view that organizations will be able to convert to electronic filing at a reasonable costs and that the benefits to the IRS and filers substantially outweigh the expenses.

The IRS is required to prescribe regulations providing the standards for determining which returns must be filed on magnetic media or in other machine-readable form; the agency is not authorized to require electronic filing of returns by individuals, estates, and trusts.[114] Also, the agency may not require any person to file returns on magnetic media unless the person is required to file at least 250 returns during the calendar year.[115] Further, the IRS must, in this regard, take into account the ability of organizations to comply at reasonable cost with the requirements of the regulations.[116]

(i) Mandatory Filing. The IRS, in early 2005, issued temporary and proposed regulations that require certain large tax-exempt organizations to electronically file their annual information returns beginning in 2006.[117] The basic rules are:

- Tax-exempt organizations with assets of at least $100 million and that file at least 250 returns,[118] which are required to file annual information returns, must file them electronically beginning with tax years ending on or after December 31, 2005.

- Tax-exempt organizations with assets of at least $10 million and that file at least 250 returns, which are required to file annual information returns, must file them electronically beginning with tax years ending on or after December 31, 2006.

---

[113] The returns that may be electronically filed are Forms 990, 990-EZ, 990-PF, 1120-POL, and 8868. The Form 990-T may not be electronically filed at this time. Generally, PDF attachments are not permitted, with exceptions for items such as copies of third-party documents (for which XML cannot be used).

[114] IRC § 6011(e)(1).

[115] IRC § 6011(e)(2)(A).

[116] IRC § 6011(e)(2)(B).

[117] Reg. §§ 1.6033-4T, 301.6033-4T (T.D. 9175, REG-130671-04).

[118] This includes income tax, excise tax, and employment tax returns, as well as other information returns (such as Forms W-2 and 1099).

- Private foundations and split-interest charitable trusts (irrespective of asset size) and that file at least 250 returns must file them electronically beginning with tax years ending on or after December 31, 2006.

The determination as to whether an entity is required to file at least 250 returns is made by aggregating all returns that the entity is required to file in the course of the calendar year involved.[119]

The IRS accepts returns directly from tax-exempt organizations or via a third-party preparer; however, an IRS-approved e-file provider must be used. Tax professionals who plan to file these returns electronically are required to submit a new or revised electronic IRS e-file application.[120] This is a one-time registration; application must be made at least 45 days before electronic filing.

(ii) Waivers. The IRS may waive the requirements to file electronically in 2006 in cases of undue economic hardship or technology issues; the agency believes that electronic filing will not impose significant burdens on filers; thus, waivers of the electronic filing requirement will be granted only in "exceptional cases."

The IRS issued guidance as to the procedures to be followed by tax-exempt organizations that wish to request a waiver of the requirement to electronically file their annual information return.[121] These rules permit the agency to waive the electronic filing requirement if the organization demonstrates that undue hardship would result if the entity were required to file its return electronically.

The IRS announced that it will approve or deny requests for a waiver of the electronic filing requirement on the basis of each organization's "particular facts and circumstances." The agency will consider an organization's "ability to timely file its return electronically without incurring an undue economic hardship." The IRS will generally grant these waivers where the requisite undue hardship is shown, "including any incremental costs to the filer." Mindful of the "software and technological issues" in filing electronically, the IRS generally will grant waivers where "technology issues prevent" the organization from filing its return electronically.

To request a waiver, an exempt organization must file a written request containing:

- A notation at the top of the request stating, "in large letters," either "Form 990 e-File Waiver Request" or "Form 990-PF e-File Waiver Request"
- The organization's name, tax identification number, and mailing address
- The type of form for which the waiver is requested
- The tax year for which the waiver is requested
- The value of the organization's total assets at the end of the tax year as reported (or to be reported) on the entity's Form 990 or 990-PF

---

[119] This electronic filing requirement is determined annually; thus, an exempt organization may have to e-file in one year but not the next (such as because in the next year it filed less than 250 returns).
[120] This is done by means of Form 8633.
[121] Notice 2005-88, 2005-48 I.R.B. 1060.

- A "detailed statement" that lists:
  - The steps the organization has taken in an attempt to meet its requirement to timely file its return electronically
  - Why these steps were unsuccessful
  - The undue hardship that would result by complying with the electronic filing requirement, including any incremental costs (that is, costs that are above and beyond the costs to file on paper) to the organization of complying with the requirements, with these costs supported by a "detailed computation"
- A statement as to the steps the organization will take to assure its ability to file electronically in the future
- A penalty-of-perjury statement signed by an officer of the organization

Organizations are encouraged to file electronic filing waiver requests at least 45 days prior to the due date of the return, including extensions. This filing should be sent to the Ogden Submission Processing Center.

(iii) Electronic Mail Box. A unique feature of the MeF program is the "Fed/State System" component of the program. Beginning in 2006, the IRS will serve as an electronic mail box for exempt organizations that file with one or more states, permitting transmitters to submit multiple federal and state returns within one transmission. (This assumes that the state(s) involved elect to cooperate with the IRS in this regard.) Exempt organizations will be able to electronically file Form 990-like forms, annual reports, charitable solicitation filings, and more via this IRS feature. The IRS will also file Form 990s with the states where that filing by exempt organizations is mandated by state law. The IRS is working with the National Association of State Charity Officials and the National Association of Attorneys General to ensure that state reporting requirements for exempt organizations are considered.

§ 10.2 FEDERAL DOCUMENT AVAILABILITY REQUIREMENTS

These documents containing information about tax-exempt organizations generally must be filed with the IRS: the application for recognition of tax exemption and supporting documents (such as governing instruments, exhibits, and legal memoranda), any statements as to changes in material facts, and annual information returns. Another pertinent document is, of course, any ruling as to exempt (and, where applicable, public charity/private foundation) status.

(a) Availability Through IRS

Generally, the IRS must disclose the text of any written determination and any background file document relating to such a determination.[122] A *written determination* is a ruling, determination letter, technical advice memorandum, or chief

---

[122] IRC § 6110(a).

counsel advice.[123] The term *background file document* includes the request for the determination, any written material submitted in support of the request, and certain communications between the IRS and other persons.[124] Before the IRS makes a written determination public, the agency is required to delete (redact) certain identifying information, including the "names, addresses, and other identifying details of the person to whom the written determination pertains."[125]

This body of law does not, however, apply to all written determinations from the IRS. For example, the general disclosure rule does not apply to "any matter to which section 6104 . . . applies."[126] That section of the Internal Revenue Code makes available for public inspection tax information relating to specified entities.

One of the provisions of this law requires the IRS to disclose documents relating to tax-exempt organizations, including applications or recognition of exemption, supporting materials, and IRS determinations granting the exemptions.[127] This body of law does not contain a requirement that identifying information be redacted.[128] The tax regulations accompanying this statutory regime are based on the premise that the more specific rule[129] applies to all determinations concerning tax-exempt status.[130]

Thus, the application for recognition of tax exemption and any supporting documents filed by most exempt organizations[131] must be made accessible to the public by the IRS where a favorable determination letter is issued to the organization.[132] Where there is no prescribed application form, the documents filed with the IRS that led to the issuance of an exemption ruling become publicly available under these rules. These rules are triggered by a finding that an organization is exempt for any year, even though the organization may subsequently lose its exemption.

Information contained in the application or supporting documents may relate to a trade secret, patent, process, style of work, or apparatus. An organization, the application for recognition of exemption of which is open to public inspection, may request in writing that this information be withheld. The information will be withheld from public inspection if the IRS determines that disclosure of it would adversely affect the organization.[133] A *written determination* is a

---

[123] IRC § 6110(b)(1)(A).

[124] IRC § 6110(b)(2).

[125] IRC § 6110(c).

[126] IRC § 6110(l)(1).

[127] These rules also apply with respect to notices filed by political organizations (see § 23.6, *infra* § viii).

[128] A different disclosure regime is applicable with respect to pension, profit-sharing, and like plans (IRC § 6104(a)(1)(B)). This rule requires disclosure of applications and written determinations regarding tax exemptions for the funds underlying these plans. This provision references "any applications" filed with the IRS, which encompasses those that result in a grant or denial of the application (and perhaps revocation of exemption).

[129] That is, IRC § 6104.

[130] Thus, the regulations associated with IRC § 6110 state that matters within the ambit of IRC § 6104 include applications and related documents pertaining to the granting, denying, or revoking of tax-exempt status (Reg. § 301.6110-1(a)).

[131] That is, those entities described in IRC § 501(c) or 501(d).

[132] IRC § 6104(a)(1)(A). This disclosure requirement is confined to papers submitted in support of the application by the organization (Reg. § 301.6104(a)-1(e)). It does not apply to papers submitted by any other person, such as a member of Congress (Lehrfeld v. Richardson, 132 F.3d 1463 (D.C. Cir. 1998)).

[133] Reg. § 301.6104(a)-5.

ruling, determination letter, technical advice memorandum, or chief counsel advice.[134] The term *background file document* includes the request for the determination, any written material submitted in support of the request, and certain communications between the IRS and other persons.[135] Before the IRS makes a written determination public, the agency is required to delete (redact) certain identifying information, including the "names, addresses, and other identifying details of the person to whom the written determination pertains."[136]

Once an organization's application for recognition of exemption, and related and supporting documents, become open to public inspection, the determination letter (ruling) issued by the IRS also becomes publicly available. Also open to inspection under these rules are any technical advice memoranda issued with respect to any favorable ruling. A favorable ruling recognizing an organization's tax-exempt status may be issued by the National Office; these rulings and the underlying applications for recognition of tax exemption are available for inspection in the IRS Freedom of Information Reading Room in Washington, D.C.[137]

According to the tax regulations, certain determinations issued by the IRS in the tax-exempt organizations context, however, are not open to public inspection. These include (1) unfavorable rulings issued in response to applications for recognition of exemption, (2) rulings revoking or modifying a favorable ruling, (3) technical advice memoranda relating to a disapproved application for recognition of exemption, and (4) any letter filed with or issued by the IRS relating to an organization's status as a nonprivate foundation or as a private operating foundation.[138] A federal court of appeals held that the IRS and a tax-exempt organization are not required to disclose the contents of a closing agreement[139] between them.[140]

The foregoing statutory and regulatory framework was found to be faulty by a federal court of appeals, with the court voiding the regulations prohibiting disclosure of denials or revocations of exemption, on the ground that these regulations are in conflict with the statutes.[141] The IRS asserted that the general disclosure rule[142] is "ambiguous" and that the regulations reflect a reasonable interpretation of the statutory scheme. The appellate court disagreed, "discern[ing] no ambiguity" in the statute; the provision was held to be "straightforward."[143] The exception provision was held to be applicable only with respect to *tax-exempt* organizations; the court of appeals wrote that the provision "says nothing about documents relating to non-exempt organizations."[144] The IRS argued that its interpretation of the law leads to a conclusions by means of

---

[134] IRC § 6110(b)(1)(A).

[135] IRC § 6110(b)(2).

[136] IRC § 6110(b)(2).

[137] Notice 92-28, 1992-1 C.B. 515.

[138] Reg. § 301.6104(a)-1(i). Also Christian Coalition Int'l v. United States, 90 A.F.T.R. 2d 6010 (E.D. Va. 2002).

[139] Closing agreements are the subject of IRC § 7121.

[140] Tax Analysts v. Internal Revenue Service & Christian Broadcasting Network, Inc., 410 F.3d 715 (D.C. Cir. 2005).

[141] Tax Analysts v. Internal Revenue Service, 350 F.3d 100 (D.C. Cir. 2003), *rev'g* 215 F. Supp. 2d 192 (D.D.C. 2002).

[142] That is, IRC § 6110.

[143] Tax Analysts v. Internal Revenue Service, 350 F.3d 100, 103 (D.C. Cir. 2003).

[144] *Id.*

"negative implication" that Congress did not intend disclosure of documents involving denials or revocations of exemption.[145] To counter this, the court observed that "Congress knew exactly how to refer to denials and revocations when it so intended,"[146] referring to the rules concerning pension and like plans.[147] The appellate court thus concluded that the IRS must disclose determinations denying or revoking tax exemptions but do so in redacted form.[148]

An application and related materials may be inspected at the appropriate IRS service center. Inspection may also occur at the National Office of the IRS; a request for inspection should be directed to the Assistant to the Commissioner (Public Affairs), 1111 Constitution Avenue, N.W., Washington, D.C. 20224.[149]

The excise tax return filed by private foundations (Form 4720) is disclosable to the public.[150] This return as filed by a person other than a foundation (as well as one filed in the intermediate sanctions context) is not disclosable. Therefore, if disclosure of the return filed by a person other than a private foundation is not desired, the person should file separately rather than jointly with the foundation, inasmuch as the joint filing is disclosable.[151]

These document availability rules are applicable to the notice that must be filed by political organizations to establish their tax-exempt status[152] and to the reports that they must file.[153]

The IRS is required to make publicly available, at its offices and on the Internet, a list of all political organizations that file this notice, and the name, address, electronic mailing address, custodian of records and contact person for these organizations.[154] This information must be made available not later than five business days after the notice is received.

If the IRS assesses a fee in connection with the production of this information (including photocopying), the fee may not be in excess of the fee that would

---

[145] *Id.*

[146] *Id.*

[147] See text accompanied by *supra* note 128.

[148] The IRS, in compliance with this appellate court order, commenced disclosure of what it termed Exemption Denial and Revocation Letters; after a few months, it ceased issuing these letters by that name and began issuing them as private letter rulings.

Despite this appellate court holding, it appears, by application of standard rules of statutory construction, that Congress intended that IRC § 6104(a)(1)(A) be its sole statement as to what exempt organization written determinations are to be made public. Also, in 2000, the staff of the Joint Committee on Taxation made recommendations as to tax law disclosures, including a proposal that the IRS make exempt organization revocation and denial rulings open to the public (see XVII *Nonprofit Counsel* (No. 4) 4 (April 2000)); obviously, that recommendation would have been unnecessary had this court of appeals been correct. The Senate passed legislation to make IRC § 6110 applicable to written determinations and related background file documents relating to tax-exempt organizations, including determinations denying recognition of exempt status (Charity Aid, Recovery, and Empowerment Act of 2003 § 201 (S. 476, 108th Cong., 1st Sess. (2003)); again, if this decision were correct, the Senate legislation would be superfluous. In general, Hogan, "What's CARE Got to Do with It? *Tax Analysts v. Internal Revenue Service* and the CARE Act of 2003," 57 *Tax Law.* (No. 4) 921 (Summer 2004); Dobrovir, "Anatomy of a Regulation: How Far the IRS Will Go to Hide Its Law," 44 *Exempt Org. Tax Rev.* (No. 2) 179 (May 2004).

[149] Reg. § 301.6104(a)-6.

[150] Reg. § 1.6033-2(a)(ii)(j).

[151] T.D. 7785, 1981-2 C.B. 233.

[152] See *Tax-Exempt Organizations* § 23.6.

[153] See *id.* § 24.3(d).

[154] IRC § 6104(a)(3).

be assessed under the fee schedule promulgated pursuant to the Freedom of Information Act.[155]

(b) Disclosure by Exempt Organizations

A tax-exempt organization is required to disclose, and generally is required to disseminate, its most recent three annual information returns and application for recognition of exemption, although there are exceptions from the document dissemination rules.[156]

(i) General Rules. Under the law in effect before 1999, the general rules were that a tax-exempt organization[157] must make its application for recognition of exemption[158] available for public inspection without charge, during regular business hours, at its principal, regional, and district offices.[159] In addition, it must make its annual information returns available for public inspection without charge, during regular business hours, in the same offices.[160] Each return must be made available for a period of three years, beginning on the date the return is required to be filed or is actually filed, whichever is later.[161]

In addition, as of the 1999 effective date, the general rule is that a tax-exempt organization must provide a copy without charge, other than a reasonable fee for reproduction and actual postage costs, of all or any part of any application for recognition of exemption or return required to be made available for public inspection to any individual who makes a request for the copy in person or in writing.[162]

Subsequently, these rules were made applicable to private foundations. Separate regulations to this end became final in early 2000,[163] making foundations subject to these disclosure requirements as of March 13, 2000.[164]

---

[155] Reg. §§ 301.6104(a)-6(d), 301.6104(b)-1(d). Generally, this rate currently is $.20 per page.

[156] IRC § 6104(d); Reg. § 301.6104(d)-1(h)(1). Generally, the names and addresses of donors need not be disclosed (IRC § 6104(d)(3)(A)) (but see *infra* note 168) and certain information can be withheld from public inspection, such as trade secrets and patents (IRC § 6104(d)(3)(B), (a)(1)(D)).

[157] That is, an organization described in IRC § 501(c) or (d).

[158] See §§ 2.2, 2.3. This requirement embraces papers submitted in support of the application and any documents issued by the IRS with respect to the application (IRC § 6104(d)(5)).

[159] IRC § 6104(d)(1)(A). This requirement is inapplicable with respect to an application filed before July 15, 1987, unless the organization that filed it had a copy of it on that date (Reg. § 301.6104(d)-1(b)(3)(iii)(B)).

[160] IRC § 6104(d)(1)(A).

[161] IRC § 6104(d)(2). IRS rules (Notice 88-120, 1988-2 C.B. 454) reinforce the point that exact copies of these documents are required. This means that, for charitable (IRC § 501(c)(3)) organizations, the compensation of key employees must be disclosed.

Organizations that are covered by a group exemption (see *Tax-Exempt Organizations* § 23.7) and do not file their own annual information returns, and that receive a request for inspection, must acquire a copy of the group return from the central organization and make the material available to the requestor within a reasonable amount of time (Notice 88-120, 1988-2 C.B. 454). Alternatively, the requestor can request, from the central organization, inspection of the group return at the principal office of the central organization (*id.*). Similar rules apply with respect to the document dissemination requirements (Reg. § 6104(d)-1(f)).

[162] IRC § 6104(d)(1)(B); Reg. § 301.6104(d)-1(d).

[163] T.D. 8861.

[164] Reg. § 301.6104(d)-1(h)(2). In contrast to the general rule (see *supra* note 155), private foundations are required to disclose information as to their donors.

(ii) Rules as to Inspection. A tax-exempt organization must make its application for recognition of exemption available for public inspection without charge at its principal, regional, and district offices during regular business hours.[165] Likewise, an exempt organization must make its annual information returns available for public inspection without charge in the same offices during regular business hours.[166] Each annual information return must be made available for a period of three years.

(iii) Rules as to Copies. Generally, a tax-exempt organization must provide copies of the documents, in response to an in-person request, at its principal, regional, and district offices during regular business hours. Also generally, the organization must provide the copies to a requestor on the day the request is made.[167]

In the case of an in-person request, when unusual circumstances exist so that fulfillment of the request on the same business day places an unreasonable burden on the exempt organization, the copies must be provided on the next business day following the day on which the unusual circumstances cease to exist or the fifth business day after the date of the request, whichever occurs first. *Unusual circumstances* include receipt of a volume of requests that exceeds the organization's daily capacity to make copies, requests received shortly before the end of regular business hours that require an extensive amount of copying, and requests received on a day when the organization's managerial staff capable of fulfilling the request is conducting special duties. *Special duties* are activities such as student registration or attendance at an off-site meeting or convention, rather than regular administrative duties.[168]

If a request for a document is made in writing, the tax-exempt organization must honor it if the request:

- Is addressed to, and delivered by mail, electronic mail, facsimile, or a private delivery service to a principal, regional, or district office of the organization

- Sets forth the address to which the copy of the document should be sent[169]

A tax-exempt organization receiving a written request for a copy must mail the copy within 30 days from the date it receives the request. If, however, an exempt organization requires payment in advance, it is only required to provide the copy within 30 days from the date it receives payment. An exempt organization must fulfill a request for a copy of the organization's entire application or annual information return or any specific part or schedule of its application or return.[170]

A tax-exempt organization may charge a reasonable fee for providing copies. The photocopying fee that may be charged by an exempt organization is not

---

[165] Reg. § 301.6104(d)-1(a).
[166] *Id.*
[167] Reg. § 301.6104(d)-1(d)(1)(i).
[168] Reg. § 301.6104(d)-1(d)(1)(ii).
[169] Reg. § 301.6104(d)-1(d)(2)(i).
[170] Reg. § 301.6104(d)-1(d)(2)(ii).

reasonable if it is in excess of the comparable fee assessed by the IRS.[171] It can also include actual postage costs. The requestor may be required to pay the fee in advance.[172]

(iv) Failure to Comply.   If a tax-exempt organization denies an individual's request for inspection or a copy of an application or return, and the individual wishes to alert the IRS to the possible need for enforcement action, he or she may send a statement to the appropriate IRS district office, describing the reason why the individual believes the denial was in violation of these requirements.[173]

(v) Widely Available Exception.   A tax-exempt organization is not required to comply with requests for copies of its application for recognition of exemption or an annual information return if the organization has made the document widely available.[174] The rules as to public inspection of the documents nonetheless continue to apply.

A tax-exempt organization can make its application or a return *widely available* by posting the document on a Web page that the organization establishes and maintains. It can also satisfy this exception if the document is posted as part of a database of similar documents of other exempt organizations on a Web page established and maintained by another entity.[175]

The document is considered widely available only if:

- The Web page through which it is available clearly informs readers that the document is available and provides instructions for downloading it.

- The document is posted in a format that, when accessed, downloaded, viewed, and printed in hard copy, exactly reproduces the image of the application or return as it was originally filed with the IRS, except for any information permitted by statute to be withheld from public disclosure.

- Any individual with access to the Internet can access, download, view, and print the document without special computer hardware or software required for that format, and can do so without payment of a fee to the exempt organization or to another entity maintaining the Web page.[176]

The organization maintaining the Web page must have procedures for ensuring the reliability and accuracy of the documents that it posts on the page. It must take reasonable precautions to prevent alteration, destruction, or accidental loss of the document when printed on its page. In the event a posted document is altered, destroyed, or lost, the organization must correct or replace the document.[177]

---

[171] Reg. §§ 301.6104(a)-6(d), 301.6104(b)-1(d). See text accompanied by and text of *supra* note 154.
[172] Reg. § 301.6104(d)-1(d)(3).
[173] Reg. § 301.6104(d)-1(g).
[174] IRC § 6104(d)(4); Reg. § 301.6104(d)-2(a).
[175] Reg. § 301.6104(d)-2(b)(2)(i).
[176] *Id.*
[177] Reg. § 301.6104(d)-2(b)(2)(iii).

(vi) Harassment Campaign Exception.   If the IRS determines that a tax-exempt organization is the subject of a harassment campaign and that compliance with the requests that are part of the campaign would not be in the public interest, the organization is not required to fulfill a request for a copy that it reasonably believes is part of the campaign.[178]

A group of requests for a tax-exempt organization's application or returns is indicative of a harassment campaign if the requests are part of a single coordinated effort to disrupt the operations of the organization, rather than to collect information about it. This is a facts-and-circumstances test; factors include a sudden increase in the number of requests, an extraordinary number of requests made by means of form letters or similarly worded correspondence, evidence of a purpose to deter significantly the exempt organization's employees or volunteers from pursuing the organization's exempt purpose, requests that contain language hostile to the organization, direct evidence of bad faith by organizers of the purported harassment campaign, evidence that the organization has already provided the requested documents to a member of the purported harassment group, and a demonstration by the exempt organization that it routinely provides copies of its documents on request.[179]

A tax-exempt organization may disregard any request for copies of all or part of any document beyond the first two received within any 30-day period or the first four received within any one-year period from the same individual or the same address, irrespective of whether the IRS has determined that the organization is subject to a harassment campaign.[180]

There is a procedure to follow for applying to the IRS for a determination that the organization is the subject of a harassment campaign. (There is no form.) The organization may suspend compliance with respect to the request, as long as the application is filed within 10 days after harassment is suspected, until the organization receives a response from the IRS.[181]

(vii) Penalties.   A person failing to allow inspection of an organization's annual information returns is subject to a penalty of $20 per day for each day the failure continues, absent reasonable cause, with a maximum penalty per return of $10,000.[182] A person failing to allow inspection of an organization's application for recognition of tax exemption must, absent reasonable cause, pay $20 per day for each day the failure continues.[183] A person who willfully fails to comply with these inspection requirements is subject to a penalty of $5,000 with respect to each return or application.[184]

---

[178] IRC § 6104(d)(4); Reg. § 301.6104(d)-3(a).
[179] Reg. § 301.6104(d)-3(b).
[180] Reg. § 301.6104(d)-3(c).
[181] Reg. § 301.6104(d)-3(d), (e).
[182] IRC § 6652(c)(1)(C), (3).
[183] IRC § 6652(c)(1)(D), (3).
[184] IRC § 6685. In general, Sullivan, "New IRS Regulations Will Make Information About Nonprofit Health Care Providers Widely Available," 24 *Exempt Org. Tax Rev.* (No. 2) 307 (May 1999); Ellingsworth & Horning, "New Public Disclosures Rules Present Opportunities and Challenges to Exempt Organizations," 23 *Exempt Org. Tax Rev.* (No. 1) 55 (Jan. 1999).

(viii) Political Organizations. These document availability rules are applicable to the notice that must be filed by political organizations to establish their tax-exempt status[185] and to the reports that they must file.[186]

(ix) Return Preparation. With the annual information return a public document, it is important that it be prepared accurately and completely. This is easier to state than to do, for the preparers of today's annual information return often are expected to make determinations as to which there is little guidance, in law and in accounting, as to how to do them. These judgments include functional accounting of expenses,[187] allocations as between types of legislative activities,[188] separation of related and unrelated activities,[189] and the availability of a host of exceptions to unrelated income taxation.[190] Nonetheless, the annual information return is an excellent means by which to present an organization's programs and other activities in the best possible light to the public, the media, and the IRS (perhaps thereby avoiding an audit). The return also is an effective tool for the management of a tax-exempt organization to use to assess the programmatic and financial circumstances and progress of the organization.[191]

§ 10.3 DISCLOSURES REGARDING CERTAIN INFORMATION OR SERVICES

A tax-exempt organization[192] must pay a penalty if it fails to disclose that information or services it is offering are available without charge from the federal government.

Specifically, this penalty may be imposed if (1) a tax-exempt organization offers to sell (or solicits money for) specific information or a routine service for any individual that could be readily obtained by the individual without charge (or for a nominal charge) from an agency of the federal government; (2) the exempt organization, when making the offer or solicitation, fails to make an "express statement (in a conspicuous and easily recognizable format)" that the information or service can be so obtained; and (3) the failure is due to "intentional disregard" of these requirements.[193]

This requirement applies only if the information to be provided involves the specific individual solicited. Thus, for example, the requirement applies with respect to obtaining the social security earnings record or the social security

---

[185] See *Tax-Exempt Organizations* § 23.6.

[186] See *id.* § 24.3(d).

[187] See § 10.5(c).

[188] See *Tax-Exempt Organizations*, Chapter 20.

[189] See Chapter 5.

[190] *Id.*

[191] In early 2000, the staff of the Joint Committee on Taxation issued a report containing a massive set of proposals to substantially expand the disclosure requirements imposed on tax-exempt organizations. In general, Faber, "The Joint Committee Staff Disclosure Recommendations: What They Mean for Exempt Organizations," 28 *Exempt Org. Tax Rev.* (No. 1) 31 (April 2000).

[192] That is, an entity described in IRC §§ 501 (c) or (d) and exempt from federal income tax under IRC § 501(a), or a political organization as defined in IRC § 527(e).

[193] IRC § 6711(a). IRS guidelines (Notice 88-120, 1988-2 C.B. 454) state that if materials and/or services are available from the federal government for less than $2.50 (including postage and handling costs), the materials are considered by the IRS as being available from the federal government at a nominal charge.

identification number of an individual solicited, while the requirement is inapplicable with respect to the furnishing of copies of newsletters issued by federal agencies or providing copies of or descriptive material on pending legislation. Also, this requirement is inapplicable to the provision of professional services (such as tax return preparation, grant application preparation, or medical services), as opposed to routine information retrieval services, to an individual even if they may be available from the federal government without charge or at a nominal charge.[194]

The penalty, which is applicable for each day on which the failure occurred, is the greater of $1,000 or 50 percent of the aggregate cost of the offers and solicitations that occurred on any day on which the failure occurred and with respect to which there was this type of failure.[195]

§ 10.4 STATE LAW REQUIREMENTS

A tax-exempt business league is likely to be required to file annual reports in compliance with the law of the state in which it was formed, the state in which it is headquartered (if different), and any other state in which it does business. This reporting requirement is far more likely if the business league is formed as a corporation.

These same requirements are likely to be applicable to a foundation that is related to the exempt business league.[196] There may be separate reporting requirements in the case of a related foundation that is soliciting charitable contributions.[197]

State reporting requirements are likely to be applicable to other entities affiliated with a tax-exempt business league, such as a political action committee,[198] a for-profit subsidiary,[199] and/or a joint venture in which the business league (or a related entity) is a member or other participant.[200]

§ 10.5 SPECIFIC REPORTING REQUIREMENTS OF ASSOCIATIONS

Certain portions of the basic federal annual information return (Form 990) are particularly or uniquely applicable to tax-exempt business leagues.

(a) Web Site Address

The opening portion of the annual information return requests the filing organization's Web site address.[201] Inasmuch as officials of the IRS, other governmental officials, representatives of the media, and many other persons visit these sites, it

---

[194] Notice 88-120, 1988-2 C.B. 454.
[195] IRC § 6711(b).
[196] See Chapter 8.
[197] See Chapter 9.
[198] See § 4.7.
[199] See Chapter 6.
[200] See Chapter 7.
[201] Form 990, item G.

is important that these organizations be certain that material posted on their Web sites does not contravene the federal tax and other laws.

(b) Revenue

Tax-exempt organizations are required, in preparing the annual information return for submission to the IRS, to report their items of revenue. For exempt associations, the items to report that are likely to be the most pertinent are membership dues and assessments[202] and program service revenue.[203] Associations can have, of course, other forms of revenue, such as interest,[204] dividends,[205] and rent.[206] Associations are unlikely to receive contributions[207]; they may receive grants from governmental entities.[208]

(c) Statement of Functional Expenses

All tax-exempt organizations are required to report their expenses on the annual information return.[209] Unlike exempt charitable and social welfare organizations, however, exempt business leagues are not required to report their expenses on a functional basis.[210]

(d) Program Service Accomplishments

All tax-exempt organizations are required to describe, in a "clear and concise manner," their exempt purpose achievements.[211] Unlike exempt charitable and social welfare organizations, however, exempt business leagues are not required to report any amount of grants or allocations to others, nor are they required to report their program service expenses.

In this portion of the return, an exempt business league inventories the principal services provided to its members, such as conferences and seminars, publications, advocacy efforts, and community outreach programs.[212] This analysis should include the number of members served by the organization's programs.

(e) Changes in Operations and Documents

The reporting business league is asked whether it engaged in any activity not previously reported to the IRS and, if so, to attach a "detailed description" of each activity.[213] This requirement, however, is confined to the reporting of operational changes that are material. Thus, an association that has undertaken one or more substantive programs not reflected in its application for recognition of

---

[202] *Id.*, Part I, line 3.

[203] *Id.*, line 2.

[204] *Id.*, line 4.

[205] *Id.*, line 5.

[206] *Id.*, line 6.

[207] *Id.*, line 1.

[208] *Id.*, line 1c.

[209] *Id.*, Part II, column (A).

[210] That is, exempt business leagues are not required to complete Form 990, Part II, columns (B)–(D).

[211] Form 990, Part III.

[212] See §§ 1.3, 2.4.

[213] Form 990, Part VI, line 76.

exemption (if any)[214] or subsequently reported to the IRS as part of a previous annual information return or other separate filing should submit a description of these programs with the return. The same is true if the association ceased operation of one or more substantive programs.

The business league is also asked whether any changes were made in its "organizing or governing documents" not previously reported to the IRS and, if so, to attach a "conformed copy" of the changes.[215] Again, an association with changes in its documents of this nature should submit them with the return.

(f) Unrelated Business Activity

If a tax-exempt association has gross unrelated business income[216] of at least $1,000, it should so state as part of the return.[217] In this case, it is required to file an unrelated business income tax return for the year[218] and thus be able to indicate, on the annual information return, that it complied with that requirement.[219]

(g) Related Organizations

Tax-exempt associations are often related to one or more exempt and/or nonexempt organizations. This relatedness usually is manifested through an interlocking directorate, a membership, or stock. (This rule does not extend to situations where the association is a member of an association, such as a state association as a member of a national association.) These related entities may include a related foundation,[220] a political action committee,[221] and/or a for-profit subsidiary.[222] The reporting association should, if there is one or more related organization, report that information on the return, identifying the entity or entities by name and indicating whether the entity is tax-exempt or nonexempt.[223]

(h) Political Expenditures

If an association has made, directly or indirectly, any political expenditure during the reporting year, that fact should be reflected on the return.[224] A *political expenditure* is an expenditure intended to influence the selection, nomination, election, or appointment of one or more individuals to a federal, state, or local public office.[225] It is irrelevant as to whether the attempt was successful. The

---

[214] See § 2.2.
[215] Form 990, Part VI, line 77.
[216] See Chapter 5.
[217] Form 990, Part VI, line 78a.
[218] See § 10.7.
[219] Form 990, Part VI, line 78b.
[220] See Chapter 8.
[221] See § 4.7.
[222] See Chapter 6.
[223] Form 990, Part VI, line 80.
[224] *Id.*, line 81a.
[225] See § 4.7(a). An expenditure includes a payment, distribution, loan, advance, deposit, or gift of money or anything of value. It also includes a contract, promise, or agreement to make an expenditure, whether legally enforceable or not.

association should also indicate whether it filed a Form 1120-POL for that year.[226]

(i) Public Inspection Requirements

Associations and similar organizations are subject to public inspection requirements as to their application for recognition of exemption and recent annual information returns.[227] Compliance with this body of law should be reported on the annual information return.[228]

(j) Deductibility of Dues

The annual information return poses questions as to the deductibility of dues under circumstances where a tax-exempt association (or like entity) engaged in attempts to influence legislation and/or political activities during the reporting year.[229] This portion of the return is applicable to exempt business leagues and similar organizations,[230] exempt social welfare organizations,[231] and exempt labor organizations.[232]

The two exceptions to these rules are reflected on the return: where (1) substantially all of the dues are nondeductible by the association's members[233] and/or (2) the organization made only in-house lobbying expenditures of no more than $2,000.[234] If either of these exceptions applies, the association should not complete the balance of the annual information return on this subject, unless it received a waiver for proxy tax owed for the prior year.

Otherwise, the association is required to provide the total amount of dues, assessments, and similar amounts from members.[235] The term *dues* means the amount the organization requires a member to pay in order to be recognized as a member. Payments that are *similar* to dues include members' voluntary payments,[236] assessments to cover basic operating costs, and special assessments to conduct lobbying and/or political activities.

---

[226] Form 990, Part VI, line 81b. If a tax-exempt business league establishes and maintains a separate segregated fund (political organization), it is the responsibility of the fund to file Form 1120-POL (assuming the fund is required to file that form). Nonetheless, if an exempt business league (or most other exempt organizations) transfers its own funds to a separate segregated fund for use as political expenses, the business league must report the transferred funds as its own political expenditures on its Form 990.

[227] See § 10.2(b).

[228] Form 990, Part VI, line 83a.

[229] Form 990, Part VI, line 85. See §§ 4.2, 4.5.

[230] That is, organizations described in IRC § 501(c)(6) and tax-exempt by reason of IRC § 501(c)(6).

[231] See § 1.6(a).

[232] See § 1.6(c).

[233] Form 990, Part VI, line 85a.

[234] *Id.*, line 85b.

[235] *Id.*, line 85c.

[236] It is unlikely that a member of a business league or similar entity would make a contribution to the organization. If this is done, a business expense deduction is not available (Reg. § 1.162-15(b)). Also, if the amount of this type of gift is in excess of the federal gift tax annual exclusion amount (currently $11,000) (IRC § 2503), there is potential gift tax exposure for the excess amount (e.g., Priv. Ltr. Rul. 200533001). See *Charitable Giving* § 8.2(h).

Absent the availability of one of these exceptions, the association must report the amount of any lobbying and/or political expenditures.[237] These are expenses paid or incurred during the reporting year in connection with:

- Attempting to influence legislation
- Participating or intervening in a political campaign on behalf of or in opposition to a candidate for a public office
- Attempting to influence a segment of the public with respect to elections, legislative matters, or referenda
- Communicating directly with a covered executive branch official in an attempt to influence the official actions or positions of such official

Also, the association should report:

- Excess lobbying and political expenditures carried over from the preceding tax year
- An amount equal to the taxable lobbying and political expenditures reported[238] for the preceding tax year, if the organization received a waiver of the proxy tax imposed on that amount

The association should not include in this reporting:

- Any direct lobbying of a local council or similar governing body with respect to legislation of direct interest to the organization or its members
- In-house direct lobbying expenditures, if the total of these expenditures is no more than $2,000 (excluding allocable overhead)
- Political expenditures for which the political organizations tax has been paid[239]

The association is required to report the total amount of dues and the like allocable to the reporting year that members were notified were nondeductible.[240] Also to be reported is the taxable amount of lobbying and political expenditures.[241]

The organization must indicate whether it is electing to pay the proxy tax.[242] The organization also must respond to the question as to whether, if dues notices were sent, the organization agrees to add the taxable amount of lobbying and political expenditures to its reasonable estimate of dues allocable to nondeductible lobbying and political expenditures for the following tax year.[243]

---

[237] Form 990, Part VI, line 85d. See Chapter 4.
[238] That is, reported on Form 990, Part VI, line 85f (see text accompanied by *infra* note 240).
[239] This tax is reported and paid by means of Form 1120-POL.
[240] Form 990, Part VI, line 85e.
[241] *Id.*, line 85f. This is the amount on line 85d (see text accompanied by *supra* note 236) less the amount on line 85e (see text accompanied by *supra* note 239).
[242] Form 990, Part VI, line 85g.
[243] *Id.*, line 85h.

(k) Income-Producing Activities

A tax-exempt association is required to report and characterize the various sources of its income.[244] For exempt associations, the most likely of these entries are program service revenue,[245] membership dues and assessments, and investment income.

(l) Subsidiaries and Disregarded Entities

Tax-associations are required to report information concerning their use of taxable subsidiaries and/or entities that are disregarded for federal tax purposes.[246]

§ 10.6   SPECIFIC REPORTING REQUIREMENTS OF ASSOCIATION-RELATED FOUNDATIONS

Certain portions of the basic federal annual information return (Form 990) are particularly or uniquely applicable to association-related foundations.

(a) Recapitulations

Some of the items summarized in the preceding section are also applicable with respect to association-related foundations: the matter of the Web site address, reporting of expenses on a functional basis, program service accomplishments, changes in operations and documents, unrelated business activity, related organizations, compliance with the public inspection requirements, reporting of income-producing activities, and use of subsidiaries and/or disregarded entities.[247]

(b) Revenue

For tax-exempt association-related foundations, the items of revenue to be reported, that are likely to be most pertinent, are contributions and grants,[248] program service revenue,[249] and investment income.[250] These foundations may also report revenue from special fundraising events.[251]

(c) Fundraising Expenses

Association-related foundations are likely to have fundraising expenses. Professional fundraising fees are required to be identified.[252] All other fundraising expenses are reported on a functional basis.[253] The IRS is likely to be concerned if a charitable organization reports a large amount of contributions and grants and little or no fundraising expenses.

---

[244] *Id.*, Part VII.
[245] *Id.*, line 93.
[246] *Id.*, Part IX.
[247] See § 10.5(a), (c)–(g), (i), (k), and (l), respectively.
[248] Form 990, Part I, line 1.
[249] *Id.*, line 2.
[250] *Id.*, lines 4–8.
[251] *Id.*, line 9.
[252] *Id.*, Part II, line 30.
[253] *Id.*, columns (A), (D).

(d) Other Information

An association-related foundation presumably will not have any political expenditures to report.[254] Such foundations may have occasion to report the value of donated services and/or the use of materials, equipment, or facilities[255]; compliance with the *quid pro quo* contributions rules[256]; taxes paid for excessive lobbying expenditures[257]; and/or information about its involvement in one or more excess benefit transactions.[258] The filing of Schedule A is required and presumably Schedule B is as well.[259]

§ 10.7 UNRELATED BUSINESS INCOME TAX RETURN

Revenue and expenses associated with unrelated business activity[260] by a tax-exempt organization are reported to the IRS on Form 990-T.[261] This form is a *tax return*, rather than an *information return*.

A tax-exempt organization with unrelated business taxable income must file, in addition to Form 990 or Form 990-EZ (or, in the case of a private foundation, Form 990-PF), Form 990-T. It is on this form that the source (or sources) of unrelated income is reported and any tax computed.[262]

Tax-exempt organizations must report their unrelated trade or business income.[263] These reporting obligations are less where the unrelated trade or business gross income is no more than $10,000.

All forms of unrelated trade or business gross income must be reported, along with associated deductions.[264] Separate schedules pertain to rental income,[265] unrelated debt-financed income,[266] investment income of those organizations that must treat that type of income as unrelated business income,[267] income (other than dividends) from controlled organizations,[268] exploited exempt activity income (other than advertising income),[269] and advertising income.[270]

The unrelated business income tax return is due on or before the 15th day of the fifth month following the close of the tax-exempt organization's tax year.[271]

---

[254] *Id.*, Part VI, line 81. See *Tax-Exempt Organizations*, Chapter 21 § 10.5(h).

[255] *Id.*, line 82.

[256] *Id.*, line 83b. See § 9.5.

[257] Form 990, Part VI, line 89a. See *Tax-Exempt Organizations* § 20.6.

[258] Form 990, Part VI, line 89b.

[259] See § 10.1(a)(ii), (iii).

[260] See Chapter 5.

[261] IRC § 6012(a)(2)(4); Reg. §§ 1.6012-2(e), 1.6012-3(a)(5), 1.6033-2(i). This form is reproduced in Appendix F.

[262] Reg. § 1.6012(e).

[263] See § 5.1.

[264] Form 990-T, Parts I, II.

[265] Form 990-T, Schedule C. See § 5.8(g).

[266] Form 990-T, Schedule E. See § 5.9.

[267] Form 990-T, Schedule F. These organizations are social clubs (see § 1.6(f)), voluntary employees beneficiary associations (see § 1.6(h)), and supplemental unemployment benefit trusts (see *Tax-Exempt Organizations* § 16.4).

[268] Form 990-T, Schedule G. See § 5.10.

[269] Form 990-T, Schedule H. See § 5.7(e).

[270] Form 990-T, Schedule I. See § 5.8.

[271] IRC § 6072(e); Reg. § 1.6033-2(e). In general, see *Unrelated Business*, Chapter 11.

CHAPTER ELEVEN

Summary of Non–Tax Association Law

The law pertaining to tax-exempt associations involves more than the federal tax law. A summary of some of these other bodies of law follows.

§ 11.1 CORPORATE GOVERNANCE

The sweeping subject of corporate governance of nonprofit organization, traditionally nearly the sole province of state law, today is in the forefront of existing and developing federal law. Included are topics such as the composition, functions, and responsibilities of members of the governing boards of these organizations. The impetus for this potential expansion of this aspect of the law is, in part, scandals in the nonprofit, mostly charitable, sector and the enactment of corporate governance legislation pertaining to for-profit corporations.

Historic federal accounting reform and corporate responsibility legislation—the Sarbanes-Oxley Act—was signed into law in 2002. This measure is focused on publicly traded companies and large accounting firms, not tax-exempt organizations. The emergence of this law, however, raises a number of questions for exempt organizations, and leaders of these organizations often are voluntarily adopting many of its precepts.

(a) Terminology

Certain terms are essential to understand to appreciate the scope of this body of law as it relates to tax-exempt organizations.

An *audit committee* is a committee established "by and amongst" the board of directors of an issuer for the purpose of overseeing the accounting and financial reporting processes of the issuer and audits of the financial statements of the issuer.

An *audit report* is a document prepared following an audit performed for purposes of compliance by an issuer with the securities laws, and in which a public accounting firm either states the opinion of the firm regarding a financial statement, report, or other document, or asserts that such an opinion cannot be expressed.

A *code of ethics* means standards that are reasonably necessary to promote (1) honest and ethical conduct, including the handling of conflicts of interest;

(2) full, fair, accurate, timely, and understandable disclosure in reports of an issuer; and (3) compliance with applicable governmental rules and regulations.

A *financial expert* is an individual who has (1) an understanding of generally accepted accounting principles and financial statements; and (2) experience in the preparation or auditing of financial statements, the application of these principles, experience with internal accounting controls, and an understanding of audit committee functions.

An *issuer* is a for-profit corporation, the stock of which is registered pursuant to the federal securities laws, and that is otherwise required to comply with those laws, including the filing of reports (also known as a *public company*).

The term *nonaudit services* means any professional services provided to an issuer by a registered public accounting firm, other than those provided to an issuer in connection with an audit or review of the financial statements of an issuer.

A *public accounting firm* is a legal entity (such as a corporation or partnership) that is engaged in the practice of public accounting or preparing or issuing audit reports. A *registered public accounting firm* is a public accounting firm that is registered with the new Oversight Board.

(b) Principal Features of Law

(i) Public Company and Accounting Oversight Board. The Public Company and Accounting Oversight Board ("Board"), the members of which are appointed by the Securities and Exchange Commission ("SEC"), was established. The Board has five full-time members, with five-year terms, two of whom may be certified public accountants. These members must be "prominent," of "integrity and reputation," have a "demonstrated commitment to the interests of investors and the public," and have an "understanding of the responsibilities for and nature of the financial disclosures required of issuers under the securities laws and the obligations of accountants with respect to the preparation and issuance of audit reports with respect to such disclosures."

The purpose of this Board is to "oversee the audit of public companies that are subject to the securities laws, and related matters, in order to protect the interests of investors and further the public interest in the preparation of informative, accurate, and independent audit reports for companies the securities of which are sold to, and held by and for, public investors." The Board is required to submit an annual report to the SEC.

The Board is not part of the federal government but rather is a District of Columbia nonprofit corporation. Only Congress, however, can dissolve it. It is empowered to accept contributions. The statute is silent as to the tax-exempt status of the Board (the act is not tax legislation).

The Board's duties include: (1) registration of public accounting firms that prepare audit reports for issuers; (2) adoption of auditing, quality control, ethics, independence, and other standards relating to the preparation of audit reports for issuers; (3) conduct inspections of registered public accounting firms; (4) conduct investigations and disciplinary proceedings concerning, and impose sanctions on registered public accounting firms and persons associated with these firms; (5) otherwise promote "high professional standards among, and improve the quality of audit services offered by, registered public accounting firms and associated persons thereof"; and (6) enforce compliance with this law, rules of the Board, and related securities laws.

(ii) Board Funding. The Board established an "annual accounting support fee" for purposes of establishing and maintaining the Board. These fees (and fees to fund an accounting standards setting body) are paid by and allocated among issuers.

Funds collected by the Board from the assessment of penalties are used to fund a "merit scholarship program" for undergraduate and graduate students enrolled in accredited accounting degree programs. The board or an entity selected by it administers this program.

(iii) Registration with the Board. It is unlawful for a person that is not a registered public accounting firm to prepare or issue, or to participate in the preparation or issuance of, an audit report with respect to an issuer. The legislation detailed the contents of the application for registration, which includes a listing of clients (issuers) and the fees paid by them for audit and other services. These applications generally are publicly available.

Each registered public accounting firm pays a registration fee and an annual fee.

(iv) Standards. The Board established "auditing and related attestation standards, . . . quality control standards, and . . . ethical standards" used by registered public accounting firms in the preparation and issuance of audit reports.

These rules include a seven-year records retention requirement, a rule as to second partner review of audit reports, and rules describing in each audit report the scope of the auditor's "internal control structure and procedures of the issuer."

In this connection, the Board may establish advisory groups. It is to "cooperate on an ongoing basis" with these groups and with professional groups of accountants.

(v) Inspections. The Board conducts a "continuing program of inspections" to assess compliance by registered public accounting firms (and associated persons) with this law, rules of the SEC and the Board, or professional standards, in connection with its performance of audits, issuance of audit reports, and related matters.

If a firm regularly provides audit reports for more than 100 issuers, the inspection must be annual. Otherwise, the review must be at least once every three years. The board can adjust this inspection schedule and conduct special inspections.

(vi) Investigations. The Board established "fair procedures" for the investigation and disciplining of registered public accounting firms (and associated persons). These investigations pertain to alleged violations of this law, Board rules, and securities laws pertaining to the preparation and issuance of audit reports.

The statute detailed the procedures these investigations are to follow, including disciplinary procedures, sanctions, and suspensions.

(vii) Nonaudit Services.   The law amended the securities laws to generally make it unlawful for a registered public accounting firm, that performs for an issuer an audit, to provide to that issuer, contemporaneously with the audit, any nonaudit service. The Board has the authority to grant exemptions.

These services include bookkeeping services, financial information systems design and implementation, appraisal services, fairness opinions, actuarial services, internal audit outsourcing services, investment adviser services, and legal services.

(viii) Audit Partner Rotation.   The statute amended the securities laws to make it unlawful for a registered public accounting firm to provide audit services to an issuer if the lead (or coordinating) audit partner, or the audit partner responsible for reviewing the audit, has performed audit services for that issuer in each of the five previous fiscal years of the issuer.

The statute provides for a study of mandatory rotation of registered public accounting firms.

(ix) Audit Committees.   The law in essence mandated the creation and functioning of audit committees of issuers. This is done, in part, by requiring the SEC to in turn direct the national securities exchanges and associations to prohibit the listing of the securities of issuers who fail to establish and use these committees.

The audit committee of an issuer must be directly responsible for the appointment, compensation, and oversight of the work of a registered public accounting firm employed by the issuer for the purpose of preparing or issuing an audit report or related work. Each such registered public accounting firm must report directly to the audit committee.

Each member of an audit committee must be a member of the board of directors of the issuer involved. He or she may not accept any consulting, advisory, or other compensation from the issuer.

The SEC issued rules to require each issuer to disclose whether, and if not why not, the audit committee of the issuer is comprised of at least one member who is a financial expert.

(x) Corporate Responsibility.   The law requires the principal executive officer and principal financial officer of an issuer to certify each annual or quarterly report filed by the issuer in compliance with the securities laws. This includes certification that the report does not contain any untrue statement of a material fact or failure to state a material fact "necessary in order to make the statements made . . . not misleading."

If an issuer is required to prepare an accounting restatement due to the "material noncompliance" of the issuer, as a result of misconduct, with a financial reporting requirement under the securities laws, the chief executive officer and chief financial officer of the issuer must reimburse the issuer for any bonus or other incentive-based or equity-based compensation received by that individual from the issuer during a prior 12-month period. This disgorgement rule can also encompass profits realized from the sale of stock of the issuer.

It is generally unlawful for an issuer to extend or maintain credit in the form of a personal loan to or for any director or executive officer of that issuer. This includes the use of a subsidiary for this purpose.

A person who is the beneficial owner of more than 10 percent of any class of a registered equity security must file a statement with the SEC. This includes nonprofit organizations.

The SEC issued rules requiring each issuer to disclose whether, and if not why not, the issuer has adopted a code of ethics for senior financial officers.

(xi) Lawyers. The SEC, in accordance with this statute, issued rules setting forth minimum standards of professional conduct for lawyers practicing before the SEC. These rules require a lawyer to report evidence of a "major violation of securities law or breach of fiduciary duty or similar violation by the company" to the chief legal counsel or the chief executive officer of the company.

If there is not an appropriate response to the evidence presented, including remedial measures, the lawyer is to report the evidence to the audit committee of the issuer or another committee of the board.

(xii) Disgorgement Funds. If the SEC obtains a disgorgement order against a person for violation of the securities laws, and that includes a civil penalty, the penalty is to be added to and become part of a disgorgement fund for the benefit of the victims of the violation.

The SEC is authorized to accept and utilize gifts, bequests, and devises for one or more of these funds. (The law does not address the point, but these contributions are deductible as charitable gifts.)

(xiii) Real-Time Disclosures. This law amended the securities to require reporting issuers to disclose to the public, on a "rapid and current basis," additional information concerning material changes in the financial condition or operations of the issuer, in "plain English." This type of disclosure may include "trend and qualitative information and graphic presentations."

(xiv) Other Provisions. The SEC, pursuant to this law, issued rules for the disclosure of material off-balance sheet transactions. An accountant who conducts an audit of an issuer is required to maintain all audit or review work papers for five years. A criminal law provision concerns the knowing destruction or falsification of corporate records with intent to impede or influence a federal investigation.

(c) Import of Law for Tax-Exempt Organizations

This body of law does not, as noted, apply to tax-exempt organizations (other than the criminal law rule concerning destruction of evidence). Again, it applies to, and with respect to, *issuers* and *public accounting firms*.

Nonetheless, those who manage associations and other tax-exempt organizations, and perhaps those who make contributions to them, may want to give consideration to some or all of these points: whether (1) the accounting firm retained by an exempt organization should be a registered public accounting firm; (2) an exempt organization should have an audit committee or similar body; (3) an exempt organization should develop a code of ethics for its senior officers (this would go beyond a conflict-of-interest policy); (4) an exempt organization should require certification of its financial statements and/or annual information returns by its executive; (5) an exempt organization should have a policy of prohibiting loans to its senior executives; (6) in an instance of a need for an accounting restatement by an exempt organization, due to some form of misconduct, any bonuses and/or the like to executive personnel should be reimbursed; (7) an exempt organization should follow the rules as to audit partner rotation; (8) an exempt organization should separate audit and nonaudit service providers; (9) an exempt organization's lawyers should be required to report breaches of fiduciary responsibility to its executive; and (10) there should be a rule requiring real-time disclosures by tax-exempt organizations.

Congress may well enact corporate responsibility legislation applicable to tax-exempt organizations. Also, corporate responsibility principles applicable to exempt entities are embedded, directly or indirectly, in the application for recognition of exemption filed by charitable organizations[1] and annual information return.[2] The revisions of these documents reflect corporate responsibility concepts, such as the adoption of conflict-of-interest policies and governing board practices as to the setting and review of compensation arrangements with senior executives.

§ 11.2 BOARD MEMBER RESPONSIBILITIES AND DUTIES

In today's litigious society, avoidance of a lawsuit cannot be guaranteed. Rules prohibiting frivolous lawsuits are not fully enforced. There are, however, a number of steps that members of the board of a tax-exempt association can take to minimize the likelihood of a lawsuit against the organization—and against themselves.[3]

(a) Form

Every member of the board of a tax-exempt association should understand the form of the entity.[4] The board member should also know what is required to maintain that form—and see to it that the necessary action (or actions) is taken. For example, an organization that is incorporated can lose its corporate status if it fails to timely file annual reports with the state in which it is incorporated.

Moreover, if the association is not incorporated, it is incumbent on each board member to understand why that is the case. If the entity is to remain unincorporated, the board member should be satisfied by being provided (by a lawyer) at least one good reason for its status. An unincorporated organization almost always can become incorporated.

---

[1] Form 1023. See § 2.2.
[2] Form 990. See § 10.1; Appendix E.
[3] This analysis is equally applicable with respect to boards of association-related foundations (see § 8.8).
[4] See *Tax-Exempt Organizations* § 4.1.

(b) Organization's Purposes and Mission

The board member should understand, and be able to articulate, the tax-exempt association's mission. This entails knowledge of the organization's *purposes*. For this, the individual should read the statement of purposes contained in the entity's articles of organization. If the purposes are not understood, a suitable explanation should be obtained.

(c) Organization's Activities

Just as the board member should understand the association's purposes, the member should understand the association's *activities*.

With regard to program activities, the board member should understand and remain informed as to each of them. The member should be able to explain what they are and why they are conducted. The member should know the connection between the association's operations and furtherance of its purposes.

The association's activities may include lobbying.[5] If so, the board member should be satisfied that the lobbying is appropriate for the organization and that such activity is not jeopardizing the organization's tax-exempt status. The same is true with respect to any political campaign activities.[6]

If the association engages in fundraising activities, either directly or by means of an association-related foundation,[7] the board member should understand what they are. The member should make some effort to be satisfied that the organization is using the types of fundraising that are suitable for it and its objectives. Fundraising is not program, however; rather, it is a means to advance program and should be kept in that perspective.

The association may conduct one or more unrelated businesses.[8] There is nothing inherently wrong with unrelated activity, but the board member should know why the business is being conducted, be certain it does not detract from program undertakings, and be satisfied that the organization's tax-exempt status is not being endangered.

(d) Articles of Organization

The board member should understand each article of the association's articles of organization—what it means and why it is in the document. Of particular importance are the statement of purposes and any dissolution clause.

Other provisions to review and understand are those describing the organization's membership and provisions in the document that are reflective of federal tax law requirements and limitations.

(e) Structure and Bylaws

The board member should understand the association's bylaws. This document spells out (or should spell out) the entity's basic governance and operational

---

[5] See § 4.1.
[6] See § 4.3.
[7] See Chapters 8, 9.
[8] See Chapter 5.

structure. Items to check are: (1) the origin, composition, and stated duties of the organization's directors; (2) the origins and duties of the organization's officers; (3) the qualification and functions of any members; (4) the rules as to conduct of meetings (such as notice, quorum, voting); (5) the organization's committee structure; (6) provisions as to any indemnification (although state law may require that the provisions be in the articles); and (7) provisions as to any immunity (again, the language may have to be in the articles).

(f) Other Documents

The board member should understand the reason for, and the content of, other documents published by and/or prepared for the association. These include annual reports, promotional materials (brochures, pamphlets), fundraising materials, newsletters, and journals. Of course, if a program activity of the organization is publishing, it is not necessary that the board member read every book or other publication of the organization.

There are other documents—those that have some import in the law—that the board member should understand. They include any documents that are required to be filed with a state, such as annual reports and reports filed pursuant to one or more charitable solicitation acts.

(g) Related Entities

A tax-exempt association often is not a solitary entity; it may be a part of a cluster of entities. For example, a membership association may have a related foundation,[9] a political action committee,[10] and/or a for-profit subsidiary.[11] The board member should understand why these discrete entities exist, what their functions are, and how the relationships are structured. Other entities that may be involved are partnerships, limited liability companies, and/or other forms of joint ventures.[12]

In the case of multiple related entities, what has just been said is true for all of them. For example, the board member may be well advised to review and understand the documents pertaining to each of these entities.

(h) Doing Business Rules

The board member should know the jurisdiction(s) in which the association "does business." (That term, while sounding as though it applies only to commercial enterprises, also applies to nonprofit organizations.) Certainly the organization is "doing business" in the state in which its offices are located.

An exempt organization, however, may also be doing business in one or more other jurisdictions. An obvious illustration of this is an office or some other manifestation of a physical presence in another state. These precepts vary from state to state, however, and an organization can be deemed to be doing business

---

[9] See Chapter 8.
[10] See § 4.7.
[11] See Chapter 6.
[12] See Chapters 6, 7.

in a state where there is less of a presence than a formal office. If the organization is doing business in other jurisdictions, the board member should be advised of those locations and understand why the organization is deemed to be engaged in business.

(i) Public Charity Status

If the association is a charitable one, and/or if there is an association-related foundation,[13] the board member should know whether it is a public charity or a private foundation.[14] If it is a public charity, the board member should know the organization's classification for this purpose. The principal choices in this context are: (1) a *publicly supported organization*, with its support derived from gifts, grants, and/or exempt function (program service) revenue; or (2) a *supporting organization*.

Much of the law pertaining to private foundations focuses on transactions with, or in relation to, disqualified persons. In many instances, however, it is necessary that a public charity understand who the disqualified persons are with respect to it. The most obvious example in that regard is the intermediate sanctions rules.[15] Each board member should know who the association's and/or related foundation's disqualified persons are.

(j) Perspective

The premise of the foregoing discussion is that the member of the board of directors of a tax-exempt association who understands the legal aspects of the organization's structure and operations is far less likely to attract legal liability than the board member who acts (or fails to act) with lack of knowledge of these points.

§ 11.3 BOARD MEMBER LIABILITY

Actions by or on behalf of a tax-exempt association can give rise to personal liability. The term *personal liability* means that one or more managers of an exempt organization (its trustees, directors, officers, and/or key employees) may be found personally liable for something done (commission) or not done (omission) while acting in the same name of the organization. Some of this exposure can be limited by incorporation, indemnification, insurance, and/or immunity.

(a) Incorporation

The matter of incorporation has been discussed earlier, in the context of choice of form.[16] To reiterate, a corporation is regarded in the law as a separate legal entity that can attract legal liability. This liability generally is confined to the organization and thus does not normally extend to those who set policy for or manage the organization. (This is one of the principal reasons a tax-exempt association should be a nonprofit corporation.)

---

[13] See § 8.8.
[14] See Chapter 8.
[15] See § 3.8.
[16] See § 11.2(a).

(b) Indemnification

Indemnification occurs (assuming it is legal under state law) when the organization agrees (usually by provision in its bylaws) to pay the judgments and related expenses (including legal fees) incurred by those who are covered by the indemnity, when those expenses are the result of a misdeed (commission or omission) by those persons while acting in the service of the organization. The indemnification cannot extend to criminal acts; it may not cover certain willful acts that violate civil law.

Because an indemnification involves the resources of the organization, its efficacy depends on the economic viability of the organization. In times of financial difficulties for a tax-exempt organization, with little in the way of assets and revenue flow, an indemnification of its directors and officers can be a classic "hollow promise."

(c) Insurance

Insurance (directors' and officers' [D&O] insurance) has features somewhat comparable to indemnification. Instead of shifting the risk of liability from the individuals involved to the nonprofit organization (indemnification), however, the risk of liability is shifted to a (usually independent) third party—an insurance company. Certain risks, such as criminal law liability, cannot be shifted by means of insurance (because it would be contrary to public policy). The insurance contract will likely exclude from coverage certain forms of civil law liability, such as defamation, employee discrimination, and/or antitrust matters.

Even where adequate insurance coverage is available, insurance can be costly. Premiums can easily be thousands of dollars annually, even with a sizable deductible.

A tax-exempt organization can purchase insurance to fund one or more indemnities it has made of its directors and officers.

(d) Immunity

Immunity is available when the law provides that a class of individuals, under certain circumstances, is not liable for a particular act or set of acts or for failure to undertake a particular act or set of acts. Several states have enacted immunity laws for directors and officers of nonprofit organizations, protecting them in case of asserted civil law violations, particularly where these individuals are functioning as volunteers.

The board member who is knowledgeable about the tax-exempt organization's programs and other operations is a board member who is not likely to do or not do, or say, something that will result in legal liability, for the organization or personally. Following are some practical steps board members can take to enhance this knowledge and minimize the prospects of legal liability.

(i) Create a Board Book. Each board member should have, and keep up to date, a board book. It need not be particularly formal or fancy; a simple three-ring binder will suffice. In the book should be, at a minimum: the board address list (discussed next), the association's (and/or foundation's) articles of organization, its bylaws, any other documents with legal overtones (such as a mission statement or conflict-of-interest policy), recent board meeting minutes, a copy of the ruling from the IRS recognizing the organization as a tax-exempt entity, the most recently filed state report, the most recent financial statement, and the most recent three annual information returns.

Other documents that may be included are recent committee reports, a copy of the organization's application for recognition of tax exemption, and the most recent unrelated business income tax return (if any).

(ii) Board Address List.   Each member of the board should have, and keep in the board book, a current list of the organization's board members. This list should contain each individual's mailing address, telephone numbers (office, home, cell, car, pager), fax number, and e-mail address.

(iii) E-Mail Communication System.   There should be a system by which the board members can communicate by e-mail. Each member should have a group listing of all of the board members. These individuals should communicate by e-mail to the extent practicable.

(iv) Minutes.   Careful consideration should be given to board meeting minutes. There should be minutes of every board meeting. The minutes should be prepared with a heavy dose of common sense and perspective. These documents are not transcripts of the proceedings but are summaries of important actions, perhaps accompanied by resolutions.

It is difficult to generalize about the length and contents of board meeting minutes. Usually, whether something should have been in the minutes and is not, or whether something should not have been stated in the minutes and is, is determined in hindsight. The best practice is to be certain that all material decisions and actions are reflected and to be careful that nothing damaging to the organization is in the document.

A board member who opposes a majority board action on a matter, and is sufficiently concerned about the seriousness of the issue, should be certain that this opposition is reflected in the minutes, perhaps coupled with an explanation of the board member's position.

A good practice is for the secretary to provide a draft of the minutes to legal counsel for review and, if necessary, revision, before they are circulated to the board members for their review and adoption.

In general, solid and current minutes are one of the most important of the "corporate" formalities to observe.

(v) Attend Meetings.   It is critical that the board member attend each of the meetings of the board. Obviously, there will be occasional schedule conflicts; if the board member cannot attend a meeting, the minutes should reflect that fact and why. A board member cannot exercise the requisite degree of fiduciary responsibility without attending meetings and interfacing with the other members.

The director should actively participate in the decision-making process. Silence is deemed to be concurrence. If a director is opposed to an action to be undertaken by the organization at the behest of the board, the director should speak up and, as noted, be certain to have his or her dissent noted in the minutes.

(vi) Understand What Is Going On. A summary of the aspects of an organization's structure and operations, involving legal matters, that a board member should know was provided earlier.[17] This understanding needs to be ongoing, as purposes are revised or expanded, programs change, and documents are amended. It is essential that the board member know these basics and then build on that base of knowledge as the organization evolves.

(vii) Ask Questions. Probably one of the worst nonactions of a board member is failure to ask questions. The board member who merely pretends to understand what is taking place is only fooling himself or herself and is placed in a position to cause harm—to the organization and/or personally.

Questions may be asked of other board members, the organization's officers, and the staff. Questions may be posed during the course of a board meeting or on other occasions. Inquiries usually can be made by e-mail, although caution should be exercised as to how those messages are framed. Questions can be asked of lawyers and other professionals.

This opportunity to pose questions at a board meeting is why some boards of tax-exempt organizations do not meet without the organization's lawyer present. Others make decisions conditioned on legal advice.

(viii) Board Oversight of Staff. The board should oversee the activities of the organization's staff. Although board members should refrain from micromanaging, they should have sufficient knowledge of the role of each staff member and a general understanding as to their performance.

How this works in practice will vary considerably. If the organization has an executive director, that individual should provide most of this information. (Again, questions should be asked.) Some boards prefer to meet only when the organization's executive director is present. (Indeed, in some instances, the executive director is a member of the board, perhaps a nonvoting member.) Others do that but reserve some time to meet without that individual (or other staff) present.

(ix) Conflict-of-Interest Policy. While for the most part it is not required as a matter of law, a nonprofit organization—particularly a charitable one—should give serious consideration to adoption of a conflict-of-interest policy. For one thing, the IRS is pushing this as a condition of tax-exempt status. More important, this type of policy enables an organization to identify its disqualified persons and to know about any potential conflict at the time it is entering into transactions with such persons.

(x) Intermediate Sanctions Compliance. Board members of tax-exempt organizations that are charitable or social welfare in nature certainly want to be aware of

---

[17] See § 11.2.

the intermediate sanctions rules.[18] This is the case if only because the penalties for violation of these rules are imposed not on the organization but on the disqualified persons with respect to the organization. The disqualified persons with respect to the organization almost certainly will include members of the organization's board. Even if these rules are not directly applicable, as in the case of business leagues, some of their principles should be followed as a matter of good management.

(xi) Read Materials About Nonprofit Boards.　An immense amount of literature concerns the role of members of the board of tax-exempt organizations, including material on the operations of exempt organizations as such. Board members are well advised to read as much of this literature as possible.

(xii) Attend Seminars.　Seminars are of considerable utility to individuals in their capacity as board members of tax-exempt organizations. Just as publications are recommended, so too are seminars of this nature—at least one annually.

(xiii) Retreats.　The board of directors of a tax-exempt organization should consider having a periodic—perhaps even annual—board retreat. This is an opportunity for the board members to escape their employment and family responsibilities and focus—if only for a few hours—on the mission and goals of the organization. This experience can help place the nonprofit organization's activities in perspective—and help the board member understand more fully the organization's structure and operations.

At this retreat, various outside consultants can appear, share their expertise, give the board members the opportunity to ask questions, and provide the board a sense of the state of the organization. The board should consider use of a consultant for this purpose, to enhance the retreat with an outside perspective and a more directed focus.

(xiv) Overall Authority.　The board should not exceed its authority. The members of the board serve as overseers. Their role is to make extraordinary, not ordinary, decisions. Day-to-day management of the organization should be left to the officers and the executive staff.

§ 11.4 POSTAL LAW

Fundraising and other activities undertaken by tax-exempt organizations by means of the U.S. mail system is regulated to various extents by the federal postal laws. This regulation is largely accomplished by enforcement of the law concerning special mailing rates that are limited to use by qualified organizations when they are mailing eligible matter.

Only qualified organizations that have received specific authorization from the Postal Service may mail eligible matter at these specific rates of postage. These organizations cannot be organized for profit, and none of their net income may accrue to the benefit of persons in their private capacity.[19]

---

[18] See § 3.8.
[19] See Chapter 3.

(a) Determination of Postal Rates

Rates for all classes of mail are determined in rate cases, which are public proceedings administered by the Postal Rate Commission (PRC). The congressional mandate for the Postal Service is recovery of all of its operating costs from the rates it charges. This rate-making consists of assigning the Postal Service's projected costs in two categories of costs to each class of mail; combining the categories yields the rates. These categories are (1) *attributable costs,* which are costs that are directly measurable and traceable to a particular class of mail (such as nonprofit organization mailings), and (2) *institutional costs,* which are the overhead costs of the Postal Service, recovered by being assigned to each class in the form of a *markup,* stated as a percentage of the attributable cost.

The preferred rate for nonprofit tax-exempt organizations has existed because Congress, in 1970, undertook to provide the Postal Service an annual appropriation (*revenue forgone*) in lieu of the markup that nonprofit organizations would otherwise pay. That is, nonprofit organizations paid the attributable cost portion only (which became the nonprofit rate), and the federal government absorbed the institutional costs.

Throughout the 1980s, a steady increase in the volume of mail sent by nonprofit organizations helped to increase the need for revenue forgone; this was true for all postal rate classes, which reached nearly $1 billion for the government's fiscal year 1995. Congress became reluctant to appropriate the funds necessary to support the revenue forgone subsidy. Absent full funding of revenue forgone, the Postal Service was authorized to raise the nonprofit organizations' postal rates.

In the intervening years, nonprofit organizations faced ongoing uncertainty as to the levels of the postal rates. There were increases from rate cases (at approximately three-year intervals) and struggles with Congress over appropriations to avoid annual increases in the nonprofit rates. Congress threatened changes in the eligibility rates; two were enacted after 1990.

By 1992, a solution was clearly necessary. Congress and the Postal Service did not want any more pressure from the nonprofit community as to the revenue forgone amounts. Commercial mailers using the third-class rates were fearful that they would bear the burden of rate increases. Nonprofit organizations were weary of these uncertainties and were concerned about the prospects of a severe increase in the applicable postal rates.

Compromise legislation was enacted in 1993. This measure—the Revenue Forgone Reform Act—eliminated the concept of revenue forgone and ensured continued preferred rates by establishing a favorable markup for nonprofit organizations. For the federal government's fiscal year 1994 and thereafter, the markup for each class of nonprofit rates was set at one-half of the comparable commercial markup amount. This legislation provided a phasing-in schedule to cushion nonprofit organizations from the effects of the new system. This schedule produces annual increases in the range of 2 to 3 percent (unless or until the intervention of a PRC rate case).

The special rate for nonprofit organizations is termed by the Postal Service the *nonprofit standard mail rate.* This rate provides authorized organizations an opportunity to realize significant savings in postage compared with that charged at the regular standard bulk mail rates.

(b) Qualifying Organizations

The nonprofit standard mail rates are available to qualified nonprofit organizations. As noted, an organization may be authorized to mail at the nonprofit standard mail rates if it is not organized for profit and one of its net income accrues to the benefit of persons in their private capacity. A qualifying organization must have a primary purpose relating to at least one of these categories: religious, educational, scientific, philanthropic (charitable), agricultural, labor, veterans, or fraternal ends. Also, certain political organizations can qualify for the nonprofit standard mail rates. Business leagues and the like do not qualify for these rates.

This purpose must be reflected in the manner in which the organization is organized and operated. Nonprofit organizations that occasionally or incidentally engage in qualifying activities are not eligible for the special mailing rates.

§ 11.5 FEDERAL ELECTION LAW

In addition to the considerable amount of federal tax law concerning political activities by tax-exempt organizations, the federal election laws restrict and regulate political election-related activities by exempt organizations.

The federal election laws operated largely independently of the federal tax laws. Consequently, conduct by certain types of exempt organizations that may be prohibited under the federal election laws may be permissible under the federal tax laws; the reverse may also be the case. Thus, an exempt organization engaging in advocacy that may be or is political campaign activity should take the federal election law requirements and limitations into consideration.

(a) Federal Election Commission

The Federal Election Commission (FEC) is composed of six members appointed by the president, by and with the advice of the Senate. No more than three of these members may be affiliated with the same political party. Each member of the FEC serves for a single term of six years. These members are to be chosen on the basis of their experience, integrity, impartiality, and good judgment. They are to be full-time employees of the federal government.

The FEC has the responsibility for administering, enforcing, and formulating policy with respect to the federal election laws, principally the Federal Election Campaign Act ("FECA"), which was substantially amended in 2002 by the Bipartisan Campaign Reform Act ("BCRA"). The FEC is charged with preparation of rules to implement these policies and for the conduct of its activities. It is authorized to conduct investigations and participate in the litigation.

(b) Involvement of Corporations in the Election Process

In general, a corporation may not make a contribution or expenditure of corporate treasury funds in connection with a federal election. This prohibition, which applies to nonprofit corporations, applies to contributions of money as well as to loans, advances, contributions of services, and gifts of anything of value. There are special rules for applicable electioneering communications.

The federal election laws permit, subject to limitations, uses of corporate facilities and assets. Shareholders and employees may make incidental use of corporate facilities for individual volunteer activities. *Incidental* use means use that does not interfere with the normal operations of the corporation. Activity that does not exceed one hour a week or four hours a month is considered incidental. Certain reimbursement requirements apply for more than occasional, isolated, or incidental use. If a corporation regularly makes rooms available for civic or community groups, it may offer rooms to political candidates on a nonpartisan basis on the same terms.

A corporation may communicate with its executive or administrative personnel and their families on any subject, as well as to nonpartisan registration and get-out-the-vote campaigns aimed at these individuals. A corporation may establish, administer, and solicit contributions for an affiliated political committee. These exceptions also apply in connection with labor organizations and their members and their families.

(c) Separate Segregated Funds

Despite the federal election law prohibitions on corporations from using corporate treasury money to make contributions or expenditures in connection with federal elections, a corporation may use treasury funds to establish and administer a political committee. These political committees may solicit and receive contributions from the restricted class and, in turn, make contributions and expenditures to influence federal elections. Committees of this nature are referred to as *separate segregated funds* (otherwise often known as *political action committees*). The funds of these committees, consisting of lawful contributions, are kept separate—segregated—from the sponsoring organization's treasury funds. Treasury funds include money obtained from commercial transactions, dues, and other membership fees.

(i) Contributions by a Separate Segregated Fund.   A contribution from a separate segregated fund (SSF) usually entails the giving of money to one or more candidate committees, the purchase of goods or services on behalf of a candidate ("in-kind contributions"), or giving money to another political committee, such as a party committee, that in turn supports candidates. Contributions to and by these funds include gifts of money and property, in-kind contributions, and loans, endorsements, and guarantees of loans; they also can receive sales proceeds.

(ii) Solicitation of Contributions to an SSF.   A corporation or its separate segregated fund may solicit only its *restricted class*, that is, its stockholders and executive and administrative personnel and their immediate families. An incorporated membership organization, including a trade association, cooperative, and corporation without capital stock and its SSF may solicit contributions from its noncorporate members and their families to a fund for political purposes. Noncorporate members include individuals and partnerships. With the exception of trade associations, a membership corporation may not solicit the employees of its members.

(iii) Definition of *Member.* An organization's *members* include all persons who currently satisfy the organization's requirements for membership. The courts and the FEC have attempted to clarify this vague definition.

(d) Limitations on Contributions and Expenditures

There are limitations on the level of contributions that persons may make to candidates, political committees of candidates, and political committees of national political parties with respect to elections for federal office. For example, a person may not make contributions to a candidate and his or her political committee, in connection with a federal election, in excess of $2,000. Likewise, contributions to a political committee maintained by a national political party may not, in a calendar year, exceed $25,000.

There are limitations and restrictions on the expenditures made, in connection with the general election campaigns of candidates for federal office, by the national committee of a political party and a state committee of a political party.

Generally, *expenditures* are any purchase, payment, distribution, loan, advance, deposit, or gift of money or anything of value made by any person for the purpose of influencing any election for federal office, as well as any written agreement or promise to make an expenditure. The 2002 revisions of the FECA did not amend the definition of the term *expenditure* but categorized certain election-related activities into *federal election activity* and *electioneering communications.*

(e) Soft-Money Restrictions

Contributions for federal election purposes generally must be made with funds that are subject to the FECA's disclosure requirements, and source and amount limitations. These funds are known as *federal* or *hard* money. The term *contribution* is defined to include gifts, loans, advances, or like transfers of anything of value made by any person for the purpose of influencing any election for *federal* office. Contributions made solely for the purpose of influencing state or local elections are, therefore, unaffected by the FECA's requirements and prohibitions.

Prior to the enactment of the BCRA, federal law permitted corporations and unions, as well as individuals who had made the maximum permissible contributions to federal candidates, to contribute *nonfederal* or *soft* money to political parties for activities intended to influence state or local elections. In the case of contributions intended to influence both federal and state elections, the FEC ruled that political parties could fund mixed-purpose activities, including get-out-the-vote drives and generic party advertising, in part with soft money. This was done by means of establishment by these parties of federal and nonfederal accounts. Thereafter, the FEC concluded that the parties could also use soft money to defray the costs of *legislative advocacy media advertisements,* even if the advertisements mentioned the name of a federal candidate, as long as they did not expressly advocate the candidate's election or defeat. This solicitation, transfer, and other use of soft money—what the Supreme Court would later portray as the "FEC's allocation regime"[20]—thus enabled parties and candidates to circumvent the FECA's limitations on the source and amount of contributions in connection with federal elections.

Congress, in 2002, as the Supreme Court observed, made an "effort to plug the soft-money loophole."[21] The FECA, as amended by the BCRA, prohibits national party committees and their agents from soliciting, receiving, directing, or spending soft money. State and local party committees are prohibited from using soft money for activities that affect federal elections. The Supreme Court observed that the "core [of this second rule] is a straightforward contribution regulation: It prevents donors from contributing nonfederal funds to state and local party committees to help finance 'federal election activity.'"[22] The Court noted that this rule arose out of congressional recognition of the "close ties between federal candidates and state party committees."[23]

Federal election activity encompasses four discrete categories of activities: (1) voter registration activity during the 120 days preceding a regularly scheduled federal election; (2) voter identification, get-out-the-vote, and generic campaign activity that is conducted in connection with an election in which a candidate for federal office appears on the ballot; (3) a public communication that refers to a clearly identified federal candidate and that promotes, supports, attacks, or opposes a candidate for that office; and (4) the services provided by certain political party committee employees. In finding these rules to be constitutional, the Supreme Court referred to these four types of activities collectively as *electioneering*.

These federal election activities are nearly identical to the mixed-purpose activities that were allowed by the FEC before enactment of the BCRA. Political parties are prohibited from soliciting and contributing funds to tax-exempt organizations that engage in electioneering activities. Federal candidates and officeholders are prohibited from receiving, spending, or soliciting soft money in connection with federal elections. This limits their ability to do so in connection with state and local elections. Circumvention of the restrictions on national, state, and local party committees is prevented by prohibiting state and local candidates from raising and spending soft money to fund advertisements and other public communications that promote or attack federal candidates.

(f) Solicitations for, Contributions to, Expenditures by Tax-Exempt Organizations

The FECA, as amended by the BCRA, prohibits national, state, and local party committees and their agents or subsidiaries from soliciting funds for, or making or directing any contributions to, any tax-exempt organization that makes expenditures in connection with an election for public office or to any exempt political organization "other than a political committee, a State, district, or local committee of a political party, or the authorized campaign committee of a candidate for State or local office."

---

[20] McConnell v. Federal Election Commission, 540 U.S. 93, 131 (2003).
[21] *Id.* at 133.
[22] *Id.* at 161–162.
[23] *Id.* at 161.

The purpose of this law is to prevent circumvention of the FECA limits on contributions of soft money to national, state, and local party committees. The Supreme Court found it constitutional, by narrowly construing the prohibition to apply only to the donation of funds not raised in compliance with the FECA.

The FECA, as amended by the BCRA, also prohibits national, state, and local party committees from making or directing any contributions to tax-exempt political or other organizations. The Supreme Court, to render this rule constitutional, narrowly construed the ban to apply only to donations of funds not raised in conformity to the FECA's prohibitions and limitations. Thus, the Court wrote that "political parties remain free to make or direct donations of money to any tax-exempt organization that has otherwise been raised in compliance with [the] FECA."[24]

The FECA, as amended by the BCRA, regulates the raising and soliciting of soft money by federal candidates and officeholders. It prohibits federal candidates and officeholders from soliciting, receiving, directing, transferring, or spending any soft money in connection with federal elections. It also limits the ability of federal candidates and officeholders to solicit, receive, direct, transfer, or spend soft money in connection with state and local elections. Among the exceptions to these rules is that federal candidates and officeholders may make solicitations of soft money to tax-exempt organizations (1) the primary purpose of which is not to engage in *federal election activities* as long as the solicitation does not specify how the funds will be spent, (2) the primary purpose of which is to engage in federal election activities as long as the solicitations are limited to individuals and the amount solicited does not exceed $20,000 per year per individual, and (3) for the express purpose of carrying out federal election activities as long as the amount solicited does not exceed $20,000 per year per individual. The Supreme Court found these rules to be constitutional because, unlike an outright ban on solicitations to exempt organizations, this law permits "limited" solicitations of soft money, thereby "accomodat[ing] individuals who have long served as active members of nonprofit organizations in both their official and individual capacities."[25]

The FECA, as amended by the BCRA, generally prohibits corporations and unions from using their general treasury funds to make election-related advertising expenditures, including the financing of electioneering communications. The Supreme Court founds this ban constitutional, in that corporations and unions remain free to organize and administer separate segregated funds for that purpose.

(g) Advocacy and Electioneering

The BCRA introduced the term *electioneering communication*, which encompasses any "broadcast, cable or satellite communication" that refers to a clearly identified candidate for federal office; is made within 60 days before a general, special, or runoff election for the office sought by the candidate or 30 days before a primary or preference election, or a convention or caucus of a political party that

---

[24] *Id.* at 181.
[25] *Id.* at 183.

has the authority to nominate a candidate, for the office sought by the candidate; and in the case of a communication that refers to a candidate (other than one for president or vice president) that is targeted to the relevant electorate. The term is utilized in two contexts: There are disclosure requirements for persons who fund electioneering communications, and there are restrictions on the ability of corporations and unions to fund electioneering communications. This term was created, the Supreme Court observed, "to replace the narrowing construction of [the] FECA's disclosure provisions adopted" by the Court previously.[26] The Court wrote that "that construction limited the coverage of [the] FECA's disclosure requirement to communications expressly advocating the election or defeat of particular candidates."[27]

This aspect of the law has generated considerable confusion as to what the Court meant in its earlier pronouncement. The thinking in many quarters for years was that the Court drew a constitutionally mandated distinction between *express advocacy* and *issue advocacy*, with persons having an inviolable First Amendment right to engage in the latter category of speech. The challenge to this portion of the BCRA was predicated on the view that Congress cannot constitutionally require disclosure of, or regulate expenditures for, electioneering communications without making an exception for communications that do not involve express advocacy. "That position," the Court wrote, "misapprehends our prior decisions, for the express advocacy restriction was an endpoint of statutory interpretation, not a first principle of constitutional law."[28]

In the earlier decision, the Court examined prior law restricting election-related expenditures and found some of the phraseology to be impermissibly vague. The Court cured the defect by interpreting the rule as being limited to communications that include explicit words of advocacy of election or defeat of a candidate. The express advocacy limitation, then, was the product of statutory interpretation; it "nowhere suggested that a statute that was neither vague nor overbroad would be required to toe the same express advocacy line."[29] Thus, the "concept of express advocacy and the concomitant class of magic words were born of an effort to avoid constitutional infirmities."[30] The Court's prior decisions "in no way drew a constitutional boundary that forever fixed the permissible scope of provisions regulating campaign-related speech."[31]

Aside from the Court's prior holdings, it concluded that it was not persuaded that the First Amendment "erects a rigid barrier between express advocacy and so-called issue advocacy."[32] The Court wrote of its "long-standing recognition that the presence of absence of magic words cannot meaningfully distinguish electioneering speech from a true issue ad."[33] Proclaiming the "magic-words requirement" to be "functionally meaningless," the Court wrote

---

[26] *Id.* at 189.
[27] *Id.*
[28] *Id.* at 190. Also Wisconsin Right to Life, Inc. v. Federal Election Commission, 126 S. Ct. 1016 (2006).
[29] McConnell v. Federal Election Commission, 540 U.S. 93, 192 (2003).
[30] *Id.*
[31] *Id.* at 192–193.
[32] *Id.* at 193.
[33] *Id.*

that the "express advocacy line, in short, has not aided the legislative effort to combat real or apparent corruption, and Congress enacted [the] BCRA to correct the flaws it found in the existing system."[34]

The term *electioneering communication* was found by the Court to not be vague, with its components "easily understood and objectively determinable."[35] This portion of the FECA, then, is constitutional.

(h) Political Organizations

Certain political organizations must file a statement of organization (register) with the FEC within certain time frames. These entities are authorized campaign committees, separate segregated funds, and certain other political committees.

An *authorized campaign committee* is the principal campaign committee or any other committee authorized by a candidate for federal office to receive contributions or make expenditures on behalf of the candidate. A *separated segregated fund* is a fund utilized for political purposes by entities such as corporations, labor organizations, and other membership organizations.

For federal election purposes, a *political committee* includes any group of persons that receives contributions aggregating more than $1,000 in a calendar year or that makes expenditures aggregating more than $1,000 during a calendar year. The term also includes certain *separate segregated funds* and certain local committees of a political party.

The Supreme Court narrowed the definition of the term *political committee*, stating that the term "need only encompass organizations that are under the control of a candidate or the major purpose of which is the nomination or election of a candidate" and that the term does not "reach groups engaged purely in issue discussion." The FEC applies the *major purpose test* when assessing whether an organization is a political committee.

The federal election law subjects political committees to record-keeping and reporting requirements that are inapplicable to organizations that are not political committees. It also imposes limitations and prohibitions on the contributions they receive and make.

Thus, some political organizations are recognized as such for federal tax purposes but are not recognized as political entities by the FEC (and thus do not have to register with the FEC). These *nonconnected 527 organizations* may nonetheless be required to register with the IRS.

§ 11.6 ANTITRUST LAW

The federal antitrust laws are, in certain respects, applicable to nonprofit organizations. The principal law in this regard, the Sherman Act, prohibits contracts, combinations, and conspiracies that unreasonably restrain trade. The Supreme Court wrote that "[t]here is no doubt that the sweeping language of section 1 [of the Sherman Act] applies to nonprofit entities." Civil actions under the antitrust laws may be brought by the Antitrust Division of the Department of Justice, the

---

[34] *Id.* at 194.
[35] *Id.*

Federal Trade Commission (FTC), or private plaintiffs. The federal government can also bring criminal actions against entities and individuals for certain antitrust actions.

(a) Fundamental Principles

Among the most common antitrust law violations are concerted or collusive activities involving two or more competitors. Thus, the nonprofit organizations usually involved in antitrust law matters are business or professional associations. These entities have the interesting feature—as mandated by federal tax law requirements—of being composed of members that are competitors.

Consequently, an association constitutes what may be termed *a convenient vehicle* by means of which collusive activities may be undertaken. The law is clear that agreements relating in any way to prices or to fees, even agreements that affect prices or fees merely indirectly, are illegal *per se*. This standard means that there is no need to prove any actual injury to competition resulting from this type of an agreement. The simple existence of the anticompetitive agreement is sufficient to establish illegality. In one instance, an engineering society's ethical canon, which prohibited members from discussing prices with potential customers until there was an initial selection of an engineer, was held to be a *per se* violation of the Sherman Act.

Another context in which the antitrust laws can be applicable to nonprofit organizations is standard-setting. An example of this application of the antitrust laws is a court decision that an association that promoted harness racing did not violate these laws by standardizing the design of the two-wheeled vehicle (sulky) pulled by horses in this type of racing. In another case, the claim that an organization was attempting to monopolize the market of occupational therapy certification in violation of the Sherman Act was rejected. In still another instance, an act violation claim was rejected in a dispute over the criteria used to determine that a laboratory must use reagent water produced on site for laboratory tests generated a lawsuit by a company that produced this type of water in bottled form.

Membership associations are vulnerable to antitrust allegations in still another context: member expulsion. If not undertaken for reasonable cause, an expulsion of this nature can be a *converted refusal to deal* or a *group boycott*. For an association to engage in this type of illegal conduct, however, it must have the requisite *market power*; that is, membership in it has to be the exclusive access to some necessary element of the business involved. In one case, an expelled member failed to convince a court of antitrust wrongdoing by an association, inasmuch as the association lacked market power: Of about 500 firms in the industry, only 85 were association members.

Restraints of trade that are not illegal *per se* are reviewed pursuant to a *rule of reason* standard. Application of this standard entails a full economic analysis of the practice(s) involved. This process can be time consuming and expensive.

A third approach has evolved: the *quick look*. Here, although the restraint in question is found to not be a *per se* violation, if there is anticompetitive effect, the practice is determined to be a sufficiently apparent transgression of the antitrust laws as to not warrant a rule-of-reason analysis. As the Supreme Court stated, the quick look is appropriate when an "observer with even a rudimentary understanding of economics could conclude that the arrangements in question would have an anticompetitive effect on customers and markets." If a quick look is inconclusive, a full economic analysis may follow.

The Court considered a case involving the code of ethics of an association of dentists; at issue were restrictions on price advertising. The FTC determined that these restrictions were a form of price-fixing and thus constituted a *per se* violation of the antitrust law. A court of appeals agreed but ruled that the practices were to be evaluated using the quick-look test. The Court was troubled with the standard of review, with the majority expressing the view that there may have to be a type of review that is more extensive than a quick look but less encompassing than a rule-of-reason analysis.

(b) Federal Trade Commission Jurisdiction

The scope of the jurisdiction of the FTC over nonprofit organizations is not clear. The Federal Trade Commission Act prohibits "unfair methods of competition." This act's phraseology encompasses not only all Sherman Act violations but also any other restraints of trade that are contrary to the policy or spirit of the antitrust laws.

The FTC has the authority to prevent "persons [that is, individuals], partnerships or corporations" from engaging in unfair competitive methods and unfair or deceptive acts or practices. The definition of the term *corporation* in this context includes any company or association, "incorporated or unincorporated, without shares of capital or capital stock, except partnerships." The law that authorizes the FTC to investigate and discipline organizations states that the agency may only investigate an "entity which is organized to carry on business for its own profit or that of its members."

Therefore, the FTC has jurisdiction over nonprofit trade, business, and professional associations—where they have for-profit members and where the economic benefits that are provided are substantial. Where the economic benefit is insubstantial, the agency lacks jurisdiction. The Supreme Court has observed that an organization "devoted solely to professional education may lie outside the FTC Act's jurisdictional reach, even though the quality of professional services ultimately affects the profits of those who deliver them." At any rate, *pure charity* is beyond the ambit of the antitrust laws.

§ 11.7 SECURITIES LAW

At the federal level, the principal securities laws are the Securities Act of 1933, the Securities Exchange Act of 1934, and the Investment Company Act of 1940. These laws are administered and enforced by the Securities Exchange Commission ("SEC"). Generally, this body of law is designed to preserve a free market in the trading of securities, provide full and fair disclosure of the character of securities sold in interstate commerce and through the mails, and prevent fraud and other abuse in the marketing and sale of securities. State securities laws have the same goal.

The federal securities law broadly defines the term *security* as including not only stocks and bonds but also notes, debentures, evidences of indebtedness, certificates of participation in a profit-sharing agreement, investment contracts, and certificates of deposit for securities. It is rare for a charitable organization to offer a financial benefit or package to the general public where that benefit or package is considered a security, but some nonprofit organizations offer *memberships* that, technically, constitute securities. There are, however, exceptions from the federal securities laws for these types of securities.

Nonetheless, a charitable organization may find itself at least within the potential applicability of the securities laws if it maintains one or more *charitable income funds*. The federal securities laws include rules that are designed to shield charities against the allegation that these funds are investment companies subject to the registration and other requirements of the Investment Company Act. This legislation, introduced by the Philanthropy Protection Act of 1995, provides exemptions under the federal securities laws for charitable organizations that maintain these funds.

A charitable income fund is a fund maintained by a charitable organization exclusively for the collective investment and reinvestment of one or more assets of a charitable remainder trust or similar trust, a pooled income fund, an arrangement involving a contribution in exchange for the issuance of a charitable gift annuity, a charitable lead trust, the general endowment fund or other funds of one or more charitable organizations, or certain other trusts in which the remainder interests benefit or are revocably dedicated to one or more charitable organizations. The SEC has the authority to expand the scope of these exemption provisions to embrace funds that may include assets not expressly defined.

A fund that is excluded from the definition of an investment company must provide at the time of the contribution, to each donor to a charity by means of the fund, written information describing the material terms of operation of the fund. This disclosure requirement, however, is not a condition of exemption from the Investment Company Act. Thus, a charitable income fund that fails to provide the requisite information to donors is not subject to the securities laws, although the fund may be subject to an enforcement or other action by the SEC.

This exemption is also engrafted onto the Securities Act and the Securities Exchange Act. Thus, for example, the exemption in the Securities Act (from registration and other requirements) is available for "any security issued by a person organized and operated exclusively for religious, educational, benevolent, fraternal, charitable, or reformatory purposes and not for pecuniary profit, and no part of the net earnings of which inures to the benefit of any person, private stockholder, or individual."

The Securities Exchange Act provides that a charitable organization is not subject to the act's broker-dealer regulation rules solely because the organization trades in securities on its behalf, or on behalf of a charitable income fund, or the settlers, potential settlers, or beneficiaries of either. This protection is also extended to trustees, directors, officers, employees, or volunteers of a charitable organization, acting within the scope of his or her employment or duties with the organization.

Exemption similar to those available in the broker-dealer setting are provided for charitable organizations and certain persons associated with them, in connection with the provision of advice, analyses, or reports, from the reach of the Investment Advisors Act.

Interests in charitable income funds excluded from the definition of an investment company, and any offer or sale of these interests, are exempt from a state law that requires registration or qualification of securities. A charitable organization or trustee, director, officer, employee, or volunteer of a charity (acting within the scope of his or her employment or duties) is not subject to regulation as a dealer, broker, agent, or investment advisor under any state securities law because the organization or person trades in securities on behalf of a charity, charitable income fund, or the settlers, potential settlers, or beneficiaries of either.

§ 11.8 INTELLECTUAL PROPERTY LAW

The U.S. legal system provides rights and protections for owners of property that result from the "fruits of mental labor." This type of property is referred to as *intellectual property*. Rights and protections of owners of intellectual property are based on patent, trademark, copyright, and state trade secret laws, affording protection to profit-motivated, as well as nonprofit, entrepreneurs. In general, patents protect inventions of tangible things, copyrights protect various forms of written and artistic expression, trademarks/service marks protect a name or symbol that identifies the source of goods or services, and trade secrets protect know-how that provides a competitive advantage.

(a) Copyrights

A copyright is a statutory property right that grants to authors, artists, composers, photographers, or other creative parties exclusive rights in their creations (that is, books, graphics, sculptural works, music, paintings, computer programs) for a limited duration. A copyright arises upon fixation of a work in a tangible medium of expression and endures for the life of the author plus 70 years. A copyright applies to both published and unpublished works. Registration of a copyright with the Copyright Office in Washington D.C. is not required for the existence of a copyright or for the use of the copyright symbol (© 2006 John Doe); however, registration is a prerequisite to a lawsuit for copyright infringement and to the recovery of statutory damages and attorneys' fees. Copyrights are registered in the Copyright Office in the Library of Congress.

The U.S. copyright laws have historically favored the creative party who actually develops the work product. One exception arises in the employer-employee relationship. Employers, under the *work made for hire* doctrine, own works that are created by employees within the scope of their employment. Conversely, works created by independent contractors or freelancers are owned by the creators of such works, even though the commissioning party has actually paid for such work product, unless the creative parties assign or relinquish their rights in the work by a written instrument, or the commissioning parties contribute separately copyrightable subject matter, in which case the work may be jointly owned. Associations and charitable organizations that hire advertising agencies, artists, or designers to create copyrightable subject matter, such as greeting card designs, ad campaigns, or other graphic works, should require such parties to assign their copyright interests in the work product to the non-profit entity as part of the engagement or commissioning process.

(b) Trademarks

A trademark is a word, phrase, symbol, or design, or combination of words, phrases, symbols, or designs, that identifies and distinguishes the source of the goods or services of one party from those of others. A service mark is the equivalent of a trademark except that it identifies and distinguishes the source of a service rather than a product. The purpose of a trademark or service mark is to identify the origin of goods or services and not simply to describe the underlying goods or services. Trade identity rights are valuable for nonprofit entities as well as for-profit entities. In general, a mark for goods is affixed to the product or on its packaging, whereas a service mark appears in advertising for the services. Trademark rights arise from either actual use of the mark or the filing of a proper application to register a mark in the U.S. Patent and Trademark Office. The holder of an unregistered mark may use the symbol "™" to denote its claim of rights in a trademark or "ˢᵐ" to signify its claim of rights in a service mark. Only the holders of a federally registered mark may use the registration symbol (®) in connection with their use of trademarks or service marks, however. Unlike patents or copyrights, trademark rights can last indefinitely if the owner continues to use the mark to identify its goods or services. The initial term of a federal trademark registration is 10 years, with 10-year renewal terms. Between the fifth and sixth year after the date of initial registration, an affidavit must be filed, setting forth certain information to keep the registration alive. Failure to file this affidavit results in cancellation of the registration.

While rights in a mark are established by use and adoption, maintaining or protecting rights in a mark depends partly on whether the mark is distinctive, suggestive, descriptive, or generic. Distinctive marks are the strongest marks, often because the words are coined, arbitrary, or fanciful. EXXON® is a coined phrase used by an oil company and is considered a strong, inherently distinctive mark. OLD CROW® for whiskey is an example of an arbitrary mark because, although the words may be common, when used with the goods in question the mark neither suggests nor describes any ingredient or characteristic of the product. STRONGHOLD® for nails is a suggestive mark because the word suggests the nature of the products without actually describing them. TENDER VITTLES as applied to cat food draws attention to the ingredients, quality, or nature of the product and is therefore descriptive. Generic words are synonymous with the name of the product, such as "facial tissue" or "butter."

Generic terms are always, and descriptive marks are usually, denied trademark protection. Descriptive words may be afforded protection upon proof of "secondary meaning"—an ambiguous phrase that indicates that the mark has acquired source-indicating significance and distinctiveness, even though it is descriptive. Suggestive marks are stronger than descriptive marks, although the classification of marks as either suggestive or descriptive is often blurry. Distinctive marks are regarded as the strongest source identifiers.

Trademark infringement requires proof of *likelihood of confusion* in the relevant marketplace, which does not necessarily require actual confusion. Actual confusion, however, is often the best evidence of likelihood of confusion. Marks can infringe based on similarity of appearance, sound, or connotation. Although actual competition is not required, the likelihood of confusion increases when the goods sold under similar marks are competing or closely related. Trademark holders may enforce their rights in goods or services that represent a natural line extension of their brands. Infringement often is proven by consumer surveys and the testimony of marketing experts. Infringement cases involving nonprofits often position a national charity, such as the YMCA, against a dissident local chapter, which has fallen out of favor with the national organization but still uses the national organization's marks without authorization. The local chapter usually is held liable for creating a false association and misappropriation of the trademark holder's trade identity, as well as for diluting the value of the marks.

(c) Patents

A patent for an invention is a grant of a property right by the U.S. Patent and Trademark Office that grants to its owner (or heirs or assigns) a legally enforceable right to exclude others from practicing the invention described and claimed in the patent. The term of a patent is 20 years from the date on which the application for the patent was filed in the United States, subject to the payment of maintenance fees. Like other forms of property, the rights symbolized by a patent can be inherited, sold, rented, mortgaged, and even taxed.

Congress has specified that a patent will be granted if the inventor files a timely application that adequately describes a new, useful, and unobvious invention of proper subject matter. To be timely, an application must be filed *within one year* of any act that reduces the invention to practices.

Patents usually are granted to individual inventors, who typically assign their patents to their employers. If the inventors discovered the topic of the invention during the course of their employment, but fail to assign the patent to their employers, the employers may be deemed to have acquired a "shop right," entitling the employers to use the patent internally as part of their business operations, without owing a royalty to the inventors. Many employers require their employees to assign any developments or patentable discoveries to the employer to avoid any ownership controversies.

A patent does not necessarily have to cover a machine or a new gadget— many items can be patented, including business methods, carpet designs, clothing accessories and designs, computer software, fabrics and fabric designs, food inventions, jewelry, plants, and much more.

(d) Trade Secrets

Trade secrets embody all forms and types of financial, business, scientific, technical, economic, or engineering information, including patterns, plans, compilations, program devices, formulas, designs, prototypes, methods, techniques, processes, procedures, programs, or codes, whether tangible or intangible, and whether or how stored, compiled, or memorialized physically, electronically, graphically, photographically, or in writing if: (1) the owner has taken reasonable measures to keep such information secret; and (2) the information derives independent economic value, actual or potential, from not being generally known to, and not being readily ascertainable through proper means by, the public. Trade secrets usually are protected from misappropriation or unauthorized disclosure by specific state statutes or agreements by and between employers and employees or independent contractors restricting use of such trade secrets.

Trade secrets for nonprofit organizations might include confidential lists of donors and fundraising techniques, long-range strategic plans, acquisition strategies, and much more.

(e) Licensing

Licensing is the grant of the right to another party to use of an idea, trademark, patent, or copyright in exchange of bargained-for consideration. The licensor retains the rights to the idea, trademark, patent, or copyright. Assigning is selling the rights to the idea, trademark, patent, or copyright outright.

A licensing agreement usually provides the owner of intellectual property with royalties based on fixed or variable rates. The licensor must reserve the right to control or inspect the licensee's activities with respect to the nature and quality of the goods or services marketed or sold, or the idea, mark, or copyright may be deemed abandoned or forfeited. Licensing arrangements have been utilized by nonprofit entities to reinforce the affinity relationship between the organization, its members, and certain providers of goods or services. For example, many charities (such as the Sierra Club) offer affinity credit cards whereby a portion of the funds charged is donated to the charity. Under the federal tax law, a passive royalty from the card issuer is regarded as nontaxable income, but the provision of any ancillary services by the charity may result in the characterization of the royalty proceeds as unrelated taxable business income.[36]

(f) Unfair Competition

Unfair competition consists of acts or practices, in the course of trade or business, that are contrary to honest practices, including, in particular: (1) acts that may cause confusion with the products or services, or the industrial or commercial activities, of an enterprise; (2) false allegations that may disparage or discredit the products or services, or the industrial or commercial activities, of an enterprise; (3) indications or allegations that may mislead the public, in particular as to the manufacturing process of a product or as to the quality, quantity, or other characteristics of products or services; (4) acts in respect of unlawful acquisition, disclosure, or use of trade secrets; and (5) acts causing dilution or other damage to the distinctive power of another's mark or taking unfair advantage of the goodwill or reputation of another's enterprise. Unfair competition sometimes is referred to as *business torts*. Although the Lanham Act, the federal trademark

---

[36] See § 5.9(f).

statute, has broadened into a federal law of unfair competition, various state laws also address unfair competition. Unfair competition claims are not limited to commercial enterprises. On the contrary, nonprofit businesses are vulnerable to unfair and deceptive trade practices, especially unscrupulous fundraisers who try to confuse the public by adopting names or marks that are confusingly similar to well-known, respected charities.

§ 11.9 EMPLOYEE BENEFITS LAW

The law of tax-exempt organizations and the law of employee benefits are inextricably intertwined. This is because the funding underlying the various forms of employee benefits plans is derived from assets contributed to and held for investment in a trust or fund; these funds are exempt from federal income tax exemption, so as to maximize the resources available to provide the benefits.

This interrelationship is also reflected in the organization of the IRS. A component of the agency is the Tax Exempt and Government Entities Division. This division serves three IRS "customer segments": tax-exempt organizations, government entities, and employee (public and private retirement) plans.

The tax-exempt organizations aspect of the law of employee benefits is reflected in the opening passage of the statutory law of tax-exempt organizations, where it is provided that organizations referenced in the rules concerning retirement, profit-sharing, and similar plans[37] are exempt from federal income taxation.[38] That section makes reference to trusts that are part of qualified stock bonus, pension, or profit-sharing plans.

(a) Compensation Fundamentals

Basically, employees—whether of nonprofit, for-profit, or governmental employers—are individuals who provide services to an employer. That is, these individuals are provided compensation, in a context where they are not functioning as independent contractors, in exchange for their services. There are employees of nonprofit, tax-exempt associations and other organizations who choose to earn less than what they would receive were they working in a for-profit sector, but for the most part those who work for nonprofit organizations (other than volunteers) expect and must have remuneration for their services. Indeed, the law is clear that an individual need not necessarily accept reduced compensation merely because he or she renders services to an exempt, as opposed to a taxable, organization.

Compensation in general is provided in three forms: current, deferred, and retirement. Each of these forms of compensation is available to employees of tax-exempt associations. Whatever the mode of compensation—be it wages, salaries, bonuses, commissions, fringe benefits, deferred compensation, and/or retirement benefits—most exempt organizations are constrained by the doctrines of private inurement, private benefit, and/or the intermediate sanctions rules.[39]

---

[37] IRC § 401(a).
[38] IRC § 501(a).
[39] See Chapter 3.

This essentially means that all compensation, no matter how determined or whatever the form, must, for the employer to be or remain exempt, be *reasonable*.

(b) Current Compensation in General

A nonprofit association may pay a salary or wage. This is a form of *current*, as opposed to *deferred*,[40] compensation. Generally, the payments must be reasonable, largely using the community's standard, taking into account factors such as the nature of the tax-exempt organization, the value of the services being rendered, and pertinent experience.[41] (The same rule essentially applies with respect to for-profit employers, in that, to be deductible as a business expense, a payment of compensation must be ordinary and necessary.) For this purpose, reasonable current compensation includes appropriate salary increases based on merit and appropriate cost-of-living adjustments.

Nonprofit organizations may pay bonuses. A bonus amount also is subject to the standard of reasonableness. A bonus, however, is likely to be more closely scrutinized than regular current compensation, because it is additional compensation and thus more susceptible than regular compensation to the allegation that it is excessive or otherwise a form of inurement of net earnings. The sensitivity is increased where a bonus is paid to one who is a director, officer, key employee, or similar insider with respect to the nonprofit organization.[42]

In many respects, commissions are subject to the same rules as bonuses, in that both are forms of incentive compensation. Commissions and other forms of percentage-based compensation can, however, result in heightened inquiry, because they are, by definition, computed using percentages and thus tend to approximate, if not constitute, private inurement. Consequently, the IRS and/or a court may scrutinize compensation programs of tax-exempt organizations that are predicated on an incentive feature where compensation is a function of revenues received or guaranteed, or is otherwise outside the boundaries of conventional compensation arrangements.

(c) Fringe Benefits

Federal tax and other laws do not prohibit the payment of fringe benefits by tax-exempt organizations. A *fringe benefit* usually is a form of noncash compensation to an employee, although it may well entail a cash outlay by the employer. Once again, a fringe benefit (or a package of them), paid by an exempt employer to an employee, usually must be reasonable to preserve the tax exemption of the employer.

Typically, an employer that is a tax-exempt organization will pay for fringe benefits such as health insurance, medical insurance, dental insurance, disability insurance, and perhaps travel insurance. For the most part, exempt organizations can pay for one or more of these benefits without tax law difficulties.

Other common forms of fringe benefits paid (either directly or by reimbursement) by employers in general are entertainment costs, costs of an automobile,

---

[40] See § 11.9(d).
[41] See § 3.4(a).
[42] See § 3.3.

moving expenses, costs of attending conventions and/or educational seminars, costs of parking, club memberships, and costs of certain professional fees (such as physicians' charges for physical examinations, financial planning fees, and stress management expenses).

These latter types of fringe benefits may cause tax law problems for the tax-exempt organizations that pay them. Some exempt entities may be able to pay moving expenses, continuing education expenses, and perhaps automobile and parking expenses, without attracting too much investigation by the IRS. Generally, however, an exempt organization will be suspect, in the eyes of legislators and regulators (and perhaps the general public), if its employees are granted fringe benefits such as country club memberships, financial planning services, or substantial entertainment allowances.

(d) Deferred Compensation

Tax-exempt organizations commonly provide *deferred compensation* to their employees. Many unique tax and other issues arise when exempt employers provide deferred compensation arrangements. As with current compensation, deferred compensation is subject to the rule of reasonableness.

Deferred compensation programs may take many forms, including retirement plans and profit-sharing plans. (A nonprofit organization can maintain a profit-sharing plan; the words *excess of revenue over expenses* are used instead of *profit*.) These plans are usually subjected to the law laid down by the Employee Retirement Income Security Act of 1974 (ERISA), as well as subsequent enactments, such as those extending rules of nondiscrimination.

Legislation enacted in 2004 affected many deferred compensation arrangements, including executive salary deferral, elective bonus deferral, supplemental executive retirement, deferred severance, tax-exempt "option" plans, and deferred bonus plans. The IRS was given the power to impose taxes, penalties, and interest on violations of this tax law; primarily, recipients of deferred compensation will bear the brunt of these sanctions. Failure to abide by these requirements may result in the current inclusion of all amounts that would otherwise be deferred in the individual's gross income, a tax equal to 20 percent of the amount included in gross income, and interest at the underpayment rate plus 1 percent.

The law prohibits employers and employees from accelerating the distribution of benefits. Distributable events are limited to separation from service, disability, death, occurrence of an unforeseen emergency, or a time specified in the plan. Distributions may also take place in connection with a change in control of the employer. Individual elections to defer the receipt of compensation must be made before the year in which the services are performed.

Deferred compensation plans are basically divided into qualified and nonqualified plans.

(e) Qualified Plans

A *qualified plan* is a plan that satisfies a variety of tax law requirements as to coverage, contributions, other funding, vesting, nondiscrimination, and distributions.

For for-profit organizations, it is desirable for a plan to be a qualified one, to enable employer contributions to the plan to be deductible as business expenses. This, of course, is not of relevance to tax-exempt organizations. Another consideration of a qualified plan is that the income and capital gains from the assets underlying the plan are not subject to federal income tax, in that they are held in an exempt trust.

Qualified plans may be either defined benefit plans or defined contribution plans; the latter also are referred to as individual account plans.

(i) Defined Benefit Plans. A *defined benefit plan* is a plan established and maintained by an employer primarily to systematically provide for the payment of definitely determinable benefits to the employees over a period of years, usually life, following retirement. Retirement benefits under a defined benefit plan are measured by and based on various factors, such as years of service rendered and compensation earned by the employee. The determination of the amount of benefits and the contributions made to the plan is not dependent on the profits of the employer. Under a defined benefit plan, the benefits are established in advance by a formula and the employer contributions are treated as the variable factor.

Any plan that is not a defined contribution plan is a defined benefit plan.

(ii) Defined Contribution Plans. A *defined contribution plan* is a plan that provides an individual account for each participant and bases benefits solely on the amount contributed to the participant's account and any expense, investment return, and forfeitures allocated to the account.

This type of plan defines the amount of contribution to be added to each participant's account. This may be done in one of two ways: by directly defining the amount the employer will contribute on behalf of each employee or by leaving to the employer's discretion the amount of the contribution but defining the method of allocation. The individual accounts must receive, at least annually, their share of the total investment return, including investment income received and realized, and unrealized gain.

Ordinarily, all of a defined contribution plan's assets are allocated to the individual accounts of plan participants. If a participant terminates his or her employment before becoming vested, the nonvested portion of the account balance is forfeited and is applied either to reduce future employer contributions or to increase the accounts of other participants. When a participant becomes eligible to receive a benefit, his or her benefit equals the amount that can be provided by the account balance. The benefit may be paid in the form of a lump-sum distribution, a series of installments, or an annuity.

Defined contribution plans may be structured in many ways. Where the undertaking is to set aside periodic contributions according to a predetermined formula, the plan is referred to as a *money purchase pension plan*. Employer contributions to a money purchase pension plan are mandatory and generally are expressed as a percentage of each participant's compensation. A *target benefit plan* is a money purchase pension plan that sets a targeted benefit to be met by actuarily determined contributions. Special antidiscrimination rules apply to target benefit plans.

Another type of defined contribution plan is a *profit-sharing plan*. A profit-sharing plan is one established and maintained by an employer to provide for participation in profits by employees or their beneficiaries. The sponsor of this type of a plan must make substantial and recurring contributions, but unlike money purchase pension plan contributions, employer contributions to a profit-sharing plan may be discretionary. The plan must have a definite, predetermined formula for allocating any contributions made under the plan among the participants and for distributing the funds accumulated under the plan after a fixed number of years, the attainment of a stated age, or on the prior occurrence of an event, such as layoff, illness, disability, retirement, death, or severance of employment. A profit-sharing plan may, but is not required to, have a definite, predetermined formula for computing the amount of annual employer contributions.

Tax-exempt employers (other than governmental employers) also may sponsor *cash or deferred arrangements*, also known as *401(k) plans*. A 401(k) plan is a qualified profit-sharing or stock bonus plan pursuant to which participants may choose to reduce their current compensation and have that amount contributed to the plan. These contributions, and any earnings or losses on them, are excluded from the participant's taxable income until they are distributed to the participant. Distributions generally may not be made without penalty until the participant retires, becomes disabled, dies, or attains age 59½.

Other defined contribution plans (some of which are profit-sharing plans) include stock bonus plans, employee stock ownership plans, and simplified employee pension plans (which can be a form of individual retirement accounts).

(iii) Funding Mechanism. The usual method of funding a pension or profit-sharing plan is through a tax-exempt trust. A trusteed plan uses a trust to receive and invest the funds contributed under the plan and to distribute the benefits to participants and/or their beneficiaries. In order for a trust forming part of a pension, profit-sharing, or like plan to constitute a qualified trust, (1) the trust must be created or organized in the United States and must be maintained at all times as a U.S. domestic trust; (2) the trust must be established by an employer for the exclusive benefit of the employees and/or their beneficiaries; (3) the trust must be formed or availed of for the purpose of distributing to employees and/or their beneficiaries the corpus and income of the fund accumulated by the trust in accordance with the plan; (4) the trust instrument must prohibit any use of the trust's corpus or income for purposes other than the exclusive benefit of employees and/or their beneficiaries; (5) the trust must be part of a plan that benefits a nondiscriminatory classification of employees under IRS guidelines and provides nondiscriminatory benefits; and (6) the plan of which such trust is a part must satisfy various other federal tax law requirements.

The tax advantages of a qualified plan can be obtained without the use of a trust through an *annuity plan*, under which contributions are used to purchase retirement annuities directly from an insurance company. An annuity contract is treated as a qualified trust if it would, except for the fact that it is not a trust, satisfy all the requirements for qualification. In that case, the annuitant is treated as if he or she were the trustee.

A segregated asset account of a life insurance company can be used as an investment medium for assets of a qualified pension, profit-sharing, or annuity plan. Assets of a qualified plan may be held in this type of account without the use of a trust.

A custodial account can be another nontrusteed funding device. Under this approach, the employer arranges with a bank or other qualified institution to act as custodian of the plan funds placed in the account. Although a custodial account is not a trust, a qualifying custodial account is treated for tax purposes as a qualified trust.

(f) 403(b) Plans

Another form of deferred compensation arrangement in the tax-exempt organizations context is the tax-sheltered (or tax-deferred) annuity. This is an annuity paid out of a *403(b) plan*. A tax-sheltered annuity is treated as a defined contribution plan, but it is not a qualified plan because it is not subject to the general qualified employer benefit plan requirements.

Tax-sheltered annuity programs are available only to employees of charitable organizations and employees of public educational institutions. Essentially, if a qualified employer makes contributions toward the purchase of an annuity contract for an employee, then, to the extent that the amounts do not exceed federal tax law limits for the tax year of the employee, the employee is not required to include the amounts in gross income for the tax year. These plans usually are represented by an individual annuity contract purchased by the employee or a group annuity contract with the employer where a separate account is maintained for each participant. As an alternative, funding may be through a custodial account.

Contributions to a tax-sheltered annuity plan—usually made on a salary reduction basis—are excluded from the employees' taxable income, with certain limitations. Generally, elective (employee) contributions may not exceed an annual dollar limit set forth in the statutory law; that limit is $15,000 in 2006. The funds contributed to a tax-sheltered annuity accumulate without taxation.

As a consequence of this legislation, tax-sheltered annuity (as well as 401(k) plans) may permit any employee who will reach age 50 by the end of the year, and who has already made the maximum contribution permitted under the terms of the plan and the law, to make an additional (or catch-up) contribution for that year. The maximum additional contribution is $5,000 in 2006. Amounts contributed by an employee to a tax-sheltered annuity plan are not required to be included in the employee's gross income to the extent that such contributions do not exceed a limit set forth in federal tax law.

Tax-sheltered annuity plans generally are subject to less federal regulation than other employee benefit plans. Many of these plans are exempt from the ERISA requirements. In general, this exemption applies if an employer makes no contributions of its own to the plan, limits its involvement with the plan, and affords employees a reasonable choice of funding media. If the employer's role is more extensive, however, various provisions of this law apply, as do many of the nondiscrimination, distribution, and other limitations (including restrictions on loans) on qualified plans.

Distributions from a tax-sheltered annuity plan are taxed in the same way as are periodic distributions from qualified plans.

(g) Nonqualified Plans

Nonqualified plans are used as a means to provide supplemental benefits and/ or to avoid the technical requirements imposed on qualified plans. The advantages of nonqualified plans for many employers (particularly for-profit ones), however, have been substantially eroded in recent years. Yet nonqualified plans are of great importance to tax-exempt employers.

The federal tax consequences of nonqualified plans in general vary, depending on whether the plan is funded or unfunded. Where the plan is funded, contributions by an employer to a nonexempt employees' trust are includable in an employee's gross income in the first tax year in which the rights of the individual having the beneficial interest in the trust are transferable and are not subject to a substantial risk of forfeiture. Unfunded plans are those plans that do not constitute qualified employees' trusts or certain nonqualified annuity contracts. The tax consequences to an employee under an unfunded arrangement are determined by application of the doctrines of constructive receipt or economic benefit.

Nonqualified deferred compensation programs afford tax-exempt employers an additional means of compensating certain of their top executives. In order to avoid the strictures of the law, which generally restricts an employer's ability to tailor a benefit plan in a manner that favors highly paid employees, nonqualified plan benefits under an unfunded plan must be provided solely to a "select group of management or other highly compensated employees." This group often is referred to as a "top-hat" group and these programs as "top-hat" programs. Although the Department of Labor has not formally defined the contours of the top-hat group, its most authoritative statement on the subject limits the group to individuals who by virtue of their position or compensation level have the ability to affect or substantially influence, through negotiation or otherwise, the design and operation of their deferred-compensation plan, taking into consideration any risks attendant thereto, and [who], therefore, would not need the substantive rights and protections of ERISA.

Two types of top-hat plans are available to tax-exempt employers. Both of these methods of providing nonqualified, unfunded deferred compensation receive favorable tax treatment under the federal tax law, and they are referred to as *457 plans*. These plans also are available to employees of state and local governments (although the rules are different).

A 457 plan enables an employee to defer the current taxation of income. In exchange for this favorable tax treatment, however, the employee's deferrals must be unfunded and thus remain subject to the claims of the employer's general creditors in the event that the employer becomes insolvent. The employee's only assurance of receiving the benefits from such a plan is the employer's contractual promise to pay.

(i) 457(b) Plans. Top-hat plans that are *457(b) plans* generally provide more favorable tax treatment than the other type of top-hat plan available to tax-exempt employers. A 457(b) plan may allow each executive to defer up to $15,000 per year (in 2006) on a tax-deferred basis. Under some circumstances, catch-up deferrals are permitted, up to twice the annual limit that would otherwise apply. Deferral of the tax on 457(b) plan contributions continues even after the contributions become vested. An executive is not taxed on these deferrals, or earnings on the deferrals, until he or she receives a distribution from the plan.

Distributions from a 457(b) plan cannot be made before the earlier of the date the employee has a severance from employment, attains age 70½, or is faced with an unforeseeable emergency.

Legislation enacted in 2001 made 457(b) plans even more advantageous for employees of tax-exempt employers. Previously, 457(b) plan deferrals counted against the dollar limit on elective contributions to 403(b) plans, with the reverse also true. Thus, there had been little incentive for an employer to maintain both types of plans. This coordination requirement was repealed, however, beginning in 2002, making it possible for an employee who participates in both a 403(b) plan and a 457(b) plan to defer much more compensation.

(ii) 457(f) Plans.   A *457(f) plan* is a top-hat plan that does not satisfy the requirements applicable to 457(b) plans. The tax advantages attendant to 457(f) plans are far more limited than those accorded 457(b) plans. Although participants in 457(f) plans may defer an unlimited amount of their compensation, these deferrals are taxed as soon as they become vested, as are any earnings that have accumulated prior to the vesting date. Earnings that accrue after the deferrals are fully vested are not taxed until the participant has an immediate right to receive them, such as at a specified retirement age.

(iii) Rabbi Trusts.   Although both 457(b) plans and 457(f) plans generally must be unfunded in order to avoid regulation by ERISA and preserve their principal tax advantages, the assets of these plans may nevertheless be held in a particular form of trust fund. This type of trust—commonly referred to as a *rabbi trust* because the first such trust for which the IRS issued a private letter ruling involved the payment of deferred compensation to a rabbi—essentially is treated as a mere extension of the sponsoring employer. The trust document must provide that deferred amounts will remain subject to the claims of the employer's general creditors in the event of the insolvency of the employer. Any income, deductions, or credits attributable to such a trust are treated as being attributable to the employer for tax purposes. The primary advantage of a rabbi trust is that plan participants are protected against losing their benefits on account of most corporate events short of insolvency.

(h) Options for Tax-Exempt Employers

When Congress relaxed the rules that had prohibited tax-exempt organizations from sponsoring 401(k) plans, it caused these organizations to consider more carefully which type of deferred compensation arrangement best suits the needs of their employees. Each plan—401(k), 403(b), 457(b), or 457(f) type—comes with its own set of advantages and drawbacks. Often the suitability of a particular deferred compensation arrangement depends on the nature of the employer.

A noncharitable tax-exempt employer generally is limited to a 401(k) plan or a 457 plan. For these employers, a 401(k) plan may be preferable, inasmuch as 457 plans receive less protection from the operation of the constructive receipt doctrine than do 401(k) plans, and because 457 plans must be unfunded and restricted to a small group of management employees.

In addition to a 401(k) plan and a 457 plan, a charitable tax-exempt employer also may sponsor a 403(b) plan. Although the attributes of 401(k) plans and 403(b) plans are similar, 401(k) plans afford broader investment flexibility than do 403(b) plans. The assets of 403(b) plans must be held in either annuity contracts or mutual funds, while 401(k) plans can permit participants to invest their accounts in commons stocks, limited partnerships, and other investment options. That flexibility as to investment, however, comes at a cost. A 401(k) plan must comply with nondiscrimination requirements that may limit the contributions that can be made to highly compensated employees and also is subject to regulation by the Employee Retirement Income Security Act. A 403(b) plan may be structured so that it need not comply with these rules.

(i) Perspective

The law in this field is complex, with Congress repeatedly visiting the subject. The enactment of ERISA in 1974 brought a vast amount of statutory law on the subject, for tax-exempt and for-profit employers alike. In 1986, Congress, as noted earlier, extended deferred compensation plan rules for the benefit of employees of tax-exempt organizations and made it clear that exempt organizations can maintain qualified profit-sharing plans. In 1996, Congress decided that exempt organizations may maintain the qualified cash or deferred arrangements known as 401(k) plans. The year 2001 brought even more changes to the rules governing retirement arrangements sponsored by tax-exempt employers. Congress, Treasury, and the IRS will assuredly add more law in this field in the coming years—much of it of direct applicability in the exempt organizations context.[43]

§ 11.10   INTERNET LAW

Associations function in a digital age; the proliferation of the Internet signifies a revolution in the way of doing business. E-commerce is the wave of the future. The Internet is a powerful medium that will someday affect virtually all persons within its path. The Internet and e-commerce present wonderful new marketing opportunities and horizons for profit-motivated, as well as nonprofit, entrepreneurs. Consumers have overcome their initial fears of privacy and security issues and are now purchasing millions of dollars of goods and services regularly through the Internet.

---

[43] In general, Pianko & Samuels, *Nonprofit Employment Law: Compensation, Benefits, and Regulation* (New York: John Wiley & Sons, 1998).

(a) Internet/E-Commerce

The Internet is a global telecommunications network, connecting computer networks and users. The Internet permits immediate, global communication and transmission. Part of the excitement (as well as the challenge) of using the Internet effectively is acknowledging that persons around the world may access content and information that is posted. In fact, international boundaries and local jurisdiction dissolve, to some extent, in cyberspace. The interplay between enforcement of local, state laws over Internet transmissions, and disputes will be one of the hotly contested legal issues at the start of the twenty-first century. For example, many entrepreneurs attempt to increase Web site visits by sponsoring sweepstakes or contests. Unfortunately, overeager entrepreneurs sometimes fail to recognize that individuals residing in remote, far-off countries can access the sweepstakes just as readily as residents of the United States. State laws, as well as the laws of many foreign countries, regulate games of chance, and the unwary entrepreneur may have violated laws in many jurisdictions governing lotteries or gambling.

(b) Web Site Use and Management

In order to maintain a presence on the Internet, a business or enterprise must first establish a Web site. A Web site is an electronic location on the World Wide Web that may contain text, graphics, visual images, or sound. The site is accessed by a unique uniform resource locator (URL) or domain name, which is the equivalent of a telephone number or address for the site. Domain names are applied for and issued by domain name registration services, such as Network Solutions, Inc. (Internic), which, for some time, held an exclusive right to allocate domain names. Today 29 organizations have the right to allocate top-level domain names, ending in the now-common .com, .net, .org, .edu, and .gov, and other domain name strings will soon be available. Although the .org suffix initially was reserved for charities, the distinction among .com, .net, and .org has blurred to the degree that .org is no longer synonymous with a charitable venture.

The single most important aspect of Web site management is to take appropriate precautions to ensure that the developer of the Web site, usually an independent contractor, assigns and relinquishes ownership in and to the site and its hypertext markup language (html) to the commissioning party. As noted elsewhere, in the absence of such written assignment, the Web site developer could claim ownership of the Web site and its content. The Web site's owner should consider using disclaimers or a statement of terms and conditions governing access to the Web site, alerting the user to any rules or regulations governing use of the site and/or its content. It is becoming common for such disclaimers and policy statements to require the user to click on an "I Accept" icon, to create an evidentiary record of consent, before being permitted to access the site any further. The user should also be warned that transmissions across the Internet are not secure and that there should be no expectation of privacy in any information transmitted (or even in the user's access to the site).

The Web site owner should be cautious about using "links"—connections from one site to the site of another party. Linking can create liability if the user is deceived or confused about the origin of a site or association between the owners of two sites. A link could also be construed as an endorsement of another party's goods or services.[44]

§ 11.11   MANAGEMENT OF INSTITUTIONAL FUNDS ACT

The board of a charitable organization may, pursuant to the Uniform Management of Institutional Funds Act, appropriate for expenditure for the purposes for which an endowment fund is established so much of the net appreciation, realized and unrealized, in the fair value of the assets of the fund over the historic dollar value of the fund as is prudent. This rule does not apply if the gift instrument involved indicates the donor's intention that net appreciation shall not be expended.

The board may invest and reinvest an institutional fund in any real or personal property deemed advisable by it, whether it produces a current return or not, including mortgages, stocks, bonds, and debentures. It may retain property contributed by a donor to an institutional fund for as long as it deems advisable. The board may include all or any part of an institutional fund in a pooled or common fund maintained by the institution.

Unless the law or the gift document provides otherwise, the board may delegate to its committees, officers, or employees of the institution or the fund, or agents, the authority to act in place of the board in investment and reinvestment of the organization's funds. It may contract with independent investment advisors, investment counsel or managers, banks, or trust companies for this purpose. It is authorized to pay compensation for investment advisory or management services.

In the administration of its powers in this regard, the members of the board are required to exercise ordinary business care and prudence under the facts and circumstances prevailing at the time of the action or decision. In so doing, they are to consider long- and short-term needs of the organization in carrying out its charitable purposes, its present and anticipated financial requirements, expected total return on its investments, price level trends, and general economic conditions.

§ 11.12   OTHER LAWS

There are, of course, many other bodies of law applicable to nonprofit organizations, some more directly applicable than others and often with unique variances or special rules for nonprofit entities. Included are laws concerning banking, bankruptcy, bond financing, communications, consumer protection, criminal activities, education, employment, environmental matters, estate administration, federal contracts and grants, gambling, health, housing, insurance, international relations, labor, transportation, trust administration, and welfare.

---

[44] In general, Hopkins, *The Nonprofits' Guide to Internet Communications Law* (Hoboken, NJ: John Wiley & Sons, 2003).

Appendices

APPENDIX A

Sources of the Law

The law as described in this book is derived from many sources. For those not familiar with these matters and wishing to understand what "the law" regarding tax-exempt associations is, the following explanation should be of assistance.

FEDERAL LAW

At the federal (national) level in the United States, there are three branches of government, as provided for in the U.S. Constitution. Article 1 of the Constitution established the U.S. Congress as a bicameral legislature, consisting of the House of Representatives and the Senate. Article II of the Constitution established the presidency. Article III of the Constitution established the federal court system.

Congress

Congress has created and continues to create the legal structure (statutes) underlying the federal law for nonprofit organizations in the United States. Most of this law is manifested in the tax law and thus appears in the Internal Revenue Code (which is officially codified in Title 26 of the United States Code and referenced throughout the book as the "IRC" (see § 1.1, note 6)).

Tax laws for the United States must originate in the House of Representatives (U.S. Constitution, art. I § 7). Consequently, the members and staff of the House Committee on Ways and Means often initially write the nation's tax laws pertaining to associations and other tax-exempt organizations. Frequently, these laws are generated by work done at the subcommittee level, usually the Subcommittee on Oversight or the Subcommittee on Select Revenue Measures. Nonetheless, it is becoming common for tax legislation to originate in the Senate; these measures are subsequently added to a House tax bill.

Committee work in this area within the Senate is undertaken by the Committee on Finance. The Joint Committee on Taxation, consisting of members from both the House of Representatives and the Senate, also provides assistance in this regard. Nearly all of this legislation is finalized by a House-Senate conference committee, consisting of senior members of the House Ways and Means Committee and the Senate Finance Committee.

A considerable amount of the federal tax law for associations and other tax-exempt organizations is found in the legislative history of these statutory laws.

Most of this history is in congressional committee reports. Reports from committees in the House of Representatives are cited as "H. R. Rep. No." (see, e.g., § 5.9(a), n. 272); reports from committees in the Senate are cited as "S. Rep. No." (see, e.g., § 2.5(a), n. 90); conference committee reports are cited as "H. R. Rep. No." (see, e.g., § 2.5(a), n. 90). Transcripts of the debate on legislation, formal statements, and other items are printed in the *Congressional Record* (Cong. Rec.). The *Congressional Record* is published every day one of the houses of Congress is in session and is cited as "[number] Cong. Rec. [number] (daily ed., [date of issue])." The first number is the annual volume number, the second number is the page in the daily edition on which the item begins. Periodically, the daily editions of the *Congressional Record* are republished as a hardbound book, which is cited as "[number] Cong. Rec. [number] ([year])." As before, the first number is the annual volume number and the second is the beginning page number. The bound version of the *Congressional Record* then becomes the publication that contains the permanent citation for the item (see, e.g., § 2.5(b), n. 103).

A Congress sits for two years; each of these years is termed a *session*. Each Congress is sequentially numbered. For example, the 109th Congress is meeting during the calendar years 2005–2006. A legislative development that took place in 2006 is referenced as occurring during the 109th Congress, 2nd Session (109th Cong., 2nd Sess. (2006)).

A bill introduced in the House of Representatives or Senate during a particular Congress is given a sequential number in each house. For example, the 1,000th bill introduced in the House of Representatives in 2006 is cited as "H.R. 1000, 109th Cong., 2nd Sess. (2006)"; the 500th bill introduced in the Senate in 2006 is cited as "S. 500, 109th Cong., 2nd Sess. (2006)."

Executive Branch

A function of the executive branch of the United States is to administer and enforce the laws enacted by Congress. This executive function is performed by departments and agencies, and "independent" regulatory commissions (such as the Federal Trade Commission or the Securities and Exchange Commission). One of these functions is the promulgation of regulations, which are published by the U.S. government in the *Code of Federal Regulations* ("CFR"). When adopted, regulations are printed in the *Federal Register* ("Fed. Reg."). The federal tax laws are administered and enforced by the Department of the Treasury.

One of the ways in which the Department of the Treasury executes these functions is by the promulgation of regulations ("Treas. Reg." or simply "Reg."), which are designed to interpret and amplify the related statute (see, e.g., § 1.1, n. 8). These regulations (like rules made by other departments, agencies, and commissions) can have the force of law, unless they are overly broad in relation to the accompanying statute or are unconstitutional, in which case they can be rendered void by a court (see below).

Within the Department of the Treasury is the Internal Revenue Service ("IRS"). The IRS is, among its many roles, a tax-collecting agency. The IRS, though headquartered in Washington, D.C. (its "National Office"), has regional and field offices throughout the country.

The IRS (from its National Office) prepares and disseminates guidelines interpreting tax statutes and tax regulations. These guidelines have the force of law, unless they are overbroad in relation to the statute and/or Treasury regulation involved, or are unconstitutional (see below). IRS determinations on a point of law are termed *revenue rulings* ("Rev. Rul."); those that are rules of procedure are termed *revenue procedures* ("Rev. Proc.").

Revenue rulings (which may be based on one or more court opinions) and revenue procedures are sequentially numbered every calendar year, with that number preceded by a four-digit number reflecting the year of issue. For example, the 50th revenue ruling issued in 2006 is cited as "Rev. Rul. 2006-50." Likewise, the 25th revenue procedure issued in 2006 is cited as "Rev. Proc. 2006-25."

These IRS determinations are published each week in the *Internal Revenue Bulletin* (I.R.B.). In the foregoing examples, when the determinations are first published, the revenue ruling is cited as "Rev. Rul. 2006-50, 2006-__ I.R.B. ____," with the number after the hyphen being the number of the particular issue of the weekly *Bulletin* and the last number being the page number within that issue on which the item begins. Likewise the revenue procedure is cited as "Rev. Proc. 2006-25, 2006-__ I.R.B. ____." Every six months, the *Internal Revenue Bulletins* are republished as hardbound books; these publications are termed the *Cumulative Bulletin* (C.B.). The *Cumulative Bulletin* designation then becomes the permanent citation for the determination. Thus, the permanent citations for these two IRS determinations are "Rev. Rul. 2006-50, 2006-1 C.B. ___" (see, e.g., § 1.4, n. 48) and "Rev. Proc. 2006-25, 2006-1 C.B. ___" (see, e.g., § 5.9(p), n. 528), with the first number being the year of issue, the second number (after the hyphen) indicating whether the determination is published in the first six months of the year ("1," as in the example, or the second six months of the year ("2")), and the last number being the page number within that semiannual bound volume at which the determination begins.

The IRS considers itself bound by its revenue rulings and revenue procedures. These determinations are the "law," particularly in the sense that the IRS regards them as precedential, although they are not binding on the courts. Indeed, the courts generally treat an IRS revenue ruling as merely the position of the IRS with respect to a specific factual situation.

By contrast to these forms of "public" law, the IRS (again, from its National Office) also issues private or nonprecedential determinations. These documents principally are private letter rulings ("Priv. Ltr. Rul."), technical advice memoranda ("Tech. Adv. Mem."), and chief counsel advice memoranda ("Chief Counsel Adv. Mem."). These determinations may not be cited as legal authority (IRC § 6110(j)(3)). Nonetheless, these pronouncements can be valuable in understanding IRS thinking on a point of law, and, in practice (the statutory prohibition notwithstanding), these documents are cited in court opinions, articles, and books as IRS positions on issues.

The IRS issues private letter rulings in response to written questions (termed *ruling requests*) submitted to the IRS by individuals and organizations. An IRS field office may refer a case to the IRS National Office for advice (termed *technical advice*); the resulting advice is provided to the IRS district office in the form of a technical advice memorandum. In the course of preparing a revenue ruling, private letter ruling, or technical advice memorandum, the IRS National Office may seek legal advice from its Office of Chief Counsel; the resulting advice may be provided in the form of a chief counsel advice memorandum (see below). These documents are eventually made public, albeit in redacted form.

Private letter rulings and technical advice memoranda for years were identified by seven-digit numbers, as in "Priv. Ltr. Rul. 9826007" (see, e.g., § 2.4(b), n. 77). (A reference to a technical advice memorandum appears in § 2.3, n. 40.) Beginning in 1999, however, the IRS began using a nine-digit numbering system, as in "Priv. Ltr. Rul. 200626007 (e.g., § 1.4, n. 40). The first four numbers are for the year involved (here, 2006), the second two numbers reflect the week of the calendar year involved (here, the 26th week of 2006), and the remaining three numbers identify the document as issued sequentially during the particular week (here, this private letter ruling was the seventh one issued during the week involved). General counsel memoranda (now Chief Counsel Adv. Mem.) are numbered sequentially in the order in which they are written (e.g., Gen. Couns. Mem. 39457 is the 39,457th general counsel memorandum ever written by the IRS's Office of Chief Counsel). A reference to a general counsel memorandum appears in § 1.4, n. 38.

In the tax-exempt organizations area, the IRS was ordered by a federal court of appeals to release rulings denying or revoking exempt status; these were initially termed exemption denial and revocation letters ("Ex. Den. & Revoc. Ltr."). An example appears in Chapter 3, n. 13. Today, however, the IRS issues these rulings in the form of private letter rulings.

Judiciary

The federal court system has three levels: trial courts (including those that initially hear cases when a formal trial is not involved), courts of appeal (*appellate courts*), and the U.S. Supreme Court. The trial courts include the various federal district courts (at least one in each state, the District of Columbia, and the U.S. territories), the U.S. Tax Court, and the U.S. Court of Federal Claims (formerly the U.S. Claims Court). There are 13 federal appellate courts: the U.S. Courts of Appeals for the First through the Eleventh Circuits, the U.S. Court of Appeals for the District of Columbia, and the U.S. Court of Appeals for the Federal Circuit.

Cases concerning the tax law for associations and other tax-exempt organizations at the federal level can originate in any federal district court, the U.S. Tax Court, or the U.S. Court of Federal Claims. Under a special declaratory judgment procedure available only to charitable organizations (IRC § 7428), cases can originate only with the U.S. District Court for the District of Columbia, the U.S. Tax Court, or the U.S. Court of Federal Claims. Cases involving tax-exempt organizations are considered by the U.S. courts of appeal and the U.S. Supreme Court.

Most opinions emanating from a U.S. district court are published by the West Publishing Company in the Federal Supplement series. Thus, for many years, a citation to one of these opinions appeared as "[number] F. Supp. [number]," followed by an identification of the court and the year of the opinion. The first number is the annual volume number; the second number is the page in the book on which the opinion begins (see, e.g., § 1.1, n. 11). In early 1998, West began publishing the Federal Supplement Second series (once volume 999 of the Federal Supplement series was published); thus, citations to subsequent opinions from the U.S. courts of appeal appear as "[number] F. Supp. 2d [number]" (see, e.g., § 1.6(a), n. 72). Some district court opinions appear sooner in Commerce Clearing House or Prentice-Hall publications (see, e.g., § 2.8, n. 165); occasionally these publications will contain opinions that are never published in the Federal Supplement reporter.

Most opinions emanating from a U.S. court of appeals are published by the West Publishing Company in the Federal Reporter Second series (F.2d). Thus, a citation to one of these opinions appears as "[number] F.2d [number]," followed by an identification of the court and the year of the opinion. The first number is an annual volume number, the second number is the page in the book on which the opinion begins (see, e.g., § 1.1, n. 12). In early 1994, the Federal Reporter Third series was started (once volume 999 of the Federal Reporter Second series was published); thus, citations to subsequent opinions from the U.S. courts of appeal appear as "[number] F.3d [number]" (see, e.g., § 1.6(a), n. 76). Appellate court opinions appear sooner in Commerce Clearing House or Prentice-Hall publications; occasionally these publications will contain opinions that are never published in the Federal Reporter series. Opinions from the U.S. Court of Federal Claims are also published in Federal Reporter Second (and Third) series.

Opinions from the U.S. Tax Court are published by the U.S. government and are often cited as "[number] T.C. [number]," followed by the year of the opinion (see, e.g., § 1.1, n. 11). As always, the first number of these citations is the annual volume number; the second number is the page in the book on which the opinion begins. Other opinions from this court, deemed by the court to be of lesser import, are memorandum decisions; these are cited as "[number] T.C.M. [number]," followed by the year of the opinion (see, e.g., § 2.3, n. 21).

U.S. district court and Tax Court opinions may be appealed to the appropriate U.S. court of appeals. For example, cases in the states of Maryland, North Carolina, South Carolina, Virginia, and West Virginia, and the District of Columbia are appealable (from either court) to the U.S. Court of Appeals for the Fourth Circuit. Cases from any federal appellate or district court, the U.S. Tax Court, and the U.S. Court of Federal Claims may be appealed to the U.S. Supreme Court.

The U.S. Supreme Court usually has discretion as to whether to accept a case. This decision is manifested as a "writ of certiorari." When the Supreme Court agrees to hear a case, it grants the writ (*"cert. granted"*); otherwise, it denies the writ (*"cert. denied"*).

In this book, citations to Supreme Court opinions are to the United States Reports series published by the U.S. government, when available ("[number] U.S. [number]," followed by the year of the opinion) (see, e.g., § 1.1, n. 10). When the United States Reports series citation is not available, the Supreme Court Reporter series, published by the West Publishing Company, reference is used ("[number] S. Ct. [number]," followed by the year of the opinion (see below). As always, the first number of these citations is the annual volume number; the second number is the page in the book on which the opinion begins. There is a third way to cite Supreme Court cases, which is by means of the United States

Supreme Court Reports—Lawyers' Edition series, published by the Lawyers Co-Operative Publishing Company and the Bancroft-Whitney Company, but that form of citation is not used in this book. Supreme Court opinions appear earlier in the Commerce Clearing House or Prentice-Hall publications.

Courts are often called on to review a Department of the Treasury regulation or an IRS public pronouncement. The fundamental question for a court reviewing an agency's construction of a statute that it administers is whether the agency's position is based on a permissible interpretation of the statute (Chevron U.S.A., Inc. v. Natural Res. Def. Council, Inc., 467 U.S. 837 (1984)). This level of deference, however, is limited to those cases where it "appears that Congress delegated authority to the agency generally to make rules carrying the force of law, and that the agency interpretation claiming deference was promulgated in exercise of that authority" (United States v. Mead Corp., 533 U.S. 218, 226–227 (2001)). "Otherwise, the interpretation is 'entitled to respect' only to the extent it has the 'power to persuade'" (Gonzales v. Oregon, 126 S. Ct. 904, 914–915 (2006)) (quoting Skidmore v. Swift & Co., 323 U.S. 134, 140 (1944)).

Thus, a court generally will defer to an agency's position only where the interpretation at issue is a "fruit[] of notice-and-comment rule making" (United States v. Mead Corp., 533 U.S. 218, 230). Otherwise, an agency's positions do not carry the force of law; that is, they "do not warrant *Chevron*-style deference" (Christensen v. Harris County, 529 U.S. 576, 587 (2000)). Thus, a court will defer to an interpretation proffered by an agency only to the extent it finds that construction of the law to be persuasive.

For example, a federal court of appeals voided the tax regulations that prohibited the IRS from disclosing denials or revocations of tax exemption on the ground that the interpretation was in conflict with the statutes (IRC §§ 6104(a)(1)(A), 6110) (Tax Analysts v. Internal Revenue Service, 350 F.3d 100 (D.C. Cir. 2003)). This appellate court also held that IRS Field Service Advice Memoranda are not protected from disclosure by the federal tax law (Tax Analysts v. Internal Revenue Service, 117 F.3d 607 (D.C. Cir. 1997)). Yet this court agreed with the IRS that it and the tax-exempt organization involved were not required to disclose the contents of a closing agreement between them (Tax Analysts v. Internal Revenue Service and Christian Broadcasting Network, Inc., 410 F.3d 715 (D.C. Cir. 2005)). Nonetheless, other law may be involved. For example, a court held that IRS "informal" chief counsel advice documents are not exempt from disclosure pursuant to the federal tax law but concluded that the documents were protected from public inspection because of the "deliberative process privilege" found in the Freedom of Information Act (5 U.S.C. § 552(b)(5)).

STATE LAW

Legislative Branches

Statutory laws in the various states are created by the state legislatures.

Executive Branches

The rules and regulations published at the state level emanate from state departments, agencies, and the like. For charitable organizations, these departments are usually the office of the state's Attorney General and the state's Department of State. There are no references to state rules and regulations in this book.

Judiciary

Each of the states has a judiciary system, usually a three-tiered one modeled after the federal system. Cases involving charitable organizations are heard in all of these courts. There are few references to state court opinions in this book (see, e.g., § 2.5(b), n. 95).

State court opinions are published by the governments of each state, and the principal ones are also collected and published by the West Publishing Company. The latter sets of opinions (referenced in this book) are published in "reporters" covering court developments in various regions throughout the country. For example, the *Atlantic Reporter* contains court opinions issued by the principal courts in the states of Connecticut, Delaware, Maine, Maryland, New Hampshire, New Jersey, Pennsylvania, Rhode Island, Vermont, and the District of Columbia; the *Pacific Reporter* contains court opinions issued by the principal courts of Arizona, California, Colorado, Idaho, Kansas, Montana, Nevada, New Mexico, Oklahoma, Oregon, Utah, Washington, and Wyoming.

PUBLICATIONS

Articles, of course, are not forms of "the law." However, they can be cited, particularly by courts, in the development of the law. Also, as research tools, they contain useful summaries of the applicable law. In addition to the many law school "law review" publications, these periodicals (not an exclusive list) contain material that may be helpful in following developments concerning tax-exempt associations and affiliated entities:

Bruce R. Hopkins' Nonprofit Counsel (John Wiley & Sons)

The Chronicle of Philanthropy (The Chronicle of Higher Education)

Daily Tax Report (Bureau of National Affairs)

Exempt Organizations Tax Review (Tax Analysts)

Foundation News (Council on Foundations)

The Journal of Taxation (Warren, Gorham & Lamont)

The Journal of Taxation of Exempt Organizations (Faulkner & Gray)

The Philanthropy Monthly (Non-Profit Reports)

Tax Law Review (Rosenfeld Launer Publications)

The Tax Lawyer (American Bar Association)

Tax Notes (Tax Analysts)

Taxes (Commerce Clearing House)

Form 1024

Form **1024** (Rev. September 1998) Department of the Treasury Internal Revenue Service	**Application for Recognition of Exemption Under Section 501(a)**	OMB No. 1545-0057 If exempt status is approved, this application will be open for public inspection.

Read the instructions for each Part carefully. **A User Fee must be attached to this application.**
If the required information and appropriate documents are not submitted along with Form 8718 (with payment
of the appropriate user fee), the application may be returned to the organization.
Complete the Procedural Checklist on page 6 of the instructions.

Part I. Identification of Applicant (Must be completed by all applicants; also complete appropriate schedule.)
Submit only the schedule that applies to your organization. Do not submit blank schedules.

Check the appropriate box below to indicate the section under which the organization is applying:

a ☐ Section 501(c)(2) — Title holding corporations (Schedule A, page 7)

b ☐ Section 501(c)(4) — Civic leagues, social welfare organizations (including certain war veterans' organizations), or local associations of
employees (Schedule B, page 8)

c ☐ Section 501(c)(5) — Labor, agricultural, or horticultural organizations (Schedule C, page 9)

d ☐ Section 501(c)(6) — Business leagues, chambers of commerce, etc. (Schedule C, page 9)

e ☐ Section 501(c)(7) — Social clubs (Schedule D, page 11)

f ☐ Section 501(c)(8) — Fraternal beneficiary societies, etc., providing life, sick, accident, or other benefits to members (Schedule E, page 13)

g ☐ Section 501(c)(9) — Voluntary employees' beneficiary associations (Parts I through IV and Schedule F, page 14)

h ☐ Section 501(c)(10) — Domestic fraternal societies, orders, etc., not providing life, sick, or accident, or other benefits (Schedule E, page 13)

i ☐ Section 501(c)(12) — Benevolent life insurance associations, mutual ditch or irrigation companies, mutual or cooperative telephone
companies, or like organizations (Schedule G, page 15)

j ☐ Section 501(c)(13) — Cemeteries, crematoria, and like corporations (Schedule H, page 16)

k ☐ Section 501(c)(15) — Mutual insurance companies or associations, other than life or marine (Schedule I, page 17)

l ☐ Section 501(c)(17) — Trusts providing for the payment of supplemental unemployment compensation benefits (Parts I through IV and Schedule J, page 18)

m ☐ Section 501(c)(19) — A post, organization, auxiliary unit, etc., of past or present members of the Armed Forces of the United States (Schedule K, page 19)

n ☐ Section 501(c)(25) — Title holding corporations or trusts (Schedule A, page 7)

1a Full name of organization (as shown in organizing document)	2 Employer identification number (EIN) (if none, see **Specific Instructions** on page 2)
1b c/o Name (if applicable)	3 Name and telephone number of person to be contacted if additional information is needed
1c Address (number and street) Room/Suite	
1d City, town or post office, state, and ZIP + 4 If you have a foreign address, see **Specific Instructions** for Part I, page 2.	
1e Web site address 4 Month the annual accounting period ends	5 Date incorporated or formed

6 Did the organization previously apply for recognition of exemption under this Code section or under any other section of the Code? .... ☐ Yes ☐ No
If "Yes," attach an explanation.

7 Has the organization filed Federal income tax returns or exempt organization information returns? .... ☐ Yes ☐ No
If "Yes," state the form numbers, years filed, and Internal Revenue office where filed.

8 Check the box for the type of organization. ATTACH A CONFORMED COPY OF THE CORRESPONDING ORGANIZING DOCUMENTS TO THE
APPLICATION BEFORE MAILING.

a ☐ Corporation — Attach a copy of the Articles of Incorporation (including amendments and restatements) showing approval by the appropriate
state official; also attach a copy of the bylaws.

b ☐ Trust — Attach a copy of the Trust Indenture or Agreement, including all appropriate signatures and dates.

c ☐ Association — Attach a copy of the Articles of Association, Constitution, or other creating document, with a declaration (see instructions) or
other evidence that the organization was formed by adoption of the document by more than one person. Also include a copy
of the bylaws.

If this is a corporation or an unincorporated association that has not yet adopted bylaws, check here .... ▶ ☐

I declare under the penalties of perjury that I am authorized to sign this application on behalf of the above organization, and that I have examined this
application, including the accompanying schedules and attachments, and to the best of my knowledge it is true, correct, and complete.

**PLEASE
SIGN
HERE** ▶

_____   _____   _____
(Signature)   (Type or print name and title or authority of signer)   (Date)

For Paperwork Reduction Act Notice, see page 5 of the instructions.

ISA
STF FED2181F.1

APPENDIX B

Part II. Activities and Operational Information (Must be completed by all applicants)

1   Provide a detailed narrative description of all the activities of the organization — past, present, and planned. Do not merely refer to or repeat the language in the organizational document. List each activity separately in the order of importance based on the relative time and other resources devoted to the activity. Indicate the percentage of time for each activity. Each description should include, as a minimum, the following: **(a)** a detailed description of the activity including its purpose and how each activity furthers your exempt purpose; **(b)** when the activity was or will be initiated; and **(c)** where and by whom the activity will be conducted.

2   List the organization's present and future sources of financial support, beginning with the largest source first.

STF FED2181F.2

■   434   ■

Part II. Activities and Operational Information (continued)

3   Give the following information about the organization's governing body:

a Names, addresses, and titles of officers, directors, trustees, etc.	b Annual compensation

4   If the organization is the outgrowth or continuation of any form of predecessor, state the name of each predecessor, the period during which it was in existence, and the reasons for its termination. Submit copies of all papers by which any transfer of assets was effected.

5   If the applicant organization is now, or plans to be, connected in any way with any other organization, describe the other organization and explain the relationship (e.g., financial support on a continuing basis; shared facilities or employees; same officers, directors, or trustees).

6   If the organization has capital stock issued and outstanding, state: **(1)** class or classes of the stock; **(2)** number and par value of the shares; **(3)** consideration for which they were issued; and **(4)** if any dividends have been paid or whether your organization's creating instrument authorizes dividend payments on any class of capital stock.

7   State the qualifications necessary for membership in the organization; the classes of membership (with the number of members in each class); and the voting rights and privileges received. If any group or class of persons is required to join, describe the requirement and explain the relationship between those members and members who join voluntarily. Submit copies of any membership solicitation material. Attach sample copies of all types of membership certificates issued.

8   Explain how your organization's assets will be distributed on dissolution.

STF FED2181F.3

Part II. Activities and Operational Information (continued)

9 Has the organization made or does it plan to make any distribution of its property or surplus funds to shareholders or members? . . . . ☐ Yes   ☐ No
If "Yes," state the full details, including: **(1)** amounts or value; **(2)** source of funds or property distributed or to be distributed; and **(3)** basis of, and authority for, distribution or planned distribution.

10 Does, or will, any part of your organization's receipts represent payments for services performed or to be performed? . . . . ☐ Yes   ☐ No
If "Yes," state in detail the amount received and the character of the services performed or to be performed.

11 Has the organization made, or does it plan to make, any payments to members or shareholders for services performed or to be performed? . . . . ☐ Yes   ☐ No
If "Yes," state in detail the amount paid, the character of the services, and to whom the payments have been, or will be, made.

12 Does the organization have any arrangement to provide insurance for members, their dependents, or others (including provisions for the payment of sick or death benefits, pensions, or annuities)? . . . . ☐ Yes   ☐ No
If "Yes," describe and explain the arrangement's eligibility rules and attach a sample copy of each plan document and each type of policy issued.

13 Is the organization under the supervisory jurisdiction of any public regulatory body, such as a social welfare agency, etc.? . . . . ☐ Yes   ☐ No
If "Yes," submit copies of all administrative opinions or court decisions regarding this supervision, as well as copies of applications or requests for the opinions or decisions.

14 Does the organization now lease or does it plan to lease any property? . . . . ☐ Yes   ☐ No
If "Yes," explain in detail. Include the amount of rent, a description of the property, and any relationship between the applicant organization and the other party. Also, attach a copy of any rental or lease agreement. (If the organization is a party, as a lessor, to multiple leases of rental real property under similar lease agreements, please attach a single representative copy of the leases.)

15 Has the organization spent or does it plan to spend any money attempting to influence the selection, nomination, election, or appointment or any person to any Federal, state, or local public office or to an office in a political organization? . . . . ☐ Yes   ☐ No
If "Yes," explain in detail and list the amounts spent or to be spent in each case.

16 Does the organization publish pamphlets, brochures, newsletters, journals, or similar printed material? . . . . ☐ Yes   ☐ No
If "Yes," attach a recent copy of each.

Form 1024 (Rev. 9-98)   Page **5**

Part III. Financial Data (Must be completed by all applicants)

Complete the financial statements for the current year and for each of the 3 years immediately before it. If in existence less than 4 years, complete the statements for each year in existence. **If in existence less than 1 year, also provide proposed budgets for the 2 years following the current year.**

A. Statement of Revenue and Expenses

Revenue	(a) Current Tax Year From ___ To ___	3 Prior Tax Years or Proposed Budget for Next 2 Years			(e) Total
		(b) ___	(c) ___	(d) ___	
1 Gross dues and assessments of members					0.00
2 Gross contributions, gifts, etc.					0.00
3 Gross amounts derived from activities related to the organization's exempt purpose (attach schedule) (Include related cost of sales on line 9.)					0.00
4 Gross amounts from unrelated business activities (attach schedule)					0.00
5 Gain from sale of assets, excluding inventory items (attach schedule)					0.00
6 Investment income (see page 3 of the instructions)					0.00
7 Other revenue (attach schedule)					0.00
8 Total revenue (add lines 1 through 7)	0.00	0.00	0.00	0.00	0.00
Expenses					
9 Expenses attributable to activities related to the organization's exempt purposes					0.00
10 Expenses attributable to unrelated business activities					0.00
11 Contributions, gifts, grants, and similar amounts paid (attach schedule)					0.00
12 Disbursements to or for the benefit of members (attach schedule)					0.00
13 Compensation of officers, directors, and trustees (attach schedule)					0.00
14 Other salaries and wages					0.00
15 Interest					0.00
16 Occupancy					0.00
17 Depreciation and depletion					0.00
18 Other expenses (attach schedule)					0.00
19 Total expenses (add lines 9 through 18)	0.00	0.00	0.00	0.00	0.00
20 Excess of revenue over expenses (line 8 minus line 19)	0.00	0.00	0.00	0.00	0.00

B. Balance Sheet (at the end of the period shown)

Assets		Current Tax Year as of ___
1 Cash	1	
2 Accounts receivable, net	2	
3 Inventories	3	
4 Bonds and notes receivable (attach schedule)	4	
5 Corporate stocks (attach schedule)	5	
6 Mortgage loans (attach schedule)	6	
7 Other investments (attach schedule)	7	
8 Depreciable and depletable assets (attach schedule)	8	
9 Land	9	
10 Other assets (attach schedule)	10	
11 **Total assets**	11	0.00
Liabilities		
12 Accounts payable	12	
13 Contributions, gifts, grants, etc., payable	13	
14 Mortgages and notes payable (attach schedule)	14	
15 Other liabilities (attach schedule)	15	
16 **Total liabilities**	16	0.00
Fund Balances or Net Assets		
17 Total fund balances or net assets	17	
18 **Total liabilities and fund balances or net assets** (add line 16 and line 17)	18	0.00

If there has been any substantial change in any aspect of the organization's financial activities since the end of the period shown above, check the box and attach a detailed explanation .... ▶ ☐

STF FED2181F.5

Form 1024 (Rev. 9-98)   Page 9

| Schedule C | Organizations described in section 501(c)(5) (Labor, agricultural, including fishermen's organizations, or horticultural organizations) or section 501(c)(6) (business leagues, chambers of commerce, etc.) |

1   Describe any services the organization performs for members or others. (If the description of the services is
    contained in Part II of the application, enter the page and item number here.)

2   Fishermen's organizations only. — What kinds of aquatic resources (not including mineral) are cultivated or harvested
    by those eligible for membership in the organization?

3   Labor organizations only. — Is the organization organized under the terms of a collective bargaining agreement? . . . . ☐ Yes   ☐ No

    If "Yes," attach a copy of the latest agreement.

STF FED2181F.9

APPENDIX C

Form 4720

Form **4720** Department of the Treasury Internal Revenue Service	**Return of Certain Excise Taxes on Charities and Other Persons Under Chapters 41 and 42 of the Internal Revenue Code** (Sections 170(f)(10), 4911, 4912, 4941, 4942, 4943, 4944, 4945, 4955, and 4958) ▶ See separate instructions.	OMB No. 1545-0052 2**005**

For calendar year 2005 or other tax year beginning	2005, and ending	20

Name of foundation or public charity	Employer identification number

Number, street, and room or suite no. (or P.O. box if mail is not delivered to street address)	Check box for type of annual return: ☐ Form 990 ☐ Form 990-EZ
City or town, state, and ZIP code	☐ Form 990-PF ☐ Form 5227

		Yes	No
A	Is the organization a foreign private foundation within the meaning of section 4948(b)?		
B	Has corrective action been taken on any taxable event that resulted in Chapter 42 taxes being reported on this form? (Enter "N/A" if not applicable)		

If "Yes," attach a detailed description and documentation of the corrective action taken and, if applicable, enter the fair market value of any property recovered as a result of the correction ▶ $ _____ . If "No," (i.e., any uncorrected acts, or transactions), attach an explanation (see page 3 of the instructions).

Part I **Taxes on Organization** (Sections 170(f)(10), 4911(a), 4912(a), 4942(a), 4943(a)(1), 4944(a)(1), 4945(a)(1), and 4955(a)(1))

1	Tax on undistributed income—Schedule B, line 4	**1**
2	Tax on excess business holdings—Schedule C, line 7	**2**
3	Tax on investments that jeopardize charitable purpose—Schedule D, Part I, column (e) .	**3**
4	Tax on taxable expenditures—Schedule E, Part I, column (g)	**4**
5	Tax on political expenditures—Schedule F, Part I, column (e)	**5**
6	Tax on excess lobbying expenditures—Schedule G, line 4	**6**
7	Tax on disqualifying lobbying expenditures—Schedule H, Part I, column (e)	**7**
8	Tax on premiums paid on personal benefit contracts	**8**
9	**Total** (add lines 1–8).	**9**

Part II-A **Taxes on Self-Dealers, Disqualified Persons, Foundation Managers, and Organization Managers** (Sections 4912(b), 4941(a), 4944(a)(2), 4945(a)(2), 4955(a)(2), and 4958(a))

	(a) Name and address of person subject to tax	(b) Taxpayer identification number
a		
b		
c		
d		

	(c) Tax on self-dealing—Schedule A, Part II, col. (d), and Part III, col. (d)	(d) Tax on investments that jeopardize charitable purpose—Schedule D, Part II, col. (d)	(e) Tax on taxable expenditures—Schedule E, Part II, col. (d)	(f) Tax on political expenditures—Schedule F, Part II, col. (d)
a				
b				
c				
d				
Total				

	(g) Tax on disqualifying lobbying expenditures—Schedule H, Part II, col. (d)	(h) Tax on excess benefit transactions—Schedule I, Part II, col. (d), and Part III, col. (d)	(i) Total—Add cols. (c) through (h)
a			
b			
c			
d			
Total			

Part II-B **Summary of Taxes** (See **Tax Payments** on page 2 of the instructions.)

1	Enter the taxes listed in Part II-A, column (i), that apply to self-dealers, disqualified persons, foundation managers, and organization managers who sign this form. If all sign, enter the total amount from Part II-A, column (i)	**1**
2	**Total tax.** Add Part I, line 9, and Part II-B, line 1. (Make check(s) or money order(s) payable to the United States Treasury.)	**2**

For **Privacy Act and Paperwork Reduction Act Notice, see page 8 of the instructions.**   Cat. No. 13021D   Form **4720** (2005)

SCHEDULE A—Initial Taxes on Self-Dealing (Section 4941)

Part I   Acts of Self-Dealing and Tax Computation

(a) Act number	(b) Date of act	(c) Description of act
1		
2		
3		
4		
5		

(d) Question number from Form 990-PF, Part VII-B, or Form 5227, Part VI-B, applicable to the act	(e) Amount involved in act	(f) Initial tax on self-dealing (5% of col. (e))	(g) Tax on foundation managers (if applicable) (lesser of $10,000 or 2½% of col. (e))

Part II   Summary of Tax Liability of Self-Dealers and Proration of Payments

(a) Names of self-dealers liable for tax	(b) Act no. from Part I, col. (a)	(c) Tax from Part I, col. (f), or prorated amount	(d) Self-dealer's total tax liability (add amounts in col. (c)) (see page 4 of the instructions)

Part III   Summary of Tax Liability of Foundation Managers and Proration of Payments

(a) Names of foundation managers liable for tax	(b) Act no. from Part I, col. (a)	(c) Tax from Part I, col. (g), or prorated amount	(d) Manager's total tax liability (add amounts in col. (c)) (see page 4 of the instructions)

SCHEDULE B—Initial Tax on Undistributed Income (Section 4942)

1	Undistributed income for years before 2004 (from Form 990-PF for 2005, Part XIII, line 6d)	1	
2	Undistributed income for 2004 (from Form 990-PF for 2005, Part XIII, line 6e)	2	
3	Total undistributed income at end of current tax year beginning in 2005 and subject to tax under section 4942 (add lines 1 and 2)	3	
4	**Tax**—Enter 15% of line 3 here and on page 1, Part I, line 1	4	

Form **4720** (2005)

SCHEDULE C—Initial Tax on Excess Business Holdings (Section 4943)

Business Holdings and Computation of Tax

If you have taxable excess holdings in more than one business enterprise, attach a separate schedule for each enterprise. Refer to the instructions on page 4 for each line item before making any entries.

Name and address of business enterprise

Employer identification number . . . . ▶

Form of enterprise (corporation, partnership, trust, joint venture, sole proprietorship, etc.) . ▶

		(a) Voting stock (profits interest or beneficial interest)	**(b)** Value	**(c)** Nonvoting stock (capital interest)
1	Foundation holdings in business enterprise	1 %	%	
2	Permitted holdings in business enterprise	2 %	%	
3	Value of excess holdings in business enterprise	3		
4	Value of excess holdings disposed of within 90 days; or, other value of excess holdings not subject to section 4943 tax (attach explanation)	4		
5	Taxable excess holdings in business enterprise— line 3 minus line 4	5		
6	Tax—Enter 5% of line 5	6		
7	**Total tax**—Add amounts on line 6, columns (a), (b), and (c); enter total here and on page 1, Part I, line 2	7		

SCHEDULE D—Initial Taxes on Investments That Jeopardize Charitable Purpose (Section 4944)

Part I   **Investments and Tax Computation**

(a) Investment number	(b) Date of investment	(c) Description of investment	(d) Amount of investment	(e) Initial tax on foundation (5% of col. (d))	(f) Initial tax on foundation managers (if applicable)— (lesser of $5,000 or 5% of col. (d))
1					
2					
3					
4					
5					

Total—column (e). Enter here and on page 1, Part I, line 3 . . . .

Total—column (f). Enter total (or prorated amount) here and in Part II, column (c), below . . .

Part II   **Summary of Tax Liability of Foundation Managers and Proration of Payments**

(a) Names of foundation managers liable for tax	(b) Investment no. from Part I, col. (a)	(c) Tax from Part I, col. (f), or prorated amount	(d) Manager's total tax liability (add amounts in col. (c)) (see page 6 of the instructions)

Form **4720** (2005)

SCHEDULE E—Initial Taxes on Taxable Expenditures (Section 4945)

Part I Expenditures and Computation of Tax

(a) Item number	(b) Amount	(c) Date paid or incurred	(d) Name and address of recipient	(e) Description of expenditure and purposes for which made
1				
2				
3				
4				
5				

(f) Question number from Form 990-PF, Part VII-B, or Form 5227, Part VI-B, applicable to the expenditure	(g) Initial tax imposed on foundation (10% of col. (b))	(h) Initial tax imposed on foundation managers (if applicable)—(lesser of $5,000 or 2½% of col. (b))
Total—column (g). Enter here and on page 1, Part I, line 4		
Total—column (h). Enter total (or prorated amount) here and in Part II, column (c), below		

Part II Summary of Tax Liability of Foundation Managers and Proration of Payments

(a) Names of foundation managers liable for tax	(b) Item no. from Part I, col. (a)	(c) Tax from Part I, col. (h), or prorated amount	(d) Manager's total tax liability (add amounts in col. (c)) (see page 7 of the instructions)

SCHEDULE F—Initial Taxes on Political Expenditures (Section 4955)

Part I Expenditures and Computation of Tax

(a) Item number	(b) Amount	(c) Date paid or incurred	(d) Description of political expenditure	(e) Initial tax imposed on organization or foundation (10% of col. (b))	(f) Initial tax imposed on managers (if applicable) (lesser of $5,000 or 2½% of col. (b))
1					
2					
3					
4					
5					
Total—column (e). Enter here and on page 1, Part I, line 5					
Total—column (f). Enter total (or prorated amount) here and in Part II, column (c), below					

Part II Summary of Tax Liability of Organization Managers or Foundation Managers and Proration of Payments

(a) Names of organization managers or foundation managers liable for tax	(b) Item no. from Part I, col. (a)	(c) Tax from Part I, col. (f), or prorated amount	(d) Manager's total tax liability (add amounts in col. (c)) (see page 7 of the instructions)

Form **4720** (2005)

SCHEDULE G—Tax on **Excess Lobbying Expenditures** (Section 4911)

1	Excess of grassroots expenditures over grassroots nontaxable amount (from Schedule A (Form 990 or 990-EZ), Part VI-A, column (b), line 43). (See page 7 of the instructions before making entry.)	**1**
2	Excess of lobbying expenditures over lobbying nontaxable amount (from Schedule A (Form 990 or 990-EZ), Part VI-A, column (b), line 44). (See page 7 of the instructions before making entry.)	**2**
3	Taxable lobbying expenditures—enter the larger of line 1 or line 2	**3**
4	**Tax**—Enter 25% of line 3 here and on page 1, Part I, line 6	**4**

SCHEDULE H—**Taxes on Disqualifying Lobbying Expenditures** (Section 4912)

Part I Expenditures and Computation of Tax

(a) Item number	(b) Amount	(c) Date paid or incurred	(d) Description of lobbying expenditures	(e) Tax imposed on organization (5% of col. (b))	(f) Tax imposed on organization managers (if applicable)— (5% of col. (b))
1					
2					
3					
4					
5					

Total—column (e). Enter here and on page 1, Part I, line 7 . . . . .

Total—column (f). Enter total (or prorated amount) here and in Part II, column (c), below . . . .

Part II Summary of Tax Liability of Organization Managers and Proration of Payments

(a) Names of organization managers liable for tax	(b) Item no. from Part I, col. (a)	(c) Tax from Part I, col. (f), or prorated amount	(d) Manager's total tax liability (add amounts in col. (c)) (see page 7 of the instructions)

SCHEDULE I—**Initial Taxes on Excess Benefit Transactions** (Section 4958)

Part I Excess Benefit Transactions and Tax Computation

(a) Transaction number	(b) Date of transaction	(c) Description of transaction
1		
2		
3		
4		
5		

(d) Amount of excess benefit	(e) Initial tax on disqualified persons (25% of col. (d))	(f) Tax on organization managers (if applicable) (lesser of $10,000 or 10% of col. (d))

Form **4720** (2005)

APPENDIX C

Form 4720

Form **4720** Department of the Treasury Internal Revenue Service	**Return of Certain Excise Taxes on Charities and Other Persons Under Chapters 41 and 42 of the Internal Revenue Code** (Sections 170(f)(10), 4911, 4912, 4941, 4942, 4943, 4944, 4945, 4955, and 4958) ▶ See separate instructions.	OMB No. 1545-0052 **2005**

For calendar year 2005 or other tax year beginning	2005, and ending	20

Name of foundation or public charity	Employer identification number

Number, street, and room or suite no. (or P.O. box if mail is not delivered to street address)	Check box for type of annual return: ☐ Form 990 ☐ Form 990-EZ ☐ Form 990-PF ☐ Form 5227
City or town, state, and ZIP code	

		Yes	No
A	Is the organization a foreign private foundation within the meaning of section 4948(b)?		
B	Has corrective action been taken on any taxable event that resulted in Chapter 42 taxes being reported on this form? (Enter "N/A" if not applicable)		

If "Yes," attach a detailed description and documentation of the corrective action taken and, if applicable, enter the fair market value of any property recovered as a result of the correction ▶ $ _____ . If "No," (i.e., any uncorrected acts, or transactions), attach an explanation (see page 3 of the instructions).

Part I Taxes on Organization (Sections 170(f)(10), 4911(a), 4912(a), 4942(a), 4943(a), 4944(a)(1), 4945(a)(1), and 4955(a)(1))

1	Tax on undistributed income—Schedule B, line 4	**1**	
2	Tax on excess business holdings—Schedule C, line 7	**2**	
3	Tax on investments that jeopardize charitable purpose—Schedule D, Part I, column (e) . .	**3**	
4	Tax on taxable expenditures—Schedule E, Part I, column (g)	**4**	
5	Tax on political expenditures—Schedule F, Part I, column (e)	**5**	
6	Tax on excess lobbying expenditures—Schedule G, line 4	**6**	
7	Tax on disqualifying lobbying expenditures—Schedule H, Part I, column (e)	**7**	
8	Tax on premiums paid on personal benefit contracts	**8**	
9	**Total** (add lines 1–8)	**9**	

Part II-A Taxes on Self-Dealers, Disqualified Persons, Foundation Managers, and Organization Managers (Sections 4912(b), 4941(a), 4944(a)(2), 4945(a)(2), 4955(a)(2), and 4958(a))

	(a) Name and address of person subject to tax	(b) Taxpayer identification number
a		
b		
c		
d		

	(c) Tax on self-dealing—Schedule A, Part I, col. (d), and Part III, col. (d)	(d) Tax on investments that jeopardize charitable purpose—Schedule D, Part II, col. (d)	(e) Tax on taxable expenditures—Schedule E, Part II, col. (d)	(f) Tax on political expenditures—Schedule F, Part II, col. (d)
a				
b				
c				
d				
Total				

	(g) Tax on disqualifying lobbying expenditures—Schedule H, Part II, col. (d)	(h) Tax on excess benefit transactions—Schedule I, Part II, col. (d), and Part III, col. (d)	(i) Total—Add cols. (c) through (h)
a			
b			
c			
d			
Total			

Part II-B Summary of Taxes (See **Tax Payments** on page 2 of the instructions.)

1	Enter the taxes listed in Part II-A, column (i), that apply to self-dealers, disqualified persons, foundation managers, and organization managers who sign this form. If all sign, enter the total amount from Part II-A, column (i)	**1**	
2	**Total tax.** Add Part I, line 9, and Part II-B, line 1. (Make check(s) or money order(s) payable to the United States Treasury.)	**2**	

For Privacy Act and Paperwork Reduction Act Notice, see page 8 of the instructions.   Cat. No. 13021D   Form **4720** (2005)

APPENDIX D

Form 1023

Schedule D. Section 509(a)(3) Supporting Organizations

Section I　Identifying Information About the Supported Organization(s)

1　State the names, addresses, and EINs of the supported organizations. If additional space is needed, attach a separate sheet.

Name	Address	EIN

2　Are all supported organizations listed in line 1 public charities under section 509(a)(1) or (2)? If "Yes," go to Section II. If "No," go to line 3.　　　　☐ **Yes**　☐ **No**

3　Do the supported organizations have tax-exempt status under section 501(c)(4), 501(c)(5), or 501(c)(6)?　　　　☐ **Yes**　☐ **No**

If "Yes," for each 501(c)(4), (5), or (6) organization supported, provide the following financial information:

- Part IX-A. Statement of Revenues and Expenses, lines 1–13 and
- Part X, lines 6b(ii)(a), 6b(ii)(b), and 7.

If "No," attach a statement describing how each organization you support is a public charity under section 509(a)(1) or (2).

Section II　Relationship with Supported Organization(s)—Three Tests

To be classified as a supporting organization, an organization must meet one of three relationship tests:

Test 1: "Operated, supervised, or controlled by" one or more publicly supported organizations, or

Test 2: "Supervised or controlled in connection with" one or more publicly supported organizations, or

Test 3: "Operated in connection with" one or more publicly supported organizations.

1　Information to establish the "operated, supervised, or controlled by" relationship (Test 1)

Is a majority of your governing board or officers elected or appointed by the supported organization(s)? If "Yes," describe the process by which your governing board is appointed and elected; go to Section III. If "No," continue to line 2.　　☐ **Yes**　☐ **No**

2　Information to establish the "supervised or controlled in connection with" relationship (Test 2)

Does a majority of your governing board consist of individuals who also serve on the governing board of the supported organization(s)? If "Yes," describe the process by which your governing board is appointed and elected; go to Section III. If "No," go to line 3.　　☐ **Yes**　☐ **No**

3　Information to establish the "operated in connection with" responsiveness test (Test 3)

Are you a trust from which the named supported organization(s) can enforce and compel an accounting under state law? If "Yes," explain whether you advised the supported organization(s) in writing of these rights and provide a copy of the written communication documenting this; go to Section II, line 5. If "No," go to line 4a.　　☐ **Yes**　☐ **No**

4　Information to establish the alternative "operated in connection with" responsiveness test (Test 3)

a　Do the officers, directors, trustees, or members of the supported organization(s) elect or appoint one or more of your officers, directors, or trustees? If "Yes," explain and provide documentation; go to line 4d, below. If "No," go to line 4b.　　☐ **Yes**　☐ **No**

b　Do one or more members of the governing body of the supported organization(s) also serve as your officers, directors, or trustees or hold other important offices with respect to you? If "Yes," explain and provide documentation; go to line 4d, below. If "No," go to line 4c.　　☐ **Yes**　☐ **No**

c　Do your officers, directors, or trustees maintain a close and continuous working relationship with the officers, directors, or trustees of the supported organization(s)? If "Yes," explain and provide documentation.　　☐ **Yes**　☐ **No**

d　Do the supported organization(s) have a significant voice in your investment policies, in the making and timing of grants, and in otherwise directing the use of your income or assets? If "Yes," explain and provide documentation.　　☐ **Yes**　☐ **No**

e　Describe and provide copies of written communications documenting how you made the supported organization(s) aware of your supporting activities.

Schedule D. Section 509(a)(3) Supporting Organizations *(Continued)*

| Section II | Relationship with Supported Organization(s)—Three Tests *(Continued)* |

5 Information to establish the "operated in connection with" integral part test (Test 3)

Do you conduct activities that would otherwise be carried out by the supported organization(s)? If "Yes," explain and go to Section III. If "No," continue to line 6a. ☐ Yes ☐ No

6 Information to establish the alternative "operated in connection with" integral part test (Test 3)

a Do you distribute at least 85% of your annual **net income** to the supported organization(s)? If "Yes," go to line 6b. (See instructions.) ☐ Yes ☐ No

If "No," state the percentage of your income that you distribute to each supported organization. Also explain how you ensure that the supported organization(s) are attentive to your operations.

b How much do you contribute annually to each supported organization? Attach a schedule.

c What is the total annual revenue of each supported organization? If you need additional space, attach a list.

d Do you or the supported organization(s) **earmark** your funds for support of a particular program or activity? If "Yes," explain. ☐ Yes ☐ No

7a Does your organizing document specify the supported organization(s) by name? If "Yes," state the article and paragraph number and go to Section III. If "No," answer line 7b. ☐ Yes ☐ No

b Attach a statement describing whether there has been an historic and continuing relationship between you and the supported organization(s).

| Section III | Organizational Test |

1a If you met relationship Test 1 or Test 2 in Section II, your organizing document must specify the supported organization(s) by name, or by naming a similar purpose or charitable class of beneficiaries. If your organizing document complies with this requirement, answer "Yes." If your organizing document does not comply with this requirement, answer "No," and see the instructions. ☐ Yes ☐ No

b If you met relationship Test 3 in Section II, your organizing document must generally specify the supported organization(s) by name. If your organizing document complies with this requirement, answer "Yes," and go to Section IV. If your organizing document does not comply with this requirement, answer "No," and see the instructions. ☐ Yes ☐ No

| Section IV | Disqualified Person Test |

You do not qualify as a supporting organization if you are **controlled** directly or indirectly by one or more **disqualified persons** (as defined in section 4946) other than **foundation managers** or one or more organizations that you support. Foundation managers who are also disqualified persons for another reason are disqualified persons with respect to you.

1a Do any persons who are disqualified persons with respect to you, (except individuals who are disqualified persons only because they are foundation managers), appoint any of your foundation managers? If "Yes," (1) describe the process by which disqualified persons appoint any of your foundation managers, (2) provide the names of these disqualified persons and the foundation managers they appoint, and (3) explain how control is vested over your operations (including assets and activities) by persons other than disqualified persons. ☐ Yes ☐ No

b Do any persons who have a family or business relationship with any disqualified persons with respect to you, (except individuals who are disqualified persons only because they are foundation managers), appoint any of your foundation managers? If "Yes," (1) describe the process by which individuals with a family or business relationship with disqualified persons appoint any of your foundation managers, (2) provide the names of these disqualified persons, the individuals with a family or business relationship with disqualified persons, and the foundation managers appointed, and (3) explain how control is vested over your operations (including assets and activities) in individuals other than disqualified persons. ☐ Yes ☐ No

c Do any persons who are disqualified persons, (except individuals who are disqualified persons only because they are foundation managers), have any influence regarding your operations, including your assets or activities? If "Yes," (1) provide the names of these disqualified persons, (2) explain how influence is exerted over your operations (including assets and activities), and (3) explain how control is vested over your operations (including assets and activities) by individuals other than disqualified persons. ☐ Yes ☐ No

Form **1023** (Rev. 10-2004)

APPENDIX E

Form 990

Form **990**	**Return of Organization Exempt From Income Tax**	OMB No. 1545-0047
	Under section 501(c), 527, or 4947(a)(1) of the Internal Revenue Code (except black lung benefit trust or private foundation)	**2005**
Department of the Treasury Internal Revenue Service	▶ The organization may have to use a copy of this return to satisfy state reporting requirements.	**Open to Public Inspection**

A For the 2005 calendar year, or tax year beginning _____ , 2005, and ending _____ , 20 ____

B Check if applicable:	Please use IRS label or print or type. See Specific Instructions.	**C** Name of organization		**D** Employer identification number
☐ Address change				:
☐ Name change		Number and street (or P.O. box if mail is not delivered to street address)	Room/suite	**E** Telephone number ( )
☐ Initial return				
☐ Final return		City or town, state or country, and ZIP + 4		**F** Accounting method: ☐ Cash ☐ Accrual
☐ Amended return				☐ Other (specify) ▶
☐ Application pending				

● Section 501(c)(3) organizations and 4947(a)(1) nonexempt charitable trusts must attach a completed Schedule A (Form 990 or 990-EZ).

H and I are not applicable to section 527 organizations.
H(a) Is this a group return for affiliates? ☐ Yes ☐ No
H(b) If "Yes," enter number of affiliates ▶ ....
H(c) Are all affiliates included? ☐ Yes ☐ No
(If "No," attach a list. See instructions.)
H(d) Is this a separate return filed by an organization covered by a group ruling? ☐ Yes ☐ No
I Group Exemption Number ▶
M Check ▶ ☐ if the organization is not required to attach Sch. B (Form 990, 990-EZ, or 990-PF).

G Website: ▶

J Organization type (check only one) ▶ ☐ 501(c) ( ) ◀ (insert no.) ☐ 4947(a)(1) or ☐ 527

K Check here ▶ ☐ if the organization's gross receipts are normally not more than $25,000. The organization need not file a return with the IRS; but if the organization chooses to file a return, be sure to file a complete return. Some states require a complete return.

L Gross receipts: Add lines 6b, 8b, 9b, and 10b to line 12 ▶

Part I — Revenue, Expenses, and Changes in Net Assets or Fund Balances (See the instructions.)

1	Contributions, gifts, grants, and similar amounts received:			
a	Direct public support	1a		
b	Indirect public support	1b		
c	Government contributions (grants)	1c		
d	**Total** (add lines 1a through 1c) (cash $ _____ noncash $ _____)		1d	
2	Program service revenue including government fees and contracts (from Part VII, line 93)		2	
3	Membership dues and assessments		3	
4	Interest on savings and temporary cash investments		4	
5	Dividends and interest from securities		5	
6a	Gross rents	6a		
b	Less: rental expenses	6b		
c	Net rental income or (loss) (subtract line 6b from line 6a)		6c	
7	Other investment income (describe ▶)		7	
8a	Gross amount from sales of assets other than inventory	(A) Securities	(B) Other	
		8a		
b	Less: cost or other basis and sales expenses	8b		
c	Gain or (loss) (attach schedule)	8c		
d	Net gain or (loss) (combine line 8c, columns (A) and (B))		8d	
9	Special events and activities (attach schedule). If any amount is from **gaming**, check here ▶ ☐			
a	Gross revenue (not including $ _____ of contributions reported on line 1a)	9a		
b	Less: direct expenses other than fundraising expenses	9b		
c	Net income or (loss) from special events (subtract line 9b from line 9a)		9c	
10a	Gross sales of inventory, less returns and allowances	10a		
b	Less: cost of goods sold	10b		
c	Gross profit or (loss) from sales of inventory (attach schedule) (subtract line 10b from line 10a)		10c	
11	Other revenue (from Part VII, line 103)		11	
12	**Total revenue** (add lines 1d, 2, 3, 4, 5, 6c, 7, 8d, 9c, 10c, and 11)		12	
13	Program services (from line 44, column (B))		13	
14	Management and general (from line 44, column (C))		14	
15	Fundraising (from line 44, column (D))		15	
16	Payments to affiliates (attach schedule)		16	
17	**Total expenses** (add lines 16 and 44, column (A))		17	
18	Excess or (deficit) for the year (subtract line 17 from line 12)		18	
19	Net assets or fund balances at beginning of year (from line 73, column (A))		19	
20	Other changes in net assets or fund balances (attach explanation)		20	
21	Net assets or fund balances at end of year (combine lines 18, 19, and 20)		21	

(Revenue — lines 1–12; Expenses — lines 13–17; Net Assets — lines 18–21)

For Privacy Act and Paperwork Reduction Act Notice, see the separate instructions. Cat. No. 11282Y Form **990** (2005)

Form 990 (2005)

Part II	**Statement of Functional Expenses**	All organizations must complete column (A). Columns (B), (C), and (D) are required for section 501(c)(3) and (4) organizations and section 4947(a)(1) nonexempt charitable trusts but optional for others. *(See the instructions.)*

Do not include amounts reported on line 6b, 8b, 9b, 10b, or 16 of Part I.		**(A)** Total	**(B)** Program services	**(C)** Management and general	**(D)** Fundraising
22	Grants and allocations (attach schedule) . . (cash $ _____ noncash $ _____) If this amount includes foreign grants, check here ▶ ☐	22				
23	Specific assistance to individuals (attach schedule)	23				
24	Benefits paid to or for members (attach schedule)	24				
25	Compensation of officers, directors, etc. . .	25				
26	Other salaries and wages	26				
27	Pension plan contributions	27				
28	Other employee benefits	28				
29	Payroll taxes	29				
30	Professional fundraising fees	30				
31	Accounting fees	31				
32	Legal fees	32				
33	Supplies	33				
34	Telephone	34				
35	Postage and shipping	35				
36	Occupancy	36				
37	Equipment rental and maintenance	37				
38	Printing and publications	38				
39	Travel	39				
40	Conferences, conventions, and meetings .	40				
41	Interest	41				
42	Depreciation, depletion, etc. (attach schedule)	42				
43	Other expenses not covered above (itemize):					
a	....	43a				
b	....	43b				
c	....	43c				
d	....	43d				
e	....	43e				
f	....	43f				
g	....	43g				
44	**Total functional expenses.** Add lines 22 through 43. (Organizations completing columns (B)-(D), carry these totals to lines 13-15)	44				

Joint Costs. Check ▶ ☐ if you are following SOP 98-2.

Are any joint costs from a combined educational campaign and fundraising solicitation reported in **(B)** Program services? . ▶ ☐ **Yes** ☐ **No**

If "Yes," enter **(i)** the aggregate amount of these joint costs $ _____; **(ii)** the amount allocated to Program services $ _____;

(iii) the amount allocated to Management and general $ _____ ; and **(iv)** the amount allocated to Fundraising $ _____

Form **990** (2005)

Part III **Statement of Program Service Accomplishments** *(See the instructions.)*

Form 990 is available for public inspection and, for some people, serves as the primary or sole source of information about a particular organization. How the public perceives an organization in such cases may be determined by the information presented on its return. Therefore, please make sure the return is complete and accurate and fully describes, in Part III, the organization's programs and accomplishments.

What is the organization's primary exempt purpose? ▶ ....

	Program Service Expenses (Required for 501(c)(3) and (4) orgs., and 4947(a)(1) trusts; but optional for others.)

All organizations must describe their exempt purpose achievements in a clear and concise manner. State the number of clients served, publications issued, etc. Discuss achievements that are not measurable. (Section 501(c)(3) and (4) organizations and 4947(a)(1) nonexempt charitable trusts must also enter the amount of grants and allocations to others.)

a ....
....
....
....
(Grants and allocations $) If this amount includes foreign grants, check here ▶ ☐

b ....
....
....
....
(Grants and allocations $) If this amount includes foreign grants, check here ▶ ☐

c ....
....
....
....
(Grants and allocations $) If this amount includes foreign grants, check here ▶ ☐

d ....
....
....
....
(Grants and allocations $) If this amount includes foreign grants, check here ▶ ☐

e Other program services (attach schedule)
(Grants and allocations $) If this amount includes foreign grants, check here ▶ ☐

f **Total of Program Service Expenses** (should equal line 44, column (B), Program services).   .   .   .   . ▶

Form **990** (2005)

Part IV	Balance Sheets *(See the instructions.)*			

Note: *Where required, attached schedules and amounts within the description column should be for end-of-year amounts only.*

				(A) Beginning of year		**(B)** End of year
Assets	45	Cash—non-interest-bearing			45	
	46	Savings and temporary cash investments			46	
	47a	Accounts receivable	47a			
	b	Less: allowance for doubtful accounts	47b		47c	
	48a	Pledges receivable	48a			
	b	Less: allowance for doubtful accounts	48b		48c	
	49	Grants receivable			49	
	50	Receivables from officers, directors, trustees, and key employees (attach schedule)			50	
	51a	Other notes and loans receivable (attach schedule)	51a			
	b	Less: allowance for doubtful accounts	51b		51c	
	52	Inventories for sale or use			52	
	53	Prepaid expenses and deferred charges			53	
	54	Investments—securities (attach schedule) ▶ ☐ Cost ☐ FMV			54	
	55a	Investments—land, buildings, and equipment: basis	55a			
	b	Less: accumulated depreciation (attach schedule)	55b		55c	
	56	Investments—other (attach schedule)			56	
	57a	Land, buildings, and equipment: basis	57a			
	b	Less: accumulated depreciation (attach schedule)	57b		57c	
	58	Other assets (describe ▶ ....)			58	
	59	**Total assets** (must equal line 74). Add lines 45 through 58.			59	
Liabilities	60	Accounts payable and accrued expenses			60	
	61	Grants payable			61	
	62	Deferred revenue			62	
	63	Loans from officers, directors, trustees, and key employees (attach schedule)			63	
	64a	Tax-exempt bond liabilities (attach schedule)			64a	
	b	Mortgages and other notes payable (attach schedule)			64b	
	65	Other liabilities (describe ▶ ....)			65	
	66	**Total liabilities.** Add lines 60 through 65			66	
Net Assets or Fund Balances		Organizations that follow SFAS 117, check here ▶ ☐ and complete lines 67 through 69 and lines 73 and 74.				
	67	Unrestricted			67	
	68	Temporarily restricted			68	
	69	Permanently restricted			69	
		Organizations that do not follow SFAS 117, check here ▶ ☐ and complete lines 70 through 74.				
	70	Capital stock, trust principal, or current funds			70	
	71	Paid-in or capital surplus, or land, building, and equipment fund			71	
	72	Retained earnings, endowment, accumulated income, or other funds			72	
	73	**Total net assets or fund balances** (add lines 67 through 69 **or** lines 70 through 72; column (A) **must** equal line 19; column (B) **must** equal line 21)			73	
	74	**Total liabilities and net assets/fund balances.** Add lines 66 and 73.			74	

Form **990** (2005)

APPENDIX E

Part IV-A Reconciliation of Revenue per Audited Financial Statements With Revenue per Return *(See the instructions.)*

a	Total revenue, gains, and other support per audited financial statements		**a**	
b	Amounts included on line **a** but not on Part I, line 12:			
1	Net unrealized gains on investments	**b1**		
2	Donated services and use of facilities	**b2**		
3	Recoveries of prior year grants	**b3**		
4	Other (specify):	**b4**		
	Add lines **b1** through **b4**		**b**	
c	Subtract line **b** from line **a**		**c**	
d	Amounts included on Part I, line 12, but not on line **a**:			
1	Investment expenses not included on Part I, line 6b	**d1**		
2	Other (specify):	**d2**		
	Add lines **d1** and **d2**		**d**	
e	**Total revenue** (Part I, line 12). Add lines **c** and **d** ▶		**e**	

Part IV-B Reconciliation of Expenses per Audited Financial Statements With Expenses per Return

a	Total expenses and losses per audited financial statements		**a**	
b	Amounts included on line **a** but not on Part I, line 17:			
1	Donated services and use of facilities	**b1**		
2	Prior year adjustments reported on Part I, line 20	**b2**		
3	Losses reported on Part I, line 20	**b3**		
4	Other (specify):	**b4**		
	Add lines **b1** through **b4**		**b**	
c	Subtract line **b** from line **a**		**c**	
d	Amounts included on Part I, line 17, but not on line **a**:			
1	Investment expenses not included on Part I, line 6b	**d1**		
2	Other (specify):	**d2**		
	Add lines **d1** and **d2**		**d**	
e	**Total expenses** (Part I, line 17). Add lines **c** and **d** ▶		**e**	

Part V-A **Current Officers, Directors, Trustees, and Key Employees** (List each person who was an officer, director, trustee, or key employee at any time during the year even if they were not compensated.) *(See the instructions.)*

(A) Name and address	(B) Title and average hours per week devoted to position	(C) Compensation (If not paid, enter -0-.)	(D) Contributions to employee benefit plans & deferred compensation plans	(E) Expense account and other allowances
....				
....				
....				
....				
....				
....				
....				
....				
....				
....				
....				
....				

Form **990** (2005)

APPENDIX E

| | | Page **6** |

Part V-A Current Officers, Directors, Trustees, and Key Employees *(continued)* | | Yes | No |

75a Enter the total number of officers, directors, and trustees permitted to vote on organization business at board meetings . . . . ▶ . . . .

b Are any officers, directors, trustees, or key employees listed in Form 990, Part V-A, or highest compensated employees listed in Schedule A, Part I, or highest compensated professional and other independent contractors listed in Schedule A, Part II-A or II-B, related to each other through family or business relationships? If "Yes," attach a statement that identifies the individuals and explains the relationship(s) . | 75b | |

c Do any officers, directors, trustees, or key employees listed in Form 990, Part V-A, or highest compensated employees listed in Schedule A, Part I, or highest compensated professional and other independent contractors listed in Schedule A, Part II-A or II-B, receive compensation from any other organizations, whether tax exempt or taxable, that are related to this organization through common supervision or common control? | 75c | |
Note. Related organizations include section 509(a)(3) supporting organizations.

If "Yes," attach a statement that identifies the individuals, explains the relationship between this organization and the other organization(s), and describes the compensation arrangements, including amounts paid to each individual by each related organization.

d Does the organization have a written conflict of interest policy? . . . . | 75d | |

Part V-B Former Officers, Directors, Trustees, and Key Employees That Received Compensation or Other Benefits (If any former officer, director, trustee, or key employee received compensation or other benefits (described below) during the year, list that person below and enter the amount of compensation or other benefits in the appropriate column. See the instructions.)

(A) Name and address	(B) Loans and Advances	(C) Compensation	(D) Contributions to employee benefit plans & deferred compensation plans	(E) Expense account and other allowances

Part VI Other Information *(See the instructions.)* | | Yes | No |

76 Did the organization engage in any activity not previously reported to the IRS? If "Yes," attach a detailed description of each activity . . . . | 76 | |

77 Were any changes made in the organizing or governing documents but not reported to the IRS? . . . . . | 77 | |
If "Yes," attach a conformed copy of the changes.

78a Did the organization have unrelated business gross income of $1,000 or more during the year covered by this return? . . . . | 78a | |
b If "Yes," has it filed a tax return on **Form 990-T** for this year? . . . . | 78b | |

79 Was there a liquidation, dissolution, termination, or substantial contraction during the year? If "Yes," attach a statement . . . . | 79 | |

80a Is the organization related (other than by association with a statewide or nationwide organization) through common membership, governing bodies, trustees, officers, etc., to any other exempt or nonexempt organization? . . . . | 80a | |
b If "Yes," enter the name of the organization ▶ . . . .
. . . . and check whether it is ☐ exempt **or** ☐ nonexempt

81a Enter direct and indirect political expenditures. (See line 81 instructions.) . . | 81a |
b Did the organization file **Form 1120-POL** for this year? . . . . | 81b | |

Form 990 (2005)   Page **7**

Part VI	Other Information *(continued)*		Yes	No

82a Did the organization receive donated services or the use of materials, equipment, or facilities at no charge or at substantially less than fair rental value? **82a**

   b If "Yes," you may indicate the value of these items here. Do not include this amount as revenue in Part I or as an expense in Part II. (See instructions in Part III.) **82b**

83a Did the organization comply with the public inspection requirements for returns and exemption applications? **83a**

   b Did the organization comply with the disclosure requirements relating to quid pro quo contributions? . . **83b**

84a Did the organization solicit any contributions or gifts that were not tax deductible? **84a**

   b If "Yes," did the organization include with every solicitation an express statement that such contributions or gifts were not tax deductible? **84b**

85 *501(c)(4), (5), or (6) organizations.* **a** Were substantially all dues nondeductible by members? **85a**

   b Did the organization make only in-house lobbying expenditures of $2,000 or less? **85b**

   If "Yes" was answered to either 85a or 85b, **do not** complete 85c through 85h below unless the organization received a waiver for proxy tax owed for the prior year.

   c Dues, assessments, and similar amounts from members **85c**

   d Section 162(e) lobbying and political expenditures **85d**

   e Aggregate nondeductible amount of section 6033(e)(1)(A) dues notices . . **85e**

   f Taxable amount of lobbying and political expenditures (line 85d less 85e) . . **85f**

   g Does the organization elect to pay the section 6033(e) tax on the amount on line 85f? **85g**

   h If section 6033(e)(1)(A) dues notices were sent, does the organization agree to add the amount on line 85f to its reasonable estimate of dues allocable to nondeductible lobbying and political expenditures for the following tax year? **85h**

86 *501(c)(7) orgs.* Enter: **a** Initiation fees and capital contributions included on line 12 . . . . **86a**

   b Gross receipts, included on line 12, for public use of club facilities . . . **86b**

87 *501(c)(12) orgs.* Enter: **a** Gross income from members or shareholders . . . **87a**

   b Gross income from other sources. (Do not net amounts due or paid to other sources against amounts due or received from them.) **87b**

88 At any time during the year, did the organization own a 50% or greater interest in a taxable corporation or partnership, or an entity disregarded as separate from the organization under Regulations sections 301.7701-2 and 301.7701-3? If "Yes," complete Part IX **88**

89a *501(c)(3) organizations.* Enter: Amount of tax imposed on the organization during the year under:
section 4911 ▶ _____ ; section 4912 ▶ _____ ; section 4955 ▶ _____

   b *501(c)(3) and 501(c)(4) orgs.* Did the organization engage in any section 4958 excess benefit transaction during the year or did it become aware of an excess benefit transaction from a prior year? If "Yes," attach a statement explaining each transaction **89b**

   c Enter: Amount of tax imposed on the organization managers or disqualified persons during the year under sections 4912, 4955, and 4958 . . . . ▶ _____

   d Enter: Amount of tax on line 89c, above, reimbursed by the organization . . . . ▶ _____

90a List the states with which a copy of this return is filed ▶ ....

   b Number of employees employed in the pay period that includes March 12, 2005 (See instructions.) **90b**

91a The books are in care of ▶ .... Telephone no. ▶ (.......) ....
Located at ▶ .... ZIP + 4 ▶ ....

   b At any time during the calendar year, did the organization have an interest in or a signature or other authority over a financial account in a foreign country (such as a bank account, securities account, or other financial account)? **91b**
If "Yes," enter the name of the foreign country ▶ ....
See the instructions for exceptions and filing requirements for **Form TD F 90-22.1,** Report of Foreign Bank and Financial Accounts.

   c At any time during the calendar year, did the organization maintain an office outside of the United States? **91c**
If "Yes," enter the name of the foreign country ▶ ....

92 *Section 4947(a)(1) nonexempt charitable trusts filing Form 990 in lieu of Form 1041*—Check here . . . . . . ▶ ☐
and enter the amount of tax-exempt interest received or accrued during the tax year . . . ▶ **92**

Form **990** (2005)

Part VII — Analysis of Income-Producing Activities (See the instructions.)

Note: Enter gross amounts unless otherwise indicated.

		Unrelated business income		Excluded by section 512, 513, or 514		(E)
		(A) Business code	**(B)** Amount	**(C)** Exclusion code	**(D)** Amount	Related or exempt function income
93	Program service revenue:					
a						
b						
c						
d						
e						
f	Medicare/Medicaid payments					
g	Fees and contracts from government agencies					
94	Membership dues and assessments . . .					
95	Interest on savings and temporary cash investments					
96	Dividends and interest from securities . .					
97	Net rental income or (loss) from real estate:					
a	debt-financed property					
b	not debt-financed property					
98	Net rental income or (loss) from personal property					
99	Other investment income					
100	Gain or (loss) from sales of assets other than inventory					
101	Net income or (loss) from special events					
102	Gross profit or (loss) from sales of inventory					
103	Other revenue: a					
b						
c						
d						
e						
104	Subtotal (add columns (B), (D), and (E)) .					
105	**Total** (add line 104, columns (B), (D), and (E)) . . . . ▶					

Note: Line 105 plus line 1d, Part I, should equal the amount on line 12, Part I.

Part VIII — Relationship of Activities to the Accomplishment of Exempt Purposes (See the instructions.)

Line No. ▼	Explain how each activity for which income is reported in column (E) of Part VII contributed importantly to the accomplishment of the organization's exempt purposes (other than by providing funds for such purposes).

Part IX — Information Regarding Taxable Subsidiaries and Disregarded Entities (See the instructions.)

(A) Name, address, and EIN of corporation, partnership, or disregarded entity	**(B)** Percentage of ownership interest	**(C)** Nature of activities	**(D)** Total income	**(E)** End-of-year assets
	%			
	%			
	%			
	%			

Part X — Information Regarding Transfers Associated with Personal Benefit Contracts (See the instructions.)

(a) Did the organization, during the year, receive any funds, directly or indirectly, to pay premiums on a personal benefit contract? ☐ Yes ☐ No

(b) Did the organization, during the year, pay premiums, directly or indirectly, on a personal benefit contract? ☐ Yes ☐ No

Note: If "Yes" to (b), file Form 8870 and Form 4720 (see instructions).

Please Sign Here ▶

Under penalties of perjury, I declare that I have examined this return, including accompanying schedules and statements, and to the best of my knowledge and belief, it is true, correct, and complete. Declaration of preparer (other than officer) is based on all information of which preparer has any knowledge.

▶ Signature of officer	Date
▶ Type or print name and title.	

Paid Preparer's Use Only

Preparer's signature ▶	Date	Check if self-employed ▶ ☐	Preparer's SSN or PTIN (See Gen. Inst. W)
Firm's name (or yours if self-employed), address, and ZIP + 4 ▶		EIN ▶	
		Phone no. ▶ ( )	

Form **990** (2005)

Form 990-T

Form **990-T**	**Exempt Organization Business Income Tax Return** (and proxy tax under section 6033(e))	OMB No. 1545-0687
Department of the Treasury Internal Revenue Service	For calendar year 2005 or other tax year beginning ...., 2005, and ending ...., 20 ..... ▶ **See separate instructions.**	**2005**

A ☐ Check box if address changed		Name of organization (☐ Check box if name changed and see instructions.)	**D Employer identification number** (Employees' trust, see instructions for Block D on page 7.)
B Exempt under section ☐ 501( ) ( ) ☐ 408(e) ☐ 220(e) ☐ 408A ☐ 530(a) ☐ 529(a)	**Print or Type**	Number, street, and room or suite no. (If a P.O. box, see page 7 of instructions.)	**E New unrelated bus. activity codes** (See instructions for Block E on page 7.)
		City or town, state, and ZIP code	

C Book value of all assets at end of year | **F** Group exemption number (See instructions for Block F on page 7.) ▶

G Check organization type ▶ ☐ 501(c) corporation ☐ 501(c) trust ☐ 401(a) trust ☐ Other trust

H Describe the organization's primary unrelated business activity. ▶

I During the tax year, was the corporation a subsidiary in an affiliated group or a parent-subsidiary controlled group? . ▶ ☐ Yes ☐ No
If "Yes," enter the name and identifying number of the parent corporation. ▶

J The books are in care of ▶   Telephone number ▶ (   )

Part I	**Unrelated Trade or Business Income**		(A) Income	(B) Expenses	(C) Net
1a	Gross receipts or sales				
b	Less returns and allowances c Balance ▶	**1c**			
2	Cost of goods sold (Schedule A, line 7)	**2**			
3	Gross profit. Subtract line 2 from line 1c	**3**			
4a	Capital gain net income (attach Schedule D)	**4a**			
b	Net gain (loss) (Form 4797, Part II, line 17) (attach Form 4797)	**4b**			
c	Capital loss deduction for trusts	**4c**			
5	Income (loss) from partnerships and S corporations (attach statement)	**5**			
6	Rent income (Schedule C)	**6**			
7	Unrelated debt-financed income (Schedule E)	**7**			
8	Interest, annuities, royalties, and rents from controlled organizations (Schedule F)	**8**			
9	Investment income of a section 501(c)(7), (9), or (17) organization (Schedule G)	**9**			
10	Exploited exempt activity income (Schedule I)	**10**			
11	Advertising income (Schedule J)	**11**			
12	Other income (See page 9 of the instructions—attach schedule.)	**12**			
13	**Total.** Combine lines 3 through 12	**13**			

Part II	**Deductions Not Taken Elsewhere** (See page 9 of the instructions for limitations on deductions.) (Except for contributions, deductions must be directly connected with the unrelated business income.)		
14	Compensation of officers, directors, and trustees (Schedule K)	**14**	
15	Salaries and wages	**15**	
16	Repairs and maintenance	**16**	
17	Bad debts	**17**	
18	Interest (attach schedule)	**18**	
19	Taxes and licenses	**19**	
20	Charitable contributions (See page 11 of the instructions for limitation rules.)	**20**	
21	Depreciation (attach Form 4562) **21**		
22	Less depreciation claimed on Schedule A and elsewhere on return . . **22a**	**22b**	
23	Depletion	**23**	
24	Contributions to deferred compensation plans	**24**	
25	Employee benefit programs	**25**	
26	Excess exempt expenses (Schedule I)	**26**	
27	Excess readership costs (Schedule J)	**27**	
28	Other deductions (attach schedule)	**28**	
29	**Total deductions.** Add lines 14 through 28	**29**	
30	Unrelated business taxable income before net operating loss deduction. Subtract line 29 from line 13	**30**	
31	Net operating loss deduction (limited to the amount on line 30)	**31**	
32	Unrelated business taxable income before specific deduction. Subtract line 31 from line 30 . .	**32**	
33	Specific deduction (Generally $1,000, but see line 33 instructions for exceptions.)	**33**	
34	**Unrelated business taxable income.** Subtract line 33 from line 32. If line 33 is greater than line 32, enter the smaller of zero or line 32	**34**	

For Privacy Act and Paperwork Reduction Act Notice, see instructions.   Cat. No. 11291J   Form **990-T** (2005)

Part III Tax Computation

35 **Organizations Taxable as Corporations.** See instructions for tax computation on page 13.
Controlled group members (sections 1561 and 1563)—check here ☐. **See instructions** and:

a Enter your share of the $50,000, $25,000, and $9,925,000 taxable income brackets (in that order):
(1) |$ _____| **(2)** |$ _____| **(3)** |$ _____|

b Enter organization's share of: **(1)** Additional 5% tax (not more than $11,750) |$ _____|
(2) Additional 3% tax (not more than $100,000) . . . . |$ _____|

c Income tax on the amount on line 34 . . . . ▶ | **35c** |

36 **Trusts Taxable at Trust Rates.** See instructions for tax computation on page 14. Income tax on
the amount on line 34 from: ☐ Tax rate schedule or ☐ Schedule D (Form 1041) . . . . ▶ | **36** |

37 **Proxy tax.** See page 14 of the instructions . . . . ▶ | **37** |

38 Alternative minimum tax . . . . | **38** |

39 **Total.** Add lines 37 and 38 to line 35c or 36, whichever applies . . . . | **39** |

Part IV Tax and Payments

40a Foreign tax credit (corporations attach Form 1118; trusts attach Form 1116) | **40a** |

b Other credits (See page 14 of the instructions.) . . . . | **40b** |

c General business credit—Check here and indicate which forms are attached:
☐ Form 3800 ☐ Form(s) (specify) ▶ .... | **40c** |

d Credit for prior year minimum tax (attach Form 8801 or 8827) . . . . | **40d** |

e **Total credits.** Add lines 40a through 40d. . . . . | **40e** |

41 Subtract line 40e from line 39 . . . . | **41** |

42 Other taxes. Check if from: ☐ Form 4255 ☐ Form 8611 ☐ Form 8697 ☐ Form 8866 ☐ Other (attach schedule) | **42** |

43 **Total tax.** Add lines 41 and 42 . . . . | **43** |

44a Payments: A 2004 overpayment credited to 2005 . . . . . . | **44a** |

b 2005 estimated tax payments. . . . . | **44b** |

c Tax deposited with Form 8868 . . . . | **44c** |

d Foreign organizations—Tax paid or withheld at source (see instructions) | **44d** |

e Backup withholding (see instructions) . . . . | **44e** |

f Other credits and payments: ☐ Form 2439 _____
☐ Form 4136 _____ ☐ Other _____ Total ▶ | **44f** |

45 **Total payments.** Add lines 44a through 44f . . . . | **45** |

46 Estimated tax penalty (See page 4 of the instructions.) Check ▶ ☐ if Form 2220 is attached | **46** |

47 **Tax due.** If line 45 is less than the total of lines 43 and 46, enter amount owed . . . . . ▶ | **47** |

48 **Overpayment.** If line 45 is larger than the total of lines 43 and 46, enter amount overpaid . ▶ | **48** |

49 Enter the amount of line 48 you want: **Credited to 2006 estimated tax ▶** | Refunded ▶ | **49** |

Part V Statements Regarding Certain Activities and Other Information (See instructions on page 16.)

		Yes	No
1	At any time during the 2005 calendar year, did the organization have an interest in or a signature or other authority over a financial account in a foreign country (such as a bank account, securities account, or other financial account)?		
	If "Yes," the organization may have to file Form TD F 90-22.1. If "Yes," enter the name of the foreign country here ▶		
2	During the tax year, did the organization receive a distribution from, or was it the grantor of, or transferor to, a foreign trust? If "Yes," see page 5 of the instructions for other forms the organization may have to file.		
3	Enter the amount of tax-exempt interest received or accrued during the tax year ▶ $		

Schedule A—Cost of Goods Sold. Enter method of inventory valuation ▶

1	Inventory at beginning of year.	**1**		**6**	Inventory at end of year	**6**		
2	Purchases	**2**		**7**	**Cost of goods sold.** Subtract line 6 from line 5. Enter here and in Part I, line 2			
3	Cost of labor	**3**				**7**		
4a	Additional section 263A costs (attach schedule)	**4a**		**8**	Do the rules of section 263A (with respect to		Yes	No
b	Other costs (attach schedule).	**4b**			property produced or acquired for resale) apply			
5	**Total.** Add lines 1 through 4b.	**5**			to the organization?			

Under penalties of perjury, I declare that I have examined this return, including accompanying schedules and statements, and to the best of my knowledge and belief, it is true, correct, and complete. Declaration of preparer (other than taxpayer) is based on all information of which preparer has any knowledge.

**Sign
Here**

▶ _____   ▶ _____

Signature of officer   Date   Title

May the IRS discuss this return with the preparer shown below (see instructions)? ☐ Yes ☐ No

Paid Preparer's Use Only	Preparer's signature ▶		Date		Check if self-employed ☐	Preparer's SSN or PTIN
	Firm's name (or yours if self-employed), address, and ZIP code ▶				EIN	
					Phone no. ( )	

Form **990-T** (2005)

Form 990-T (2005)

Schedule C—Rent Income (From Real Property and Personal Property Leased With Real Property)
(See instructions on page 17.)

1 Description of property

(1)

(2)

(3)

(4)

	2 Rent received or accrued	
(a) From personal property (if the percentage of rent for personal property is more than 10% but not more than 50%)	**(b)** From real and personal property (if the percentage of rent for personal property exceeds 50% or if the rent is based on profit or income)	**3** Deductions directly connected with the income in columns 2(a) and 2(b) (attach schedule)
(1)		
(2)		
(3)		
(4)		
Total	Total	

Total income. Add totals of columns 2(a) and 2(b). Enter here and on page 1, Part I, line 6, column (A) . . . ▶

Total deductions. Enter here and on page 1, line 6, column (B). . . ▶

Schedule E—Unrelated Debt-Financed Income (See instructions on page 17.)

1 Description of debt-financed property	2 Gross income from or allocable to debt-financed property	3 Deductions directly connected with or allocable to debt-financed property	
		(a) Straight line depreciation (attach schedule)	**(b)** Other deductions (attach schedule)
(1)			
(2)			
(3)			
(4)			

4 Amount of average acquisition debt on or allocable to debt-financed property (attach schedule)	5 Average adjusted basis of or allocable to debt-financed property (attach schedule)	6 Column 4 divided by column 5	7 Gross income reportable (column 2 × column 6)	8 Allocable deductions (column 6 × total of columns 3(a) and 3(b))
(1)		%		
(2)		%		
(3)		%		
(4)		%		
			Enter here and on page 1, Part I, line 7, column (A).	Enter here and on page 1, Part I, line 7, column (B).

Totals. . . . . ▶

Total dividends-received deductions included in column 8 . . . . ▶

Schedule F—Interest, Annuities, Royalties, and Rents From Controlled Organizations (See instructions on page 18.)

		Exempt Controlled Organizations			
1 Name of Controlled Organization	2 Employer Identification Number	3 Net unrelated income (loss) (see instructions)	4 Total of specified payments made	5 Part of column (4) that is included in the controlling organization's gross income	6 Deductions directly connected with income in column (5)
(1)					
(2)					
(3)					
(4)					

Nonexempt Controlled Organizations

7 Taxable Income	8 Net unrelated income (loss) (see instructions)	9 Total of specified payments made	10 Part of column (9) that is included in the controlling organization's gross income	11 Deductions directly connected with income in column (10)
(1)				
(2)				
(3)				
(4)				
			Add columns 5 and 10. Enter here and on page 1, Part I, line 8, column (A).	Add columns 6 and 11. Enter here and on page 1, Part I, line 8, column (B).

Totals . . . . ▶

Form **990-T** (2005)

APPENDIX F

Schedule G—Investment Income of a Section 501(c)(7), (9), or (17) Organization
(See instructions on page 19.)

1 Description of income	2 Amount of income	3 Deductions directly connected (attach schedule)	4 Set-asides (attach schedule)	5 Total deductions and set-asides (col. 3 plus col. 4)
(1)				
(2)				
(3)				
(4)				
Totals ▶	Enter here and on page 1, Part I, line 9, column (A).			Enter here and on page 1, Part I, line 9, column (B).

Schedule I—Exploited Exempt Activity Income, Other Than Advertising Income
(See instructions on page 19.)

1 Description of exploited activity	2 Gross unrelated business income from trade or business	3 Expenses directly connected with production of unrelated business income	4 Net income (loss) from unrelated trade or business (column 2 minus column 3). If a gain, compute cols. 5 through 7.	5 Gross income from activity that is not unrelated business income	6 Expenses attributable to column 5	7 Excess exempt expenses (column 6 minus column 5, but not more than column 4).
(1)						
(2)						
(3)						
(4)						
Totals ▶	Enter here and on page 1, Part I, line 10, col. (A).	Enter here and on page 1, Part I, line 10, col. (B).				Enter here and on page 1, Part II, line 26.

Schedule J—Advertising Income (See instructions on page 19.)

Part I   Income From Periodicals Reported on a Consolidated Basis

1 Name of periodical	2 Gross advertising income	3 Direct advertising costs	4 Advertising gain or (loss) (col. 2 minus col. 3). If a gain, compute cols. 5 through 7.	5 Circulation income	6 Readership costs	7 Excess readership costs (column 6 minus column 5, but not more than column 4).
(1)						
(2)						
(3)						
(4)						
Totals (carry to Part II, line (5)) ▶						

Part II   Income From Periodicals Reported on a Separate Basis (For each periodical listed in Part II, fill in columns 2 through 7 on a line-by-line basis.)

(1)						
(2)						
(3)						
(4)						
(5) Totals from Part I						
Totals, Part II (lines 1-5) ▶	Enter here and on page 1, Part I, line 11, col. (A).	Enter here and on page 1, Part I, line 11, col. (B).				Enter here and on page 1, Part II, line 27.

Schedule K—Compensation of Officers, Directors, and Trustees (See instructions on page 20.)

1 Name	2 Title	3 Percent of time devoted to business	4 Compensation attributable to unrelated business
		%	
		%	
		%	
		%	
Total. Enter here and on page 1, Part II, line 14 ▶			

Form **990-T** (2005)

Tables

Table of Cases

Table of IRS Revenue Rulings and Revenue Procedures Cited in Text

Revenue Rulings	Book Sections	Revenue Rulings	Book Sections
54-73	5.9(i)	67-109	5.7(a)
54-170	7.1	67-139	1.4
54-369	7.1	67-175	2.8
54-442	4.1	67-182	2.10(c)(ii)
55-715	2.10(c)(ii), 2.12	67-218	5.9(g)(i)
55-749	5.9(r)	67-219	2.8, 5.9(n)(i)
56-65	2.4(b), 2.10(c)(ii)	67-252	3.5
56-84	2.10(c)(ii)	67-264	2.6
56-138	3.4(b)(vi)	67-295	2.8
56-152	3.5, 5.9(m)	67-296	3.5
56-486	1.4	67-297	5.9(c)
56-511	5.2(d)	67-343	2.6
57-493	2.10(c)(ii)	67-344	2.8
58-224	2.8, 5.9(n)(i)	67-367	3.4(b)(viii)
58-294	2.7(b)	67-393	2.4(b)
58-482	5.9(g)(i)	67-394	2.4(b)
58-502	3.5	68-14	3.6(a)
59-91	5.2(e)	68-182	2.7(b)
59-234	2.10(c)(ii)	68-207	2.5(b)
59-391	2.4(a)(iii), 2.6, 2.11	68-264	2.10(c)(iv)
60-143	1.4	68-265	2.8, 2.10(c)(iv)
60-206	5.9(g)(i)	68-296	6.1(a), 7.7
61-170	2.10(c)(ii), 3.4(b)(viii)	68-373	3.4(b)(viii), 5.9(i)
61-177	2.8, 4.1	68-422	3.4(b)(vi)
62-23	8.2(b)	68-432	9.4
64-128	8.2(b)	68-504	3.6(a)
64-195	4.2(a)(iv)	68-505	5.5(b)
65-1	3.4(b)(viii)	68-536	5.4, 5.9(k)
65-164	2.8	68-550	5.7(d)
65-244	2.10(c)(ii)	68-657	2.8
66-179	1.4, 2.7(a)	69-66	3.4(b)(vii)
66-222	3.5	69-69	5.9(g)(i)
66-223	2.8	69-106	2.8
66-259	3.3, 3.4(b)(x)	69-162	5.9(f)
66-260	2.8	69-175	3.4(b)(viii)
66-323	5.2(c)	69-176	3.4(b)(x)
66-338	2.10(c)(ii)	69-178	5.9(g)(i)
66-354	2.10(c)(ii)	69-179	5.9(f)
67-8	3.4(b)(viii)	69-188	5.9(c)
67-72	3.6(a)	69-256	3.4(b)(viii)
67-77	2.7(b)	69-383	3.3

TABLE OF IRS REVENUE RULINGS AND REVENUE PROCEDURES CITED IN TEXT

Revenue Rulings	Book Sections	Revenue Rulings	Book Sections
69-387	2.4(b)	74-229	8.6
69-430	5.9(f)	74-308	2.10(c)(ii)
69-574	5.2(d)	74-361	5.9(m)
69-575	6.2	74-553	2.4(c)
69-632	2.4(b), 2.7(c), 3.4(b)(viii)	74-572	8.2(c)
69-634	2.4(b)	74-614	5.2(c)
70-31	2.4(a)(ii)	75-196	3.6(a)
70-79	4.2(a)(iv)	75-200	5.8
70-81	2.11	75-201	5.8
70-186	3.4(b)(viii), 3.6(a)	75-286	3.6(a)
70-244	2.7(a)	75-287	2.4(b)
70-591	2.8	75-435	8.3(a)
70-641	2.6, 2.9	75-436	8.6(g)
71-97	1.4	75-437	8.6(g)
71-155	2.8, 2.10(c)(ii)	75-492	8.2(b)
71-311	5.10	75-516	5.9(n)(i)
71-395	3.4(b)(viii)	75-517	5.9(n)(i)
71-504	2.9	75-518	5.9(n)(i)
71-505	2.9	75-519	5.9(n)(i)
71-506	1.4, 2.9	75-520	5.9(n)(i)
71-529	5.2(c)	76-32	8.6(g)
71-580	3.4(b)(viii)	76-38	2.10(c)(ii)
72-101	3.6(a)	76-93	5.8
72-124	5.2(c)	76-94	5.7(b)
72-147	3.4(b)(viii)	76-95	5.10
72-211	2.4(b), 2.10(c)(i)	76-167	2.3, 8.2(b)
72-391	3.4(b)(viii)	76-206	3.1
72-430	8.2(b)	76-207	2.8, 2.11
72-431	5.9(r)	76-208	8.6(g)
72-521	5.9(d)	76-296	5.9(i)
73-45	5.2(c)	76-297	5.9(f)
73-126	3.4(b)(vi)	76-354	5.10
73-127	5.7(b)	76-384	8.2(b)
73-128	5.7(b)	76-400	2.8
73-193	5.9(f)	76-401	8.7
73-386	5.7(b)	76-402	5.7(d)
73-411	2.11, 4.12	76-409	2.10(c)(ii)
73-424	5.5(a), 5.8	76-410	2.4(b)
73-434	8.2(b)	76-416	8.3(a)
73-439	3.4(b)(ix)	76-440	8.4(c)
73-452	2.4(b)	76-441	3.4
73-567	2.4(c)	76-452	8.2(c)
74-27	5.9(d)	77-72	5.10
74-38	5.8	77-112	2.4(a)(i)
74-81	2.10(c)(ii)	77-116	8.3(c), 8.5(c)
74-116	2.7(c)	77-162	10.1(vi)
74-147	2.4(b), 2.7(c)	77-206	3.5, 3.6(a)
74-197	5.10	77-232	2.9
74-228	2.10(c)(ii)	77-255	8.3(a)

TABLE OF IRS REVENUE RULINGS AND REVENUE PROCEDURES CITED IN TEXT

Revenue Rulings	Book Sections	Revenue Rulings	Book Sections
77-365	5.7(d)	80-301	3.4(b)(viii)
77-366	2.3	80-302	3.4(b)(viii)
78-70	2.12	80-305	8.6(g)
78-82	8.2(b)	81-29	5.2(c)
78-88	5.2(d), 5.9(d), 5.10	81-43	8.6(c)
78-98	5.7(d)	81-60	3.5
78-144	5.9(m)	81-94	3.4(b)(vii)
78-145	5.2(c), 5.3	81-95	4.3
78-225	2.11	81-101	5.8
78-232	3.4(b)(vii)	81-138	2.11
78-240	5.9(n)(i)	81-174	2.10(b), 2.10(c)(ii)
78-309	8.2(b)	81-175	2.10(b), 2.10(c)(ii)
78-428	5.2(c)	81-178	5.9(f)
79-17	5.2(c)	82-138	2.4(a)(ii)
79-18	5.2(c)	83-164	2.7(c)
79-19	5.2(c)	85-123	5.9(h)(i)
79-31	5.3	86-98	2.10(c)(ii)
79-122	5.10	95-8	5.10
79-197	8.6(c)	97-21	3.4(a)(iii)
79-349	5.9(c), 5.10	98-15	3.6(b), 7.2(a), 7.4(b)
79-370	5.8	2002-55	6.2
80-207	8.6(g)	2002-67	9.4
80-287	2.10(c)(ii)	2003-49	4.7(a), 10.1(d)
80-294	3.5	2004-6	4.4
80-297	5.7(d)	2005-51	7.5
80-298	5.7(d)	2004-112	5.9(n)(i), 5.9(n)(ii)

Revenue Procedures	Book Sections	Revenue Procedures	Book Sections
73-29	10.1	95-53	5.9(q)
76-9	10.1(a)(viii)	96-59	5.9(q)
79-2	10.1(a)(viii)	97-12	5.9(p)
81-7	8.4(c)	97-57	5.9(p), 5.9(q)
83-23	10.1(b)	98-61	5.9(p), 5.9(q)
85-58	10.1(a)(viii)	99-42	5.9(p), 5.9(q)
92-58	5.9(q)	2001-13	5.9(p), 5.9(q)
92-102	5.9(q)	2001-59	5.9(p), 5.9(q)
93-49	5.9(q)	2002-70	5.9(p), 5.9(q)
94-17	10.1(b)	2003-21	10.1(b)
94-72	5.9(q)	2003-85	5.9(p), 5.9(q)
95-21	5.9(p)	2004-71	5.9(p), 5.9(q)
95-35	4.2(b)(ii)	2005-70	4.2(a)(ix), 5.9(p), 5.9(q)
95-48	10.1(b)		

Table of IRS Private Determinations Cited in Text

	Book Sections		Book Sections
7806039	5.9(m)	8822096	8.3(a), 8.4(d)
7820057	7.7	8825116	8.6
7820058	7.2(a)	8833038	7.3
7823062	5.7(e)	8925092	7.6
7826003	5.7(d)	8938001	7.2
7840072	5.7(d)	8939002	6.5
7905129	5.5(a)	8950072	5.2(e)
7908009	5.7(d)	9003045	2.4(b)
7921018	7.2(a)	9016072	6.1(a)
7922001	2.8	9021060	8.6(g)
7924009	5.9(i)	9032005	2.4(b)
7926003	5.9(f)	9050002	2.4(b)
7936006	5.9(i)	9108021	5.9(c)
7948113	5.8	9128003	2.10(c)(iv)
7952002	7.2(a)	9130002	3.1, 3.4(b)(iii), 7.2
8006005	5.9(f)	9147007	5.5(d), 9.3(a)
8020010	5.7(d)	9242038	6.3(b)
8024001	5.7(d)	9242039	6.3(b)
8040014	5.9(m)	9245031	6.2, 6.3(a)
8041007	5.9(m)	9246032	5.9(g)(i)
8128004	5.9(r)	9247038	5.9(h)(i)
8203134	5.5(b)	9249026	7.3
8211002	5.9(m)	9302023	5.9(m)
8234084	3.4(b)(iii)	9305026	6.3(a), 6.6(b)
8244114	5.9(a)	9308047	6.1(a), 6.3(c)
8304112	6.1(a)	9316032	5.2(e), 5.2(g)
8338127	7.2(a)	9316052	3.4(a)(iii)
8347010	7.7	9320042	5.7(d)
8422170	2.4(b)	9345004	5.9(p)
8433010	5.9(m)	9352030	6.5
8505044	6.3(a)	9416002	5.9(p)
8521055	7.3	9425030	5.5(a)
8524006	2.10(c)(i), 2.10(c)(iii)	9429016	4.2(a)(ix)
8541108	7.2(b)(i)	9434041	8.6(b)
8602001	5.9(o)	9438013	8.6(b)
8621059	7.3	9438029	6.8
8638131	6.5	9438030	7.2(b)(i)
8706012	6.1(a)	9442025	8.6(b)
8708031	5.9(f)	9448036	3.5
8709051	6.3(a)	9450028	5.9(f)
8715055	7.7	9451001	3.4(a)(ii)
8817039	7.3	9502009	5.9(r)
8818008	7.3	9505020	5.2(e)

TABLE OF IRS PRIVATE DETERMINATIONS CITED IN TEXT

	Book Sections		Book Sections
9509002	5.9(f)	200151061	5.7(a)
9530032	3.4	200202077	6.10(d)
9535023	5.7(b)	200203069	6.0
9539016	3.4(a)(i)	200223067	2.6
9544029	5.9(m)	200225046	6.0
9550001	2.8, 2.10(c)(i)	200227007	6.3(a)
9608039	7.2(a), 8.3(b), 8.4(a)	200244028	3.8(d)(i), 3.8(e)
9612003	5.2(d)	200246032	5.2(e)
9615030	3.6(a)	200247055	3.8(d)(i)
9615045	5.9(g)(iii)	200249014	6.10(d)
9619069	5.2(e), 5.9(h)(i)	200249043	6.2
9629030	5.2(e)	200303062	5.8
9635001	5.9(r)	200304036	6.10(d)
9637050	6.1(b), 7.3	200304041	6.10(c)
9637051	6.6(b)	200314031	5.9(g)(iii)
9645004	5.3, 5.7(d)	200326035	6.0
9645017	6.6(b), 6.8	200328042	5.2(g)
9702004	5.3	200332018	3.8(d)(i)
9709014	7.4(a)	200333031	6.10(c)
9712001	5.5(d)	200335037	3.8(d)(i)
9715031	6.2, 7.4(a)	200341023	6.10(d)
9719002	5.4	200351033	7.5
9722006	6.2	200404057	5.9(g)(iii)
9740032	5.9(g)(i)	200405016	6.2
9742001	5.9(p)	200411044	6.10(c)
9751001	5.9(p)	200413014	3.8(e)
9802045	3.8(d)(i)	200421010	3.8(d)(i)
9835001	3.3	200425050	6.0
9839039	7.3, 7.7	200431018	6.10(d)
199938041	6.1(a)	200431023	3.8(f)
200003005	9.4	200435005	6.8
200020056	2.4(a)(iii)	200435018	3.8(d)(ii)
200020060	3.4(a)(ii)	200436022	6.10(d), 7.5, 7.7
200021056	2.3, 5.2(b), 5.3, 5.6, 5.7(a)	200437040	2.3, 6.4
200033049	5.3	200439043	1.4
200044040	6.10(c)	200444044	6.0
200047049	5.2(e), 5.2(g), 5.4	200446025	3.4
200101036	5.8	200447050	3.6(c)
200102052	6.10(c)	200450041	2.3
200103083	3.6(a)	200501017	5.9(d)
200114040	3.6(a)	200501020	5.2(b)
200117043	7.3	200509027	3.4
200118054	6.10(c), 7.5	200510029	5.2(e)
200119061	5.2(e), 5.3	200512025	5.3, 5.7(d)
200124033	6.10(d)	200522022	2.10(c)(ii), 2.10(c)(iii)
200128059	5.5(c)	200531024	10.1(a)(vi)
200131034	5.2(d)	200533001	10.5(j)
200132040	6.2	200535029	3.1
200134025	6.10(b), 6.10(d), 10.1(c)	200544020	1.6(a)
200151045	7.2, 7.2(b)(ii)		

Table of Cases Discussed
in *Bruce R. Hopkins' Nonprofit Counsel*

The following cases, referenced in the text, are discussed in greater detail in one
or more issues of the author's monthly newsletter, as indicated.

Case	Book Section	Newsletter Issue
Aid to Artisans, Inc. v. Comm'r	2.3, 3.6	Mar. 1987, Feb. 1991
Airlie Found. v. Internal Revenue Service	5.2(b)	Nov. 2003
Airlie Found., Inc. v. United States	3.3	Oct. 1992, July 1993
Alabama Central Credit Union v. United States	5.10	Jan. 1987, June 1987
Alumni Ass'n of Univ. of Ore., Inc. v. Comm'r	5.9(f)	Apr. 1996, Dec. 1999
American Academy of Family Physicians v. United States	5.2(a), 5.2(d), 5.4	June 1995, Oct. 1996
American Bar Ass'n v. United States	5.8	Mar. 1984
American Campaign Academy v. Comm'r	3.3, 3.6(a), 3.7, 8.2(b)	July 1989
American College of Physicians v. United States	5.8	Oct. 1984, Aug. 1985, June 1986, Nov. 1986, Dec. 1986
American Hosp. Ass'n v. United States	5.8	May 1987, Oct. 1989
American Inst. for Economic Research, Inc. v. United States	2.3	Jan. 1991
American Medical Ass'n v. United States	5.8	Oct. 1987, Nov. 1987, Sep. 1988, Oct. 1988, Dec. 1989, Jan. 1990
American Soc'y of Ass'n Executives v. United States	4.6	Jan. 1999, Jan. 2000
Anclote Psychiatric Center, Inc. v. Comm'r	3.4(b)(iii), 3.8(d)(i)	June 1992, Sep. 1998
Arkansas State Police Ass'n, Inc. v. Comm'r	5.9(f)	Apr. 2001, May 2002
Better Business Bureau of Washington, D.C. v. United States	2.3, 6.0	Jan. 1991
Bob Jones Univ. v. United States	8.2(b)	July 1984, Aug. 1984, Nov. 1984, July 1985, July 1987, Oct. 1988, Dec. 1990, May 1993
Callaway Family Ass'n, Inc., The v. Comm'r	3.4(b)(viii)	Jan. 1990
Camps Newfound/Owatonna, Inc. v. Town of Harrison, Maine	8.4	May 1994, July 1997, Sep. 1997
Caracci v. Comm'r	3.4(b)(iii), 3.8, 3.8(d)(i)	Feb. 2000, July 2002
Carolinas Farm & Power Equip. Dealers Ass'n, Inc. v. United States	5.2(d), 5.4	June 1985
Centre for Int'l Understanding v. Comm'r	6.8	April 1985
Chicago Metropolitan Ski Council v. Comm'r	5.8	May 1995
Christian Coalition Int'l v. United States	10.2(a)	Nov. 2002

Case	Book Section	Newsletter Issue
Christian Stewardship Assistance, Inc. v. Comm'r	3.4(b)(viii)	Feb. 1991
Christie E. Cuddeback & Lucille M. Cuddeback Memorial Fund v. Comm'r	8.6(g)	Feb. 2003
Church by Mail, Inc. v. Comm'r	3.4, 7.2(a)	Oct. 1984, Sep. 1985, Dec. 1985, Apr. 1989, June 2001
Church of Eternal Life & Liberty, Inc., The v. Comm'r	3.4(b)(vii)	June 1986, Nov. 1986
Church of Ethereal Joy v. Comm'r	3.6	Sep. 1984
Church of Modern Enlightenment v. Comm'r	3.4(b)(vii)	Sep. 1988
Clarence LaBelle Post No. 217, Veterans of Foreign Wars of the United States v. United States	5.9(o)	Mar. 1987
Cline v. Comm'r	10.1(a)(vii)	Oct. 1988
Cockerline Memorial Fund v. Comm'r	8.6(c)	Feb. 1986
Columbia Park & Recreation Ass'n, Inc. v. Comm'r	3.3	Feb. 1987, Mar. 1988
Common Cause v. Comm'r	5.9(f)	Aug. 1999
Comm'r v. Groetzinger	5.4	Nov. 1988, Mar. 1989, Aug. 1989
Copperweld Steel Co.'s Warren Employees' Trust v. Comm'r	3.4(a)(iii)	Feb. 1991
Credit Union Ins. Corp. v. United States	2.4(a)	July 1995, Sep. 1996
Devine Brothers, Inc. v. Comm'r	3.4(a)(ii)	Mar. 2003
Disabled American Veterans v. Comm'r	5.9(a), 5.9(f), 5.9(r)	Apr. 1990, Aug. 1991, July 1993, Nov. 1994
Disabled American Veterans v. United States	5.9(r)	July 1986, Aug. 1986, Sep. 1986, Sep. 1990, Aug. 1991
Dzina v. United States	3.8	Apr. 2003, July 2005
Edgar v. Comm'r	2.3	June 1987
E.J. Harrison & Sons, Inc. v. Comm'r	3.4(a)(vii)	Sep. 2005
Engineers Club of San Francisco, The v. United States	1.1, 2.4(a), 2.10(c)(ii)	Aug. 1986
est of Hawaii v. Comm'r	7.2(a)	June 2001
Estate of Clopton v. Comm'r	10.1(a)(vi)	Nov. 1989, June 1990
Exacto Spring Corp. v. Comm'r	3.4(a)(ii)	June 2000
Executive Network Club, Inc. v. Comm'r	5.9(m)	Mar. 1996
Fides Publishers Ass'n v. United States	2.3	Jan. 1991
Florida Trucking Ass'n, Inc. v. Comm'r	5.8	Dec. 1986
Founding Church of Scientology v. United States	3.3, 3.4(a)(ii), 3.4(b)(i), 3.4(b)(ii)	July 1992
Fraternal Med. Specialist Sev., Inc. v. Comm'r	2.9	Mar. 1985
Fraternal Order of Police, Illinois State Troopers Lodge No. 41 v. Comm'r	5.8, 5.9(f)	Nov. 1986
Freedom Church of Revelation v. United States	3.4(b)(vii)	Sep. 1984
Gemological Inst. of America v. Comm'r	3.2	Feb. 1984

Case	Book Section	Newsletter Issue
Goldsboro Art League, Inc. v. Comm'r	3.6	July 1985, Oct. 1985
Haffner's Service Stations, Inc. v. Comm'r	3.4(a)(ii)	June 2003
HCSC-Laundry v. United States	2.1	Feb. 1984, Oct. 1986
Henry E. & Nancy Horton Bartels Trust for the Benefit of the Univ. of New Haven v. United States	8.6(b)	July 2000
Housing Pioneers, Inc. v. Comm'r	7.2, 7.2(a)	June 1993, Aug. 1993, Apr. 1995, Sep. 1995
IHC Health Plans, Inc. v. Comm'r	1.6(a)	Dec. 2001, June 2003
IIT Research Inst. v. United States	5.9(i)	Dec. 1985
Incorporated Trustees of the Gospel Worker Soc'y, The v. United States	3.4(a)(ii), 5.2(f)	April 1984, Jan. 1986, Feb. 1991
Independent Ins. Agents of Huntsville, Inc. v. Comm'r	5.9(j)	Oct. 1993
Industrial Aid for the Blind, Inc. v. Comm'r	3.1	Feb. 1991
Junaluska Assembly Housing, Inc. v. Comm'r	5.2(e)	Aug. 1986, Feb. 1991
Kentucky Bar Found. v. Comm'r	2.3, 2.9	Mar. 1985
LabelGraphics, Inc. v. Comm'r	3.4(a)(ii)	Oct. 2000
Laborer's Int'l Union of North America v. Comm'r	5.2(a), 5.4, 7.3	Oct. 2001
LAC Facilities, Inc. v. United States	3.4(a)(ii)	Jan. 1995
Lapham Found., Inc. v. Comm'r	8.6(g)	Feb. 2003
Lehrfeld v. Richardson	10.2(a)	Mar. 1998
Leonard Pipeline Contractors, Ltd. v. Comm'r	3.4(a)(ii)	June 1998, July 2001
Lintzenich v. United States	3.8(i)	Dec. 2005
Living Faith, Inc. v. Comm'r	5.2(b), 5.7(b)	Nov. 1990, May 1991, Feb. 1992
Louisiana Credit Union League v. United States	2.10(c)(ii), 5.4, 5.7(a)	Sep. 1993
Manning Ass'n v. Comm'r	3.4(b)(viii)	Jan. 1990
Media Sports League, Inc., The v. Comm'r	2.3	Jan. 1987
Menard, Inc. v. Comm'r	3.4(a)(ii)	Nov. 2004
Miller v. Internal Revenue Service	9.1(a)	Nov. 1987
Miller & Son Drywall, Inc. v. Comm'r	3.4(a)(ii)	Aug. 2005
Nat'l Found., Inc. v. United States	3.4(a)(iii)	Aug. 1984
Nat'l League of Postmasters v. Comm'r	5.9(p)	June 1995, Sep. 1996
Nat'l Water Well Ass'n, Inc. v. Comm'r	5.9(f)	Mar. 1989, Sep. 1990
North Carolina Citizens for Business & Industry v. United States	5.8	Oct. 1989
Ocean Cove Corp. Retirement Plan & Trust v. United States	5.10	June 1987
Ohio Farm Bureau Fed., Inc. v. Comm'r	5.5(b)	June 1996, Apr. 1997
Orange County Agric. Soc'y, Inc. v. Comm'r	2.3, 6.0, 6.2	Oct. 1988, Mar. 1990
Oregon State Univ. Alumni Ass'n, Inc. v. Comm'r	5.9(f)	Mar. 1996, April 1996, Dec. 1993
People of God Community v. Comm'r	3.2, 3.4(a)(iii)	Feb. 1984, Dec. 1986
Peters v. Comm'r	3.4(a)(ii), 3.8(d)(ii)	Dec. 2000
Plumstead Theatre Soc'y, Inc. v. Comm'r	7.2(a)	Jan. 1984

Case	Book Section	Newsletter Issue
Policemen's Benevolent Ass'n of Westchester County, Inc. v. Comm'r	2.3	June 1987
Presbyterian & Reformed Publishing Co. v. Comm'r	5.2(f)	April 1984, Oct. 1984, Nov. 1984, Aug. 1987, Feb. 1991
Pulpit Resource v. Comm'r	2.3	Mar. 1987, Feb. 1991
Quality Auditing Co. v. Comm'r	3.7, 8.9	Sep. 2000
Rapco, Inc. v. Comm'r	3.4(a)(ii)	Aug. 1996
Redlands Surgical Services v. Comm'r	3.6, 3.6(a), 7.2(a) 7.4(b)(iv)	Sep. 1999, May 2001, June 2001, July 2004
Regan v. Taxation With Representation	4.6	Nov. 1984
Riley v. Nat'l Fed'n of the Blind of North Carolina, Inc.	9.7(h)	Sep. 1988, Feb. 1989, Jan. 1990, Feb. 1990, July 1991, Aug. 1992
Robertson v. United States	9.1(a)	Jan. 1985
Roe Found. Charitable Trust v. Comm'r	8.6(g)	Dec. 1989
Scripture Press Found. v. United States	2.3	Jan. 1991
Secretary of State of Maryland v. Joseph H. Munson Co., Inc.	9.7(h)	Aug. 1984, Jan. 1985, Mar. 1985, July 1985, May 1987, Mar. 1988, June 1988, Sep. 1988, Feb. 1989, Jan. 1990, July 1991, Aug. 1992
Senior Citizens of Missouri, Inc. v. Comm'r	3.4(a)(viii)	Mar. 1989
Sierra Club, Inc. v. Comm'r	5.9(a), 5.9(f), 5.9(r)	July 1993, Sep. 1993, Oct. 1994, April 1996, Aug. 1996, May 1999
Sound Health Ass'n v. Comm'r	3.3	Feb. 1987, Mar. 1993
South Community Ass'n v. Comm'r	5.9(m)	Feb. 2006
St. David's Health Care System, Inc. v. United States	7.2(a), 7.4(b)(iv)	Aug. 2002, Jan. 2004, May 2004, July 2004, Aug. 2004
St. Joseph Farms of Ind. Bros. of the Congregation of Holy Cross, Southwest Province, Inc. v. Comm'r	5.9(m)	Aug. 1985
Stanbury Law Firm, P.A. v. Internal Revenue Service	8.1	Oct. 2000
Steamship Trade Ass'n of Baltimore, Inc. v. Comm'r	5.2(d), 5.4	June 1985
Strawbridge Square, Inc. v. United States	7.2(a)	Jan. 1984
Tax Analysts v. Internal Revenue Service	10.2(a)	Nov. 2002
Tax Analysts v. Internal Revenue Service & Christian Broadcasting Network, Inc.	10.2(a)	Aug. 2005, Sep. 2005
Texas Farm Bureau, Inc. v. United States	5.9(f)	June 1993, Sep. 1993, Aug. 1995
Trust U/W Emily Oblinger v. Comm'r	5.9(g)(ii), 7.1	May 1999
United States v. Powell	3.8(i)	Dec. 2005
Universal Church of Jesus Christ, Inc. v. Comm'r	6.2	Sep. 1988

Case	Book Section	Newsletter Issue
Vigilant Hose Co. of Emmitsburg v. United States	5.2(a), 5.2(d), 7.3	Aug. 2001
Village of Schaumberg v. Citizens for a Better Environment	9.7(h)	Aug. 1984, Jan. 1985, Mar. 1985, July 1985, May 1987, Mar. 1988, June 1988, Sep. 1988, Feb. 1989, Jan. 1990, Feb. 1990, July 1991, Aug. 1992
Vision Service Plan v. United States	1.6(a)	Feb. 2006
Waco Lodge No. 166, Benevolent & Protective Order of Elks v. Comm'r	5.9(m), 5.9(n), 10.1(a)(vi)	Aug. 1985
Wendy L. Parker Rehabilitation Found., Inc. v. Comm'r	3.4(b)(viii)	Nov. 1986
West Va. State Medical Ass'n v. Comm'r	5.4	Nov. 1988
World Family Corp. v. Comm'r	2.3, 3.4(a), 3.4(a)(iii)	Nov. 1985, Dec. 1986

Table of IRS Revenue Rulings and Revenue Procedures Discussed in *Bruce R. Hopkins' Nonprofit Counsel*

Revenue Ruling	Book Sections	Newsletter Issue
71-504	2.9	June 1989
71-505	2.9	June 1989
73-567	2.4(c)	June 1989, Dec. 2004
74-147	2.4(b), 2.7(c)	Oct. 1987
75-516	5.9(n)(i)	Sep. 1985
75-517	5.9(n)(i)	Sep. 1985
75-518	5.9(n)(i)	Sep. 1985
75-519	5.9(n)(i)	Sep. 1985
75-520	5.9(n)(i)	Sep. 1985
78-232	3.4(b)(vii)	Nov. 1984
81-94	3.4(b)(vii)	July 1989
81-178	5.9(f)	Aug. 1991
86-98	2.10(c)(ii)	Sep. 1986, June 2005
95-8	5.10	Feb. 1995, Feb. 2002
97-21	3.4(a)(iii)	June 1997
98-15	3.6(b), 7.2(a), 7.4(b)	May 1998, Apr. 2001, June 2001, Feb. 2004, Nov. 2004
2002-55	6.2	Nov. 2002, Sep. 2005
2002-67	9.4	Jan. 2003
2003-49	4.7(a), 10.1(d)	July 2003
2004-6	4.4	Mar. 2004
2005-51	7.5	July 2004, Sep. 2005
2004-112	5.9(n)(i)	Feb. 2005

Revenue Procedure	Book Sections	Newsletter Issue
73-29	10.1	Nov. 1989
93-49	5.9(q)	Jan. 1994
94-17	10.1(b)	Mar. 1994
94-72	5.9(q)	Jan. 1995
95-21	5.9(p)	May 1995
95-48	10.1(b)	Aug. 1998
95-53	5.9(q)	Feb. 1996
97-12	5.9(p)	Mar. 1997
97-57	5.9(p), 5.9(q)	Feb. 1998
99-42	5.9(p), 5.9(q)	Jan. 2000
2002-70	5.9(p), 5.9(q)	Dec. 2002
2003-21	10.1(b)	Mar. 2003
2003-85	5.9(p), 5.9(q)	Jan. 2004
2004-71	5.9(p), 5.9(q)	Feb. 2005

Table of IRS Private Determinations Discussed in *Bruce R. Hopkins' Nonprofit Counsel*

The following IRS private letter rulings and technical advice memoranda, referenced in the text, are discussed in greater detail in one or more issues of the author's monthly newsletter, as indicated.

Private Determination	Book Sections	Newsletter Issue(s)
8505044	6.3(a)	May 1985, June 1985
8521055	7.3	Aug. 1985
8541108	7.2(b)(i)	Sep. 1985, Dec. 1985, Oct. 1986
8621059	7.3	Aug. 1986
8706012	1(a)	Apr. 1987
8925092	7.6	Aug. 1989
9021060	8.6(g)	July 1990
9130002	3.1, 3.4(b)(iii), 7.2	Nov. 1991
9302023	5.9(m)	Apr. 1993
9305026	6.3(a), 6.6(b)	Apr. 1993, Feb. 1997, Apr. 1997
9316052	3.4(a)(iii)	Jan. 1994
9434041	8.6(b)	Oct. 1994
9438013	8.6(b)	Nov. 1994
9438029	6.8	Nov. 1994, Jan. 1995, Feb. 1997
9438030	7.2(b)(i)	Nov. 1994, Dec. 1994
9442025	8.6(b)	Oct. 1994, Dec. 1994
9448036	3.5	Jan. 1985
9530032	3.4	Nov. 1995
9608039	7.2(a), 8.3(b), 8.4(a)	Apr. 1996
9615030	3.6(a)	June 1996
9615045	5.9(g)(iii)	July 1996
9619069	5.2(e), 5.9(h)(i)	Aug. 1996
9637050	6.1(b), 7.3	Nov. 1996
9637051	6.6(b)	Apr. 1997
9645017	6.6(b), 6.8	Feb. 1997, Apr. 1997
9722006	6.2	Nov. 2002
9740032	5.9(g)(i)	Dec. 1997
9839039	7.3, 7.7	Dec. 1998
199938041	6.1(a)	May 2000, Feb. 2002
200033049	5.3	Oct. 2000
200101036	5.8	Mar. 2001
200114040	3.6(a)	June 2001
200117043	7.3	July 2001
200118054	6.10(c), 7.5	July 2001
200119061	5.2(e), 5.3	Aug. 2001
200128059	5.5(c)	Sep. 2001
200132040	6.2	Nov. 2001
200134025	6.10(b), 6.10(d), 10.1(c)	Nov. 2001

TABLE OF IRS PRIVATE DETERMINATIONS IN *NONPROFIT COUNSEL*

Private Determination	Book Sections	Newsletter Issue(s)
200151061	5.7(a)	Mar. 2002
200223067	2.6	Aug. 2002
200225046	6.0	Sep. 2002
200247055	3.8(d)(i)	Sep. 2003
200303062	5.8	Mar. 2003
200304041	6.10(c)	Apr. 2003
200314031	5.9(g)(iii)	June 2003, Aug. 2003
200326035	6.0	Sep. 2003
200332018	3.8(d)(i)	Oct. 2003
200333031	6.10(c)	Oct. 2003
200335037	3.8(d)(i)	Nov. 2003
200341023	6.10(d)	Dec. 2003
200351033	7.5	Feb. 2004
200405016	6.2	Apr. 2004
200411044	6.10(c)	May 2004
200413014	3.8(e)	June 2004
200421010	3.8(d)(i)	July 2004
200425050	6.0	Aug. 2004
200431018	6.10(d)	Oct. 2004
200436022	6.10(d), 7.5, 7.7	Nov. 2004
200439043	1.4	Dec. 2004
200450041	2.3	Mar. 2005
200501017	5.9(d)	Mar. 2005
200501020	5.2(b)	Mar. 2005
200510029	5.2(e)	May 2005
200512025	5.3, 5.7(d)	June 2005
200522022	2.10(c)(ii), 2.10(c)(iii)	Sep. 2005
200531024	10.1(a)(vi)	Oct. 2005
200533001	10.5(j)	Nov. 2005
200544020	1.6(a)	Feb. 2006
200602039	6.7(b)	Apr. 2006

Table of IRS Private Letter Rulings, Technical Advice Memoranda, and General Counsel Memoranda

The following citations, to pronouncements from the Internal Revenue Service issued in the context of specific cases, are coordinated to the appropriate footnotes (FN) in the suitable chapters.

Citations are to IRS private letter rulings, technical advice memoranda, and general counsel memoranda, other than those specifically referenced in footnotes, that are directly pertinent to the material discussed in the text. Nine- and seven-number items are either private letter rulings or technical advice memoranda; items that end with an "E" are exemption denial and revocation letters (now issued as private letter rulings); five-number items are general counsel memoranda.

While these pronouncements are not to be cited as precedent (IRC § 6110(k)(3)), they are useful in illuminating the position of the IRS on the subjects involved.

Chapter 2

FN	Private Letter Rulings, etc.
48	200020056
51	9517036
74	20044041E
80	9349022
105	39721
158	9029035
180	20044007E, 20044031E, 20044042E, 20044043E
197	9645027
239	37853
248	8826004
249	9645027
257	20044001E, 200444024
269	9429002, 9429003
271	9124004

Chapter 3

FN	Private Letter Rulings, etc.
10	200446025
21	9338043
59	9525056
78	9231045, 9621035
80	200447047, 200508021, 200532051
81	20042703E, 20044004E, 20044032E, 200511016

88	9112006, 9201035
108	20044013E
118	8731032
122	38394
125	35638
139	8838047
146	20044033E
180	8807081, 8808070
185	9025089, 37180, 38283, 39670
186	32518, 35865
208	20044004E, 20044032E, 200447050
236	9428035
252	39876
262	9530024-9530026
273	20044004E, 20044032E, 200511017, 200524029

Chapter 4

FN	Private Letter Rulings, etc.
69	9510047, 9534021, 9602026, 9636016
72	199919038

Chapter 5

FN	Private Letter Rulings, etc.
5	9120029
10	200027056
29	8722082, 9735047, 32896, 36827
30	9217001
34	9325061
52	9401031
57	9242035
58	8822057
59	8840020, 8841041
60	8806056, 9318047
67	9042038
70	8852002
82	9616039, 9619068, 9619069, 9630031, 9631025, 9631029, 9652028, 9704010, 9745025, 200246032
99	9438040, 9505020, 9509041, 9510039, 200148085, 200328045, 200328046, 200328048
108	36827
110	9720035
120	8852002
134	8651086, 8708052, 8841041
135	8829003, 8932004, 9309002
137	8717002, 8717063, 8733037, 8734005, 8901064, 8934050, 8936013, 9003059, 9017058, 9018049, 9240937, 9337027, 9340061, 9340062, 9349022

138	9425031
158	8922064, 9407005, 9413020
159	9417003
164	9137002, 9417003, 9509002, 9721001
172	8641001
176	9302023, 9539005
182	8819005, 9723046
187	9535023
193	9750056
194	9641011, 9728034, 9715041
196	8732029, 9041045, 9350045
225	9014069
227	9137002, 9147054, 9205037, 39860
230	8947002, 9044071, 9234002, 9304001, 9345004, 9724006
232	9023003, 199914035
233	9302035
235	8932004
240	8726069, 9302023
249	9023001, 9023002, 9204007, 9402005
252	9247001
253	8834006, 8835001, 9023001, 9023002, 9217002, 9402005, 9419003, 9734002
254	8403013
256	9248001
269	9042038
272	8836037
280	9826046
282	200315028, 200315032, 200315034
285	199914042, 199928042
297	9030048
329	9231045
335	9151001, 9309002, 9306030, 39827
347	8839016
350	9346014
352	8827017
356	9316045, 9319042, 9419033, 9503024, 9552019
359	8222066, 8645050, 8717066, 8717078, 8721102, 8728060, 8808002, 8808003, 8810097, 8824054, 8828011, 8845073, 8846005, 8922084, 8941011, 8941062, 8948023, 9015038, 9023091, 9024026, 9043039, 9108021, 9316052, 9404003, 9404004, 9417036, 9417042, 9417043, 9419033, 9436001, 9440001, 9441001, 9450028, 9703025, 9705001, 9709029, 9714016, 9723001, 9724006, 9810030, 9816027, 200046039, 200149035, 200149043, 200119037, 200225046, 39615
362	9139029, 9212030, 9231045, 9234043, 9551019, 35957, 39568
363	9450045, 200041031, 200147058, 200148057, 200148074
365	8950072, 9139029, 9141051, 9146047, 9702003
366	8445005, 8720005, 8802009, 8925029, 39825
273	9450045

380	8713072, 8822096, 8932042
392	9245036, 9246032, 9246033, 9301024, 9315021, 9703025, 9850020
393	8822057, 9551019
403	200032050
407	9108034, 9108043, 9127045, 9128030, 9132040, 9132061, 9144032-9144035, 9150047, 9204048, 9247038, 9252028, 9547040, 9551021
409	9619068
413	9108034, 9108043, 9128030, 9132040, 9132061, 9144032, 9144035, 9150047, 9252028 (modified by 9248037), 9308040, 9316032, 9319044, 9401029, 9407005, 9411018, 9411019, 9412039, 9414002, 9432019, 9629032, 9651014, 9803024, 9826046, 9844004, 9853034, 199952071, 200041038, 200151046, 200151062, 200219037, 200237027
423	8201024
467	39786
469	8832043, 39752
489	39734
502	9302035, 9303030
528	9847001
555	8044023, 8104098, 8107114, 8110164, 8338138, 8738006, 8807082, 9031052, 9407023, 9703026, 200041038, 200233032
557	9010025, 9431001, 9533014
561	9533014
565	8822057
567	9042043, 9108021, 9110012, 9527033, 9743054, 200150040, 200233023, 200449033, 39826
568	9012001
574	8945038
582	8818008, 8923077, 9031052, 9047069, 9218006, 9218007
584	9450045, 200137061
585	9508031, 200318076
595	9128020
598	9002030
599	200224014, 200351032
604	8721104, 8721107, 9042038
606	9619077
607	9637053, 9642051
609	9717004

Chapter 6

FN	Private Letter Rulings, etc.
7	9308047
13	8606056, 8705087, 8706012, 8709071, 8720048, 8749058, 8749059, 8805059, 8810082, 8811003, 8819034, 8821044, 8833002, 8840056, 8846053, 8901012, 8901050, 8903083, 8909029, 8925051, 8934064, 8952076, 9005068, 9024068, 9024026, 9024086, 9030063, 9033069, 9108016, 9119060, 9131058, 9245031, 9308047, 9311031, 9316052, 9341024, 9346013, 9402031-9402933, 9408026, 9417036, 9417042, 9417043, 9421006, 9438041, 9447043, 9523027, 9528020, 9530009,

13 *(continued)*	9535022, 9539014, 9542045 (amended by 9720036), 9547039, 9626021, 9630014, 9637051, 9705028, 9721038, 9726010, 9720031, 9722032, 199941048
27	8934064, 9242038, 9408026, 9421006, 199941051
33	39598, 39646, 39866
34	199929006
37	39776
38	8625078, 8720048, 8732040, 8743070, 8840056, 8934064, 9027050, 9305026, 9734026, 9734027, 9734036, 9734037, 9734039, 9734040, 199938041, 200037050, 200130048, 200130049, 200130055, 200132040, 200149043
49	8839002
50	8709051, 9305026
95	199941048
103	8729005, 8832084, 8833002, 8903083, 8922047, 9010073, 9045003, 9108016, 9308047, 9324026, 9404004, 9438029, 9506046, 9535022, 9547039, 9601047, 9642054, 9705028, 200132040
112	8849072, 9136032, 9148051
152	200325003, 200325004, 200327065, 200327067
153	200102053
155	200304042
158	200333032, 200333033

Chapter 7

FN	Private Letter Rulings, etc.
21	9230001, 9350044
50	8628049, 8705089, 8715039, 9715040, 8717057, 8723065, 8724060, 8727080, 8806057, 8807012, 8814047, 8817039, 8818008, 8820093, 8833009, 8901054, 8909036, 8912003, 8912041, 8915065, 8917055, 8931083, 8936047, 8936077, 8938002, 8939024, 8940039, 8941006, 8942099, 8943050, 8943064, 9021050, 9029034, 9109066, 9122061, 9122062, 9122070, 9147058, 9318033, 9319044, 9323030, 9345057, 9349032, 9352030, 9438030, 9502035 (updating 8528080), 9603839, 9642051, 9736039, 9736043, 9739001, 9709014, 9718036, 9722032, 39732
51	200211052
73	8925052, 8945063
76	8621060, 8903060, 8912003, 8925052, 8936073, 8945063, 9029034, 9035072, 9105029, 9105031, 9215046, 9308034, 9323030, 9352030, 9407022, 9518014, 9517029, 200206058
77	9637050, 9645018, 9739036-9739039
80	8925051, 9547039
84	200044040
108	8921203, 8932085, 8941006, 8949034, 9001030, 9521013

Index